AN EDGEFIELD PLANTER AND HIS WORLD

A welcome and important contribution to the history of South Carolina and the United States in the 1840s, the journals of Whitfield Brooks offer historians a glimpse into the world view of this vital player. These journals bring to light the essential ways in which Brooks viewed the cultural mores and religious sensibilities of his day. With remarkable depth and insight, James Farmer places the man in the context of his time. Farmer's introduction and annotations fill in the tantalizing details of other persons of interest. This is an essential primary source for those interested in the history of this period.

—Orville Vernon Burton, Matthew J. Perry
Distinguished Professor of History,
Clemson University

The journals of Whitfield Brooks are the 'white whale' of Southern scholarship—a mammoth historical resource that surfaced and resurfaced without ever being seen whole, leaving historians to tell tall tales from their armchairs. James Farmer has finally caught the source in his editorial net, and it is everything we could have imagined. Here is a planter's whole world—his dreams, decency, and struggles, not least his struggles with his disappointing son, who did more than any one man to bring on the Civil War. Farmer spent years chasing these journals, and it has all been worth it. The resulting book is a towering achievement of historical reclamation and editing.

— Stephen Berry, Gregory Professor
of the Civil War Era,
University of Georgia

James Farmer's editing and noting unwraps the many treasures found in the journals of Whitfield Brooks, a large slaveholder and planter in South Carolina's Edgefield district, a devout Christian who pursued many avenues for potential economic gain, often with success, and father of Congressman Preston Brooks, infamous for his caning of Charles Sumner on the floor of the United States Senate in 1856. A leading expert on pre-civil war South Carolina, Farmer provides the expertise to help readers develop an understanding of Brooks' large network of connections and he contextualizes Brooks' life with consummate skill. These are content-rich journals edited with knowledge and aplomb.

—Lacy K. Ford Jr., dean of
the College of Arts and Sciences,
University of South Carolina

James Farmer is a master of his sources and a meticulous editor, and in the daily journal of this upper-class planter he has found a treasure worthy of his talents. This insightful and perceptive journal is an open door to the lives of the planter nabobs of the antebellum South, especially since it comes to us from that crucible of Southern history that is Edgefield County, South Carolina.

—Philip Racine, Kenan Professor
of History Emeritus,
Wofford College

AN EDGEFIELD PLANTER AND HIS WORLD

The 1840s Journals of Whitfield Brooks

James O. Farmer Jr.
Editor

MERCER UNIVERSITY PRESS
Macon, Georgia
1979–2019
40 Years of Publishing Excellence

MUP/ H968

Published by Mercer University Press
1501 Mercer University Drive
Macon, Georgia 31207

9 8 7 6 5 4 3 2 1

Books published by Mercer University Press are printed on acid-free paper that meets the requirements of the American National Standard for Information Sciences—Permanence of Paper for Printed Library Materials.

Printed and bound in the United States.

This book is set in Adobe Caslon.

ISBN 978-0-88146-692-8
Cataloging-in-Publication Data is available from the Library of Congress

To Bettis, and to Mary Jane

"A patriot should be accustomed to tolerate every political party, to stand true to his own, and to attack his antagonist with eagerness yet without personal animosity. Political antagonists should regard each other like the officers of two opposing armies who do their best to wound and kill each other yet all in honor."

—Whitfield Brooks
From a fugitive sheet among
papers in Brooks family's possession

"Our decision was to fight."

—Brooks Journal, June 27, 1841

"At one time my life was dispaired of and I thought I should certainly die but I felt not the slightest alarm. I had endeavoured to come to God through Christ, humbly & deeply repenting the commissions of my manifold sins and putting my trust for salvation in Christ and not in any merit of my own."

—Brooks Journal, July 30, 1845

"I thank God for all his mercies & blessings and pray for the aid of his almighty grace to enable me to keep his commandments, & to increase in every christian Virtue."

—Brooks Journal, February 5, 1842

"Religion is built on humility, honour on pride; how to reconcile them must be left to wiser heads than mine."

—Bernard deMandeville
Fable of the Bees, 1714

CONTENTS

PREFACE

The book before you has a long history, involving both Brooks' journals themselves and my editorial relationship with them. I first encountered Whitfield Brooks (1790-1851) in the early 1990s, when Edgefield, South Carolina businessman and historian Bettis C. Rainsford showed me photocopies of two manuscript volumes of Brooks' 1840s journal. My friendship with Bettis began in 1992 when I was appointed the first June Rainsford Henderson Professor of Southern and Local History at the University of South Carolina Aiken. In endowing the chair Bettis paid homage to his beloved Aunt June and showed his commitment to advancing scholarship on the history of his native county and region. In accepting the appointment I welcomed Bettis' intention that my research would give priority to the "Old Edgefield District," and the counties created entirely or in part from it.[1]

Soon after arriving I presumed to offer, in Edgefield, a continuing education class on the county's history. The fifty or so class members, all white, most born before 1940, and many sprung from old Edgefield roots, taught me as much as I did them, and reminded me about the staying power of tradition. (I attributed the absence of African-Americans to the awkwardness that black Edgefieldians could anticipate in addressing sometimes racially charged content with white neighbors.) When the class ended, a remnant of die-hards continued to gather on Sunday afternoons. Long led by Bettis—a walking encyclopedia of Edgefield history--they have produced a helpful visitors' guide and illustrated history of the town and county.[2]

The class was enhanced by Bettis' familiarity with the voluminous primary sources housed in the Edgefield County Archives, the Tompkins (genealogical) Library, and his own extensive collection. Among the latter were the photocopies of Brooks' 1840s journals. Sampling them, I was intrigued by the diarist's occasional mentioning of his son, future Congressman Preston Smith Brooks, remembered for one of the most dramatic events in American political history--his caning of Massachusetts Senator Charles Sumner on May 22, 1856.

Note: Only short titles and citations are used throughout the footnotes; however, full source information can be found in the bibliography.

[1] Created in 1785, the "Old Edgefield District" was the political and judicial district bounded by the Savannah and Saluda Rivers and Abbeville, Newberry, Lexington, Orangeburg, and Barnwell Districts of South Carolina. It included, in addition to modern Edgefield and Saluda Counties, parts of modern McCormick, Greenwood, and Aiken Counties.

[2] Rainsford et al., *The Story of Edgefield.* The vast Old Edgefield District was "more a region than a county" (Burton, *In My Father's House,* 14).

The attack was Brooks' response to Sumner's vituperative "Crime against Kansas" speech. In it he condemned the ongoing proslavery violence in the Kansas territory, where the question of slavery's future remained undecided.[3] Offensive as this was to Congressman Brooks, he was further enraged by the tasteless insults Sumner directed at his state and his Edgefield first cousin once removed, the absent and enfeebled Senator Andrew Pickens Butler. Of Brooks' frenzied response, Orville Vernon Burton, an authority on both Edgefield and the caning, writes, "[f]ew individual acts in American history have done more to change the course of national events." Sumner, previously seen by many, North and South, as a self-absorbed fanatic, became in northern eyes a symbolic martyr in the causes of human rights and free speech. Meanwhile Brooks, thanks in part to the enthusiastic endorsement he received in the South, symbolized for those above the Mason-Dixon Line the very brutality of which the Senator spoke. Thus did "Bully Brooks" highlight the growing distance between the sections and stimulate the growth of the infant Republican Party. And thus was the stage set for the election of Abraham Lincoln, secession, and the Civil War.[4]

Knowing this, the historian who opens the journals kept by Preston Brooks' father while his son was in his twenties anticipates that beyond their value in documenting elite antebellum life, it may be a source of insight into the father-son relationship and young Preston's much-analyzed personality. But there was a fly in the ointment; a big piece of the puzzle was missing. The two journal volumes, one beginning in November, 1840 and the other ending in May, 1849, were separated by a gap of more than two years. The middle volume's location, even its existence, was uncertain. I dismissed any notion of editing and publishing the extant volumes.

After retiring in 2008 I began work on a general history of Edgefield County. Its theme seemed obvious. An early twentieth century observer wrote, with only mild hyperbole, that "Edgefield has had more dashing, brilliant, romantic figures, statesmen, orators, soldiers, adventurers and daredevils than any other county in South Carolina, if not any rural county of America." This celebratory pronouncement, while missing its well documented underside of murder and mayhem, captures the county's

---

[3] Abolitionist John Brown's "Pottawatomie Massacre," retaliation for the "Sack of Lawrence," by pro-slavery men, occurred May 24–25.

[4] Burton, *The Age of Lincoln*, 50. Burton's many contributions to Edgefield studies are led by the indispensable *In My Father's House Are Many Mansions.* On the caning, see Donald, *Charles Sumner*; Gienapp, "The Crime Against Sumner"; Benson, ed., *The Caning of Senator Sumner;* Hoffer, *The Caning of Charles Sumner*; Puleo, *The Caning;* Freehling, *Road to Disunion*, vol. 2, ch. 6; Sinha, "The Caning of Charles Sumner"; Deitreich, "'Ever Able, Manly, Just, and Heroic"; Deitreich, "The Sly Mendacity of Hints"; Mathis, "Preston Smith Brooks: The Man and His Image"; Berry and Welborn, "The Cane of His Existence"; and Graden, "Losing Control."

larger-than-life image, its collective panache. Summing up Edgefield's place in southern history, Lacy Ford writes succinctly, "Among historians, Edgefield's reputation precedes it."[5]

The subject matter was compelling, and the raw materials for a history were rich and accessible. A generous grant from the Watson-Brown Foundation eased financial concerns. Then, after several months of research, Whitfield Brooks reentered the picture in the form of an email message from Jane Aldrich, archivist at the South Carolina Historical Society in Charleston. The Society had recently acquired and transcribed a volume of Whitfield Brooks' journal.[6] Even more interesting, its dates indicated that the volume filled the void between the two photocopied volumes in Bettis Rainsford's files. Together, the three volumes covered almost completely the period between November, 1840 and May, 1849. Since Brooks' health was declining when the third volume ended, and he died on December 28, 1851, his journal keeping may have ended with the third volume. I would later learn that, other than a few fugitive excerpts, no earlier Brooks journals are known to have survived.

In short order my excitement about the Brooks journal trumped my county history plans. The decade it covered, the 1840s, though calmer than the nullification and secession eras that preceded and followed it, was a critical one in the history of South Carolina and the United States, and the journal's author was a significant yet largely unknown figure. The second-generation pillar of "one of the most influential planter families in antebellum South Carolina," Brooks was one of Edgefield's largest planters, owning at times over one hundred slaves and real estate valued at $20,000 ($648,500 in 2017 dollars). He was an advocate and practitioner of progressive farming methods, a lawyer and jurist, a state legislator and an unsuccessful candidate for Congress. A founding member and along with his wife and mother-in-law a generous supporter of Edgefield's Trinity Episcopal Church, he was an intriguing mixture of piety and pride. Educated and well connected, he was, as his journals reveal, capable

---

[5] Ball, *The State That Forgot*, 22; and Ford, "Origins of the Edgefield Tradition." Ford acknowledges that the county was "a cradle of political insurgency" but rejects, as does Burton, the view that it was "a singularly radical locale." That view was fostered by Brown, "South Carolina Extremism and Its Violent Origins." See also Simkins, *Pitchfork Ben Tillman*, 25; and Burton, *In My Father's House*, xvii–xviii, 20–21. For an overreaching but powerful portrait of Edgefield's nationally significant violent history, see Butterfield, *All God's Children.* Dated but still essential is Chapman, *History of Edgefield County.* Edgefield's list of "ten governors" includes men born elsewhere who resided in the district for varying lengths of time, and others born there who were associated with other places as well. Among its political luminaries are George McDuffie, Louis T. Wigfall, Pierce Mason Butler, Andrew Pickens Butler, Francis W. Pickens, Martin W. Gary, Ben Tillman, and Strom Thurmond. For an extended discussion of the cultural roots of backcountry violence, including Edgefield, see Fischer, *Albion's Seed*, 605–782, especially 770–71. See also Williams, *Vogues in Villainy*, 4 and *passim*.

[6] While it is clearly authentic, the provenance of this volume is obscure.

of introspection.[7] Although his journals don't show it, he was also capable of the sort of impetuous acts associated with the stereotypical southern male of his era. Thus publication of his journal could add another layer of variety and complexity to the still disputed image of the patriarchal Old South planter. If it also provided evidence for or against the insights of historians about his intriguing son, so much the better.[8]

Several crucial steps still lay ahead. I had to verify that the manuscript journal held by the South Carolina Historical Society was authentic and that its transcriber had done her job well. Examining it the Fireproof Building in Charleston, I found that although its covers were gone and condition was worse than the first and third volumes, both the handwriting and the style of this journal were Whitfield Brooks'. Placing the transcription beside the manuscript, I saw that the transcriber had produced a reliable copy. The second hurdle disappeared when the Watson-Brown Foundation's board graciously gave their approval for me to apply the grant funds to editing the Brooks Journal.

The third hurdle was removed when I received permission from the owners of the first and third volumes of the journal to publish them. Bettis Rainsford introduced me to two great-grandchildren of Whitfield Brooks, Mary Jane Brooks Mobley and Emmett Brooks of Greenwood, South Carolina. They graciously granted me permission, soon joined by that of their siblings, to pursue publication. Director Faye Jensen granted The South Carolina Historical Society's permission to publish the middle volume.

Months of transcribing the first and third volumes followed, using the photocopies in Bettis office and expedited somewhat by voice-recognition software. But photocopy imperfections (and my accent) left many uncertainties. Fortunately Mary

---

7 Barney, "Preston Smith Brooks." The best contemporary profile of WB is O'Neall, *Biographical Sketches of the Bench and Bar,* vol. 2, 473–75. John Belton O'Neall and Brooks were college classmates and lifelong friends. See also U. R. Brooks, *South Carolina Bench and Bar,* vol. 1, 106–107, edited by a grandson of the diarist. An essay on his famous son, Preston, published within a month of his shocking January 1857 death, proclaims that WB was "a gentleman of fine intellect, a lawyer by profession, of signal virtues, and distinguished in the history of the district, as one of her most upright, useful, and public spirited citizens" (*Southern Quarterly Review* 2 [1857]: 348–70). The unsigned author was Maximilian LaBorde, a close associate of WB. On money values over time, see www.measuringworth.com/.

8 Intellectual historian Michael O'Brien might have cringed at this paragraph and the preceding note, since he wrote that too many "[b]iographers, like introducers, seem to be terrified that the audience will be insufficiently impressed, or rather they believe that it is wise to persuade the audience of the merit of the lecturer, in case it proves less than self-evident in the case of the lecture" (O'Brien, *Placing the South,* 89). I have tried to be mindful of this pitfall in the introduction that follows. For a broad-ranging study of the "great planters" of the Old South, see Scarborough, *Masters of the Big House.* While Scarborough's subjects exceeded Brooks in numbers of slaves, many of his observations apply to him. For a brief overview of the planter class and the scholarly controversies they have inspired, see Boney, *Southerners All,* ch. 1, "The Aristocrats." Boney's collective portrait actually describes Brooks reasonably well.

Jane Mobley and her husband, Dr. Mims Mobley, invited me to make several visits to their home to examine the manuscript volumes in her possession. They also showed me other Brooks artifacts and even included me in family lunches on several occasions, but made no attempt to influence my perspective on Mary Jane's ancestor. After correcting errors and acknowledging uncertainties in my transcription at the Mobleys' dining table, I began discussions with academic publishers, which focused on the length of the manuscript. At 235,000 words (983 manuscript pages), it was considered too long to publish in its entirety, especially with substantial ancillary material. I resisted cutting it because of the damage deletions would do to the integrity of the journal, and because I dreaded having to make the editorial decisions on what words to sacrifice. Surely another editor would choose differently, and readers might wonder if I had allowed the person portrayed in his whole text to survive my editorial scissors. Time reconciled me to reality, especially as I wanted to include a lengthy introduction and extensive notes. What remains is about eighty-five percent of the whole, and, for what it is worth, I think Whitfield Brooks survived the process.

Brooks' Journal and Others

In recent decades historians have become bolder in their efforts to explore the psyches of the people they write about. It helps of course to have a subject who cooperated by leaving manuscripts that reveal something of his or her inner life. Two somewhat contradictory perspectives present themselves here, both offered by scholars familiar with historical diaries. Stephen Berry notes that the Old South offered men little encouragement toward introspection. "[Southern] [m]en of the nineteenth century were encouraged to cloak their hearts and stifle their doubts, to so carefully groom their public persona as to become it," Berry writes. "The result is a staggering amount of evidence dedicated to the public, external, and projected aspects of men's lives and significantly less dedicated to the private, internal, and introspective." Yet whatever their tendencies to cloak and stifle, men who ran plantations needed to at least make a record of the weather and their daily farm-related activities, and thus periodically engaged in a writing ritual in which some level of self-examination was possible, and for those so inclined, likely. Since no two of them approached that task with the same eagerness or perceptiveness, and since some planters kept two records – one for their farming business and one for their social and personal lives--planters' diaries offer a range of insights for their modern readers.[9]

Michael O'Brien addressed the diary form itself and its complex usages among antebellum southern men and women. He writes that diaries, like letters, while considered private, and thus appropriate for the introspective nineteenth century, "could be public things, to be read out in the parlor or placed on a table for family viewing." Yet, he adds, while writing the diarist might "forget the distant prospect of publicity"

---

[9] Berry, *All That Makes a Man*, 11.

so that candor might overcome caution. There were, however, limits. "Diaries dealt with venial, not mortal sins." O'Brien notes that the diary form was especially appealing to the young, as a tool in their self-definition, to the religious for the same reason, to those like Mississippian Henry Hughes, with a need to vent, or fantasize, or the elderly, like Edmund Ruffin of Virginia, who wanted to look back. Understandably considering the scale of research undertaken in his book project, O'Brien's monumental study of antebellum southern thought doesn't treat plantation diaries.[10]

Whitfield Brooks must have kept plantation records, and perhaps personal journals, from the time he began managing a farm, around the time of his marriage to Mary Parsons Carroll in 1818. Fugitive fragments belonging to descendants indicate that he made at least sporadic entries in a journal or journals well before the ones published here. The earliest I have seen are dated 1833. These include revealing religious and scientific references. Brooks also kept a record of a trip to Florida with Mary between November 14, 1845 and January 7, 1846 in a separate volume filling ninety-seven pages.[11]

Readers of Brooks' Journal who are unfamiliar with this genre may wonder how his compares with those of other antebellum planters.[12] Published journals comparable to Brooks' were kept by two near-contemporary South Carolinians, his acquaintance and sometime political ally, Barnwell and Edgefield District planter/politician James Henry Hammond (1807-1864), and lowcountry planter Thomas B. Chaplin (1822-1890).[13] Hammond kept a separate plantation record, so his "diaries" could serve as vehicles for personal reflection and for venting frustrations. Thus these documents revealed, sometimes with surprising candor, aspects of his inner self. Chaplin's "journal" comes closer to Michael O'Brien's definition of a journal. Although it contains attacks on his stepfather, whom he considered a gold-digger, and on others he felt had wronged him, in general it focuses rather unselfconsciously on his mundane activities and interactions with others, including his slaves. These two records are as different as the men who kept them, but each is an extremely valuable historical resource. Hammond's diaries provide a unique psychological study, mesmerizing and

---

[10] O'Brien, *Conjectures of Order*, vol. 1, 456, 459, 462–63.

[11] The length of this project precluded including it here. It may be examined in transcription at the South Carolina Historical Society in Charleston.

[12] These men used the labels "journal" and "diary," without implying anything about their contents. Although the standard definitions of diary and journal are essentially interchangeable, Michael O'Brien makes a distinction, describing a journal as a record of "the weather, the crops, or the beaux," and adding that "however introspective or discursive a diary might become, it was far more common for it to be called a journal than a diary" (O'Brien, *Conjectures of Order*, vol. 1, 456–57).

[13] Bleser, ed., *Secret and Sacred: The Diaries of James Henry Hammond;* and Rosengarten, *Tombee: Portrait of a Cotton Planter*.

at times appalling. Chaplin's journal is a less introspective summary of a more ordinary life.[14]

The first and third volumes in which Brooks made his daily entries have "Private Journal" stamped on their spines, and so bear that label here. Part of the appeal and value of his journals is that they provide a blend of the two kinds of records left by Hammond and Chaplin. They cannot compete with Hammond's diaries for dazzling mental acuity or melodrama. Nonetheless, they allow the reader as satisfying a view of his world as Chaplin's does, and often more of his mind and heart.

The Brooks journals do have their shortcomings from the historian's point of view. Careful readers will notice occasional entries (only rarely acknowledged by the diarist) that were made some time after the fact. Such entries must suffer from the delay. While portraying his wife Mary very favorably and their marriage as essentially happy, though plagued by the loss of three infant children and their beloved son Whitfield, he reveals little about her. There is also a frustrating lack of elaboration on potentially revealing events. Does "I went to the village to meet with the Sheriff on a matter of business" denote an ordinary legal matter, or something he preferred not to reveal? Couldn't he have elaborated on "The overseer reports that Toney ran away yesterday"? He must have expected that others, if only his kin, would be curious about his journal, and there are occasions, such as young Whitfield's suspension from the South Carolina College, when circumspection trumped candor. He also wrote, without elaboration and without obvious reason, that his father must never read the journal. Only once did a page in his journal prove too revealing for his or his family's comfort. It was cleanly cut out, possibly by him, but more likely by Mary or a descendant after his death. But a candid entry on his disappointment with Preston on Nov 17, 1846, survived the journal's reading by family members.

Since the first volume published here was begun, as Brooks states, to make a record of his family's feud with young Edgefieldian Lewis (later Louis) T. Wigfall, it seems odd that his account omits significant details. The feud was highlighted by two duels – one involving Brooks' brother-in-law James Parsons Carroll and the other his son Preston. The journal includes only the second. It is also silent on two of Wigfall's acts. He fatally shot young Thomas Bird, son of Brooks' sister Lucinda and Daniel Bird, and he apparently challenged Brooks himself, whose rejection precipitated the two duels mentioned above. Less surprising is the omission of the diarist's reaction to Wigfall's challenge, which a contemporary cited as an example of Brooks' impulsiveness. (See Introduction). The explanation could be that he had recorded at least some of these events in the last pages of the previous journal volume, now lost. In any case, the journals we do have are both illuminating and frustrating.

---

[14] Ayers, "Everyman as Master." See also www.vqronline.org/articles/1987/summer/ayers-everyman-as-master/.

Editorial Method

In transcribing the first and third journal volumes my task was to make a complete and accurate copy and to address any uncertainties resulting from Brooks' handwriting or the condition of the manuscript. To give readers a sense of the journals as Brooks created them I left the entries for the first two months, November and December, 1840, intact. Beginning with January, 1841, I deleted what seemed the least essential material, starting with most of Brooks' daily weather reports. While appreciating U. B. Phillips' famous assertion about the importance of weather and climate for understanding the Southern past, I have generally retained Brooks' weather reports only when they were unusual or described weather that altered his plans. Beyond that, my intent was to make deletions based on the priority of enabling readers to understand Whitfield Brooks and his world. Redundancies were thus generally deleted.[15]

Ellipses were used to indicate omitted words or phrases. An ellipsis on a separate line indicates omission of one or more daily entries, as the retention of Brooks' dates confirms. Beyond deletions, Brooks' writing has been generally unaltered except for the sake of clarity. Misspellings, especially of names, were corrected when the reader might not guess correctly. Necessary commas were added silently, although his superfluous commas were generally left alone. Where I had to guess, I bracketed the dubious word or phrase and added a question mark. Except in the middle volume, superscripts were generally brought down to the line, and words he marked through were deleted, except where preserving them might suggest Brooks' thinking. Inadvertent errors such as repeating a word (often at a page break, common at that time) were silently corrected. Words I inserted in the interest of clarity were placed in brackets and italicized. Brooks' page numbers were deleted. His &C was changed to etc. and his cursive *a* (meaning and) to &.[16]

Journal footnotes record basic information about every person mentioned by Brooks (roughly 600) whom I could identify. The notes are appended at the first mention of the name, so those so identified can be located by the first page number after the name in the Index. In compiling these data I relied on the federal census of 1850, Bettis Rainsford's Edgefield history files, the Tompkins Library files, the *Edgefield Advertiser*, John Chapman's *History of Edgefield County* and other secondary sources, and the internet including Ancestry.com. and Newspapers.com. The biggest challenge here was Brooks' practice, in many cases, of identifying people only by their

[15] The opening sentence in *Life and Labor in the Old South*, "Let us begin by discussing the weather," would be understood by anyone who has spent a few hours outdoors during a southern summer, and especially by farmers (Phillips, *Life and Labor in the Old South,* 1). For farmers' perspective on this, see Loehr, "Farmers' Diaries: Their Interest and Value as Historical Sources," 285, AgHist.online.

[16] The transcriber of the second volume generally retained more of Brooks' wording, symbols, and punctuation.

surnames. When the name was common among Edgefieldians it was often impossible to identify with confidence. In such cases I generally relied on age and wealth as indicated in the census record. A question mark in a note alerts readers to my uncertainty, but no doubt I made errors that are not so marked.[17] I greatly appreciate Mercer University Press' policy of using footnotes rather than endnotes for this information.

Acknowledgments

Bettis Cantelou Rainsford introduced me to Whitfield Brooks and many other Edgefieldians, past and present, encouraged me in this project, provided access to his large collection of Edgefield documents, and through innumerable conversations and emails made suggestions and answered questions about the project. If all this were not enough, he coordinated fund-raising for the publisher's subvention. Tricia Price Glenn, who was the Edgefield County Archivist during most of the time I worked on the journal, and Tonya Browder Guy and Vernon Miller of Edgefield's Tompkins Library provided friendly assistance with research materials, as did staff members at the South Carolina Historical Society, the South Caroliniana Library, and the Southern Historical Collection at UNC Chapel Hill. Library staff at Duke University were helpful via their online information system, and the library staff at the University of the South cheerfully made available their rare copies of the early years of the *Edgefield Advertiser*.

Mary Jane Brooks Mobley, Emmett F. Brooks, and their siblings gave me permission to edit and publish the Journal volumes in her possession, and bore with me while the project consumed far too much time. Faye Jensen of the South Carolina Historical Society granted permission to publish the middle volume. The South Carolina State Museum and the McKissick Museum at the University of South Carolina allowed me to include images from their collections. Tim Belshaw made the map. Others who helped in various ways include Tom Baleerski, Steve Berry, Vernon Burton (who made excellent suggestions on the Introduction), Terrence Finnegan, Lacy Ford, Alexia Helsley, Vernon Miller, Dot Mims, David Moltke-Hansen, Mary Allison Brooks Pettigrew, John Pettigrew, Allen Stokes, James "Tray" Welborn, and the "Edgefield History class." Members of the St. George Tucker Society listened to my thoughts about the Brooks Journal and shared theirs. The Watson-Brown Foundation provided a generous research grant. The following Brooks descendants made generous financial contributions toward publication: Carroll H. Brooks, Emmett F. Brooks and Edith B. Brooks, Richard W. Van Gurp, E. Cantey Haile, Jr., E. Mims Mobley and Mary Jane Mobley, Jon and Nancy Newton, John W. Pettigrew and

[17] Alphabetical Excel files of the 1850 census for Edgefield District were kindly provided by Vernon Burton and Terrance Finnegan.

Mary Allison Brooks Pettigrew, Lilla D. McCutchens Richards, and Karen Whitfield. My wife Judy provided equal portions of patience and encouragement throughout the long process that culminated in this book. She may not fully appreciate its keeping me from being an ever-present retired spouse. Mercer University Press was willing to publish a large book not likely to make the bestseller lists. Particular thanks go to Director Marc Jolley, Marsha Luttrell, and Mary Beth Kosowski. To all of these, and any others that I may have overlooked, many thanks. Any editorial errors that eluded detection are my responsibility.

Abbreviations for Journal of Whitfield Brooks

Adv.	Edgefield Advertiser
APB	Andrew Pickens Butler
ECH	Edgefield Court House
FWP	Francis Wilkerson Pickens
m.	Married
MPCB	Mary Parsons Carroll Brooks
PSB	Preston Smith Brooks
SCDAH	South Carolina Department of Archives and History
SCHS	South Carolina Historical Society, Charleston
SCL	South Caroliniana Library, University of South Carolina, Columbia
WB	Whitfield Brooks

INTRODUCTION

Whitfield Brooks' lifetime witnessed the transformation of the South Carolina backcountry, and his life illustrates the effects of that transformation on a man positioned to take advantage of it. At his birth in 1790 most backcountry residents lived hard lives, subsisting on what could be grown, bartered, shot, or caught for their own consumption. With the state's commercial center, Charleston, more than a week away, the occasional peddler and the trading posts in Campbelltown and Augusta were the only sources of commercial goods. By Brooks' fiftieth birthday, in the year these journals began, this scene had been replaced by one of massive cotton farming, a slave labor system whose disappearance whites could imagine only with horror, and an entrenched planter elite whose lives mimicked those of the Lowcountry gentry. At his death in 1851, a decade-long cotton recession had been replaced by a boom, and many in his region were embracing railroads and banking, engines of growth that Brooks had long advocated.[1]

During Brooks's boyhood, the backcountry still lived with the effects of three harrowing events. The Cherokee War of 1760-61, though devastating to the Indians, terrorized the early white settlers. The vigilante "Regulator" movement of the late 1760s turned neighbor against neighbor, often violently. And the Whig-Tory bloodletting of the War for Independence intensified those divisions and left a residue of resentment and suspicion. The result was a legacy of violence that would mark the region for generations. But change was underway. The restraints of civil authority, almost nonexistent before, became more of a reality in the mid-1780s when the legislature divided the vast Ninety Six District into six counties (soon districts). These included Newberry, where Zachariah Smith Brooks (1765-1848) lived as a youth and where his first child, Whitfield, was born, and Edgefield, to which the family moved during the 1790s. By that time, though the majority of Upcountry families continued to subsist in a virtually cashless economy, some, including Zachariah, were acquiring large tracts and a growing number of slaves, and were producing tobacco for European

---

[1] French immigrant Pierre LaBorda opened the first store on ECH around 1800. The following sources will aid readers who want to explore the Brooks Journals' context more deeply: Burton, *In My Father's House Are Many Mansions,* is a comprehensive analysis of 19th-century Edgefield social history based on massive computer-generated data. Its first chapter is the best introduction to the antebellum district. Ford, *Origins of Southern Radicalism,* is an excellent treatment of the antebellum South Carolina Upcountry's evolving economy and politics. Klein, *Unification of a Slave State*; and Downey, *Planting a Capitalist South,* the latter focusing on Edgefield and Barnwell Districts, together cover a century of upcountry development. An older work by a knowledgeable amateur that remains an essential reference is Chapman, *History of Edgefield County. The Story of Edgefield* includes a timeline of Edgefield's history. Wyatt-Brown, *Southern Honor;* and Stowe, *Intimacy and Power,* provide interpretive background on a larger scale.

markets as well as a variety of crops for local consumption. Meanwhile a coarse culture lacking strong community life began yielding to the evangelical intensity of the "Second Great Awakening" of the early 1800s. As Baptist and Methodist churches sprang up, their influence, after briefly challenging slavery and class privilege as inconsistent with the Gospel, shifted to saving souls and smoothing the rough edges of backcountry culture.[2]

By the time Brooks was ready to join the junior class at the South Carolina College in 1810, Eli Whitney's improved cotton gin, patented in 1793, cotton-friendly soil, and an expanding slave labor force had transformed the economy of the lower Upcountry, including the Edgefield District. Now short-staple cotton was king, and a growing number of families were entering the planter class with twenty or more slaves. But, leaving aside the consequences for victims of the African slave trade and their descendants, this was problematic in the long term for South Carolina whites. It mechanized the cleaning of the cotton (removing seeds and husks from the precious fiber), but it *increased* the need for slaves to hand pick the cotton bowls. The resulting rise of the slave population was cause for whites' anxiety, especially when it surpassed the white, as it did in Edgefield District during the 1820s. To this concern a second was added as the southwestern frontier rolled back, expanding cotton's habitat ultimately into Texas. The outmigration of white families and their slaves almost offset South Carolina's natural population increase and created an economic crisis in the Palmetto State.[3]

But in the short run the new technology seemed heaven-sent. Families who had subsisted on small plots could plant cotton, haul it to the closest gin and then across the Savannah to Augusta for sale, and become part of the cash economy. Soon land

---

[2] In labeling the hilly northwestern region of South Carolina, I follow Lacy Ford's usage, in which the frontier "backcountry" evolved into the cotton-dominated "Upcountry" (Ford, *Origins of Southern Radicalism,* viii, 5). The most detailed source on the settlement of the backcountry is still Meriwether, *The Expansion of South Carolina, 1729–1765*, available online via Google Books. See also Edgar, *South Carolina, A History*, 204–207, 211–16, 231–44. On Edgefield's violent culture, see Brown, "South Carolina Extremism and Its Violent Origins," in Brown, ed., *The Strain of Violence*, 67–90. On the brutality of the revolution in South Carolina, see Royster, *Light-Horse Harry Lee,* 34–35. Brannon, *From Revolution to Reunion,* deepens our understanding of the healing of societal wounds in the post-war era. On the brief tobacco boom in Edgefield and the vicinity, see Downey, *Planting a Capitalist South,* 18–19. Z. S. Brooks almost certainly used tobacco profits to buy most of the eight slaves he owned in 1790. On the evolving impact of evangelical Christianity, see Heyrman, *Southern Cross.*

[3] On the chronology of the planters' appearance in the back country and cotton's dramatic impact on their numbers, see Klein, *Unification of a Slave State,* 16, 19, 29, 32, 248–57. Edgefield population figures from the censuses of 1790 and 1830 are in footnote 17. The inaugural issue of *The Edgefield Advertiser*, Feb. 11, 1836, reprinted an article from *The Southern Agriculturalist* (Orangeburg) entitled "The West," which bemoaned the lure of the region "that drains away our population and harms our economy." Robert Mills noted this "push-pull" phenomenon and its effect on Edgefield District's population in *Statistics of South Carolina*, 527.

and slaves, cash and credit, were the *sine qua non* for an increasing number. The cotton factories of England and the New England states were insatiable, and men who kept them fed were able to buy more land and slaves, gain wealth, and possibly join the expanding planter elite. Those less fortunate, or less motivated, either followed the same path on a smaller scale with few if any slaves, forming the yeoman class, or remained outside both the market economy and the social and political world of their "betters."[4]

Aware of their lack of polish, first-generation planters, including Zachariah Brooks, usually provided their children with formal education, land and slaves with which to strive for planter status, and some of the social graces which emulated those of the Lowcountry gentry. If a spouse from an elite Lowcountry family could be acquired, as Whitfield Brooks was fortunate to do, so much the better. Thus, as Brooks vividly revealed in his journal, by the 1840s these changes had produced a cultivated society for those able to enter it, but had yet to banish either the meticulous protocol of the cult of honor among elite men, or the quick resort to ruder violence among those beneath them.[5]

In migrating from Virginia and settling near the Little Saluda River, the Brooks family and their Butler kin followed an established pattern. Others had begun arriving in the late 1740s when treaties with the Cherokee Indians eased fears, prematurely as it turned out, about native resistance to white encroachment. Lured by the colony's offer of free land, they traveled south, most from Virginia and many via the Great Wagon Road, clustered around its temporary terminus, Goudey's trading post at Ninety Six, and spread south and west from there. Other early arrivers included Swiss settlers of New Windsor Township, French Huguenots who settled on Long Cane Creek, and German Palatines on Hard Labor Creek. Meanwhile English colonists migrated

---

[4] Whitfield Brooks' obituary, *Edgefield Advertiser*, Jan. 22, 1852; Klein, *Unification of a Slave State*; and Burton, *In My Father's House Are Many Mansions*, 57–79. Cotton production in the Upcountry rose from a few thousand pounds in 1793, the year Whitney patented his gin, to some 30,000,000 pounds in 1811, and continued upward (Ford, *Origins of Southern Radicalism*, 7–14). A classic description of the rise of a "typical" South Carolina Upcountry planter and wife is Cash, *The Mind of the South*, 15–17. The political consequences of South Carolina's economic crisis of the 1820s are treated in Freehling, *Prelude to Civil War*.

[5] On the evolution of Upcountry agriculture and society, see Ford, *Origins*, pt. 1; Harris, *Plain Folk and Gentry*; and Burton, *In My Father's House*, 14–147. On the role of honor in that society and beyond, see Wyatt-Brown, *Southern Honor*. On its Edgefield manifestations, see Burton, 90–95; and Welborn, "Drinkin', Fightin', Prayin'." On less "honorable" violence, see Gorn, "Gouge and Bite, Pull Hair and Scratch." On planters as parents, see Glover, *Southern Sons*; Censer, *North Carolina Planters and Their Children*; and Williams, *Intellectual Manhood*. Zachariah Brooks' generosity toward his son is documented on his tombstone, which, after praising his honesty, patriotism, and simple tastes, affirms that "to the education and advancement of his children he bestowed his means with judicious liberation" (Z. S. Brooks' grave, Butler United Methodist Church cemetery, Saluda County SC).

from the Carolina Lowcountry, mixing, sometimes uneasily, with the larger numbers of Scots-Irish and others who had moved South. Other English émigrés to the young colony of Georgia came up the Savannah to the fortified settlement at Augusta (founded 1737), and some crossed the river into South Carolina from its western flank. African slaves soon completed the ethnic mix.[6]

Whitfield Brooks' grandfather Elisha Brooks descended through his father Richard's line from ancestors that had been in Virginia for generations. He was born before 1734 in Lunenburg (later Mecklenburg) County, near the North Carolina border. In the spring of 1765 he made preparations for a move, selling a black man and four horses and "the rest of my estate" for £200, along with 600 acres, "all the land he owns on Allen's Creek."[7] He soon left the county owing money to David Christopher and two other men. Since the couple's youngest child Zachariah Smith Brooks was born May 18, 1765, there is room for doubt as to where he first saw the light of day. In 1766 Elisha filed a petition for 400 acres on the south side of "Saludy River" in South Carolina, downstream from "Maxwell's Neck," a horseshoe bend identified on Thomas Anderson's 1817 map of Edgefield District.[8] (See map.)

The family evidently moved soon thereafter. In September, 1767, Elisha was one of three men owning land adjacent to a tract granted to John Walker "on a branch of Cuffytown Creek of Savannah River" (near the later Edgefield - Abbeville District

[6] On Indian deprivations along the Saluda River, see Motes and Motes, *Laurens and Newberry Counties,* 18; Burton, *In My Father's House,* 18–19; and Meriwether, *Expansion of South Carolina,* 66–72, 117–35, 160–62, 251–57. See also Wallace, *The History of South Carolina*, vol. 2, 41–46; Edgar, *South Carolina,* 50, 54–56; and Cashin, *The Story of Augusta*, 13. On the Great Wagon Road, see Breen, "The Great Wagon Road." On the Scots-Irish influence on the piedmont and mountain South, see Fischer, *Albion's Seed,* 605–782.

[7] Mecklenburg County [Virginia] Deed Book 1, page 375. Research in the Brooks genealogy has produced two conflicting family trees, resulting in a perplexing mess that I have not been able to resolve. Katherine B. Elliott, *Early Settlers of Mecklenburg County Virginia* (Southern Historical Press, 1965), has yielded an online genealogical forum, www.genealogy.com/forum/surnames/topics/brooks/11450/, and is the basis for the account that follows here. An alternate version is found in Donna Yarborough, "It All Began with Moses," typescript in the Tompkins Library, Edgefield SC, which names Z. S. Brooks' parents as James Brooks and Elizabeth Smith. See also www.findagrave.com/cgi-bin/fg.cgi?page=gr&Grid=54961027. Thomas Stallworth's and Ida Brooks Kellam's research on the Brooks family and others supports this ancestry. See Brooks file in Tompkins Library. I find the first account more convincing, although the Yarborough record offers an explanation for the source of Zachariah Smith Brooks' middle name (or was Elisha's wife Frances also named Smith, or was he married twice?). Another confusing issue is Zachariah's birthplace (Mecklenburg County, Virginia, Chatham County, North Carolina, or Newberry and Edgefield South Carolina). The spottiness of migration records from this period allows the disputes to continue, as with the longstanding one between the Carolinas over the 1767 birthplace of the most famous of these migrants, Andrew Jackson.

[8] On Elisha Brooks' first South Carolina land grant, see Holcomb, "Petitions for Land from the South Carolina Council Journals," 39.

line). And in November, 1769 Elisha and Frances Brooks "of South Carolina" sold 300 acres, "part of 400 acres, originally granted to Brooks on February 13, 1768 . . . on 96 Mile Creek." Presumably farming while land-speculating, Elisha soon added wagon building to his business interests. He and a partner, John Satterwhite, also from Lunenburg County, co-owned a "waggoning" business from 1773 to 1779. He no doubt continued to plant, but in diversifying his financial interests he likely served as a model for later members of the Brooks family. He died in 1782, leaving an estate of which Frances was administrator, that, if records are correct, was massive for its time.[9]

Elisha and Frances Brooks' sons William Elisha (called Elisha), Bartley, Dudley, and Zachariah, came with their parents. Zachariah made his first mark in South Carolina during the Revolution, as an impetuous junior member of a militia company on the eastern side of the Saluda River (in modern Newberry County). Joining at about sixteen, in 1781, he soldiered for at least a year, and earned notice by his brash courage. While serving under Major Samuel Hammond (1757-1842) he volunteered for a risky assault against an enemy force, but was likely saved from injury or death when Hammond overruled another officer and forbad the maneuver. Brooks rose to the rank of lieutenant by the end of the war, and was a militia colonel during the War of 1812.[10]

In 1786, Zachariah, now twenty-one, bought from the state two tracts of land in modern Newberry County. The first was a horseshoe shaped 1,112 acre tract bordering the Saluda River on its eastern side for which he paid £25, 18s, 11d. The plat shows it to be the Maxwell's Neck tract, a mile upstream from "Chappel's Ferry" and near the land his father had obtained twenty years earlier. The second tract, 240 acres, was on "Both Sides of Little River Waters of Saludy" a tributary that enters the river from the north, downstream from the first. In 1789 Brooks married Elizabeth Butler (1766-1802), a daughter of James Butler and Mary Simpson who had also migrated from Virginia. The family is recorded as living in Newberry District in 1790, the year of Whitfield Brooks' birth, but sometime in the 1790s they moved across the Saluda to the Edgefield District. Now parents of a son, Whitfield, and three daughters, they were apparently "squatting" for a few years. An 1804 grant of 127 ½ acres "on the waters of Big Creek" in northern Edgefield District, near where some of the Butlers

---

[9] See wc.rootsweb.ancestry.com/cgi-bin/igm.cgi?op=GET&DB=wgbrooks&id=16267. Could the date 1768 on this entry be a typographical error and the tract be Brooks' original 400 acres granted in 1766? The 400 acres suggests a family of six: 100 acres each for two adults and 50 for each of four children. The £14,000 value of his estate may be a clerical error.

[10] See Zachariah Smith Brooks' pension application S9294, Nov. 31, 1832, SCDAH; and Chapman, *Edgefield County,* 44, 47, 56. His service in the cause of independence may be appreciated from the fact that he was asked by Hammond to vouch for the reliability of that war hero's pension application, because "the hand of time" had not been kind to the documents Hammond submitted in October 1832. Copy of Hammond's application in files of Bettis C. Rainsford, Edgefield. On Hammond, see Chapman, *Edgefield County,* 130–39.

had settled, made Zachariah a landowner there. He was still living at "Brooks Hill" on Big Creek, near its confluence with Persimmon Creek, when he died in 1848.[11]

Zachariah's bride had lost her father, Captain James Butler, in a merciless episode of Revolutionary War blood-letting, on November 17, 1781. Although not yet recovered from his imprisonment by British authorities in the Provost Dungeon in Charleston, where he was held for refusing to sign a pledge to oppose the revolution, he volunteered for militia duty at the urging of his son James. Celebrating at a tavern on Cloud's Creek after their success against a Tory force – ignoring Butler's advice that they push on – the company was surprised by "Bloody Bill" Cunningham's Tory Brigade. Father and son were among twenty-eight men massacred after trying to surrender. Elizabeth's brother, Captain William Butler, led the force that defeated Cunningham's Brigade, though its commander eluded them.[12] This likely gave Butler, an uncle of Whitfield Brooks, the edge needed to win a seat in the United States House of Representatives.[13]

Zachariah's older brother Elisha, born in 1761, had married Nancy Butler, Elizabeth's sister, in Edgefield County in 1786, so Zachariah's and Elizabeth's wedding wove these families together with double strands. Elisha and Nancy were living in northern Newberry District in 1790, where he owned five slaves. They would give Whitfield several cousins who would reside in Newberry and Abbeville Districts. He saw them infrequently, but was happy to renew those ties. The Butler family would produce cousins who connected Whitfield to generations of South Carolina military and political leaders, adding luster to the Brooks name as well.[14]

---

[11] Deeds and grants with plats showing Z. S. Brooks held tracts on both sides of the Saluda are in State Grants, vol. 15, 148; State Plats, vol. 1, 35; State Grants, vol. 15, 232; State Plats, vol. 9, 511; State Grants, vol. 50, 288; and State Plats, vol. 40, 256; SCDAH. The Census of 1800 lists Zachariah Brooks among residents of Edgefield District. The 1817 Thomas Anderson map of Edgefield District, improved by Robert Mills in 1825, which identifies the tract Brooks bought in 1786 as "Maxwell's Neck," shows the "Col. Z. S. Brooks" residence, near the fork of Big Creek and Persimmon Creek, some four miles from the Saluda River, and two Butler residences a mile away across Big Creek. See Chapman, *History of Edgefield*, 173, on the Butlers' residence; and 191, on Maxwell's Neck. On "Brooks Hill," see Motte Yarborough, "Some of James Butler's Descendants," Brooks file, Tompkins Library, Edgefield. The Butler homesite was where the Butler United Methodist Church, northeast of Saluda, South Carolina, on Highway 194, now stands.

[12] O'Neall, *Biographical Sketches of Bench and Bar*, 473; and Lumpkin, *From Savannah to Yorktown*, 52–53. See also Chapman, *History of Edgefield County*, 30–41.

[13] Chapman, *Edgefield*, 68–71; and Butler, *Biographical Directory of the United States House of Representatives*, 929.

[14] On the illustrious Butler family's place in Edgefield and South Carolina history, which almost led to Saluda County being named Butler, see Chapman, *Edgefield*, 30–46, 66–70, 171–72. U.S. Census, 1790, Newberry County. Elisha Brooks, Sr., died before May 1782 in what would soon be Edgefield County, and his wife Frances before August 1791 in Edgefield or Newberry.

Zachariah's and Elizabeth Brooks' family included, in addition to Whitfield, three girls who survived to maturity, Lucinda, Behethland, and Nancy. A fourth, Eliza, died in 1802 before her fourth birthday. Elizabeth died in childbirth in 1802 or 1803, about a year after the loss of Eliza, bringing grief and a burden all too common for families of that era. If Zachariah was seeking to ease that burden by marrying again, he must have been disappointed. Whitfield's stepmother remains mysterious. She is identified in some records as Lucretia Bell and in others as Frances (no surname), and there is a mention of a "marriage settlement Feb. 3, 1824" in one genealogical account. Whatever the story behind this, Whitfield never mentions a stepmother in his journal, but it is full of veneration for his "Aunt Butler," who apparently became his surrogate mother. She was Behethland Foote Moore, wife of General William Butler, pursuer of "Bloody Bill" and Congressman. Their children included Congressman William Butler (1790-1850) Senator Andrew Pickens Butler (1796-1857) and Governor Pierce Mason Butler, (1798-1847). Their mother is described in accounts of the Butler family as an extraordinary woman.[15]

Living through most of the backcountry—Upcountry transition described above, the Butler-Brooks generation preceding Whitfield Brooks likely shared their neighbors' resentment of the dismissive attitudes of many Lowcountry nabobs toward backcountry grievances. Those memories kept the vast majority of backcountry men on the sidelines in the fight for independence until Redcoat and Tory brutality drove many into the rebel ranks. A few years later the diarist's forebears joined most of their neighbors in opposing the United States Constitution, in contrast to the largely federalist views of the Lowcountry gentry. Whitfield Brooks' generation would return to this theme of fear of power in faraway hands with the nullification and secession movements.[16]

---

[15] Elliott, *Early Settlers of Mecklenburg County;* and www.genealogy.com/forum/surnames/topics/brooks/11450/. The Butler Methodist Church cemetery inventory gives Elizabeth's death date as 1802. The Brooks family Bible states that she "departed this life in the autumn of 1803." Copy in files of Bettis Rainsford. A genealogical account titled "Descendants of Elisha Brooks," while confusing at some points, states that Z. S. Brooks also married Lucretia Bell (1757–1822), daughter of Benjamin Bell, and adds that Lucretia is buried next to her first husband, William Daniel, at the Daniel home place in Saluda County. Also verifying a second wife are WB's obituary, *Advertiser*, Jan. 22, 1852, which refers to Elizabeth Butler as Z. S. Brooks' first wife. See also John and Charles Bulow to Major Zack S. Brooks, Dec. 15, 1808 (several years after Elizabeth's death), mentioning cotton of "Mrs. Brooks," in Chapman, 410. The lost child was named William Butler. On Behethland Foote Moore Butler, for whom Zachariah and Elizabeth Brooks named a daughter, see "Who Is Behethland Butler?" at www.lchr.org/a/35/bw/butler.html.

[16] Brown, *The Regulator Movement;* Edgar, *South Carolina,* 203, 215, 223, 251–53; and Chapman, *Edgefield,* 188. Among the Anti-federalist delegates to the 1788 convention, which

With the explosion in Upcountry cotton production and slave ownership, the interests and values of the leading men in the two sections became more closely aligned, and differences faded. Edgefield District census figures between 1790 and 1830 reflect, as dramatically as those of any Upcountry district, the rise of the cotton plantation and the planter class. In 1790 Zachariah Brooks' eight slaves placed him among the fifty largest Newberry District slaveholders. The largest owned twenty-four. By 1800 his work force numbered twelve. In December, 1808, in the only such record known, he consigned, in one lot, fifteen cotton bales weighing 4,679 pounds, eight of which belonged to the mysterious second "Mrs. Brooks," to be sold by Charleston merchants John and Charles Bulow, and ordered from them "sundry store goods" costing a substantial £55, 11s, 6d. By 1820 his household, likely depleted by a gift of slaves to the recently wedded Whitfield, included twenty-four male and sixteen female slaves.[17]

These assets enabled the elder Brooks to enjoy a lifestyle shared by few in the Upcountry. Although his son described his tastes as "simple," John Chapman recalled from his youth that Zachariah Brooks had "the only carriage" in his neighborhood. "It seemed to me to be a very grand sort of life to be able to ride to church in a two horse carriage with a servant driving," he added. "And when the carriage stopped to have him let the steps down and help the master out!" Chapman added, "[h]e was in partnership with James Abney in a store."[18]

Seeing such changes, the Lowcountry leaders became more amenable to Upcountry demands and loosened their hold on political power during the early 1800s. Those concessions went far to mend intrastate animosity, and the rise of North-South tensions over federal tariffs and slavery fostered a siege mentality which drew the state's two regions together against a common antagonist. Whitfield Brooks' journal suggests that by the 1840s little of the earlier tension remained.[19]

---

ratified the U.S. Constitution, were William Butler and Arthur Simkins, who is regarded as the founder of the town of Edgefield.

[17] In 1790 the Edgefield District had 9,605 white and 3,684 black residents, the latter virtually all slaves. Those numbers for Newberry were 8,198 and 1,144 (Pope, *History of Newberry County,* vol. 1, 58). In 1830 Edgefield's numbers were 14,957 and 15,522 (Burton, *In My Father's House,* 20). Only Fairfield District, east of Newberry, had a larger percentage of blacks among Upcountry Districts in 1830 (Ford, *Origins of Radicalism,* 45). Klein, *Unification of a Slave State* describes this process in detail. Zachariah Brooks' census slave numbers are available online at FamilySearch.org. See for 1790 Newberry County SC, page 76; for 1800 Edgefield County SC, page 137; and for 1820 Edgefield County SC, page 48. For his cotton consignment and purchases, which would have included 55 pounds of salt had the price been acceptable, see Chapman, *Edgefield,* 410. (The cotton shipment and the goods with the merchants' reply were delivered by Brooks' slave "Saint.")

[18] Chapman, *History of Edgefield County,* 50. Unsigned biographical sketch of ZSB in Brooks file, Tompkins Library.

[19] Sellers, *The Market Revolution,* treats this process on the national level. Concessions to the rising Upcountry included moving the State House from Charleston to Columbia, more

* * *

Zachariah's only son, Whitfield's prospects were enhanced by two advantages denied to his father—a college and legal education and a Lowcountry wife who brought social and financial assets to their marriage. Starting at an "old field school," he progressed to the respected Methodist-supported Mt. Bethel Academy in Newberry District, then headed by Elisha Hammond, father of James Henry Hammond. "For a year [he] read law in the office of his uncle, Stanmore Brooks Butler, then Clerk of Edgefield." Next he prepared for the South Carolina College at Willington Academy in western Abbeville District (now McCormick County), "the greatest and most famous of all the academies in South Carolina." There he was subjected to the Spartan regimen and rigorous academics imposed on a long list of future state leaders by the Rev. Moses Waddel (1770-1840).[20]

The Willington springboard gained Whitfield admission to the junior class at the South Carolina College in 1810, and he finished near the top of the class of 1812. College classmates included congressman and *Charleston Mercury* founder Henry Laurens Pinckney, Edgefield lawyer, congressman, governor and senator George McDuffie, and Brooks' lifelong friends John Belton O'Neall of Newberry and William Campbell Preston of Virginia (later Columbia). O'Neall rose to be chief justice of the state, and was a courageous Unionist and temperance reformer. Preston, briefly a Whig, became a U.S. senator and South Carolina College president. Brooks presumably named his first son for him.[21]

---

fairly distributing seats in the lower house, extending voting rights to all adult white males, and establishing the South Carolina College in Columbia so Upcountry planters' sons could be educated beside those of rice nabobs. This resulted in many intersectional alliances. On the further unifying effect of upcountry-lowcountry marriages, see Klein, *Unification of a Slave State*, 266–67.

[20] Vernon Burton describes the rise of Edgefield's antebellum elite from two starting points: the Middle Atlantic colonies and the South Carolina Lowcountry. See *In My Father's House,* 65–66; on Brooks' path, see his obituary, *Edgefield Advertiser,* January 22, 1852. See also, Meriwether, *History of Higher Education in South Carolina,* 37–40. For a hint as to Zachariah Brooks' capacity for providing his son with advantages, see Chapman, *History of Edgefield,* 410. Mt. Bethel, opened by Bishop Francis Asbury in 1795, had some seventy-five students in its prime and provided all of the students in the original class at the South Carolina College. Kibler, *Our Fathers' Fields*, 30. *SC Encyclopedia*, 120.

[21] Brooks' obituary, *Advertiser*. See also LaBorde, *History of the South Carolina College*, 531. On McDuffie, see O'Neall, *Biographical Sketches,* vol. 2, 463–68. On O'Neall, see SC Ency., 683–84. On Preston, see *SC Ency.,* 754. Other Willington boys who were admitted to college as juniors included Augustus Longstreet (Yale), Patrick Noble (Princeton), George McDuffie, David and Francis Wardlaw, and James Petigru (South Carolina). Brooks' cousins Andrew Pickens Butler and Pierce Mason Butler also studied at Willington, as did his son Preston. David and Robert Means were in the S.C. College class of 1813, so Brooks was ac-

The War of 1812 briefly preempted Brooks' career plans as he became a state militia officer, but by 1815 his studies at Litchfield Law School in Connecticut (following the example of Calhoun and others), his family's connections, and further legal training in the office of Congressman Eldred Simkins in Edgefield led to his election by the state legislature to a newly created judicial position. In 1814 the legislature created a new circuit, based in Edgefield, for Commissioners in Equity who "heard petitions from individuals who alleged that the normal judicial procedures had failed to treat them fairly." Their courts operated "parallel to, but distinct from the courts of law," and rather than being bound by precedent, decided based on "rules of equity and good conscience."[22] Election so young to such a position suggests that Brooks had, in addition to good connections, an early reputation for wisdom and fairness. He held the post until 1832, when health concerns led him to resign, and was, according to a fellow jurist, "a model commissioner."[23]

In addition to his official duties, Brooks practiced law, first in partnership with his cousin George Butler (1786-1826), son of General William Butler and his wife Behethland, (who may have provided the first home of newlyweds Whitfield and Mary—see below) and then with his neighbor, future Chancellor Francis Hugh Wardlaw (1800-1861). His legal practice introduced him to attorneys in surrounding districts, lifting his profile among influential men beyond Edgefield. Some of these would be in the state House of Representatives with him in the early 1830s. By 1840, when he began the first surviving volume of his Journal, his law practice had become less active as his farming interests expanded.[24]

---

quainted with Preston's two fathers-in-law. There was a Preston Brooks in the Newberry District census of 1790, so the assumption about W. C. Preston is uncertain (Meriwether, *History of Higher Education*, 40–42; and www.genealogytrails.com/scar/1805to1905USC.htm).

[22] On Eldred Simkins, see Chapman, *Edgefield*, 188–90. On the office of Commissioner in Equity, see Helsley and Stauffer, *South Carolina Court Records: An Introduction for Genealogists,* SCDAH, 17–18. Commissioners were required, under risk of forfeiture of a $20,000 bond "provided by three to five sureties," to "make all sales ordered by the…court, and execute conveyances pursuant thereto" (*Statutes at Large of South Carolina, 1840,* 119). See also https://archive.org/details/statutesatlargeo07edit. On Litchfield Law School, see www.litchfieldhistoricalsociety.org/ledger/students/432.

[23] O'Neall, *Biographical Sketches*, vol. 2, 473–75. Such praise should be balanced with the recollection of an *Edgefield Advertiser* writer of an old Edgefield hotel "of some thirty years ago [when] Butler and Wardlaw and Griffin and McDuffie and Jeter…and Brooks and Addison…sowed their wild oats" (*Adv.*, 1851, quoted in *The Story of Edgefield*, 59). Not everyone approved of the equity courts. To Governor John Lide Wilson, they were "that Hydra of despotism" in a "contest for supremacy" with the "courts of common law" (Wilson, Message No. 1, Nov. 22, 1824, Governors' Messages, SCDAH).

[24] Brooks' obituary. His journals, while full of farm doings, rarely summarize a year's production. But see the entry for Feb. 25, 1841, and the description of his plantation in the *Proceedings of the Agricultural Society of South Carolina*, 1845, Appendix.

Brooks "followed the script" of second generation elite Upcountry scions in another way. Following the example of John C. Calhoun, he married Lowcountry heiress Mary Parsons Carroll (1800-1870) on June 16, 1818. The wedding took place in St. Paul's Episcopal Church, a new house of worship in the Radcliffeborough neighborhood of Charleston.[25] It was a major social event, for the Carrolls were well connected and well heeled, and Mary was quite a catch. Her great-uncle, Irish-born James Parsons (1724-1779) had been a member of the Council of Safety and the crucial Committee on Correspondence (with other colonies). He was Speaker of the Assembly in the critical year 1776, and briefly the Vice President of South Carolina under President John Rutledge in 1777-78. He held over 22,000 acres in royal grants, and died without surviving children, leaving an estate valued at £1,981,331. Mary's mother, Mary Giles Carroll, (1782-1851) benefited financially from her marriage into this family; she was a large slaveholder.[26]

In courting Mary, Whitfield no doubt had stiff competition from the sons of the Lowcountry elite. His father, impressive as his rise to planter status had been, would not have had entre into Charleston society, where "No gentleman was ever born above tidewater" was once a given. How he beat out Mary's other suitors we cannot know, although appointment to the office of Commissioner in Equity at twenty-four was in his favor. As to how they met and his opportunity to court her, that may be surmised from James Parsons' vast Upcountry land holdings – at least sixteen in the old Ninety Six District. One of these, "Mount Parsons," is mentioned in Brooks' Journal among his holdings. Historian John Edmunds, who researched portions of Brooks' journal in the 1980s, found evidence that the Carroll family summered in Edgefield, offering Whitfield opportunities to court Mary.[27]

Though they make clear his devotion to her, Brooks' journals are disappointingly cryptic about Mary. We may catch a sense of her upbringing from the epitaph of her mother Mary Giles Carroll, who came to Edgefield soon after her husband's death and lived next door to Whitfield and Mary for some thirty years. Conforming to the extravagant verbal taste of that day, her tombstone inscription conveys a striking image: "A masculine intellect, an admirable judgment, an extraordinary energy

---

[25] Brooks family Bible, photocopy in files of Bettis Rainsford. St. Paul's would become known as "the planters' church." See also www.charlestonfootprints.com/charleston-blog/st-luke...st-pauls.../13/.

[26] Edgar et al., *Biographical Directory of the South Carolina House of Representatives,* vol. 3 (1775–1790), 195, 539, 667. Rogers, ed., *Papers of Henry Laurens,* vol. 7, 135; Chesnutt, ed., *Papers of Henry Laurens*, vol. 11, 196 n. 2, 463. Wallace, *History of South Carolina*, vol. 3, 496. Mary Giles Carroll owned seventy-three slaves in 1850 (1850 slave census, Edgefield District).

[27] For the snobbish quotation, Wright, *The Atlantic Frontier,* 292. Bettis Rainsford found in the Edgefield County Archives sixteen land transactions in which James Parsons obtained property in Ninety Six District. Emily Strother Dunovant McCutcheon (1915–1997), a great-granddaughter of Ellen Brooks Dunovant, told Rainsford that the property the Brookses named "Roselands" had been granted to James Parsons and inherited by Mary (https://archives.org/.../2015.117527). On John Edmunds' research, see *Advertiser,* Feb. 17, 1988.

and dignity...a Christian humility, and...a maternal love the truest and tenderest." The most detailed published description of Mary Brooks portrays her as an aged widow plantation mistress. It is in a paean to the Old South and The Confederacy, "'Old Miss' on the Old Plantation," by her grandson Ulysses R. Brooks. Here she serves as an epitome of the elite white women of the South who through acts of religious obligation lifted an inferior race to a modicum of civilization. She heard the complaints and supplications of her work force, then asked for the overseer, saying "I will tell him what to do." She conducted Sunday School, including catechism memorization, for the plantation children in the "big house," using biscuits as rewards for good students. When war came she outfitted two companies for the Confederate forces, both raised by her son Hampden.[28]

Mary seems to have exemplified the classic southern lady whose identity and role was rooted in her family and community. Her piety was remarked on by her contemporaries, while one upcountry woman faulted her for being an overly refined Charleston lady. Her artistic talent is revealed in the flag she made for the Edgefield Huzzars during the near-military encounter with Andrew Jackson's U.S. government over Nullification, in artistic sketches, including an impressive one of a horse, and the small Church of the Redeemer whose construction at Roselands she oversaw. She had practical abilities as well. She and Whitfield must have talked extensively about his farming operations, and probably about slave management as well, for she carried out those responsibilities, with the help of an overseer, for the eighteen years between his death and hers, including the war and post-war eras, "making money every year." Relatives recalled that other widowed plantation mistresses sought her advice, and her slaves revered her.[29]

In another nostalgic look back at Mary she is described as "a woman of discernment, shrewd business tact, and of large sympathies" about whom "traditions...linger yet in the community more than 50 years after her death." The writer added that her youngest son "Ham Brooks always told me that he owed everything to his mother's training." Describing the couple's last home, Roselands, "eight or nine miles below Old Ninety Six," the writer drew a charming picture of "[t]he large plantation house [facing] a flower garden, once tenderly cared for and exquisitely kept," and went on to portray a veritable showplace—testimony to Mary's love of natural beauty.[30]

---

[28] Mary Giles Carroll's tombstone, Willowbrook Cemetery, Edgefield. See U. R. Brooks, *Stories of the Confederacy*, 44–50. Her grandson wrote that during and after the war other widows sought Mary's advice on plantation management. On widowed planter wives generally, see Wood, *Slaveholding Widows*.

[29] Fox-Genovese, *Within the Plantation Household;* Cantey Haile personal collection; and U. R. Brooks, *Stories of the Confederacy*, 44–50. Mary's photograph is on page 45. WB's reliance on Mary is clear from his Journal, in one instance in particular.

[30] Unsigned article, *Advertiser*, Nov. 22, 1922 (http://newspapers.com/image/72158796). Davidson, *The Last Foray*, 155, includes "Roselands" on a list of the most impressive upcountry plantations, along with F. W. Pickens' "Edgewood" and J. H. Hammond's "Redcliffe." All three survive, though Edgewood has been moved to the campus of USC Aiken and altered.

The newlyweds began married life in Edgefield. Their first residence may have belonged to Whitfield's cousin Stanmore Butler, who owned several Edgefield houses at that time. Their second home, now known as the Brooks-Tompkins House, was their base from 1825 to 1849. Young lawyer Waddy Thompson, Jr. (1798-1868), husband of Whitfield's cousin Emmala Butler (1800-1848), bought the Cambridge Road lot in 1820 and built the impressive house, between present-day Brooks and Carroll Streets. He sold it, with 9 ¾ acres, to Whitfield after deciding to return to his boyhood home, Greenville, where his political gifts led him to Congress and to diplomatic service in Mexico. The Brooks home and others with classical elements, including Halcyon Grove, Holmewood, Carroll Hill and the Adams-Mims House, would later earn the street the label "the Appian way."[31]

Two of Brooks' sisters would be among his and Mary's Cambridge Road neighbors, at least for a few years. Behethland Brooks Simkins (1793-1864) bought a house on the street in 1822 after the death of her husband, Jesse Simkins. Lucinda Brooks (1791-1826) became her sister's next door neighbor in 1825 when her husband, lawyer and large landowner Daniel Bird, Jr. (1784-1865) built the "magnificent mansion" later known as Halcyon Grove. After Lucinda's tragic death in 1826, leaving Bird with four small children, he found a new wife next door, marrying Behethland in 1827, forming a family with eight children. The extended family enclave was broken in 1829 when Bird sold Halcyon Grove to Francis W. Pickens. Within a few years the Birds moved to Jefferson County, Florida. They would return and Bird would build another of Edgefield's iconic houses, Oakley Park, on the southeastern edge of town, in 1835, only to leave permanently for Florida in the late 1840s.[32]

Whether Zachariah Brooks helped Whitfield in the purchase of his house has not been determined, although the appreciative words on his father's grave marker and in his journal suggest this. As a lawyer and Commissioner in Equity for a decade

---

[31] Rainsford, *Halcyon Grove,* n. 19; Brooks family Bible, photocopy in files of Bettis C. Rainsford, Edgefield; Preston Smith Brooks' grave marker, stating that he was born in Edgefield in 1819, Willowbrook Cemetery, Edgefield; and Rainsford, *Celebrating Halcyon Grove,* 11–12. Waddy Thompson would become a three-term Whig Congressman and Minister to Mexico, and opponent of the U.S.-Mexican War (*South Carolina Encyclopedia*, 958–59). Rainsford suspects that one of Edgefield's early-mid-20th-century historians, Hortense Woodson or Mamie Tillman, gave the street its Roman appellation, or it could have been local editor James T. Bacon.

[32] Rainsford, *Halcyon Grove,* 14–16, 19–22. Whitfield Brooks acted as a trustee for his sister Behethland's property in a marriage contract between the couple, probably to protect his sister's rights (*Halcyon Grove*, 20 n. 93). In a similar act of neighborliness, Brooks became the guardian of Edmund Bacon's minor children after his death in 1826 (Dorothy Mims to Bettis Rainsford, Jan. 7, 1996, Rainsford's file on James Parsons Carroll). The departure of the Birds illustrates the interest in new frontiers among that generation of South Carolinians. Between 1800 and 1850, roughly half of the whites born there moved away (Tommy Rogers, "The Great Population Exodus from South Carolina, 1850–1860"). Halcyon Grove was the home of former governor Andrew Pickens Jr. during the 1830s.

Whitfield could have contributed substantially in any case. There is less uncertainty about paternal generosity regarding the nineteen slaves that Whitfield owned two years after his marriage. And that number, more than a household would need, indicates that while practicing law he was operating a farm, probably on land provided by either his father or mother-in-law, or both.[33]

To a reader of his Journals, Whitfield Brooks' interest in religion is clear, as is his Episcopal identity, though his early influences were primarily Methodist. His father was "a regular attendant" at Persimmon Creek (later Zoar) Methodist Church, probably took Whitfield and his sisters to that church, and may have named his only son for the charismatic and controversial English evangelist George Whitefield. In October, 1831 Whitfield joined his brother-in-law Daniel Bird, Jr., "a leader of the Methodist Church in the region," and three other prominent Edgefieldians, in calling for bids on constructing a new Edgefield Methodist church, replacing the small one in Pottersville. Before that, the only house of worship in the village was the Baptists,' constructed in 1823 during the ministry of the soon-to-be prominent Rev. Basil Manly (1802-1845). Whether or not Brooks' signature beneath the call for bids indicates, as some surmise, that he was a deacon in that congregation, he clearly endorsed that expansion of religious life in his community. As the Methodists were one of the two dynamic evangelical denominations, along with the Baptists, in the early nineteenth century, Brooks' early exposure to that powerful religious current should be taken into account when considering the religious element of his Journal.[34] His

---

[33] In 1820 Whitfield Brooks' household included eleven male and eight female slaves, some he almost certainly could not have bought (U.S. Census of 1820, Edgefield District, 48, www.FamilySearch.org).

[34] If Chalmers Davidson and Edward Crowther are correct, Brooks was a typical Carolina planter in being religious (Davidson, *The Last Foray,* ch. 3); Crowther, "Holy Hornet." See also, Chapman, *History of Edgefield County,* 50, 295; Brooks' obituary; and the Brooks family Bible. Zachariah and Elizabeth Brooks' graves, in the Butler family section of Butler United Methodist Church cemetery in Saluda County, hint at their denominational affiliation. A Brooks cousin was named John Wesley Brooks, a stronger hint. JWB's impressive 1815 house, Scotch Cross, stands on US 25 two miles south of Greenwood, South Carolina (*The Carolinian*, Oct. 22, 1831, cited in Rainsford, "Celebrating Halcyon Grove," 21–22). As a youth Whitfield probably heard sermons by George Daugherty, Lewis Myers, or Reddick Pierce, Presiding Elders of the Saluda Methodist Circuit, and possibly by the celebrated itinerate Lorenzo Dow. Daugherty was once "mistakenly" identified as anti-slavery (as many early Methodists were) and almost drowned by a Charleston mob (Chapman, *Edgefield County,* 290–95). See also, Hortense Woodson, *History of the Edgefield Baptist Association,* 211–213.

On George Whitefield (1714–1770), sometimes "Whitfield" and pronounced as such, a Calvinist Anglican associate of John Wesley who defended slavery and preached in South Carolina intermittently, see Fox-Genovese and Genovese, *The Mind of the Master Class*, 232, 328, 506. Another possible namesake is Capt. George Whitefield, Jr., a nephew of the evangelist. He prudently surrendered British Fort Charlotte on the Savannah to James Mayson's Whig militia force on July 12, 1775. Mayson later wrote: "Capt. Whitefield did everything an officer religious sensibility is also evident in his reading tastes. The journal mentions published sermons and theological essays most often, along with Shakespeare, James Fenimore Cooper, Alexis de Tocqueville, Charles Dickens, Eugene Sue, and lives of Revolutionary War heroes Charles Lee and Nathaniel Greene.[35]

In the early 1830s Rev. Edward Ford, rector of St. Paul's Episcopal Church, Augusta, began holding quarterly services in Edgefield, and in 1833 Rev. Christian Hanckel of St. Pauls, Charleston, Mary's family's church, visited and encouraged the election of wardens and a vestry. These included Brooks, Edmund B. Bacon, John S. Jeter, Francis Pickens, and Arthur T. Wigfall (brother of Lewis Trezevant Wigfall). Soon after its sanctuary's completion a visitor to Trinity Church declared "the interior of this little Church is surpassed in beauty and effect by none in the upper sections of our state...." In its first few years the small congregation was served intermittently by clergymen including Wigfall (one month, April, 1840), Carter Page, R. D. Shindler, Edward Reed, (a Brooks favorite) and E. T. Walker. Rev. Bruce Walker offered the first stable leadership, pastoring from 1845 to 1849. Brooks' journal sheds light on these men and his perspective on their service.[36]

---

could do without Power and he Submitted...with a grace that will do him honour—his Centiments (sic) seem to be much in favour of the...Council of Safety" (*South Carolina Historical & Genealogical Magazine* 1/1 [January 1900]: 45). See also, Logan, *History of the Upper Country of South Carolina*, vol. 1, 315–17. The 1790 census lists this George Whitfield as a resident of Abbeville District, with a household of nine and 24 slaves (*The* [Edgefield] *Carolinian*, Oct. 22, 1831, cited in Rainsford, "Celebrating Halcyon Grove," 21–22). See also Woodson, *History of the Edgefield Baptist Association*, 211–13. For whatever reason, WB attended the Baptist church more than the Methodist when no service was held at Trinity Episcopal.

[35] Historians' assessment of the Old South's reading and thinking has become more positive, but the well-read southerners pointed to are mainly ministers, teachers, and lawyers. Michael O'Brien observes that with rare exceptions planters seemed to agree that they had "no business with books" (O'Brien, *All Clever Men Who Make Their Way*, 19–20, 311). For an examination of the Old South's intellectual class, see O'Brien's two-volume *Conjectures of Order*. For the broader world of Southern thought, see Fox-Genovese and Genovese, *The Mind of the Master Class*.

[36] Dalcho, *The Protestant Episcopal Church in South Carolina*, 550. "At a meeting of the vestry on Saturday, April 11, 1840, present Messrs. Brooks, Wardlaw, Carroll, Means, Meigs, and Terry, the Rev. Arthur Wigfall was unanimously elected to take charge of Trinity church.... Tue. May 5, 1840, Wigfall submitted his resignation...to Whitfield Brooks in order to accept an invitation from the Parish of Clarendon. Accepted" (Sarah R. Collett, "Trinity Episcopal Church in Edgefield," *Advertiser*, Feb. 12 1936 [centennial issue]). Alvy King's assertion that Lewis Wigfall's feud with the Brooks family resulted from his belief that they blocked his brother's path to the Trinity pulpit may be correct, but not if A.W. wanted to move or his bishop reassigned him. WB's comments in his Journal are not conclusive. On Trinity's history, see the late Dorothy Mims' files in possession of the Lovick Mims family, Edgefield, and files of Bettis C. Rainsford, Edgefield. Although Brooks was a long-time vestryman and warden, he was not confirmed as a member until late in life, not unusual in that day. Mary

Whitfield and Mary worshiped weekly in Edgefield throughout the years covered by his journal, unless prevented by weather or health. When no priest was available at Trinity they attended the Baptist or Methodist services. (Somewhat curiously, Edgefield District, with a smaller percentage of Scots-Irish or Huguenot settlers than other Upcountry Districts, had no Presbyterian church until 1877). Edgefield Baptist was served during the 1840s by denominational luminary William Bullein Johnson, the last president of the General [American] Baptist Convention (1841-44) and the first of the Southern Baptist Convention (1845-51). He was a supporter of education and a founder of what became Furman University, originally located in Edgefield village. Clearly no mean figure, he more than once left Brooks bemoaning what he considered a rudimentary sermon or a repulsive bigotry. While Brooks' presence in these houses of worship speaks loudly on the place of Christianity in his life, these and other disparaging journal observations offer telling commentary on his taste and theology.[37]

Upcountry Baptist and Methodist churches attracted worshipers of all social strata and both races, so Brooks saw some of his social peers when he attended these churches. But the larger number of yeomen and poor white worshipers were often ambiguous, if not hostile, toward what they saw as the materialism and condescension of planter families. For some, it followed that the economic changes outlined above, which had produced the materialism if not the condescension, were impediments to true Christian living, and therefore evil. Thus Brooks may have seemed an alien amongst the simpler and more passionately spiritual evangelicals. But the confidence they had as beloved children of a God who was no respecter of earthly status, a rising standard of living that cotton could provide, hope that cotton might bring a planter's life within reach, and Brooks' evident piety, likely blunted any discomfort his presence might have caused.[38]

Brooks, her mother Mary Giles Carroll, and her brother James Parsons Carroll (1809–1883) were also very supportive of Trinity.

[37] Brooks Journal, *passim*; and Chapman, *Edgefield*, 299. Bettis Rainsford surmises that numbers explain the absence of a Presbyterian church (Woodson, *Giant in the Land, passim).* Wyatt-Brown, *Southern Honor*, 100–112, describes how the Second Great Awakening (early 1800s) affected some southern men's sense of their religious nature and obligation. He cites John Belton O'Neall among his examples.

[38] On the evolution of evangelical churches in the antebellum South, see Mathews, *Religion in the Old South*; and Heyrman, *Southern Cross.* Slaves, who likely outnumbered whites in the evangelical churches he visited, would also have noticed Brooks, but their reactions are more difficult to imagine. On slaves' complex relationship with owners and other whites, the best source is Genovese, *Roll, Jordan, Roll.* As to the contest between Christian values and the Old South's un-Christ-like cult of honor, one scholar could have had Edgefield in mind when he wrote, "Although [antebellum southern] Christians made significant gains in terms of church membership, and although their influence spread before the Civil War, southern churches were not the preeminent formulators of a southern identity. That remained the prerogative of the white male, who, in the context of a slave-based economy remained convinced

* * *

Whitfield Brooks began planting under trying circumstances. The Panic of 1819 hit the year after his marriage, ushering in a decade in which cotton prices fell 72% while soil erosion depleted the fields, hurting yields. Meanwhile, newly cleared acres to the Southwest were producing higher quality crops. Brooks did not succumb to the lure of those virgin fields, but he must have struggled to offset the conditions he faced. In 1825 he joined with other concerned farmers to form an agricultural society at Pottersville, and was appointed, with others, to contact other societies and successful planters across the state for advice on increasing the quality and quantity of crops and livestock. In querying the very wealthy Sumter District planter Richard Singleton (1794-1844), he demonstrated his own keen understanding of farming issues. Brooks clearly weathered the 1820s better than most. By the end of the decade he had been able to increase his work forces to sixty-two slaves.[39]

Smaller scale farmers mostly retained their independence of the market, pointing with alarm to the Panic and the unreliability of banks and prices. But by 1830 the depression was over, and the continuing explosion of demand and the erratic but always rebounding price of cotton enticed most of them, and planters like Brooks, into a compromise that historians have come to call "safety-first" farming. They grew some cotton, but relied on a range of crops and livestock as a hedge against the unreliability of the cotton market.[40]

Within the safety-first school was a range of practice, from the cautious whose emphasis was on self-sufficiency to the more adventurous who were eager to attain the living standard and social status of planters. The former adhered, as best they could, to the admonition of Brooks' friend John Belton O'Neall, that "[t]rue independence is to be found in the abundance of your own farms. Raise...your own hogs,

---

that honor stood as the underlying principle of any proper society. True, antebellum ministers did fashion themselves as honorable men, but they were only marginally successful in convincing southern men that Christianity was an honorable faith.... It was the Civil War experience that fused honor and Christianity, thus confirming the South and southerners as quintessentially Christian, and creating the 'Bible Belt.'" (Berends, "Confederate Sacrifice and the 'Redemption' of the South," in Schweiger and Mathews, eds., *Religion in the American South*, 104). Edward Crowther argued for a more symbiotic relationship between Christianity and honor in the Old South in "Holy Honor."

[39] Freehling, *Prelude to Civil War*, 36. See also, WB to Richard Singleton, Nov. 1, 1825, Singleton Papers, Duke University. Singleton was the father-in-law of George McDuffie, a college acquaintance of WB who, like him, was mentored in the law by Congressman Eldred Simkins of Edgefield. This letter indicates that Brooks read one or more of the southern agricultural journals. He was later active in the Cambridge and South Carolina Agricultural Societies, and was called "a man of science" in Preston Brooks' obituary (*Advertiser,* Feb. 11, 1857). Roselands was chosen the state's best managed plantation in 1844 (*Proceedings of the State Agricultural Society*, 1844, 385–89). See Appendix Roselands Plantation – Cambridge – Greenwood County. SKIWAY.net, LLC.

[40] Ford, *Origins of Southern Radicalism*, 49–73.

sheep, [etc.] Clothe your own households by domestic wheel and loom...supply your own tables...and you can bid defiance to all the tariffs in the world." [41]

Brooks belonged to the latter group, more willing to take risks by borrowing to add acres and slaves and ride the cotton market to greater prosperity. While agreeing with O'Neall's advice, and balancing his cotton acres with grains and livestock, he prioritized cotton so as to support a rapidly growing workforce. The 1830s saw it expand to 100. He was now a leading figure among his state's agriculturalists, and, as his journal shows, was accustomed to keeping his eye out for land parcels and slaves made available by others' hard times, death, or departure to the southwestern or Florida frontiers. Many others were following the same path. As they did so, those who lived in the southwestern half of Edgefield District, including Edgefield Court House, were drawn into the commercial orbit of Augusta and its upstart rival, Hamburg. [42]

Augusta's location, below the fall line on the west bank of the Savannah, was for centuries a focal point of Indian travel and commerce. Founded in 1737, by the mid-18th century it was the commercial hub of the region.[43] The topography of southern Edgefield District invited travelers and trade goods to follow a ridge running just west of Horse Creek, which flows southward into the Savannah, roughly along the route of present US Highway 25, toward Augusta some twenty-five miles south of Edgefield Court House.[44]

In the late 1700s Leroy Hammond's Campbelltown (modern North Augusta), and Augusta were the markets for Edgefield's tobacco. Augusta would later become the second largest inland cotton market in the world, trailing only Memphis. Its hinterland, which reached thirty or more miles in all directions, included much of the

---

[41] O'Neall, "An Address Delivered Before the State Agricultural Society, 11 September 1844," in Ford, *Origins*, 53.

[42] Downey, *Planting a Capitalist South*, 20; and Ford, *Origins*, ch. 2. The Cross Index to Deeds, 1787–1839 in the Edgefield County Archives, page 57, lists Brooks 41 times as purchaser of land, beginning in 1814. He sold some of these tracts. He was "requested to take the chair" and named to the agenda committee at the first meeting of the South Carolina Agricultural Society on November 25, 1839. He was also elected a vice president of the society (*Proceedings of the State Agricultural Society,* 1846, 9, 21, https://catalog.hathitrust.org/Record/005947125). A resolution he introduced decried the harmful effects of a two-currency system—one based on gold and silver and thus reliable, and the other based on paper and therefore wildly erratic. It called on the legislature to remedy this problem, which particularly plagued cotton growers (see page 22). As evidence of his interest in crop diversity, Brooks authored a report on corn for the Cambridge Agricultural Society in 1842 (Agricultural Society of Cambridge, "Report...1842").

[43] Cashin, *The Story of Augusta,* 3–4.

[44] Burton, *In My Father's House,* 18.

Edgefield District.[45] Wade Hampton I built the first of many short-lived bridges spanning the Savannah in 1791. A covered toll bridge, built by eccentric German entrepreneur Henry Shultz and his partner Lewis Cooper, went up in 1814. Shultz soon opened his Bridge Bank in Augusta, and formed a company which built "the city's first decent wharf" in 1816. Steamboats were now reaching Augusta from Savannah, and carrying cotton bales on the return trip. In 1819 Shultz sold all of his assets, some on credit, planning to return to his German home, Hamburg. But the Panic of 1819 greatly reduced the value of his bank and bridge, and the bank's new owners lost it to the Bank of the State of Georgia. Furious, Shultz would fight that bank in court for the rest of his life.[46]

In 1821 Shultz challenged Augusta's commercial supremacy by establishing the town of Hamburg on the Savannah's opposite bank.[47] So seductive was Shultz's vision and energy that in less than a decade Hamburg boasted 1200 inhabitants and some sixty stores, dwarfing Edgefield Courthouse in both respects. The cotton boom made both rival markets flush, and created a corresponding boom in Savannah, at the river's mouth. Alarmed Charleston merchants financed the South Carolina Railroad, completed in 1833, linking Hamburg and Charleston and making the latter the destination of choice for western Carolina and northeastern Georgia cotton crops, undercutting river traffic to Savannah. But Hamburg was an equal beneficiary, as it now lured more of the upriver cotton trade away from Augusta. Hundreds of wagons delivering, by one account, 70,000 pounds of Edgefield and Abbeville cotton to Hamburg in the late fall, jammed the poor roads and often bogged down in the mud, until a twenty-six mile plank road (now US 25) was built in the 1850s. In 1835 the Bank of Hamburg, whose charter Brooks supported as a state representative, began competing with Augusta's financial institutions. Only the fifth bank chartered by the state, (Edgefield Courthouse had none) its capital stock totaled $300,000.[48]

---

[45] Downey, *Planting a Capitalist South*, 18. See also, "Cotton Exchange Sent Crop to World," *Augusta Chronicle*, August 8, 2010, www.augustacottonex.html, www.historic-memphis.com/Memphis-historic/frontstreet.

[46] Cashin, *The Story of Augusta*, 50, 70, 71–72. Eldred Simkins, and later Whitfield Brooks' brother-in-law James Parsons Carroll, were Schultz's lawyers (Bettis Rainsford file on Hamburg).

[47] Downey, *Planting a Capitalist South*, 67–73. See also, Burton, *In My Father's House*, 29. Shultz requested a $50,000 loan from the state, which was granted in December 1821 after commissioners, including Eldred Simkins, John Jeter, and Sampson Butler, were appointed to approve the securities he put up (*Acts and Joint Resolutions of the General Assembly of the State of South Carolina*, 1821, 80, accessed from Google Books).

[48] Burton, *In My Father's House*, 30. Earlier attempts to open a bank in Hamburg had fizzled (Downey, *Planting a Capitalist South*, 151). This one, headed by Hiram Hutchinson, flourished, except for short periods following national panics in 1837 and 1857 (Downey, *Planting a Capitalist South*, 135, 151–53, 187–88). On the scale of the cotton delivered to Hamburg, see Chapman, *Edgefield County*, 237; and *Advertiser*, August 7, 1851. Hamburg's growth to an 1830 population of 1,200 doesn't seem to have hurt Augusta much. Its population

Thus, although Edgefield Courthouse was the political and social center of the District, Hamburg surpassed it as a commercial center. Hamburg's bright prospects were threatened, however, first by floods during the 1840s, then by the Augusta canal (1845), which bypassed the rapids north of Augusta, accelerating river traffic, and finally by a railroad trestle spanning the Savannah in 1853, eliminating the need for train traffic from its east to stop in route to the Georgia side. Although his main plantation was at the opposite edge of Edgefield District, a day's travel from Hamburg, Brooks sold his cotton there, and he and his family regularly traveled there from Edgefield Court House on business or to shop. Often they also visited Augusta, whose stores Mary and daughter Ellen preferred.[49]

As long as cotton ruled, agriculture would remain the preferred route to prosperity for most Edgefield men. Also important to men reared on the Jeffersonian "country-republican ideology" were the societal benefits that farming was thought to provide. Brooks spoke for the typical planter when he lauded "the Agricultural class . . . [as] the only sure and permanent foundation of all government, and upon which civil society and government must, in truth, depend for their continued support and preservation." Commerce itself did not threaten farming's position as society's cornerstone; growers needed buyers and shippers. But expanding trade and improved infrastructure fostered the entrepreneurial spirit in some Edgefieldians, and with their backing manufacturing also became more prominent in Edgefield District.[50]

The earliest significant industry in Edgefield District was utilitarian alkaline-glazed stoneware pottery, for which the district later became famous. Finding the clay in the southern Edgefield District especially good for making stoneware, Dr. Abner Landrum (1785-1859) a student of Moses Waddel, free-thinker and creative genius, established Pottersville 1.5 miles north of the Court House in 1809, and built the first alkaline glazed pottery factory in America soon after. David ("Dave") Drake (1800-1879?), a slave who worked at his factory and others, has gained fame for the size and gracefulness of his pots and the verses and signatures he incribed on some of them. Recent archeological research has suggested that the Pottersville kiln (c1810-1850s)

---

rose from 2,476 in 1810 to 6,403 in 1840 and an estimated 12,000 in 1850 (Cashin, *The Story of Augusta*, Appendix B). On Hutchinson and other entrepreneurs, see Ford, Jr., "The Tale of Two Entrepreneurs," 198–224.

[49] The Saluda River, which flowed to the Saluda cotton factory (1830) and Columbia, passed a few miles from Roselands, but was too obstructed to carry commercial goods (SC Ency.). A road linked Ninety Six to Ridge Spring and thence to Columbia, but was a longer trip (Colton's 1861 map of NC and SC). See also, Burton, *In My Father's House*, 28, 29; Derrick, *Centennial History of the South Carolina Railroad*; Ford, *Origins*, 64, 177–81, 324–28; *South Carolina Encyclopedia*, 44–45; and "Augusta Canal, A Self-Guided Adventure." WB never mentions shipping cotton anywhere but Hamburg. A son and/or slave often drove the wagons.

[50] *Edgefield Advertiser*, May 6, 1841, quoted in Downey, *Planting a Capitalist South*, 30–31. On the country ideology, to which Brooks was alluding here, see *South Carolina Encyclopedia*, 234. Lacy Ford and others call it the republican ideology.

ultimately reached the length of 105 feet. This confirms the enormous scale of Landrum's operation, which employed men of both races. Landrum also published *The Edgefield Hive*, a Unionist paper for which his slave Dave worked, until he sold the pottery and took the paper to Columbia in 1831. Other potteries, one operated by Rev. John Landrum, brother of Abner, opened around the District, making it a major center for production of utilitarian vessels into the later decades of the nineteenth century when glass containers replaced clay. Whitfield Brooks occasionally mentioned passing Pottersville on his way to his plantation, or other destinations.[51]

Despite concerns about creating a dependent factory class—labeled "wage slaves" by some antebellum writers—it was only a matter of time before the idea of turning the ever-increasing bales of locally-grown cotton into cloth near its source bore fruit. In the late 1820s a small group of Edgefield planters, led by German immigrant Christian Breithaupt and including Congressman George McDuffie, built the Vaucluse cotton mill on Horse Creek in southern Edgefield District. It experienced setbacks, underwent reorganization under the leadership of William Gregg, and survived to the end of the antebellum era. Two decades after its founding its difficulties provided a cautionary tale for Gregg, whose vision of cotton manufacturing on the New England mill village model became reality when the Graniteville Mill, among the Old South's largest, began production in 1849, downstream from Vaucluse on Horse Creek. The factory and its mill village were twenty miles south of Edgefield Courthouse. Controversy arose over the social and political implications of this heretofore primarily northern phenomenon, and the effects of long hours in poorly ventilated factory buildings and the regimented lifestyle were too much for some operative families. Yet the Graniteville Company brought an important industrial dimension to the Edgefield District's and the region's economy. Gregg moved from Charleston to the railroad town of Aiken in the early 1850s to better supervise the mill and monitor the lives of its employees, and dabbled in politics. Brooks' journal reveals that he and Gregg were acquainted, although some mentions of "Col. Gregg" in his journal may be of future Confederate General Maxcy Gregg of Columbia.[52]

---

[51] Stoneware was impervious to liquids, so these pots held meats, butter, pickled vegetables, and anything else people needed to store (Mills, *Statistics of South Carolina*, 523–24; www.histarch.illinois.edu/Edgefield/). See also, Todd, *Carolina Clay;* Horne, ed., *Crossroads of Clay*; *Story of Edgefield,* 4, 88, 90; and Burton, *In My Father's House,* 34, 181, 346 n. 52. On the range of Landrum's interests and talents, see http://dexterpottery.com/2010/06/14/dr-abner-landrum/. *The Hive* got its name from Landrum's nickname, "the learned bee" (Todd, *Carolina Clay,* 46). Old Edgefield stoneware is highly prized by museums and collectors.

[52] Downey, *Planting a Capitalist South*, 123–44, 220. See also, Mitchell, *William Gregg*. Apparently, Brooks was not involved in either of these enterprises. Given his belief in farming as the best foundation for a healthy society, he likely had misgivings, but he generally supported economic growth. Oddly, especially since he (once) owned a large tract almost adjacent to it, Brooks' Journal is silent on the Graniteville mill, which was under construction when his jour-

The record of Whitfield Brooks' life between his college and legal training years and 1840 is limited to his marriage and the births of his children, newspaper mentions of his public service, the Journal of the state House of Representatives during his two terms, his land transactions, census records, and a few scraps of an apparent earlier diary. The diary fragments show his scientific and theological curiosity during the early 1830s; he commented on "[Justus von] Leibeg's [1803-1873] Organic Chemistry," (a natural interest for a progressive farmer), Sir Francis Bacon, and the Christian heresy, Arianism. His daily routine must have been dominated by his duties as Commissioner in Equity, which contemporaries said he took very seriously, his law practice, and the management of his increasingly far-flung farming operations. No comprehensive list of his properties has been compiled, but the 1850 census for Edgefield District recorded that his holdings were worth $20,000, which suggests that he owned at least 6000 acres. That year his work forces totaled ninety-three slaves, down from 100 in 1840, before he gave some to sons Preston and James around the time of their weddings. The South Carolina Archives has records of only three of his land acquisitions, all occurring between 1826 and 1830, and totaling 2,951 acres, but the Edgefield County Archives lists forty-one acquisitions over some twenty-five years. Since Brooks was continually looking for tracts and open to offers on some of his own, assessing his total holdings at any one time would be a complex task.[53]

Considering the family legacy of public service, it was natural for Brooks to involve himself in the public life of his community. He could not remember a time when one or more of his kin were not in prominent civic or military positions. He no doubt listened to stories about the experiences of his father and uncles during the Revolutionary War. His generation has been portrayed by some scholars as struggling to somehow live up to the reputations of their heroic fathers. Whether or not this

---

nal ended. In the 1850s Gregg and Brooks' brother-in-law James Parsons Carroll would compete for a seat in the state Senate, with Carroll winning. Both were elected to the Secession Convention in 1860.

[53] Brooks' children's birth dates: Preston Smith, August 6, 1819; James Carroll, January 27, 1821; Mary Elizabeth, August 6, 1822 (lived two weeks); George Butler, June 18, 1824 (died Oct. 5, 1825); Whitfield Butler, December 28, 1825; Ellen Sophia, January 23, 1829; John Hampden, September 6, 1833; and William Butler, October 4, 1840 (died Oct. 15) (Brooks family Bible, diary fragment in family's possession). Brooks' land included unnumbered acres Mary had inherited. In antebellum South Carolina "only single women and widows could own property and sign contracts" (SC Ency., 1038). See also, 1850 census, Edgefield District, 69, line 8, visitation order 534, Brooks, Whitfield, usgwarchives.net/sc/sca_edge.html). See also, Neuffer, ed., *Names in South Carolina,* vol. 14, 47; and Watson, *Greenwood County Sketches,* 165–66. SCDAH, Plats for State Land Grants, Series 213792, vol. 48, 43, 129; and vol. 49, 247. Two of these three tracts were on Ninety Six Creek, one likely an addition to the Roselands plantation tract. The third was on Bridge Creek, a tributary of Big Horse Creek, just above Graniteville. As Commissioner in Equity, Brooks' name is on uncounted numbers of deeds where a controversy was settled by his ruling (Edgefield County Archives, Deed Books).

applies to him, Brooks was keenly aware of the service performed by Zachariah, whom he helped prepare and submit a pension application in the mid-1830s.[54]

Other kin only heightened his sense of public obligation. His uncle, General William Butler (1759-1821), one of those war heroes and husband of Whitfield's "Aunt Butler," was an anti-federalist member of the state convention that ratified the US Constitution in 1788, and of the state constitutional convention of 1790. He led the committee that escorted President Washington as his southern tour passed through Edgefield District in 1791. As sheriff of Ninety Six District beginning in 1794, he "always presided...during the sitting of the [District] Court." William's brothers Thomas and Stanmore had been his deputies. As a Congressman in 1807 he chaired the House committee to investigate General James Wilkinson for complicity in the "Burr conspiracy" proceedings, but resigned when Wilkinson, citing his militia rank, challenged his fairness. Resigning his seat in 1813, he commanded the defense of Charleston during the War of 1812.[55]

William Butler's sons, cousins of Whitfield, honored their father's legacy. James was sheriff of Edgefield District, George was an army major during the War of 1812, and William, an army surgeon, served a term in Congress. Pierce Mason Butler was a regular army officer, president of the Bank of the State, governor 1836-38, and commander of the Palmetto Regiment in the war with Mexico. Andrew Pickens Butler was a judge and U. S. Senator. Emmala, the only daughter who survived to adulthood, was the wife of Congressman Waddy Thompson, Jr.[56]

Brooks entered adult life amid local clashes that left him with few illusions about politics. In the period after the War of 1812, a time when "one did not have to go far [in Edgefield] to find either a fight or a frolic," there arose a contest between the "old and new parties of Edgefield," which included a hotly contested election between Congressman William Butler and Edmund Bacon. Though hard feelings were later assuaged, the campaign "was bitter and led to many painful controversies." Among these was an 1825 brouhaha that was whipped up by men who resented "the influence of the Butler and Simkins families in the county...thinking that they were getting rather more offices than they were fairly entitled to." The dispute was initiated by a pamphlet published by Catlett Connor, "a celebrated character of that day" who lived near Ninety Six, and "ably seconded" by Matthew Jones of "The Ridge" section. "Party feeling ran...so high that Mr. Matthew Jones and Colonel [Zachariah] Smith

---

[54] Glover, *Southern Sons,* discusses the burden that awareness of ancestors' Revolutionary War service placed upon men of Brooks' generation (Pension Application of Zachariah Smith Brooks, S9294, fn 36SC, South Carolina Dept. of Archives and History).

[55] Chapman, *Edgefield*, 34–44. Tales about his uncle William's pursuit of the notorious Tory "Bloody Bill" Cunningham must have thrilled young Whitfield all the more because their horserace ended at Lorick's Ferry on the Saluda, near where he grew up.

[56] Chapman, *Edgefield*, 44–45. Brief sketches of several prominent Butlers are in the online National Register of Historic Places Inventory – Nomination Form for Butler Family Cemetery, Dec. 31, 1974, Saluda County SC.

Brooks had a fight about the election at Mount Willing in which, it was said, that Colonel Brooks got the worst of it." His son's distaste for the bare-knuckled style of politics was thus formed at close hand. In a fugitive page found among his papers he expressed his aspiration, not always honored, in this regard. "A patriot should be accustomed to tolerate every political party, to stand true to his own and to attack his antagonist with eagerness yet without personal animosity. Political antagonists should regard each other like the officers of two opposing armies who do their best to wound and kill each other yet all in honor." [57]

By 1823, while still a young family man, Brooks was already a Commissioner of Roads and trustee of the Edgefield Village Academy. He continued in the latter role into the early 1840s. In 1827 he was a District Commissioner along with Benjamin Frazier, Christian Breighthaupt, and Allen B. Addison, advertising in the *Augusta Chronicle* that they had appropriated three thousand dollars for repairs and improvements on the Court House. The following year he wrote a report to the General Assembly on behalf of the "Commissioners to Consider Dividing Edgefield District...Recommending Division and Proposing Boundary Lines." A referendum was said to have revealed "great discontent" among a majority due to distances from the court house, and the delays caused by lengthy dockets in so large a district. Brooks' report endorsed creating "Butler District" which would be formed from the northeastern third of Edgefield District, and transferring the Beech Island area (east and south of Horse Creek) to Barnwell District. Nothing came of this at the time, but the issues cited in the Report were resolved with the formation of four new counties beginning in 1870. Brooks' public offices also included Commissioner of the Free Schools in the District in 1835, and Commissioner of Public Buildings in 1836.[58]

Beginning in the early 1830s, debilitating migraine headaches would plague Brooks for the rest of his life and hinder his participation in Edgefield's social and

---

[57] Chapman, *History of Edgefield County*, 44, 54–55. It was in 1825 that O'Connor defeated Brooks' mentor Eldred Simkins for the state Senate. The erosion of civility in South Carolina politics was noticed and disparaged as early as 1810. A Scottish visitor observed that "[n]o human invention is too gross or too indecent to be made use of on these occasions [elections]" (Mohl, ed., "The Grand Fabric of Republicanism: A Scotsman Describes South Carolina, 1810–1811," 180). WB's personal relationships were sorely tested when men he was close to became adversaries (Edmunds, *Francis Pickens*, 36–37). WB's "Political Maxim" is quoted in front matter of Edmunds' *Pickens.*

[58] Woodson, "William Bullein Johnson, Baptist Leader," ch. 9, www.smalltowngems.com-EdgefieldSC-History. See also, *Advertiser,* October 4, 1883, and Misc. Communications to the General Assembly, Series S, 165029, Nov. 12, 1828, SCHAH. New counties were Aiken in 1870, Saluda in 1896, Greenwood in 1896, and McCormick in 1916. These divisions shrunk the Old Edgefield District to a small fraction of its original size, but increased its residents' voices in the state senate substantially (draft of WB entry in Biographical Directory of the South Carolina House of Representatives [unpublished] in the editor's files). See also, O'Neall, *Bench and Bar,* vol. 2, 473–75.

civic life. In 1832 he resigned as Commissioner in Equity, likely because of his headaches, but also perhaps because he anticipated what would occur during the upcoming state legislative session. In his first bid for the legislature he was elected to one of Edgefield's six seats in the House of Representatives. The delegation included his friend Francis Pickens, among the youngest members at twenty-five but soon to take a leadership role, and his brother-in-law Maximilian LaBorde. Normally the legislature met for only a few weeks in the late fall, but it convened earlier than usual, on October 22, 1832, in response to Governor James Hamilton's call for an extraordinary session on the state's response to the federal tariffs of 1828 and 1832.[59]

Brooks had supported, along with the vast majority of Edgefield's public figures, South Carolina's power struggle with President Jackson and the federal government over protective tariffs. The Palmetto State alone would "nullify" these two tariff laws, and Jackson's bellicose response put state and country on a collision course. Mary Brooks and Mrs. Nathan Lipscomb Griffin made a flag for the Edgefield Hussars, a unit of the state's defenses against federal forces that Jackson threatened to use to crush the "Nullies."[60]

The new member of the General Assembly was not an outsider. His law practice had introduced Brooks to several legislators, and two of his college friends were House leaders. Henry Laurens Pinckney was elected Speaker for the 1832 term, and William Campbell Preston was chairman of the key committee on federal relations. An early order of business was the authorization of a Convention of the People to nullify the protective tariffs within the bounds of the state. Supporters of this action held a two-thirds majority, so the outcome was clear. Brooks voted consistently with the majority in favor of calling the nullification Convention. That body, easily dominated by "Nullies," including Brooks, declared both tariff acts null and void.[61]

Among the few House votes taken on nullification in which members' votes were recorded, Brooks voted for a bill to provide for the security and protection of the state, for a bill requiring the governor to swear to enforce the nullification ordinance (countering President Jackson's request for authorization to enforce collecting tariffs in the state), and for a bill asking the Governor to warn the citizens "against the insidious attempt by the president to seduce them from their allegiance to the State" (Jackson's December 10th "Proclamation to the People of South Carolina"). Brooks also supported a resolution "that the paramount allegiance of the citizens of this State…is of right due to the state," and all such bills where a voice vote is recorded,

---

[59] On the beginning of his migraines, see Brooks Journal, January 16, 1846. Manuscript Journal of the South Carolina House of Representatives, SCDAH.

[60] The 1832 election for the state legislature yielded 1,629 Edgefield votes for Nullifiers and 640 for Unionists (Sinha, *The Counter-Revolution of Slavery*, 45). Fairfield was even more one-sided, with a vote of 1,747 to 103. For Abbeville the totals were 1,666 and 946 (ibid.).

[61] All information on Brooks' role as a member of the House is taken from the Manuscript Journal of the South Carolina House of Representatives for the years 1832–1835, SCDAH (*SC Encyclopedia*, 112).

including "the right to cecede" (sic). The crisis was averted in early 1833 by a compromise including reduced tariff rates and South Carolina's rescinding of its Ordinance. On a less weighty matter, Brooks voted for the election of tax collectors by the people, which failed.[62]

In the 1833 session, "Mr. Brooks introduced a bill to authorize the formation of a Company to construct a Rail Road from Aiken in Barnwell District to the Village of Edgefield." Its defeat began an on-again off-again campaign toward that goal that extended beyond Brooks' lifetime. He was against a bill to re-charter the Bank of the State, which also failed. He backed a bill "more effectively to provide for defence of the state," which passed. On December 11 "Mr Brooks submitted a resolution, which was...agreed to and ordered to be sent to the Senate...that Rhydon Mays, Larkin Griffin, John Bowie, Richard Griffin, and Simeon Christie be appointed commissioners whose duty it shall be personally to inspect and examine the condition of the public way leading from Cambridge to Charleston beginning at the branch near the residence of the late William Burton deceased to its intervention with the Island Ford Road...."

Also in the 1833 session, on a successful motion to strike a portion of a funding bill imposing a tax on income from stock held in banks not incorporated by the state, Brooks voted yea. When a Senate bill that would ban teaching slaves to read or write came to the House floor, Thomas Nixon of Edgefield offered an amendment that "It shall not be lawful for any free person of colour to preach, lecture or give religious instruction in any occasion to coloured persons, unless there shall be present...at least five respectable white persons, who shall be owners of slaves." Brooks, a paternal master in his own eyes, voted yea. His colleague Francis Pickens voted nay. The amendment failed 33–64, but the bill without the amendment passed 51-34, with both men voting yea.[63]

The pending retirement of Congressman George McDuffie led Brooks to consider running for his seat in 1834. A possibly pivotal moment in his political life was short-circuited, however. John C. Calhoun learned of McDuffie's plans early that year, and encouraged his young cousin Francis Pickens to run, correctly assuring him that "Mr. Brooks will retire" from the race. Thus began Pickens' roller-coaster political ride as one of Calhoun's acolytes, while Brooks settled for a second term in the state House.[64]

---

[62] House Journal, 1832 session, 182.

[63] House Journal, 1833. The anti-slave literacy bill died in the Senate on a vote to postpone, which passed 20-17. Brooks' cousin Andrew Pickens Butler voted with the majority. Senator Whitemarsh Seabrook, a leading opponent of slave literacy and the "mission to the slaves," considered the outcome a victory for the naïve advocates of paternalism (Ford, *Deliver Us from Evil,* 467–69).

[64] Edmunds, *Francis W. Pickens*, 19–20. This had no apparent effect on their friendship. "Whitfield Brooks...and James Parsons Carroll...were Pickens' closest friends; along with M. L. Bonham, N. L. Griffin, and Arthur Simkins, they comprised Pickens' Edgefield junto" (Edmunds, *Pickens,* 126).

In the 1834 session, no longer a back-bencher, he chaired the agriculture committee and served on the internal improvements committee, indications of his reputation as a planter and his interest in improved infrastructure. His neighbor, previous law partner and sometime political enemy Francis Hugh Wardlaw presented the proceedings of public meeting in Edgefield on building a railroad from Aiken to Edgefield. A few days later "An act to authorize the formation of the Edgefield Rail Road Company," which Wardlaw had introduced, passed both houses. Nothing came of it, however. Brooks supported spending up to $20,000 on repairing buildings at the South Carolina College. A bill to amend the 1812 "act to prevent the pernicious practice of dueling" passed without a recorded vote.[65]

During the 1835 session, his last, Brooks presented the report of the Commissioners of Free Schools of Edgefield District with a memorial recommending amendments to the system. A resolution that "Leonard Dozier has committed a gross breach of the privileges of this House" in wounding a member with words spoken in debate, and that he be committed to the gaol of Richland district until Dec. 5," passed 60-46 with Brooks voting in the affirmative. Speaker Patrick Noble of Abbeville ordered the punishment carried out. Brooks' last, and perhaps most satisfying, presentation, was a petition of the Vestry and Wardens of Trinity Protestant Episcopal church, Edgefield, for incorporation, which passed. Two matters relating to Hamburg were presented. The first was a memorial of Henry Shultz, indicative of his ambition, to establish a trading company between Hamburg, by the way of Charleston, and the kingdoms of Russia, Sweden, Denmark, and Holland. It was referred to committee on incorporation. On a bill to establish and incorporate a bank in Hamburg, which passed, Brooks voted yea.[66]

Based on the recorded votes cited above, and his view of the positive role that government could play in economic development, one might expect him to be drawn into the nascent Whig Party. At different times there were two Whig Congressmen, Waddy Thompson and William Butler, in his extended family, and a third in his old friend Senator William Campbell Preston. But Edgefield was overwhelmingly Democratic, and Brooks was opposed to the views of Whig national leader Henry Clay.[67]

The 1830s saw several local developments that Brooks supported, and some in which he was active. The village of Edgefield was incorporated by the state legislature in 1830, an action that Brooks surely supported, along with the founding of the

[65] House Journal, 1834.

[66] House Journal, 1835. Brooks did not run for another term.

[67] An excellent discussion of the ideology of the antebellum Whigs in the context of today's liberal and conservative ideologies is found in Ford, "Henry Clay, American Commerce and the Public Option." Brooks states his opposition to Clay, whose political skills he acknowledged, in his Journal. In 1840 the Democratic ticket bested the Whigs by 4 to 1 in Edgefield District (Ford, *Origins*, 171). Brooks would later reveal his anti-Whig bias in the context of his support for the war with Mexico. He asked Congressman James A. Black, "Why did the Whig Party vote men and money to carry it on" if they thought it unconstitutional (WB to Black, Jan. 12, 1848, PSB papers, SCL)?

Edgefield District Poor House the following year. Also, since Abner Landrum enjoyed the patronage of the Simkins family in his pottery operation, and Eldred Simkins had helped Brooks in the first years of his legal career, he likely looked favorably on the founding of Landrum's paper, *The Hive,* in 1827, which succeeded *The South Carolina Republican (1824-1827).* But *The Hive's* editorial policy was Unionist, and showed sympathy for "mechanics" (skilled laborers). Thus Brooks likely shed few tears when Landrum moved it to Columbia in 1831, as *The Carolinian* (1829-1836) published by F. H. Wardlaw and S. W. Mays, filled the void. In turn, it was reincarnated as *The Edgefield Advertiser* in 1836, an event Brooks heartily endorsed in the paper itself. Signing himself "a planter," he penned a long letter in the premier issue, February 11, 1836, appealing for support of what he described as an essential enterprise. He emphasized that its editors, Maximilian Laborde (his brother-in-law) and General James Jones, were natives of the district, graduates of the South Carolina College, and "true and staunch states rights men." The times, he added, presented "a question involving not only our rights but our social and political existence," and he urged "every man who can read and spare three dollars" [per year] to subscribe.[68]

Among his public services in these years, he was a member of the commission to oversee construction of the new District Court House, which the *Edgefield Advertiser* called "an ornament to the village," in 1838-39. On March 29, 1839 he gave an address in the new building, "full of research," which continued his support for the ongoing "Southern Commercial Conventions" movement. As he had done three years earlier, he argued for opening direct trade between the southern states and Europe, in hopes of "Emancipating the South from...dependence upon the North...." The gathering approved sending a delegation to the upcoming southern commercial convention in Charleston. Also in 1839 he was reelected a trustee of the Edgefield Male Academy, and one of five vice presidents of the newly organized State Agricultural Society.[69]

Non-political developments may have affected Edgefield's citizens almost as much as the nullification drama. The Edgefield Baptist Association's congregations

---

[68] Burton, *In My Father's House*, 68, 72. See also, *Chronicling America*, Library of Congress database of U.S. newspapers, 1836–1922: http://chroniclingamerica.loc.gov/lccn/sn85042804/. "For much of its existence The *Advertiser* has served as a barometer of the influence of agrarian elites on government and society in South Carolina" (ibid.). *Advertiser*, February 11, 1836; note on the *Pottersville Hive* in Bettis C. Rainsford files. The national issue he referenced was the future legality of slavery in the District of Columbia.

[69] *Advertiser,* February 21, 1839, April 4, 1839, April 5, 1836, and January 1, 1840; and also, Brooks Journal, Dec. 30, 1840. Among Edgefield's delegates to the 1839 commercial convention were John Bauskett, Milledge Bonham, Whitfield Brooks, Dr. Harwood Burt, A. P. Butler, James Parsons Carroll, James Jones, John Wever, and Lewis Wigfall (*Advertiser*, April 4, 1839). On the ongoing campaign for direct trade with Europe, see *Debow's Review* 4/2 (Oct. 1847): 208–226. The contractor for the courthouse, Charles Beck, had been associated with the architect Robert Mills ("History of the South Carolina State Fair and History of Agriculture in South Carolina," 1). Also see, http://scstatefair.org/fair/field-to-fair/intro.php.

experienced a spiritual revival "like a mighty earthquake" in August, 1831, and the state's Methodist Conference established its first congregation in the village, erecting a church (Brooks was actively involved as noted above) on the newly renamed Buncombe Street, formerly the Road to Cambridge. That year cotton prices fell to nine cents a pound, and news reached the Palmetto State of a terrifying slave uprising in southeastern Virginia, led by a slave named Nat Turner. Edgefield whites, some recalling a rumor of such an uprising in their district some twelve years earlier, must have shuttered.[70]

In 1842 Brooks made his last bid for political office, seeking the Congressional seat being vacated by his friend Francis Pickens. He lost to Armistead Burt of Abbeville, whom he had encountered before as an ally of Lewis Wigfall. It is clear from his Journal that while flattered by signs of popular support, and pushing himself to travel the district campaigning, he found electioneering distasteful. To his misfortune, his opponent did not. Brooks carried his home District but lost badly outside of it. Considering his health, perhaps his defeat was a blessing in disguise.[71]

Meanwhile, members of his extended family were involved in a range of activities, some dangerous. His cousin James Butler Bonham died during the siege of the Alamo, fighting for Texan independence from Mexico, which would allow slavey there, in March, 1836. Another first cousin, Pierce Mason Butler, was elected governor in the same year, and led Edgefield troops and others as a lieutenant colonel in the Second Seminole War of the late 1830s and early 1840s. Edgefield's Peurifoy family moved to Florida as missionaries to the Indians, and Brooks' niece Louisa Bird Peurifoy was caught up in the violence of the Seminole War. Her husband, Rev. Tillman Dixon Peurifoy was away on church business on a Sunday in 1836 when Louisa was attacked in their home, shot, stabbed, beaten and left for dead. She was found the next day and survived after suffering for many weeks. The bodies of her two children were found in the ruins of the house. The family moved to Georgia and in 1849 returned to Edgefield District, settling near Butler Church. Brooks' journal mentions them rarely, but with feeling.[72]

Narrowing the focus to Brooks himself, and acknowledging that a diary or journal is a translucent window and other readers may reach different conclusions, the following is a distillation of impressions from his Journal. Brooks was a progressive farmer who

---

[70] Chapman, *Edgefield County*, 84, 197; and Burton, *In My Father's House*, 21–28, 57–61.

[71] Burt, a friend of Lewis Wigfall from their days at the University of Virginia, was asked by Wigfall early in the 1840 gubernatorial campaign to pressure the Brooks clan to support John P. Richardson instead of James Hammond. That experience, and the link between Burt and the Brooks nemesis Wigfall, must have added spice to the congressional campaign (Wigfall to John L. Manning, Jan 29, 1840, Williams-Chesnut-Manning Papers, SCL). On Burt, see *SC Ency.*, 109.

[72] *SC Encyclopedia*, 113; and Chapman, *Edgefield*, 198–200. Louisa was a daughter of Daniel Bird and Lucinda Brooks Bird.

took pride in maximizing the quantity and quality of his yields, but he may have appreciated the South Carolina Agricultural Society's award for the best managed plantation more than getting top dollar for his cotton. He hired overseers to manage his larger holdings, and thought the results were mixed. Considering distances requiring several hours of travel, he was "hands on" in managing his farms. He was well informed on public affairs, and, within limits imposed by his age and health, involved in them. He allied himself with other public men, including Francis Wilkerson Pickens, James Henry Hammond, his brothers-in-law James Parsons Carroll and Maximilian Laborde, and his cousins Andrew Pickens Butler and Pierce Mason Butler. Less political than Hammond or Pickens, he bemoaned the continuing trend toward soliciting votes and the character of some office seekers. The slight success he had in that arena raises the question how much broader might his political horizon have been, had he not been hindered by debilitating headaches.[73]

Brooks was a family man, happiest when all of his family members were under his roof. He was an affectionate and appreciative husband and loving father to his wife, five children, and daughters-in-law (whom he also called his daughters) and grandchildren. The couple suffered at least their portion of grief, losing three children in infancy and their grown son Whitfield in a faraway battle. His deeply religious sensibility was likely shaped by the influence of his pious wife. In this regard Brooks presents a sharp contrast with James Hammond, his distant neighbor and occasional guest and host. He seems a model of the religiously inspired "paternalistic" planter.[74]

A convivial man, Brooks and his wife hosted and were hosted by Edgefield's elite men and their families, and enjoyed community gatherings. Kate Wigfall Cheatham, niece of Brooks' young nemesis Lewis T. Wigfall, reminiscing in later years about the hospitality of Old Edgefield families, listed the Brookses first along with "the Griffins, the Nicholsons, the Bonhams, the Abneys, the Blockers, the Pickenses, the Bacons, the Simkinses, the Wardlaws" and others. His journal brings home the reality of his agonizing headaches, as he often found it necessary to retreat to his room while family and invited guests enjoyed themselves within his hearing, or to decline social invitations for the same reason. His journal provided a means of giving

---

[73] Burton, *House*, 73; Downey, *Planting a Capitalist South*, 145–48; and Ford, *Origins*, 160–75. See "To the People of Edgefield" by "No Candidate" (possibly Brooks) suggesting that candidates be nominated from each legislative district by Militia Battalions—acting for the residents—at their Spring Musters, and that all agree to support the choices of the other Musters, thus removing "the cruel and laborious task of electioneering" (*Advertiser*, February 13, 1840).

[74] Davidson, *The Last Foray*, 83. On the religiosity of the planter class generally, see Fox-Genovese and Genovese, *The Mind of the Master Class*, ch. 13 and ch. 14; and Wyatt-Brown, *Southern Honor*, ch. 3. On the evolution of the paternalistic ideal and the complex reasons for this, see Ford, *Deliver Us from Evil*, especially ch. 5 and ch. 17. See also Wyatt-Brown, *Shaping of Southern Culture*, pt. 2.

vent to his resulting disappointment as well as his pain, and he expressed self-pity, heroic fortitude, and pious submission in about equal measure.[75]

Brooks also enjoyed associations with a range of acquaintances in Edgefield Village, at nearby Hamburg and Augusta, at South Carolina's premier spa Glenn Springs in Spartanburg District, and, less often, at Columbia and Charleston. He liked playing the tourist in the mountains of the Carolinas, Charleston and Savannah, and in northern Florida. Accustomed to a certain level of cleanliness and comfort, he was put off when the accommodations available to him were lacking in that regard. Able to afford better amenities than the average traveler, he was frugal and expressed his ire at what he considered unreasonable rates.

A pious Episcopalian who enjoyed few things more than a long conversation with a learned clergyman, Brooks was a founder of two Episcopal Churches, Trinity in Edgefield and, during the years covered here, Calvary at Glenn Springs. He evinced some of the evangelical perspective of his Baptist and Methodist neighbors, while disdaining their sometimes narrow sectarianism and, to his mind, their misguided theology and prosaic sermons. Holding himself to a high standard of decency and propriety (as defined in his culture of honor) and supporting reforms such as temperance and education, he must have struck some contemporaries as prudish. He lamented the shortcomings he observed among the local populous, but did not spare himself. He enjoyed sharing good food and drink with friends, especially at the lavish affairs provided by Francis Pickens. Watching young people having a good time, including dancing, an activity some believed sinful, gave him pleasure.[76]

In his own eyes Brooks was a paternalist both within his family and on his plantations, and his journal does little to undermine that self-image. In it he never boasts of his dominance over his household, and only rarely shows frustration over the willfulness of his charges, but the sense of his authority as natural needed no journal affirmation. Readers might expect more attention to his many slaves in the Journals, but he was typical in almost ignoring them there.[77] On the whole Brooks' slaves, who infrequently caused him grief, were valued for their contribution to his family's economic well being, while a few of them, like Joseph, who accompanied his sons to Mexico and Young Whitfield's body back home, were especially depended upon and valued more personally. He was willing to unite a black family by the purchase of a neighbor's slave, but he appears to have also separated family members in selling or

---

[75] Cheatham, "The Old South and Beloved Old Edgefield"; and WB Journal.

[76] Some may detect a self-congratulatory tone in his comments on the religion of these congregations. Brooks endorsed the temperance movement and may have written letters to the *Advertiser* noting its merits. See the letter by "No Candidate," January 23, 1840, which irritated one reader (the responding letter's tone suggests Wigfall) by its "vanity and arrogance" (*Advertiser*, February 13, 1840). On Calvary Church and Glenn Springs, which he visited regularly and eventually built a small house nearby, see his Journal comments.

[77] Historian Steven Stowe, after reading hundreds of planter letters, was "struck by how seldom these letters make mention of black people…even familiar, personal servants" (Stowe, *Intimacy and Power*, xvi).

conveying one or more. When any of them frustrated his management he tried, at least in instances mentioned in his journal, to find non-corporal means of "correction." As to his assumption about the use of the lash, some indication may be found in his son Preston's disclaiming the House of Representatives' right to punish him for a violent act occurring beyond the confines of that chamber. If it assumes that power, it could also punish him for "directing that his slave be "flogged." His father, we may conclude, was a man of his time, typifying slaveholders who saw their property as monetized laborers, and their sometimes frustrating behavior as proof of African inferiority.[78]

In short, Whitfield Brooks fits the image of the antebellum southern man of genteel honor. "Gentility," writes Bertram Wyatt-Brown, "was a . . . specialized, refined, form of honor, in which moral uprightness was coupled with high social position." One can see this refined form of honor repeatedly in Brooks' behavior. His social position was insured by his family connections and great planter status, but those were augmented by his diligence in fulfilling his civic and professional duties, and his piety as a churchman. These made him a natural leader in community development and mediator in disputes within and even beyond his community, roles he seems to have taken as an obligation dictated by his social standing.[79]

But there is another side of the man, without which any portrait of him would be incomplete. When he, or anyone close to him, was involved in a dispute, the benign bearing could quickly fall away, as the Journal's opening episode shows. While Preston, in his twenties during the Journal's decade, frustrated his father more than once by his recklessness and lack of maturity, the apple seems not to have fallen far from the tree. Whitfield had, according to his friend John Belton O'Neall, one notable fault. "[H]e was too impulsive." Brooks acknowledged this with regret in his journal, but if he berated himself on that score, he made no apology for actions taken in defense of his or his family's honor. While he faulted Edgefieldians' proclivity for violence, for him moral uprightness did not preclude the use of force when appropriate.[80]

---

[78] His will suggests paternal concern for, as well as complete control of, his slaves, as he disbursed them among his heirs and ordered them shuffled to balance the monetary value received by each, but instructed Mary that those left to her receive annual gifts according to his instructions (Edgefield County Archives). See also Burton, *In My Father's House*, 174. For Preston Brooks' address to the House, see *Congressional Globe*, 34th Congress, 1st session, 832.

[79] Wyatt-Brown, *Southern Honor*, 88, 104–105. For an example of these qualities on an even grander scale, see Scarborough, *The Allstons of Chicora Wood: Wealth, Honor, and Gentility in the Carolina Lowcountry*.

[80] O'Neall, *Biographical Sketches of Bench and Bar*, vol. 2, 474. O'Neall added, "but his impulses were generally right." James Hammond saw him (and Preston) differently, calling him a "particular friend" (strong supporter) who was "always moving in the wrong time and place" and whose "doings in my behalf have cost me no little in many ways" (Bleser, ed., *Secret and Sacred*, 140). Some of the language in WB's letters to the *Edgefield Advertiser* during the tempestuous 1840 campaign suggest a failure to maintain his usually genteel version of honor,

When Whitfield Brooks began a new volume of his journal in early November, 1840, his country was reconfiguring its politics with the establishment of a second two-party system, and his state was seeking political unity after a decade of turmoil. For the United States, the election of 1840 signified the Whig party's parity with the Jacksonian Democrats. After Andrew Jackson's eight years as president, his designated successor Martin Van Buren had held off three Whig "favorite sons" in 1836 thanks to a loyal organization and a gift for electoral politics that earned him the nickname, the "Little Magician." In 1840, thanks in part to economic depression that followed the Panic of 1837, Van Buren would lose to the Whig candidate, General William Henry Harrison, whose Jacksonesque "log cabin campaign" was boosted by his handle, "Old Tippicanoe." The new politics of party discipline and mass electioneering had triumphed over that of deference to founding era leaders. Brooks lamented this, but publicly supported Van Buren and the "sub-treasury plan" over Harrison, whose views on slavery were considered suspect.[81]

In South Carolina, where the previous five candidates for the largely honorific office of governor had all been ex-Nullifiers elected by the legislature without opposition, an actual contest emerged in 1840, thanks to the obstinacy of ex-Congressman James Henry Hammond, whose Barnwell District plantation lay just below Edgefield District. Hammond, a former Nullifier, seemed not to have "gotten the memo" when several among the state's political leadership, taking Senator John C. Calhoun's cue, had agreed upon a strategy to reunite the Nullifiers and Unionists. Their bitter contest a decade earlier had left wounds that were still raw.[82]

The plan, hatched by Robert Barnwell Rhett, Franklin Elmore, and others, and announced in the *Charleston Mercury* in January, 1840, was to support ex-unionist John Peter Richardson, whose election would signify the end of the disunity that was felt to hamper the Palmetto State's opposition to protective tariffs and to the ominous tide of northern abolitionism. But the brilliant Hammond, whose ambition needed little stimulus, had been encouraged by friends, including two Edgefieldians, former Governor Pierce Mason Butler and Congressman Francis Pickens, both Brooks allies,

---

as Alvy King notes in his biography of Louis Wigfall. Compared with a description of the typical planter by Eugene Genovese, Brooks seems within the norm, but far from its extreme: "They were tough, proud, and arrogant; liberal-spirited in all that did not touch their honor; gracious and courteous, generous and kind, quick to anger and extraordinarily cruel" (Genovese, *Roll, Jordan, Roll*, 96–97). WB confessed to his Journal his sometimes unruly temper.

[81] Wilentz, *The Rise of American Democracy*, ch. 15–16. The sub-treasury, or independent treasury, was a compromise that provided some elements of central banking without reestablishing the Bank of the United States. Brooks made his support for Van Buren, the Sub-Treasury, and James Hammond clear in a public letter to Hammond, to which was appended Hammond's letter concurring with Brooks, in the *Advertiser*, June 18, 1840.

[82] Faust, *James Henry Hammond and the Old South*, 212–23. For a conservative's perspective on the change in state politics, see "The Next Governor," by "Turnbull" [Brooks?], *Advertiser*, March 26, 1840, 3.

to allow his name to be put forward in the press. Since he knew Pickens was an intimate of Calhoun, the virtual master of South Carolina's political life, Hammond consented to be nominated. Confronted with the Richardson candidacy, he would not yield to what he saw as a cabal of third-rate men, even after Pickens, presumably speaking for Calhoun, asked him to do so.[83]

Events in Brooks' home district of Edgefield demonstrated how hot the gubernatorial campaign could become. In an era when newspapers nominated as well as endorsed candidates, The *Edgefield Advertiser*, now edited by Pierre LaBorde, younger brother of Brooks' brother-in-law Maximilian, was the object of a power struggle between supporters of the two candidates. Beginning with a mild endorsement of Richardson, the paper retreated from that stance and endorsed Hammond. Throughout spring and summer 1840 it featured thrusts and counterthrusts by Hammond supporters, led by the Brooks family (including LaBorde and James Carroll) and Congressman Pickens, and the backers of Richardson, whose sharpest voice was that of young Edgefield attorney and militia colonel Lewis (later Louis) Trezevant Wigfall. The brilliant, pugnacious Wigfall got the better of it, using money from Richardson's nephew John Lawrence Manning to add pro-Richardson subscribers to the paper while his compelling letters and editorials stirred up support. He bedeviled the Brookses and humiliated Laborde, who resigned due to ill health, making Wigfall for a while the default editor. As the journalistic jousting escalated during the summer and fall, personal and family animosities fueled increasing tensions between those on opposing sides. More than once during the verbal jousting, a line, difficult to locate in a community where every man had his own sense of what constituted an unbearable affront, was crossed.[84]

---

[83] Faust, *Hammond*, 209, 219; and Wiltze, *John C. Calhoun, Nullifier*, 394. See also, Ford, *Origins of Radicalism*, 160–76. Richardson won the governorship by a legislative vote of 104–47, and Hammond succeeded him in 1842 (Bleser, ed., *Secret and Sacred*, 31, 60–62, 66). WB, a cousin of Butler and neighbor of Pickens, also supported Hammond. As governor, Hammond would make Preston Brooks his aide-de-camp (Bleser, 131).

[84] Letters from Wigfall to John L. Manning, his best friend at the time, are the basis for much of this story. See Jan. 9, 17, 29; Feb. 20, 21, 27; Mar. 3, 10, 19; June 10, 1840; and several undated, W-C-M papers, SCL. On Wigfall's tactics and the *Advertiser*'s uneasy position, see King, *Wigfall*, 26–27; and *Advertiser*, January 16 and 30, 1840. The Brooks family became embroiled in this donnybrook, in part at least, through a letter in late winter 1840, from Francis Pickens to his good friend James P. Carroll. Pickens had seemed headed for the U.S. House Speakership until derailed by his rivals Rhett and Elmore in late 1839. He vented his spleen in letters to Hammond and Carroll, and word of this reached Rhett and Elmore in Washington. "Carroll had shown the letter to his brother-in-law Whitfield Brooks and his son Preston." Though Preston assured him that he had kept the letter in confidence, Lewis Wigfall told Manning that Preston had told him (Edmunds, *Pickens*, 50–54). Exchanges continued to their October–November climax, described below. But serious bullet wounds were not enough to end matters and the feud extended well into the next year. WB may have taken some pleasure (see journal) in Wigfall's financial straits in the mid-1840s (Burton, *In My Father's House*, 72–73). On Wigfall's early life and this episode, see King, *Wigfall*, ch. 1–2, especially 25–26; and

At one of these points, in July, 1840, a duel was averted through a conference at Limestone Springs, east of Spartanburg. A court of honor including some of the state's most prominent citizens labored to find a way out of the verbal thicket woven by hot-heads Lewis Wigfall and Preston Brooks. They apparently succeeded, but with combatants still on edge a truce was not a peace treaty. Preston Brooks claimed that Wigfall had avoided a duel by backing down on the points of contention. Wigfall took to the *Advertiser* with his version, which included inflammatory attacks on the Brooks family. When Whitfield Brooks' strongly worded account of the settlement, refuting Wigfall's version, appeared in the *Advertiser*, Wigfall challenged his elder opponent to a duel.[85]

In retrospect this may all seem predictable, but the usually proper and composed Brooks appears to have been caught off guard. Old enough to be Wigfall's father, he was infuriated because he felt—surprisingly to those who read some of his published statements—that he had treated the young hotspur with due circumspection. When he received the challenge, his immediate response was to "thrust the head of the bearer, a young lawyer, through a window pane."[86] Yet his sense of dignity, his secure

Cooper, *Wigfall*, ch. 2. On Laborde's resignation, see *Advertiser*, Feb. 27, 1840. For examples of the back-and-forth between Wigfall and the Brooks family (including Preston), see *Advertiser*, March 19; June 18, 25; July 9; Oct. 22, 29; and Nov. 5, 1840.

A letter (Aug. 4, 1840) from Maxcy Gregg to John L. Manning recounts the growing animosity between Preston Brooks and Wigfall, placing the heavier burden on young Brooks (W-C-M papers, SCL, quoted in Cooper, *Wigfall*, 10–11). Wigfall biographer Alvy King suggests that Whitfield Brooks and his son bore at least as much blame as Wigfall, and Cooper, relying on Maxcy Gregg's account, reaches the same conclusion. Be that as it may, it was the gifted but immature Wigfall who lumped all members of the Brooks clan together and took his beef with Whitfield Brooks to its potentially lethal stage (King, 20, 22, 29–30). On Old Edgefield's larger-than-life personality, of which Wigfall may be the best exemplar, see Ball, *The State That Forgot*, 22, quoted in Burton, *In My Father's House*, 74–75. That Wigfall's personality changed little as he grew older is borne out by Russell in *My Diary North and South*, 86–89.

[85] King, *Wigfall*, 32, 33 n. 28; and WB to Hammond, July 2, 1840, Hammond Papers, Library of Congress. Assuming that King's labeling of WB's account as "scurrilous" refers to the *Advertiser* article on Oct. 29, I disagree with that description. Brooks wagged a figurative finger in his young adversary's face, but did not use vulgar or abusive language (King, *Wigfall*, 28, 32).

A manual on the proper procedure for a duel, *The Code of Honor*, had been published two years earlier by former South Carolina Governor John Lyde Wilson. Its purpose, in part, was to reduce the likelihood of duels by providing a protocol that would offer each man opportunities to satisfy his and his rival's honor short of violence. In this instance that purpose seems to have been pursued as fully as could be expected.

[86] U. R. Brooks, *South Carolina Bench and Bar*, vol. 1, 106–107. There is some reason to doubt this story. Its source is the memorial sketch of James Parsons Carroll, Brooks' brother-in-law, by his law partner, Edgefield attorney John Edmund Bacon (1827–1897). Bacon's step-father was Wigfall's brother, Rev. Arthur Wigfall. The anecdote was published by Brooks'

standing in the community, and his open opposition to dueling, abetted by his advanced age and poor health, led him to ignore the challenge. Thus did Whitfield Brooks exhibit his particular blend of impulsiveness and self-control, which, along with geniality, were hallmarks of the antebellum southern gentleman. When reputation and family loyalty were involved, he might lose control, but only briefly. He would not face his challenger on the field of honor.[87]

However, community norms and family loyalty among Brooks relatives impelled matters toward resolution. Brooks' brother-in-law, thirty-year-old James Parsons Carroll, who had grown up in his household and was his protégé in the law, accepted Wigfall's challenge in his place. On October 30, 1840, Wigfall, following custom, posted a notice at the Court House, calling Brooks a coward for refusing to duel with him. Carroll and Brooks' nephew Tom Bird arrived soon thereafter, and Carroll defiantly tore the placard down. Here accounts vary, and the *Advertiser,* in whose pages this melodrama had played out over several months, judiciously declined to provide details. What is known is that Tom Bird was fatally shot by Wigfall in an exchange of fire. Carroll's condemnation of Wigfall as a murderer elicited the predictable reaction.[88]

The Carroll-Wigfall duel, the opening event in the Journal pages that follow, came off without injury to either man, which typically would have sufficed to settle the dispute. But the twenty-one-year-old Preston, expelled just short of graduation from the South Carolina College a year earlier for trying to break his younger brother out of a Columbia jail at gunpoint, insisted that the matter was not yet satisfactorily resolved. He issued a challenge to Wigfall. His father, despite his general opposition and personal fears, accepted that decision and watched the ensuing duel, in which both men received near-fatal wounds. Yet even this did not end the controversy, as Brooks' journal reveals.[89]

---

grandson U. R. Brooks after the passing of forty-seven years, yet I choose to accept the story as based on fact. An unsigned account in the Anderson SC *Intelligencer*, May 1, 1914, which focuses on Preston Brooks, gives the name of the young lawyer as Coleman, says that WB responded to the challenge by "beating Coleman severely with his cane," and that Coleman "left the country after reporting to Wigfall." This sketch also explains Preston's absence at the time of Wigfall's challenge by citing a courtship with a lady from Fairfield, plausible since he married Caroline Means of that district within a year (King, *Wigfall,* 32).

[87] Brooks' perspective is clear in the opening pages of his Journal. While such reticence may seem contrary to the image of the honor-bound southern elite, in fact most confrontations never reached the stage of a formal challenge, and those that did were settled short of bloodletting more often than not. One insightful young southerner observed in 1843, "There is a great difference between a desire for honor and a desire to deserve honor" (Berry, *All That Makes a Man*, 20).

[88] *Advertiser,* Nov. 5, 1840. A charge of murder against Wigfall was dismissed (King, *Wigfall,* 33–34). Both Preston and his brother James were away at that time.

[89] The younger brother was either James, who received the Bachelor of Arts in 1842, or Whitfield, who may have been in Columbia in 1839, although he only reached the age of 14

Whitfield Brooks began a new journal volume on November 3, 1840, stating his purpose (in part) to leave an account of these events. Oddly it would seem, he failed to mention the October 15 death of his infant son William or that of his nephew Tom Bird, shot by Wigfall. Perhaps he was too distressed in the days leading to the duels and too anxious about Preston's tenuous health in the weeks that followed. However these omissions more likely point to the existence of a previous journal volume, since lost, whose closing pages treated these events while chronicling the 1840 gubernatorial campaign and its verbal bombast from one combatant's viewpoint. In any case, Brooks did leave a daily account of his next eight and one-half years, in which he recorded the joys and sorrows of his family's life, his social activities, his agricultural and occasional civic efforts, his travels, and his ruminations on politics, personalities, religion, the weather, and himself. However great the loss of earlier journals, the three volumes presented here form an engaging personal narrative and a window into a world that fascinates and charms, even as it perplexes and, occasionally, appalls.[90]

When the last of three extant journal volumes came to an abrupt end on May 10, 1849, the episode with which it began seemed all but forgotten. A decade of political turmoil had ended in December, 1840 with the legislature's gesture of reconciliation in choosing John Peter Richardson over James Henry Hammond as governor. Wigfall, soon married and with a growing family, accumulated debts that led to the loss of his property in sheriff's auctions. He left Edgefield in 1846 and, with the help of his relative, former South Carolina governor James Hamilton, began climbing the ladder of Texas politics.[91]

---

on Dec. 28, 1839. He was an SC College senior in 1845, but was expelled before graduation (Hollis, *University of South Carolina*, vol. 1, 138; and "Roll of Students of the University of South Carolina College, 1805–1905," http://genealogytrails.com/scar/1805to1905USC.htm). Wigfall changed his name from Lewis to Louis when he moved to Texas. Two other factors contributed to the intensity of the Brooks-Wigfall feud. Wigfall suspected that the Brookses had opposed the assignment of his brother, Arthur, who had recently abandoned the law for the priesthood, to Edgefield's Trinity Church. Church records suggest that he was mistaken or confused, for as noted above, Rev. Wigfall was installed as rector of Trinity in April 1840, but left for another parish one month later. He would return to fill the pulpit occasionally, as on January 16, 23, and 30, 1842 (WB Journal). A brother of the Wigfalls died from a duel, and Arthur preached against dueling (Wigfall manuscript sermons, Bettis Rainsford collection). The second factor was an Augusta woman whom both Wigfall and Preston Brooks fancied (King, *Wigfall*, 29). On the longevity of the dispute, see James Hammond's observations in summer 1841 in Bleser, ed., *Secret and Sacred*, 60–61, 66; and Faust, *Hammond*, 219–20. Readers baffled by such "touchiness" regarding honor may find the essay on the subject in the *Encyclopedia of Southern Culture* (1483–484), helpful.

[90] William Butler Brooks was born Oct. 4 and died Oct. 15, 1840 (Brooks family Bible, photocopy in Bettis Rainsford files).

[91] King, *Louis T. Wigfall, passim;* and Cooper, *Wigfall, passim.*

Other family tragedies superseded those of 1840, as Brooks' journal painfully reveals. Preston, who was set up by his father with land and slaves at his marriage, lost his wife Caroline Means in childbirth, then married her cousin, Martha, who ultimately gave him four children. The self-esteem he must have gained by a term in the state house of representatives (1844-1846) was likely reduced by his failure to win a second term.[92] James, the second oldest child, graduated from the South Carolina College and received gifts equal to Preston's. He married Sarah Robert of Barnwell District and settled there, and after a few years returned to northern Edgefield, inheriting land from his grandfather. His father doted on his children. Young Whitfield, unmarried, died a hero's death from wounds received in the Battle of Churubusco in 1847. (See below). Ellen, the only daughter, was educated in Charleston and Columbia, and married former physician and Mexican war veteran Robert G. M. Dunovant, a union not entirely suitable to her father apparently. The youngest, Hampden, was schooled in Greenwood and, after the journals end, at the South Carolina College. He and James were Confederate army officers.

In early 1849 Whitfield and Mary left their Edgefield home to Preston and his family and, after making improvements, settled permanently at Roselands. Although his journal records Mary's love of gardening before the move, it was doubtless then that Mary began turning the property into the showplace that visitors would remember. As a nostalgic scribe later described it,

"The large plantation house faced a flower garden....The road wound by the dwelling in a crescent...from end to end shaded by oaks. In open spaces, Bermuda and blue grass grew; back of the grove of big trees behind the house, the land fell away to a spring, pure and sweet, whose flow was carried off in a branch into the wilds of Half-way swamp." Another branch fell off toward what was known as "the territory, where it joined Ninety Six Creek. . . . The upper and lower verandas were festooned with vines. In season the whole place was glorified with roses. . . . The grove was always alive with squirrels, many albinos among them. . . . The family chapel was just off the highway, to the right as you went toward Edgefield." Inside, "[t]he wide hall had the drawing room on the right, its walls ornamented with ancestral portraits, and the dining room on the left, where the wide sideboard knew and did its duty."[93]

Whitfield Brooks died on December 28, 1851, a little over a month shy of his sixty-second birthday. Had he lived another year he would have relished, Preston's election to the U.S. House seat vacated by his rival Armistead Burt. Brooks' long-time friend and political ally Francis W. Pickens was among the losing candidates, so death spared Whitfield the awkwardness of that intra-clique contest. No doubt his victory

---

[92] All district seats were filled by at-large votes.

[93] "Paladins of South Carolina: John Hampden Brooks," *Advertiser*, Nov. 22, 1922, reprinted from *The State*. At Mary's death in 1870, John Hampden ("Ham") inherited Roselands. Today Tillman Territory Road crosses SC 246 south of the town of Ninety Six.

gave Preston some feeling of vindication, but he could hardly have imagined the challenge to his family's honor that this would present to him. Five more years would have allowed Whitfield to share in his son's achievement of a fame—and a notoriety—attained by no other Edgefieldian, not even Ben Tillman or Strom Thurmond. Preston's caning of Senator Charles Sumner of Massachusetts, a physical response to what was to him an unbearable verbal provocation, ratcheted up sectional hostility and nourished the nascent Republican Party. Had he lived, the adulation of southerners might have carried Preston to the upper echelons of the Confederacy.[94]

We are left with two questions. First, how was Preston Brooks, the scion of the Brooks clan, affected by his relationship with his proud but sometimes disappointed father? As William Freehling , who labeled him "the essential South Carolinian [of his day]," observed a decade ago, "[t]he great biography of Preston Brooks has yet to be written; it will demonstrate the more personal reasons why [he] demonstrated South Carolina's more general hot and cold aggressiveness." The studies by William-James Hull-Hoffer and Stephen Puleo, published since Freehling's prediction, while valuable, have likely not preempted more thorough attempts. The historiographical foundation has been laid by Lloyd Benson, Stephen Berry, Vernon Burton, Jane Turner Censer, Lorri Glover, Harlan Joel Gradin, Steven Stowe, Bertram Wyatt-Brown, and others, all pointing to the complex relationship of planter fathers and sons and the need sons felt to merit their parents' approval and uphold family honor by demonstrating courage and "manliness."[95]

While his daily life provided a mixture of evidence by which his father could gauge his maturity, four dramatic episodes allowed Preston Brooks opportunities to earn fatherly approval: his duel with Lewis Wigfall and its extended epilogue of verbal

---

[94] On Preston's election to Congress, see Edmunds, *Pickens*, 124–26. On the historiography of the Brooks-Sumner affair, see preface, note 4. An essay on Preston Brooks, appearing only a few weeks after his death in the *Southern Quarterly Review,* gushed with superlatives and ventured that "it was his fortune [fate] to become the standard bearer of one of the great parties of the country" (*SQR*, Series 3, 2/2 [Feb. 1857]: 348). Since James Hammond wrote to the prolific William Gilmore Simms on Jan. 31, 1857, and mentioned Preston Brooks, I suspected Simms as the author (Bleser, ed., *Hammonds of Redcliffe*, 23–24). But Maximilian LaBorde is identified as the author in a sketch on him in his *History of the South Carolina College*, xxiii. The *Review's* editor at that time was James Thornwell, who knew LaBorde well as a former faculty colleague at the college, and LaBorde, of course, knew Preston well. Also on PSB's prospects, see Chapman, *Edgefield,* 265–66. On the caning's national impact, which included further enflaming the anti-slavery violence of John Brown in Kansas, see Puleo, *The Caning*, ch. 13; and Gienapp, "The Crime Against Sumner." Preston Brooks died on Jan. 27, 1857.

[95] William W. Freehling, *The Road to Disunion: Secessionists Triumphant, 1854–1860,* 81, 546–47 n. 36. Like WB, many antebellum parents felt "anxiety" that their children were "incapable of controlling their urges and unwilling to accept responsibility" ("Mothers and Children of the Present Day," quoted in Berry, *All That Makes a Man*, 32. See also, Stowe, *Intimacy and Power.* An interpretive study of Preston Brooks, Harlan Joel Graden, "Losing Control," is unpublished.

jousting in 1840-1841; his volunteering, despite Wigfall's bullet lodged in his hip, to command Company D of the Palmetto Regiment during the U.S.—Mexico War (1846-48); his July, 1849 affair of honor with cousin Milledge Bonham; and, after his father's death, his May 22, 1856 response to Senator Sumner's speech.[96]

The first of these may have accomplished the young man's hopes, although at the expense of great parental anxiety and extensive effort on the part of his father and prominent friends, as the Brooks Journals indicate, to mediate the ongoing controversy between two equally combative hotspurs. It was Wigfall, after all, who "left the field," emigrating in disgrace to Texas a few years later (young Brooks seriously considered moving to Florida about the same time). The second, commanding Company D of the Palmetto Regiment, surely seemed to be the ultimate opportunity. But the long march inland from Vera Cruz with every step made more difficult by Wigfall's bullet, weakened him, and typhoid got him sent home before any real test of courage under fire. His aborted campaign was unavoidably contrasted with that of his father's cousin, Pierce Mason Butler, and his younger brother, Whitfield. Butler, a former South Carolina governor and the commander of the Palmetto Regiment, died on the battlefield at Churubusco, and Whitfield succumbed to wounds received during a heroic assault there after his commander assured him that he had acted like a man. This brought deep grief, mixed, possibly, with envy, to Preston.[97]

Preston surely sensed that Whitfield was his father's favorite. Brooks' journal entry in which he responds to the news of his namesake's death is especially revealing on this point. The brothers' grandfather Zachariah Brooks left young Whitfield his gold watch in his 1846 will. As a witness to the document, Preston's knowledge of this may have compounded his sense of need, as the eldest son, to merit the elder Brooks' favor.[98] Young Whitfield's impressive funeral, Preston's maddening inability

---

[96] Isolated incidents do not necessarily define a life; Robert Mathis observed that Preston Brooks was not generally inclined toward violent outbursts, and sometimes found ways to avoid them (Mathis, "Preston Smith Brooks," 296). Another discussion of these episodes is in Deitreich, "Ever Able, Manly, Just, and Heroic," 30–31.

[97] "Preston Smith Brooks," *SC Ency.*, 100. Also see, Gradin, "Losing Control," 157–67. As was the norm, PSB was elected captain by his company. WB supported the war against Mexico (*Journal*; Lander, *Reluctant Imperialists*, 15; and Edmunds, *Pickens,* 101). Afterwards he would write, "It would be difficult to find a man, the blood of whose family had been poured out more copiously or freely on the soil of Mexico" (WB to Congressman James Black, Dec. 20, 1847, PSB Papers, SCL). The loss of his beloved son, in addition to a cousin and a nephew (and the wounding of two other kinsmen) was a blow from which his wife felt Whitfield never recovered. (Brooks' obituary, *Advertiser*, Jan. 1, 1852; and O'Neall, *Biographical Sketches of Bench and Bar*, vol. 2, 373–75).

[98] Will of Zachariah Smith Brooks, Edgefield County Archives. Editor's copy. Preston Brooks' name appears as a witness on a typescript copy of the will. Zachariah survived his grandson Whitfield's death, so the original will was revised by a codicil. On his father's dashed hopes for his lost son, Preston's anxiety over missed opportunities, and his desire to repair what

to achieve a proud war record, and the apparent suspicion among Edgefield wags as to his courage, compounded the older brother's frustration and self-doubt. After recuperating at home as an only moderately successful recruiter, Preston, aided by his father, pleaded for a second chance, and was returned to his company, but too late for honor-restoring duty. He came home to raised eyebrows over questions about his conduct. He was not included in the July 4, 1849 parade of Edgefield veterans, nor did he receive one of the presentation swords given to several of these men. A July 4, 1849 oration provided him what he apparently saw as a third opportunity. He reacted to the slight by throwing suspicion on his cousin Milledge Bonham's war experience. (He had missed action as well, after shooting himself in the foot). Bonham's concern for his honor led him to insist that Brooks acknowledge their equality. Brooks' frustrating replies might have driven them to the dueling ground but for the intercession of friends on both sides.[99] However, his restrained if frustratingly evasive letters in the exchanges that followed showed maturity (contrasted with his behavior in the Wigfall affair nine years earlier) as he proceeded with care and accepted the aid of friends as mediators. The result was that Bonham was satisfied, and the relationship was healed in less than a month.[100]

Had Preston lived long enough, a final opportunity to vindicate his honor would have come with his state's secession and military mobilization, but his death in January 1857, before reaching the age of forty, preempted that. Instead, in May 1856 Congressman Brooks faced what was to be the last major test of his honor. His violent response to the extraordinary "Crime Against Kansas" speech in which Senator Charles Sumner condemned slavery, demeaned white southern values, and mocked the absent Senator Andrew Pickens Butler, can best be understood in the context of his Edgefield roots, his complete identification with the South's slave system, and, perhaps foremost, his obligation to defend his family. Brooks' explanation, that after carefully reading Sumner's speech "I had no alternative" but to redress "a personal wrong," left the senator, assuming he read it, baffled. (He apparently did not know of

---

he felt was a damaged reputation, see WB to Representative James A. Black, Dec. 20, 1847, PSB Papers, SCL, USC.

[99] PSB to Adj. Gen. R. Jones, July 2, 1847; PSB to Dr. James Davis (Surgeon of Palmetto Regiment), Aug. 26, 1847; copy of Davis' letter documenting PSB's condition on the march, Oct. 7, 1847; and WB to Congressman James A. Black, 20 Dec., 1847, PSB Papers, SCL, USC. On recognition of young Whitfield's heroic end, see W. G. Simms, "Young Whitfield Brooks," and "Oh! Stern Was the Voice of That Anguish," *Lays of the Palmetto*, 30–32. On Preston-bashing by Edgefieldian "Bill Jones" in summer 1847, see Abner Blocker (his cousin) to PSB, Jan. 4, 1848 (PSB Papers, SCL). Letters between Brooks and Bonham, July 14–26, 1849, are in the PSB Papers and M. L. Bonham papers, SCL. On this episode, see Stowe, *Intimacy and Power*, 30–33.

[100] Letters dated July 13, 14, 16, 17, 18 (2), 19 (2), 20, 21, 25, 26 (3), Milledge Luke Bonham papers, SCL. See also, Stowe, *Intimacy and Power*, 30–33.

the Butler-Brooks kinship.) Sumner's first comment on the attack, "I could not believe that a thing like this was possible," dramatizes the cultural distance between the two men.[101] The kinship was strong. A. P. Butler was the congressman's first cousin once removed, a brother of Preston's Palmetto Regiment commander Pierce Mason Butler, and a cousin his father had grown up with. Senator Butler's mother, Behethland Foote Moore Butler, then three years dead, was Whitfield Brooks' much venerated "Aunt Butler," who, after the death of his mother in 1802, had virtually raised him along with her own eight children. Given these ties and obligations, not to have "chastised" Sumner would have been, in Preston's eyes and the eyes of many if not most of his constituents, to disgrace himself.[102]

There remains another layer of context and possible motivation, harder to assess but more profound if real. The Brooks journal reveals the complex father-son relationship of Whitfield and Preston, and invites conjecture as to the son's still-unresolved need to prove his mettle to the doubting shade of his then dead father. The point should not be pushed too far, for the evidence is complex. In the diary that Preston kept during the early and mid-1850s, at least in excerpts, copied by his wife Martha for their children, there is nothing that suggests anything but an ideal father-son relationship. And in his resignation speech in the House of Representatives he made no mention of his father. But what might Martha have omitted, and what might Preston have *felt* as he delivered his remarks?[103]

At least Preston Brooks need not have worried about his state's impression of him. His first two elections to the House, 1853 and 1855, had surely made an impression beyond his district. The moderate stance—by South Carolina standards—he had taken on sectional issues provided a backdrop for his immoderate response to Sumner's speech, possibly presenting the caning in a more acceptable light for some. While many wished he had reacted differently, an unprecedented multitude feted him in the town of Ninety Six. He received journalistic support and commendations from across the South, a silver cup from admirers in Columbia, and an unknown number of new canes, one inscribed "Hit him again!" As icing on the cake, a virtually unanimous constituency returned him to Congress after his resignation following the House of Representatives vote to reprimand, but not to expel him, and elected him again in the fall. His death on January 27, 1857, after a short illness announced as croup or laryngitis, elicited grief, more honors, and varying theological inferences. On November 26, 1857, Governor R. F. W. Allston reminded legislators that "Since your last session…The Honorable Preston S. Brooks, while in the midst of active public

---

[101] Donald, *Sumner*, 297; Benson, *The Caning*, 135. See also, Brooks' written statement to the Senate.

[102] On WB's appreciation of PMB, see *Journal*, April 14, 1845.

[103] In remarks at his trial he did mention his mother (Benson, *The Caning*, 198–99). For his resignation speech, see Benson, 149–54. The unedited diary is evidently still in private hands. Tom Balcerski kindly shared with me his transcript of portions of the Preston Brooks papers at the SCL, which I also examined.

duty, engaged in a course of usefulness and honor, and winning by his manly conduct and sterling worth, the confidence and admiration of members, was removed to another sphere." But readers of Whitfield Brooks' journal may wonder how much comfort Preston, troubled as he may have been as to his father's perception of his behavior, could have taken in such public tributes.[104]

A second question, while unanswerable, invites speculation encouraged by the historiography on honor in the Old South. How would a more long-lived Whitfield Brooks have reacted to his son's attack on Sumner? Surely he would have felt pride, but also dismay. Brooks was uneasy about democratic politics, especially the demagoguery prompted by a lust for office, and the public's tendency toward political idolatry. One imagines him greeting the flattery heaped upon Preston in the Southern press, and the tumultuous reception given him at Ninety Six, first with family pride—Sumner had it coming, he would have thought, and cousin Pickens Butler didn't deserve Sumner's vitriol—but also with dismay. "Will my boy be able to keep his head amidst all this?" he would have wondered. Preston's violent encounter with George Dionysus Tillman over a card game a few weeks after the caning could only have increased Whitfield's concern on that account.[105]

One aspect of Preston's response to the outpouring of adulation from around the South might have eased his father's anxiety. In a letter to his brother "Ham" he lamented having "lost my individuality in my representative capacity...as an exponent of the South..." In his son's "struggle to adapt to his new identity as an icon of sectionalism," Whitfield would have seen a welcomed sign of mature self-awareness. Yet Preston would yield to the mob-spirit at least once, saying, falsely, to the multitude at Ninety Six, "I have been a disunionist since the time I could think." Hearing that, Whitfield Brooks would have shaken his head again. But he might also have recalled

---

[104] Devereaux, *Life and Times of R. F. W. Allston,* 206. A second loss cited by the governor was "the late Judge [Senator Andrew Pickens] Butler," for whom "the labors of the last Congress had proved too much." The inscription on Preston Brooks' monument in Edgefield's Willowbrook Cemetery reinforces the view that he was a hero in the eyes of his constituents. His mother provided another tribute, a marble plaque, first displayed in the family chapel at Roselands, and now at the South Caroliniana Library, University of South Carolina. A contrary view was expressed by Rev. Basil Manly, a former pastor of Edgefield Baptist Church and now at the Wentworth Street Church, Charleston. He called Brooks' untimely death "a very impressive event," and noted "how differently God sees from ourselves! When all were admiring, and some envying, - God 'changes his countenance' and sends him away" (Fuller, *Chaplain to the Confederacy*, 348). Another southern clergyman who saw Brooks' conduct in an unfavorable light was Virginia Presbyterian Robert Lewis Dabney (Hobson, *Tell About the South*, 95).

[105] Simkins, *Pitchfork Ben Tillman,* 32. Tillman was Ben's older brother, and a future Congressman. Simkins provides no details, but the Tillmans' violent reputation could have eased fatherly concerns. In 1853 Preston had publicly challenged an anonymous letter-writer who backed his congressional opponent, Francis Pickens, to a duel. Pickens had disavowed his candidacy, then reversed himself (Edmunds, *Pickens,* 125–26).

his father's fury at Catlett Connor and brawl with Mathew Jones, or his own window-breaking moment.[106]

[106] Hull Hoffer, *The Caning of Charles Sumner*, 92–93; and Benson, *The Caning of Senator Sumner,* 197. Robert Mathis wrote that this was the only time Brooks made that statement (Puleo, *The Caning,* 185). Congressman Brooks was allied with Democratic nationalist James L. Orr (Benson, *The Caning*, 27–28). He had once called disunion "a fearful catastrophe," but at Ninety Six was heard to say "the Constitution of the United States should be torn to fragments." Virginia Congressman J.M. Botts thought the praise and abuse Brooks received had combined to "bewilder and mislead his judgment" (Puleo, *The Caning*, 184–85). On PSB's relative moderation, see Edmunds, *Pickens*, 124–25. An example is his speech on the Kansas-Nebraska Act (Benson, *The Caning*, 28–33). Dozens of editorials from Northern and Southern newspapers are accessible from Furman University Dept. of History, online "Secession Era Editorials Project," http://history.furman.edu/editorials/see.py. Select "Sumner."

ILLUSTRATIONS

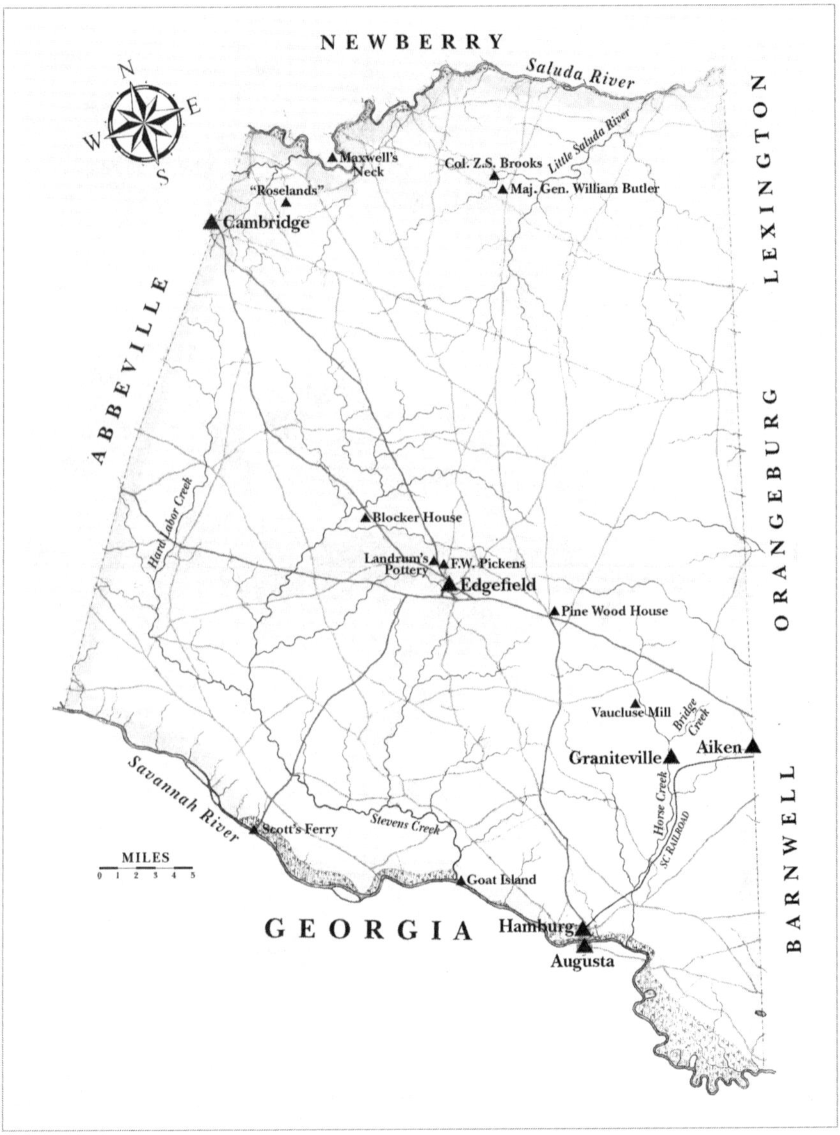

Map of the Old Edgefield District, based on Thomas Anderson's 1817 survey, improved for Robert Mills' *1825 Atlas of the State of South Carolina*. Alterations by Tim Belshaw.

Map used with permission of South Carolina Department of Archives and History.

Whitfield Brooks (1790–1851).
Portrait by William Harrison Scarborough, 1844.
Copy in the Edgefield Discovery Center, image by Haigh Reiniger.

Mary Parsons Carroll Brooks (1800–1870).

Portrait by William Harrison Scarborough, 1844.

Courtesy of descendant Mary Jane Brooks Mobley.

Preston Smith Brooks (1819–1857).
Portrait by William Harrison Scarborough, 1844.
Courtesy of and photograph by McKissick Museum, University of South Carolina.

Whitfield Brooks house (built ca. 1820) on Buncombe Street in Edgefield was aquired by Brooks in 1825. The portico was likely added later. Later the house burned and was rebuilt substantially as before but with wider portico.

Trinity Episcopal Church, Simkins Street, Edgefield.
Organized 1835, sanctuary built 1836.
Original portico replaced by a tower in 1886; current steeple 1951.

Front porch of Roselands plantation house (built ca. 1849), northern Edgefield District as seen today.
Courtesy of James Farmer.

Behethland Foote Moore Butler (1764–1853).
Wife of Revolutionary War General and Congressman William Butler;
Whitfield Brooks' much-admired aunt;
mother of Andrew Pickens Butler and Pierce Mason Butler.
Artist unknown. Courtesy of South Carolina State Museum, photograph by Hunter Clarkson.

Andrew Pickens Butler (1796–1857).
State legislator, judge, U.S. Senator from 1846–1857.
Artist unknown. Courtesy of South Carolina State Museum, photographed by Hunter Clarkson.

Pierce Mason Butler (1798–1847).
Soldier, Bank of South Carolina president, governor,
and Commander of the Palmetto Regiment, Mexican-American War.
Artist Jacob Eichholtz, ca. 1821.
Courtesy of South Carolina State Museum, photograph by Hunter Clarkson.

AN EDGEFIELD PLANTER
AND HIS WORLD

THE JOURNALS OF WHITFIELD BROOKS
NOVEMBER, 1840 – MAY, 1849
VOLUME I

I

November 1840

Tuesday 3rd Clear & cool. I left home this morning in company with Doct. Cain & Col. Carroll[1] for Hamburg[2] to witness a hostile meeting between the latter gentleman and L. T. Wigfall Esq.[3]

Wednesday 4th. The meeting between Col. Carroll and Wigfall took place about 1 ocl on an island in the Savannah River a few miles above Augusta, Genl. Jones[4] acting as the second of Carroll & Mr. Manning[5] of Wigfall. They exchanged shots without effect – when a reconciliation was brought about by the seconds and they left the ground & we all returned to Hamburg. Here my son Preston[6] challenged Wigfall, which was accepted.

---

[1] Dr. S. V. Cain (–1859), a favored companion of WB, lived near Cambridge and was active in the Cambridge Agricultural Society. James Parsons Carroll (1809–1883), brother-in-law and law protégé of WB, a member of his household from age nine. Lawyer, SC house and senate, Chancellor 1859–1868, secession convention. Married Eliza, a daughter of Senator John M. Berrien of Georgia, led investigation into burning of Columbia in 1865. Retired as the "most distinguished member of the Columbia bar."

[2] Market town on the Savannah River opposite Augusta. See introduction.

[3] Edgefield native Lewis (later Louis) Trezevant Wigfall (1816–1874), a brilliant but self-destructive lawyer and political operative. Marriage settled him somewhat, but he moved to Texas in 1846 after losing his property in sheriff's sales. There his "fire-eater" flamboyance led him to the U.S. Senate in 1859, and then into the Confederate government, where he clashed with President Jefferson Davis.

[4] General James Jones (1805–1865). Born in Ridge Spring. Lawyer, brother-in-law of industrialist William Gregg. Partner/manager of Vaucluse cotton mill, Captain in Seminole War, co-founded *Edgefield Advertiser* with WB ally Maximillian LaBorde. Adjutant and Inspector General of SC, Chair, Board of Visitors, The Citadel 1842–1865, directed construction of State House, Colonel in Civil War, recognized authority on the Code Duello who was successful in averting some duels.

[5] John Laurence Manning (1816–1889). Clarendon District native, son of Governor Richard I. Manning. Lewis Wigfall's friend and idol as a young man. A Unionist in the Nullification era. Governor 1852–1854, signer of Ordinance of Secession. Owned over 600 slaves in 1860. "The handsomest man alive," according to Mary Boykin Chesnut. Barred by the U.S. Senate from taking a seat in 1865.

[6] See introduction.

Thursday 5th. We left Hamburg and returned to Edgefield. The weather mild and pleasant.

Friday 6th. I went to my plantation[7] and gave directions about sowing wheat, etc.

Saturday 7th. Rode over my plantation, inspected the crop & selected the ground for the wheat & rye. The day cloudy, cool and some rain. Kennerly[8] passed the day and night with me. Directions given to overseer to begin to sow wheat on Monday.

Sunday 8th. Mild & pleasant. I returned home.

Monday 9th. Clear and seasonable weather.

Tuesday 10th. The weather still mild. Col. P. M. Butler[9] arrived from Columbia in the stage to act as the second for Preston. He, Preston, Carroll, and Doct. Cain left the Village at 2 oclock for Doct Geiger's[10] where they remained all night. The week devoted to sowing wheat.

Wednesday 11th. I left home after an early breakfast and came up with my friends at the fork of the road near Peggy Clark.[11] Here we met Mr. Manning, who informed us, that the meeting between my son and Wigfall was appointed to take place at some point near to Col. Bausketts[12] plantation. This information forced the party to make a rapid drive in order to reach the place in time. We arrived at 2 ocl. at Bauskett's plantation and partook of the remains of a very good dinner prepared by the wife of the overseer. In a short-time, the parties took their departure for the place, selected for the hostile meeting. This was a small, sterile & bleak island in the [Savannah] River, called goat island, containing about one acre of land & having no accommodations but its insulated situation which protected the party from interruption. The principals, seconds, physicians, and three friends on each side rowed over in a small boat to the island. The parties were soon posted in a position, where they could be distinctly seen from the shore. The first fire was ineffectual, Wigfall miss-

---

7 "Roselands" plantation, a few miles southeast of the village of Cambridge, was a half-day's carriage ride from Edgefield Courthouse. See map.

8 Rev. S. W. Kennerly. Possibly Shearried (*sic*) Kennerly, born Aug. 3, 1804.

9 Pierce Mason Butler (1898–1847), son of William Butler and Behethland Moore, cousin of WB. U.S. Army 1819–1829, plantation near Columbia. President, Columbia branch, Bank of the State of SC, 1833–1836. Co-author Ordinance of Nullification. Seminole War, Governor 1836–1838, Commander Palmetto Regiment, Mexican-American War. Killed at Churubusco Aug. 20, 1847.

10 Dr. William W. Geiger, began medical practice in area around Cherokee Ponds, eight miles from Hamburg, in 1837. After several years became commission merchant in Hamburg.

11 Margaret Clark, age c.36 (1850 census).

12 John Bauskett (1794?–1867), Newberry native, lawyer, legislator, planter on Beaver Dam Creek with over 2,000 total acres. Part-owner Vaucluse Mill. Ferry and bridge owner (Stevens Creek). Two hundred twenty-one slaves in 1850, real and personal estate $161,000 in 1860. Married Roman Catholic Sophia Crozon and converted. Preston Brooks' congressional colleague Lawrence Keitt married daughter Susan.

ing Preston and the ball of the latter passing through the coat & waistcoat of Wigfall over his breast but not touching the skin. At the second fire both were wounded and both fell. I saw my son fall. My feelings at that occurrence, may be more easily conceived than described. I crossed over to the island in a few minutes & upon witnessing an examination of his wound discovered that the ball had entered near the spine, passing through the fleshy part of the left hip and touching the bone, & then passing through the left arm, shattering one of the bones. Wigfall was shot through both thighs. Owing to the situation of the island, & the want of accommodations in the neighborhood, they were forced to remain on the island during the night, on the very spots, where they fell. It was after nine ocl before we could procure either bed or covering for Preston, until which time he lay with nothing but a cloak around him. He was hurried into the fight without the necessary preparation. A light shower of rain fell about 10 ocl. which rendered his situation still more uncomfortable. After making a tent of blankets for him, providing as well for his comfort as I could, I left him for the night in the care of Col. Butler, Carroll & his physician Doct. Cain, who is a good fellow but not a very skillful surgeon.

Thursday 12th I left Bauskett's this morning for Hamburg, having first heard from the parties on the island. I arrived in Hamburg about 12 oclock, and the wounded party, who came by water in an open boat, about 10 ocl. Preston was carried to Hubbards,[13] in a state of much exhaustion & some fever. He had a bad night.

Friday 13th The morning cold and clear. Doct. Dugas[14] was employed this morning to attend on Preston, when Doct. Cain and our friends took their departure for Edgefield and Columbia. Preston's fever assumed the type of pneumonia & presented some alarming symptoms this day.

Saturday 14th A change in the weather and rain during the day. Preston was very ill today.

Sunday 15th Cold and clear. Preston was too ill for either his mother, grandmother or myself to leave him long enough to go to church. Preston still very ill.

Monday 16th Very cold & heavy frost & ice. Preston somewhat better.

Tuesday 17th Very cold & clear. Preston still mending.

Wednesday 18th No change in the temperature of the weather. Heavy rain.

Thursday 19th Cloudy in the morning but clear by 9 ocl. I returned to Edgefield

---

[13] An inn run by Mr. and Mrs. Hubbard. WB stayed there on several trips to Hamburg, which was too far from ECH for a round trip.

[14] Louis Alexander Dugas (1806–1884), internationally known surgeon, founder and professor at the Medical College of Georgia, Augusta. Published over 100 medical treatises. During the first outbreak of Yellow Fever in Augusta in 1839, he alone attributed it to a pathogen brought by the new railroad. Its transmission by infected mosquitoes was established in 1900.

with Mr. Carroll. Miss Sarah Jeter[15] was married to a Mr. Harris from N. Carolina. Judge Butler[16] took tea with me & returned from the wedding and remained with me till after breakfast next day.

Friday 20th. I returned to Hamburg with Col. Carroll & Abner Blocker[17] in the carriage with me. I sent my nephew to the Georgia railroad depository on his way to Alabama. He is a manly, promising boy, and I shall be disappointed if he does not make an energetic, influential & honorable man. I found Preston much improved so far as the fever had affected him & his wounds gradually mending. The early part of the week very cold.

Saturday 21. Clear and mild. I crossed the River to Augusta & saw at the Hampton race course the celebrated race horse Boston[18] & his rival [Gant?]. They are large, tall, & powerful made horses.

Sunday 22nd. I returned to Edgefield to day with Hampden.[19] The day cold & the night very cold.

Monday 23rd. Very cold. I went in the afternoon to Major Blocker's[20] & staid all night. The family were well. I here met my daughter,[21] who was staying with the

[15] Sarah Jane Jeter, daughter of Sabra Simkins Jeter and John Speed Jeter (1789–1847), WB neighbor, lawyer, legislator, solicitor, nullifier, state senator, who served with WB on local boards and commissions. During the Revolution his father was captured and tortured by British soldiers wanting his gold. Sarah married William A. Harris.

[16] Andrew Pickens Butler (1796–1857), "Pickens." Brother of P. M. Butler, cousin of WB. Lawyer with large practices in several districts, state legislator, circuit and appeals court judge 1833–1846, U.S. Senate 1846–1857. Nullifier, Cooperationist in 1850s. After two brief marriages he lived with his widowed mother Behethland Butler, WB's venerable aunt. A target of Senator Sumner's "Crime Against Kansas" speech.

[17] Abner Blocker, son of Bartley and Nancy Blocker, nephew of WB. Bartley married WB's sister Nancy. After the Mexican War, Abner Blocker wrote to PSB about "slanderous" remarks being made in Edgefield regarding his service.

[18] "Boston," 1833–1850, considered the first great racehorse in the U.S. In 1839 he ran in nine races, winning eight. In 1840 he was unbeaten in seven starts. His owner was sometimes paid not to enter him, thus encouraging more owners to compete.

[19] John Hampden Brooks (1833–1911) was WB's youngest child. Married two daughters of Governor James Hopkins Adams, Captain in Civil War. Inherited Roselands after Mary Carroll Brooks' death, active in opposing "Radical" regime during Reconstruction.

[20] Bartley Blocker (1790–1849) son of John Blocker, Sr., builder of the Blocker House. The "intellectual" of this prominent family. Married Nancy, sister of WB, who brought a dower of slaves from their father Zachariah. Son Wm. Butler killed in Mexican War. Named another son Whitfield Brooks.

[21] Ellen Sophia Brooks (1829–1870), only daughter of WB and Mary, married Robert Gill Mills Dunovant (General, Civil War) on June 21, 1849. Named first son Whitfield. Mother-in-law of suffragist Emma Anderson Dunovant (1866–1956).

family for a few days, during the absence of her mother.[22] I left Major Blocker's for the plantation neighbours Messrs Griffith[23] & Kay, on a hunting excursion. All well.

Wednesday 25. Cloudy & a light rain in the morning. That afternoon pretty clear.

Thursday 26. Clear & cold day. A very heavy frost & ice. I rode over to Prestons place[24] with Ellen & Hampden, who were delighted with the extensive prospect from the eminence, on which I am now erecting houses.

Friday 27th. Clear & cold. We returned home.

Saturday 28th. Clear & mild. I went to the Village.[25] I saw some of the good people & a few of the canting hypocrites. Col. Frazier[26] had just returned with his third wife, a Miss Harris of Abbeville, a very distant relation of mine.

Sunday 29th. Warm, clear, & pleasant day. I paid a visit to my Aunt Butler,[27] whom I found in fine health and greatly interested for Preston. Took tea with Mrs. Carroll[28] in the evening.

Monday 30th. Clear and pleasant. I returned to Hamburg prepared for the removal of Preston, whom I found out of all danger & in a convalescent state and in a situation which would allow of his removal. The last day of November was a bright and cheerful one, to all, who were in health and prosperity. About one half of the month was mild and clear, and the other and latter half exceedingly cold. Very little rain fell during the month. It has been to me a month of trial, suffering & solicitude of a painful nature, beyond any thing that I have encountered in all my past life. One man,[29] has caused me more grief, vexation and suffering than I have had to bear from all the other crosses losses or misfortunes of a life of fifty years. May God take

---

[22] Mary Parsons Carroll Brooks (1800–1870), daughter of James Parsons Carroll and Mary Giles, grand-niece of James Parsons, Vice President of SC 1776. See introduction.

[23] William Griffith, 1850 census: age 53, real estate value $3,000.

[24] Leaside, PSB's plantation, was adjacent to WB's Roselands plantation. Both were a few miles south of the village of Ninety Six. Preston would marry Caroline Means within a few months.

[25] WB's home on Cambridge Road (now Buncombe Street) was less than a mile from the Edgefield courthouse; he refers here to the village center.

[26] Col. Marshall B. Frazier (1806–1870), planter, m. Sara Ann Harris of Abbeville, Nov. 24, 1840. In 1850 he opened a dry goods and grocery store in ECH.

[27] Behethland Foote Moore Butler (1764–1853). Born in Virginia. Rev. War heroine. Wife of Capt., later General, William Butler (1759–1821). Several sons prominent in politics and/or military. See introduction.

[28] Mary Giles Carroll (1782–1851), mother of WB's wife. Born in Cork, Ireland, m. Irish immigrant James Parsons Carroll, Sr., in Charleston in 1797. Moved to Edgefield soon after his death and lived adjacent to WB and MPCB. Supporter of Trinity Church, Edgefield. Daughters Sophie and Elizabeth m. Dr. Maximilian Laborde. At death owned 54 slaves.

[29] Lewis [later Louis] Trezevant Wigfall (1816–1874). See introduction.

mercy on him for the mischief he has done & correct the error of his ways, & may he have mercy upon me and forgive whatever faults and sins I may have committed in the unpleasant warfare with this rash & msguided young man, which has been forced upon me and upon my family. I hereby attest, in the presence of Heaven, that a quarrel with that young man was not sought by me, nor was it acceptable to my wishes and purposes. I was willing to do every thing consistent with truth and honor to avoid any hostility with him. He was not in my way, he did not cross my path or that of my family; I had no unkind feeling toward him but on the contrary he had my best wishes for his success. In an unguarded hour, however, he suffered himself to be seduced into the support of a cause, which finally absorbed all his thoughts & engrossed all his wishes & hopes & in defence of which, he was prepared to sacrifice all the social relations of life, with the feelings of kindness and sympathy to which they usually give birth. I leave this record to vindicate myself, when the passing of the hour shall have passed away & when truth may claim her empire, with some hopes of being heard and respected.

December 1. 1840

Tuesday 1. A mild & clear day. At 11 oclock in the morning Preston left Hamburg for home in a close[d] waggon, which I had procured for the occasion. He came as far as Doct. Guiger's, at which place I & his mother overtook him at night and found him in a comfortable state, having sustained no injury from the ride.

Wednesday 2. We left Dr. Guiger's about 10 ocl. and arrived at home near 4 ocl. Preston was suffering from fatigue & debility. The day rather cold and cloudy.

Thursday 3rd. The weather variable with clouds and sunshine & brisk wind. Preston not so well as we could desire. He has fever & but little appetite. His wounds do not give him much pain yet he is very feeble.

Friday 4th. Heavy rain and high wind from 5 o'clock in the morning until 10 ocl. Preston still has fever & a full pulse. His removal from Hamburg has evidently been free of injury so far. I should do injustice to the good people of Hamburg, if I failed here to bear testimony to the uniform and unremitted kindness & attention paid to my son & his family, while he was confined there with his wounds. I have never been thrown among a kinder or more obliging people or a community, who without exception and at all times, manifested greater solicitude for the sufferings of my son or greater anxiety for his recovery. I offer this tribute with pleasure & here take occasion to record an expression of my sincere and grateful thanks for all their kindness & attention. This has proved the most inclement day since the commencement of the fall season. Rain at 4 ocl. P.M. wind from N.E.

Saturday 5th Cold & cloudy through the day with light drizzle. Therm.t 35°.

Sunday 6th Cloudy in the morning but clear at 11 oclock. Therm.t 33° at sunrise. Preston is gradually mending & is now entirely free from fever, & his wounds are healing. Col. Carroll returned from Columbia today but brought no political news, other than that contained in the papers. Our son James[30] writes that he passed his examination & is now a junior.

Monday 7th. Clear, mild and lovely morning by 8 ocl. Therm.t 34°. Several negroes and tracts of land were sold by the Sheriff; the negroes at rates somewhat reduced but the land at fair prices. A likely negro boy 18 years of age sold for $660 & a girl about 15 years old sold for $441. The concourse of persons rather more numerous than is usual at this season of the year. Nothing of interest occurred.

Tuesday 8th. Cloudy & cool in the morning but clear and mild by 10 ocl. I met the trustees of the academy[31] but we adjourned without coming to any determination.

Wednesday 9th. No change in the weather. I went to my plantation where I found a very sick negro.

Thursday 10th. Very warm & clear. I devoted the day to an examination of the plantation

Friday 11th. Still clear & warm. I sold about 200 acres of the Howle tract of land to Elijah Holloway[32] for $725.

Saturday 12th. A cold & inclement day & rain falling in light showers during the greater part.

Sunday 13th. Cloudy in the morning but clear and mild in the afternoon. I returned home to dinner. Saw some half dozen persons from the Village, who called to see Preston.

Heard that Mr. Jno Smyley was married to a doughter of A. Bland[33] and that the election for Governor had resulted in the choice of John P. Richardson[34] by a very large majority, 104 to 47. I sent in my resignation as trustee of the male academy.

Monday 14. Cool morning with a thick fog, which obscured the sun until 10 ocl.

Tuesday 15th. Clear and cold. I went to my plantation, taking Hampden with me.

Wednesday 16th. Clear & mild. I examined my stock & the progress made in the erection of some houses for Preston.

Thursday 17th. No change in the weather. I rode to Cambridge[35] and passed a short time with the few persons whom I saw.

---

[30] James Carroll Brooks (1821–1899), second son of WB. SC College. m. Sarah Crawford Robert of Barnwell Nov. 20, 1843, and lived for several years on a plantation there, then moved to a 950-acre farm on Center Springs Road 5.5 mi. north of ECH, given by his mother. Family tradition says it was a grant to James Parsons. Did not volunteer for service in war with Mexico (two young children) but served in Confederate forces.

[31] Edgefield Male Academy organized 1811. WB was chairman of the board. Subject at issue likely replacing principal teacher.

[32] 1850 census: 53 years old, real estate worth $1,000, 22 slaves.

[33] Avory Bland, 1850 census: age 58, real estate value $40,000, 41 slaves.

[34] See introduction.

[35] Formerly Ninety Six (see introduction), renamed by the legislature in 1797.

Friday 18th. Cold and clear. I was engaged in visiting Preston's new establishment and laying off different portions of land to be cleared.

Saturday 19th. Very cold with fresh wind. I returned home to dinner, finding the family very well except Preston, who is slowly mending.

Sunday 20th. A cold and disagreeable day. Judge Butler & Col. Carroll dined with me.

Monday 21. Clear and pleasant. I rode over my pine land with my neighbor Kirksey[36] and then to the Village. My young friends Davis and Harper from Fairfield are now on a short visit to my son Preston.

Tuesday 22nd. Cold frosty morning but cloudy & mild at night. I sent for my overseer and purchased a quantity of pork for my plantation at 5 cts. I also dined with Col. Carroll, where I met Judge Butler, McClintock[37] and several other gentlemen with whom I passed an agreeable afternoon. Genl. McDuffie[38] and his daughter left us this morning for Mr. Singleton's [his father-in-law, see xxxv]. He was in rather indifferent health but in good spirits.

Wednesday 23rd. A cold and disagreeable day. Very cloudy at sunset and every appearance of snow but clear by 9 ocl. Messrs. Davis and Harper left us this morning on their return to Fairfield & Whitfield returned from his visit to the same District.

Thursday 24th . Clear and cold. Therm.t 18° at sun rise. Ice one inch thick in vessels in the house and the streams of water frozen over.

Friday 25th. A clear and mild day. I dined with Mr. Wardlaw[39] in company with a number of gentlemen. The dinner & wine were excellent but the company rather dull. Preston suffered much yesterday & today from fever and recovers very slowly.

Saturday 26th. Clear & mild with high winds from S.W. Our relation Mrs. Thomp-

---

36 John Kirksey, 1850 census: age 77, 42 slaves, real estate value $2,500.

37 Henry King McClintock (1787–1848), born in Providence, R.I. Brown University. Taught in southern schools 26 years, the last 4 in Edgefield where he died. Lived next door to WB.

38 George McDuffie (1790–1851), Georgia native who was rescued from poverty by the Calhouns. Waddel's academy and SC College (1813). Law partner of Eldred Simkins. SC House 1818–1820, U.S. House 1821–1834. At first a nationalist, he shifted to states rights and was "a living embodiment of the wrath of the nullifiers." (Freehling) Governor 1834–1836. U.S. Senate 1842–1846. Bullet wounds from early duels plagued him until death.

39 Francis Hugh Wardlaw (1800–1861), Abbeville Dist. native, SC College top graduate 1816, settled in ECH 1822 to practice law with WB. Later with brother David and Wm. C. Moragne. Null. Conv., state house, chancellor, secession conv. (purported author of Ordinance). Friend and neighbor of WB. Lived across Buncombe Street. House burned 1846, purchased Holmewood.

son[40] called to see us with her two pretty girls, etc. I have suffered more or less from head aches for several days.[41] My waggons returned from Hamburg, bringing me the intelligence that cotton had sold as high as $10 ¼ per 100 lb. The Season has been for the last two weeks, fine open weather, cold but clear & dry.

Sunday 27th. Partially cloudy and mild in the morning but high No. West wind by 12 ocl. and cold at night. In the afternoon I called to see Mrs. Nicholson[42] who is in a low and declining state of health.

Monday 28th. Clear and cold. Therm.t 20° at sun rise. I recollect no period of this season of the year when there were so many heavy white frosts without rain.

Tuesday 29. Cloudy and cold. Therm.t 32°. Rain stirring & the smoke from the chimneys ascending in a perpendicular line, which I regarded as unusual for so cloudy a day. I went to my plantation, taking Whitfield with me.

Wednesday 30th. Mild and clear. I devoted the day to business. Cloudy at night & light rain before day.

Thursday 31st. No change in the weather from yesterday. The negroes engaged in making a fence next to Mrs. Matthews. Cloudy at night & a light rain. The old year departed in clouds and gloom and during the night, moistened the earth with a gentle shower.

---

[40] Emmala Butler Thompson (1800–1848), only daughter of Wm. and Behethland Butler, cousin of WB, m. Congressman Waddy Thompson of Greenville, Minister to Mexico and Whig political nemesis of Calhoun.

[41] Migraine headaches, beginning about 1833, plagued WB for the rest of his life.

[42] Georgiana Blocker (1813–1841), m. Benjamin F. Nicholson (1810–1841), Brigade Major in Seminole War, in 1830. Four children.

II

January 1841

Friday 1st. The new year was ushered in with heavy clouds and gentle showers of rain, which continued to fall until 10 Oclock. Brisk wind from the South, which gradually changed to the N. West with increase of cold....

Saturday 2nd....I returned home, where I arrived at 2 Ocl. I found Preston much better. The other members of the family were well....

Sunday 3rd....Therm.t down to 16', being the coldest morning during the Winter so far. Ice in great quantities and the day so cold as to freeze in the shade at the warmest part of it. It was too inclement to go to church. Many of the neighbors called to see Preston, during the day, who is gradually on the recovery.

Monday 4th. . . A large concourse of persons, collected in the Village, some on business,some from curiosity, and some from a spirit of speculation. Considerable property was sold by the Sheriff, consisting of lands, negroes, horses, wagons, etc., at pretty fair prices considering the state of the money market. A negro man sold for $700 and a woman for $500. The assemblage of persons, altho numerous, exhibited a sober, well dressed & well behaved population, who live wholly free from want, but in the enjoyment of ease and independence. The harmony of the day was not disturbed by a word of passion or anger, or the slightest incident of an unpleasant kind, except the loss of a pocket book with its contents by Benj. Roper[1] ....

Tuesday 5....Engaged both here & at the plantation in saving pork lard &C which is both an indispensable but dirty & disagreeable employment at this season of the year. In the afternoon I attended the burial of Mrs. Georgiana Nicholson, consort of Benj. Nicholson, who died the previous night of a painful & protracted illness. This lady was distinguished by many high qualities & endeared to her relatives by the exercise of many virtues during her short life.

Wednesday 6th....In the afternoon I rode out to Judge Butler's & brought the [Thompson] girls home with me.

Thursday 7th....Mrs. Thompson & daughters, Judge Butler & several other friends dined with us, with whom our time passed pleasantly & profitably.

....

Monday 11th....I was confined both yesterday and today with violent head ache....

Tuesday 12th....Our servant Sally very ill of typhus fever. I heard that two young & valuable fellows at the plantation were dangerously ill.

Wednesday 13....An election has been going on for the last two days for the clerk of

---

[1] Benjamin Roper (1798–1841): His widow Emily Cogburn (1812–1852) married John Harwood Burt.

the Court in which the people seem to take but little interest, as is apparent from the small vote polled at every part of the District.

Thursday 14th....This is the tenth day successively when rain has fallen. Miss E. Addison[2] & Doct. E. Mims[3] were married by the Revd. Wm. B. Johnson.[4] I & my family were too indisposed to attend. We are informed that the party was large & agreeable & that the arrangements for the supper were most tasteful....

Friday 15th..... My old student at law and friend John Addison[5] with several others called to see us during the day.

Saturday 16th....The present has been to me a week of suffering from my old disease, and by which I am at the moment suffering pain in the head & sick eructations[6] from the stomach. The inclement weather & indisposition have not only prevented me from visiting my plantation, but have confined me to the house since Sunday last....

....

Monday 18th....I am more exempt from pain than I have been for the last eight days. My sufferings yesterday and last night were almost insufferable. Altho feeble and far from being well, my business requires that I should go to my plantation, for which place I set off at 10 oclock. I arrived about 4 ocl. somewhat fatigued but free from head ache. . .

....

Wednesday 20th. This was among the coldest and most gloomy days I ever saw. The surface of the earth and trees were covered with ice....a piercing wind from the N.East. I was confined to the house & passed my time in reading Shakespeare & Cooper,[7] both agreeably and profitably. The sick on my plantation had generally become convalescent.

....

---

[2] Emmeline Sara Addison (1821–1876), daughter of Genl. Allen Bartlett Addison (1788–1850) and Ann Patience Youngblood.

[3] Dr. Edward Jones Mims (1812–1880), son of Matthew Mims (1770–1848). In 1839 built a house at 409 Main St. Friend and partner of Dr. Maximilian LaBorde in a drugstore. Married Emmeline Addison Jan. 14, 1841. His plantation became site of town of Johnston, east of ECH.

[4] William Bullein Johnson (1782–1862), Baptist divine with little formal education who pushed for a more educated clergy. Pastored First Baptist Savannah 1811–1815, First Baptist Greenville, and Edgefield Baptist, 1830–1853. Principal of Edgefield Female Acad. President, SC Bapt. Conv. 1825–1851. First president of Southern Baptist Convention, 1845–1851, although he had worked for sectional cooperation earlier.

[5] John A. Addison (1806?–1841), Commissioner in Equity for Lexington Dist., 1841.

[6] Belching.

[7] James Fenimore Cooper (1789–1851), popular author of the Leatherstocking Tales. WB was probably reading *The Last of the Mohicans* (1826) or *The Pathfinder* (1840).

Friday 22nd. This was a bright & lovely day. The sun rose clear & bright & imparted to all inanimate nature the most brilliant appearance. The grass in the fields & the woods with their covering of ice & pendant icicles & heavy hoar[8] frost exhibited a rich & splendid view. Nature seemed covered with sparkling gems of brilliant white....Saturday 23rd. The same beautiful day as yesterday. I returned home & found the family well. Our daughter Ellen attained 12 years of age, & celebrated her birth by having a few of her juvenile companions to take tea with her.

Sunday 24....I attended for the first time in two years the performance of divine service in the Babtist church. Mr. Johnson was sensible but cold & formal as usual.

Monday 25th....I dined with Col. Carroll where I met Judge Butler, Capt. Bonham,[9] Mrs. Thompson & daughters Miss Thompson & Miss Butler --.

Tuesday 26th....I began this morning to sow oats....

....

Thursday 28th....I labored about three hours in the garden & until I became much fatigued....

....

Saturday 30th. Warm & cloudy at day light. Therm.t 53°. About 8 oclock, the wind changed to the West & it gradually became clearer & cooler. At 12 ocl. the wind had shifted to the North & the sun shown bright & clear & there was every appearance of some settled weather but by night it had veered round to the East & by 9 ocl. it became cloudy. I paid a visit to Major Blocker, where I met my father.[10]

Sunday 31....We had with us at dinner my father, B. M. Blocker, Jr. from Columbia, his two sisters[11] & Miss [H.?] Butler. Since Sale day last there has been but three clear & pleasant days and not more than five without rain. The first week was tolerably clear & cold, the second cloudy & cool & the following week cloudy & warm. For ten days the Therm.t ranged from 32° to 45 & a part of the time up to 56° & at one time to 63°. Then there were three days of intense cold with rain & sleet, which were succeeded by three days of brilliant sun shine & mild temperature. It then became cloudy and so continued from Tuesday the 26th of the month, with occasional light showers & a Therm.t varying from 46° to 52°. The earth is thoroughly saturated with water & the roads in bad condition. Very little plowing has yet been done by planters & no spring oats yet put in the ground. The cotton mar-

---

8 White frost formed on vegetation, fences, etc. in calm weather.

9 Milledge Luke Bonham (1813–1890), soldier, lawyer, planter, politician. Brother of Alamo defender James Butler, cousin of WB. Seminole, Mexican, and Civil Wars. SC house and senate, U.S. house 1857–1860, succeeding PSB. m. Ann Patience Griffin 1845, owned Darby Plantation south of ECH.

10 Zachariah Smith Brooks (1765–1848). See introduction.

11 Julia and Elizabeth, daughters of Bartley and Nancy Blocker.

ket is improving and prime lots now command in Hamburg 11 ¼ cts and very choice 11 ½ cts. Corn is cheep, 45 cts per bushel. In fact provisions are abundant and cheep of every description. The cotton crop is however short – being not much above half the crop of last year, to wit – the year 1839. Money is consequently scarce & in great demand. In fact I have seldom known such a pressure in the money market & so little in circulation. I understand that 15 per cent can be easily obtained for the loan of cash or in a discount of notes of hand. The District is somewhat in debt & I fear that there will be a good deal of sueing.

February 1st 1841

Monday 1st....This was sale day & brought a goodly number of persons to the Village notwithstanding the inclemency of the weather. The crowd was peaceable, altho I saw an unusual number in a state of intoxication in the afternoon, which has been an unfailing cause of quarrel & violence heretofore. Property sold at fair prices.

Tuesday 2nd....I devoted the morning to my father's business & in the afternoon we rode out to Judge Butler's to see our venerable relation Mrs. Butler, who was suffering from a slight attack of nervous affection in the face.

Wedneday 3rd....My father left us after breakfast & I departed to the plantation. I commenced sowing oats this morning.

Thursday 4th....I rode over part of my plantation & examined the state of the fences, ditches &C & also gave directions to Jester[12] in regard to sowing of oats & as to the manner of running the fence around the houses &C. My overseer was sowing some lots in oats for the hogs & breaking up stubble land for cotton. I was rather pleased with the state of the plantation as everything seemed to be pretty well attended to.

Friday 5th....I came by John Stedham's to attend the sale of Robins and Deen's property by the Sheriff. I met with some 20 persons but as I saw nothing which I wished to purchase, I set off home at which I arrived at 4 oc....I was 51 years old today.

Saturday 6th....Such a continuation of wet & cloudy weather has not occurred for years. I have not been able to run the plow for more than three days in thirty, nor have there been but three clear days since sale day in January....

Sunday 7th....We attended in the Epis. church and heard a sermon from the Revd. Mr. Pinckney.[13] The roads to the church presented a mass of mud and water, which made it difficult to pass over them in any vehicle. I had Mr. P. & some friends to take tea, with whom I passed a pleasant evening.

Monday 8th....For the last month there has been a remarkable uniformity both in

---

[12] Overseer.

[13] Rev. Charles Cotesworth Pinckney (1812–1899). Born in Beaufort, ordained as a priest in 1836, served Christ Church Greenville in early 1840s.

the weather & the temperature of the air. It has been cool & cloudy with damp atmosphere even when not raining & the Therm.t varying from 42° to 50° & once or twice up to 60°. The planters are behind with their plowing.

....

Thursday 11 ....I am sowing oats but I fear at the hazard of losing seed by rotting in the ground....

Friday 12th. This was one of the brightest & coldest mornings that has occurred this year. Therm.t 16°. Preston left home yesterday on his way to the plantation & went as far as Major Blockers. I am to meet him today at Jas. Dorn's.[14]

I set off for my plantation & arrived there in the afternoon having suffered considerably by cold. The extreme cold prevented Preston from leaving Major Blockers & he returned home. The earth was frozen to the depth of several inches.

Saturday 13th....I visited old Cambridge to attend a meeting to which, I had been invited, for the purpose of forming an agricultural society. I was called to the chair when Genl. Gillam submitted a resolution for the appointment of a committee to report a constitution, etc. Upon the report of the constitution by the committee, of which the Genl. was chairman, the same was adopted & an election gone into for officers, which resulted in the election of Genl. G as president & myself as V. Pres. I was also elected to deliver an address in May next at the first quarterly meeting of the Society[15]....

Sunday 14. Upon waking this morning I discovered that a snow had fallen, during the night, of one inch in depth....

Monday 15th....I was prevented by the inclemency of the weather from attending to my business as I could have desired....

Tuesday 16 ....I returned home & learned at Dr.[John] Nicholson's,[16] that he was extremely ill & not expected to live many days. He is a most excellent man & his loss would be irreparable to his family & greatly felt in his neighborhood. I found all well at home.

....

Thursday 18....Dr. Laborde[17] arrived from Columbia & passed the night with me.

---

[14] James Dorn (1808–), 1850 census: age 42, $10,000 real estate, 41 slaves.

[15] In 1844 Cambridge Agricultural Society nominated WB's plantation Roselands as best managed in SC, and he won the prize. Description of the plantation by the judges is in the Appendix.

[16] John Oliphant Nicholson (18?? –184?), husband of Elizabeth Threewits, physician, member SC House.

[17] Maximilian LaBorde, M.D. (1804–1873), brother-in-law of WB with his marriage to Sophie Carroll (d. 1841) and after her death Elizabeth Fickling Carroll (1816–1857), sisters of MPCB. Parents emigrated from San Domingue during slave uprising. Studied law

A servant to Mrs. Means arrived with a letter to Preston upon private business. [n.19]

Friday 19th....Finished sowing oats at the plantation.

....

Sunday 21....Heard with much gratification that Doct. Nicholson was so much better as to inspire hopes of his recovery. The cotton market dull & a general stagnation of business, owing to the embarrassed condition of the banks, all of which were required and did attempt to [resume?] the payment of specie on the first of this month[18]....Mrs. Brooks spent the day with our worthy & venerable Aunt Butler, and returned at night, finding me in bed, as a consequence of a violent attack of head ache, from which I got no relief until after 2 ocl. in the morning.

Monday 22nd....Doct. LaBorde took dinner with us.

Tuesday 23rd....Preston, with Ellen in company left us this morning on a visit to Fairfield.[19]

Wednesday 24th....I left home for my plantation by the way of Major Blocker's where I took dinner and arrived at my plantation about sun set, having Wm Blocker and his pack of hounds in company.

Thursday 25....Ascertained from my overseer that he had finished sowing oats about the 20th & that he was thru breaking up stubble land for cotton. He had broken up about 160 acres & expected to finish his stubble land next day. My crop of small grains consists of 20 acres of wheat, about 14 acres of rye, 40 acres in oats for pasturage for the hogs and 100 acres for the sythe. I expect to plant from 250 to 275 acres in cotton and from 170 to 180 acres in corn. I went with the overseer and laid off a dividing line between me and Preston, on which a fence is to be run. I then rode to his place & back home, inspecting the state of the plantation the stock of all kinds, the provisions etc. I saw that manure had been carried to the cotton field, sufficient for the manuring of 20 to 30 acres.

Friday 26th....I went out for a short time, hunting rabbits but the rain drove me to the house.

Saturday 27th....I traded a young sorrel horse to Lewis Matthews[20] for a large black horse. My horse was too light for a plough and had not sufficient action for a saddle horse; I had therefore no inducement to keep him. I rather think that I gave however too much to boot i.e. $30. After an early dinner I set off home, stopping on the

---

with E. Simkins and G. McDuffie, then medicine at MCSC. Co-founder *Advertiser*, taught several subjects as Prof. SC College.

[18] With the effects of the Panic of 1837 still lingering, banks throughout the country were resuming, then suspending specie payment at this time, due to inability to meet the demand for coins in exchange for paper currency.

[19] PSB would marry Caroline Means of Fairfield on March 11, 1841.

[20] Lewis Matthews, 1850 census: age 40, real estate value $1,500.

way to see Doct. Nicholson, who is daily recovering from his attack. I was truly gratified to find this amiable and estimable gentleman on the recovery. Edgefeld could illy spare so worthy a citizen & to his family his death would have been the most serious calamity....

Sunday 28th ....From 12 oclock until night I was confined to my bed with another attack of head ache. In the afternoon my worthy neighbor Mr. Terry[21] called and set with me until 10 ocl.

March 1841

Monday 1st....This being sale day & the . . . day preceding the return of the Court of Common Pleas, a number of persons were collected together. A good deal of property was sold, land, negroes, horses, mules & other kinds of personal property at very reasonable prices & in some instances at low prices. The house & lot formerly belonging to Col. Simkins[22] & built by him for a storehouse was sold for $1050. Thos. Bacon[23] gave for the same not more than two years ago upwards of $3300. Money has never been scarcer in this place & I believe over the District.

Tuesday 2nd....About 8 ocl. at night Joseph[24] arrived with intelligence, that a couple of young horses had refused to draw & that my waggoner could not get on without other horses. I sent these to his assistance....

Wednesday 3rd....We have been prevented by the rain from setting off to Augusta. It is impossible to plough & will be so throughout the week, from present appearances. About 10 oclock there were appearances of clear weather but the clouds soon collected again & continued pour down rain the entire day. My waggon has been on the road since tuesday morning, & has been delayed by stalling & turning over, so much so on the road as only to have reached Major Nicholsons, in two days. I would not have subjected my horses to the fatigue and injury and my negroes to the exposure, scarcely for the load of cotton.

Thursday 4th. At 4 oclock I awoke and found the moon shining brightly. It had become perfectly clear. I called on my man Barnett[25] & started him for Cambridge for

---

[21] James Terry succeeded WB as Commissioner in Equity for Edgefield in 1832. He hosted Edmund Ruffin when the agricultural reformer, hired by Governor Hammond, investigated farming conditions and practices in South Carolina in June 1843.

[22] Eldred Simkins (1779–1831), son of Edgefield founder Arthur Simkins (1749–1826), law partner of George McDuffie and Francis W. Pickens. Mentor of WB. Cedar Fields and Cane Break plantations, 116 slaves. Lt. Gov. 1812–1814, U.S. House 1818–1821, SC Senate and House 1820s. Named son for John C. Calhoun, who called him "my dearest and best friend." Daughters married Pickens, A. P. Butler, and James E. Calhoun.

[23] Thomas Glasscock Bacon (1812–1876), lawyer, 1st Seminole War, Clerk of Edgefield Dist. Court 1845–1860; 1850 census: real estate value $2,000, personal $3,000, 43 slaves. Civil War colonel, raced horses until corruption in the sport repulsed him.

[24] One of WB's most trusted slaves.

[25] A trusted slave.

a recruit of 32 mules....The friends of Genl. Harrison[26] will have a lovely & propitious day for the inauguration of the new President. If the morning shall turn out a true type of his administration, it will be both fortunate & popular. The political sun of Mr. Van Buren set in murky clouds, dark & chill & watery & that of Genl. Harrison has risen in brightness & serenity tho not in spendor. About 12 ocl I left home for Hamburg with Mrs. Brooks, at which we arrived at sun set, encountering the worst road, that I have ever traveled over to Hamburg.

Friday 5th....I was engaged with Mrs. Brooks in shopping the greater part of the day. Sold 6 bags of cotton to Sibley[27] for 10 cts. It being the last of my crop & laid out a bill for groceries with him....I met at the tavern in Hamburg Genl. McDuffie and several other friends, with whom I passed a pleasant afternoon.

Saturday 6th....The streets of Hamburg covered with mud and water. We left Hamburg at 10 oclock. I have never had to bear greater suffering than during the whole way from Hamb to Edgefield, arising from sick stomach and pain in the whole head & eyes....Mrs. Patterson & her sister Miss Smith came in company with us from Hamburg & staid with us at night.

Sunday 7th..... The Revd. Mr. [Charles] Pinckney preached in the Episcopal church.

Monday 8....We were engaged in making preparations for a trip to Fairfield.

Tuesday 9th....We set off for Fairfield & arrived at my father's in the afteroon....heavy rain from about midnight.

Wednesday 10th....a continued fall of rain through the entire day. The water courses appeared considerably swollen in the morning & discouraged me from prosecuting my trip to Faifield. Preston had gone the day before as far as Mr. Herbert's in Newberry, taking with him Misses Carroll & Blocker with the expectation of reaching Fairfield on the afternoon of this day. About 10 oclock I consented with reluctance to take the road, and about 11 ocl we left my father's, with the design of reaching Newberry C[ourt] House. I found the roads in bad order & the water courses very full, yet we reached the village in good time and without any accident. We took lodging at the Brick Tavern, where I fortunately met Major Davis[28] from Fairfield, a very worthy & clever gentleman, in whose company I passed a pleasant evening.

Thursday 11....rain from morning until night. About 8 ocl. we left Newberry with Major Davis as a pilot and traveling through the rain, arrived about 12 ocl at the

---

[26] William Henry Harrison was the first Whig to win the presidency, but died within a month of taking office and was succeeded by Vice President John Tyler. See introduction.

[27] Hamburg merchants. Josiah Sibley (1809–1888), Mass. native, moved to Georgia in 1821 to join brothers in business. Store moved to Augusta in 1855. He invested in land, railroads, banking, etc. Said to have freed slave Seaborn Evans, who was an early colonist in Liberia. Opposed secession but supported CSA financially. Sibley Cotton Mill (1882–2012) named for him.

[28] Possibly William K. Davis, a planter near Montecello, "very intelligent and well read," who married a Miss Zimmerman of Darlington.

cross roads near to Ashfords ferry.[29] Here we learned that we could not get over the river at this ferry. Upon this information we turned toward Hovie ferry & upon reaching the river was informed by the ferry man that there was no passing the river with the boat but that he could carry us over in a canoe or small battoe [bateau] without much hazard. We at last determined to pass over in this way & made arrangements to leave the servants with the horses & carriages in the care of a gentleman on this side of the River. Major Davis & my son Whitfield[30] first passed over & Mrs. Brooks & myself followed. Just as we had crossed over, a cotton boat was passing up the River on its return from market & upon applying to the patron I was informed that he could transport the carriage & horses over the River. I offered him $5 for which he undertook and soon succeeded in getting both horses & carriages over the river without much trouble & apparently without the slightest danger. After stopping for a short time at Mr. Hovie's, to whose house we had been carried in his private carriage, waiting for the carriages, & partaking of the kind lady's hospitality in a good cup of coffee by a warm fire, upon the arrival of the carriages we continued our journey & arrived at Major Davis about sun set. We met with a kind and hospitable reception from Mrs. D & were entertained by her & the Major with great civility and cordiality. They are exceedingly clever people & we were pleased with the opportunity of adding them to the list of our acquaintances.

Friday 12th....another cold & rainy day. We set off for Mrs. Means about 10 ocl & arrived about 12 ocl. We here met the members of the Means family, who had collected at a dining party, given to the young married pair. The marriage ceremony between our son Preston and Miss C. Means[31] had been solemnized the previous evening, so that we were a day "after the fair," occasioned by the high waters. I . . . was much pleased with the family circle into which our son had married....

Saturday 13th....We passed the day at Mrs. Means, the widow of the Revd. Robt. Means[32], where we met a number of our friends, with whom I passed a pleasant day and partook of an excellent dinner.

Sunday 14....We attended church & heard a well written sermon by the Revd. Mr. Ketchum. I dined in company of a number of gentlemen with Major Means[33], who

---

[29] Crossed the Broad River northeast of the town of Newberry.

[30] Whitfield Butler Brooks (Dec. 28,1825–Oct. 2, 1847), WB's third son. See introduction.

[31] Caroline Harper Means (1819–1843), daughter of David Harper Means (1794–1840) and Frances Coulter (1800–1868).

[32] Robert Means (1796–1836), Presbyterian clergyman. SC College 1813. Rev. Dr. George Howe wrote that only advancing blindness kept him from being appointed to the faculty of Columbia Seminary. Author of *Sermons, and an Essay on the Pentateuch* (Boston, 1836). The Meanses were parents of Martha Caroline Means, a cousin of Caroline Harper Means, who would be the second wife of PSB.

[33] Major Thomas Means, unmarried father figure to children of his deceased brothers David and Robert.

gave us good viands & excellent wine.

Monday 15....I visited Mr. Edward Means & also Wm Means & returned to Mrs. Means to dinner. I here met Doct. & Mrs. Davis[34] with whom we returned in the afternoon on our way home. Doct. Davis is an intelligent & independent planter, who takes a deep interest in agriculture & to whom the District in indebted for the introduction of some of the most approved breed[s] of cattle, hogs & other live stock. He lives in great abundance & in handsome style & he and his amiable & kind lady dispense the offices of hospitality with good taste & urbanity.

Tuesday 16....We left the Doct's after breakfast, Miss Carroll & Miss Blocker in company & arrived at my father's about dark, having made a hard day's travel. I found my father well & very glad to see us.

Wednesday 17....went to my plantation....

Thursday 18....I rode over my plantation & inspected the state of preparation for a crop & attended to the manuring and planting of a small field of corn, which was the first planting this spring.

Friday 19th....I returned home & found the family well. No news except what related to the late high waters and the damage done in various places. This freshet wanted about 4 feet of being as high as that of last May. The damage to Hamburg was inconsiderable but great to the rail road.

Saturday 20th....I inspected my farm[35] in the morning & in the afternoon paid a visit to Major [Benjamin] Nicholson, who lies very ill of fever.

Sunday 21....Attended the babtist church in the morning & visited Major Nicholson in the afternoon. He was reported to be a little better. Called to see Doct. Mays[36] & family, who had returned from Florida, through whom I heard from my relations[37] in that Territory. The Doct. is pleased with the territory for a planting interest & for a residence in winter but not in summer.

Monday 22....The Court of Com. Pleas commenced its Spring session today, under

---

[34] Dr. James B. Davis (1809–1861), noted agricultural reformer and a leader in the State Agricultural Society. "Minister of Agriculture to Turkey" 1845–1849, afterwards known in Fairfield as "Turkey Jim." Married Mary Elizabeth Scott of Richland Dist.

[35] A small farm near ECH.

[36] Dr. Rydon G. Mays, clerk of Sardis Baptist Church in northern Edgefield District. Neighbor of WB while owner of "Holmewood," 1836–1846.

[37] Daniel Bird (1784–1867) and Behethland Brooks Bird (1793–1864) and family. She was WB's sister. Bird was earlier married to Lucinda Brooks (1791–1826), also WB's sister. There were nine children in the blended family. Louisa Ann Bird, wife of Rev. Tilman Peurifoy (1809–1872), and her children were victims of a brutal attack in 1836 during the Seminole Wars. Bird was Clerk of Court 1822–1830. Built "Halcyon Grove" and "Oakley Park" mansions 1835. Moved to Florida in the late 1840s after death of son Tom in shootout with Lewis T. Wigfall.

Judge Evans.[38] The return of cases to this court has been larger than for several past years & I observed in the court room an unusual number of lawyers, some from Abbeville, Newberry, Hamburg, Aiken, Augusta & one from Charleston. The assemblage of persons was not large but they exhibited a well dressed & well behaved population. I called on Judge Evans at the tavern in the morning & visited the courtroom in the afternoon.

Tuesday 23....I rode out to see our venerable Aunt Butler & called on Col. Pickens.[39] Preston returned this evening from Fairfield with his wife.

Wednesday 24....Mr. [David] Lewis Wardlaw[40] & his lady passed the night with us. He is a well educated and intelligent gentleman, of considerable reputation as a lawyer & of high standing in the state. His lady is accomplished, affable & intelligent, & is a very agreeable & desirable acquaintance. She has a good share of what the world calls looks.

Thursday 25....I remarked that very few persons were in attendance on court, from which I infer that there is not much litigation or otherwise the planters were engaged in planting their crops. Judge Evans labors most faithfully to get through the docket, opening the court at 9 ocl. and adjourning at 5 ocl. in the afternoon.

....

Saturday 27th. This was a mild & agreeable day. I went into court this morning with Aunt Butler & attended on the Judge, to have an oath administered to her. Met my old acquaintance Major Jeter & resumed our relations of amity by shaking hands with each other. In the afternoon had a small party of friends, with whom we passed a few delightful hours.

Sunday 28th....I called to see Major Nicholson whom I found extremely ill. Dined with Mrs. Carroll....

Monday 29th....I left home for my plantation with Preston in company by the way of Major Blocker's, with whom we dined. Reached the plantation before night. Major Nicholson died about 1 oclock. He had many good & strong points in his character & was calculated to exert considerable influence in his circle of acquaintances. I be-

---

[38] Josiah James Evans (1786–1858), Justice of State Supreme Court 1829–1852. U.S. Senator 1853–1858.

[39] Francis Wilkinson Pickens (1807–1869), son of Gov. Andrew Pickens, Jr. Married a daughter of his law mentor, Eldred Simkins, and his third wife was the famous beauty Lucy Holcombe of Texas. Major land owner in SC, AL, and MS, and owned 276 slaves at one point. An early advocate of nullification, he was close to Calhoun personally and politically, as he was to WB. U.S. House 1834–1842, SC Senate 1844–1846, Minister to Russia 1858–1860, Governor 1860–1862.

[40] David Lewis Wardlaw (1799–1873) of Abbeville. Brother of Francis Hugh Wardlaw, law partner of WB. SC House speaker 1836–1842. Circuit Judge and Supreme Court Justice. Shouted down by a large gathering in Nov. 1860 when he warned against seceding unless four other states joined. Helped draft the SC "Black Codes" in 1865.

gan to plant corn.

Tuesday 30th. I rode with Preston to his place, where he left me for Fairfield, on a trip of business.

Wednesday 31....I rode over my plantation & was somewhat surprised to find that the small shower which fell at Edgefield on Sunday night was a heavy rain, and so wetting as to render all my bottom land unfit for the plow. My crop so far is well planted & the preparation for the residue meets my approbation....The negroes were generally well. The stock of horses & hogs were in good order & the cattle looking pretty well for the season of the year.

April 1841

Thursday 1st. The first day of this mild & pleasant month was as bright & balmy, as mild & serene as heart could desire. I saw the corn coming up in the field on the branch.[41]

Friday 2nd....I returned home & found all well. In the afternoon I rode out to my farm. My servants were about finishing the planting of a field in corn of something like 30 acres which had been commenced on Monday. I rode to the Village & got my papers & letters &C. No news of any importance either foreign or domestic.

Saturday 3rd....Preston returned with the Misses Means from Fairfield.[42]

....

Monday 5....The attendance of persons at the Village was unusually small for sale day. Some property was sold at very moderate prices....We spent the evening at Mrs. Carroll. The company was select, intelligent & agreeable to the taste of [Miss?] Carroll.[43] About 2 ocl. a company of gentlemen called at my house and serenaded the young married people. The music was of very high order, for skillful execution, tasteful selection & the harmony of the tones of the different instruments. Mr. Arthur Simkins[44] sung several songs in admirable style —

....

Wednesday 7th....We had a large party in honor of our Sons marriage, & were gratified with the belief that our guests enjoyed themselves to a late hour in mirth & glee & song without an occurrence to mar the hilarity of the occasion. I was exceedingly

---

[41] Branch of Ninety Six Creek.

[42] WB is referring to his daughter-in-law by her maiden name, or Caroline had two sisters.

[43] Presumably Mary Carroll's daughter Elizabeth (1816–1857), WB's sister-in-law and future wife of Maximilian LaBorde.

[44] Arthur Simkins (1819–1863), son of Eldred Simkins. Lawyer-planter, brother-in-law of A. P. Butler and F. W. Pickens. Pickens bought land from him and loaned him large sums. SC House 1846–1847. Ed. of *Advertiser* 1850s. Family lore says he died while drinking from the faucet of a barrel of brandy. Known for his singing voice.

sick with headache & was confined to my bed, but I could hear the cheerful tongues & joyous laugh, bearing uninterrupted testimony that the hearts of all were light & cheerful & merry. We heard this afternoon the mournful tidings of the death of Genl. Harrison which occurred on the 4th of April at 35 minutes past midnight.[45]

....

Friday 9th....The three last weeks have presented the most uniformly mild & growing weather, of which I have any recollection. Vegitation has advanced in that time with unusual rapidity. The Spring could not be more favorable to the planter & his crop has the promise of a fine "stand". We left home at 10 ocl. in company with the Misses Means, to dine with Major Blocker. Passed a pleasant day with the Major & returned home to tea....Recd. a letter from my overseer by Preston, informing me of the progress of planting cotton at the plantation. He began on Tuesday 7th.

Saturday 10th....Mrs. Brooks & the young people spent the evening at Col. Pickens. I was prevented from going by indisposition. They report favorably of the hospitality & cleverness of the gentleman & his estimable lady, and of the agreeable manner in which they passed their time....

....

Tuesday 13th....I left home for my plantation with Preston & his wife & the two Misses Means in company. We arrived in the afternoon and found all pretty well. The girls were delighted with the appearance which the place exhibited at this beautiful season of the year.

Wednesday 14th....I met my father at a place of John Inlow's about seven miles from my plantation & rode with him over the tract of land which Inlow was offering for Sale. There was a larger portion of good land than I expected but it lies in detached and small bodies which impairs the value of the tract. I parted with my father at 1 ocl. & rode home in a state of great suffering from headache, which continued with unabated violence until 10 ocl. at night.

Thursday 15th....\\ Preston & his party left me this morning on their return to Fairfield. His wife is a charming & most estimable lady, sensible & discrete, gentle in her manners, amiable in her disposition & affectionate and kind in the temper of her mind. His choice for a wife seems to be a fortunate one and I trust that happiness & prosperity may be their portion through life. The young ladies rival their sister in all their excellent qualities. They are in all soberness very lovely girls.

Friday 16th....I returned home & . . . found my family well & letters from Col. Butler & Preston, informing me of the final adjustment of the difficulty between Pres-

---

[45] News of President Harrison's death could not have reached ECH by the 7th, so this must have been added later.

ton & Wigfall.[46]

Saturday 17th....At my plantation the crop of corn is principally planted & up. By the close of this day the overseer will have planted about 220 acres of cotton. I shall be able to finish the planting of both corn & cotton next week. I shall complete the labor of planting corn at home today & also a lot in vines & vegetables &C. Mr Giles Mims was married to Miss Waldo on Thursday night last.[47] They are clever young folk but not well matched as I think them dissimilar in character & disposition.

Sunday 18th....Shelton[48] returned from Fairfield bringing a letter from Preston, informing us of their safe arrival & continued good health.

Monday 19th....I commenced today to replant and plow my corn at the farm.

Tuesday 20th....We were prevented by indisposition from attending a party last evening at Mr. Pope's[49] & this evening by the inclemency of the weather from another at Mr. Lipscomb's.[50] Most of these parties are dull things without music & the dance.

Records Mother's birthday [someone else's hand - pencil]

....

Thursday 22....Vegitation advances rapidly but the coming up crops of corn and cotton appear of a pale and rather sickly color owing to the cold in the mornings & the bleak wind.

Friday 23rd....Mrs. Brooks attained her 41st year, on this her birthday. She is in good health & I hope will live, God bless her, some thirty or forty years more.

Saturday 24th....I set off to my plantation by the way of Major Blockers, where I dined. His son Abner was sick of fever but not dangerously ill.

Sunday 25. Rode in the morning to see Jester[51] but found that he was from home and in the afternoon to see my neighbor King, whose lady is very unwell....

Monday 26th. Rode over my plantation. The corn very promising[,] the oats pretty good but the wheat indifferent. Cotton coming up & promising a good stand. My

---

[46] Further mediation led by P. M. Butler had resolved differences, or so WB hoped.

[47] Col. Giles Mims (1815–1884) owned a plantation near modern north Augusta, and co-chaired the ceremony for the return of the body of Whitfield Butler Brooks from Mexico and the committee for the celebration of the Ninety Six Boys' return from the war.

[48] A slave belonging to WB.

[49] James Pope was elected to the state house. George Pope was clerk of court, 1836–1844.

[50] John Lipscomb (1789–1856) was a planter who owned a store at White Hall on Hard Labor Creek. Large landowner in Florida but kept a house in Edgefield. In 1836 he bought "Halcyon Grove" property from Andrew Pickens II. Sister Ann m. John Wesley Brooks, WB's cousin, who built "Scotch Cross" house near Greenwood for her.

[51] Overseer.

entire crop has been well planted.

Tuesday 27th....I devoted the greater part to business & the balance to writing.

....

Thursday 29th. This was a remarkable & memorable day. Cool at day light with wind from the East. Mild at 9ocl. with the wind from the South & warm by 11 ocl with wind from the West. Heavy clouds were running during this time from the various directions, to which the wind shifted, being from East to West within space of 5 hours. There were occasional fitful appearances of the sun. At 11 oclock several heavy showers of rain fell and about 1 ocl. it began to clear & to be very warm. At about 2 the wind rose & blew briskly from the West & continued to increase in violence until night. A more violent & boisterous blow I have never seen at this season of the year. The road was covered with leaves and small twigs whipped off from the forests & the atmosphere filled with particles of matter which was very annoying to the eyes. I returned home in the afternoon and found all well. No event had occurred during my absence but the death of poor Mary Dunton by a rapid consumption.[52] When I left my plantation my overseer had finished the planting of his crop of corn & cotton, the cotton on Wednesday in the low fields with the ditch, and the corn this day in the new ground on the branch. He had plowed over about 100 acres of corn & howed over the Williams field of about 55 acres. The corn in this field looked exceedingly well. He will get over his corn with the plow this week and be ready for the cotton the ensuing.

Friday 30th....I rode out to inspect my farm & also to the Village. My overseer finished plowing 150 acres of corn the first time being an entire crop except twenty acres of low ground & some small lots of new grounds. He had run the harrows over about 100 acres of cotton. While at my plantation I had the sheep sheered between 50 & 60 in number. Cotton was coming up & looking well when the rain fell but I fear the wind & cold have greatly injured & even killed much of it that was up. The European news in regard to cotton rather unfavorable & a small decline in our markets in consequence. Not more than 10½ cts can be got for the best lots. The State of the money market in London & New York more easy than it had been tho trade continued in a languid state & some of the manufacturies working short time, only four days in the week....I understand that a slight frost was seen on some humid spots.

May 1st 1841

Saturday 1....I visited Judge Butler at whose house I met Col. P. M. Butler from Columbia. I passed a pleasant day with the gentlemen....

Sunday 2....We paid a visit to Major Blocker, to see his son Abner, who is danger-

---

[52] Mary Dunton (c.1785–1841), wife of Hollis Dunton. Large family; 8 slaves, 4 in agriculture (1840 census).

ously ill of fever. His situation is critical & alarming. He is a noble boy and I should lament his fate, if he should be cut off so young & so full of life & hope as he was a few weeks since.

Monday 3rd....Few persons for sale day were in the Village. Some property in both land & negroes sold by the Sheriff at fair prices. A general complaint from all quarters of the District in regard to the prospect of the cotton crop, owing to the cold & wind, which is killing much of that which is up.

Tuesday 4th....Saw at the Village & had a few minutes conversation with W[hitemarsh]. Seabrook & Chs. Furman.[53]

Wednesday 5th....I left home with the family for the plantation where we arrived in good time after being caught in a shower of rain.

Thursday 6th....I rode over & inspected my plantation. The corn very superior & in good order. The prospect of a cotton crop absolutely alarming from the bad stand. I was much discouraged from an apprehension that I should not have a stand of cotton to more than half the crop. Preston & his wife arrived in the evening.

Friday 7th. I attended a meeting of the agricultural society at Cambridge. There were thirty or forty members & from fifty to sixty persons present. I delivered an address. It was recd. well as I was informed. Several reports from committees were read & a good deal of other business done, during the day....I sent my waggon & cart for cotton seed for M. Mims[54], of whose overseer I purchased a load. I was also fortunate in getting gratis a load from a Mr. Clark & one from Mr. John Foy.[55]

Saturday 8th. I was busily employed in superintending the replanting of cotton. I plowed up & replanted about 40 acres, principally on old land.

....

Monday 10th....We parted with our Son Preston & his wife, we on our return to the Village & he for Fairfield. We found all well at home & the garden exhibiting a richness in the shrubbery absolutely refreshing to the sight & feelings. I began this day to work over the cotton at the plantation, plowing & chopping out. Finished plowing & hoeing the corn the first time on Friday the 7th and also two or three small pieces of new ground, being low land. My observation for the last two years has satisfied me that my low grounds ought not to be planted in either corn or cot-

[53] Whitemarsh Seabrook (1793–1855), Edisto Island cotton planter who helped form the State Agricultural Society in 1839. Wrote in defense of slavery and states' rights. State legislature, Lt. Governor. Supported the Bluffton Movement of 1844. As Governor, 1848–1850, he urged that SC prepare for secession and military defense. Charles Manning Furman (1797–1872), son of Rev. Richard Furman, lawyer-planter, state house, director of SCRR, Charleston City Council, State Treasurer, President of the Bank of the State of SC 1850–1865.

[54] Matthew Mims (1780–1848), son of Drury Mims, married Elizabeth Perrin Tutt. A charter member of Edgefield Baptist Church in 1823.

[55] John Foy, under 30 years old, married, 47 slaves and 1 free black.

ton before the last of April. The crop will do well if planted by the 10th of May. If planted before the last of April the seed will rot & not germinate.

Tuesday 11th....I inspected my farm. It is in good order & the corn pretty good. It is much missing owing to the ravages of the bug & birds & worms. My crop of oats is promising. Visited the Village & heard that Genl. Thos. Glascock[56] had been killed by a fall from his horse.

....

Thursday 13th ....Corn planted in stubble land, looks unusually unpromising & much of it has been distroyed in the bud by a small black bug. This insect was very destructive 10 or 12 years past to young corn on stubble land. The bugs are also distructive to young vines, such as cucumbers, melons, & also to beans. If the appearance of the little black bug be any indication of the character of the coming seasons, this should be a favorable crop year for corn as the one on which they last made their appearance was a fine crop year....

Friday 14th....Attended the performance of divine service in the episcopal church & heard a sort of political Sermon from the Revd. Mr. Shindler,[57] delivered in compliance with the request of the President of the U. States [John Tyler], that the day might be observed by the people as one of fasting & humiliation on account of the death of Genl. Harrison. The sermon altogether was rather a strange medley but portions of it were sensible & philosophical....

....

Sunday 16th. Still clear & cool. Therm.t 48°. We attended church & heard a sensible sermon from Mr. Shindler. There was a freshness & boldness in conducting the argumentative part of his sermon, that pleased me. In the afternoon I rode up to Major Blockers to see my father. He returned & passed the night with me....

Monday 17th....I commenced this morning to plow over my corn [on the farm] the second time. Heard from the overseer that he was plowing over the corn the second time & chopping out cotton. Major Blocker & lady dined with us.

Tuesday 18th....My father reached this day his 76th year & entered upon his 77th. His health is good for his age. He left us this morning on his return home. I began to plant cow peas this morning at my farm.

Wednesday 19th....I was exceedingly unwell & had to remain in bed for several hours

---

56 Genl. Thomas Glascock, Jr. (1790–1841): His father was guardian of Edmund Bacon (1776–1826); m. Harriet Hatcher Hays. Portrait owned by Edgefield County Historical Society.

57 Rev. Robert D. Shindler (1814–1874), native of Virginia. Principal of Cheraw Male Academy 1837. Tutored in home of Judge Josiah Evans 1838–1839. Pastor (Deacon) of Trinity Church Edgefield 1841–1842. Ordained as a priest in 1844. Served other SC churches until moving to Maryland in 1850.

....

Friday 21....I went to my plantation at which I arrived at 1 ocl.

Saturday 22nd....I rode over my plantation. My stand of cotton pretty good, the corn crop very fine & the small grain tolerably good. My overseer had chopped over about 150 acres of cotton & was going over his corn the second time. The negroes in pretty good health. Preston's crop is about an average one so far.

Sunday 23rd....I returned home. In the afternoon went to church & heard a sermon from Mr. Shindler, also paid a visit to Col. Pickens, who is on the eve of departure for Washington. We met there Mr. & Mrs. J. E. Calhoun,[58] Mr. & Mrs. A[rthur]. Simkins, & Mrs. Martin. Our Congressman was exceedingly cordial & civil & his lady gentle & courteous as she usually is.

....

Tuesday 25th....Vegitables & the oat crop begin to suffer for rain. I was afflicted yesterday & today with head ache. No news other than that furnished by the Charleston papers of a large political meeting at which Col. Preston[59] spoke with great elat.

Heard of the deaths of Capt. Weaver,[60] Elijah Watson[61] & Genl. Thos. Glascock.

....

Friday 28th....I visited Major Blocker & family & called at Major Hughes[62] on my return.

Saturday 29th....The papers give a glowing account of a Calhoun meeting in Charleston, at which the great statesman was present and addressed the assembled crowd of citizens both male & female.

Sunday 30th....We attended worship at the Epis. Church.

Monday 31....I went to Hamburg with Mrs. B. We spent the afternoon & night

---

[58] James Edward Calhoun (1796–1889), brother-in-law of John C. Calhoun. Married Maria Simkins (1816–1889), daughter of Eldred Simkins. Millwood Plantation, Abbeville Dist., 25,000 acres total.

[59] William Campbell Preston (1794–1860), son of a distinguished Virginia family. SC College 1812, U. Edinburgh law. Settled in Columbia 1824 in partnership with Wm. Harper. SC House 1828–1833; U.S. Senate 1833–1842. A moderate nullifier, his opposition to Jackson led him into the Whig Party. Opposition to the subtreasury widened his breach with Calhoun, whose influence crushed the SC Whigs in 1840 and led Preston to resign in 1842. President and prof. of belles lettres, SC College 1846–1851.

[60] Jonathan Weaver/Wever (c.1769–1841), known for his great wealth.

[61] Elijah Watson (1775–1841), Nullification convention 1832. Early settler at Ridge Spring. 1840 census: 63 slaves.

[62] John Halhead Hughes (1801–1871), Cedar Grove plantation, m. Martha Bones, sister of John, of Augusta 1831. Active Methodist.

with the Revd. Mr. Ford.[63]

June 1841

Tuesday 1 ....I returned to Hamburg & sold a lot of 60 bales of cotton to D. Adams for 9 5/8 for which I could have received 10 4/8 in the month of Feby. The intelligence from Europe has been unfavorable for the last two arrivals & fearing a further fall in the price of cotton I determined to sell. We returned home in the afternoon & I was compelled to take my bed on account of a severe attack of headache.

Wednesday 2nd....I am still suffering with headache.

Thursday 3rd....I went to my plantation....

Friday 4th....I rode over my plantation & found my crop in good order. Both corn & cotton are rather smaller than usual at this season of the year but are nevertheless very promising....The wheat looks well but has some rust.[64] The rye & oats are pretty good but want rain. In the afternoon I took an excursion to the neighboring plantations & passed by Payne, Mims, Griffin, Martin, & P.S. Brooks....the crops were small & backward.

Saturday 5th....I returned home to dinner & found all well. Therm.t in an open piaza 92ϒ[,] in a cool room on the mantelpiece 82°. In the passage at Mrs. Carroll's 87°.

Sunday 6th....Attended divine service in the Epis. Church. Major & Mrs. Blocker called to see us. Therm.t 95° 84° & 89° in the situations above stated....Recd. & read the Presidents [Tyler] message. It is a plain, sensible & frank communication of his opinions upon the topics introduced....Genl. [Waddy] Thompson arrived at my house & remained with us. It is reported that Mr. Wardlaws house was struck with lightning & that some injury was sustained by the family.

Monday 7th....The court of equity commenced its annual session at 11 ocl, Judge David Johnson[65] presiding. The assemblage of persons to attend the Court & on business was rather less than usual. Some property was sold by the Shff at fair [to?] average prices. About 3 ocl at night our Son James arrived from Columbia, bringing the melancholy intelligence of the death of our very dear relative Mrs. Laborde.[66]

---

[63] Rev. Edward Eugene Ford, D.D. (1795–1862), rector of St. Paul's Augusta, had conducted services in Edgefield from 1832, encouraging establishment in 1836 of Trinity Episcopal Church.

[64] Rust-colored parasitic fungus caused by potassium deficiency.

[65] David Johnson (1782–1855), judge, governor 1846–1848. A Unionist, he, with Judge O'Neall, ruled unconstitutional the 1833 militia test oath adopted by the nullifier-dominated legislature, leading it to abolish the Court of Appeals. WB had briefly backed Johnson for governor in 1840. As governor (1846–1848), he led efforts to support the Palmetto Regiment, although he did not favor war with Mexico.

[66] Maximilian LaBorde's wife Sophia Parsons LaBorde, daughter of James Parsons Carroll, Sr., and Mary Giles Carroll, and sister of MPCB, born Dec. 22, 1806.

She died at her residence near Columbia on Monday afternoon at 8 oclock the 7 day of June.

Tuesday 8th. It was on this Tuesday night that James Brooks arrived from Columbia. Doct. Laborde & Mrs. Carroll left Columbia at 8 ocl in the morning with the corpse & arrived at Edgefield at half past 3 ocl. only a short time after James' arrival....Wednesday 9th....I rode at day light & called to see Mrs. Carroll & Doct. Laborde. Went at an early hour & marked out the spot for the grave of Mrs. Laborde. At 5 ocl. in the afternoon the funeral service was read by Revd. Mr. Shindler in the Epis. Church & immediately afterwards, she was interred by the side of her children in the burial ground adjoining the babtist church. The assemblage of persons at the burial was large & embraced nearly all of the villagers.

Thursday 10th....I began yesterday to plow over my corn the 3rd time at my farm.

....

Saturday 12th....The Court of Equity adjourned this morning after a laborious session.

Sunday 13th....I was too sick to attend church.

....

Tuesday 15th....I went to my plantation in the forenoon & in the afternoon rode over a part of my crop ....My crop of corn & cotton rather promising. The oat crop will be very light & the wheat crop will turn out almost worthless from the rust. Rain wanted.

Wednesday 16th....I rode over Preston's crop. It is pretty good & in very fine order. Joseph arrived from Fairfield with a letter from Preston, which determined me to leave for home, to let his mother know that he was well & in good spirits.

....

Friday 18th....I had a violent attack of headache after my visit to Judge Butler.

....

Sunday 20th....I was unwell in the forenoon & prevented from attending church. Preston & his lady returned from Fairfield about 3 ocl.

Monday 21....Recd. a messenger from Col. [P. M.] Butler. [See below]

Tuesday 22....I rode out to Judge Butlers in company with Preston ....

Wednesday 23. I paid a visit to Major Blocker & passed the day with him....

Thursday 24th....The Villagers endeavored to get up a whortleberry[67] party, which was partly defeated by the rain.

Friday 25....We called to see Capt. Bird & family who had returned from Florida.

---

[67] A small blue or red berry resembling a blueberry, used in desserts, jams, and jellies.

We found my sister[68] & two of the children sick in bed. Our Son James returned from College in good health....

Saturday [June] 26th....Col. Butler arrived from Columbia & dined with me....

Sunday 27 ....Judge Butler, Col. Butler, Laborde, Blocker & Carroll dined with me. We had a question under consultation, in which our son Preston was mainly concerned & on which there finally was little or no difference among us. Our decision was to fight.[69]

Monday 28th....I passed the evening with Major Jeter with a small party....

Tuesday 29th....I left home in company with Preston for the plantation ....

Wednesday 30th. I visited old Mr. Rogers,[70] living on Halfway swamp on business. He was an active soldier in the Revolution & now receives a pension from the Genl. government. He is 82 years of age & still enjoys pretty good health altho feeble. I returned by Prestons plantation and examined his & my crop. The corn crops of each of us are good and the cotton pretty good....Both the corn & cotton crops through the District are backward from a week to 10 days. I saw cotton blooms but they were not more numerous than is usual about the 18th of this month. My corn was tasseling and shooting. The cotton varied in height from half leg to half thigh high.

July 1st 1841

Thursday 1....We returned home in the afternoon.

Saturday 3rd....I attended the delivery of an oration, intended to be in commemoration of the 4th of July, by young Mr. Spann[71] at Durisoes[72] about a mile of the Village. The oration was appropriate in sentiment & thought to the occasion, in style & composition decidedly creditable to the young Speaker & the manner of delivery very good. The auditory consisted of ladies & gentlemen from 50 to 75 in number, most of whom partook of a barbaque (sic) dinner, furnished gratis by Mr. Durisoe & a few neighbors. I was too indisposed to remain to dinner. At 10 ocl. at night my

---

68 Behethland Brooks Simkins Bird.

69 The Brooks-Wigfall feud had flared up again. Does the omission of Preston's name indicate that he was not present?

70 Likely the former owner, or son of the owner, of land called "Rogers' Old Field," near the town square in Edgefield, and thought by some to be the origin of the name "Edgefield."

71 Henry R. Spann was admitted to practice law in Edgefield in 1841. See n. 79.

72 William Francis Durisoe (1790–1874), son of refugees from San Domingue. Apprentice printer in Savannah, ran away to ECH. With Pierre LaBorde, he bought the *Advertiser* from M. LaBorde in 1839 and ran it until 1859. Strong states rights advocate.

worthy and respected friend Mr. Hankle [Hanckel][73] arrived at my house from Charleston.

Sunday 4th....In the forenoon I attended church & heard a very sensible & orthodox sermon from Mr. Hankle. He administered the communion.

Monday 5th. Mr Hankle left us this morning at an early hour on his return to Charleston, in company with Mr. Jas Jervey,[74] who came with him. Their object in coming to this place at this time was to interpose their kind offices, in terminating a private quarrel, which has continued to agitate the society of this place for the last twelve months. I am sure that they did no good, & I fear they may have made matters worse.

Genl. [Hugh] Means & Mr. Thos. Means arrived at my house on Sunday about 3 ocl. The assemblage of persons in the Village on sale day was not large. Not much property sold.....

Tuesday 6th....We called at Judge Butlers on Mr. Alex Taylor & lady. We also met Col. P. M. Butler & family at the judges.

Wednesday 7th....Judge Butler, Col. Butler & several other gentlemen spent the day with me pitching quoits,[75] a recreation & exercise now very fashionable with the gentlemen. My enjoyment of the company was much marred by a headache, which confined me in bed during the greater part of the day....

Thursday 8th....At 3 ocl. in the afternoon I set off for Cambridge in company of Genl. Means & Thos. Means & Preston. We arrived at my Plantation at dark....

Friday 9th....We rode over my plantation and Prestons and inspected the crops. [T]hey have failed to improve in appearance for the last week & are now suffering for the want of rain. Genl. & Thos. Means expressed the most favorable opinion of my plantation & also of Prestons. Our friends left us at 12 ocl. on their return to Fairfield & we took our departure for home after early dinner. On arriving at home I found my father & Mr Jos Davenport at my house.

....

Sunday 11....We attended service at the Epis. church.

Monday 12....Therm.t 93° in the vestibule & 96° in the piaza towards the kitchen. It was above 95° in the passage at Judge Butler's....

Tuesday 13th....In the afternoon we rode out with Father to Judge Butler's to see

---

[73] Rev. Christian Hanckel, D. D. (17?? –1870), ordained as a deacon in 1813. Taught at SC College before becoming rector of St. Paul's, Charleston, Mary Brooks' former parish. Visited Trinity Church in 1833 and held services. At his suggestion wardens and vestrymen were elected, including WB.

[74] James C. Jervey was president of the "State Bank" in Charleton and a customs official.

[75] A game similar to horseshoes, using an iron ring instead of a horseshoe.

Col. P. M. Butler & family.

Wednesday 14th....Father left us this morning about sunrise on his return home.

Thursday 15th. Clear & exceedingly hot till 2 ocl. when a very heavy rain commenced falling. I have not been able to ascertain, whether it extended to any distance. Rain is greatly wanted in various parts of the District & especially at & near my plantation.

Friday 16th....I joined a party in the afternoon in a visit to Judge Butler, with whom part of my family had dined and passed the day. I had a severe headache at night.

Saturday 17th....Col. Butler & family passed the day with us.

Sunday 18th....I was very unwell & did not attend church.

....

Tuesday 20th....I wrote a letter on business to F. W. Pickens, Esq....

Wednesday 21. I left home with my family for the plantation....On arriving at my plantation I found that . . . drought was doing severe injury to my crop.

Thursday 22. Rode over my plantation & inspected my crop & that of Preston. My corn crop was pretty good, much being planted in the swamp, where less rain was required to mature a crop. The cotton in low or fresh land was fair but on the old red land was unusually small & unpromising. I cannot make a full crop. Col. Butler arrived on a visit to me this afternoon.

Friday 23rd. In company with Col. Butler & Preston I rode over my plantation & exhibited a view of my crop to the Col. He was greatly pleased with my plantation & praised my crop with faint praise.

Saturday 24. My friend Col. Butler left me for Abbeville Courthouse. My overseer is engaged in getting out wheat,[76] of which I shall make but a poor crop, owing to the injury sustained by it from rust....

....

Monday 26....Dark & promising clouds would rise in every quarter of the heavens but as they would approach my plantation, the total dryness of the earth seemed to repel them & they would pass away with only a few drops & sometimes with a very light shower.

....

Wednesday 28th. This was a remarkable day. In the morning there was a light fog, which passed away by 9 ocl. when it became clear. At 12 ocl. the clouds began to form & the thunder to roll in terrific peels. For one hour there seemed to be waged an awful strife with elements, manifested by incessant thunder, & vivid flashes of lightning, & which terminated in torrents of rain & severe gusts of wind....After it ceased I rode into my plantation, which in several places exhibited a sea of water. I

[76] Separating the wheat kernels from the straw or chaff.

found my cotton fields washed & the corn lying prostrate on the ground torn up in many places by the roots.

....

Friday 30th....I rode through the neighborhood & saw a few of my neighbors crops, which are not very good. In the afternoon there was a heavy shower of rain on the lower part of my plantation but very little at the house.

Saturday 31. We returned home....My ride was not the most agreeable as I was exposed to the sun the entire way....The crops of corn in the vicinity of the Village are very good & equal to any for the last ten years. The cotton crops are not very promising in any part of the District that I have see especially on old land. The rain & cold in the Spring rendered old, and especially red land so dead & inert, that cotton failed either to come up or to grow to any size & the washed & galled [eroded] spots in the fields now exhibit a bald & arid appearance.

August 1. 1841

Sunday 1....We attended at the Epis. church & heard a sermon from an aged & infirm minister by the name of Dellavoe.[77]

Monday 2....This was a quiet day for the Village for a public occasion. [sheriff's sale] The assemblage of persons was not large. Very little property was sold & the crowd dispersed by 4 oclock.

....

Thursday 5th....The crops near the Village have not been better for years. I left home for my plantation.

Friday 6th. Attended a meeting of the Agricultural Society at Cambridge & read my report on the cultivation of corn. The meeting was well attended & afforded both interest & instruction.

....

Sunday 8th. I left the plantation for my fathers by the way of Chapman's steam saw mill[78] & reached his house at 2 ocl. in the midst of a heavy shower of rain. In the afternoon went to old Mr. Herberts in Newberry.

Monday 9th....I arrived at Mrs. Means in Fairfield & met a warm reception from the family.

Tuesday 10th. I passed the day at Mrs. Means. I met at dinner most of the male members of the family to wit, Genl. M.[,] Major M[,] W. E. Means & Mr. Har-

---

[77] Francis Padmore Delavaux (1780–1855), born in England. Longtime rector of St. Bartholomew's Parish.

[78] Probably John Nathan Chapman (1788–1854), who made cotton gins. He was father of John Abney Chapman (1821–1906), historian of Edgefield and Newberry Counties.

per.[79] In the afternoon Judge Harper & lady called to see me....

Wednesday 11th. I rode with W. E. Means to his plantation & inspected his crop & stock of cattle. His stock of cattle is superior in size and appearance to any in the upper Country, being a cross of the Durham on Taylors English breed. From the view of the crops on the road I formed the opinion that the cotton was very fine & the corn pretty good in Fairfield. In the afternoon I went to Genl. Mean's in company with Preston Brooks & wife, W. E. Means & Jas. Brooks & passed the night there.

....

Friday 13. Still very cloudy & the atmosphere dark & humid. I left Mrs. Means for the Glenn Springs,[80] accompanied by our Son James, crossed the Broad River at Shelton's & arrived at night at the Revd. Mr. Jennings.

Saturday 14th. Left Mr. Jennings & passing through the Village of Union, arrived at Glenn Spring about 12 ocl. I was forced to take a bed, from which I did not arise until next morning in consequence of a violent paroxism of headache –

Sunday 15th....Most of the Visitors at the Springs went to a camp meeting in the neighborhood but indisposition prevented me from going. The company at the Springs was rather larger than usual at that [not THIS. Writing later?] season, being on a average for 10 days from 130 to 150.

Monday 16th....I passed the day in reading, riding and conversing with all who came in my way, who manifested a disposition to be sociable, not neglecting the regular use of the water.

Tuesday 17th....The company at the Springs cheerful & agreeable.

....

Thursday 19th. No change except that produced by the departure of some & the arrival of others.

Friday 20th. Warm & clear weather & favorable to the crops of cotton, which had sustained some injury from the excessive rains of the previous week –

Saturday 21. Some sensation was produced by the intelligence from Washington that the President would place his veto upon the bill, establishing a bank of the

---

[79] Chancellor William Harper (1790–1847), lawyer, trustee of SC College, interim U.S. Senator 1826, Speaker of SC House 1827–1828, Judge, Chancellor.

[80] John B. Glenn opened an inn by a sulphur spring in southern Spartanburg District in 1825. In 1838 the Glenn Springs Company built an impressive hotel with fine furnishings, gardens, a ballroom, and a first-class kitchen. Cottages provided an option when crowds filled the hotel. South Carolina's elite, including the governor, gathered there in summer, and matchmaking competed with "healthful" water as an attraction. In 1850 an Episcopal church was built, with WB among its founders. See also online Inventory-Nomination Form, National Register of Historic Places, Glenn Springs Historic District, SC, 1982; "A Tourist's View of Glenn Springs, 1847," *Upper South Carolina Genealogy and History* 2/1 (Feb. 2006).

United States.

Sunday 22nd....The Revd. Mr. Lee from Talihassee in Florida performed divine service in the hall of the public house & delivered an interesting sermon. Some thought the Revd. gentleman eloquent. Preaching again at night by the same gentleman.

Monday 23rd....I passed through Laurens on my way to Capt. Cunninghams but was forced by headache to stop at Mr. Boyds.

Tuesday 24. This was a day of incessant rain in light showers. I arrived at my plantation at 2 ocl & met my two sons Preston & Hampden. The crop of cotton had grown very much during my absence & looked pretty well. The negroes were reported to be doing pretty well & two of the females were in their confinement with each a fine child. About two thirds of my fodder was gathered & saved without rain.

Wednesday 25....continued rain. I reached home to dinner & found all well. No news except the removal of our nearest neighbor Mrs.Wagner & the confinement of Mrs. Eldred Simkins by a son.

Thursday 26th....I rode to Mr. Mays and went over a portion of his crop which is promising.

Friday 27....I rode to my farm but I was deprived of the pleasure of a careful inspection of my crops by the wet condition of the corn & the miry state of the earth....

Saturday 28th....A protracted meeting with the Babtists began this morning.

Sunday 29th. Clear & pleasant morning. Attended divine service in the Epis. church. Therm.t 90°.

Monday 30th. Warm & sultry. The protracted meeting going on but not much excitement.

Tuesday 31st....Both yesterday & today I was confined to my bed by headache. Preaching still continued in the babtist church with no excitement except among the little girls, who are as sinless, I presume, as the preachers yet they are encouraged by both parents & the old members of the church to march up to the altar & prostrate themselves & ask the prayers of the ministers in their behalf. These little girls of 10 to 12 years of age cannot have any just notion of sin & certainly none of the plan of salvation. Yet they are encouraged by those, who preach repentance for sin & faith in the mediation of Christ as the necessary prerequisite to regeneration, things utterly incomprehensible to these children—My great objection to these public exhibitions by children is that it places them in an unnatural position, which they soon feel to be both false and embarrassing & which too generally ends in open apostacy or in hypocrisy, either of which has a pernicious effect upon the young mind. I hope good may spring from the meeting now being held here & that my fears all prove imaginary.

September 1st 1841

Wednesday 1st....I went morning & night to the babtist church, in which preaching had been regularly had since Friday night last. The ministers are good men but without education or intelligence. [in another hand: J.H.B W.B.B. J.C.B. P.S.B. E. L. D. JHB = John Hampden WBB = Whitfield Butler JCB = James Carroll Brooks PSB = Preston E(S?) D = Ellen Dunovant. (Mary Jane Mobley reads them thusly.]

Thursday 2nd....I went to my plantation where I met my Son Preston – In the afternoon I rode over my cotton crop, which has greatly improved within the last three weeks. The abundant rains for the last 20 days have caused a too rapid & vigorous growth to my crop of cotton & while the weed looks promising, it will be found on examination too full of sap to bear well or mature quickly.

Friday 3rd. I devoted this day to superintending the raising of Preston's house....

Saturday 4th. I returned to Prestons place & attended to the raising of his house. I rec.d through Preston from Genl. John Means, a very likely bull calf, a half blooded Durham & also from Major Thos. Means a ram & ewe of mixed blood, being a cross of the Southdown with the . *[he leaves space]* & of superior form & appearance. It was gratifying to receive these presents from the gentlemen as I regard them the evidences of respect & friendly feeling from the respected donors toward me, for which I return them many thanks.

Sunday 5th....I returned home & found all well....

Monday 6th....Our Son Hampden entered his ninth year. To mark the progress, which he has made in his books, I will state that he spells & reads with some ease & correctness. This is sale day & so very clear & inviting that I anticipated a large gathering at the Village. The concourse was small & very little business done or property sold. Some few cases of drunkenness in the afternoon....

Tuesday 7th....Mrs. Brooks & Miss Carroll called this evening on Mrs. Benj. Yancy,[81] a young bride from Georgia. She is a clever & well educated lady, of pleasing manners & improved mind. The Revd. Mr. Capers[82] preached in the Methodist church but I was too unwell to attend. In fact I had a bad night by diarreaha, which produced great debility.

Wednesday 8th ....I was very sick in the afternoon & suffered great pain until after 12 ocl. at night.

---

[81] Sarah Paris Hamilton. Benjamin Cudworth Yancey, Jr. (1817–1891), University of Georgia, Harvard Law, practiced in Hamburg 1841–1850, served in SC House, then moved to Alabama and elected to U.S. House. Brother of "fire-eater" secessionist William Lowndes Yancey of Alabama.

[82] William Capers (1790–1855), converted to Methodism at a camp meeting in 1808. Led movement to evangelize Creek Indians and slaves. In 1844 supervised 80 missionaries. Editor of *Southern Christian Advocate.* Supported 1844 schism in American Methodism and was an early Bishop of the M. E. Church, South.

Thursday 9th....I went in the afternoon to my plantation, rather improved altho fatigued by the ride.

Friday 10th Rode to Prestons plantation & through a part of the plantation in the morning & over the balance in the afternoon. I sold to Saml March[83] 20 head of cattle for $145. Saw James Vaughn & had some conversation with him in regard to his employment as an overseer.

Saturday 11. Returned home in the forenoon. The day warm & clear. Rec.d a request from my father that he wished me to sell his cotton in Hamburg, for which an offer was made the same day by letter of 8 4/8. [*8 ½ cents per pound*]

Sunday 12th....Attended in the Epis. Church & heard a sermon from Mr. Shinler....Set off for Hamburg at 3 ocl & reached Doctr. Guiggers [*Geiger's*].

Monday 13th. Set off from Dr. Guiggers at sunrise & arrived at Hamburg to breakfast. Sold to Doct. Stokes a lot of 99 bales of cotton at 8 4/8, which belonged to my father – purchased a few articles, settled a little business & at 2 ocl set off for home, at which I arrived at dark, after a warm & fatiguing ride ....

....

Wednesday 15th....We are preparing to go to the plantation, for which place we set off & at which we arrived in the afternoon....

....

Friday 17....A great freshet in all the streams both large & small. The creeks about Cambridge higher than they were ever known to be. Immense damage was sustained by the crops & also by the bridges & mills. Saluda River was very full, doing much injury to both corn & cotton on the low grounds. A small branch of half-way swamp rose so rapidly as to wash a waggon of Col. R[ichard?] Griffin while in the act of crossing considerably below the ford, to the great danger of the mules & the driver. The waggon body was separated from the wheels & a new saw gin was considerably injured. The overseer & the negro driver remained on the creek the whole night from an inability to get away, owing to the exceeding darkness, which rendered the road invisible.

Saturday 18th....I parted with my family at the plantation & set out for the Glenn Spring. Mrs. Brooks & the children went to Doct. Barretts[84] on a visit. On arriving at Wilson's creek, I ascertained that I could not pass on account of the high water,

---

[83] Samuel Marsh (1813–1848), nephew of Baptist clergyman of same name who helped found several churches. His plantation, "Marshfields," was about five miles east of ECH.

[84] John Perkins Barrett (1795–1859), English-born physician, naturalist, versatile intellect, agricultural leader. President of Abbeville District Med. Soc. 1835. Friend of Louis Agissiz and John James Audubon. He outlined a theory of serial evolution and foretold airplanes and lunar trips. Married Lavinia Brooks, child of Wm. Elisha Brooks and Nancy Butler, thus a cousin of WB. His home south of Greenwood was the home of congressman William Jennings Bryan Dorn in the mid-20th century.

the bridges being washed away as far up the creek as Doct. Logan's mill. I then turned my course to Doct. Barretts, passed through Cambridge & joined my family in the afternoon. My Aunt Brooks came to the Doct.s in the afternoon to see us. We passed an agreeable night with the family. Mrs. Barrett is a kind, affectionate and sensible lady & the Doct. is both kind, hospitable & intelligent. He is a gentleman of literary taste & of some scientific attainments in the departments of geology, mineralogy, astronomy, botany & chemistry. His collection of shells, minerals & flowers, both exotic & indigenous is large & varied, far beyond what is found in the possession of a private gentleman. He has also a taste for orthinology & has made a collection of the principal birds & animals, found in his section of the Country. I saw but little of the Doctr. as he was busily engaged in the discharge of his professional duties. The neighborhood was sickly.

Sunday 19th....We left the Doctr. to return to my plantation by the way of Fellowship church, at which a protracted meeting was being held.

Monday 20th....I left the plantation at an early hour for the Glenn Spring, leaving my family to return to the Village. I arrived at night at Godfrey's about midway to the Springs, where I recd. good accommodations. The roads were much washed & impassible in many places for carriages of any kind. The water courses in Laurens had been high & had caused much injury to the crops.

Tuesday 21....I arrived at the Glenn Spring about sunset [and] procured a comfortable cabbin to which I retired at an early hour. There were about Sixty persons at the Spring of all classes & sizes, constituting a mixed society.

Wednesday 22....I commenced this morning the systematic arrangement of my time, devoting the mornings & afternoons to exercise on horseback & the other portions of the day to reading & conversing & visiting the Spring.

Thursday 23....I went through the usual routine.

Friday 24th....I rode by Mr. [Benjamin?] Hatcher to Mrs. Brooks.

Saturday 25....I dined with Doctr. Moore in the company of a few gentlemen. The Doctr. is a good host & gave us an excellent dinner & some laughable anecdotes. Mrs. Moore is a perfect lady both in manners & education.

Sunday 26th....I had a return of headache, which confined me on the bed throughout Sunday & until next morning. Most of the visitors called to see me.

Monday 27. Still clear & mild. I used the water this morning freely with an infusion of table salt....

Wednesday 30th....I rode to two or three places in the neighborhood & procured some choice peach stones for a nursery. I made preparations to leave the Springs the ensuing morning. I passed my time pleasantly enough for a watering place. The landlord Mr. Mourman[?] was attentive & polite & maintained a good table. I felt improved in health by the use of the water, exercise &C – The month of September has been unusually wet, with more frequent freshets in the water courses than I recollect ever to have seen. At no time was there more than 4 or 5 clear days. Some of these however, were clear bright & lovely. The season unfavorable for cotton. Fever of various types is prevailing in various parts of the District & some deaths have taken place. This year has been particularly fatal to old persons – Capt. Weaver, Elijah Watson, Benj. Lindsey, Mr. Noble, Peter Hilliard, Jas. Graham, old Mr. Thurmond & wife, very aged persons, have all died within the last three months.

October 1st 1841

Friday 1....I left the Springs on my return home, passed through the Village of Laurens & reached Mr. Fullers at dark....

Saturday 2....I left Mr. Fuller's at half past 3 ocl. & rode through the rain to Mr. Vaughn's, where I arrived at dark.

Sunday 3rd....I crossed Saluda River at the Island ford & reached my plantation at 12 ocl. finding the negroes in health & everything in pretty good order. In the afternoon I returned home & found my family in excellent health with my father at my house on a visit.

Monday 4....A light frost was observable this morning....There was a large concourse of persons in the Village. Several tracts of land & 2 or 3 negroes were sold at fair prices....

[missing] ....on business with John Weaver[85] & returned to dinner.

Wednesday 6th....My father left us this morning. He was very feeble & I fear is in a declining State. I began today to gather corn in the church field. It yielded about 175 bushels.

Thursday 7th....I went to the plantation & on arriving there I met my Son Preston. His health was somewhat infirm & that of his wife is improving. All my negroes were well. In fact I have been fortunate in not having fever on my plantation, during the year.

Friday 8th. Rode over my plantation & ascertained that my corn crop was daily sustaining injury from the wet weather. Much of it has been blown on the ground & is now rotting. This fact forces me to neglect my cotton in order to save my corn. Preston returned to Fairfield.

Saturday 9th....I returned home & found all well. I was not well during the whole afternoon....

Sunday 10th....I attended preaching in the morning at the Episcopal & in the even-

---

[85] General John Ryden Wever [sometimes Weaver] (1820–1874), son of Capt. Jonathan Weaver. m. Sarah Eliza Dunton. Bought the "Pine House" in 1847, substantially rebuilt it and sold to Benjamin Bettis in 1858. Had several convictions and fines from one to 50 dollars, including shooting at Peter LaBorde. Ran unsuccessfully for sheriff, known for opulent lifestyle, died poor.

ing at the Methodist church. Also assisted in the burial of the infant daughter of Mr. Kennerly in the afternoon. He is also in a low state of health, having been attacked by a violent [congestive?][86] fever.

Monday 11th....We paid a visit to Col. Pickens & lady, who had returned from Washington.

Tuesday 12th....I paid a visit to Major Blocker on my way to the plantation & dined with the family. I was attacked on my way by a violent head ache with great nausia at the stomach which caused me such intense pain, that I was forced to stop and lie on the ground for some time & until by [caseading?][87] I was partially relieved....

Wednesday 13th....I rode over my crop & attended to the gathering of corn....

Thursday 14. Clear & cool with brisk wind. I rode through a portion of the neighborhood & called at some half dozen houses. The health of this part of the District is very good. Crops of corn inferior.

Friday 15th....a light hoar frost. Its effects were visible at several places on the road to the Village, particularly near Stephens Creek. I returned home to dinner & in the afternoon called to see Capt. Bird, who has the fever.

Saturday 16th....I called to see Capt. Bird, who was ill of chill & fever & also the Revd. Mr. Barnwell[88] from Charleston. We attended the performance of divine service at night by Mr. Barnwell at the Episcopal church. He gave us an impressive exhortation & performed in a very solemn manner the ordinance of Baptism to Genl. Jn. W. Wimbush, who united himself to the church.[89]

Sunday 17....We attended in the Episcopal church & heard a very impressive sermon from Mr. Barnwell on the ordinance of taking the sacrament.

Monday 18th....I sent Whitfield to Hamburg to sell two loads of cotton. The Court of Com[mon] Pleas began its autumnal session, Judge ONeal[90] presiding. I understand that there is more business on the criminal docket than usual. There was a large assemblage of persons in attendance upon the Court, whose deportment during the day was quiet & peaceable. They departed in the afternoon with few cases of intoxication.

---

[86] Earliest use cited in OED 1846. Some sources say it was a 19th-century synonym for malaria.

[87] Caseate: A salt or caseic acid (OED).

[88] Rev. William H. Barnwell (1806–1863), Beaufort and Charleston. Brother of Senator and SC College president Robert Woodward Barnwell. St. Peter's Episcopal Church, Charleston.

[89] John W. Wimbush, son of the above most likely, was Ensign of Capt. James Jones' company of volunteers for service in the Seminole War in 1836.

[90] John Belton O'Neall (1793–1863), Newberry native, lifelong friend of WB since college. Major General of SC militia, Speaker of SC House, staunch Unionist, appeals court judge, Chief Justice of SC. Author of *Biographical Sketches of Bench and Bar of SC.* Baptist leader, champion of temperance, female education, agricultural reform. Successful planter.

Tuesday 19th....Vegitation remains unkilled by the frost. In fact the effect of frost here is scarcely visible.

Wednesday 20th....I called to see Doct. Gillison[91] & family.

Thursday 21....For the last ten days the therm.t has ranged in the morning from 40° to 50°, more frequently about 45°. My waggons passed in their return from market – I received for two loads of cotton (20 bales) $572 – my niece Mary Bird was married to Doct. Gillison of Beaufort by the Reverend Mr. Johnson.

Friday 22....The wedding party & a few friends passed the evening with us.

Saturday 23rd. A severe & killing frost was visible this morning over all the fields. Vegitation generally is killed.

Sunday 24th....We attended service in the Epis. Church both morning & evening and I listened with some interest to two pretty able but somewhat controversial sermons by Mr. Schindler. Received a letter from our son Preston informing us of the serious indisposition of his wife. Called to see our friends at Capt Birds in the afternoon among whom was Jas. Treadwell Esq.[92]

Monday 25....Ice & frost in abundance. Mrs. Brooks with Ellen & Hampden set off this morning for Fairfield to see our daughter in law Mrs. Preston Brooks. Heard this morning that our acquaintance Mr. Dow died last night at 10 o'clock. He was a gentleman of some good qualities. He was frank, liberal and just in his dealings with men, of a kind & social disposition, which created for him a feeling of goodwill & esteem among his neighbors. He was buried today at 5 o'clock. This has been the coldest day for the month of October that I have ever experienced....

Tuesday 26th....Therm.t down to 27. being a degree of cold greater than I have ever known in this month. I & Whitfield went to the plantation. Mild in the afternoon.

Wednesday 27....I passed the day in inspecting the plantation, crop, etc.

....

Saturday 30th....I rode through a part of the neighborhood and ascertained that the health of the people was good except on the waters of Cuffee Town & Wilson's Creeks, where ague & fever and bilious fever prevailed.

Sunday 31. Very warm & cloudy....I returned home by the way of Major Blockers where I drank a tumbler of milk which made me very sick, & to pass a night of intense suffering. I took my bed about sundown & counted the hours by the clock

---

[91] William David Gillison, M.D. (1817–1887), Yale, Med. College SC, m. WB's niece Mary Simpson Bird Oct. 12, 1841. Army surgeon in Mexican War, Civil War. 1850 census: Beaufort, 22 slaves.

[92] James Douthit Treadwell (1810–1880), Columbia SC, m. Elizabeth Christiana Boatwright (1811–1854), Columbia. She was a relative of the Boatwrights and Watsons of Ridge Spring, SC.

until 2 o'clock when after throwing up repeatedly & taking a dose of peters pills[93] I fell into a sleep & rested pretty well until morning. On arriving at home I learned that Preston's wife must have recovered from her illness as he was in Columbia on the 28th. Mrs. Brooks & the children are still at Fairfield & I therefore had a large & cheerless house to myself during my suffering. I am inclined to believe from all the intelligence, that I have received that the crops of corn are pretty good but inferior to those of last year & that the crops of cotton although somewhat better, will fall below the general calculation.

November 1, 1841

Monday 1....This was sale day. The concourse of persons was not large. An unusual quantity of land was sold by the Comm in Equity[94] and some little by the sheriff & very fair prices. I learned from the papers the death of the Honorable Jno. Forsythe[95] & heard of the death of my warmhearted friend Jno. Addison Commr. in Equity for Lexington....

Tuesday 2. A clear, mild & lovely morning with an atmosphere as balmy & soft as the month of May. I returned to my plantation & sent Whitfield to Hamburg to sell three loads of cotton.

Wednesday 3rd....I devoted the day in riding over my plantation & visiting Preston's place in company with Mrs. Brooks, Ellen and Hampden, who had met me at the plantation on their return from Fairfield the previous evening.

Thursday 4th....My attention was primarily devoted to the sowing of wheat. The overseer began the preparation of land on Monday morning. I finished sowing about 20 acres on Saturday & began to sow rye, which will finish on Monday.

Friday 5. Very cold & a little cloudy. Mrs. Brooks left for the Village & I repaired to Cambridge to attend the meeting of our agricultural society. Several persons joined the society & among the number was Dr. Barrett an eccentric, learned & clever gentleman. He both amused & edified us with his remarks on manures & animal physiology.

Saturday 6th....Mr. Lowry[96] paid me a visit, whom I engaged as an overseer & we exchanged written memorandums of our agreement. I deferred returning to

---

[93] Dr. Peter's Pills, called "the medicine of medicines," was a widely advertised remedy for a variety of ailments in the 1800s.

[94] James Terry was elected by the Senate for a term as Commissioner in Equity beginning in Nov. 1839.

[95] John Forsyth (1780–1841), Virginia native, lawyer in Augusta, Georgia, U.S. House 1813, Senate 1818. Negotiated 1819 Adams-Onis Treaty conveying Florida from Spain to the U.S. Governor, then returned to U.S. Senate. Opposed GA nullification of the tariffs. Jackson named him Sec. of State and Van Buren kept him in that post.

[96] Likely either James, age about 30, or Conrad, about 44.

Edgefield on account of my anxiety to repair a small injury to the machinery of the gin, on which I had a Mr. E. Brooks[97] engaged.

Sunday 7th....I returned to the village and found all well. Attended church in the afternoon and heard a sermon by Mr. Schindler.

Monday 8th....My son Whitfield handed me the returns of the sale of 28 bags of cotton, which he had sold in Hamburg on the third instant. He sold 25 bags for 9 cts & three do [ditto] for 8 ½. which was a good sale. He sold two loads in October for which he got 8 ½ . 8 bales of the last lot belonged to Preston –

Tuesday 9th ....I sent Whitfield to the plantation with instructions to go to Fairfield with a letter to Preston if he did not meet him at the plantation.

Wednesday 10th....About seven o'clock the wind rose and blew briskly from the N.East, when it became cool & cloudy & remained with partial sun shine throughout the day. I attended a sale at Mrs. Burne's, of the estate both real & personal. It generally sold at fair prices & the negroes at very high prices.

Thursday 11....On this day twelve months past my son Preston and Wigfall had a hostile meeting in the Savannah River an account of which is given at the beginning of this book. So far the day resembles the one on which they met. My situation & feelings are however widely different. I & my family are now in the enjoyment of health & contentment. I thank God that my worldly condition is easy & my worldly prospects as cheering & as prosperous as I have reason to expect or as falls to the lot of most men. I desire in the spirit of humility to return thanks and adoration to God for his many mercies & privileges. We have but one cause of uneasiness at this moment & that is the health of Preston's wife.

Friday 12....It is milder than the corresponding day last year but not so clear. I rode to Mr. Miles[98] below the Pine House[99] and on my return I saw what I had not seen for years, a matched cockfight with murderous gafts[100] on the cocks. I should consider it very poor amusement & a barbarous mode of betting.

Saturday 13th....I passed the evening at Colonel Pickens where I met Mr. James Calhoun[101] from Ala.

Sunday 14....My father and Preston arrived at 2 oclock. Preston reports his wife as being in a convalescent state –

....

---

[97] Likely Esau Brooks (c.1815–1852) of Kirksey's Crossroads, a distant relative. Appears to have had a part interest in a pottery factory on Martintown Road.

[98] Lewis Miles, potter, owner of Stoney Bluff Pottery, 11 miles east of ECH. Son-in-law of Rev. John Landrum. Owned slave potter Dave Drake.

[99] At intersection of US 25 and SC 19, Trenton SC. See Weaver/Wever.

[100] Gaffs: Spur-like blades attached to a fighting cock's feet.

[101] James Martin Calhoun (1805–1877), nephew of JCC. Husband of F.W. Pickens' sister Susan. Migrated from SC to AL c.1831. Planter and lawyer. Owned 54 slaves 1840.

Tuesday 16th....Therm.t below 28°. Heavy white frost.

Wednesday 17. Clear & somewhat milder. Therm.t 32°. Another heavy white frost. It has been so far a remarkably clear, & dry fall & very favorable to the agriculturalist. A drove of Kentucky hogs are now in the village & selling at 4 cts gross.[102] I went to the plantation with Preston, Whitfield and David Means in company....

Thursday 18th....Rode over the plantation and to Prestons new building. Gave directions to alter the chimneys, etc.

Friday 19th....Rain began to fall about 11 ocl. and on returning from Prestons place I became a little wet. My screw gave way this morning while packing cotton.

Saturday 20th....I returned home and was forced to take my bed in consequence of a headache. No news in the village except the marriage of William Glover with a Miss Collier.

Sunday 21....In the morning I was too much indisposed to attend church but did so in the afternoon and heard a sermon from Mr. Schindler, in which he gave the character and influence of the Jesuits by way of illustrating his text, "We trust we have a good conscience."

Monday 22. Rain...in the night and from 6 to 8 ocl. it fell in heavy & washing showers. Very warm & some thunder. I set off for Columbia at 1 ocl & arrived at dark at Mr. Watsons, where I remained through the night.

Tuesday 23rd. A cold & rainy day with some thunder. I arrived in Columbia about 6 ocl & took lodgings at Mabens. At night I attended a meeting of the State agricultural Society & heard an interesting an instructive report from the President on the subject of the cultivation of cotton.

Wednesday 24th. This was a cloudy & disagreeable day....In the yard in the rear of the Statehouse the competitors for prizes collected their stock for exhibition & a finer sight of the kind I have never seen. The yard was full of spectators all of whom seemed to be animated by anxious desires for the success of the society. The exhibition consisted of horses, colts, cattle, hogs & sheep & a few superior mules & mule colts. The cattle were of the Durham Devonshire Airshire & crosses of these different breeds. The sheep were principally of the Bakewell & one flat tail ram & the swine entirely Birkshire. It affords me pleasure to record the fact that Captain Ward[103] of this District received a silver cup for the second best bull of the Durham breed. He also exhibited a very pretty heifer.

Thursday 25th....The Society held it's fourth & last meeting this afternoon, at which

---

[102] KY was a large exporter of hogs to the cotton states. Gross meant on the hoof; gross weight.

[103] Likely Richard Ward (1802–1879), father of Clinton Ward, founder of the town of Ward, modern Saluda County.

General Hammond[104] delivered a very able & instructive address. The society made a new election of officers. Mr. Seabrook was reelected, upon which he delivered a short but spirited and impressive address.

Friday 26....I left Columbia on my return home & reached Mrs. Lees[105] at night. I met here a drover of hogs who asked 4 cts for his pork.

Saturday 27....some appearance of snow but clear & mild by 12 ocl. I reached home at 2 ocl. & found all well. I learned that a drove of hogs had been sold at 3 cts to the Villagers.

Sunday 28. The snow was falling at daylight & continued till 9 ocl. but it melted nearly as fast as it fell....I have no recollection of the fall of snow at so early a period of the year. I wish that it may be the harbinger of a mild winter but I fear it will prove the admonitory sign & warning of a severe winter. I shall endeavor to profit by the hint & prepare for the rigors of an inclement season. When I left Columbia it was rumored that Judge Gantt[106] had been compelled to promise to resign in order to avoid proceedings for his removal from the judicial bench on the ground of age and incompetency. D. L. Wardlaw will be elected to succeed him....

Monday 29th. Clear & very cold in the morning. Therm.t 26°. I purchased 20 hogs of a Kentuckian at 3 cts per pound. They weighed 5722 lbs & brought $171.66. I sent them to the plantation. I succeeded in obtaining an order from the ordinary for my appointment of Administrator to the estate of Captain [Jonathan] Weaver, which [his son] John Weaver had been maneuvering with the ordinary (as I have grounds to suspect) to prevent. After defeating the opposition, I determined to have nothing to do with the estate. I now predict that the estate will ultimately ruin both John Weaver and the ordinary, Olv. Towles Esq.[107]

Tuesday 30th....I went to my plantation. The very inclement weather & heavy rains had prevented the negroes from doing much. My Waggons passed on to Hamburg with 20 bales of cotton. The cotton crops in the vicinity of Cambridge will be considerably less than was anticipated two months since & the corn crops less than they were last year.

---

[104] James Henry Hammond (1807–1864), brilliant son of New Englander Elisha and Catherine Fox Spann of Edgefield. SC College, studied law with Wm. Harper and W. C. Preston. Acquired Silver Bluff plantation through marriage to Catherine Fitzsimmons, 1831. Nullifyer, U.S. House. Defeated for governor 1840, elected 1842. Scandal derailed his political career until election to U.S. Senate 1857. Built "Redcliffe," perhaps the grandest house in Upcountry SC. In a pro-slavery speech in the Senate he proclaimed "Cotton is King." His diary is among the most important documents from the Old South.

[105] Present-day Leesville.

[106] Richard Gantt (1767–1850), born in MD. SC House 1804–1818. Edgefield District Judge, resigned Dec. 1841. A "teetotaler."

[107] Oliver Towles (1800–1851), planter, militia colonel Saluda regiment. District Ordinary (judge) 1835–1844.

December 1841

Wednesday 1st. This was a cold & disagreeable day with high winds....I passed the day in riding to Preston's place, seeing the progress of his workmen on his house & examining the line of a ditch, which I am engaged in having dug, to turn the creek & drain some land in the swamp near the Corley field. I am to pay at the rate of 75 for every rod [*i.e.*] 16 ½ feet long, 4 feet wide & 3 feet deep. The ditcher takes two fellows to work with him & their labor is estimated of the same value as his & I am therefore to pay him half price for the ditch.

Thursday 2....In the afternoon the rain fell in torrents & soon rendered the creeks impassible. Rain fell through the night.

Friday 3. Very heavy rain in the morning. High winds in the afternoon & a gradual clearing....About four ocl. I rode in my plantation & as far as Preston's pond field, where my mare got away from me & from which I had to walk the distance of near three miles through mud & mire & across the branches, that I found it difficult to get over. I bore it with a good deal of philosophy & made my way through the cotton & cornfields & over branches & through mud & mire with a patience & perseverance becoming a good tempered man, to which quality I am sorry to say, I have no right to alledge any just claim as the general temper of my disposition.

Saturday 4th....I parted with Preston & returned home. I found the roads in a very muddy state but not very bad. The watercourses had been very high & impassable for about 12 hours. On reaching home I learned from the papers, that Judge Gantt had resigned his office of judge & that Lewis Wardlaw was elected in his place. Mr. Wm. Colcock was elected Speaker of the house of representatives to fill the vacancy, occasioned by the promotion of Mr. Wardlaw.

Sunday 5th....Rheumatism in the arm prevented me from attending church, so I sat by the fire the greater part of the day. I attended church in the afternoon and heard one of Mr. Schindler's doctrinal sermons on the subject of faith & works.

Monday 6....Therm.t 26° at Sun rise. This being sale day, a number of persons collected from all quarters of the district. In the afternoon there were several cases of drunkenness but the companies dispersed without any violence or break of the peace –

Tuesday 7th....We passed the day with our good aunt Butler, whom we found in fine health & spirits for one of her age. She gave us a cordial reception & made the day pass away pleasantly by her cheerful conversation. For strength of mind, soundness of judgment and equanimity of temper, she is remarkable at her time of life, being now in her 77th or 78th year.

Wednesday 8th....I attended the sale of Benj[amin F.] Nicholsons property at his late residence. Corn sold from 38 to 40 cts fodder for 50 cts per 100 lbs. The horses mules & cattle sold at fair prices and the negroes at very high rates. One negro fellow sold for $1000 and others from 850 to 960. A young woman with two children brought upwards of $1000 & one other with two children & pregnant with the third brought $1145. I heard from Watson's sale & the properties sold 25 prcent lower than at Nicholsons. Field hands fully grown sold for $750 to 775.

Thursday 9th....My waggons arrived on their way to market with 20 bales of cotton.

Friday 10th....I killed 11 hogs this morning for home use & have 10 more to be killed next week.

....

Sunday 12....Therm.t 38° at sunrise. Heard from the plantation, that Chancy was very sick.

Monday 13th....I went to my plantation, taking Whitfield & Hampden in with me. Some of the negroes were still sick, particularly the woman Chancy.

Tuesday 14th....I visited Preston's place & rode over a part of my plantation.

Wednesday 15....overcast & rain from three o'clock till night. I was attacked with headache & had to take my bed.

Thursday 16th....I killed 28 hogs this morning weighing on an average 200 pounds nett to each hog. I sent 10 to the village for consumption for my family. At 10 ocl my head ache returned & continued through the day & night. For twenty four hours I endured more entense & overpowering agony than I before ever suffered for the same space of time. The night was cold & exceedingly boisterous after a heavy shower of rain.

Friday 17th....I returned home being both feeble & and indisposed. I found all well.

Saturday 18th....Therm.t at sunrise 25°. I paid a visit to the Village but heard no news. The papers give discouraging accounts of the markets in Europe and also of the distresses & sufferings of the people in England, Scotland and Ireland for the want of food. My overseer will finish the business of picking out the cotton crop sometime during this day. The crop will be a short one, not exceeding 95 bales & some 10 or 15 of these much stained & injured. The Revd. Mr. Ford arrived in the afternoon from Augusta with whom I passed a pleasant evening in social conversation. For purity of principle & kindness of disposition there can be no better man. To these he unites gentleness of manners and the attainments of a well cultivated mind.

Sunday 19th. Heavy hoarfrost in the morning. Therm.t 32°. Mr. Ford performed divine service & administered the sacrament in the Epis. Church....

Monday, December 20....The Revd. Mr. Ford left us on his return to Augusta.

Tuesday 21. I attended a sale of Caleb Mitchell.[108] The property brought fair prices. One negro boy about 18 years of age sold for $865. Corn at 48 to 49 ct. Fodder

---

[108] Caleb Mitchell, Oliver Towles, and Bailey Corley signed a notice promoting Pottersville Academy's exercises and terms (*Adv.*, Dec. 28, 1840).

from 60 to 65 cts per 100 lb. I heard of the death of Colonel John Key,[109] who for the last two years has been suffering from paralysis, accompanied with great feebleness & melancholy. He was in many respects a man of high character though greatly deficient in education. He was frank, independent, hospitable & public spirited & filled several offices in the district with great fidelity & to the approbation of the people.

Wednesday 22....It is warm enough to endanger pork. In twenty minutes a most extraordinary change took place. The winds suddenly veered to the east, it became cloudy & in a short time a light mist began to fall. The balance of the day was gloomy & inclement, though not unpleasantly cold.

Thursday 23rd....Rain in the afternoon & night. I suffered greatly by an attack of headache & was confined to my bed the greater part of the day.

Friday 24th....The members of the Epis. Church collected at the church & decorated it with evergreens for the services of Christmas Day. For Christmas Eve it is unusually calm & quiet, no music, no noise nor the least note of a merry festival at hand. The children are anticipating Christmas morn as an occasion for looking into their stockings for gifts &C. & the cooks prepairing good things to eat.

Saturday 25th....A light snow about 12 o'clock but melted as it fell to the ground. The religious services of the day were performed by Mr. Schindler in the Episcopal Church, which had been draped for the occasion and looked very pretty. We dined with Mrs. Carroll & passed a very agreeable day with the family & our estimable friend Doct. Laborde.

Sunday 26....Attended divine service in the Epis. church in the morning. Very cold & disagreeable in church. Judge Butler dined with me.

Monday 27th....I went to the sale of the estate of Captain Weaver. The concourse of persons was very large.

Tuesday 28th. Still cold & cloudy & occasionally light showers of rain. I returned to the sale. The real estate was sold the first day at very good prices & the stock, furniture, provisions &C. today at fair prices.

Wednesday 29th. This was a rainy & disagreeable day. The sale took place at Stephens Creek & every article sold high. On returning from the sale one of the wheels of my father's carriage broke to pieces & we were forced to walk for half a mile through the mud to get to Geo. Outs[110] [Outz] & then to borrow Mrs. Struthers carriage in order to be conveyed home. There was a disgusting exhibition of drunkenness at the sale among the crowd generally & many instances among the self-righteous baptists.

---

[109] Col. John Key (1784–1841), planter, militia company commander War of 1812. SC House 1820s. Null. Conv. Died Dec. 19, 1841, leaving second wife Mary Ann Merriwether pregnant and with 10 children.

[110] George Outz (1808–1880), planter; 1850 census: 22 slaves.

Thursday 30th....This was the day assigned for the sale of Capt. Weaver's negroes. My father & Preston attended the sale but in consequence of bad weather & fatigue, I declined to go. Corn sold from 37½ to 43 cts per bushel. Fodder at 50 ct per 100 lbs. Cattle from $5 to 6 per head. Oats at something like 50 cts & other articles at corresponding prices. Mules from $55 to 135 & horses from $10 to 130.

....

III

January 1842

Saturday 1st. The morning of the new year was mild & almost clear. Therm.t 32°. Every member of my family are well & the negroes are in good health both at home & at the plantation. We have no family affliction or cause of sorrow, that I am aware of, & we all enjoy enough of the good things of this earth to contribute to comfort & happiness. With these a reasonable mind should be content & should be especially thankful to the great Giver of every good gift, that our lot has been cast in a land of plenty & of social, religious and political liberty. If we will perform our part & faithfully employ our time in the attainment of moral & intellectual excellence there can be no doubt, that we shall enjoy our due share of the happiness, prosperity & success, that crown the labors of the deserving & meritorious in this life. At least let my household be thankful to God for what we are & for what we have & let each one renew his covenant, to invigorate & not relax his efforts in the way of well doing, so that our evening of life may be calm & unclouded and the morning of our resurrection bright & cheering. Our Son Whitfield left us this morning for the Greenwood Academy in Abbeville Dist. It is the first time, that he left home for the purpose of going to school. In the evening Col. Pickens & family, & a few friends and neighbors took tea with us.

Sunday 2nd....My father, Major Blocker & wife, Mr. Carroll & family & Dr. Laborde dined with us. We passed with our friends a very pleasant day.

Monday 3....very wet and disagreeable particularly in the roads & streets. It was a busy and exciting day in the Village, occasioned by the sale of property by the Commissioner in Equity & by the Sheriff & also by the hiring of negroes, trafic in horses, etc. The concourse of persons was numerous & the day passed without any unusual incident.

Tuesday 4....The sale of Mr. Dowd's personal estate, commenced to day. There were from 150 to 200 persons in attendance & all anxious to purchase. I have never known the mania for trading, buying & speculating in every way & in almost every article prevail so generally & with all classes. The hardness of the times seems to have stimulated the people to venture into debt with a blind disregard of the consequences. Every species of property sells higher than it did two years ago & higher than when cotton brought $.10. I predict that many will be broken up & rendered bankrupt in two years.

Wednesday 5....I left home for my plantation at 12ocl. & arrived before dark.

Thursday 6th....I devoted today to the business of giving directions to Mr. Lowry, my new overseer and pointing out the fences to be run & the new ground to be cleared. In the afternoon I rode to Preston's place with him.

....

Saturday 8th....I was very much indisposed this morning, notwithstanding I ventured to set off home. I suffered much on the way & had an unspeakable attack of pain in the head at night attended with sick stomach. On my arrival at home I was informed that one of the negro women, Clarissa, had lost her infant child that morning. It was supposed that its death was caused by her lying on it & smothering it. The poor creature seemed greatly afflicted at the loss of her child.[1]

Sunday 9th....We attended the performance of divine service in the Methodist church & heard a sermon from the Revd. Mr. Wallace of Columbia, who is performing a tour through the state for the purpose of forming Bible societies. He succeeded in forming a small society on this occasion, consisting of 20 or 30 persons. The Revd. Jos. Moore[2] Presidt. --

....

Wednesday 12th....The earth very wet & the roads exceedingly cut up & muddy. Very few waggons passing to market.

Thursday 13th....I was notified to appear before the Town Council for running a fence across a road. I claimed the right to stop the road upon the ground, that it was a private way & not a street or public highway. We agreed to submit the question to gentlemen learned in the law.[3]

Saturday 15. Clear & mild as an April morning. I have no recollection of as warm a January, so far, since 1824. The temperature of the air, appearance of the Sun & the smoke give to the morning the precise appearance of spring. Thermt. 42°.

Sunday. [16th] ....Went to the Epis. Church & heard a sermon from A[rthur] Wigfall.[4] His manner is artificial, his emphasis often misplaced & his gesticulation vio-

---

[1] Studies of infanticide in other cultures have led some scholars of slavery in the American South to explore this controversial topic. High infant mortality and what masters saw as indifference among some enslaved mothers raised suspicions. Eugene Genovese's majesterial *Roll, Jordan, Roll,* 495–97, offers a cautious assessment, which concludes that infanticide was extremely rare among antebellum slave mothers. WB's acceptance of this report was likely warranted.

[2] Joseph Moore (1767–1851) was born in VA and spent some 65 years in the ministry, retiring in Edgefield in 1833. In 1841 he deeded the land where Edgefield Methodist Church stands to nine trustees.

[3] Fences were controversial since the free-range method of raising livestock had been the norm. Thus, crops were vulnerable unless fenced in. Not until the 1880s would state "fence laws" mandate fences to restrain livestock. Whether this was the issue here is unknown.

[4] Arthur Wigfall (1805–1865), older brother of Lewis T. Wigfall. Married Sarah, daughter of Edmund Bacon, in 1833. Edgefield newspaper editor, lawyer, then Episcopal clergyman who was briefly the rector at Trinity Church in April 1840. While pastoring the church in Grahamville, Beaufort County, published *A Sermon Upon Dueling* in 1856, eloquently condemning the practice.

lent & out of time. He is not an agreeable speaker but I believe him to be an honest Christian & a clever gentleman.

Monday 17th....The Court of com. Pleas commenced an extra session this morning, Judge [John Belton] O'Neall presiding: not many persons in attendance.

....

Wednesday 19th. Rather warmer than yesterday. I began to sow oats on Monday morning. The earth is in fine order & the weather favorable to sowing but I am somewhat fearful, that the cold weather may injure the oats.

Thursday 20th....I saw a short time after sunrise a rainbow in the West, which is said to be a sure sign of rain. Rain began to fall in showers about 10 ocl. & continued until 1 o'clock. I set off for the plantation at 1 ocl. & arrived at dark, cold & sick.

Friday 21....I inspected the work done by the overseer & also the state of the ditches, none being dug. Negroes all well but I regret to have to record the fact that two of them had left the plantation. My new overseer so far has proven himself to have energy, decision & industry with very good judgment & is getting along with his work exceedingly well.[5]

Saturday 22nd....I returned home to dinner & found the family pretty well. In the evening we had a few friends to tea, Judge Oneal & lady among the number. The Court of Common did not adjourn before 9 ocl. It was occupied to this late hour in trying a case between a Mr. Belk against Benj. Tillman[6] & others for inflicting Linch's law upon him. The jury gave a verdict for damages of $1500. A very proper & just verdict. It is reported on all hands that [J. P.] Carroll made an admirable argument.

Sunday 23rd....I felt slightly unwell & did not attend church. I have heard from several that Mr. Wigfall preached two touching and affecting sermons. He has much ardor in the good cause.

Monday 24....I had my plows breakup stubble land at the farm.

Tuesday 25....I met Judge Wardlaw in the Village on his way to the Court in the District of Beaufort. He seemed in fine spirits & health. I saw several of the Villagers depart for Hamburg, to attend the sale of Mr. Shultz[7] real estate, which is advertised to take place tomorrow.

....

[5] Were the two slaves unhappy with Mr. Vaughn's workpace? See Feb. 11, 1842.

[6] Benjamin Ryan Tillman (1802–1849), m. Sophia Hancock 1823, added 1,864 acres to the family land in southern Edgefield District, and operated an inn in their home between ECH and Augusta. Killed a man in 1847, not prosecuted. Owned 49 slaves in 1850. Father of governor and senator B. R. Tillman and Congressman George D. Tillman.

[7] Henry Shultz (1776–1851). See introduction. His ongoing efforts to develop Hamburg led several creditors to obtain judgments against him.

Friday 28th. Temperate & clear & therm.t about 32°. So far the month has been unusually mild with more than the ordinary portion of clear weather at this season. It has been favorable to the planter & has admitted of the breaking up of the greater part of stubble land.

....

Sunday 30th....Heard a sermon in the morning from the text "take this in remembrance of me" by the Revd. Mr. Wigfall. He is a very zealous Christian and an animated speaker but his animation appears to me to be forced & assumed & not natural. His manner is too dramatic & fails to affect me strongly. Heard through Preston from my plantation.

Monday 31. This is as dark & gloomy a morning as yesterday was bright & clear. Rain began to fall about day light and continued without abating with occasional heavy showers. E. Glascock[8] died last night at his uncle E. Simkins[9] & was buried this afternoon in the Epis. burial ground – He died of consumption.

February 1. 1842

Tuesday 1....This morning is the perfect contrast of yesterday, mild clear & bright with light & sometimes brisk wind. It is as pleasant as an April morning. The earth is very wet & the roads in very bad condition. The intelligence from England is favorable & is generally regarded as encouraging. A member of the Com[mission] house of Baring & Co.[10] has been sent on a special embassy to this government, to settle existing differences with the British government. This is regarded as favorable to peace. The cotton market is steady. This fact has given confidence to dealers & an advance is anticipated....

Wednesday 2. Dark & cloudy & every appearance of snow. Therm.t 46°. The changes in the weather pass from one extreme to the opposite in 24 hours.

Thursday 3rd....I devoted the day to the graves of our children,[11] and causing work of brick to be erected for the preservation & identification of the spots, where their bodies lie interred. Heavy cloud & storm of wind & rain at night.

....

---

[8] Edmund A. Glascock, son of Gen. John S. Glascock (1788–1822). Volunteered for the state forces during the Seminole War, 1836.

[9] Eldred James Simkins (1802–1845), grandson of Arthur Simkins, "founder of Edgefield."

[10] Powerful London financial institution earlier known as the sixth most powerful entity in Europe, the first five being its leading nations. Alexander Baring, 1st Lord Ashburton, came to negotiate with Sec. of State Webster the disputed boundary between the U.S. and Canada. This led to "54-40 or fight."

[11] Mary Elizabeth died age 2 weeks, 1822; George Butler died age 15 months, 1825; William Butler Oct. 4–14, 1840. Grave locations unknown.

Saturday 5. Clear, bright & cheering morning as mild as Spring. I am this day 52 years of age and enjoying better health & feeling more strength than I have enjoyed for the last ten years. I thank God for all his mercies & blessings and pray for the aid of his almighty grace to enable me to keep his commandments, & to increase in every christian Virtue. My family are in good health & they are now exempt from all cause of pain or suffering or anxiety except what is incident to the state of life in all its gradations & conditions.

Sunday 6th....A Mr. Berry preached in the Epis. Church. He is a native of the West Indies but in language, manners & appearance so nearly resembles those of an American that he would not be taken for a foreigner. His voice & manner are good & the matter of his sermon sound & sensible. In truth he is superior to 7 out of ten of even the Episcopal ministers.

Monday 7th....Rain began to fall at day light & continued through the greater part of the day. The concourse of persons in the village was small. Some 10 or 15 negroes were sold by the Shff at very fair prices – I purchased a boy at $610 & sold him in the afternoon for $640. A negro fellow brought over $700.

Tuesday 8th. Clear & cool. Therm.t 33°. We are greatly concerned at the intelligence recd. yesterday of the illness of Preston's wife. He was sent for in great haste. I attended the Shffs. sale at the courthouse & purchased two negroes – I sold a little girl at a profit of $50....

Wednesday 9th....Therm.t at sunrise 20°....a good deal of ice. I left home for my plantation & went by Major Blockers, where I took dinner.

Thursday 10th. Clear & much milder. I visited Preston's place & examined my own plantation during the day.

Friday 11th....rain . . . continued to fall in light showers, through the day. I inspected my stock of all kinds & found them in good order. From the work done since Christmas, I must think that my overseer is a pushing, industrious & energetic man. To these qualities he unites judgment.

Saturday 12th....I left my plantation at 9 ocl....heavy showers . . . continued with but little intermission until I reached home – All well at home –

Sunday 13th....Attended service in the Epis church & heard a sermon by Mr. Berry. He is an interesting preacher. Recd. a letter from Preston informing us that his wife was better. The arrival of Mr. [Charles] Dickens from England & his reception at Boston & New York is the only subject which at present excites public attention.[12] The eyes of the people of this country are now drawn in the direction of Washington city by the eccentric & unpardonable course of Mr. [John Quincy] Adams Ex

---

[12] Dickens, then 30 and known mainly for *Oliver Twist*, drew large crowds as he visited major cities of the NE and Midwest, but grew more disillusioned as he went.

Presid.t on the subject of the right of petition in connection with abolition.[13]

Monday 14th....I met my waggons near Outz's on their way to market. The roads almost impassable.

Tuesday 15th....I went to Hamburg, which, after passing over the worst road I ever saw, I reached at 3 oclock. The cotton market very dull and low. Not more than 7 7/8 could be obtained for the best lots of cotton....

Wednesday 16th....My waggons arrived about nine oclock in the morning & although suffering the most agonizing pain I was compelled to attend to the purchase of various articles & to the loading of the waggons. There were 15 bales of cotton on the wagons, which I had sold to Messrs. Penn's[14] & for which 5 cts. only was offered. They were put in store. I sold in the afternoon 40 bales of cotton to Mr. Adams[15] for 7 5/8, the highest price I could get for a lot of cotton, equal to any, made on my plantation this year. There is a general stagnation in the trading community & great difficulty is encountered in making sale of all articles or property except cotton & provisions. These sell readily but at low prices. The scarcity of money is clearly proven by the price of articles in market. Butter 12 ½ cts pr. lb. Eggs 10 cts pr. doz. Poultry correspondingly low. Chickens 12 pr. & turkeys 1.25 pr. pair. Corn 56 to 60 cts. Bacon from 4 to 6 cts pr lb.

Thursday 17th....A good deal of ice. I passed over to Augusta after breakfast & purchased such articles as I could not get in Hamburg. Businesses seemed to be dull & very few waggons in the street. I left Hamburg for home at 12 ocl. and arrived before Sunset. All well.

Friday 18th....The waggons left here for the plantation with every thing in good order. Rain began to fall at Sunset & a more boisterous & inclement night has not occurred this winter....

....

Sunday 20th....Recd. a note from my overseer in which he informs me that a heavy storm of wind & rain had prevailed at my plantation, blowing down fences & inundating the creeks, to the serious injury of the ditches, which have been lately opened through my fields for the purpose of changing the course of the creeks & of draining the land.

Monday 21....Therm.t 26° in the morning. Wind from the North – I began this morning to carry out manure to the church field. The land too wet to plough.

---

[13] Adams, then a representative from MA, unsuccessfully opposed the annual adoption of the "gag rule," which blocked admission of anti-slavery petitions. Congressman Henry L. Pinckney, a college mate of WB, had led the 1836 effort to have such petitions automatically "tabled."

[14] George Penn and son Edmund were later leading merchants in ECH.

[15] Adams & Thew, Hamburg merchants. David Adams was a Hamburg banker. In later years WB visited his home in the Augusta suburb of Summerville.

Tuesday 22....Therm.t 28°. Mild & pleasant at midday. Doct. Wm. Burt[16] arrived in the village yesterday with his bride. She is a daughter of Dawson Atkinson of Beech Island. General W[addy]. Thompson has recd. the appointment of minister to Mexico.

Wednesday 23....I was indisposed and confined myself to the house through the greater part of the day.

Thursday 24th. Mild & clear. Thermometer 38°. I set off for my plantation at 1 ocl & arrived before dark.

Friday 25th....I rode with Preston over a part of my plantation & then to his. I had reason to be satisfied with the condition of the plantation. My overseer is an energetic & industrious man, with very good judgment for one so young and the general management of a plantation.

Saturday 26th....I again rode over & inspected every part of my plantation, having my son Whitfield in company, for whom I had sent to Greenwood the previous afternoon.

Sunday 27. Clear & warm. I parted with my two sons Preston & Whitfield after breakfast & returned home. On my way home I met my neighbor Thomas Payne[17] on his return from Hamburg, to which place he had gone in pursuit of a runaway, who had taken one of [his] best horses, saddle & bridle on the Wednesday night preceding. He learned at Hamburg that the boy with the mare had been taken up by some waggons & taken to Hubbards,[18] who after an examination of the boy & a consultation with the Marshall of the Town & others, discharged & gave him a pass to return home. The boy belonged to me, and represented to the gentleman, that I had sent him in pursuit of my carriage horses, that had strayed from home & that after leaving home, his hat was blown off his head by the wind by which he lost his pass. Such was the credulity of his examiners, that they credited this improbable story & not only dismissed him with the horse but imprudently gave him a pass. This transaction does not certainly bear very high testimony in favor of the sagacity & intelligence of the good folk of Hamburg. It is not very complimentary to their understanding to be outwitted by a negro boy not more than 18 to 20 years of age. I reached home at three o'clock & found all well—

Monday 28....I went to the Village to inquire about my runaway but recd. no information....I recd. a notice from Council of their determination to refer our controversy in regard to a road "to the court of sessions." In reply I informed them that I should indict them for a neglect of duty in not keeping the roads in repair. This was an incident for the current month of some little moment.[19]

---

[16] William Burt (1815–), one of three brothers who were Edgefield physicians.

[17] Thomas Payne (c. 1800–), 41 slaves in 1850.

[18] A Hamburg inn run by the Hubbards, husband and wife. WB sometimes a guest.

[19] See January 13, 1842.

March 1st.

Tuesday 1....I finished, sowing oats at my farm yesterday & began this morning to sow the field around the garden in oats for a pasture for hogs.

Wednesday 2....The weather could not be more favorable to the young vegetation & the grain crops. Preston arrived from the plantation.

Thursday 3rd....Mrs. Brooks & Preston left home for Augusta. In the afternoon I dispatched Barnett [a trusted slave] to meet Preston's waggon from which I had heard no tidings. I rode as far as Turkey Creek to meet it & upon meeting a gentleman coming to the village, was informed by him that my waggon was stopped at the hill near Rocky Creek & that the mules refused to draw – I returned home & passed the night alone with Hampden. I had consented for Ellen to go with her mother.

Friday 4th....I sent another horse this morning to meet the waggon. It is a singular coincidence that I started my waggon last Spring to Market on the same day that Preston started his. That my waggon was delayed two days on the road & did not reach my house until the third. Preston has been two days on the road already & has been "stalled" as mine was & nearly at the same point. My waggon was sent to market to make some preparation for his wedding & encountered the most discouraging incidents. Preston's waggon has been sent to market in anticipation of his removal to his own house & to make preparations for this event & it has been stuck in mud holes more than half the time since its departure. The elements appear to war agt. my son & to interpose difficulties in the way of his happy removal to his own home. I am not superstitious & yet I am impressed with the coincidence of events, which happened to me last year & are now happening to my son and this on precisely the same days of the month – I trust a bad beginning will have a good ending. At least let us all strive to do our duty & trust to the goodness of a wise & merciful God, while we implore his aid to guide & direct us. The waggon reached my house at 1 o'clock. I went to meet it & found it stopped in the road, the horses refusing to draw – I got a negro man belonging to the estate of Col. Simkins to drive the horses & under his management, they got off so easily, that I exchanged Preston's driver for him, to go on to Hamburg. He left my house at two ocl. & was going on finely when an axle of the waggon broke & he returned to inform me of it – such a succession of disasters overcame all my fortitude for a moment. I gave him my two horse waggon & dispatched two men with him to assist in transferring the cotton to the small waggon. They had not left my house exceeding one half hour before there commenced falling one of the heaviest rains, we have had this year. The exposure of the negroes, loss of time, injury to the horses & breaking of the waggon, are more than an equivalent for the price of the cotton. About 10 o'clock at night my negroes returned & reported to me that they had arranged everything to set off in the morning. I am very sure that I & Preston have ample cause to dread the [2?] March.

Saturday 5th....Mrs. Brooks returned from Augusta late in the evening & informed that she passed Preston's cotton near Hamburg. I was in bed suffering the most intense agony from headache & sick stomach.

Sunday 6th....Preston returned to dinner & his waggon in the afternoon in good order.

Monday 7th....This morning is as warm & as fragrant with the odour of flowers as a May morning. The peach trees are in full bloom & the elm & many other trees, shrubbery & plants are putting forth their leaves & blossoms. Preston left us after breakfast for the plantation – this was Sale day & much property was sold by the Sheriff at prices from 25 to 30 per cent cheaper than the same would have commanded at Christmas.

....

Wednesday 9th....I met the town council & came to an amicable arrangement with them in regard to my road, in despite of the prejudiced & ill natured opposition of Doct. E. Mims, whom I regard as a low spirited & vindictive man. E. Youngblood[20] behaved with firmness & impartiality & had the cooperation of Peter [Pierre] Laborde[21] & B. Bryan.[22]

Thursday 10th....I was confined on the bed from 12 o'clock until friday morning with a distressing attack. Mr. F.H. Wardlaw with Mrs. Stark[23] & [?] spent the evening with Mrs. Brooks but I was unable to see them.

Friday 11th....The thermt. has been as high as 80° for several days. I have never known vegetation advance so rapidly. The two last days exhibit a perfect contrast to the same period last year. It was then cold with an unceasing fall of rain for three days, causing the roads & water courses to be almost impassable. It is now one year since Preston was married & he has not yet gone to his own house. The ill health of his wife prevents his removal.

Saturday 12....I went in the forenoon to Judge Butlers to call upon Genl. [Waddy] Thompson, lately appointed minister to Mexico & now on his way to that Country. I found the Genl. in good health & spirits....Major Blocker & my Sister [Nancy] & my father arrived & passed the night with us.

Sunday 13th....In the afternoon my sister Mrs. Blocker returned home & I & my father rode out to Judge Butlers to pay a visit to him & his guests. Light mist fell

---

[20] Erasmus J. Youngblood (1800–1887), grandson of Arthur Simkins. His wife Eliza was sister of Arthur and Louis Wigfall. Princeton grad. Congressman PSB endorsed his son as officer in the U.S. Marines.

[21] Pierre Fabian LaBorde (1807–1850), brother of Maximilian. Briefly ed./pub. of the *Advertiser*, in which he promoted high culture and strict states-rights politics. Intendant of the village 1840. In poor health much of his life.

[22] B. C. Bryan (1812–1885), 22 slaves in 1850.

[23] "Miss Stark" ran a school for girls in Columbia, which WB's daughter Ellen attended.

occasionally during the day –

Monday 14th....There was an application before the Ordinary to set aside the Will of Elijah Watson which brought a number of persons to the Village.

....

Thursday 17th....I was confined in bed through the greater part of the day with an unusually severe attack of sick headache & Stomach. I certainly never suffered such agony for 36 hours. It made me almost wish for death.

Friday 18th....I am partially relieved of head ache but am very feeble. Spring is rapidly advancing & is now as forward as is common by the middle of April. Even forest trees are putting forth their leaves.

Saturday 19th. This is as clear, mild & cheering a morn as ever was seen in the month of April. The balmy atmosphere, the singing of birds, the verdent appearance of the shrubbery and the veried hues of flowers all together constitute it one of the sweetest mornings of this delightful season –

Sunday 20....Mr. Berry preached in the Episcopal Church. His sermons are sensible & well composed & his style chaste & lucid. He is in fact an interesting preacher.

Monday 21....I went to my plantation & on the way was exposed to a light rain. I met Preston, who had that evening returned from Fairfield.

Tuesday 22....I rode over my plantation & inspected the general state of affairs. My overseer was engaged in planting corn –

Wednesday 23rd....I devoted the day to riding over to Wash. Holloways on business & to the further inspection of the plantation & stock, etc.

Thursday 24th....I returned home to dinner & found all well. My overseer had planted about 175 acres in corn & had about 100 acres ready bedded for cotton – on my return home I saw at the former plantation of Capt. Weaver corn up, large enough to admit the plow – the overseer Murphy was planting cotton.

Friday 25th....I began to plant corn in the church field, first manuring in the hill.

Saturday 26th. A clear, spring morning. I am engaged with all my force in planting corn. Some of the forest trees are in full leaf –

Sunday 27th....There has been service in the Epis. Church every day, during the past week & again this morning at sunrise. If people are sincere, they cannot be too zealous in the cause of religion. We should not neglect to employ every means that is calculated to improve the heart & to purify it from the low passions & desires, which a love of this world & its treasures is sure to inspire. One distinguishing difference between a good & bad man is, that the good man mortifies & controls his passions while the bad yields to & is governed by them.

Monday 28th....The Court of Common Pleas began its spring session this morning,

Judge Richardson[24] presiding. About the usual number of persons were in attendance on Court.

Tuesday 29th....The roads are becoming dusty & the earth somewhat too dry & hard for the plow. I am engaged in planting the Church field in corn & expect to finish it this evening. I have manured nearly the whole field in the check & covered the corn with the plough. The business of Court progresses slowly –

Wednesday 30th....Judge Richardson came over & passed the evening with us.

Thursday 31....It is very dry & the atmosphere is becoming charged with smoke – no political news of importance except the expected invasion of Texas by the Mexicans under Genl. Arista. Meetings are being held in different cities for the purpose of aiding the Texians. I do not feel much interest in the contest between Mexico & Texas except that it is a contest between liberty & despotism. My sympathies both from principle and education would be given to my people, struggling for independence but towards the people of Texas I entertain not the most favorable opinions. The inhabitants consist of a heterogeneous population, gathered there from all quarters of the Globe & consisting of all classes and descriptions of character with no identity of interest or feeling or purpose. The largest part of the people are adventurers, who have left their former homes in quest of better fortunes & a large portion of the remainder are renegades from Justice or bankrupts, who have fled to save a remnant of property from their creditors. For such a people I cannot entertain a very high regard or take a very lively interest.

April 1, 1842

Friday 1st....I have again to remark that I have never seen vegitation, so far advanced at this period of the year. The leaves of many of the trees are nearly full-grown & the general appearance of the forest would indicate the last of this month.

Saturday 2nd....I left home with Mrs. Brooks & Miss Carroll for Augusta on our way to Savannah & arrived about sunset at Mrs. Camfield's.[25]

Sunday 3rd. No change in the weather. We set off after early breakfast for Savannah in the steam boat Mary Somers. I was much indisposed all day & confined to my birth, consequently saw very little of the land & scenery on the banks of the river. We had a good run & got within one hundred miles of Savannah when the Capt. stopped the boat & lay by for the night. Cloudy & a light rain in the afternoon.

Monday 4th. We arrived in Savannah about 5 oclock & took lodgings at the Pulasky

---

[24] John Smythe Richardson (1777–1850), Sumter Dist. Judge of Court of Common Pleas.

[25] Rebecca Longstreet (1786–1876) of Augusta, m. Ariel Camfield III, 1809. He died 1827. Her father William invented a steam engine. She was sister of Augustus Baldwin Longstreet, and aunt of Gen. James Longstreet (CSA).

house[26]....

Tuesday 5th....I visited the courthouse and inspected a sale of part of a large gang of negroes, belonging to Thos. Butler King[27] by the US Marshall & also of other property by the Shff of the County. I thought the negroes brought fair prices but horses & carriages sold at about half prices. I inspected a portion of the Town & some of its public buildings. The Town is laid out with great regularity, the streets running parallel with each other in a line with the river & crossed by parallel streets, forming squares. Portions of the squares are reserved for public grounds, and closed & set out in trees, principally elm[,] laurel, Pride of India & the flowering locust. These cool & verdant spots, add much to the beauty, comfort & health of the Town. The Town stands upon an elevated sand bluff, from 30-40 feet (I should judge), above the level of the River. It is a coarse, dry & porous sand & the heat in Summer would be intolerable but for the number of shade trees, that line their streets and abound in the public grounds & private enclosures. It is altogether a handsome & pleasant City.

Wednesday 6th. I devoted the day in looking around the Town & in receiving the visits of gentlemen. We spent the preceding evening with Mr. & Mrs. Burrows, where we met Miss Eliza Berrien, who's approaching nuptials with our brother Col. Carroll was the occasion of our visit to Savannah I called this morning with Miss Carroll at the Judges & met Mrs. Berrien & the two sisters, Eliza & Willy with whom we were pleased. They are well bred Yankees and sensible ladies & courteous & affable and their manners – we flatter ourselves that Col. Carroll has been fortunate in his selection of a lady who is to become the partner of his fortunes in this life. She appears of mild & gentle disposition, of easy & pleasing manners & of a well cultivated understanding, with which there is a seeming blending of a sweet & benevolent temper of mind & feeling. We took tea with our old acquaintances Doct. & Mrs. Griffin & went with them to hear Bishop Elliott,[28] who was to preach in his chapel a sort of farewell sermon in anticipation of a short tour of duty through the interior of the State. The bishop is a very interesting preacher & has already acquired a high reputation for so young a man. He possesses advantages, which are allowed to few men in the distribution of the gifts of God – he has a fine & commanding person, a grave & dignified manner & a voice full & impressive & capable of great compass & modulation, assisted by a clear, distinct & composed delivery & the sanctified manner of a humble & ardent Christian. Such a man can-

---

[26] Pulaski House, a grand hotel at Johnson Square, Savannah, est. 1835. Named for Casimir Pulaski, hero of the American Revolution, who is buried in Savannah. First in the South with gas heat and lights.

[27] 1800–1864. Planter-politician on St. Simons Island. MA native, inherited father-in-law's Retreat plantation, added other properties then lost most of them when long-staple cotton mkt. fell in 1830s. A Whig, he supported railroads and port improvements.

[28] Stephen Elliott (1806–1866), First Bishop of Georgia, 1841–1866. Beaufort SC native, Harvard and SC College, lawyer. Converted, ordained 1836. Prof. SC College 1835–1841.

not fail to "win hearts" & be the instrument of much good –

Thursday 7th. I went this morning to the top of the City exchange, from which I enjoyed an interesting panoramic view of the City, the River & the surrounding Country. The view from this elevation is very fine – in the afternoon I was confined to my bed by headache & in the evening we all repaired to Judge Berrien's[29] to witness the nuptials of our relations. The marriage took place as all marriages do, by the young couple pledging their troth to each other, under the direction of the Revd. Bishop, who performed the marriage ceremony – Then there followed the usual kissing & congratulations by Sisters & Aunts & friends &C, the eating of cake with a glass of wine or cordial then supper with its beauties & its viands & sparkling champagne and lastly bowing & shaking hands on leave taking, which is the most troublesome & least agreeable of all the ceremonies of a marriage occasion.

Friday 8th. We left Savannah in the rail road cars at 7 ocl. on our return home, having Col. Carroll & Lady & Bishop Elliott & Lady & many others in company. I was exceedingly sick during the day & was compelled to lie down, so that I neither saw the country or enjoyed the company. We took the stage at the 80 mile station & arrived at Augusta about 2 ocl at night – it was a day & night of agony to me. Heavy rain during the day.

Saturday 9th....We left Augusta at 11 ocl & reached home at 5. We found all well & the garden & surrounding woods looking more beautiful than ever. We went to take tea with Mrs. Carroll & to tell her of the marriage & its incidents, of her daughter & her good qualities & of all the other little matters connected with our trip to Savannah –

Sunday 10th....I was deprived of the privilege of going to church by headache. My daughter informs me that George Addison[30] was at church with his bride. He was married to Miss [Rebecca] Harris of Abbeville on Thursday night –

Monday 11th. . .. The season for the last 20 days has been mild & uniform & more favorable to vegetation than I ever knew at the same time of the year. The foliage of the trees is nearly full grown & vegetation is nearly a month in advance of ordinary seasons. The Spring so far has been rather dry for the planter, his land at times being hard & difficult to break. I went to my plantation in the afternoon.

Tuesday 12th....I rode over my plantation & inspected the state of my crop. My corn crop is planted & most of it up. It looks well. I have upwards of 100 acres of cotton planted & about 40 acres ready for planting. The wheat & small grain tolerably good. The preparation of the land & the general condition of the plantation is creditable to the skill & industry of my overseer. I visited my Son Preston at his house,

---

[29] John Macpherson Berrien (1781–1856), New Jersey native. Broke with Jackson over Peggy Eaton scandal. Supported the American (know-nothing) party in mid-1850s. Lawyer, judge, U.S. Att. Gen. under Jackson, Whig, and U.S. Senator.

[30] Major George A. Addison (1816–1871), son of Allen Bartlett Addison and Patience Youngblood Butler; 1850 census: $6,000 real estate, 22 slaves.

where I met him & his wife, they having moved home in a few days before my arrival. I felt peculiar gratification in seeing my children in their own house & looking as contented & happy as love & confidence in each other, are qualified to make the most favored in this life. On returning home, I visited my sick negroes, examined my cribs & stables, the condition of the horses, milk cows &C. I also traded horses with a man from Alabama & gave $15 between one of my old carriage horses, that had broken down & a young mare. Whitfield arrived from Greenwood....

Wednesday 13th....Preston & his Wife came over & took breakfast with me. At 8 ocl I left the plantation & returned home, accompanied by Caroline & Whitfield. We went over & dined with Mrs. Carroll where we met the Col. and his lady, who had arrived the preceding evening – I passed a very pleasant afternoon with our relations. Col. Carroll's Lady is a very agreeable & interesting woman, of gentle manners & of a [?] & affectionate disposition – ....The night was exceedingly dark & disappointed me in attending a party at Mr. Addison's,[31] given to his son George on the occasion of his marriage –

....

Friday 15th....I attended a large party in the evening at Mr. Griffin's,[32] given in complement to Mr. George Addison & his bride. The supper was sumptuous & elegant, our host & his lady affable & courteous & the company cheerful & talkative. There was neither wine or other strong drink & neither seemed to be necessary to the comfort of the company. It is a good example & I am tempted to follow it. There would be more honor in the observance than in the break of it.

Saturday 16th....Mrs. Carroll & family & Colonel Carroll & Lady dined with us....

Sunday 17th....The earth pretty thoroughly wet from the rain of last night. Pleasant afternoon. Heavy rains at night with thunder & lightning.

Monday 18th....Heavy rain & thunder in the afternoon, which prevented many of our neighbors from being with us & participating in the social pleasures of a party, given to Colonel Carroll & his lady. The company was large enough to pass off the time agreeably & they did not depart until after 12 ocl.

Tuesday 19th....Preston & his Wife with Whitfield left us this morning, the two first on their return home & Whitfield to school.

---

31 Now the Addison-Jennings House. Built 1824 on lower Buncombe St. Home of John Kemp Antiques (2018).

32 Nathan Lipscomb Griffin (1803–1853), prosperous lawyer-planter-legislator; m. Ann Patience Butler 1824. Read law under A. P. Butler, practiced with him, then Armistead Burt (1802–1883) until 1843. Intendant of ECH 1844. SC House and Senate. Daughter Ann m. M. L. Bonham. Bought Darby Plantation in 1847 and built a large house. At his death it passed to his son-in-law, M. L. Bonham. WB owned adjacent land. 1850 census: $27,000 and 124 slaves. At death, owned c. 5,000 acres. Popular and widely admired. Temperance advocate. House, on Main St., demolished 1968.

Wednesday 20th....I heard from my plantation, where the rains have been abundant. The earth too wet for the plough. I was engaged in replanting & thinning corn.

Thursday 21....I made a second planting of the potatoes & commenced replanting corn in the field to the East of my house. Ellen commenced taking lessons in music under E. Bacon[33] this morning.

Friday 22nd....In the afternoon we called on Mr. Pickens & Lady. He has left Washington on a short visit to his family. We found him courteous & cordial and his manners & free and communicative in his conversation –

Saturday 23rd....A brighter or more genial Sun never rose upon the natal day of any human being nor did a more balmy & refreshing air brace & cheer & elevate the feelings. Mrs. Brooks is forty two (42) years of age this morning & is, I am happy to say, in good health bright and cheering from the light of a clear moon at full orb. It was a most lovely day & night in this most lovely season.

Sunday 24th....The foliage of the trees is already full grown & the appearance of the woods & the gardens would suggest the month of June instead of April. Went to the Babtist Church & heard a very sensible & Orthodox sermon from Mr. Johnson upon the omnipotence and omniscience of God & the free agency of Man. Altho these subjects [are?] beyond our comprehension & the limited minds of man can not reconcile the apparently contradictory propositions, yet the learned & revend Doctor insisted that both were true & that our duty required us to believe altho we could not understand them ....

Monday 25th....It is difficult to conceive of milder & fairer & lovelier weather. Therm. at 3 oc. 86°....Began to plow over my corn in the Church field. It looks very promising. Spent the evening at Col. Pickens, who had invited a few families to a social party & with whom I passed a few pleasant hours.

Tuesday 26th....My runaway Abram and a young Durham bull were both brought to me this afternoon.

....

Saturday 30th....Rain in gentle showers would be of advantage as the surface of the earth has been rendered dry & hard by the clear Sun & brisk winds, which have prevailed for the last three days. This is a remarkable Spring. Vegitation of all kinds, the foliage of the forests, fruit & flowers & the herbage of the fields are from 20-30 days in advance of any Spring, of which I have any recollection. The present time might well be taken for the last of May to judge from the general appearance of things. Notwithstanding the forward spring in the vegitable kingdom, the planters

---

[33] Edmund Burke Bacon (1805–1885), son of noted attorney Edmund (1776–1826), who was A. B. Longstreet's model for "Ned Brace" in *Georgia Scenes.* A founder of Trinity Church. Taught music in ECH and was later organist at Christ Church Episcopal, Greenville. His home, where he taught piano, became rectory of Trinity Episcopal for over a century.

are rather behind with their crops of corn & cotton. This is owing to the character of the weather from the first of January until the first of April, which was unfavorable to work on account of the heavy rains. They retarded the business of plowing & planting. This season of wet weather was succeeded in the beginning of April by two weeks of dry weather, during which time the land became too hard to admit of the plow & planters were forced to suspend planting cotton until rain which fell in heavy showers about the 17th & 18 & this caused a further suspension of 3 or 4 days. So that between the first planted & last of the cotton crop there is a space of two weeks. I believe the stands of corn & cotton to be pretty good throughout the District. The entire month of April has been mild & generally clear. It has been a sweet month. It has cheated May of her usual display of rich & beautiful & fragrant flowers. For several successive days a more brilliant sun or a clearer or more cerulean sky never was presented to the admiring eyes of mortal man. Oh! How beautiful all the works of God & how loudly do they proclaim him to be a God of love & mercy. Sin alone mars & deforms this beautiful universe.

May 1, 1842

Sunday 1st....We heard a sermon in the Babtist church from a very dull preacher from Aiken.

Monday 2nd....Very few persons in the Village & I believe no property was sold. The day passed off quietly & rather dully. I had an interview with Major Hibler[34] and announced to him my determination of not being a candidate for a seat in the Senate branch of the legislature. He seemed unaffectedly desirous that I should be a candidate stating at the same time, that if I declined, he should be, and accordingly he announced himself in the course of the day. My old acquaintance & neighbor Major Jeter is indiscrete in again presenting himself as a candidate & under the circumstances the chances of a success are against him. No consideration can save his election but the want of education & business habits on the part of his opponent. I am rejoiced that I am out of the contest & feel that I have decided wisely.

Tuesday 3rd....We are now preparing for our departure, on a short Visit to the plantation to which place we set off about 9 ocl....

Wednesday 4th....I rode over the plantation & to Prestons in the morning. My crop looks tolerably well & the greater part in good order. Preston & his wife came over & passed the night with us. I found several of the negroes still sick.

Thursday 5th....Preston & his wife spent the day with us. In the afternoon he & I rode to Wash. Holloway's, thence by Mr. Mims & Griffins plantations & through my plantation home.

Friday 6th....I went to Cambridge to attend the anniversary meeting of the agricul-

[34] Thomas J. Hibler was SC House member in 1830s. Isaac Hibler (c. 1802– ?), 1850 census: 52 slaves.

tural Society. The meeting was large & respectable. Several members were added to the Society. The address was delivered by Dr. Cain. It was sensible & apparently well written but badly delivered. I read as chairman of a committee a report upon the subject of manure. After the adjournment of the society there was an exhibition of Stock. Returned to my plantation, calling at Preston's, where I saw Mrs. Means & a part of her family who had come on a visit to him & his Wife –

Saturday 7. Preston & wife & Mrs. Means, Thomas & Mariah dined with us at the plantation. In the afternoon rode over my crop, accompanied by Thomas Means, Preston & the overseer.

Sunday 8th. We left the plantation at 9 ocl. on our return home, stopped at Stevens Creek to attend preaching & dined with Doct. [John] Nicholson. We parted in the morning with Whitfield, who had come down from Greenwood to visit us. We had left our daughter Ellen with Doct. Johnson during our absence from the village & had Hampden alone with us. The entire week was cool & windy & unfavorable to cotton. The entire cotton crop so far as I have seen is backward & not very promising. The part up grows very slowly while at least one third can not come up on account of the dry condition of the Earth. The corn crop looks pretty well, as does the wheat but the oat crops want rain. My overseer will finish plowing & working his corn the first time the last of the week. He cannot commence his cotton until next week. Upon referring to last year, I find that I am one week behind in beginning to work the cotton. My corn crop is better & larger than it was at this time last year –

Monday 9th....Upon examining my farm, and find my crop of corn badly come up & requiring an unusual proportion to be replanted. The oats are wanting rain but look pretty well. I visited the village but heard no news.

....

Thursday 12th....The Methodists began a quarterly meeting in their church in the village, in which there was preaching morning & evening.

Friday 13th....Replanted corn & the last planting of cotton are coming up slowly and irregularly. I fear the stands of each will be bad if rain does not fall in a few days. The first planted corn looks promising & is growing rapidly. We paid a visit to Major Blocker & passed the night at his house.

Saturday 14th....We paid a visit to Mrs. Iour in the morning & in the afternoon returned home....I had a headache & took medicine.

Sunday 15....Rain is greatly needed & oats & cotton are suffering for the want of it – there is not moisture enough in the earth to bring up cotton & unless rain falls very shortly, the cotton planting will be inferior. We attended the performance of divine service in the Methodist church in the morning & heard a very good sermon from Mr. Tally.[35] He also administered the sacrament in a solemn manner to a large number of communicants. In the afternoon I heard another pretty good sermon in the same church –

Monday 16th....I had a severe paroxysm of headache, which lasted about three hours.

. . .

Tuesday 17....about dark rain began to fall very moderately & continued through the night but not wetting the earth more than one or 2 inches.

Wednesday 18th. Cloudy & light rain through the greater part of the day. Vegetation looks revived but has not yet received a tenth of the quantity of rain wanted.

Thursday 19th....Vegetation has assumed a fresh & growing appearance. Gardens are improved greatly by the rain.

Friday 20th....The rain on Tuesday last was abundant in various parts of the District & particularly on the north or Saluda river side. Oats are still suffering in this neighborhood. Thunder & lightning in the night & a very light rain about day light.

Saturday 21....I set off for [Oliver?] Towle's plantation to attend the battalion review of Major Quattlebaum.[36] I reached there at 12 ocl. in time to witness the review by Col. Denny[37] & the subsequent evolutions. The crowd of persons was large & among the number several candidates for the Legislature & for various District offices. The company dispersed at an early hour. There was no spirits for sale. I met my father, who went with me to my plantation & he & Preston & Wife passed the night with us....no rain, which is much wanted in that vicinity.

Sunday 22nd....My father left me after breakfast. I went over to dine with Preston but instead of spending a pleasant day with my children I was compelled to take a bed, on which I remained until late in the afternoon, when I returned to the plantation.

Monday 23....I returned home & was again compelled by headache to take my bed. All well & no news.

Tuesday 24....all promise of rain seems to have disappeared. In less than 30 minutes after writing the foregoing sentence, it became cloudy & in the afternoon there was much thunder & showers of rain in various parts of the neighborhood but no more than a sprinkle here.

Wednesday 25....The gardens & oat fields are suffering for the want of rain.

Thursday 26th....I began on Saturday last 21st to work over my corn the second time & I shall finish by 12 ocl. to day, the lots near the house & the field on the Acade-

---

35 Rev. Nicholas Talley was Presiding Elder of Cokesbury District, Methodist Church. Cokesbury, in Greenwood County, was home to an academy, and was named for Thomas Coke and Francis Asbury, early Methodist bishops.

36 John Quattlebaum (1807–1865).

37 David Denny, Capt. of Edgefield volunteers, Seminole War.

my branch[38] amounting to near 20 acres. The whole planted in peas & beans. My man Toney who ran from my overseer about the first of Jany last came to me yesterday morning. The quarrel between him & my overseer has lost me 5 months work beside the injury to his character in remaining so long in the woods.

Friday 27th....It would be delightful weather if we could have one good rain to lay the dust. Corn & cotton grow slowly but continue to look green & thriving.

Saturday 28th....Thick clouds and heavy thunder in the afternoon & rain in various parts of the District but none at this place.

Sunday 29th....Mr. [George] McDuffie [took?] breakfast with me on his way to Aiken. His health seems to have undergone little or no change for the last year. He is thin & feeble but in good spirits....

Monday 30th....A short time before day a light shower of rain fell, wetting the earth from 1/2 to an inch. The appearance of rain is however passing away & the sun is now shining ie 7 oc. in the morning. At 12 ocl. I set off for my plantation with Ellen in company....

Tuesday 31. I rode over my crop in the morning, with which I was pretty well satisfied. The stand of corn & cotton as good as I could have expected except in a field of 20 acres of cotton on the branch, which was planted last, where the moisture was not sufficient to germinate the seed. I rode over a part of Preston's crop & found his stand of cotton good, except on a few acres. I passed the day and dined with him. Rain had fallen in that neighborhood on both Friday & Saturday, of which I only got a moderate shower at the house & on a portion of my adjoining fields but very little in the swamp. My wheat & rye cut & in shocks. A portion of the oats (the first sowed) pretty good but the latter sowing is inferior. The wheat is clear of smut [a fungus], & black [?] but the bear[d?]ed kind is a little injured by rust. The crops of wheat, & other small grain with corn is as early as usual in this season but the cotton is backward & small. On the worn & galded places in the fields, the corn & cotton is very small, there not being moisture sufficient, to promote its growth. One benefit resulting from the dry weather is the opportunity, which it has afforded the planters, of putting their crops in fine order as is apparent in their present clean condition. They are now in fine condition to receive wet weather & would be greatly benefited by a gentle rain of two or three days duration.

June 1, 1842

Wednesday 1....After breakfast I left my plantation for Greenwood in Abbeville [District], to attend the examination of the female & male academies, taking with me my two daughters Caroline Brooks & Ellen. We arrived at 11 ocl. & I repaired to the chapel to attend the examination. I must not omit to record that Mr. Hacket

---

38 Tributary of Beaverdam Creek, crossed by the road to Cambridge (now Buncombe St.) in ECH.

gave us a most cordial reception & treated us with great hospitality during our stay. At night Mr. Chiles delivered before the Greenwood Lyceum the first anniversary address of the society to a crowded auditory. The address was sensible but rather common place in both matter & manner. Doct. Calhoun also delivered an address before the same Society upon the social & intellectual qualifications of the physician. This address was characterized by sound sense & some reflection, united with some personal feeling.

Thursday 2nd. This day was devoted to the examination of some of the classes in the english school and & also other part of Mrs. Leslie's classes in latin & Greek. At night an address was delivered by Preston S. Brooks before the Lyceum upon the advantages of the physical sciences to the interests of agriculture. To me the address was interesting not only on account of the relationship of the speaker but on account of its own intrinsic merits. I thought it contained the fruits of both reading & reflection upon the subject with an order & arrangement of ideas, that was calculated to afford entertainment & instruction. I afterwards heard that it was well recd. Three young men on the same evening delivered speeches of their own composition but the delivery was defective & awkward.

Friday 3rd. The examination of Mrs. Leslie's pupils in greek, geometry & mathematics was closed about 11 ocl. The institutions at Greenwood deserve in an eminent degree the public confidence & patronage. The boys are correctly & thoroughly taught & evinced by the manner in which they went through their examinations . . . they are making good progress under a faithful & competent teacher. At the conclusion of the scholastic exercises Col. Trotti[39] of Barnwell delivered to the patrons of the institution & to a large auditory from the neighboring Country, an address upon education. For a popular address it was respectable but a good deal was not pertinent to the subject or appropriate to the occasion. It gave general satisfaction & recd. the hearty approbation of the audience, who now dispersed for their separate homes. I dined with Col. R. Griffin & in the afternoon returned to my plantation. I was greatly gratified with my visit & cannot in terms too high bestow praise upon the trustees & inhabitants for their zeal & exertions in the cause of education & for their kindness and hospitality to all visitors upon these public occasions. Their courtesy to me was both gratifying & complimentary. They have my fervent wishes for the long & uninterrupted success of these institutions of learning. The literary society formed by the gentlemen of the place, has commenced its operations in a manner, that promises much good for the cause of intelligence among the inhabitants of the District & the peoples of the schools if not for the cause of literature generally....

Saturday 4th....I rode over my crop after breakfast & returned home to dinner. My overseer had brought my cotton almost to a stand, had ploughed over the corn the

---

[39] Francis John Andrews Trotti?, said to have inherited Briarwood plantation from his father, Gasper Trotti.

second time except about 20 acres & had cut the wheat, rye & barley. The crop looked well but wanted rain. Returned home.

Sunday 5. I went to the Episcopal Church in the morning & heard an interesting sermon from Mr. Reid, a young clergyman of great worth, who has lately returned to this place to take charge of the church.[40] In the afternoon I went with my father to Clouds near Hamburg....

Monday 6th. Left Clouds & went to Hamburg to breakfast. My father sold 60 bales of cotton to Sibley at 8 cts & six bales at $4.50 cts. I went over to Augusta & purchased a few articles. After getting through our business we set off for home, dined at Doct. Guiggers [Geiger's] & arrived at home at dark – about 10 ocl. at night we had a fine display of electricity towards the North & some thunder.

Tuesday 7th....The Court of Equity commenced its sitting for this District yesterday morning, Judge Harper presiding. In the afternoon I called upon Judge Harper & Mr. [R.H.] Wilde. [41]

Wednesday 8th....Upon examining the surface of the earth, I find it has already become dry & ashy, yet vegitation has been greatly revived by the shower of rain, which fell yesterday.

Thursday 9th....I gave a supper to the Judge & bar & had under my roof during the evening Judge Harper, Genl. McDuffie, Judge Butler, Mr. Petigrew[42] & R. H. Wilde Esq. of Augusta and the legal gentlemen of the Village. The company formed a real galaxy of talent, wit & professional reputation. Unfortunately for my enjoyment I was assailed by my old enemy & deprived of the pleasure of participating in the conversation of the evening. Harper, Petigrew & McDuffie passed the night with me. The argument of the cause of [Henry] Shultz by his trustee [John W.] Yarborough against the City Council of Augusta commenced to day – Mr. Wilde & Shultz addressed the Court.

Friday....Judge Butler gave a bar dinner but I was too indisposed to attend.

Saturday 11th. Very clear & a little cool on account of a brisk wind from the N. East. Major Burt concluded the argument of Yarborough vs the City Council &C. In the evening I attended a supper party, given by Col. Carroll to the Judge & members of the bar. We formed an agreeable party & the evening passed away pleasantly.

---

[40] Edward Reed (1812–1863), NY native, came from TN in 1842 and was Trinity's Rector until 1844 when he moved to Holy Trinity in Grahamville. Married Julia Blocker and returned occasionally to conduct services after he left.

[41] Richard Henry Wilde (1789–1847) of Augusta. Irish-born lawyer, poet, Congressman, law prof. U. of Louisiana (now Tulane U.).

[42] James Louis Petigru (1789–1863), native of the New Bordeaux area; changed from "Pettigrew." Law partner of James Hamilton in Charleston. SC Att. Gen. 1822–1830. SC House. Defended unpopular causes and opposed Nullification, the "Test Oath," and the firing on Ft. Sumter. Respected as a lonely voice.

Sunday 12th....Judge Harper left me at 5 ocl. to take breakfast with Judge Butler on his way to Preston S. Brooks. We dined with Mrs. Carroll....

Monday 13th....I have suspended the plowing of my corn the third time for the want of rain. There has not been moisture enough in the earth to bring up the crop of peas with regularity.

Tuesday 14th....Saw Judge Wardlaw yesterday on his way from Charleston, who informed me that the honorable John C. Calhoun had returned to Carolina on a short visit. He brings no news from Washington in addition to what is furnished by the papers....

Wednesday 15th....Col. E. Simkins returned from his western exploration, not pleased with the country as I am informed.

....

Friday 17th....I am engaged in cutting oats at the farm, which have been forced to maturity by the dry weather at least 10 days earlier, than they otherwise would have been.

Saturday 18th....Recd. a letter from my overseer, stating that they are suffering for rain in that quarter of the District & that the corn on old red land, looks very unpromising. Rain is greatly wanted in this vicinity & vegetables are much injured by the prolonged drought. The earth has not been wet here thoroughly since the middle of April & at no period since, has it been sufficiently wet to admit of transplanting potatoe slips[43] or vines.

Sunday 19th. Mr. Reed preached in the Ep. Church.

Monday 20th....Engaged in cutting oats at the farm.

Tuesday 21....Our Son James returned from College in good health....Rain has prevailed in all parts of the District & State so far as I have heard except at this place & near Cambridge where there has not fallen enough since April to run in the plough furrow.

Wednesday 22nd....Two fine showers of rain in the afternoon, which wet the earth in my fields more thoroughly than at any time since 15th of April.

Thursday 23rd....Crops & vegetation greatly revived.

Friday 24....We are preparing to pay a visit to the plantation, to which place we set off at 9 ocl. & arrived at 3 ocl.

Saturday 25th....I rode over my plantation & found that my crop had greatly suffered for the want of rain. My corn crop is smaller & inferior to any, made on my plantation in ten years but it is not so far exhausted not to yield well if it can get rain in time. I also rode to Preston Brooks, where I met Mrs. Harper & Miss Means & three of the boys on a visit. Preston & his wife had suffered four or five attacks of

---

[43] Shoots of a mature sweet potato from which new potatoes grow.

chill and fever & looked extremely reduced & feeble.

Sunday 26th....Preston, Wife, Mrs. Harper &C took tea with us.

Monday 27. Dry & hot. I passed by [lands of] Messrs. Payne, Holloway, Mims, Griffin, Williams & Martin Cresswell Burnett & PS Brooks & had a passing view of the crops of these persons. They are small & unpromising. Nothing short of the most favorable seasons for the next two weeks can give these planters two thirds of a crop & in some cases not over a half.

Tuesday 28....In attempting to break a young horse, my negro boys suffered him to fall with his head against a log & killed him.

Wednesday 29. Still very warm & dry. I took another excursion by Doct. Griffins, Cresswell, N. L. Griffin, & as far as Cambridge to see the state of the crops – they were not good tho better than those, which I saw the day before – I dined in Cambridge with my friend W. Chiles.[44] [O]n my return home I found my friend Capt. Lipscomb at my house on his way to Greenwood.

Thursday 30th. I left home with Mr. Lipscomb for Greenwood in Abbeville to offer our friendly mediation to effect a reconciliation between the two adverse parties at that place. We arrived at Greenwood at 11 o'clock & sought an interview first with one party & then the other & found each in a proper temper of mind, to admit of reconciliation. After hearing the statement of each party, we drew up the terms of reconciliation, to which in the end by patience & perseverance, we got them to accede, which happily terminated the dispute & adjusted all their difficulties.[45] We passed the night with Mr. Harket. In the afternoon there was a heavy cloud in the direction of my plantation & a heavy rain around Cambridge & to the West of it but none at my plantation--

July 1st 1842

Friday 1

After effecting the settlement between the gentlemen at Greenwood, Capt. Lipscomb and myself took our departure on our return to my plantation, at which we arrived at 3 ocl, when I was forced to take my bed by a violent headache....

Saturday 2. I went to a barbacue near Mr. R. Cooper's, where I passed a very dull day. On my return in the afternoon I was exposed to several showers of rain which finally wet the earth in my plantation to the depth of one or two inches. Portions of my corn seemed too much exhausted ever to recover & make a crop. I had a part of the wheat thrashed out, & the yield was pretty good.

Sunday 3rd....I returned to Edgefield in company with Preston & Whitfield & ar-

---

[44] William Chiles was Clerk of Bethany Baptist Church, 1829–1841.

[45] WB's involvement in the Brooks-Wigfall dispute two years before provided experience and a level of concern that were likely beneficial here.

rived at 12 ocl. All well. Mrs. B. & the children had returned on Saturday, leaving me & the boys to attend the barbaque. Went to church in the afternoon & while there a very heavy rain began to fall, which did not cease until in the night –

Monday 4th....The earth...very wet in this neighborhood. I heard from my plantation & learned from my overseer that a fine rain fell on Sunday evening, which thoroughly wet the earth, an occurrence, which has not happened since the 18 of April when the last rain fell, which was copious enough to run in the furrows of the plough – the Court of Common Pleas began to hold an extra session under Judge Richardson, was organized & then adjourned in consequence of the day, being our national anniversary. Their was no celebration in this neighborhood....

Tuesday 5th....The Court entered upon the business this morning. Very few persons in attendance....

Wednesday 6th....Showers of rain in the morning & also from 12 to 2 ocl. the earth very wet & the water courses full. The crops have greatly improved by the rains for the last week.

Thursday 7th....Much thunder & showers of rain about 2 ocl. The atmosphere is charged with moisture & the earth saturated with water. Heavy showers continue to fall in different places & of very limited extent. Preston & Wife left us this morning, on their return home. I heard that at my plantation the rain is now abundant. The Earth has been too wet to admit the plough since Sunday.

....

Saturday 9th. About day light a very heavy shower of rain fell ....The evening was calm & delightful. Heard from my overseer that the rain has been abundant at my plantation during the week & that the crop is improving very much.

Sunday 10th....Heard a sermon by Mr. Reed in the Episcopal Church. Judge Richardson & a few friends passed the evening with us.

Monday 11th. Clear & cool. Col. Carroll & Lady, Miss Carroll & Doct. Laborde took their departure to Aiken on their way to the North at 12 ocl. I wish them a safe, pleasant & profitable trip through our Sister States & safe return to the bosom of their family in due time. I spent the day with Judge Butler.

Tuesday....I attended a meeting of the temperance society last evening in the Courthouse at which N. L. Griffin, Doct. Burt & Doct. Mays addressed the assembly. On motion this Society was dissolved & a union formed with the new mechanic's Washingtonian abstinence Society. Some 10 or 15 persons signed the Constitution.[46]

---

[46] One of many social reform movements of this period, the Washingtonian Temperance Society, formed in May 1840 in Baltimore, was in fact an abstinence society, as WB says. It sponsored traveling speakers and pledge signing, and by 1842 had over 500,000 members. A women's society formed that year. Internal dissent over priorities and tactics ended the movement in a few years.

....

Friday 15th....Heard from Aiken that Genl. Wimbish[47] was not expected to live but a short time. His physician had written to his friends at this place that he could not survive longer than 24 hours – I was afflicted with headache.

Saturday 16th....I left home this morning with Whitfield for my plantation on his return to Greenwood – on arriving at my plantation I found all well. The crop of corn & cotton greatly improved since the rains, which began to fall on the 2 of July. By one or two more good seasons, I shall [??] a supply of corn.

Sunday 17th. I attended at the Fellowship Church & heard as dull a sermon as was ever delivered by a mortal man. I met several influential gentlemen, who declared themselves favorably to my election to Congress in the place of Mr. Pickens, who declines a reelection....

Monday 18th. I rode over my crop & a part of Preston's in the morning & in the afternoon went to Doct. Barretts. I passed my time pleasantly with the family until tuesday morning & in listening to the story of some scenes in the Revolutionary war & of family history from my old & respected Aunt Mrs. Nancy Brooks.[48] –

Tuesday 19th. I returned to Fellowship, to hear the address of Doct. Johnson to the Bible Association of Edgefield & Abbeville. It was sensible & as liberal as ought to have been expected from a rigid sectarian. In the afternoon I went to Greenwood. I arrived at Capt. Bird's about 6 o'clock & was forced to retire to bed on account of a violent headache.

Wednesday 20th. I accompanied Capt. Bird to his plantation & joined some dozen planters in riding over & inspecting his crop. It was pretty good & in tolerable order. We returned to Greenwood & took dinner at his house. Genl. Gilliam, the two Mr. Watsons, Dr. Barrett, Joel Smith & several others were of the party. I returned in the afternoon with Mr. Creswell of the Scotch X. ["Scotch Cross" - house] I recd. from most of the gentlemen encouragement to run for Congress....

Thursday 21. I called to see my relations Butler & Stanmore Brooks[49] on my way home. I returned by Cambridge & my plantation & reached home at 9 ocl at night, where I found all and good health....

....

Sunday 24th. Very warm with heavy clouds & thunder in the afternoon but not much rain near the Village. Preaching in the Episcopal Church by Mr. Reed.

Monday 25....Much thunder & heavy clouds in the afternoon but little rain, which would now benefit the crops in this neighborhood. In some parts of the District the

---

[47] John W. Wimbish, General, Abbeville District Militia. SC House, 1840.

[48] Nancy Butler, wife of William Elisha Brooks.

[49] Stanmore Butler Brooks (1801–1882) and William Butler Brooks (1806–1868) were sons of William Elisha Brooks (1761–1804), who was a brother of WB's father Zachariah Smith Brooks.

rain was abundant. A protracted meeting is now being held by the Babtists at Antioch church.

....

Thursday 28th....Fine shower of rain in the afternoon.

Friday 29....The weather has the appearance of being settled for some days at least. Reports from the greater portions of the District represent the corn crop as exceedingly abundant. On the Saluda side they are not so good from the drought in the months of May and June.

Saturday 30th....The intelligence from Washington is unfavorable & the prospect of a settlement with England of the Northeast boundary is more remote than before the negotiations with Lord Ashburton commenced. Much excitement prevails at present at the seat of government-

Sunday 31....A cloud formed suddenly about 4 ocl. which furnished a light shower.

August 1, 1842

Monday 1st....The present season will bring to maturity the entire corn crop in this part of the District & I think, it promises to be more abundant than in any year since 1819....Very few persons in the Village & only one tract of land, was sold by the Shff. I heard no news except that Wiley Freeman[50] had been lodged in the jail from which he had broken some four years ago. He had been committed for the murder of his wife & had succeeded in breaking the jail and making his escape as above stated & was pursued by John Crawford, brother of his murdered wife, who followed Freeman to New Orleans & thence to Texas & after having despaired of ever overtaking him, accidentally saw him passing by the plantation, where he had stopped for the purpose of recreating his person & supplying his purse, both of which had become exhausted by travel. This happened somewhere in Louisiana, to which state, Crawford had returned after having followed Freeman to Texas & lost his trail. It seems that Freeman had passed from this District to New Orleans, thence to Texas & then to Mexico, from which he had returned to Louisiana & was passing through the Country when destiny & retributive justice threw him in the path of Crawford by whom he was arrested & brought in irons to the jail of this District, to which he was committed to await his trial for murder....

Tuesday 2nd. This day was exceedingly cold & fire indispensable to comfort. Therm.t 56° at sun rise. High wind prevails both yesterday & today from No. East which blew down much corn. I was exceedingly sick this evening & until 3 ocl. at night slept a little. I had reason to be sick in both mind & body –

Wednesday 3rd. Very clear & cool. Therm.t 58° at sun rise. 70 at night. High wind

---

[50] The *Edgefield Advertiser,* Aug. 3, 1842, has a detailed account from the *New Orleans Picayune* of July 21.

prevailed all day.

Thursday 4th....Therm.t about 50° at sun rise. The wind was still in the morning but brisk by 10 ocl. I called to see Col. Pickens, on his return from Washington.

Friday 5. Still clear & cool. Therm.t 57°. I left home for my plantation at 8 ocl. and arrived at 1 ocl. found all well except the negro woman Franky. In the afternoon I rode over part of my crop.

Saturday 6th....I rode over & inspected my crop & a part of Preston's. The Burn's field of corn of 50 acres is very fine & the balance tolerable. The cotton crop very good –

Sunday 7....I set off home by the way of Goodhope Church, where a protracted meeting was in progress but feeling indisposed, I left at a very early period & arrived at home at 3 ocl. In the evening I called to see Col. Gregg[51] & family, who had arrived in our Village the day preceding.

....

Tuesday 9th....rain at 7 ocl., which fell in very light showers to 10 ocl....We called to see Col & Mrs. Pickens & were grieved to find Mrs. Pickens seriously ill & also her only son Eldred, a child about three years of age ill of congestive fever.

Wednesday 10th....We learned with sorrow & regret of the death of Col. Picken's child Eldred....He died at about 6 ocl. this morning. Truly our neighbor is visited with the most afflictive losses in his family. This last looks like a cruel stroke.

Thursday 11th..... Mrs. Pickens is represented to be in a very alarming situation & fears are entertained that she cannot survive till morning. The death of this amiable & most estimable lady would be an appreciable loss to her family of young children & would create a hiatus in our social circle of greater extent & influence than the death of any other lady. Her mild and benevolent disposition, gentle manners, & intelligent understanding, free from bigotry or fanaticism, constituted her a most agreeable companion, in private life & one of the most useful & respected members of our social circle. I invoke the wise & sovereign ruler of all human destinies, to grant her life to this anxious community & again to restore her to health. 9 ocl. at night. My servant has just returned from Colonel Pickens, with a message from her attending physician (Doct. Burt) that Mrs. Pickens is gradually sinking & that there

---

51 William Gregg (1800–1867), watch-maker, merchant, industry advocate. His wife Marina was a daughter of James Jones of Edgefield District. Gregg had turned the failing Vaucluse Mill around in 1838, and after prospering as a Charleston merchant for a few years, he would purchase that mill in 1843. Perhaps his visit to ECH involved negotiations for that purchase. After touring New England mills and publishing *Essays on Domestic Industry* in 1844, he founded the Graniteville Mill in 1845. Maxcy Gregg (1814–1862) of Columbia is not known to have married, so the reference to a family rules him out. Later WB visited "Col. Gregg and family" while in Columbia, indicating that WG kept a house there, where he had lived as a young man.

is little or no hope of her recovery. To her pure spirit the change can offer no terrors but on the contrary bright hopes of a happy & glorious immortality, beyond the grave.

Friday 12th. I sent at daylight a servant to inquire how Mrs. Pickens was who returned an answer that she died a short time before day. How heavily does the hand of misfortune press upon my poor neighbor Col. Pickens. Few deaths out of my own family would have afflicted me with the same degree of sympathy, sorrow & regret. It is a severe dispensation of Providence, that fills the mind with silent awe & grief & showes the utter impotency of man & the vanity of his hopes & worldly expectations. Gentle Spirit adieu – I left home for the militia encampment after early breakfast & arrived about 12 ocl. I was soon waited on by Genl. Canty[52] and invited to dine with his Excellency Gov. Richardson, with whom I passed a few pleasant hours in his tent & partook of an excellent dinner. I took supper with Genl. McDuffie & passed the night at Capt. Perrin's.[53] ....

Saturday 13th. I returned to the encampment & employed my time in witnessing the passing incidents & talking with the good folk. [campaigning] About 11 ocl. a review took place when the Governor's Staff with the Major Genl. & his staff made a good show on the field. At the close of the performance a sham fight took place between divisions of the infantry & cavalry. It was somewhat imposing to the sight. At 1 oclock the camps were struck & the emcampment dismissed by Genl. McDuffie in a short address. Immediately after dinner I set off with him for his residence at Cherry hill[54] at which we arrived in good time.

Sunday 14th....Gov. Richardson, Genl. Canty & Col. Watts[55] arrived to dinner with whom I passed an agreeable day. The Gov. is a courteous & pleasant gentleman. My old friend Watts is a good fellow & a very agreeable companion. He is a little too romantic imaginative & extravagant in his mode of thinking & acting for the common place realities of this cruel life. He never will grow old in his feelings.

Monday 15th. At an early hour we set off for Genl. McDuffie's plantation on our way to the Mineral Spring near Lowndes Ville.[56] While at the Gen.ls plantation we rode over a part of his crop. The part we saw, was good but we were informed that the greater part was inferior on account of the want of work at the proper season. The Genl. has adopted the theory that a large proportion of the usual horse power may be dispensed with & the hoe substituted in place of the plough. He has pushed

---

[52] James Willis Cantey (1794–1860) of Camden. Sheriff, Brig. Gen. of militia, Adjutant and Inspector Gen. of SC 1843. SC House 1846–1849. m. Camilla, daughter of Gov. John P. Richardson. Son J. W. Cantey III killed in Mexican War.

[53] Abner Monroe Perrin, Jr. (1798–1854), of Edgefield Dist. His son and namesake was a Brig. Gen in CSA.

[54] On the banks of the Savannah River in Abbeville Dist.

[55] Richard Watts?

[56] Between Abbeville and the Savannah in Abbeville Co.

his theory so far this summer as materially to injure his crop, portions of which are both small & foul or grassy. He has lost the labor of a large portion of his negroes from congestive fever. About 100 had been sick but none had died. In the afternoon we went to the Springs, where we arrived about sunset, after encountering severe rains & very bad roads.

Tuesday 16th....I passed the day as all loungers do at Watering places, reading, talking, walking, eating, drinking & sleeping. There were several arrivals, during the day & by night there were from 75 to 80 persons at this watering place. Among the number were Judge Wardlaw, Mr. Berrien of Georgia, Genl. [M. L.] Bonham & Capt Starnes of Augusta. Heavy rains during the day. The young people danced at night.

Wednesday 17th....the same routine of talking &C &C.

Thursday 18. The same as yesterday. One half of the company left the springs during the day. I rode with Peter Laborde to the Savannah River both in the morning & evening. The falls & islands in this river near the Springs, present a very pleasant sight & very well compensate for the ride to them. The lands adjacent to the Springs are poor & hilly but suited to small grain.[57]

Friday 19th. I left the Springs this morning on my return home, taking my friend Peter Laborde in the carriage with me. We dined at Abbe. Ct. House. & slept at Smith's on the road to Cambridge.

Saturday 20th. I paid a short visit to Greenwood to see our Son Whitfield, whom I found pretty well & then hurried to my plantation. After dinner I rode over my crop, which I found improved & equal to my expectations. One case of sickness among my negroes & every other interest in good condition. Our Son Preston came over & passed the night with me. No news of any interest –

Sunday 21. I returned home & found all well. In the afternoon Judge Butler called & remained a few hours with me....The Villagers in pretty good health.

Monday 22. I visited the Village & saw a portion of my neighbors. Learned with regret that Joseph Woods of Augusta in a fracas had shot a young man by the name of Rooney through the heart in Hamburg....We made a visit of condolence to our neighbor Col. Pickens. He appeared composed & resigned. His loss has been a heavy & grievous one.

Tuesday 23rd....a gloomy day with showers of rain.

Wednesday 24th....There was an application today before a Court of Magistrates to bail Mr. Wood of Hamburg, who had shot Jas. Marony in a fray. Sent my servant Barnett to my father's, to inform him that his runaway negroes were in the jail at Spartanburgh.

....

[57] Wheat, oats, barley, rye, rice.

Saturday 27th....Preston & James arrived to dinner bringing me intelligence from my plantation of the loss of a blooded filly by Argile, a beautiful animal.

Sunday 28....I heard two able & interesting sermons by Mr. Reed in the Epis. Church. He is an able preacher, the ablest in the State.

Monday 29th....Preston left us this morning on his return home.

Tuesday 30th....Vegetation begins to assume the appearance of Autumn. Cotton is fast opening & the planters have generally began to pick out.

Wednesday 31....I am busily engaged in sowing fodder at my farm but find the weather very unfavorable. Occasional showers of rain & floating clouds prevent the fodder from drying & also tend to enjure it. It is reported that John Key is to be married today to a Miss Ardis of Beach, Island[,] a pretty sprightly girl. Since the 2 day of July there has been an unusual quantity of rain. It has fallen at least two days in each week & occasionally and heavy showers. In various parts of the United States the floods of rain have done much damage especially in Virginia & No. Ca.

September 1, 1842

Thursday 1....heavy rain at night. It will enjure the fodder of 10 acres of land, that is now hanging on the stalk. A marriage is to take place to night between Mrs. Wallace & a young gentleman by the name of Spann a lawyer at this place.[58] There is almost too great a disparity in their ages, otherwise the match is appropriate enough. She is an industrious, energetic and exemplary lady in all that appertains to the character of a good housewife. She is good looking [,] sensible & I believe a kind hearted & clever lady. He is studious & moral & exemplary in his conduct & very attentive to his business. They have my kindest wishes for their happiness & prosperity.

Friday 2nd....Heard at night a most excellent sermon by Mr. Reed on prayer. He is the most sensible, Orthodox & interesting preacher, that I have ever heard.

Saturday 3....We called in the afternoon to see Mrs. Smith Simkins[59] (a bride from Florida, now on a visit to Capt. & Mrs. Bird). She appears to be a sensible & well educated lady, of good manners, [and] appearance. I regard her as an ellegible match for my neighbor. At night I attended preaching in the babtist church & heard a sermon from Doct. Johnson & an exhortation from Doct. Mays. I had heard extravagant accounts of the powers of the latter at exhortations but I was disappointed. His language was plain and persuasive but his ideas very commonplace.

---

[58] Henry R. Spann was admitted to the SC bar in 1842, and was the "orator of the day" for the July 4 celebrations in 1845. Mrs. H. R. Spann was a "Directress" of the Edgefield Soldiers' Relief Association, July 1861.

[59] Smith Simkins was either John Smith Simkins, born 1810, or Zachariah Smith Simkins, born 1818, both sons of Jesse Simkins (1784–1821) and Behethland Brooks (1793–1864).

He may not have let out his powers on this occasion.

Sunday 4th....Service in both the babtist church & Episcopal. The concourse of persons at the Babtist church was large. About 8 ocl. at night Col. Carroll & party returned from a visit from the North; all in a state of improved health & in very fine spirits.

Monday 5th. Protracted meeting among the babtists in progress. I attended a meeting for prayer at 8 ocl. It was conducted with order & proper solemnity. I heard at night a sermon from a Mr. Brantley from Augusta.[60] He was sensible, at times almost eloquent & occasionally graphic in his descriptions but a little too formal. There was too great an effort at fine speaking to be impressive & somewhat too theatrical to be solemn. His prayer was appropriate & impressive. At the close of the ceremonies all the little girls & one child went up to be prayed for. This was sale day but the assemblage of persons was not large. No sale by Sheriff & no news. Candidates for the Legislature were very active in courting votes....

Tuesday 6th....In going to my plantation I passed my negro man George at Geo. Outz, very ill of fever. I stopped at Doct. Nicholson's & requested the Doct. to visit him. After dining with the Doct. went to my plantation where I found 7 or 8 of my negroes sick but only one dangerously ill.

Wednesday 7th....I spent the day in assisting Preston to reraise his stables, which he had removed to a more convenient place.

Thursday 8th Rode over & inspected my plantation....

Friday 9th....My negro woman Franky quite ill. I sent for Doct. Lake[61] –

Saturday....I visited Fellowship Church, at which the Babtist Association was being held. I heard a sensible sermon by the Revd. Mr. Chiles,[62] who had that morning been elected Moderator & also a rambling & incoherent address from good old Mr. Carthage. Several friends returned with me to my plantation with whom & my boys I anticipated much satisfaction but a violent headache deprived me of all pleasure –

Sunday 11....My friends left me after breakfast for church, to which I was prevented from going by indisposition. Feeling very unwell & lonesome I determined to return home & set off at 11 ocl. The weather very oppressive. I found the family well & my Father on a visit. My man George was better & taking quinine....

Monday 12th....The weather for the last 10 days has been clear & hot, far exceeding the heat of any period, during the summer months. All vegetation is withering & the wells failing in water. The health of many portions of the District is bad &

---

[60] Wm. T. Brantley, Jr., pastor of First Baptist Augusta, 1840–1848.

[61] Dr. John Lake (1809–1884), Univ. of PA medical school; m. Sophia A. Blocker. In SC House 1848–1849, he introduced a bill to improve three roads in Edgefield Dist., with which his house calls had made him painfully familiar. His grandson was a missionary to lepers in China.

[62] Rev. James M. Chiles, pastor of Bethany Baptist Church, 1832–1844.

much sickness prevails on the Savannah River side of the District & also near Cambridge which has caused several deaths. While at my plantation, I offered my overseer 15 bales of cotton or 4500 [lbs.] of clean cotton, delivered in Hamburg, free from expence. He declined to take it. Portions of my corn crop is very fine & my cotton crop is good....

....

Wednesday 14....I am engaged in sowing rye for pastures & getting timber for house & fences.

Thursday 15....We spent a pleasant evening at E[dmund] Bacons.

Friday 16th....I was occupied in repairing the road in front of my house.

....

Sunday 18th....Attended morning & evening the performance of divine service in the Epis. Ch. & heard two capital sermons from Mr. Reed. I visited Mr. Glover, who was extremely ill of congestive fever.

Monday 19th....I devoted the day to working on the road.

Tuesday 20th....Wm. Glover[63] died at 8 ocl. He was a clever young man & more amiable than any of his brothers. He has left a young widow, without any child. It is however supposed that she is in a state of pregnancy.

Wednesday 21....I attended at Charles Glover's the funeral services over [his brother] Mr. Glover. They were performed by old Mr. [Joseph?] Moor[e].

....

Friday 23rd....Fire in the morning necessary to comfort. On Thursday evening we gave a large party to Smith Simkins and his bride . The evening was clear & mild, the company large & agreeable & the occasion passed off very pleasantly. For a miracle I was fine from headache.

Saturday 24....Julia & Elizabeth Blocker left us for home this morning.

Sunday 25. Rain from morning till night & occasionally heavy showers, so we were confined to the house. The Babtist Church was not opened in consequence of the death of young Wm Johnson, who had been living in New Orleans for the last two years.

Monday 26. Light rain in the morning after a night of uninterrupted rain with high wind from N. East. In portions of the District, the water courses were high.

Tuesday 27....I attended a meeting of the bible class, formed by Mr. Reed for instruction in the Scriptures.

....

Thursday 29th....I went to my plantation in the afternoon of Wednesday with Capt.

[63] Wm. J. Glover (1818–1842), recently elected 2nd Lt. of Cavalry, Edgefield Hussars.

Bird in company with me. We met Blair Smith Simpkins[64] & Jas Brooks, who had come by the way of my fathers, to whom they had paid a visit. Early in the morning, we rode over my crop & then to Preston's & returned to dinner. My crop is a good one & part of the cotton is very fine. I bargained with Mr. Lowry to oversee my business for the ensuing year at $1 per day & the usual provisions. I consider it a high price but he is a clever man & faithful to his business, & I was loth to part with him. He had ginned & packed 29 bales of cotton & three or four more picked out. He had gathered about 30 acres of corn & sowed in lots from 15-20 acres in small [?] for grazing lots. About half of my cotton was matured & would not suffer greatly by frost but the other half is now growing & is full of young fruit, which an early frost would destroy.

....

October 1, 1842

Saturday 1st....James left us on his return to College. He & the whole of my family are in most excellent health for which I desire to return most devout thanks to Almighty God. I rode to the Pine house on a little business. Ellick [slave] arrived at night from the plantation, bringing the intelligence that my sick negroes are getting better. We spent an agreeable evening with Capt. Bird & family.

Sunday 2....I attended at the Episcopal Church & heard an eloquent sermon by the Reverend Mr. Reed, who also administered the sacrament in a very impressive manner.

Monday 3rd. Another mild & sweet morning with a bright Sun. By reference to this day a year ago, I find there was frost. The assemblage of persons in the Village was about the usual number. The candidates to the Legislature were very busy but very little interest was manifested by the people on the subject. Very little property was sold. The crops are represented to be good over the greater part of the Dist –

Tuesday 4th. Bishop Gadson[65] & the Revd. Mr. [Lucien C.] Lance [Calvery Church, Charleston] arrived in the stage on a visit to our church. They quartered with us. The Bishop preached at night. He is a most excellent man & a sensible & well informed divine. The Revd. Mr. Lance appears to be a very agreeable gentleman & well informed on general subjects.

Wednesday 5....The bishop preached in the forenoon. We dined with Mr. Terry. Rain at night prevented service in the church.

---

[64] Possibly the Smith Simkins whose wife WB mentioned on Sept. 3, but I find no record of him.

[65] Christopher Edwards Gadsden (1785–1852), grandson of Revolutionary leader of same name. Yale class of 1804, Rector of St. Philips Charleston 1814–1852. Bishop of SC 1840–1852. Ed. of the *Gospel Messenger*. Advocated a seminary and founded a home for retired clergy.

Thursday 6th. Cool & windy. Our respected guests left us this morning, taking the stage for Pendleton & Greenville. Our Son Whitfield arrived from Greenwood, bringing the gratifying intelligence that the sick negroes at the plantation were better. My waggons returned from Market. My cotton (20 bales) was sold for 7 1/8, a price so low, that fails to remunerate the planter for the labor of making, much less for the expenses when bagging & carrying to market are added. The 20 bales sold for $484 –

Friday 7th....In looking over the garden, I discovered a second crop of rasberries of the usual size & some of them ripe. The cherry trees are in bloom & the fig trees have a second supply of leaves. It has been a remarkable fall in many respects. The greatest heat has been in September, which has caused much sickness through the District & also throughout the State –

Saturday 8th....I devoted the day to the creation of a new fence in front of the house. The present one has stood for upwards of 20 years. Heard of the death of Mrs. Sheppard.

Sunday 9th....Attended divine service in the Epis. church.

Monday 10....An election for Senator & representatives to the Legislature takes place today. I have rarely seen a more inclement day or more constant fall of rain. Not more than 50 votes were given at the courthouse, which is between 20 & 30 less than live within the corporate limits.

Tuesday 11th....I went to the Village & voted and returned to work upon my fence. Judge Butler & Major Blocker to dinner with me. I heard from my overseer that I had lost a smart boy about 10 years of age of congestive fever. He was one of Hampden's pets & called Archer.

Wednesday 12th....The votes were counted for Senator & six representatives to the legislature, which resulted in the election of Jno. S. Jeter for the Senate & M. Bonham, G. Bowell, Doct. R. Griffin. Doct. Jno. Nicholson, Wiley Harrison and Jas. Sheppard for the house of representatives. The election was conducted with order and peace and quietness, & without any of that treating & importuning for votes which has sometimes disgraced our District.

Thursday 13th....I was considerably indisposed from headache.

Friday 14th....I began yesterday to make a plank fence around the grove in front of my house to gather corn from the adjoining field. I left home for the plantation by the way of Major Blocker's, where I dined & left Hampden, who had set off with me for the plantation. I was caught in a shower of rain near Dorn's,[66] by which I was made partially wet. Arrived at the plantation before dark & learned with much

---

[66] WB would not have passed near the locally well-known William B. Dorn's place in what is now southern McCormick Co. "Billy" Dorn (1799–1876), after years of obsessive looking, found gold there in 1852, became very rich, and built Oak Grove plantation. WB likely mentions a relative.

pleasure that my sick negroes were convalescent.

Saturday 15th....I rode over my plantation & also to Preston's. My corn crop is turning out better than I expected & the cotton crop bids [fair?] to be a good one. Preston & his wife came over & spent the night with me. They are both in fine health.

Sunday 16th. Clear & mild with a very slight frost in the morning. It had no visible effect on vegetation. I returned home to dinner & found all well. Mrs. Carroll lost a small boy (Lucius) by congestive fever about 12 ocl. on Saturday night –

Monday 17....The Court of Common Pleas, commenced its Spring (sic) session, Judge Earle[67] presiding. I observed that the bar was crowded with young lawyers from various quarters of the State, one from Charleston & others from Aiken, Hamburg Abbeville, Newberry & one from Augusta. There was a large assemblage of persons & I remarked a larger number of waggons than I have seen for many years. In the Evening we called on Mr. & Mrs. Yancy[68] and on Mr. & Mrs. Burrows [Borroughs][69] from Savannah, all of whom are at present the guests of Col. Carroll.

Tuesday 18th....I was in Court for a few minutes & saw [Wiley] Freeman arraigned for the murder of his wife. He was agitated & trembled very much. In fact I have never seen a man at the bar exhibit as much alarm & agitation.

Wednesday 19th....John Johnson[70] was tried for forgery & acquitted.

Thursday 20th....My waggons passed to Market with 20 bales of cotton. I understand that in the neighborhood, frost was seen but that it did not injure vegitation. I had a few friends to dine with me. The trial of Woods was commenced for the killing of Rooney. He was acquitted.[71]

Friday 21....The frost this morning killed the cotton, potatoe vine, & young vegetation, particularly in the Northern part of the District.

Saturday 22....Wiley Freeman was tried today for the murder of his wife about five years ago & convicted. He was defended by Col. Carroll & Cunningham but the proof was so plain & undoubted, that there was but little ground on which to place an argument. The Court adjourned about dark & the Judge & a few friends passed the evening with me.

Sunday 23rd....We attended preaching at the Babtist Church & heard a sermon by

---

[67] Bayles J. Earle, Circuit Court Judge from Greenville. SC College 1811.

[68] Benjamin Cudworth Yancey, Jr. (1817–1891), brother of fire-eater William Lowndes Yancey of Alabama. Born in Charleston, father died of malaria when he was four months old. Univ. GA 1836; Harvard Law. Practiced in Hamburg 1840s. SC House 1849. Moved to Alabama, elected state senate, minister to Argentina 1858, Cobb's Legion CSA.

[69] Likely relatives of the Berrien family, of whom J. P. Carroll had become an in-law.

[70] A John Johnson volunteered for the Palmetto Regiment, Mexican War, and died in 1847.

[71] Joseph Wood of Hamburg's killing of James Rooney was ruled a justifiable homicide.

Doct. Johnson.

....

Tuesday 25....My father left us on his return home in most excellent health for a man of his age....

Wednesday 26th. E[lijah] Watson [Jr.] & his Sister Ann Barrett spent the day & night with us.

Thursday 27....A light hoar frost, which was plainly to be seen at Sun rise. The papers contained an account of a destructive fire in Liverpool, by which 40,000 bags of cotton were destroyed beside other property. The loss is valued at near $2,000,000. The manufacturing Districts have become quiet & the operatives have returned to work. Notwithstanding the loss of cotton by fire & the abundance of money, the market for cotton remained depressed. The prospect of the planter is any thing but encouraging. Cotton is from 4 ½ -7 cts.

Friday 28th....I began yesterday to dig & save the potatoe crop.

Saturday 29....The family are preparing to go to the plantation[,] for which place they set off about 10 ocl. I went in company with Col. Carroll to a battalion muster at the pine house. It was a poor throng & I passed a dull day. For the first time in many years I slept at home alone.

Sunday 30th. Rain with brisk wind from the N. East. I am now 20 miles from our family & shall in all probability be compelled to ride through the rain to get with them. Our cook Sally gave me a good breakfast this morning, which I enjoyed in silence and thankfulness. The happiness or misery of man depends more on his physical organization and temper of mind, than upon the accidental circumstances of State or conditions in which he is placed. Self possession & acquiescence amidst & to the changes and conditions of life, which lie beyond our power of prevention or control, is the best possible philosophy for the contentment or happiness of the subject.

Monday 31st....We spent the day with Preston & his wife. I also rode over a part of my crop of cotton, which was principally open yet the late fall, has been of great benefit to me.

November 1st. 1842

Tuesday 1st....I went from my plantation to Mr. Lows[72] to a regimental review. Saw & conversed with a good many, eat a pretty good dinner and returned home, at which I arrived at half after seven with a hoarseness, which forced me to speak in whispers.

---

[72] Possibly Nicholas Lowe, who bought 43 acres on Turkey Creek (tributary of Stevens Creek) in 1839.

Wednesday 2nd..... I rode over my plantation & examined my cotton crop with particularity & concluded that I should not make over 125 bales of cotton.

Thursday 3..... I rode to Cambridge to ascertain the arrangements for the succeeding day. Mr. Dubose[73] passed the night with me.

Friday 4th..... The meeting of the agricultural Society took place at Cambridge. There was a fine exhibition of stock of all kinds. The specimens of hogs, cattle & horses were very little inferior to those exhibited at Columbia in December last. The assemblage of persons were about 400 of the substantial planters of the Country, who spent the day in a very orderly & apparently agreeable way. We partook of an excellent barbacue after the adjournment of the Society & returned home at a good hour. It was a fine day for old Cambridge.

Saturday 5 ....I attended a regimental parade at Richardson's. The regiment turned out well & made a good appearance. Mr. Dubose from Columbia & Capt. Ward[74] of this District left me this morning for their respective homes.

Sunday 6th....I left the plantation at 1 ocl. for the Village under the influence of a violent headache, from which I suffered greatly. I lay in the carriage the whole way & took my bed immediately on my return.

Monday 7....More persons convened in the Village than could have been looked for on so inclement a day. Property was sold to the amount of $4 or 5000. Negroes sold from $150 to 530. A likely negro fellow brought $530. There appeared to be a good many monied men, who had come to the Village with the view of purchasing property.

Tuesday 8th....I walked to the Village for a little business & saw Doct. Stewart[75] & party at the tavern on their return to Beaufort from the Mountains. I sent by Mr. Gowdy [Goudy?] $200 to H[yrum] Hutchinson[76] to pay a note in bank of Preston's. I set off for the plantation about 12 ocl. to join my family with Mrs. Carroll & Little Oscar Laborde in company.

Wednesday 9th....We all paid a visit to Preston & his lady.

---

[73] Likely Reuben Dubose, born 1796, Richland Dist. Lived in Columbia. He and wife friends of WB. Moved to Texas in 1847.

[74] Likely Richard Ward (1802–1879). Lived on a plantation on the "Saluda side" of Edgefield Dist. Owned a stagecoach company operating between Charlotte and Augusta. Son Clinton founded the town of Ward in Saluda County.

[75] Rowland, Moore, and Rogers, *Beaufort County* does not identify a physician named Steward or the more likely Stuart, in this era, but members of the Beaufort elite summered in resorts like Pendleton SC and Flat Rock NC.

[76] Hiram Hutchinson (1790–1856), York District native. Hamburg entrepreneur with interests in the Bank of Hamburg (1835), Graniteville mill (1845), and the illusory Savannah River Railroad Co. Died in NY City. Since ECH had no bank, WB and family relied on the Bank of Hamburg or the Bank of Charleston's agency there, but given his hard money philosophy, he saw it as a last resort.

Thursday 10th....Preston & his Wife dined with us & the day passed away pleasantly. Mrs. Carroll arrived in the afternoon. Killing frost & ice.

Friday 11. We paid a visit to Cambridge & inspected the remains of the fortifications, which were thrown up by the British during the Revolutionary War.[77] I here learned that a Mrs. Smith had died the preceding night very suddenly. She felt ill at 10 ocl. & at 11 ocl. was dead. We returned to Preston's & dined with him.

Saturday 12....Mrs. Brooks, Mrs. Carroll & Young Mrs. Carroll with the children left the plantation about nine ocl. on their return to the Village. I paid a visit to our father, whom I found in most excellent health & in pretty good spirits.

Sunday 13th....I returned to the plantation by the way of Pickens & Preston Brooks plantations.

Monday 14th....I returned home & found the family well. I was however greatly shocked by the death of a little girl in the yard, who had been burnt the Friday before our return. The first site that caught my eye & ear was the appearance of my negro man Paul, hammering on a coffin, which threw a gloom over my feelings, from which I have not recovered.

Tuesday 15th....My son Whitfield left this morning for Barnwell after my runaway boy Abram.[78] ....

Wednesday 16th. An inclement day....My waggons with Preston's were on their way to market.

Thursday 17th....at night the rain fell in torrents. The waggons passed my house to market about 2 ocl. At the same hour Whitfield returned from Barnwell.

Friday 18th....I do not recollect to have witnessed so great a change in the weather as took place this day. For the last 5 or 6 days, the temperature was mild & occasionally warm but during the forenoon the Therm.t fell below the freezing point. The change was about 40° in a few hours. I left in the morning with Mrs. B. for Hamburg & arrived at 3 ocl. We did some shopping notwithstanding the cold weather....

Saturday 19th....The earth was frozen very hard. My waggons arrived & I sold 49 bales of very good cotton at 5 ¼ cts. It was as good cotton as I usually make on my plantation. The prospect of the planter was never more discouraging since the Revolutionary war. Articles of clothing have fallen in price but groceries since the passage of the tariff bill[79] have risen, particularly sugar, coffee & salt. I left Hamburg

---

[77] The "Star Fort" at Ninety Six, built by the British and besieged by Gen. Nathaniel Greene's force in May–June 1781.

[78] The same slave who had fled WB's plantation twice before. Sending 17-year-old WBB after him suggests confidence in his maturity, but WB is silent as to whether Abram was with him.

[79] A generally higher tariff enacted by the Whig majority went into effect in Sept. 1842. It marked the first increase in import taxes since 1833. Whether it was responsible for the rising prices WB mentions, is not clear.

at four ocl. & arrived at home at 9 at night. The night was very cold & clear & the reflection of the moon on the forests & fenses on the road resembled the light of fire....

Sunday 20....Preaching in the Epis church, which I attended in the morning. Preston & his wife came down on a visit –

Monday 21....I rode with Preston & Mr. Ch. Glover[80] where the tract of land, belonging to the estate of B. Wallace for the purpose of forming some opinion of its value. It was better land, than I expected.

Tuesday 22....Preston & wife left us on their return to his plantation. The present is the most inclement weather that I have ever seen in Nov., the cold being not only disagreeable but painful in the open air. I have expected to see snow for the last two days but notwithstanding the occasional heavy clouds, neither rain or snow has yet fallen.

....

Thursday 24th....Therm.t 30°....We paid a visit to Judge & Aunt Butler & also on Col. Pickens on our return.

Friday 25. This was a clear & bright morning with a heavy hoar frost on the earth, rivaling in whiteness a light snow. Therm.t below 27°. I attended the sale of Adams property at the Velito Springs[81] & went in the afternoon to my plantation. The property sold for about one half of what it would have commanded one year ago.

Saturday 26th....I returned home stopping at Adams, to select a lot of sheep, which I purchased the previous day.

Sunday 27th....Attended service in the Epis. church in the forenoon & called upon Doct. Butler[82] & Mrs. Thompson[83] at Judge Butlers in the afternoon.

Monday 28th....I set off for Columbia at 11 ocl. with Whitfield in company to apply for admission into the South Carolina College & arrived at night at Mrs. Lees [tavern] where we took quarters for the night.

Tuesday 29....I arrived at Columbia about 3 ocl. & took lodging at Maben's. At night I attended the meeting of the agricultural Society in the State house. It was not large & very little business was done. There was a short argument upon the expediency of applying to the Legislature for an appropriation to have an agricultural Survey of the state but no further action was taken on the resolution it being laid on the table.

---

80 Charles Glover (1810–1852), 1850 census: $18,000 real estate, 41 slaves.

81 Nearly halfway between ECH and Roselands.

82 William Butler (1790–1850), son of Gen. Wm. and Behethland Moore Butler. WB's cousin. Physician in Greenville SC; Navy Surgeon 1812–1819. U.S. House (Whig) 1841–1843.

83 Emmala Butler, wife of Waddy Thompson.

Wednesday 30th....this morning...the surface of the earth was saturated with water, standing in pools & puddles. I walked round the Stalls, where the stock was confined for exhibition & inspected the principal portion. The lot of Birkshire hogs of Doct. Parker were very fine. There were some good cattle, sheep, horses & mules. The premiums were principally taken by Benj Taylor, Doct. Parker & the Davises. The show of stock would have been very interesting but for the severity of the day. I dined at Doct. Gibbs[84] & met all the dignitaries of the land at table. The dinner was superb & the wine excellent. His display of paintings is very good. The little Doctor has taste & lives in great style. There was no meeting of the agricultural Society in consequence of the meeting of the trustees of the College. The price of every commodity has been reduced by the low price of cotton. Pork is $2 pr 100 lbs. Beef from 2 to 3 cts per pound. And all of the articles in the line of provisions, furnished by agriculturalists, equally low. In fact the real planter feels the present depression in the markets more sensibly than any other class of the community. I sold a lot of 40 bags of cotton of the best quality from my plantation at 5 ¼ cts. For precisely such a lot I was paid 3 or 4 years since 18 1/8 cts. more than three times the present price. The people in Columbia notwithstanding the "hard times" were gay & joyous & apparently very contented. Every body spoke of the hard times & the necessity of retrenchment yet very few exhibited any proofs of having entered upon the good work of reform.

December 1. 1842

Thursday 1....I called to see Col. Preston & family, Col. Gregg & family & Mrs. P. M. Butler. [Miranda Duval] I was invited to dine at Col. Preston's but declined in consequence of my time being occupied in preparing some business for the agricultural Society. The Society met at 6 ocl. I offered sundry resolutions in reference to the formation of auxiliary societies in the Districts & of asking the Legislature for an appropriation of $500 to be expended in offering premiums throughout the State through the medium of these Societies for agricultural productions & domestic manufactures. And I accompanied the resolutions with an explanation of their objects & the mode in which they were to [be] carried into practice when they passed with scarcely any opposition. A committee was appointed to memorialize the Legislature, of which I was chairman. Judge ONeal delivered the anniversary address. It disappointed my expectations. The President distributed the premiums, accompa-

---

[84] Robert Wilson Gibbs, M.D. (1809–1866), practiced in Columbia, taught at SC College, and researched and published in several scientific fields. He argued for the great age of the earth, which he reconciled with Scripture. His artistic interest led to a biography of SC painter James DeVeaux, and historical interest to *A Documentary History of the American Revolution* (1853), which focused on SC. He was active in the State Agri. Soc., served as mayor of Columbia, and edited the *Daily South Carolinian*. During the Civil War he was Surgeon General of SC.

nied with an address to the fortunate competitors. The house was crowded by spectators & the gallery with ladies. And the front of the Speakers seat in the Legislative hall was decorated by a collection of rare & beautiful plants, furnished by Mr.Kupal for the occasion. The evening passed away pleasantly & the Society adjourned about 9 o'clock in fine spirits. A few silk handkerchiefs of domestic manufacture were exhibited at the meeting & created a fine feeling. They were sold readily at $3 per piece. They were manufactured by Mrs. Dantzler of Spartanburgh.

Friday 2nd. I passed the greater part of the morning at the State house. Genl. McDuffie was elected in the place of Col. Preston (resigned) to serve until the 4th of March next & he was also elected US senator for six years after the 4 of March.[85] It was rumored that Mr. Calhoun intended to resign, his resignation not to take effect until after the 4th of March. In the event of his resignation there will be a half dozen candidates for the succession. There were various rumors in circulation in regard to parties & their political combinations. There is much interest felt in regard to the division of the State into Congressional Districts but no opinion can now be formed as to the allocation of the Districts. Edgefield Abbeville & Newberry will in all probability be put together. I dined today at Col. Gregg's. Mr. [Robert] Henry[86] was elected president of the College without opposition. I left the house of my good friends Mr. & Mrs. [Reuben] Dubose at 7 ocl. on my return to Edgefield. I must not omit to record that the day after my arrival in Town Mr. DuBose called on me & would take no excuse but almost forced me to take lodging under his hospitable roof. I passed my time most pleasantly with this amiable family. I arrived in the afternoon at Capt. Ward's with whom I passed the night .

Sunday 4th. Clear & very mild. I arrived at home at 12 ocl. & found all well both at my house & at Mrs. Carrolls with whom I dined.

Monday 5th....The assemblage of persons at the Courthouse was large but not much property was sold. Kentucky horses & mules were offered for sale lower than I ever knew them to be before. Kentucky pork at 2 cts per pound.

Tuesday 6th....The Sale of the estate of Mr. Wallace took place to day. The property sold at fair prices. A negro fellow was bought at $600. The house & lot in the Village sold at $2500. Preston S. Brooks gave $1950 for the tract of land adjoining Glover & Moss, called the Mims tract, containing 300 acres.

....

Thursday 8th....I finished this morning, getting in my crop. I made a more abundant crop of corn than on any previous year at my farm. The pea and potatoe crop pretty good ....Mrs. Brooks & myself for the first time in 20 years dined alone, all our

---

[85] Senator Preston's Whiggish views and political independence had cost him the support of the General Assembly.

[86] Robert Henry (1792–1856), Charleston native. Univ. of Edinburgh MA. SC College professor of logic, moral philosophy, and metaphysics. President 1842–1845, then prof. until death.

children being from home – Preston & Hampden at Cambridge, James & Whitfield in Columbia & Ellen at her grandmothers....

Friday 9th....The wind has prevailed for the last three or four days from the South. It is now blowing briskly from the S. West carrying the clouds to the N. East & occasionally dispersing them so as to show the Sun. I rode over the tract of land purchased by Preston. It is much worn & altogether he gave a high price for it.

Saturday 10th....A very bloody affair took place in the Village between Pascal Tillman & young John Tillman (uncle & nephew)[87] in which John fired a pistol without effect & then recd. some dozen severe wounds from a knife, which his uncle drew & with which he fought until they were separated – I record with pleasure that Doct. Laborde has been elected a Professor in the So. Ca. College, a situation of trust, dignity & independence. Robt. L. Pinckney is elected Secy. of State & Genl. Jas. Hammond Governor. This last election was accompanied with circumstances, which rendered it peculiarly mortifying to Hammond by the exhibition of an opposition suddenly & unexpectedly gotten up, & which would have resulted in his defeat but for the disinterested course of Col. R. H. Alston,[88] who politely in the Senate chamber declined to run & begged his friends not to vote for him. As [a] supporter of Hammond, I trust he will refuse to accept the office. I do not think that he can, under the circumstances, accept it without a sacrifice of pride & self-respect. The office of Governor is one of honor & trust, to be accepted and not to be sought after with too much avidity. It should be conferred upon some meritorious citizen as a manifestation of popular favor & public confidence. When it is grudgingly given, it loses its value.

Sunday 11th....Mr. Reed preached morning & afternoon in the church & delivered two most interesting sermons. Notwithstanding there was no service in the Babtist church, not one of its liberal & devout members made their appearance in the Epis church. They seem to act under the persuasion that there is no worship of God except in their own house & by their own Priest & no entrance into heaven except through the portals of their church....

Monday 12th....I had my farm hogs killed this morning....

Tuesday 13th....For the home consumption I killed 8 hogs, weighing from 160 to 175 lbs. and ten from the plantation weighing about 200 lbs. each & also ten hams from the plantation out of a lot of Kentucky pork, making in all about 3500 lbs. of net pork.

Wednesday 14th....I went to Preston's place & had a fellow of his removed to my house, who is very sick. Josh arrived from the plantation with pork & a letter from

---

87 Apparently not closely related to Benjamin R. Tillman's family.

88 Robert F. W. Allston (1801–1864), wealthy Waccamaw River rice planter and state senator, was put forward by legislators opposed to Hammond's presumed coronation by a clique led by R. B. Rhett and backed by Calhoun. Hammond felt humiliated by his 83-76 victory after Allston had disavowed his own candidacy, but did not do as WB hoped.

the overseer.

....

Saturday 17th....I had a severe pain in the head & passed and night of great suffering.

Sunday 18th....I was too unwell to attend church & in fact I did not go out of the yard during the day. I observe in the general orders Hammond has appointed Preston one of his aids.

Monday 19th....I left home about 9 o'clock for the plantation with Col. Simkins & James in company. My waggons passed on to market with 20 bales of cotton.

Tuesday 20th....I attended Prestons sale of corn, provisions, stock &C preparatory to his removal to the Village.[89] Corn sold from 42 to 50 cts. Cloudy in the afternoon & a good deal of rain at night with high wind.

Wednesday 21....I went to Prestons in the morning, returned to the plantation to dinner & set off for Edgefield at 3 ocl. where I arrived at half after seven at night, cold & fatigued, having passed my waggons on their return home.

Thursday 22....We witnessed the marriage of Henrietta Ioor to a Mr. Brown from Augusta[90] to which we had been invited & about 12 ocl returned to Major Blockers.

Friday 23....We spent the day at Major Blockers & returned home in the afternoon. There was a dining party at Mrs. Ioor's for the young folk. I was pleased with the young gentleman, to whom Miss Ioor was married. He appears to be a discreet, moral & unassuming gentleman, of mild & good manners & of sound & useful sense. The supper & the decorations of the table were tasteful & showy on the night of the marriage & the company both sociable & agreeable....

Saturday 24th....Col. Carroll returned from Savannah with Miss W. Berrien in company. Preaching at night in the Epis. church but we did not attend in consequence of the cold. Therm.t 22° in the morning.

Sunday 25....Christmas morn presents a dull & rather gloomy appearance. Service in the Epis. church by Mr. Reed. The congregation was larger than usual, the church handsomely ornamented, the singing very good and the sermon most excellent. We dined at Mrs. Carroll's & passed an agreeable day....

Monday 26th....I was very unwell & enjoyed not much pleasure.

Tuesday 27....This christmas presents a perfect contrast to the last in both the temperature and state of the weather....I attended a sale of the estate of Hobbs at his late residence on Beaver Dam. Property sold at fair prices.

Wednesday 28th....Col. Carroll & family, Judge Butler & numerous relations dined with us to day. I as usual was afflicted with sick headache & was forced to go to bed.

---

[89] Was PSB moving to ECH now?

[90] Emily Henrietta Ioor (1817?–1851) m. William Brown (1813–1861). Born in Ireland. She was buried in the Blocker family cemetery.

At nine the young people went out to Judge Butlers to enjoy a dance.

Thursday 29th....Capt. Bird & family & some of my neighbors passed the day with us. I again was indisposed by sick headache. From 5 ocl. to 8 I suffered great & indescribable agony. I slept from 8 to 11. & then tossed on a sleepless bed until 7 ocl.

Friday 30th....I feel great weakness & exhaustion from last nights suffering. I rode out with Preston & his wife to his plantation & rode over a part of his fields & woods....cold & bleak & windy.

Saturday 31....I set off at 10 ocl. for Lexington Ct. House & reached Mrs. Lees at night, where I met Eliza Thompson & Geo. Butler[91] on their way to Columbia. I saw some few of the inhabitants on the road, all of whom professed to be in favour of my election.

---

[91] Probably son of George Butler (1785–1827), and grandson of Gen. Wm. Butler.

IV

January 1843

Sunday 1. Still cold & clear. I arrived at Lexington at night and took lodgings at Metzs.

Monday 2....There was an immense concourse of people at the Village for the population of this District, attracted thither by various motives. About 12 o'clock I addressed the assemblage of persons in the Courthouse for about ½ hour on the subject of the election for a representative in Congress. I was informed by my friends, that I made a favourable impression & that there was a general feeling in my favour. After dinner I went to Columbia, where I arrived at dark. Doct. Laborde & my Son Whitfield met me at Mabins & remained with me until 10 ocl.

Tuesday 3rd....I breakfasted with Mr. Bauknight near the bridge and visited the Saluda Factory & passed through the fork as far as Mr. Geo. Lorick's with whom I remained at night.

Wednesday 4. I passed through the District by the way of Springhill & reached Frog level [now Prosperty] in Newberry at night, where I stopped with a Major Graham, a member of the legislature for Newberry District. He is one of the most ignorant men, whom I have ever known elected a representative of the people & keeps the dirtiest house, that I saw in either Lexington or Newberry. The floor of the room in which I slept did not appear to have been washed in ten years. He treated me well so far as he knew how.

Thursday 5th....I left Froglevel & passing by Stony battery, I crossed the river at Lees old ferry & arrived at night at Jacob Smith's[1] in Edgefield.

Friday 6th....I arrived at home in the afternoon and found all well. I learned the particulars of a most melancholy homicide committed by young Nixon on the person of Saml. Thomkins by shooting him with a pistol.[2]

Saturday 7. Cloudy & mild with occasional light showers of rain. I visited the Village & collected my store accounts for the past year, for the purpose of making arrangements for their payment. It is the first year in 24 in which I was not able to settle my debts on the first day of January – [traveling until now]. My waggons returned from market & passed on to the plantation.

Sunday 8th....I heard a most excellent sermon from Mr. Reed in the morning.

---

[1] Jacob B. Smith of the Mount Willing section. Militia Colonel, SC House; m. Matilda Youngblood, died 1853 at about age 50.

[2] On January 4 Samuel Tomkins was shot by Alexander Nixon, who fled. Nixon was charged with murder, and on March 16, after fifteen minutes, was found not guilty by a jury. For the state, Solicitor Edwards and Col. John Bauskett; for the accused, "Griffin, Burt, Wardlaw, Carroll, and Wigfall." *Adv.*, March 22, 1843.

Monday 9th. Cold & a little cloudy in the morning and as heavy a hoar frost as we had this year....I visited the Village, where I saw an unusual assemblage of persons, not to have been attracted thither by some public business or on some public occasion.

....

Thursday 12....Doct. Cain left me this morning for Hamburg.

Friday 13th. Clear & cool & brisk wind from the West. I am suffering from hoarseness, produced by exposure to the fog, which prevailed on Wednesday morning.

Saturday 14th....I learned last night, that Col. Moss[3] sustained a severe loss by the burning of his gin house, & a young negro fellow and a quantity of cotton in it. The gin took fire by friction & it is supposed while the negro man was in the cotton room, as he was found in a corner of the room. I also heard of the melancholy death of Capt. [George?] Delaughter, which resulted as it is supposed from the accidental discharge of a rifle, while hunting near his house. He was an energetic & respectable man. Within the last four years more deaths by violence and casualty have occurred in this District than in any of the old states in the Union. [*Advertiser*?] In fact the violence & bloodshed have almost rivaled the new states of Mississippi or Arkansas. Freeman killed his wife in cold blood. Wigfall shot my poor or nephew Thos. Bird in a street rencounter – Woods shot Roney in a night brawl, Nixon shot Thompkins in revenge for a most grievous injury and a dead body has been found near Clouds Creek, supposed to be robbed & murdered. The casualties by fire have been little less numerous. Two steam mills, several dwelling houses & cotton gins & numerous other improvements have been burnt & some six or seven negroes. Edmund Bacon had a negro girl, who fell & broke her neck. I left home on an excursion to the District of Abbeville & reached Pleasant Searls, with whom I remained all night. He is a man of property & influence but lives in the plainest & most economical manner, with less attention to neatness or appearance, than any man in the District of his wealth. There are but two appointments to his house. [campaigning]

Sunday 15....I left Searls & passed into Abbeville. I dined at Mr. Edmonds & reached Mr. Maragnie's at night, with whom I remained until next day. I passed by Willington[4] & staid at night with Mr. Norwood.

Monday 16th....It was on this day I passed by Willington & reached old Mr. Norwood's. I found the old gentleman polite & hospitable.

Tuesday 17th....I passed through the North West corner of the District & stopped at night at old Mr. Andersons.

Wednesday 18th. A continuation of mild weather. I passed off to a place called the

---

[3] William H. Moss (1800–?) was sheriff, 1836–1840; 1850 census: $10,000 real estate, 41 slaves.

[4] Home of the Academy where WB, PSB, and many other prominent SC men were prepared for college. See introduction.

hook, thence to due West corner & thence to the Courthouse. At due West Corner, the Society of seceders are establishing a college for the education of young men.[5] A number of buildings have been erected and several families are living at the place & form a small Village. They have now four teachers & between 50 & 60 pupils. The location is elevated & appears to be healthy.

Thursday 19th. I left the Village & passed by Genl. Bradleys & on to Len Wideman's, where I remained at night....

Friday 20th. This was a Spring morning in temperature. I left Wideman's for home and passing by Liberty hill, arrived at home at 5 ocl, where I found all well.

Saturday 21....I visited the Village & dined with Col. Carroll, where I met Judge Butler, Genl. Bonham, Mr. Terry & Col. P.S. Brooks. I passed a pleasant afternoon. In passing through Abbeville I was surprised to see so much worn & exhausted land in a waste[d] condition & exhibiting broom straw & gullies to a great extent. The removal from the low country of many families, bringing large gangs of negroes with them & the settlement of cotton plantations by numerous others has already injured the District by driving off the white population & substituting a black one in its place. The Savannah side of the District in 15 years will be cut down & worn out & the owners will be forced to seek new lands, to support their negroes.

Sunday 22....Our Son Whitfield returned from Columbia in rather a feeble state of health & reports that there is a kind of endemic prevailing in College, resembling the measles in some of its symptoms. From 10 to 15 of the students are now confined by this disease.

Monday 23rd....The Court of Common Pleas commenced this morning under an order of Judge Earle, appointing a special court, Judge Butler presiding. The case of the ordinary vs John Weaver was called & the trial entered upon in the afternoon....

....

Wednesday 25th. The argument in the case of Weaver was concluded to day & the verdict in his favour as to the right to 36 negroes. I went to Mrs. Carroll's plantation on my way to a sale in the dark Corner....

Thursday 26th. I reached old Mr. Rochel's at 11 o'clock saw about 100 of the neighbors, conversed with a number on the subject of the election, & at 2 ocl. set off for home. I flatter myself that I shall get a good vote in this part of the District....I returned to Mrs. Carroll's plantation & remained all night. Flora the cook was very attentive to me.

Friday 27....Left the plantation at day light & rode to Mr. Lowe's for breakfast. I arrived at home at 11 ocl. Visited the Village, done some electioneering, dined with Colonel Carroll at 5 ocl. entertained company at my own house until 12 oc. & then

---

[5] The Associate Reformed Presbyterian Church founded Erskine, the first denominational college in SC, at Due West in 1839. A male academy and a seminary preceded it in 1835 and 1837.

retired to rest. It was an occasion for the celebration of Ellen's birthday, and all the little girls & boys were collected together. They enjoyed themselves in playing & dancing after music on the Piano.

Saturday 28th....The Court adjourned about 2 ocl. Preston was taken very sick at the Village & was carried to my house, where he is now very unwell from fever.

Sunday 29....Preston free of fever in the afternoon & returned home....Young Nixon delivered himself a prisoner to the Sheriff & is now in jail. The sympathies of the public mind are very much in his favour but I fear he has adopted a hazardous course for his own safety. The homicide for which he is in jail, is no less than legal murder & if the public opinion should change, he must be condemned & possibly executed.

Monday 30th ....It has been clear & dry since the 12 instant being near 20 days without rain & a portion of the time almost as warm as Spring. Planters have availed themselves of this unusual season to break up their stubble and & to sow oats.

Tuesday 31st....I went to my plantation, taking Whitfield with me. The overseer reported that the negroes were generally well & that his work was progressing to his satisfaction. He had finished, sowing the oats (about 120 acres) & was engaged in making a pasture fence to enclose my hogs. The hogs, cattle & sheep looked to be in good condition. I counted 16 lambs.

February 1. 1843

Wednesday 1. This was one of the coldest & most windy & disagreeable days, that I have ever seen. I rode to Doct. Lake's to see him on business & suffered a good deal from cold.

....

Friday 3....I left the plantation for John Chappell's in Newberry District, passing through the Culbreath settlement.

Saturday 4th. This was a day of continued rain. In the afternoon I went to Doct. Moon's, taking Henry Chappell with me. The Doct. & family gave us a hospitable reception.

Sunday 5....I visited the Cross Road Church & heard a sermon from a Methodist minister Mr. Walker & also one by Mr. Williams. Returned with Doct. Moon to dinner & went in the afternoon to Newberry Courthouse.

Monday 6th....I was visited this morning by a number of the most respectable gentlemen of the District by whom I most hospitably & civilly treated. At 12 o'clock the Sheriff Genl. Kinard made proclamation that I would deliver an address in the Courthouse. The people soon collected & filled the room. I addressed them about 3/4 of an hour upon the common topics of a political canvas. I was informed that my address made a favourable impression but whether it benefit me in the canvas, is a question, which cannot now be answered. My reception at Newberry was in every respect gratifying to my feelings. I left Newberry so soon as dinner was over & arrived at night at Mr. Kinard's in Edgefield, crossing the Saluda River at McNarie's ferry.[6]

Tuesday 7th....I passed through Edgefield, into Lexington District & arrived at night at Mr. Howell's where I met Governor Hammond & several other gentlemen, with whom I passed an agreeable evening in social conversation.

Wednesday 8th....I attended the review of Col. Quattlemaum's regiment & was busily engaged during the day in forming acquaintances, among the sovereign people. In the afternoon I set off for home & reached Mr. Steadman's.[7]

Thursday 9th....reached home in the afternoon, where I found all well.

Friday 10th....I set off after dinner for Shepherds, where I arrived at dark in the rain.

Saturday 11. Clear & cool....I attended a muster at Shatterfield & met a number of friends there. In the afternoon I went to Doct. Barretts.

Sunday 12th....I reached Cokesberry in the District of Abbeville at 12 ocl. & took lodgings at Doct. Garey's.[8] In the afternoon I heard a sensible sermon by Doct. [William] Capers & at night a confused Rhapsody by Whitford Smith. The latter gentleman has imagination and volubility but no reasoning powers of mind.

Monday 13th....I left Cokesberry at 1 ocl. & came to Greenwood & remained at night with Richard White, who is as warm & true a friend as man can desire.[9] I was very sick at night & had a severe paroxysm of headache.

Tuesday 14. I passed through Cambridge on my way to my plantation, where I saw several of my warmest friends & supporters.

Wednesday 15th....I returned home by the way of Goodhope.[10]

Thursday 16th....I visited the Village &C.

Friday 17th....There was an immense concourse of persons in the Village, collected to see the execution of Wiley Freeman, who was under sentence of death for the murder of his Wife. There was a very active canvas for Congress & great efforts made by the friends of [Armistead] Burt. Freeman was executed about 1 ocl. He exhibited great composure & firmness & addressed the assemblage of persons for

---

[6] McNary's ferry, about 2 miles below confluence of the Saluda and Little Saluda Rivers.

[7] Probably Marshall Steadham, a "highly respected citizen," died in May 1866, age about 70. Also "Stedham."

[8] Dr. Thomas Reeder Gary (1802–1852), father of the unreconstructable Gen. Martin Witherspoon Gary, CSA (1831–1881).

[9] Richard M. White lived near Ninety Six. In 1872, during Reconstruction, a suspicious fire destroyed some ten bales of his cotton and a "large lot of cotton seed" (*Adv.*, Oct. 26, 1872).

[10] Good Hope Methodist Church.

some minutes on the subject of his crime & the cause of its commission. He laid the blame to Col. Thompkins.

Saturday 18th....I left home this morning & passed by Ramey's, Addison's & Posey's mills & on to Capt. Ward's, where I remained at night.

Sunday 19th....I attended divine Service at the Wateree branch church, where I saw many of the inhabitants. I dined with my friend Holson & went in the evening to Mrs. Lee's.

Monday 20....I went from Mrs. Lees to the election at Crouts. The managers told many that I had recd. the highest vote at that box. In the afternoon I returned & remained at night with Col. Bates. I heard here that I had lost only six votes at Mrs. Lee's.

Tuesday 21....I left Col. Bates, stopped for a short time at the Ridge & then returned home, where I found Preston's wife very ill of pleauracy. Heard from Various election polls in the District where the votes were more against me than I expected. I am now satisfied that I shall be defeated.

Wednesday 22 ....The votes were counted out & I recd. about 960 & Burt 670 & Caldwell 170. [in Edegfield Dist.] The extraordinary efforts by Burt's friends for the last two weeks & some [bets?] in Hamburg caused me to loose from 100 to 200 votes that I would have otherwise recd.[11]

....

Friday 24th....Returns were received from several Districts, of the votes for a member to Congress & they exhibit a large majority for Burt. I recd. about 1225 votes.

Saturday 25....I devoted the day to my farm &C. In the evening Mr. Pinckney paid me a visit & took lodgings with us. Both Preston & his wife continued indisposed.

Sunday 26....The Revd. Mr. Pinckney preached in the Episcopal church & administered the sacraments. He & Judge Butler dined with me.

Monday 27th....The Revd. Mr. Pinckney left me this morning. I set out for my plantation at 1 ocl. & after riding 13 miles, I met my waggons on their way to Market & was forced to turn back. Caroline Brooks is now quite ill & Preston is also suffering from chill & fever.

Tuesday 28....– at 1 o'clock I set out for Hamburg to meet my waggons & arrived at dark at Hubbard's. After supper I sold my two loads of cotton to Hubbard at 4 cts, neither he or my self having seen the cotton. It was the last picking....The entire month of February has been wet & cold & much more inclement than January. The planters have notwithstanding made preparations for planting as forward as usual.

[11] Vote totals in Edgefield Dist.: Brooks, 955; Armistead Burt of Abbeville, 668; Patrick Calhoun Caldwell of Newberry (incumbent), 175. For the Congressional District the totals were Burt, 2,198; Caldwell, 1,564; Brooks, 1,225. It was generally acknowledged that Burt was the best campaigner.

The last accounts from Europe in regard to the cotton crop are very discouraging. In fact the cultivators of the soil will have to exercise the most rigid economy to be able to live upon their incomes.

March 1, 1843

Wednesday 1....I was busily engaged in filling my bill of articles, of which there were between 40 & 50 articles. My waggons arrived at 3 o'clock & after seeing them partly loaded & giving directions I left Hamburg at 4 ocl. I put my note in bank & drew $1000 leaving 58 bales of cotton in the hands of Mr. Adams to pay the note. The inhabitants of Hamburg were disposed to be very civil & I endeavored to return it but it required some effort to master my feelings. On my return home I met Capt. John Weaver, who was so kind as to offer me his cloak, which in truth was a great kindness as it protected me from cold. I reached home after nine ocl. & found Caroline very little better. I saw Mr. Morris planting corn in his sandy land.

Thursday 2....Caroline is still very ill. While I was absent Col. Carroll's horses ran away with his Barouch,[12] in which were Miss Berrien & Miss Carroll. They ran from near Mr. Wardlaws, to the Village, down the cross street by County's[13] & as far as the street by Mr. Johnson's, where they were stopped by Mr. Saml. Tompkins. [Either WB was confused or there were two Samuel Tomkinses. See 94, n. 2. The 1840 census is not helful.] Very little injury was done to the Barouch & the young ladies were unhurt. The driver was thrown from his seat soon after they started, so the horses were left to take their course.

Friday 3rd....Mrs. C. Brooks better in the morning. My waggons arrived last evening with all the articles & I started them this morning to the saw mills. This day was unusually cold.

Saturday 4th....Mrs. Means & five of her children arrived at my house to see her daughter Caroline, who had been & still was very sick.

Sunday 5th....A part of the family went to Church.

Monday 6th....My father arrived last evening but in consequence of the number at my house he went to Capt. Birds. A large family or a crowded house would be to me and insupportable annoyance, if either were to continue long. Quiet & systematic habits are indispensable to my comfort but they cannot be commanded at all times & therefore I endeavor to conform to circumstances. Several tracts of land & some dozen negroes were sold by the Sheriff at fair prices....

Tuesday 7th....Snow continued to fall during the day & covered the ground to the depth of 1 inch, tho much of it melted as it fell....Gibbs, etc., at the Pottery sold out their joint property notwithstanding the inclemency of the day. I learned that al-

---

[12] Barouche: A four-wheeled carriage with a high driver's seat and facing seats under a retractable top.

[13] Charles Compty (1783–) ran a hotel on the Cambridge Road, now the corner of Buncombe and Simkins Streets, from 1843 to 1852; sold it to Lewis Covar.

most every one of the company got shamefully drunk, among whom, were some young gentleman, of whom better things & higher hopes were anticipated.

Wednesday 8th....The earth covered with snow & the heavens darkened by mirky clouds. Therm 32°. Caroline Brooks is gradually mending. Her mother with five of her brothers & sisters are still with us.

Thursday 9th....Thos. Means & Mariah left for Fairfield this morning. In the afternoon I went to my plantation.

Friday 10th. This was an inclement day ....I rode over a part of my plantation but found that the earth so wet & the creeks & branches so full of water that I found it difficult to pass through the fields. The plantation appeared to be in excellent order & the preparation for planting as forward as I expected. I examined the stock of cattle, stables &C as well as the weather would allow.

Saturday 11th....I returned home to dinner. The roads are in a bad condition & very muddy. Our daughter Caroline is gradually recovering.

Sunday 12th....The last week has been, in the language of the New Englanders, a spell of as inclement and disagreeable weather as I ever saw. Our daughter had some fever last night & still suffers from her disease. Hers seems to be a hard fate for one so young & so meek & so good. If God specially interposed his power for the good or ill of any created being, I should think that Caroline would be the object of his marked providence & grace, for if gentleness, meekness & piety, deep & fervent, can deserve the approbation of God, she may put in a claim for a "child's portion". Her case makes me in some degree skeptical & superstitious, weak points in the character of most men, which I have held in ridicule & from which I have endeavored to keep my mind free & untrammeled. Events however controll both our actions & opinions in despite of us & we have to submit to their influence.

Monday 13th....The Court of common pleas commenced its Spring session, Judge Butler presiding. I counted 23 resident & visiting lawyers and attendance on the Court. The earth is thoroughly full of water & the roads in bad order. Very little work was done last week beyond procuring wood and attending to the Stock.

Tuesday 14th....The general appearance of the weather indicates snow or sleet at this hour, to wit 8 ocl....Mrs. Means & her daughter Sarah & son Isaac left us on their return to Fairfield, having been with us for 10 days. This lady & her daughters & in fact all the family are remarkable for their amiable & affectionate dispositions and for the gentleness & forbearance of their intercourse with each other. I think them very amiable but I fear that they are a helpless family. Tenderness & sensibility of feeling in excess are virtues & are always praised & admired by the world but if they be not, in fact, bootless qualities, they at least are the source of great annoyance to the possessor by the consequent susceptibility, which they impart to the emotions of pleasure or pain, arising from the constantly shifting events of life. There is one thing certain that this excessive sensibility or show of affection will neither give food nor raiment nor advance the possessor one step in the great drama of life. It's triumphs, & honors, its high attainments & notable achievements are not advanced by that sickly sentimentality, which is too often allied to weakness if not to selfishness. I do not design to apply the last remarks to our friends, tho I could wish they had greater fortitude & hardihood of character, which would qualify them better to meet & encounter the ills of life.

Wednesday 15th....I devoted the morning to my farm & the afternoon I was confined to my bed by headache. I suffered greatly until 12 ocl. at night.

Thursday 16th....The continued wet weather in this month will delay the planters in getting their crops planted. In ten days I have not been able to run the plow for a moment. The Court is engaged to day in the trial of Young Nixon for the killing of Saml. Tompkins. The argument of counsel was able, particularly that of Col. Carroll. The jury returned a verdict of not guilty after a few minutes consultation, which produced a spontaneous burst of approbation in the crowd of spectators assembled in the Courthouse. Snow fell about 4 ocl & it became exceedingly cold.

Friday 17th. Clear & very cold....This month has abounded in colder & severer weather than either January or February. The trial of a cause of slander is to come off to day between John Hamilton & John Roundtree in which I understand that from 40 to 50 persons have been subpoenaed to attend as witnesses. The verdict of the jury was first damages, the effect of which is to make each party pay his own cost. I think the jury should have given from $50 to 75.

....

Sunday 19th....snow . . . covered the earth to the depth of 1 inch. Therm.t in the morning 32° & not above 36° during the day. Mr. Dubose from Columbia passed the day & night with me. Mr. Reed delivered in the forenoon a sensible sermon, on the practice or ceremony of the Epis. church of laying on hands and the act of confirmation by a Bishop.

Monday 20th. This is a cold & raw morning ....The snow is still lying in quantities on the ground. Very clear at night, which enabled us to have a good view of a comet[14] which made its appearance some ten days past. It resembles a transient metior, rather than a permanent body. It is in length about 25 or 30 feet & had the appearance to me of a streak of light without either head or train. It seems to exercise a baneful influence over the elements for I have no recollection of such severe & inclement & changeable weather as the entire month of March has exhibited. We have had three snows in the month, rain about every fourth day & the therm.t has repeatedly been down to 24°. Gov. Hammond passed the evening with us in company with a few friends.

Tuesday 21....snow . . . continued to fall until near 11 ocl. when I set out for my

---

[14] Between February and April the "great comet of 1843" was visible, especially in the southern hemisphere. It passed closest to the earth on March 6, was bright enough to be seen by day, and had a very long tail.

fathers. Snow fell till about 3 ocl & then light rain until night. I do not remember ever to have experienced a more uncomfortable ride, caused by the dampness & chilliness of the atmosphere & the bad condition of the roads. I reached my fathers about Sunset & found him in excellent health & spirits.

Wednesday 22nd....I attended at the house of John Inlow a sale of all his property to satisfy executions in the Sheriff's office. The assemblage of persons was numerous & the property sold at high prices. A young negro woman brought $555.00. The sale amounted to upwards of $9000. I settled for my father's demand with the Sheriff & returned to his house at night, where I was forced to take my bed on account of headache.

Thursday 23rd....I returned from my fathers & reached home at 2 ocl. having suffered from the intense cold, during the whole time, that I was on the road....There has been no colder day this year. The peach & plum blossoms seem not only killed by the cold but to have assumed a dark appearance as tho they had been scorched by fire....The oldest man in the Country has no recollection of such cold & disagreeable weather in the month of March, of a Spring when the planters were so backward and they are planting. The idle & the industrious are now on a footing and will start together in planting.

Friday 24th....The earth was so completely frozen as to prevent plowing until after 9 ocl. I think it is the coldest morning that I have noted during the Winter. All nature is now bound in the icy fetters of dead Winter instead of unfolding a rich harvest of flowers & plants, which are wont to spring from her bosom at this usually inviting season. I observe that even the english pea, has suffered from the severe cold & has assumed a sickly appearance. I rode with Preston to his house & over a part of his fields.

Saturday 25th....Therm.t was this morning above the freezing point for the first morning in weeks, 34°. Temperature at night is mild & spring like. I began to plant corn in the church field, manuring in the check & got over from 3 to 4 acres. At this time last year I had planted the greater part of my corn crop at Roselands & had ready for cotton about 100 acres. The trees were in leaf & many of them had their leaves in full growth at this season. Now there is scarcely a swelling of the buds.

Sunday 26th....Mr. Reed delivered a sermon in continuation of the subject of laying on hands in the ceremony of confirmation. He is always sensible & interesting but is censurably regardless of the beauty & force of emphasis & of the modulation of his voice in the progress of his sermons – his matter is excellent but the manner faulty & bad. His delivery is too rapid.

Monday 27th. The heavy fall of rain will so thoroughly wet the Earth, that it must necessarily be the first of April, before the planters can begin to put corn into the earth, which will be the latest period that I have ever known for planting a crop. In fact the planters have not at this time half their land broken up & many of them will be forced to plant without plowing their land in the usual way. They will be forced to check off [go ahead] & plant & then break it up at their earliest leisure....My man Kitt returned from my plantation at 8 ocl with beef, butter, etc., & a letter from my overseer in regard to the condition of the crop, stock of all kinds, & to the health of the negroes. He has planted only 75 acres of corn & has bedded about 100 acres of cotton. The night boisterous from wind[,] rain, thunder & lightning with some hail.

....

Wednesday 29th....I devoted today to my farm, putting up a pair of [barns?], ditching, etc....

Thursday 30th....Our daughter Caroline rode out for the first time since her attack of sickness, which is now six weeks. I was confined to my bed from 10 ocl. till friday morning with violent headache.

Friday 31st....Yesterday morning the Therm.t was at 40° this morning it is up to 56°. I feel as feeble as if I had suffered a severe attack of fever. This is a dark & lowering day & in fit keeping with the entire month. The whole month has been the coldest & severest wherever that we had during the winter....There have fallen 4 snows & the earth has often been frozen as hard as a rock. In some parts of the State the Therm.t has been down to 14°, in this place it was below 20°. It is remarkable that for the last four weeks I have not been able to plow more than three days. I began to plant corn on Saturday last & got over about 3 acres. The rain on Monday prevented me from plowing until yesterday....If the weather continues this unsettled & unfavorable, it will be the month of May before the crops can be planted. This is the last day of March & the face of the country & the appearance of the entire of vegitable Kingdom, look like the last of January. Spring is yet to come. From 10 oclock until after 12 ocl, the rain descended in torrents until the whole surface of the earth, presented an almost unbroken sheet of water....The Earth is now thoroughly saturated with water & I fear it will be late in the ensuing week before the business of planting corn can be resumed. The last advices from Europe with regard to the price of cotton is still unfavorable. Money is however plenty & bears a low interest compared with this country. Upon good security it can be obtained in London for 3 to 3 ½ pr.cent & in New York for 4 & 5 per centum. In this District it is customary to give 10 pr.ct. & in some cases as high as 15 pr. ct. I understand that good notes can be purchased at a discount of 12 to 15 pr.ct. Corn is selling at 50 cts. per bushel fodder at 75 cts. per 100 lbs. beans at 5 to 6 cts beef at 4 to 5 cts. per pound flour at $6 to 6 ½ per barrel. Sugar at from $5 to 12 cts. loaf sugar at 13 to 14. Poultry at 10 cts & turkeys at 50 cts. or $1 per pair. Eggs have sold as low as 5 cts. per dozen....

April 1, 1843

Saturday 1st....a bright & lovely morning, giving promise of a mild and genial day. It presents a contrast to the whole month of March. Therm.t 48°. The mild temperature for the last few days has produced a visible effect on vegitation, particularly on small grain.

Sunday 2nd....The entire day mild & Spring like.

Monday 3rd....I began for the third time to plant corn this morning in the field, opposite to the house. At half after 9 ocl. rain began to fall & continued in light showers until night. A public meeting was held in the Courthouse, at which I presided, for the purpose of taking some action in regard to the election of President of the United States. Col. Pickens, our late representative, offered a series of resolutions, which he supported in a speech of considerable animation & force. He is a sensible & impassioned speaker, who says many good & strong things, but is inelegant & ungrammatical in the construction of his sentences. Genl. Bonham also offered some resolutions providing for the appointment of delegates to a state convention, which is proposed to be held in Columbia in May next, in relation to the Presidential election. After the business of the meeting was accomplished, I requested F.H. Wardlaw to take the chair, upon which I offered a series of resolutions, in approbation of the public course of Col. Pickens as the representative in Congress from this Congress.n District. I thought that he deserved a public declaration of approval from his constituents for his zeal & fidelity in the discharge of his duties as a public servant & I therefore waived all scrupulousness & tendered him such a tribute of respect & approbation as he merited. I am always willing to render to a public servant, just so much praise as his faithfulness merits & no more. The meeting was large for the season of the year, very attentive & decorous & after manifesting great unanimity on all the matters brought before it, adjourned in good order....

Wednesday 5th. Another gloomy December looking morning with a chill & damp atmosphere. Therm.t 40°. I have for the fourth time commenced this morning to plant corn in the field opposite the house, called the church or grove field, & from present appearance, I should not be surprised if I was stopped by rain or snow before night from planting. As some evidence of the condition of the earth & state of the weather I will here record, that I began to plant corn in this field on Saturday, the 25 of March & on the fifth of April I have not planted more than 5 or 6 acres, altho I have not lost a moment when the earth was in a state to receive the corn. For the last 30 or 40 days, I have done little more than get wood for fires....

Thursday 6th. Temperate but very foggy. Therm.t 45°. There was a halo round the moon last night. Our daughter Ellen with several of the children of our neighbors commenced taking lessons in dancing at my house under a Mr. Staring. I am apprehensive that some of the more rigid Babtists will make any noise about it as two of their members have allowed with great good sense, their daughters to take lessons. One good Methodist lady, who takes an interest in the concerns of all her neighbors & who says what she pleases about every body, has already indulged her garrulity in censure and animadversions. I set out at 8 ocl for my plantation & had not ridden more than five miles, when dark clouds began to form in the West with increased cold & a bleak wind blowing directly from the North. By 10 ocl rain began to fall & the heavens assumed the appearance of heavy & continued rain, which caused me to take refuge at Doct. Nicholsons. In one hour the clouds passed away & the sun shone out & the afternoon was clear but rather cold. I have never observed a more changeable day....The alternations of sunshine & showers, like smiles & tears, proverbially characteristic of this month, differ as widely from the above recorded changes as storms & tempests from gentle breezes or refreshing zephyrs. I arrived at my plantation at 2 ocl & rode over a portion of the plantation. The negroes in pretty good health.

Friday 7th....I visited old Cambridge & attended a meeting of the Agricultural Society, which had been called by the President for the purpose of adopting some action in regard to the circular of the president of State agri Society, on the subject of the agricultural survey of the State, now being made by E. Ruffin Esq.[15] A committee was raised to invite him to meet the society in May next & to prepare a report upon the various subjects of inquiry propounded by Mr. Ruffin. I returned home in the afternoon & inspected my fields, with the barns, stable lots stock &C. I ascertained that I had by want of care or judgment lost some 10 or more head of cattle. About one half of the corn crop was planted & about the same proportion of cotton land ready for planting.....

Saturday 8th....I returned home, where I arrived at 2 ocl. All well & no news. I met a wedding party of Griffins on their way from Hamburg. While at my plantation I amused my leisure moments by reading the miscellanies of Sir Jonah Barrington.[16] Warm at night sufficiently so, to dispence with fire.

Sunday 9th....Therm.t 62°. The wind rose about 10 ocl. & blew a fresh gale through the day. I was confined to my bed a part of the day, by headache.

Monday 10th....I began to plant potatoes, for the seed of which I paid 75 cts per bushel. Vegitation is beginning to appear in the growth of grass & the swelling of the buds of the forests trees. The peach & plum trees are throwing out their leaves, together with the haw & Crabapple but none other, that I have seen.

Tuesday 11th....The last three days resemble the mild weather of March both in appearance & temperature & therefore somewhat too cool for April.

Wednesday 12th....I began to plant corn at my farm this morning....In the afternoon I rode with Col. Carroll to examine a small piece of woodland, belonging to Mr. Mims,[17] which the Col. desires to purchase & which Mr. M. offers to sell at $15 per

---

[15] Edmund Ruffin of Virginia, ed. of *The Farmer's Register*, was hired by the legislature, with the urging of agricultural societies and Gov. Hammond, to conduct an agricultural survey of South Carolina. He visited Edgefield June 17–19, 1843, and was not impressed (Mathew, ed., *Private Journal of Edmund Ruffin, 1843).*

[16] 1760–1834; Irish lawyer, judge, M.P. Author of *Historic Memoirs of Ireland* (1809) and *Personal Sketches of His Own Time* (1827). His works were "interesting, racy, and valuable."

[17] Matthew Mims (1780–1848).

acre. The land consists of rocky hills & is of very little value except for the wood & timber....

Thursday 13th....I rode with my friend the Revd. Mr. Reed to my farm. He is a very sensible & agreeable companion. He informed me that he had determined to accept the invitation from the church at Grahamville & that he would probably leave Edgefield the first of May. I could not avoid participating in the unrepressed & overflowing pleasure of two young misses, who, in some degree through my instrumentality, had received permission from their parents, to take instruction in dancing & who made their first appearance this evening.

Friday 14th....Commenced planting cotton.

Saturday 15th....I attended in the Courthouse a meeting of the philosophical Society,[18] at which Col. Pickens introduced some resolutions in relation to agricultural interests & the survey of the state by Mr. E Ruffin. I was engaged in planting corn at my farm. I visited Major Blocker in the afternoon, spent about two hours with the family & returned home in company with Mr. Reed.

Sunday 16th....The forest trees are now rapidly putting forth their young foliage. The Revd. Mr. Reed delivered a very sensible sermon upon the resurrection of Christ, peculiarly consoling & encouraging to the hopes of a Christian. This gentleman will terminate his engagement with the church at this place & remove to Grahamville in Beaufort district on the first of May. He has laboured most faithfully as the pastor of our church for the last 12 months & has not only given universal satisfaction but has exerted a happy christian influence over his congregation. He unites in his person, a higher order of intelligence, moral elevation of character & enlarged Christian piety and charity than can be found in the State and his place therefore cannot be supplied. His loss will be most sensibly felt & deeply regretted by his congregation, who nevertheless will part with him without any feeling of unkindness. He is removing to a place, where he may fill a higher destiny & enter upon a field of labour more extensive in its compass & offering more encouraging prospects of usefulness. May a kind Providence crown his labours with signal success & make him the instrument of accomplishing much good for the people, into whose service he enters as the Minister of Christ....

Monday 17th....At 2 ocl the Therm.t was 84°. In the last ten days the transition has been from dead winter to full summer heat. I finished one half of the field at the farm in corn.

Tuesday 18th....I planted about one acre in cotton & prepared another acre for planting, which I designed as an experiment to test the productiveness of my farm in this staple. Mrs. Mary Gillison [see May 15] arrived at her father's this evening with her infant on a visit to her friends. It has been about 18 months since we saw

---

[18] Little is known about this Edgefield group, but WB's circle included several likely members.

her last, which was a few days after her marriage with Doct. [Gillis?] who is about to remove to Mississippi with his family.

Wednesday 19th....I drove Mrs. Carroll & Mrs. Brooks to Preston's & on our return I was thrown from the driver's seat & fell first upon the wheel & then upon the earth with some violence. I recd. some injury in the rump & two of my fingers were sprained, all of which I deserved for my great carelessness in driving with my legs crossed, in consequence of which I lost the power of bracing & poising myself.

....

Friday 21....The forest trees with the whole vegitable kingdom is fast assuming the green costume of Spring....

Saturday 22nd....A light rain would now benefit the planters & it would hasten vegetation of all kinds....I have been engaged during the week in planting a small lot of cotton at the farm as a mere experiment & in preparing the land & planting corn....

Sunday 23....It was a sweet morning & the day mild & pleasant. We attended service in the Epis. church & heard and able sermon from Mr. Reed in proof of the eternal punishment of the impenitent hereafter. His manner of delivery was more deliberate than usual, his enunciation's distinct, his argument logical & cogent & his illustrations striking & forcible. His analogies are always, just, apposite & impressive & if he possessed the graces of elocution & the pathos of delivery he would make one of the most powerful preachers at the South. I regard him now as the ablest in all that appertains to depth of thought & power of argument. This is Mrs. Brooks birthday & I thank God, that it finds my family & friends in excellent health except our daughter in law Mrs. Preston Brooks, who continues feeble & in a state of some suffering.

Monday 24th. Mild morning with the temperature of Summer.Ther.t at 4 ocl. above 89°. I finished a 30 acre field of corn at my farm, planting it in corn. I see or hear of no news except the account of an extensive robbery of one the banks at Columbus, Georgia, in which hitherto highly respectable men, are implicated. Most of the money has [been] reclaimed & several individuals arrested.

Tuesday 25....We have just heard that a daughter of Richard Mays of Florida, died last night at her uncle's residence, Doct. Mays, of this village, in her eleventh year of age. She was sent to this place to be educated by Doct. Johnson. She did not live more than 36 hours after her first moment of indisposition. She was buried at 5 ocl. in the babtist burial ground.

Wednesday 26th....The Therm.t stood yesterday in an exposed situation at 92° & in the vestibule it was a little above 84°. I presume it would have been about 86° in a fair situation, which was very warm for the period of the year. I rode this morning to Judge Butler's & spent a few hours in agreeable conversation with him & his mother. On my return I called to see Col. Pickens but did not find him at home. I saw cotton coming up in one of his fields. A good rain would now be very inportant as it would cause corn & cotton to germinate & come up in a few days. I witnessed this afternoon the fall of two persons from their horses. Genl. Bonham in playfully pretending to ride his horse over a parcel of little girls, was thrown over the horses head, to the great amusement of the girls & without damage to the Genl....

Thursday 27th....I began to plow over corn yesterday evening in the Church field.[19] The corn has come up badly & a considerable portion of the field has to be replanted. Recd. from D[avid] L. Adams of Hamburg an account of the Sale of 58 bags of cotton at 5 1/8. which is the last of my crop. It brought about $1060.

Friday 28th. Clear & cool. Therm.t as low as 58°. I rode to my farm this morning, fed my hogs & returned before breakfast was ready. I wish my health would enable me to lead an active life & then I should have the power of making myself useful; or at least I should have the will & desire to make myself useful & the ability to make the necessary efforts. The Revd. Mr. Reed, Mrs. Carrolls family & Mrs. Birds spent the evening with us. Therm.t at 9 ocl. 56° & a fire necessary to comfort.

Saturday 29th....I again rode to my farm & attended to my stock. Preston & his wife set out for Fairfield, having gone last evening as far as Judge Butler's. The girls sent out for Solomon the fiddler, & had something of a frolic at our house. I am always pleased to see my children enjoy the pleasure arising from so healthful & innocent an amusement.

Sunday 30th....Notwithstanding the inclemency of the day we attended church & were well rewarded by a very sensible sermon from Mr. Reed....In the afternoon Mr. Reed preached his farewell sermon, which I did not hear but it was said to be able & interesting as all his sermons are.

May 1, 1843

Monday 1st....[I]t is hardly possible to conceive the idea of a brighter or lovelier day. The concourse of persons in the Village was not large altho an unusual quantity of property has been advertised for Sale. Some 10 or 12 negroes were sold at very high prices. A young negro fellow brought $565 & a young woman $528. A political meeting was held for the purpose of selecting delegates to the State convention, which is appointed to be held on the 20th instant at Columbia in reference to the election of the next President of the United States. Col. Pickens, B. C. Yancy, N. L. Griffin, Wyatt Holmes, A.J. Taylor, Doct. Thos. Lake & Jacob Smith were appointed delegates from this District. The business of the meeting was conducted with unanimity & its adjournment in great harmony.

Tuesday 2nd. Clear & cool in the morning, warm at noon and cloudy & mild in the afternoon. I began this morning to plough over my corn at the farm. I visited Preston's place & gave directions to his negroes.

Wednesday 3rd....The Revd. Mr. Reed breakfasted with me this morning & bid us

[19] Opposite WB's house. He called it "my hobby."

farewell in anticipation of his departure for Grahamville by the way of Aiken & Charleston....I went by & took dinner with Major Blocker & reached my plantation at Sunset.

Thursday 4th. I rode over & inspected my plantation & crop & found every thing in good order....The entire crop of corn & cotton was planted and about half of the cotton was up & the residue coming up....The colts & workhorses were in good order & most of the other stock except the cattle. Some of the negro women were complaining & one had a few days before suffered a miscarriage....

Friday 5th....I attended a meeting of the agricultural society at Cambridge & met a large number of my friends & acquaintances. Several interesting reports were written & other business transacted. It was determined to offer premiums for the largest product of corn wheat & oats & also for different kinds of stock. Mr. Howle my former overseer was buried at my plantation at 12 o'clock. He died the day before of fever at the plantation of N. L. Griffin Esq. He was an honest & clever man, & more faithful as an overseer than one out of fifty. He lived with me four years & I feel authorized to bear this favorable testimony to his worth.

Saturday 6th....I returned home & found all well. The earth is becoming dry & hard & small grain is wanting rain.

Sunday 7th....Attended service at the Babtist church which was performed by the Revd. Mr. Johnson.

....

Tuesday 9th....I visited Preston's place & inspected a part of his crop.

....

Thursday 11th....A gentleman from Baltimore by the name of Carey[20] has been lecturing in the Village on the subject of temperance to large audiences. I heard him on Monday night & was rather pleased with the tenor & scope of his remarks & particularly with his explanation of the principles, on which the Washingtonian temperance society was organized. It is regarded in the light of a social reform, to be affected by social & voluntary associations, disconnected & independent of both church & State. He is not however the plain, unpretending & simplehearted man, that he has been represented, who tells his story of sorrow & suffering in modest subdued & heart touching language but his vanity induces him to play the actor & occasionally to aspire to the honors of the orator. I fear that he is converting what was at first a disinterested experiment in the cause of benevolence, into a trade for making money. The moment he looses sight of his original purpose & prostitutes his powers to selfish ends, he becomes a contemptible mountebank.

Friday 12th....I am feeble to day from an attack of headache last night & am therefore unfitted to enjoy the pleasures of so bright, lovely & balmy morning. I've traded

[20] Mr. Carey was the "missionary" for the Carolinas.

for a pair of grey horses, giving my old horse Jackson & $125. On trial I was pleased with them. The squadron of Cavalry or more properly the officers, met in the Village for drill & exercise to day. I received intelligence that my son Preston had been admitted to the practice of law with 19 other young gentlemen.

Saturday 13th....The gardens & small grain are suffering for the want of rain....

Sunday 14th....My father arrived on a visit to us with my Sister & Major Blocker. The health of my father, considering his age, is very good. He will be 78 years of age on the 18 of this instant.

Monday 15th....Mrs. Mary Gillison (my niece) left us this morning, having been with us on a visit for ten days. She has an interesting infant about eight months old.

Tuesday 16th....My father left us this morning on his return home.

Wednesday 17....during the night a fine shower of rain fell ....

Thursday 18th....Upon examining the earth this morning I found that it was thoroughly wet & in order for transplanting vines and vegetables. In referring to the entry made on the corresponding day last year, I find that rain fell on the night of 17th & that the next day was cloudy. This is (I believe), my father's birthday & if so he is 78 years of age.

Friday 19th....I was attacked in the night with a slight inflammation of the bowels. Very cold & disagreeable day.

Saturday 20th....I was exceedingly sick & suffered great pain in the bowels & also from cold chills. I was confined to my room the entire day for the first time in many years [?] & was deprived of the pleasure of seeing my friends, a few of whom had been invited to a small evening party, given to Mary Gillison....

Sunday 21....I left home for Hamburg at 1 ocl & arrived at Hubbards at 7 ocl. I was feeble but able to go about, occasionally suffering pain in the abdomen.

Monday 22....I sold 23 bales of cotton for my father & purchased a bill of goods & dispatched his waggon for home before 12 ocl. I then went to Augusta to join Mrs. Brooks & Miss Carroll, who had preceded me to do some shopping. We remained in Augusta until Tuesday morning at Mrs. Canfield's private boarding house. She keeps a good table & is in every respect a good hostess. We met some few acquaintances in town & a few called to see us at the boarding house.

Tuesday 23rd....We passed over to Hamburg where I closed my business & set out for home at 9 ocl, where we arrived at 5. finding all well....Corn & oats are greatly revived & are growing finely. Altho considerably fatigued, I rode to my farm to inspect the crop & the work of my negroes, with which I was content.

Wednesday 24th....I rode to Preston's place, to inquire into the state of affairs there. All was well & his man Lewis was conducting his business on his farm very well. On my return I stopped in the Village & played loafer for one or two hours. Heard no news except in regard to a little dissatisfaction between the Temperance & non-temperance portions of the Villagers in regard to some proceeding of the former in relation to the observance, not celebration, of the 4 of July.

....

Friday 26th. I left home for my plantation, at which I arrived about 12 ocl much fatigued.

In the afternoon I rode over the greater part of my crop. A portion of the corn looked well & was from knee to half thigh high. The cotton looked well, altho small. The stand is good & most of it, had from 4 to 9 leaves. The wheat crop is promising but the oats will be inferior....

Saturday 27th. After early breakfast I again rode over my crop & on my return, I examined the corn houses, negro houses, visited the nurse house & saw the children, inspected the cows & calves, horses & colts, etc., etc. At 10 ocl. I left for Major Blockers, where I arrived at 2 ocl very much overcome by fatigue & the heat of the Sun. In the afternoon and I returned home & found all well....

Sunday 28th....In the afternoon Col. Carroll & I paid a visit to Col. Pickens. We found him sociable & communicative on the subject of the late convention in Columbia & its proceedings. I always find this gentleman cheerful & agreeable in conversation.

....

Tuesday 30....In riding over my field last evening, I observed that moisture had risen in several places to the surface....Water was also running in some drains, that were partially dry the day before. These signs indicated change in the weather. At 12 ocl. the sky was clear & of bright cerulean colour....Preston returned from Fairfield.

Wednesday 31....I rode with Preston & in company of Capt. Bird to his place & inspected his crop. It was pretty good but wanted work. Our negro woman Sally lost her infant child by inflammation of the lungs, caused by hooping cough & cold. In the afternoon I rode round the vicinity of the Village & inspected the state of the crops. Corn is from half leg to knee high, cotton has from 5 to 7 to 9 leaves but looks backward & small, oats are inferior & small.

June 1843

Thursday 1st....The entire spring has been unfavourable to crops being both cold & dry but this season has been of the most favorable kind for keeping the crops in good & clean order. Wheat is ripening and oats are beginning to head.

....

Saturday 3....In planting a bed of beans, I discovered that the earth was very dry at the surface, exhibiting little or no moisture. The papers contained a statement of the almost total destruction of Tallahassee by fire.[21]

Sunday 4th....In the forenoon I attended Doct. Johnson's church & heard a sensible sermon from the Revd. gentleman. It is to be regretted that his intolerance causes him to attack unnecessarily & too frequently the Roman Catholics & other denominations of Christians. It neither manifests good taste or Christian charity & always fails to do good. In truth I think the catholic doctrines, opinions & practices very little more unobjectionable than those of the Babtist Church. The opinions of the latter upon the subjects of grace, babtism, the final perseverance of the Saints & election are as obnoxious in my judgment as any of the dogmas of the Catholic Church. Some of them rob Deity of his highest & noblest attributes. In the afternoon I paid a visit to Judge Butler.

Monday 5th....The Court of Equity began its annual session this morning, Judge Job Johns[t]on presiding.[22] The assemblage of persons was not large. I saw Major Burt from Abbeville who informed, that a violent feud was prevailing in the Village, which would end, it was apprehended, in violence.

....

Thursday 8....Showers of rain in various parts of the District. I called to see A. Patterson Esq. of Barnwell[23] & passed several hours in conversation with him, Genl. Caldwell, Thos. Pope & Col. Wallace.

....

Saturday 10th....This season has been rendered backward by the protracted cold weather in the Spring & by the small quantity of rain, that has fallen since the month of April. Corn is from knee to half thigh high on fresh lands, cotton has squares [is progressing] but is not above 6 inches high on an average. Oats are getting in full head but are very low & have not began to change their colour. Wheat is good & is ripening generally, a good deal has already been cut & some little ground into flour. The Court of Equity adjourned today....

Sunday 11th ....We attended at the Methodist church & heard a commonplace Sermon from a young preacher. A dark cloud formed in the West while we were in church & a shower began to fall before we reached home. These continued to fall very gently until night.

Monday 12th....rain at 5 ocl. which continued to fall in gentle showers for several hours. I am now engaged in setting out potatoe slips & cabbage plants, being the only season for the last 4 weeks, that admitted of transplanting vegetables. I finished

---

[21] On May 25 most of Tallassee was destroyed by a fire that spread from one wooden structure to another. No human lives were lost.

[22] Job Johnston (1793–1862), law partner of John Belton O'Neall in Newberry. Elected Chancellor 1830. Assoc. Judge, Court of Appeals, 1859.

[23] Angus Patterson (1790–1854), Edisto River planter, NC native; lawyer, SC Senator 1822–1850, SC College trustee; 172 slaves, sawmill owner.

plowing over the corn crop the second time on Saturday last, having planted all the land in peas, which I have in cultivation. I have never witnessed the fall of more gentle showers of rain or any more thoroughly refreshing & wetting to the earth without the least washing. Recd. a letter from my overseer that I had lost a fine blooded colt which makes the fourth in number within 12 months. I think it is the last blooded colt that I shall attempt to raise....I had potatoe slips, cabbages &C set out –

Tuesday 13th....Started the plows to breaking up the lot of land, next to Mrs. Carroll, for the purpose of planting peas. All vegitation looks revived & is in a very growing state. The gentle showers of rain will greatly improve the oat crop & keep down the price of provisions. Stanmore Griffin[24] returned from College & brings the intelligence that there is much sickness among the Students. College will be prorouged on friday next, & our Son Whitfield will be expected home on Saturday. Rain . . . throughout the night in one uninterrupted & copious fall.

....

Thursday 15....I planted a field of peas & set out a small piece of ground in potatoes. My crop is in excellent order & looks promising.

Friday 16th....I called to see Mr. Thornwell,[25] one of the Professors of the South Carolina College. Rode in the afternoon to Preston's & took tea with Mrs. Carroll. This is the anniversary of our marriage, which took place 25 years ago & I thank God we are in good health & in the enjoyment of comfort & happiness. Our children are well & doing pretty well & we all are favored with as much success & prosperity in this life, as we have reason to expect. A taylor in the Village by the name of Flood, whipped his wife very severely & was committed to jail. I saw the wife endeavouring to get him discharged. It is reported that she discharged the contents of a night glass in his face, which caused him to flog her & I should think that cause a valid one.

Saturday 17th....We are preparing to go to Cambridge, to spend a week at Roselands to which place we set out at 9 ocl, attended by Cornelia & Danl. Bird[26] & arrived at the plantation about 3 ocl, having met Abner Blocker on the road & taken him with us. In the afternoon I set out to ride over the crop & was exposed to two showers of rain, which wet me to the skin.

Sunday 18th....We attended church at Fellowship [Baptist] & heard two common

---

[24] Stanmore Butler Griffin (1825–188?), son of Nathan Griffin and Ann Patience Butler; 1850 census: $2,000 real estate, 6 slaves.

[25] James Henley Thornwell (1812–1862), Presbyterian pastor/theologian/educator. In 1843 he was chaplain and prof. of sacred lit. and evidences of Christianity at SC College. He became president in 1852, and prof. of theology at Columbia Theological Seminary in 1855. An editor of the *Southern Presbyterian Review*, he was generally considered the most prominent Presbyterian in the South.

[26] Cornelia (1825–1901) was a daughter of Daniel Bird and Lucinda Brooks.

place sermons from Mr. Hill & Mr. Coleman. The congregation was large & was composed of a very well behaved & neatly dressed people. In fact a more decorous & well-dressed assembly can rarely be found in the District. Even the crowd of negroes was well dressed, & gave every evidence of a kind treatment from their owners by their fat contented faces & their clean & decent clothing. There was quite a display of carriages & fat horses.

Monday 19th. I rode over my crop in the morning, which I found in pretty good order & very good except a little backward. Doct. Cain came down & passed the day with me. I always find him a clever & companionable gentleman. Our Sons James & Whitfield arrived from the Village. In the afternoon Mrs. B & the girls with A. Blocker & Danl. Bird left the plantation on a visit to Doct. Barrett & family.

....

Wednesday 21....I passed the day in visiting the neighbours and purchasing and few chickens for immediate use.

Thursday 22....We all went on a fishing frolic & caught from 40 to 50 small fish. It was greatly enjoyed by the children, the two girls being very successful in catching a goodly number, about 20 by each of them. We had a constant supply of fish, birds & squirrels for the table, which with fat mutton & rich ham, constituted very good eating with the occasional addition of a young fowl.

Friday 23....I inspected my crop this morning. The corn & cotton had grown very much since my arrival. The corn was somewhat irregular in size but the greater part was very good & as high as my head. I saw tassels on Monday the 18th for the first. The cotton was from ankle to knee high but no blooms. I do not think that there will be blooms before the 1st of July. My wheat crop is very good & well secured in large shocks. The oat crop is a medium one, part of it good but a portion to small & thin. I visited several of the neighbours & saw their crops. I thought my own & Col. R. Griffin's the two best in the neighbourhood. I returned home at 1 ocl. and took my bed on account of an unexpected attack of my old enemy the head ache from which I had been measurably free for the last two months. I was unable to leave my bed until the next morning....I regretted to discover the insect, called the church bug[27] had made its appearance both in the small grain & corn. I caused what was on the corn to be burnt.

Saturday 24th....We set out at 8 on our return home, where we arrived at half past one ocl. I found all well. I ascertained from my overseer that he had plowed over the corn crop twice & and would this day by 12 ocl finish plowing the cotton the second time & would commence in the corn on Monday morning. Mrs. Carroll & family to tea with us. On arriving at home we learned that our son Preston had been sent for on account of the illness of his wife. It was thought by the servant that she

[27] The common wood louse, often found in churches.

could not survive until his arrival at her mothers. We are in the most painful state of anxiety to hear from her....

Sunday 25....We attended at the Methodist Church & heard a sermon from old Mr. Dunwiddie.[28] Very heavy rain & thunder from 1 to 3 o'clock. The Earth very wet.

Monday 26....I rode to Preston's place, accompanied by a number of little girls & inspected the state of his crop. It is in pretty good order & looks as promising as I was prepared to expect. His house looked cool & clean & inviting in the inside, having been newly painted & papered, but this very circumstance produced the most painful reflection, that the Mistress at that moment might be in the icy arms of death. Almighty God! Thy ways are wise & just & man the subject of thy authority & government, has no right to ask why thy dispensations are so directed as to disappoint his fondest hopes & blast his brightest prospects. During the night there fell a torrent of rain, attended by thunder & wind.

Tuesday 27th....About 2 ocl. there fell one of the heaviest rains, that has fallen this year, attended with much thunder & lightning & a light and fall of hail. The hail did no damage here but the rain must have injured the growing crops, particularly the cotton. The sun shone in the afternoon, but the weather appears still in an unsettled state. We recd. no intelligence by the mail from Columbia of our dear daughter Caroline about whom we entertained the most painful apprehensions. Dark, gloomy clouds & rain again at 6 ocl, which continued to fall in heavy showers until 10 ocl with thunder & lightning. I fear that the water courses will be very high & the fields washed.

Wednesday 28th....The earth is in a mirey state, corn blown down & the roads & fields much washed. Every thing is in direct contrast with the same period last year. The earth & the whole vegetable kingdom was then parched by an unusual long drought & now the earth is flowing with water....The paper of this morning contains two invitations to fourth of July barbacues; one from the temperance society & its friends & the other from those who are said to be in opposition. The Candidates for District offices are invited to the latter. From their number they would form a respectable company of themselves. In riding out to several of my neighbours, I learned that the rain caused most of the streams, small & large to overflow their banks, causing considerable injury to both corn & cotton. The earth is considerably washed....Whitfield returned from the plantation & informs me, that the rain there was abundant but not so heavy as to inundate the low lands or to injure the fields by washing. Doct. Barrett had visited my plantation and prescribed for two of my women, who are strangely affected, one with neuralgia of the heart & the other with hysteries of the most distressing kind.

---

[28] Methodist pastor Samuel Dunwoody "rode circuit" in Edgefield Dist. in the early 1840s. Zoar Church, then called Persimmon Creek, was "one of his churches."

Thursday 29th....I was confined to my bed by headache the greater part of the day. My hands were engaged in cutting oats & [?] from 7 to 8 acres.

Friday 30th....The papers announced the death of the Honorable Hugh S. Legare[29] at Boston of billious cholic. He had gone in company of President Tyler & several members of the Cabinet to attend a celebration of the completion of the Bunker Hill Monument & was attacked shortly after his arrival & died on the 3 day. At this moment his death will be felt as a loss to the Government & particularly to the administration of Mr. Tyler, who will have some difficulty suitably & ably to fill the office of Secretary of State & Attorney Genl. both of which are now vacant. I was occupied again to day in cutting & saving oats, of which I have made a good crop. For the first time for 3 days, I am free from headache. My fields have been too wet since Monday last for the plow & it will barely allow of their use tomorrow. Corn looks a very luxuriant & promising and the cotton is too full of sap & in a state of too rapid growth to produce much fruit. If the seasons continued favorable, the corn crop will be abundant but the cotton crop will fall below an average one. The growth of the weed will be too great. The last rains have greatly improved the crops of corn, they look promising in every case where they have recd. a due & careful cultivation. The grass has also taken a most vigorous growth & several plantations in the vicinity are already in a foul condition & some portions of the cotton almost irreclaimable.

July 1, 1843

Saturday 1. This was a mild & balmy morning & charming & delightful to the senses. The temperature was mild, the atmosphere clear & elastic & the earth & the sky exhibited that pleasing appearance, which impresses the beholder with the beauties of nature & the goodness of God, whose power created them in such rich profusion. The loveliness of such a morning can only be marred by the sloth & indolence or the wickedness of man. In riding over my farm I discovered spots of corn & a small field of cotton (say 2 acres) had suffered from the heavy rains, the growth of the corn & cotton being checked & the leaves turning red. I saw the first cotton bloom on my farm this morning & it stood "solitary & alone" on a stake, that had either been topped or broken at an early stage. My servants finished cutting & putting into small shocks my crop of oats about 1 ocl. & a better crop I have not made for years. It is more than double that of last year....

Sunday 2nd....We went to Pleasant Grove Church & heard a Sermon from Mr. Trap[p] in the forenoon. Recd. about 9 ocl. at night a letter from Preston informing us of the alarming & distressing situation of his wife. She had remained in a deliri-

---

[29] Hugh Swinton Legare (1797–1843), prominent intellectual, lowcountry planter, legislator. SC College valedictorian, 1814. Studied in Paris and Edinburgh. Unionist congressman 1836–1838 and U.S. Attorney General 1841–1843. At death, he was interim Sec. of State. Co-founded the *Southern Review*. Writings published in two volumes.

ous state for three days & on Monday morning the 26, she was delivered of a boy child, an eight months child. After the birth of the child the mother revived, was in her senses & altho feeble and prostrated, afforded some hopes, that her life may be spared. Her death would give me almost as much anguish as the loss of one of my own children. She is the mildest, most affectionate & kindest of human beings; so self-sacrificing, so benevolent, so regardful of the comfort of others & unmindful of herself; she is beloved by all, who know her.[30]

Monday 3rd....I rode to my farm before breakfast & found my servants idle & the grass growing at a rapid pace. I endeavored to apply a remedy for both. I went to the village on business & while there recd. the melancholy tidings of the death of our dear, very dear & cherished daughter Caroline, the late wife of our son Preston. Under so great & afflictive a bereavement, the heart has no language for the expression of grief. The weight & magnitude of the loss causes the tongue to be mute. I dare not murmur at God's decree & yet my heart sinks under its force.

Tuesday 4th....I rode to Preston's & gave instructions to his servants in regard to the management of the crop. On my return home saw a number of persons, coming from the neighbourhood to join in the festivities of this national anniversary, which is to be celebrated by an oration & two dinners or barbacues, one at the academy & the other at Mr. Terry's spring. Our much esteemed & valued friend, Doct. Laborde arrived by the stage from Columbia with his son Carroll.

Wednesday 5....I am getting ready to leave home for Fairfield in the company of my Wife, to pay a sad visit for the purpose of mingling our common grief with the family of our incomparable daughter for her early & melancholy death & also to see our Son & bring him back with us. We set out at 9 & arrived at Higgins about sunset.

Thursday 6th....I passed through Newberry, crossed the broad River about 1 ocl & arrived at Mrs. Means at 5th ocl. We found the family well & bearing up under their heavy affliction with a degree of resignation & fortitude, which can alone be derived from the promises & consolations of the Christian religion. The crops in the District of Newberry were not equal to my expectations. Cotton near the River & particularly on sandy, porous soils, in which mica is found, was promising, of good size & and a blooming state, but on stiff [hard] clay lands it was small & indifferent. This remark is true in regard to all the crops of either corn or cotton, which I have seen. I have never seen so great an inequality in the growth of corn & cotton, this same field exhibiting all sizes from one to six & eight feet in height & apparently of the same age.

Friday 7th....I rode with Thos. Means over his crop. The cotton is very good & the corn an average crop. Judge Harper & Col. Preston called on me this morning. Col. Preston was suffering from an injury recd. on his hands from extinguishing the cur-

[30] WB's silence regarding Caroline's pregnancy was consistent with polite notions of decorum in that day.

tains of his house which accidentally took fire. In the afternoon I rode down to Judge Harpers, where Mrs. Preston & Sally[31] were exceedingly indisposed & both under medical treatment. The family seemed alarmed about Sally & not without good cause, for I thought her very ill.

Saturday 8th. We rose early & took our leave of this most excellent & amiable family before 6 ocl., our Son Preston in company. Our visit was one of mutual grief & condolence & we had every reason to be gratified that we had made it. The members of each branch of this large family recd. us & treated us as relations. The males are all clever & worthy gentlemen, & the females gentle, pious & amiable. For high character & sterling virtue, there is no family of my acquaintance, their equal. The meekest, mildest & gentlest of her name & race has been stricken down by death & ruthlessly taken from her husband & kindred & friends in the morning of her existence and at the moment when bright hopes & sunny prospects were opening before her. God's will be done & may we [be] prepared to submit to it without rebellious murmuring. We again passed through the District of Newberry & arrived at my fathers about sunset, whom we'd found in tolerable health, tho feeble & very glad to see us....

Sunday 9th....We left my fathers at 6 ocl. & arrived at home at 1 ocl. where we found all well. Whitfield had just returned from the plantation, of which he makes a rather favourable report. Mrs. Carroll & family, Col. Carroll & family & Doct. Laborde called over & passed the afternoon & evening with us. Some clouds & heavy thunder in the evening but no rain, of the latter of which we are now in some want....

[The next page in the journal, 278, has been cut out, leaving about an inch of paper bound in the book. On this strip WB wrote:]

Monday 10th Warm, clear & dry. I am engaged in hoeing corn & hawling & housing my oats. Thermt. 91°.

Tuesday 11. No change in the weather. I find the heat relaxing & oppressive. Wind from the South. I

[The back side of this one inch strip reads:]

that man for any earthly purpose, or for any personal consideration, it will greatly impair the respect and affection, which I have always cherished for my relation. For myself, I desire to live in peace & charity with all men & to pursue that line of

[The next page, which is normal length, and is a continuation of Tuesday 11th, reads:]

conduct that is best calculated to produce this object, & I humbly pray to God, that he will impart to me his grace that I may be able to deal justly & uprightly with all men & so to act towards them as I would have them to act towards me. The Revd. Doct. Johnson called & passed some time in social conversation with me. He is a

[31] Sarah, daughter of Senator and Mrs. W. C. Preston.

sensible & well educated divine but a little too precise & formal and his manner to be very effective as a preacher. He is a skillful & successful instructor of youth & is entitled to great praise for the improvement in female education, which he has imparted to the course of instruction in all the institutions in the upper Country.

Wednesday 12th....I rode by several plantations this morning & found the crops in a grassy condition & suffering for the want of rain & work....We rode out to see Preston. He seemed pretty bowed down by grief but in health.

Thursday 13th....I left home for the plantation after 2 ocl, taking Whitfield with me. A shower of rain began to fall about 6 ocl. It extended from Jos. Stills to old Mr. Beans. Near my plantation to the North the cloud departed & passed round without giving me any rain.

Friday 14th....I rode over and inspected my crop of corn & cotton both morning & evening, also inquired into the state of my negroes health, etc., etc. The crop of corn is fine & the cotton pretty good. The cotton is from knee to half thigh high, tolerably well branched & full of squares [flower buds] & blooms. I saw several full-grown bowls. Some of the corn is in the roasting ear State. The oat crop was cut & housed & turned out pretty well. The neighborhood is healthy.

Saturday 15th....I set out at 6 ocl for home & arrived at 12. On my return I found that the rain had extended from the Matthews road to Jos. Still's, then to the Vetitoe Springs[32] dry & thence to Edgef. Ct House a refreshing shower. Very little at my farm & none at my Son Preston's. I was indisposed during the afternoon & was prevented from attending a dinner party at Col. Pickens. There was a barbacue near the Village at L[ewis?] Covars spring.

Sunday 16th....We attended divine Service at the babtist church. The Revd. Doct. was tedious, didactic & somewhat discursive & tiresome. He availed himself of the occasion to attack the Pope, who seems to enjoy his holy aversion....

....

Tuesday 18....I rode with Doct. Laborde in the morning to visit Preston. Heard that the Revd. Mr. Carthedge[33] had been thrown from his horse & killed. He has been a preacher of the gospel of Christ for about 60 years.

Wednesday 19th....The paper of this morning contains an account of a woman, who lately had at Pottersville three living children at a birth; of another who had four & of a third near Columbus in Georgia, who had five. The last were illegitimate, for whose support the neighbours had met and raised a fund by voluntary subscription.

---

[32] Spelled "Viteto" on 1817 map, "Videto" on 1871 map. Approximately halfway between ECH and Roselands.

[33] Samuel Cartledge? A Baptist preacher associated with Red Hill and Red Oak Grove Churches as early as 1812.

I paid a visit to Col. Pickens, [Benjamin?] Frazier[34] & Capt. Bird, returned home & took my bed. I suffered greatly until 9 ocl. The day was exceedingly warm. Therm 93° in one place & 91° in another. Several light showers of rain fall between 9 & 11 ocl. wetting the earth from 2 to 3 inches. Brisk wind from the north.

Thursday 20....Vegetation looks revived by the rain, which fell in the night. I have omitted to note at the proper time that old Mr. N. Lowe & his wife died last week in a very short time of each other, not more than 15 or 20 minutes between their deaths. They had lived together something like 50 years. Rain began to fall about 8 ocl & continued in gentle showers for three or four hours or longer ....

....

Saturday 22nd....The corn crops are much improved by the rain. The Augusta chronicle contains the publications of Messrs. Cunningham & Young, in which they denounce Perrin, McLockin & Wilson as cowards, etc., etc., etc.[35] It is always a matter of regret for private quarrels to be blazoned before the public in the columns of a newspaper. It is a sort of prostitution of the public Press. I heard through a servant from my plantation that a good rain had fallen there on thursday last & that all were well.

Sunday 23. Went to the Methodist Church & heard a long & dull sermon from old Mr. Dunwooddy, tho in the main it was orthodox. I passed the evening at home in company of my friends Laborde & Carroll –

Monday 24th....Heard this morning of several affairs of honor, which are expected to terminate in a fight unless compromised by friends. One between [Dr. William S.] Jones (Editor) of Augusta &[James] Gardner Atty Genl. Another between Quattlebaum & [Lartigue?] of this State....copious shower of rain at 8 ocl.

Tuesday 25th....All vegetation looks refreshed by the rain. I left home for the plantation & arrived about 12 ocl with violent headache. I met at the plantation Whitfield with Mr. Blocker & George Landrum[36] as companions.

Wednesday 26....I rode over my crop & found that it was suffering for the want of rain....It is nevertheless pretty good. I also rode & pointed out the line of a pasture fence, which I propose to erect for the benefit of my hogs & examined the stables, cribs &C &C. In the afternoon I rode through the neighbourhood & saw the crops of some half dozen of my neighbours, which were promising, particularly the corn....

Thursday 27....I left the plantation & passed down Sleepy Creek to Major Blockers, where I passed the day. The crops of corn are promising & generally in good order.

---

[34] Benjamin Frazier (1779–1844). Postmaster and hotel owner. In 1827 he was a County Commissioner, with WB and others, in charge of repair of the courthouse.

[35] Likely the Abbeville feud mentioned to WB by Armistead Burt.

[36] George W. Landrum (c. 1820–18??) was a son of Reuben and Clara [Clarissa?] Landrum.

The rains of the previous evening were heavy from the Long Cane road to Edgefield Ct. House. Both Turkey & Log Creeks were swollen & very muddy, the evidence of abundant rain towards their sources. The crops of cotton in this vicinity are suffering from excess of rain, while at my plantation they are sustaining daily injury from the want of rain. Such is the unequal distribution of this indispensable element. I reached home about 7 ocl. All well. I learned with regret that there were four or five cases of congestive fever in the Village. It is all around me but confined to the little boys, who have made a practice of going into the Creek.

Friday 28....The earth is thoroughly wet & must force the growth of cotton injuriously in this neighbourhood. Rode to my farm, to the Village, and to Preston's,[37] in the morning & to Judge Butlers in the afternoon.

....

Sunday 30th....Judge Butler & Col. Carroll returned from the babtist church and dined with me.

Monday 31....My hands summoned to work on the road. I started Kitt with the wagon & oxen to Hamburg for iron, salt, etc. Heard from my plantation, that no rain had fallen since I left it & that the crop was suffering. I also learned that rain is much wanted in several localities in the District, while in other parts, it had fallen in excess & was causing too rapid a growth in cotton. The grain crops are very good over the entire District where they have been well worked & the only exceptions are those, that have been injured for the want of work & where the grass has been allowed to grow. The corn crop on the Saluda side of the District will be greater than that of the last year but that on the Savannah River portion will be less. It is not possible at this time to form an opinion in regard to the comparative quality of the cotton crop. I think it will be much less than that of the last year. A theft was committed last night at Goodman's hotel. Patrick the Stage driver, lost from $75 to 80 & some $500 or 600 in notes. A painter & plasterer are suspected.

August 1, 1843

Tuesday 1st....This day was similar in appearance & temperature with the corresponding one last year, each being cloudy & cold & requiring fire.

Wednesday 2nd. Cool & cloudy with winds from N.East. There was a light drizzle of rain throughout the day with dense & heavy clouds. Therm.t at 3 ocl 68°.

Thursday 3. Light rain from morning until night with brisk wind from the East. The earth thoroughly wet. I hope that the rain will be abundant in every quarter of the State. Still cool enough for fire. On walking out I saw the workmen on Col. Carrolls lot preparing to commence the erection of his houses. Their commence-

---

[37] PSB, now a widower, has moved to ECH. Is he now in the house called Sweetbriar, southwest of the town?

ment has been under inauspicious circumstances for the day has been inclement & disagreeable & unsuited to all outdoor work.

Friday 4th. Warm & partially clear. Capt. Bird & I paid a visit to Preston. On my return I was forced to take my bed by headache. In the afternoon my father arrived.

Saturday 5th. A clear & mild day. I went to the Village, where the Abbeville Village quarrel & the publications in the papers were the topics of conversation in every coterie. This personal affair has assumed a very vituperative character & has already involved the families of high respectability. These personal altercations, should be excluded from the public prints, & not thrust upon the eye in disregard of all propriety & in some instances even of decency. A heavy shower of rain fell about 8 ocl.

Sunday 6th. Clear & pleasant morning after 6 ocl. A light fog & humid atmosphere early in the morning. The Revd. Mr. Reed formerly pastor of our church is on a visit and preaches today in the Episcs. Church. He delivered to excellent & Orthodox sermon. Major and Mrs. Blocker came down with a part of their family. A shower of rain fell about 3 ocl. in the vicinity.

Monday 7th....A protracted meeting is being held by the Babtists in this place but no excitement has yet been effected. This was sale day but few persons in attendance & no property sold. Warm & sultry in the afternoon & light shower of rain. Preaching at night in the babtist church & some excitement among the school girls.

Tuesday 8th....My father left us on his return home. Clear & warm at 2 ocl at which time, I set out for my plantation, where I arrived at dark, with a threatening cloud & a few drops of rain accelerating my progress for the last few miles.

Wednesday 9th....I rode over my crop & found the corn much improved & the cotton in a growing state from the last week's rains. About 10 or 15 acres of cotton had taken the rust & was much injured. The balance looked well & promised an average crop. In the afternoon I was exposed to a light rain & at 11 ocl there was a heavy shower. I visited my neighbor Wash Holloway, who was very sick.

Thursday 10th....I inspected my crop more particularly, also the stock of hogs cattle mules & horses. I counted 110 hogs & the overseer reported the number not present to be from 40 to 50. There are 82 head of cattle little & big & all in good order & not more than 2 aged. The hands were engaged in hoeing the grass and the cotton, which I find it very difficult to kill on account of the continued rains. The negroes in pretty good health. Wiley Kemp [neighbor] & my overseer kept me up till half after 11 ocl....

Friday 11....I set out for home at 7 ocl & arrived about 12 ocl. The rain on Wednesday night had been very heavy & had caused an unusual freshet in Rocky creek. The water was over the bridge. I dined at Mrs. Carroll's. A protracted meeting is still in progress here & the preachers have succeeded in scaring a few school girls & boys into a state of excitement. At night several grown persons, went up to be prayed for.

Saturday 12th....I rode out and inspected my crop at the farm before breakfast. It looks very promising, particularly a small lot of cotton & about 15 acres of corn. In the forenoon I went to Preston's & Ben Addison's[38] & in the afternoon to Judge Butlers, at whose spring, a number of gentlemen had convened to pitch [quoits?]. A heavy shower of rain fell about 6 ocl. I learned in the Village that Mr. [Benjamin C?] Yancy had cursed Mr. Wilson of Abbeville in the public square in front of Goodman's hotel & that Wilson did not resent it.

Sunday 13th....We attended the divine service at the babtist church & heard a rambling & bombastic sermon from a Mr. L[l]oyd....There has been preaching in the babtist church for ten consecutive days & nights by some three or four ignorant men. It is the saturnalia of the ancients or the carnival of the moderns under the new name of protracted meetings. This prolonged preaching is a kind of religious dysipation in which the passions are excited to a sort of frenzy, not very promotive of rational & reverential piety.

Monday 14th....I rode over & examined a tract of land, which Preston was in treaty for with Moses Swearingen[39] in company with Jas. Miller[40] & the two gentlemen [?] ....

Tuesday 15....I assisted Col. Carroll in clearing his lot of the small growth & selecting a scite (sic) for his house &C. Preaching still going on in the Babtist Church & some 10 or 15 reputed conversions.

Wednesday 16th....I began to pull fodder this morning. Finding that the poultry of all kinds were dieing, I made an experiment of running a feather down the throat of each one, wet with turpentine. It is believed that the disease of which they die, is caused by worms & the turpentine is given on the feather to clear the throat. Those, that are deceased, exhibit the appearance of being choked with worms or something else. They have ceased to die, since the administration of the foregoing remedy.

....

Saturday 19th....Two companies of the militia, mustered in the village under the drill & command of Major Posey[41]....I bargained to sell my lot opposite to my house, containing about 32 acres to Mr. Harris[42] for $1000. I felt loth to part with it but I

[38] Benjamin Addison was a son of John Addison; m. Elizabeth Waldrum.

[39] Rev. Moses Swearingen (1796–1854), Baptist pastor and farmer; son of Van Swearingen and Martha Mims; m. Rachel Cloud.

[40] Capt. James Miller (1792?–1847): m. Frances Ann Tillman, then Lucy Hatcher. His house, below the Pine House, was moved to Edgefield's Main Street and is now the front part of the Discovery Center, a museum of Edgefield County history.

[41] The 1850 census names four men whose age (deducting 7 years) made them possible militia Majors in 1843: Samuel was about 30, Daniel 48, Frank 67, and Holden 33. Another possibility is Frank's son Martin Posey, who was hanged for murder in January 1850 and thus not counted. Samuel and Holden are weaker candidates due to age.

[42] A neighbor.

considered that the amount offered for its purchase was of more value to me than the use of a lot, which was appropriated only to pasturage & corn.

Sunday 20th....for two hours a torrent of rain accompanied with thunder & lightning & wind. There has been scarcely a dry day and this month & the earth is now thoroughly saturated & the roads in a muddy condition. We attended preaching in the Babtist church & heard a sermon by Mr. Abney.[43] He seems to be a meek & devout Christian & always preaches in favour of that religion, which demonstrates its truth & value by good deeds, by the performance of our duties to God & man in conformity with the requirements of the Scriptures. I am impressed with the belief, that he is a good man & sincere Christian. The Revd. Doct. Johnson has been sick for the last two weeks of a slow fever, which has confined him to his room....

Monday 21....The Revd. Mr Hankle [Christian Hanckel] & lady arrived at Mrs. Carroll's, on a short visit to the church at this place. We called on them & found them cheerful & in good health.

Tuesday 22....I rode to Preston's & went with him to inspect the change of land, that he had made with Benj. Addison. It adds very much to the form & completeness of his tract & adds many advantages in forming fields & running fences. He has now a good track for which he has not paid a high price....Mr. Hankle preached a most interesting sermon in the Epis. church at night to a full house....

Wednesday 23rd....Mr. Hankle preached in the morning & administered the sacrament and a very impressive manner. His sermon was touching & appropriate. He also preached an admirable sermon at night to a large audience. I have rarely heard three such orthodox sensible & evangelical sermons in succession. He seems to have had his life, touched by a coal fresh from the altar of love & an unction of grace imparted to his devotions. He is a very excellent gentlemen & a sensible & pious divine....

Thursday 24....It is refreshing to the feelings to see a clear day, after so many days of rain & clouds....I called at Mrs. Carroll's & took leave of Mr. & Mrs. Hankle, who took their departure for Abbeville....

Friday 25....I took up & saved about two stacks of fodder. Our friend Laborde returned from his mountain excursion in very good health. The mortality in Mrs. B's poultry still continues & carries off some five or six every day. She has lost of turkeys ducks & chickens about 50, so that the yard is now deprived of these cheerful, busy dependents of the homestead. I joined a few gentlemen in a game at quoits at Col. Simkins.

---

[43] Rev. Mark Madison Abney (1808–1846), born near Lorick's Ferry on the Saluda River among the large and prominent Abney Clan. His grandfather Nathaniel was a militia captain during the Revolution. Studied at Furman Theological Institute. Highly regarded as a man and spiritual leader, he was a member of Antioch Church and was serving Pleasant Lane Church when he died.

....

Sunday 27th....No preaching in the Village. A protracted meeting at Antioch to which all our children went leaving Mrs. B & myself at home, where we should have dined to ourselves but for the timely visit of my most excellent friend Laborde, who came over & joined us in a plate of soup & roast beef....

Monday 28th....I shall take up & save this morning about two stacks of fodder. I observed that the cotton in this vicinity is beginning to open but an open boll is only to be seen in places or in the language of the planter "here & there". Mrs. B purchased of Capt. & Mrs. Bird a pair of arm chairs at $24.00. I rode with Col. Bauskett to ascertain a corner & line of my land, adjoining his purchase of Mr. Mims & called to see Mr. Mims in regard to the purchase of about 50 acres of his land & made him an offer.

Tuesday 29....I rose at a very early hour, preparatory for a visit to the plantation. I arrived at my plantation at 12 ocl. in the afternoon rode over my crop, which I found much improved.

Wednesday 30th....I rode to John Christie's[44] in the morning & again examined my crop in the afternoon. Very heavy rain in the neighbourhood.

Thursday 31st....I took my overseer in the morning & marked out a road from Mr. Bean's to the Edgefield road, which I directed him to have opened. In the afternoon I rode through a portion of the neighbourhood, & inspected the crops. Mr. Mims crop did not equal my expectation. His plantation has been badly managed for the last 10 years & is now much worn & exhausted....The entire month of August has been rainy & the earth almost constantly in a wet State. The seasons have been favourable to young corn & cotton has grown very fast & has done well where the rain has not been excessive. My stock of horses are in excellent order & the hogs, sheep & cattle look well. My negroes were in good health with the exception of a woman, who has some chronic [affliction?]. My woman Eliza had her first child this morning. I think it doubtful whether there has been a day in the entire month, without rain in some portion of the District & not more than four in which rain did not fall at the Village: The temperature has been mild, the Therm.t rarely above 82°. I have not gathered more than half my fodder at the plantation. Cotton is just opening.

September 1, 1843

Friday 1st....I arose at an early hour & found three of my neighbours had called on some business in regard to the robbery of Mr. Coleman's shoe shop, in which a fellow of Preston's was supposed to be concerned. I authorized them to take Daniel & try him fairly & if guilty to punish him. I left the plantation at 8 and arrived at

[44] John Christie (c. 1795– ?); 1850 census: $2,000 real estate, 41 slaves. Simeon Christie (1802–1860), sheriff 1840–1844, 1848–1852, was probably his brother.

home at 1 ocl. under a clear & burning Sun....Rode to my farm in the afternoon & returned with headache & was forced to take my bed. Whitfield & young Mr. Adams[45] returned from Hamburg, from whom I learned that the cotton market is improving. On examining the State of the crops, I think that both corn & cotton are from 3 to 4 weeks, later than ordinary years. Most planters to the north of this place only began to pull fodder the first of this week & cotton has just begun to open. Very little will be picked out before the middle of this month.

Saturday 2nd....I was confined to my bed the greater portion of the day by a violent attack of the head ache, by which I suffered unspeakable pain. An afternoon of greater suffering I have never experienced.

Sunday 3rd....Heard a sensible sermon by the Revd. Mr. Cain in the babtist church in the afternoon.

Monday 4th....The assemblage of persons was rather small at the Village for the period of the year, yet a more riotous drunken & fighting company have not been seen in the public square in five years.

Tuesday 5th....We passed the evening pleasantly at Mrs. Carroll's. I finished pulling fodder at my farm, where I have saved a quantity as good as I have ever made.

Wednesday 6th....Hampden is 10 years old this morning & is in fine health for which I desire to return devout thanks to God. My entire family are in good health.

Thursday 7....Our neighbour Mr. Lipscomb is very ill of fever, from which apprehensions are entertained for his life. He is a very honest & estimable man & his death would be a great loss both to his family & this community. Mr. Bellamy & family arrived at Capt. Birds about 6 ocl from an excursion to the mountains of Georgia & this State on account of the health of Mrs. Bel.

Friday 8th....The Revd. Doct. Henry President of the So. Carolina College arrived in the Village. My neighbour Mr. Lipscomb very ill by fever.

Saturday 9th....I called on Mr. Henry & also on Col. Pickens. Since the first of this month the weather has been clear, dry & warm & vegitation is already in want of rain....We permitted our servants to have an evening party, at which was collected by 9 ocl over 50 of the young negroes of the Village, who for two hours enjoyed themselves dancing in the yard, playing games, promenading, talking, singing & finally eating. They maintained good order & behaved with as much decorum & civility as the same number of white persons could have done. I dismissed them after 11 ocl. & retired to rest, pleased with the consciousness that I had contributed to their happiness by indulging them [in a?] few hours of innocent merriment. I felt that I had not violated the laws of social propriety or the laws of God....

Sunday 10th....Service in the Epis. church by the Revd. Mr. Henry. He delivered an interesting sermon to a goodly assemblage of persons. He, Doct. Laborde & Col.

---

[45] Possibly a son of David Addams, Hamburg merchant and sometime factor for WB.

Carroll dined with us. He again preached in the afternoon....

Monday 11....I called in the morning on Col. Berrien of Geo[rgia]. & in the afternoon with Mrs. Brooks visited Judge Butler to see our valued friend and relative Col. P. M. Butler & family. On our return we found that Mr. Shand[46] had arrived from Columbia on a visit to the church at this place. He accompanied us home & spent the balance of his time with us....

Tuesday 12th....Mr. Shand & his daughter remained with us until after dinner & then took their departure for Aiken. He is a modest & unassuming gentlemen, with pleasing and sociable manners & apparently of very meek & unostentacious christian qualities of mind. I should conjecture that he is a gentleman by education & a christian in practice....

Wednesday 13th....The temperature and appearance of the weather have assumed an autumnal character. Fire is comfortable....The Revd. Mr. Henry preached an excellent sermon to 18 persons in the Epis. church. Our good people of the Village are very religious in sectarian zeal but they are do not appear to me to abound in love & charity out of their own church, or to manifest true vital piety in their daily walk. I however forebear to judge any one, having a [festering?] & abiding sense of my own unworthiness, which should often cause me to cry out in humility & self abasement, "Lord have mercy upon me a sinner" as did the subdued publican.

Thursday 14th. Rain . . . in one continued & copious stream until night. I . . . have seldom seen a greater quantity of water fall in 12 hours. I was confined to the house & saw no person but my friend Capt. Bird, who ventured up through the rain. Young Mr. Remur arrived from Charleston with his bride....

Friday 15th....The rain of yesterday was heavy but not washing....Col. P. M. Butler, Doct. Laborde, Col. Carroll & Mr. Bellamy of Florida dined with us in company of several other friends. At 5 ocl. I was forced as usual to take my bed & a night of more agonizing suffering, no man ever experienced. I had no rest or sleep until 4 ocl. in the morning.

Saturday 16th....I was occupied in the morning in running a fence at my farm, next [to] the creek, to protect my corn from my neighbour Belcher's hogs. I was much indisposed in the afternoon & did not leave the house....

Sunday 17....The ceremony of babtism was performed by Mr. Abney on some half dozen females. In the afternoon I & Col. Carroll rode out to Judge Butler's to make a call upon Col. P. M. Butler, who was expected to take his departure for Arkansas tomorrow morning.[47] We passed a pleasant afternoon as we found the gentleman in high spirits & social temper of mind.

Monday 18th....I am engaged in the preparation of some lots for pasture, for the

---

[46] Peter Johnson Shand (1800–1886), Charleston native; rector of Trinity Episc. Church for half a century.

[47] Pierce Mason Butler was federal agent to the Cherokee, 1841–1845.

milch cows & calves-

Tuesday 19th....I attended the Review of Cheatham's regiment at Lowes. The performance was said to be good & the address of the Governor [Hammond] sensible & appropriate. Sickness prevails throughout the bounds of the regiment & several deaths have already taken place. The crops of corn & cotton not equal to those of last year, possibly one third less in the bounds of this regiment [portion of the District].

Wednesday 20th....In the forenoon I went to my plantation & in the afternoon rode over my crop, which looks very well. At night I bargained with my overseer [Mr. Lowry] to remain with me next year at $355.

Thursday 21....On my return home I came by Major Blocker's & there met some half dozen kinfolk with whom I passed a pleasant day. Mrs. Nancy Lowe, the oldest inhabitant of the Village died this morning very suddenly. She was a kind woman & obliging neighbour.

Friday 22nd....Gov.r Hammond passed the day & night with me. I had some dozen friends to dinner & in the afternoon we pitched quoits. My friends appeared to enjoy the occasion & our time passed pleasantly & even <u>hilariously</u>. It was to me an occasion of pleasure & thankfulness to God. We had all our children at table & all in health.

Saturday 23rd....Gov.r Hammond & our four boys left us at half past 7 ocl for the review at the old wells [between Augusta and the Ridge]. The performance of the regiment was very bad, which called forth a severe reprimand from the Colonel.

Sunday 24th....There was a large concourse of persons assembled in the babtist church to hear the Revd. Mr. McCain preach but to the disappointment of everyone little Billy Watkins[48] from the pinewoods was in the pulpit & held forth for upwards of one hour in empty nonsense.

Monday 25th....Daniel a negro of Mr. Mims was tried for killing his fellow servant and acquitted. My hands were engaged in pulling pea vines, etc.

Tuesday 26....Mr. Bellamy & family set out this morning on their return to Florida....

Wednesday 27....My hands began to pick cotton at my farm. I purchased of my Son Preston three negroes, two boys & one girl & swapped a boy George for his man Daniel. I gave for the 3 $1320 & $84 to boot in the swap.

Thursday 28th....I set out to my plantation & at the 4 mile post, met my boy Lewis, with a letter from my overseer, informing me that the gin wheel had given way & requesting my man Elleck to be sent up to repair, etc. I turned back and started Elleck at 12 ocl. The last advices from Europe represent trade as in a more flourish-

[48] Baptist churches pastored by William Watkins include Red Oak Grove, Chestnut Ridge, and Dry Creek in the 1830s. He was a co-founder of Red Hill Church in 1835.

ing condition & the cotton market improving. Cotton in Hamburg S Ca will bring from 8 to 9 cts.

Friday 29th....I went to my plantation taking Hampden with me. In the afternoon I rode over my plantation & found every part in good order & the crop promising. My negro man John picked out 312 lb. of cotton & several of the men had over 250 lb. Adrene, picked 216 lb. The overseer reported that the quantity picked out during the day was between 5 & 6000 lbs. There was a race among the negroes, divided into two companies for two bushels of wheat.

Saturday 30th....I returned home ....My waggons returned from mill with 20 barrels of flour of superior quality. I sold it readily at 5.50 cts per barrel. The miller wrote to me that the wheat was excellent and weighed 66 ½ lbs to the bushel. Every five bushels made a barrel of superior flower. On my return I found our Whitfield very unwell. The persons sick in the Village are represented to be better. Upon examining the state of my crop and this period the last year, I find that I was at least two weeks in advance of this. I had then upwards of 35 bags [bales?] of cotton picked out, some corn gathered & housed & lots of small grain sown. I have now not more than 25 bales picked out, no corn gathered & no lots sowed.

October 1, 1843

Sunday 1....I called to see Mr. Lipscomb and Mr. Maragnie.[49] The former is convalescing after a confinement to his bed of five weeks duration. The latter is still under the influence of fever & altho he has been ill for 18 days, he is likely to be many days still confined to his bed even if he recovers, of which I trust there are no reasonable grounds upon which to doubt.

Monday 2nd....The Court of Common Pleas commenced its fall session, Judge Evans on the bench. The attendance of the gentlemen of the bar is numerous and the assemblage of citizens very large. No news of any importance or interest. Reports from various quarters of the District represents the cotton crop, inferior to that of last year, yet I am induced to believe that the dry, warm weather in September has so hastened the maturity of the growth, as to produce at least an average crop.

Tuesday 3rd....I attended to the survey of the lot, sold to Mr. Harris. Survey by Danl. White.

Wednesday 4....I purchased of Mr. Mims about 100 acres of land for which I paid him $700.

Thursday 5th....I was engaged until 1 ocl in surveying the land bought of Mr. Mims. I am pleased with the purchase altho the price is high....

---

[49] William Caine Moragne (1818–1862), Huguenot descent. Studied in Germany, lawyer, *Advertiser* staff; m. Emma Butler. His brother John B. Moragne (1819–1847) was killed in the Mexican War.

Saturday 7th....I dined with Col. Carroll in company with the judge Josiah Evans & several members of the bar. My waggons passed to Hamburg with 20 bales of cotton the first of this crop.

Sunday 8th....At 1 ocl. I set out for Hamburg on horseback & reached Hubbards after dark....The crops on the road by Sweetwater looked indifferent. The whole country from the Village to the pineland and below Rob.t Walkers is cleared & I saw thousand[s] of acres with not enough of timber to fence it.

Monday 9th....I sold my cotton to Doct. Stokes[50] at 8 1/8 per lb. The 20 bales brought $555. I purchased a bill of articles, paid a few a/c [accounts] & set out for home at 12 ocl which I reached at sunset, considerably fatigued. No news in Hamburg.

Tuesday 10th....The Revd. Mr. Young[51] preached in the Episcopal church. The Court of Com Pleas is progressing with the second week of its session. The Revd. Bishop [Christopher] Gadsden arrived in the stage from Aiken on a visit to the church at this place. My father also arrived on his way to Hamburg in a state of considerable suffering. They are both with us.

Wednesday 11th....My father is quite ill this morning. Bishop Gadsden preached in the forenoon & afternoon & administered the rite of confirmation to some 6 or 7 persons.

Thursday 12....The bishop left us in the Stage for Abbeville. My father is better & able to walk over the house. There was rain in the neighborhood of James Dorn's.

Friday 13th....I went to the plantation in the afternoon, taking Hampden with me.

Saturday 14th....I rode over my plantation & inspected everything, of which my limited time would allow – I have picked out about 55 bags of cotton & upwards of 40 packed. I have gathered a few small lots of corn. The overseer reports that he picked from one acre on the 10th instant 1797 lb. of cotton & from the field called the grapevine corner measuring about 15 acres, he gathered on the first picking 17680 lb. & that in parts of the field not more than a half & in the balance two thirds is open. A portion of the cotton is very inferior on acct. of the rust.

Sunday 15th....A killing frost, particularly in level or low situations. I think that the cotton throughout this State, part of Georgia, Alabama Mississippi & the whole of Tennessee must be killed & all the immature fruit destroyed. We visited our Sister Mrs. Blocker, who has fever, & spent the day with the family. The measles are going through this family of which both white & black are subjects.

....

Tuesday 17th. Another clear & cold morning....I set out for Augusta at 11 ocl with

---

[50] Jerimiah W. Stokes was one of several bankers and cotton traders in Hamburg. A Whig, he supported W. H. Harrison for president in 1840.

[51] Rev. T. J. Young was asst. minister at St. Michael's, Charleston, in 1848.

Mrs. Brooks & Eliz. Carroll & arrived at Mrs. Canfield's at 6 ocl.

Wednesday 18th....I passed the day in walking through the streets and in shopping. Business appeared to be active in the streets and some improvement going on in the repair of buildings & lots &C – Augusta is made up of a mixed & heterogeneous population. It is a trading, trafficking community without much intelligence & full of prejudice both religious and political. Religious bigotry and political intolerance are their leading characteristics, nonetheless there are some honorable exceptions to this general feature and in their trading principles & practice, I find them as clever & bright & fair as any other commercial people. Party feeling is at this time much excited by the results of the recent elections in favour of the Whigs.

Thursday 19th....I crossed the River at Hamburg very early in the morning, met my waggons, ordered my cotton to the warehouse & then purchased negro shoes, blankets &C & also groceries for the family. Sold a lot of cotton for Major Blocker for 6 50/100 & made sundry purchases for his family. At 12 ocl the ladies met me from Augusta & we set out for home. I became sick soon after starting and suffered inexpressible pain on the road & through the night. We met Capt. Bird & his family on their way to Florida, from whom we learned the particulars of the elopement of his daughter Cornelia with a Mr. Charles Cross.[52] An instance of greater folly & infatuation I have never Known or read of than the connection of this young lady with that gentleman. He is a worn out & broken down debauchee, a bankrupt in fortune, with no trade or profession or employment by which he supported himself, nor has he the industry or physical strength to labour. A more gloomy & cheerless prospect never was presented to the eyes of a young bride. Her situation is so gloomy & discouraging & so hopeless, to disarm all resentment & to change into pity the feeling of indignation, which her conduct would otherwise inspire. Poor child! most bitterly will she rue the day, that she abandoned her father's house & protection for the arms of a diseased & imbecile rake, who has no shelter to offer her.

Friday 20th....I was confined to the house the greater part of the day by headache. I rode to Preston's late in the afternoon to see the progress made in the arrangement of his lot & houses. I was pleased with the manner in which he had arranged his buildings &C. Col. Carroll & lady took tea with us –

....

Sunday 22....The Revd. Mr. Scott preached in the episcopal church....

Monday 23rd....A personal rencounter took place between Billy Harris & B. M. Blocker, but no injury was sustained by either as they were separated.

---

[52] Cornelia Lucinda Bird (1825?–1902), youngest child of Daniel and Lucinda Brooks Bird; m. Charles Bardell Cross (1817– ?) in Oct. 1843 in Charleston, and they settled in Charlotte NC. Does the fact that the couple were still together two years later suggest that WB may have underestimated Mr. Cross? See WB's short summary of October 1845.

Tuesday 24....I rode to see my hogs fed at my farm & then by the Pottery, where I traded for a buggy with Caleb Mitchell[53] & returned to breakfast. At 12 ocl. I set out for my plantation, taking Whitfield with me.

Wednesday 25. I rode over my plantation. The overseer had picked out about 70 bales of cotton & had gathered something like 1000 bushels of corn. He was preparing land, in which to sow wheat....

Thursday 26. This was a day of incessant rain....Mrs. Carroll's servant Frank was exposed during the day to the rain being on his way to mill with a load of wheat, with a horse that refused to pull at every hill. He was able to progress only from W[ash] Holloways to N[athan] L. Griffin[,] about 2 miles.

Friday 27....I pursued Frank with a mule to be put in place of his baulking horse & called for a short time at Cambridge. I found the opinion general that the crop would be a short one in that section of the State, only one or two planters making a full crop of cotton. The corn crop will be an average one yet I think that the price will be high in the spring.

Saturday 28....I returned home & found the Revd. Mr. Reed at my house. In the afternoon I visited the Village & learned that Mr. Charles Cross & lady had returned to the Village & that he had assumed a hostile attitude towards the family of his Wife in all its branches, as a mode, I suppose, of making atonement for thrusting himself upon them & running off with one of their number.

Sunday 29th....Mr. Reed preached both morning and evening in the Epis. church to an unusually large congregation.

Monday 30th....Mr. Cross made a demand on our Son Preston to retract certain unspecified but alledged injurious remarks in disparagement of his character through his special & confidential friend Col. E[ldred James?] Simkins, who seems in the way of my family whenever mischief & strife are threatened. We certainly have great reason to entertain good will & kindness toward this peacemaking gentleman for lending himself to any adventurer, who happens to take offense with a member of my family.[54]

Tuesday 31....The Revd. Mr. Hankle arrived at our house from Charleston on his way to Major Blockers where he is expected to unite Mr. Reed & our niece Julia [Blocker]. In the afternoon we all left for Major Blockers, Parson[,] groom & all, & at 7 ocl. the young people were united.

---

[53] A patron of the Pottersville Academy, Mitchell signed notice promoting its exercises in December 1840.

[54] If E. Simkins was Eldred James (1792–1845), son of John (1762–1833) and nephew of Eldred (1779–1831) Simkins, law mentor/partner of WB, his hostility to the Brooks family is puzzling. And judging by WB's comment, this was not the first time.

November 1, 1843

Wednesday 1....We passed the day at Major Blocker's & returned home in the afternoon. We hope and have every reason to believe that the marriage of our niece will be an advantageous and happy one.

Thursday 2nd....I had arranged to go to my plantation but was induced to postpone my departure in the hope of seeing a settlement of the difficulty between my Son Preston & Mr. Cross. Fifteen acres of bearded wheat sowed.

Friday 3rd....I set out at 8 ocl for Cambridge to attend a meeting of the agricultural Society & reached there at 1 Oclock, in time to witness the exhibition of stock. The show of colts was fine & that of cattle, hogs & sheep very respectable. There was but one mule & that belongs to me. [half?] lots of grain sowed.

Saturday 4th....I returned home & dined with Col. Carroll. I passed the day very pleasantly. Judge Berrien & daughters, the Revd. Mr. Reed & Wife were at the table. In the evening we had a very agreeable party at our house, at which were present Judge Berrien & daughters, Col. Carroll & family, Mrs. Judge Wardlaw & daughter, the Revd. Mr. Reed, lady & her sister, Col. Pickens, & others.

Sunday 5....Mr. Reed preached morning & afternoon in the Epis. church. The Methodists are holding a quarterly meeting in their church, which was well attended, to day as I have been informed. Mr. Reed & Company left us this afternoon on their return to Log Creek.[55]

....

Tuesday 7th. Cloudy & misty in the morning. Clear & cold by 10 ocl. & through the day. Mr. Reid & Julia with Mary Blocker arrived about dark on their way to Grahamville. A somewhat novel engine was exhibited in the Village[,] being a fire engine lately purchased by the Council for the benefit of the Village.

Wednesday 8....Mr. Reed & party left us after breakfast for the low country.

Thursday 9th....Mrs. Brooks & I paid a visit to Major Blocker & family & spent the day. I finished gathering my corn this afternoon. I made about 600 bushels of corn[,]

several waggon loads of pumpkins, a pretty good crop of peas, a bale of cotton & a crop of potatoes. Upon the whole, my crop is a good one, both here and at my plantation....Heavy frost in the morning.

Friday 10th....Col. Carroll has this day closed his lot by a fence & I am now forced to quit the old way to my farm & seek a new one. He has generously given me a passage of the width of twenty 20 feet between his lot & Col. Pickens in fee simple for a passway, to my farm; for which I thank him most profoundly and for which I shall make him a more substantial return. Bye the bye take my brother in every way & he will be found a noble fellow with high qualities.

---

[55] The Blocker family home, now known as the Blocker House, was near Log Creek.

Saturday 11....I finished gathering my pea crop....

Sunday 12th....Rec.d a letter from my overseer that my beautiful heifer Columbia, the gift of my friend [Reuben] Dubose, had died a few days before from overeating of peas....

Monday 13th....My waggons arrived with 20 bales of cotton on their way to market.

Tuesday 14th....I rode out to see Thos. Means at Preston's & invited them to spend the next day with us. Col. E. Simkins & his lady left for Florida.

Wednesday 15th....Several gentlemen dined with me. I learned in the Village that cotton was selling at 8 cts in Hamburg. I was considerably indisposed a part of the day but the very reality that Col. S with his meddling pragmatical wife[56] had taken their permanent departure from our neighborhood was a sort of compensation for present suffering. This gentleman & his lady have suffered no occasion to pass where an opportunity was afforded, of exhibiting unfriendly & even hostile feeling toward me & my family. I cannot account for it for I never designed to give them cause. I am gratified at their departure but I follow them with no resentful feeling, at least I wish them no harm but rather as full proportion of Heaven's blessings, as they may hereafter merit.

Thursday 16th....I was engaged in opening a road to my farm through the land, I purchased of Mr. Mims.

Friday 17th....I was again employed in opening the road to the farm. I am greatly pleased with my purchase of Mr. Mims.

....

Sunday 19th....We attended divine service in the Babtist church in the forenoon & in the afternoon rode out to Judge Butler's to see Mrs. Thompson & family & also our good old Aunt Butler. They were all well & in good spirits.

Monday 20th....I went to my plantation, taking James Brooks with me. Rain at night.

Tuesday 21....I rode over my plantation & examined the crop &C. The negroes well except Crecy, who was in her confinement.

Wednesday 22....I went to the late residence of Roger McKinsey, to attend a sale of his personal estate. The property sold at good prices. A negro fellow sold for $603. I observed nor heard anything new or interesting or remarkable, except that there were a greater number of ugly men, than I ever saw in the same assemblage of persons. I carried home with me a Mr. McClendon who had a drove of mules & horses for Sale.

Thursday 23....I made several trades with the drover. I first swapped a bay horse for four mules, giving $230 to boot. I then traded an old mule called Cuff for a two year old mule, paying $45 to boot. I then exchanged one of a pair of gray horses, giving

---

[56] Martha Blythewood (1818–1844).

$55 to boot. So I got 5 mules & one horse & let him have two horses & a mule. I consider the trade fair on both sides. I returned home in the afternoon & found all well....A shoemaker had died in the Village of consumption during my absence.

Friday 24....My overseer reported to me that by yesterday he would have picked out 100 bales of cotton & that he supposed that there were 30 more in the fields. My crop of corn is principally gathered & it is a good one. I presume the crop is from 3500 to 4000 bushels....I was exceedingly sick of headache.

Saturday 25....We heard of the death of Mr. Reubin Landrum,[57] a very honest but somewhat eccentric man. Preston returned from Hamburg with a pair of mules in place of his five [fine?] bay horses.

Sunday 26th....Preaching in the methodist church only.

Monday 27th....I put up the hogs intended for bacon this afternoon[,] 20 in number.

Tuesday 28th. We left home at 1 ocl for Aiken on our way to Barnwell to attend the marriage of our Son James & arrived at Aiken at dark.

Wednesday 29th. At an early hour I went with the children to view the Rail road, enclined plane,[58] cars[,] fixtures &C with which they were greatly delighted. We saw the cars ascend & descend....We arrived at Barnwell about Sunset & took lodgings at Barna Browns. My four Sons, daughter & [a?] Mr. Tillman were in company with Mrs. Brooks & myself.

Thursday 30th....We left Barnwell & arrived at the residence of Capt. Ulysses Robert[59] about 4 o'clock. At the usual hour our Son James was united to the oldest daughter of Capt. Robert, Miss Sarah Robert by the Revd. Mr. Wade of Scriven County Georgia. Our son appeared to be very happy & I trust his marriage will be a fortunate and happy one. We had not known the family before except by reputation and our acquaintance gave us no grounds of dissatisfaction with the connection of our Son to the family. The company was very respectable & agreeable. The entertainment was liberal[,] tasteful & hospitable & the supper table was rich & splendid. I passed my time agreeably with a slight abatement on account of headache.

December 1, 1843

Friday 1. Rain fell from morning till night. We passed the day at Mr. Robert's & were confined to the house, so that I was deprived of seeing his plantation or any portion of the neighborhood. The day passed away pleasantly in conversation with

---

[57] Reuben Landrum (1782–1843), brother of John, Baptist pastor; and Abner, pottery manufacturer and ed. of *The Hive*. Other Landrums were also considered gifted and eccentric.

[58] From 1833 to 1852 the steam-powered inclined plane, or funicular, raised and lowered railroad trains through a 180-foot descent into Horse Creek valley southeast of Aiken.

[59] Ulysses M. Robert, planter of Mt. Pleasant, Barnwell Dist. His daughter was Sarah Crawford Robert.

the company & particularly with Col. Jones[,] an intelligent & well read gentleman from Georgia, who married the sister of Capt. Robert & also with the Revd. Mr. Wade, a shrewd & sensible Divine a member of the Meth. Church & a brother in law of Capt. Robert. The residence of Capt. Robert is strikingly beautiful & and the house large, convenient & of fine appearance. It stands on a clean looking sandhill, gently sloping on all sides but not of much elevation & is surrounded by swamps or low flatlands at the distance of fourth to a half mile, by which its health is rendered precarious in the summer.

Saturday 2....We set off for home at 9 ocl. & passed through the Village of Barnwell at 1 ocl & reached the Whiteponds [near Williston] at dark where we passed a more pleasant night than we anticipated. Our purpose was to return by the [Edisto?] River road but we passed it without observing it.

Sunday 3....We reached home in health & good condition about dark, where we found all well & no news except that Mr. [S. S.] Thompkins had been elected [by the legislature] over Mr. [James] Terry by 20 votes CommS. in Equity.

Monday 4th....A clear & cold day. There was a large concourse of persons in the Village & some property sold at fair prices. Land sold from $1 ½ to 8 pr. acre. A negro woman & Child sold for 600 & a single woman at $450. I heard no news. A good deal of sympathy is felt for Mr. Terry.[60]

Tuesday 5th....I was confined to my bed the entire day by headache. My waggons arrived on their way to market with 18 bales of cotton.

Wednesday 6....I went to Hamburg, taking Whitfield with me & arrived at Hubbards about 6 ocl....I passed an unpleasant night, occasioned by fermentations on the stomach.

Thursday 7. Rain in the morning & the cold disagreeable. My waggons got in about 9 ocl. I sold 60 bales of cotton to Mr. D. L. A[d]dams for 7 4/8 free of storage & 76 bales to Doct. Stokes for 7 3/8. Two bales of bur[?] cotton I put in the warehouse. I believed at the time that the price of cotton would be better but I preferred to sell & put the money to use. I sold also 16 shares of [Bank of?] Hamburg stock to Doct. Stokes. At 2 ocl. I left Hamburg & reached home about 7....

Friday 8th....I marked out the limits of a piece of land, to be cleared at the farm &C.

Saturday 9th....James & his Wife arrived in the afternoon from Barnwell & at night we had all of our children under our roof & in good health.

Sunday 10th....Preaching in the Methodist Church by Mr. Dunwood[y.] I rode in the afternoon for heath &C.

Monday 11....rain . . . until night. Preston set out for Columbia, taking Whitfield with him to be absent until after Christmas. I allowed Hampden to go to the plantation with [slave] Joseph. I fear that the poor boy has been thoroughly wet.

---

[60] James Terry, a neighbor of WB, had succeeded him as Commisioner in Equity.

Tuesday 12th....I went to my plantation & saw on the way a large assemblage of persons at Mrs. Stills, to attend a sale of Jos. Stills estate. I called for a few minutes and saw my overseer. I was informed that a negroe fellow sold for $710 & the others in proportion. The night exceedingly cold.

Wednesday 13....I rose in the morning with indications of headache. Sickness at the stomach increased as the day advanced & by 10 ocl my suffering was indescribable & the only relief I got was by the use of warm water, both in drinking it until I vomited & also by injections.[61] Nothing entered my mouth during the day.

Thursday 14th....The ground was frozen very hard & the ice prevailed where ever there was moisture....I returned home in a feeble state....

Friday 15th....I set out to go to Major Blockers, but meeting my father[,] the major & his family on their way to my house, I returned. They spent the day with me. The health of my father has greatly improved....I killed ten hogs this morning for family use.

Saturday 16th....My father left us this morning in excellent spirits. The warmth of the weather endangers freshly killed pork. At night the Therm.t 60.

Sunday 17th....Therm.t 60° & rain from 12 ocl till night.

Monday 18th....I learned from Col. Carroll that Ed. Frost[62] has been elected Judge of the Court of Common Pleas. He reports that the Legislature have done but little business. The bill to elect an extra Judge was lost by a very large vote, also of a bill to provide for a superintendent of free schools. I went to the village & paid the different accounts ag.t me in the stores, shops &C of all kinds, the whole amounting to over $600.

Tuesday 19....rain continued to fall without interruption. The roads are very muddy.

Wednesday 20th....My overseer sent me 18 hams, the leaf fat of 32 hogs, a few spare ribs, backbones & feet from a lot of hogs killed at my plantation. The weather is very warm & I have some apprehensions about the meat, which will be in danger of spoiling if the weather does not change.

Thursday 21....I purchased Wm. Youngbloods interest in the land on which he lives, being 1/3 of the whole & 3/7 of the remainder at the price of $500. I also attended Col. Carroll in an examination of his new house, on which I discovered as indifferent & rough work as I ever saw on any house. I fear that the entire house has

[61] Possibly by catheter. Hinged metal versions were in use by the 18th century, one invented by Benjamin Franklin.

[62] Edward Frost (1801–1868), Charleston native. Yale 1820, lawyer in Charleston, SC House, U.S. District Attorney (resigned rather than enforce tariff laws). Elected Judge of Court of Common Pleas for life in 1843; resigned after c. 10 years. President of Blue Ridge Railroad.

been badly built[63]....

Friday 22....Clear & mild in the afternoon but I could not enjoy it as I was confined by headache.

Saturday 23....I was again indescribably sick & threw up the vilest bile, I ever saw come from the stomach of any other human. I have a hard time in this life, yet I have much to be grateful for to God and many endearing ties to connect me here & to make life desirable. My waggons reached home about 9 ocl at night with 16 out of 18 bales of cotton with which they set out from the plantation on Wednesday last being 4 days on the road, in consequence of stalling & breaking a waggon. I never saw the roads in a worse condition. The delay of my waggons on the road and the neglect of my negroes to throw off a part of the load is an evidence that a negroe never reasons, among the thousand, that they furnish every year by their thoughtlessness & stupidity.

Sunday 24th....Our Son Whitfield returned from Fairfield from whom we learn that our friends in that District are well.

Monday 25....It would be difficult to imagine a more lovely day. I paid a visit to the Village where I found every person apparently cheerful & contented but I witnessed no boisterous mirth or games of play among either white or black. My family dined with Mrs. Carroll & we passed a pleasant day. I returned home at Sunset & devoted the evening to reading a number of Mr. Barnwell's[64] religious papers & making this entry. This paper is in its temper controversial & in its principles Calvinistic, neither of which suits my taste. I shall discontinue it. Received a letter from my good friend Laborde, in which he informs me that he expects to be here on Wednesday at dinner with Reverend Mr. Shand.

Tuesday 26....Last night about 11 ocl. a band of amateur musicians gave a serenade to our part of the Village & played some very pretty pieces of music in my house, in compliment to James & his bride. James Mims[65] sang two very sweet songs in good taste....We gave a party to our son & his bride, which was well attended. The young people danced to music by a negro man from Virginia, who played admirably and understood the art of directing the dance. I never saw a more joyous party where both young & old entered into the spirit of the merry making. Judges, lawmakers, grave gentlemen & even members of the church were tempted to dance. Well, if they do nothing worse, the enjoyment of this venial amusement will not exclude them from Heaven. The company broke about 1 ocl.

Wednesday 27....The Reverend Mr. Shand arrived at my house to dinner, having

---

[63] This house was "Carroll Hill," which still stands on the west side of Buncombe Street. See ch. 4, n. 3.

[64] William Hazzard W. Barnwell (1806–1863), editor of *The Episcopal Protestant.* See p. 40.

[65] James Henry Mims built the Edgefield house called East Hill.

come up with Doct. Laborde to unite him to Miss E[lizabeth] Carroll[66] in the "holy state of matrimony". About dark the groom with his attendants convened at my house & about 7 ocl we all repaired to Mrs. Carroll's, where the ceremony was soon after performed & the Doct. & Miss Carroll made man & wife. The evening was passed in animated conversation & in the young people dancing after music on the Piano. There was a peculiar fitness in the marriage & I hope the parties will be happy.

Thursday 28th. Clear & pleasant tho cold enough for frost. Doct. Laborde, his bride & daughter [with 1st wife] took their departure for Columbia about 11 ocl. & Mr. Shand for Aiken at 3 ocl. We have had the merriest Christmas that has been witnessed here in 10 years. I must begin to work tomorrow.

Friday 29th....Judge Butler gave a dancing party this evening. It was well attended & is reported to have been agreeable. My family attended but I declined to go on account of my health. They returned between 1 & 2 ocl.

Saturday 30th. Very clear & cold. Therm.t about 28°. I killed ten hogs for home consumption this morning & had them carefully salted.

Sunday 31....We attended service in the babtist church & heard a dull sermon by the Revd. Mr. Johnson & a rambling & incoherent exhortation by the Venerable neighbour Mr. [Joseph] Moore. My father arrived to dinner & in the afternoon we visited Preston's place....The last day of the year was temperate & we passed through it in the enjoyment of a calm & quiet happiness, and affectionate family entercourse. The year closed in a calm way & left our people in a much more contented & prosperous condition than they enjoyed at the close of the year previous – the general health of the District is moderately good with the exception of some instances of violent cold called grip [influenza]. Provisions are abundant & the pecuniary pressure, which was felt a year ago, is passing away & giving place to a free & ~~plentiful~~ interchange of money & a revived state of trade. Our District is generally in a prosperous condition.

[66] 1816–1857; younger sister of Mary Parsons Carroll Brooks and of Sophia Parsons Carroll, Maximillian Laborde's first wife.

V

January 1844

Monday 1....This being both new year & sale day, brought an immense concourse of persons to the Village. I have rarely ever seen a more busy throng, collected together & engaged in transacting their diversified pursuits & interests. Both real & personal property was sold to a considerable amount & at good prices. Negroes sold from $400 to 600. Young fellows hired from $70 to 80 – women from $50 to 65. & plough boys from $40 to 50. I was pleased to see that money was abundant and that there were a number of persons, present desirous of purchasing property. I believe the pecuniary pressure in this District has passed away and that very few persons will be forced to part with their property & still fewer who will submit to a Sheriff's Sale. I had Mrs. & Col. Carroll & family, Judge Butler, the Misses Berrien & all our children to dine with us. In the evening we attended a small party at Major Jeter's, which was agreeable.

Tuesday 2....Father left us on his return home. I devoted today principally to the settlement of some business in the Sheriff office, in which Major Blocker was a party.

Wednesday 3rd....I rode to the place I purchased of Wm. Youngblood & bargained for two sows & 14 pigs, three shoats & three stacks of fodder at $22. I also purchased 7 turkeys[,] three bee gums[1] & some chickens. For the turkeys I paid $3.50 & for the bee gums $2. James and his wife left us for Barnwell.

Thursday 4th....Mrs. Brooks is preparing to leave for Columbia with Whitfield & Ellen for the purpose of placing Whitfield in College & Ellen under the care of the Misses Stark. They left at 10 ocl. I gave my Son James the following property, which I value as follows –

---

[1] Sections of black gum trees in which honeybees build hives.

Black Lewis	$600	John	$450	
Joe	600	Simon	450	
Y[oung?] Lewis	800	Surry	300	
Jack --	500	Chaney	250	
Betsy & four children	1300	Carriage horses	500	
Minerva	500	Waggon & gear		
		& 4 mules	300	
Hannah	500	Cash	200	
	4800		2450	= $7250

He has the possession or the right of possession to the foregoing property. I design to add in money & other things $250 more, which will make his advancement equal to $7500. My object is to make the property given to James equal to the advancement to Preston.

Friday 5th....I had proof this morning how utterly unqualified I should be to take the charge of keeping House and carrying keys, etc., in the fact that on the first night that my wife left me, my desk was left open all night & every key belonging to the house, exposed. After discovering my neglect, I examined the pantry, safe & other places & found every thing in good condition. I already felt the loss of my Wife but what would be the extent of my misfortune if I should be deprived of her by death. The mere idea is intolerable & what would be the reality. I pray God to spare me from so great a calamity.

Saturday 6th. Light rain from 12 ocl till night. I went to the Cottage in the morning and assisted Wm. Youngblood & his Sister and taking their final departure [from property WB had purchased]. I paid him $20 for his fodder & hogs. Preston spent the night with me.

Sunday 7....Preston spent the day with me.

Monday 8th....I left home in the stage for Columbia. On the way I stopped at Watson's & voted for Sheriff & Ordinary, to wit, for [Humphrey] Boulware & Coleman. I arrived at Doct. Labordes at half past 9 ocl when I found the family & my wife in good health and all glad to see me. The Doct. and his new wife seemed to be a very rational & happy couple & gave me a most cordial reception.

Tuesday 9th. This was disagreeable & rainy day. I devoted it to purchasing some books for our daughter Ellen & in paying a visit to the Misses Stark under whose tuition we had gone down to place our daughter at School – I paid the Misses Stark $87 for one quarters tuition & board, including French & Music. We were invited to a party at Doct. Leibers[2] but declined to attend.

Wednesday 10....another rainy & unpleasant day. We were confined principally to the house. We dined at Professor [William] Ellets where we met Col. Preston & Mr. [Charles] Pelham. We passed a pleasant afternoon.

Thursday 11....Mrs. Brooks occupied the day in returning visits & purchasing a few articles. We were invited to dine with President Henry but were forced to decline. In the evening Mrs. Brooks attended a large party at Col. Prestons given in compliment to her. I was too unwell to attend which I greatly regretted. I had taken Mauphene [morphine] until I was stupefied, in order to prevent headache....I was forced to resort to medicine to relieve me from a state of distressing constipation.

Friday 12th....I prepared to leave Columbia, in opposition to the remonstrance of Doct. Laborde & our good sister Elizabeth & at 9 o'clock took our departure from the house of our very kind & worthy brother in law on the road home....At half past 6 ocl we reached Mrs. Lees in pretty good condition where we passed the night. Here I was informed that Boulware was elected Sheriff & Col. [John] Hill Ordinary, both good if not the best selections among the candidates, tho I did not vote for Hill.

Saturday 13th....We reached home between 3 & 4 ocl. & found all well. I rode to my farm to inspect the progress of the work & also the Pigeon Roost at both of which places I've found little, of which to complain....Col. Carroll has just removed to his new house on the hill to the North of us.[3]

Sunday 14th....Our son Hampden is indisposed by an attack of cold, which induced his mother & myself to remain from church, of which we had no reason for regret, as we were informed that the preacher was a missionary, belonging to the Babtist church, who said many foolish & offensive things, in regard to all other denominations....Preston & David Means passed the night with us.

Monday 15. Torrents of rain....The surface of the Earth is now fluded with Water & the roads almost impassable. The sun has only shown out, clear of clouds, one day in twelve. We could not have selected a more inclement & unfavorable season for our Visit to Columbia as the rain deprived us of much of the pleasure, of seeing our friends & acquaintances, which we should have otherwise enjoyed, as well as that of looking at the Town....

Tuesday 16....For the last 36 hours the rain has not ceased to fall except for a few hours yesterday about 12 ocl....I devoted a few hours in the afternoon to opening a

---

[2] Francis Lieber (1798–1872), native of Berlin, educated in Europe. Came to the U.S. in 1827. Ed. *Enclyclopedia Americana* 1829–1833. Prof. of History and Pol. Sci SC College 1835–1855. Kept his anti-slavery views quiet but was faulted for his nationalism; rejected for college presidency. Prof. of international law Columbia Univ.

[3] This establishes that the new house was the "Carroll Hill" of today, a few houses above the "Brooks-Tompkins House" on Buncombe Street.

road to the cottage [see 18th] but was finally driven home by the rain....

....

Thursday 18th....I learned from various Sources that the Water courses have been very full, washing away bridges & doing other injuries. Apprehensions are entertained that Hamburg may be in some danger from a freshet in the Savannah River. I completed my road to the cottage of Hawthorne Glen [acquired from Mr. Youngblood].

....

Sunday 21....I set off at 11 ocl. for my plantation & arrived at Sunset, where I found my negroes in good health.

Monday 22. I rode over my plantation and examined the condition of things. I started two waggons to market with 8 bales of cotton on each waggon. I was pleased with the examination of my stock of cattle sheep & hogs. In one lot there were about 70 sheep with 8 lambs. In another lot about 130 hogs & in the third from 55 to 60 head of cattle . . . the milk cows & oxen. My cotton crop will be larger than I expected. I shall make over 150 bales....

Tuesday 23....I left the plantation at 8 ocl. & took the Matthews road, for the purpose of looking after my waggons. I overtook them about 6 miles from the plantation, stuck fast in the mud. By great toil & labour I succeeded in getting them to Major Allen's, where I made them throw the cotton in the store house & return home to wait for clear weather & better roads. I got home at dark.

Wednesday 24....James & his wife arrived about 8 ocl from Barnwell.

Thursday 25....I wrote two letters on business, visited the Village & purchased a bill of articles for the plantation negroes. I also sent over $1100 to be deposited in Hamburg bank by Mr. Habersham for the benefit of my Sister Mrs. [Behethland] Bird.

Friday 26. Cold & clear. Ice is near half inch thick. The month of Jany has been warm & wet. There has been not more than 5 clear days, suitable for picking cotton....

Saturday 27th....The Therm.t did not rise above 30° during the day. This was James' birthday, having attained the age of 23. Preston, Dr. Means & Barkley Blocker dined with us in company with James & his Wife.

Sunday 28th....Therm.t 22°. We attended service in the Epis. Church & heard a sensible sermon from a Mr. [John] Cornish, a gentleman from the North [Michigan], but who is expected to settle at Abbv Courthouse as the pastor of a church now being erected there. I expected my waggons from the plantation but I was disappointed.

Monday 29th. Exceedingly cold & clear. Therm from 18 to 19°....

Tuesday 30th. Very cold & cloudy at day light & light flakes of snow. My waggons arrived from the plantation bringing a load of cotton seed & a family of negroes, Minter George & his family, to remain at the Youngblood place. I loaded them this morning with cotton 7 bales in each waggon & started them to Hamburg about 12 ocl. I went with them through[Benjamin?] Frazier's land & they got on without much difficulty. In going down the hill at the Academy branch, the saddle mule in Toney's waggon fell & was dragged under the tongue for 15 or 20 feet & Toney's ankle injured but I hope slightly. The mule sustained no perceivable injury. In passing at night from the Pottery to the Cottage, the mare on which George was riding got away with the bridle on her & has not yet been recovered. I have made no movement with my waggons for the last three months, that has not been attended with some accident or mishap. My luck seems to be changing for the worse. I have been fortunate for which I humbly thank God, & I now enjoy higher & greater blessings than I deserve at the hands of Providence. I rec.d a letter from Doct. Laborde informing me that Whitfield has been suspended from college for one month for some riotous conduct. I forebear to make any comment on this event which is too painful for the exercise of proper fortitude. I therefore will not trust myself to record more than the fact....

Wednesday 31....James & his Wife are preparing to leave us for Barnwell, for which place they departed at 9 ocl. The Misses Berrien also left Col. Carroll's for Augusta, taking my man Cicero[4] to drive the carriage. I began to sow oats at the Hawthorne Glen altho the earth was frozen in the morning. But the best oats I ever made, were sowed when the earth was frozen every morning.

February 1. 1844

Friday 2....My waggons returned from Hamburg with lumber & a small bill of groceries, etc....

Saturday 3rd....My waggons left for the plantation. I rose at 5 ocl this morning intending to do a good day's work but the rain has disappointed me. I shall devote it to setting out trees & shrubbery. Mrs. Carroll's servant Frank returned from Columbia & brought me a fine bull calf of the Airshire & Durham bloods as a present accompanied by a very friendly note from B. F. Taylor Esq.[5]

....

Monday 5....This is my birth day. I am now 54 years of age & in better health & having greater strength than I have enjoyed for the last 14 years. I thank Almighty

[4] A favorite slave.

[5] Benjamin Franklin Taylor (1791–1852), son of Thomas Taylor, Revolutionary-era leader whose property became the state capitol. Large planter in Richland Dist. Princeton grad. Won many prizes for examples of his plantation products. John C. Calhoun took Daniel Webster to his plantation, "Edgehill," to see slavery first-hand. Louis Agassiz had daguerreotype images made of some of his slaves for studies of "multiple creations."

God for my improved health & for all the other blessings & comforts, with which I am favored & humbly pray, that by a life of virtue & piety & active duty I may prove not totally unworthy of them. In both health & spirits I feel unusually well & cheerful this morning. There was a large concourse of persons in the Village, altho the day was inclement & rainy from morning until night. Both lands & negroes were sold at high prices. Col. Hill's property was sold, including lands negrows, horses, mules & waggons at high prices. A negro boy of about 17 years of age sold for $661. & the others in proportion....

Tuesday 6th....A good deal of property was sold by the Sheriff, both negroes & land. . .

Wednesday 7th....The inclement weather prevents & retards the operations of the planter & this whole class are unusually behind with their spring work.

Thursday 8th....Therm.t 28° in the morning. I passed today at Hawthorne Glen, in making a fire, putting up a pair of [barns?], etc.

Friday 9th. Still clear & cold. I rode in the afternoon to inspect two parcels of land, belonging to [P____] & Wells but I was not pleased with either. Went in the evening to the Village & paid $75 in the Shffs office towards some [executionary]. Abner Youngblood....

Saturday 10th....Therm.t 22° at sunrise. Two beat companies mustered in the Village but nothing occurred during the day worthy of record.

Sunday 11th....Therm.t at sunrise 26°. By 10 ocl the temperature became mild & the entire residue of the day was pleasant.

Monday 12th....I was engaged in sowing oats at Hawthorne Glen, running four plows. The earth was in fine order.

Tuesday 13th....It is very desirable to have dry weather for some 10 or 15 days, to prepare the earth for planting. We paid a visit in the morning to Judge Butlers, where we met Mrs. Thompson, the two girls & Butler. They were all in fine health but I am grieved to say that my worthy & venerable Aunt looked not only feeble but in a rapid decline under the influence of a painful neuralgia affection. I fear her time here is short. On our return we called at Col. Pickens on Mrs. Cunningham, a daughter of the lamented Govr. Noble.[6] We found the Col. clever & hospitable. In fact he is a very agreeable & civil host & dispenses his attentions & hospitality with ease & affability. His late alterations on his house are not only additions but they greatly have improved the comforts & appearence of his domicile.[7] He maintains in his furniture more style than any man in the up Country....

---

[6] Patrick Noble (1787–1840), Abbeville District. Willington Acad., Princeton, read law under Langdon Cheves and Calhoun. Twice Speaker of the SC House; president of the Senate. Governor 1838–1840.

[7] "Edgewood"; built in 1836 two miles north of ECH, the house befitted Pickens' elaborate hospitality.

Wednesday 14th....The sun exhibited for the first time since Christmas through a smoky atmosphere that red, blood like appearance, which is peculiar to the Spring season. I finished at Hawthorne Glen, sowing a field in oats from 15 to 20 acres about meridian.

Thursday 15....I was very sick by headache in the afternoon & through the whole night. On the evening of Wednesday I was so much indisposed as to be confined to bed. I was unable to enjoy the company of Col. Pickens & a few friends, who were invited to spend the evening with us.

Friday 16. This a mild & clear Spring morning. Therm.t at 10 ocl up to 48°. I employed a ditcher at Hawthorne Glen & set him to work, on the branch, near the house.

Saturday 17....I set off for Barnwell & arrived at Govr. Hammond about Sunset. I was hospitably received and entertained by the Govr. & his lady. She appears to be a lady of gentle, affable, & benevolent disposition, with good manners & very lady like appearance.[8]

Sunday 18....I left Govr. Hammond at 9 ocl & arrived at Mr. U.M. Roberts at night. Here I met my Son & his Wife. They & the family gave me a cordial reception.

Monday 19....I went to the plantation of Col. Goode, to inspect the negroes of his estate, who were for sale on the following day. Dined with Captain Whatly on my return. He & his lady are hospitable & clever.

Tuesday 20th....I attended the sale of Goode's estate & bid off one negro fellow for $645 but consented to let a gentleman take him. The negroes sold high. They were not likely....

Wednesday 21....We returned to the sale & I purchased a boy about 17 years old at $650.

Thursday 22....I made an early start from Mr. Robert on my return home. I entertain a very favourable opinion of this family. He is a gentleman of sanguine temperament, impulsive & ardent in his feelings, frank & independent in disposition but rash & thoughtless in action & conduct. He is an honorable man but an unsafe guide. Mrs. Robert is among the most exemplary ladies of my acquaintance. I arrived at Gov Hammonds at sunset by whom I was again entertained with much courtesy.

Friday 23....I left the Govr. at 9 ocl[,] passed through Augusta & arrived in Ham-

---

[8] Lowcountry heiress Katherine Fitzsimmons. Their 1831 wedding brought Hammond a large plantation, Silver Bluff, near the Savannah River in Barnwell Dist. Hammond's sexual activity with her nieces, which began by 1841, had not yet become known. Whether WB learned of this is not revealed in his journal, but it is likely. *When* would be significant in light of their warm relationship. Hammond's liaisons with two of his female slaves was still in the future and would not become public knowledge.

burg at 1 ocl. where I met my waggon, purchased a bill of articles & arrived at home at 9 ocl at night where I found all well. No local news.

Saturday 24 ....I visited Hawthorne Glenn & inspected the work of a ditcher & of my negroes. My waggon arrived from Hamburg.

Sunday 25....We attended a service in the Babtist church & heard a dull sermon from Doct. Johnson. Judge Butler, Preston, B. M. Blocker, J. Wm. Blocker & Daniel Means returned & dined with us.

Monday 26th....I went to my plantation in the afternoon, at which I arrived at dark.

Tuesday 27....I rode in the morning over the greater part of my plantation & examined the state of preparations for a crop. In the afternoon I had a severe paroxysm of headache & was forced to take Hipps & tartar [an emetic]. I remained in bed from 1 ocl till next morning. My horse fell & injured my ankle considerably.

Wednesday 28th....I returned home by the way of Richardson's[9], in order to meet my father but was disappointed. The sale of his undivided property was going on. I left at 1 ocl. & reached home before night, where all are well. Capt. Miller from Barnwell arrived about Sunset, bringing me a negro fellow, whom James had purchased for me. [see Feb. 21]

Thursday 29th. I paid Capt. Miller $650 for his negro man & took his bill of Sale. He Left me after breakfast and I went to the farm. Whitfield took his departure this morning on his return to Columbia [his suspension over]....For the last three weeks, we have had a succession of days (uninterruptedly) of mild, open & pleasant weather, with the exception of one day when it was cloudy in the afternoon & a few drops of rain fell. The farmers are preparing to plant & are greatly favoured. The news from the cotton market is not favourable. Prices are going down & speculation at a stand yet the advices from Europe are not discouraging. Money is abundant & the planting community generally in easy & safe circumstances. Provisions are abundant yet they are advancing in price. Corn is selling at 6 ½ cts per bushel, fodder at 75 cts. Bacon at $6. Oats from 37 ½ to 50 cts. The death of Col. Benj. Frazier & the ill blood among his children on account of the property is the chief subject of interest & gossip about the Village. The health of the citizens and the Village & District is generally good.

March 1, 1844

Friday 1....the entire day was as lovely & inviting as could be desired to usher in the new season of Spring. Vegitation begins to appear and invites to gardening & transplanting. I am very busy at Hawthorne Glen in clearing a branch & removing and burning the rubbish, also plowing & fencing. The place so far serves as a hobby for me & keeps me agreeably employed.

---

[9] A small settlement near Red Bank Creek, north of ECH.

....

Sunday 3rd....Attended service morning & afternoon in the Epis. church & heard two impressive sermons, altho short, by the Revd. Mr. [left blank. Cornish?]. He appears to be a sensible & well educated gentleman with very good manners. He is on a visit to the South for his health.

Monday 4....The concourse of persons in the Village was not large, notwithstanding an active speculating spirit seemed to prevail with almost every one. Both land & negroes were sold by the Sheriff at fair prices. Stanmore Brooks & Lady & two of his nieces the Misses Caldwell, arrived at our house this afternoon & passed the night with us.

Tuesday 5....I passed the greater part of the day at Hawthorne glen & returned home, experiencing a good deal of fatigue, where I met my father, who was on his way to Hamburg.

Wednesday 6th....At 9 ocl I set out with my father for Hamburg, at which place we arrived at 4 ocl. I went over to Augusta, purchased a few articles & returned to Hamburg. At 9 ocl. a fracus commenced between my father's Servant Phill and a forward Son of Hubbards, which resulted in violence to the servant by the Son & a good deal of insolence on the part of the father to me who is a drunken, cowardly beast & who has no knowledge of the conduct, due to a gentleman. He was so offensive to me that I left his house & took quarters at Hunters.[10]

Thursday 7th....I again went to Augusta & procured a title from Mrs. Youngblood to her interest in a small tract of land. Returned to Hamburg & purchased a bill of articles for my father, amounting to over $200. The cotton market was exceedingly dull & neither I nor my father offered ours for Sale. Each of us had 50 bales. I saw in the papers a confirmation of the melancholy rumor in regard to the explosion of one of the large guns on board the Steam boat Princeton & the death of Secretaries Upsher & Gilman and also of three other distinguished citizens.[11] We left Hamburg at 12 ocl & arrived at home in the afternoon.

Friday 8th....I went to Hawthorne Glen & superintended the laying of the worm of a fence [the first rails, to mark the course of the fence], etc. My sister Mrs. Blocker & part of the children arrived & passed the night with us.

Saturday 9th....My father left us after breakfast....Mrs. B. left us after dinner & must have been overtaken by a copious shower of rain accompanied with hail. At the close of the shower the earth was white with hail....We took tea with Mrs. Carroll where we met the daughter[s?] of the Revd. Mr. Johnson & of Mr. Jos. Pritchard.

---

[10] A James Hubbard, a native of Bloomfield CT, age 60, was buried in Hamburg. His marker has no birth or death dates.

[11] On Feb. 28, 1844, the explosion of a gun on the warship Princeton killed Sec. of State Abel Upshur and Thomas Gilmer, Sec. of the Navy. Calhoun would succeed Upshur on March 6.

Sunday 10th....lovely Spring morning. This spring is in advance of the last at least one month, both in the appearance of the warmth of the weather on the vegitable kingdom & in the preparation of the planting for the new crop.

Monday 11th....The Court of Common Pleas commences its Spring session under Judge Richardson who arrived on Saturday. The Abbeville Belligerents Messrs. Cunningham & McGowan with a portion of their friends are in our Village, waging a war of words & shedding of ink, which must end in a hostile meeting if the parties have the requisite pluck. It is a woman's privilege to scold & quarrel but men should either fight at once or keep the peace. I called in the afternoon on Judge Richardson & Capt. Cunningham at County's [Compty's] where I saw most of the lawyers, who are in attendance upon the Court. Capt. Ward & Preston passed the night with me....

Tuesday 12....I saw for the first time yesterday a female exhibiting in the street for money. She was about 45 years of age and appearance & had a daughter apparently 17. [i]nnocent & modest in behavior who assisted the mother in singing popular songs, the mother at the same time playing on the organ.[12]

Wednesday 13....We had a few friends at tea in complement to Mrs. Robbins & her Sister Miss Pritchard from Cheraw. It is understood that the hostile party from Abbeville have left this place for Augusta under an arrangement to fight on Saturday next with rifles. I fear that one of the combatants may be killed for the quarrel is bitter & the weapons deadly.

Thursday 14th....I rode to the farm & on my return got wet. The rain continued to fall without cessation from 10 ocl. till night. I felt considerably indisposed.

Friday 15th....The trial of Deas [Dees?] for the murder of Barefoot took place to day. I heard part of the testimony. It was a vile & cold blooded murder & of the guilt of the accused, there could be no doubt as he confessed it to many persons in Georgia detailing the place & circumstances, where & underwhich the murder was committed & the motive for it. Col. Carroll gave a dinner to the bar but I was too indisposed to attend. Deas was convicted of the murder of Barefoot.

Saturday 15th....The juries were dismissed by the Court last evening & it will only set to day to grant motions & pass sentences. No business was done on the issue docket but it is understood that no extra Court will be ordered....I learned that McGowan & Cunningham had met, fought with rifles & that McGowan was shot in the head but it was supposed not to be mortal. It is to be hoped that this quarrel will end here & further bloodshed be spared.

....

Monday 18. Clear, cold & windy, even boisterous & disagreeable until evening, when it became calm & cool....

---

[12] A hand organ or barrel organ, played by turning a crank.

Tuesday 19th. Very clear & cold. Therm.t 33°. Some frost but not destructive. We heard from our children in Columbia. They are well. Ste. Griffin & Jos. Addison arrived in the Stage from Columbia, having been dismissed from college on account of some rebellious conduct, in which the whole class was involved. The boys were wrong but not guilty of any ungentlemanly or immoral conduct. The information from Hamburg, represents Mr. McGowan as in fair way to recover from his wound which I humbly trust may take place. My sympathies have been inlisted for this young man, so far at least as to wish him to recover & do well. Our mother & sister Mrs. M[ary] & E[lizabeth] Carroll & Miss Leslie passed the evening with us in social converse.

Wednesday 20th....About 4 ocl. a dark cloud rose in the No.West & passed over with a light rain & terrible gust of wind. It blew down several treas in Mrs. B[rooks]'s garden....

Thursday 21 ....I set out at 1 ocl. for my plantation. On my arrival I found the overseer planting corn in the field at the house, called prospect field.

Friday 22....I rode over my plantation in the morning & found it in a desirable order.

I also inspected the corn cribs & stables & looked at the stock of hogs, cattle & sheep. I also saw two young kids of a goat of Hamdens. In the afternoon they commenced planting corn in the Corley field.

Saturday 23. Cold & cloudy in the morning & a light fall of snow. I set out for home after breakfast by the way of Major Blocker's, where I passed two or three hours & got my dinner. Have reached home about sunset & found all well....

Sunday 24. A severe hoar frost this morning & Therm.t down to 30°. I fear the fruit is killed. Mr. Tibbetts the painter died this morning from a fall while painting R. Mims house. He was a worthy man & and honest mechanic. I greatly regretted the death of this clever man. I was attacked about 12 ocl by headache & passed the afternoon & night in great agony. Mr. Calhoun and his lady have arrived at Col. Pickens on his way to Washington to enter upon the duties of Secretary of State [chosen by President Tyler to succeed Abel Upshur who had died].

Monday 25....Altho very feeble I rode out to my farm in the morning & in the afternoon took a ride with Mrs. B in the buggy.

Tuesday 26....I began to plant corn at my Mount Parson's farm[13] in the afternoon, from which I did not return until dark.

Wednesday 27. I am busily engaged with all hands and planting corn, manuring in the check & covering with the plough. It is reported that the difficulty between Yancy [Yancey?] & Alexander has been compromised. They raised a storm & waged a bitter war of words to the great excitement & annoyance of the public,

[13] Named for James Parsons. See introduction.

thereby giving their friends an opportunity of displaying their diplomatic ingenuity & talents of restoring sweet peace between the belligerents. It is better to waste ink than to spill blood. The repeated recurance of these personal quarrels & affairs of honor is brutalizing the feelings of our people & inculcating false tastes & principles into our children. They ought & must be discountenanced....

Thursday 28th....I rode to Preston's & went with him over a part of his plantation. On my return I took refuge from the rain at Mr. James Griffins,[14] by whom & his wife and I was treated with all the civility, of which they were capable. The old gentleman appeared much delighted with a grandchild, to whom he played nurse, during the greater part of the time, I stayed.

Friday 29. This was a warm & drizzly day. I was engaged in putting up a gate at Hawthorne Glen. I got partly wet. The reception of Mr. [Henry] Clay[15] in Augusta is represented to have been enthusiastic & emposing. He addressed the assemblage for an hour & a half in an easy & familiar style. The passage of this gentleman through the United States, attended at every town & Village with all the pageantry of processions & public addresses, must be very flattering & gratifying to the feelings of the man & the patriot. Mr. Clay is as much entitled to this distinguished attention as any man in the United States for his long & eminent public services, for his lofty & noble character & for the purity & ardour of his patriotism. I admire the character of the man but do not approve his politics.

Saturday 30th....rain has disappointed my arrangement to plant a field of corn at Hawthorne Glen, for which every preparation had been made yesterday. This rain "puts me out" as it deranges the entire plan of operation for the day....I repaired fences, cleaned the land, etc.

Sunday 31st....We visited Col. Carroll, who was indisposed from fever & cold. Preston & D[avid] Means [brother of Caroline] spent the day & night with us. This month closes with clear & seasonable weather. The foliage of the trees is fast putting forth their green buds & leaves & the earth begins to clothe itself in a mantle of green herbage & grass. Flowers are blooming & the gardens exhibit their rich stock of young & growing vegitables.

April 1st 1844.

Monday 1....This was sale day & brought together a small assemblage of persons.

---

[14] James Griffin (1782?–1855?) lived about 3 miles from ECH. His second wife was Nancy Mims, many years his junior. He was an active member of Antioch Church. His son James Benjamin Griffin (1825–1881) is the subject of McArthur and Burton, *A Gentleman and an Officer*.

[15] 1777–1852 (of KY); leader of the Whig Party and architect of the "American System" of tariffs, a national bank, and "internal improvements." Speaker of U.S. House; candidate for president 1824, 1832, 1844; J. Q. Adams' Sec. of State; Senator. Negotiated compromises in 1820, 1833, and 1850, that forestalled sectional crises.

Mr. Toomey[16] called on me this morning with a letter of introduction from Gov.r Hammond. He is the successor of Mr. Ruffin & appointed by the Governor to compile the agricultural & geological Survey of the State. I rode with him to my farm & then by the Pottery, where he inspected the specimens of soil & Clay, & took portions from my land for analysis. He is a modest unassuming & well-informed gentleman, especially so, for a son, of Erin for he reports himself as a native of the Emerald Isle. He dined with me & took his departure for Abbev[ille]

Tuesday 2nd....I finished planting a field corn at Hawthorn Glen & commenced a second. I also opened a passway from my Mount Parsons farm to Hawthorn glen & put up a gate to open the communication....

....

Thursday 4th ....The garden is vocal with the music of birds & ornamented by variety of Spring flowers.

Friday 5th....I began to plant potatoes at Hawthorn Glen & also a field of corn at the Mount Parsons farm.

Saturday 6th....I wrote to our children in Colombia [Whitfield and Ellen] & sent them $150.

Sunday 7th. No change in the weather. We spent the day with our honorable & respected Aunt Butler. We were gratified to find her in tolerable health and in very good & cheerful spirits. She is a remarkable woman for the strength of her mind & great firmness of character, to whom my father & his children are indebted for many acts of kindness & maternal care, bestowed on them at a period of time when from the loss of a mother, they were most helpless & unprotected.[17]

Monday 8....The temperature of the weather within the last ten days, has passed from the cold of December to midsummer. In consequence of which, the forests . . . have suddenly bursted forth almost into full leaf. I fear that we shall pay dearly for this unexampled fine weather, by cold frost about the full moon in May. If a frost could then fall & kill one half the growing crop of cotton in the entire cotton growing region, it would be for the good of the Country as planters would [inserted: then] substitute corn, the effect of which would be to enhance greatly the value of the cotton crop in to within one third of the value of a full one and at the same time furnish an abundant supply of provisions for home consumption. I am still planting corn.

....

Wednesday 10th....I began this morning to plant a lot of cotton at Hawthorn Glen. I also planted in a lot of Irish potatoes & water melons. Hawthorn Glen is now my

---

[16] Michael Toumey (1805–1857), born in Cork, Ireland; came to U.S. in 1830. Studied geology at Rensselaer Inst., Troy NY. SC state geologist, 1844–1847. His *Report on the Geology of South Carolina*, 1848, included Edgefield District.

[17] WB's mother Elizabeth Butler Brooks died in 1802.

hobby. It both occupies my time & interests me, which constitutes the true secret of contentment & the only infallible means of success in our affairs....

....

Friday 12th....We are preparing to pay a visit to Roselands for a few days. We set out at 10 ol. & arrived at 4 ocl. The day was very warm.

Saturday 13th....In the morning I rode over my plantation. I had all the corn planted except about 15 acres of new ground and about 175 acres of cotton planted. The corn was up & looked well generally & the cotton was planted in superior order. My overseer expects to finish his cotton on Wednesday & the balance of the corn by Saturday night. I shall plant 275 acres in cotton & 200 in corn & over 150 in small grain, to wit, wheat, oats[,] rye & barley. The earth was getting dry & hard, which would prevent corn in the stiff [hard] land from coming up. My stock of all kinds looked pretty well. I counted between 70 & 80 head of cattle & was informed by Mr. Lowry that I had 30 lambs. The negroes were all well.

Sunday 14....In the morning attended divine service at Sister Spring Church[?] & heard dull & senseless sermon from a Mr. Carter. The congregation was small & as cold as the minister was dull. In the afternoon several of our neighbors called to see us & most of our negroes called on their Mistress in their Sunday dress, with clean faces & combed heads, bringing their children with them.

Monday 15th....We set out on our return home at 7 & arrived at 12 ocl. All well. No news. We received letters from James & his Wife & also an invitation by mail to Miss L[ouisa?] Berrien's wedding in Savannah, to which Col. Carroll & lady set out on yesterday morning. Rode over my farm in the afternoon. My corn is coming out very well & I shall finish a field of about 10 acres in cotton tomorrow.

Tuesday 16th....I began to plant a lot of cotton near to Mrs. Carroll for pin money for Mrs. Brooks. Received a very sweet letter from our very dear daughter, who is at School in Columbia. Mrs. Mariah Calhoun[see below] is reputed to be very ill.

Wednesday's 17th. Warm, dry & clear. I do not recollect ever to have seen so dry & warm a month of April. There has in fact, been no spring for the change was from the cold of winter (to wit 30°) in a few days to summer heat of 82°. There has not yet fallen one April shower & the entire month more resembles a June than April. Mrs. Mariah Calhoun died this morning in giving birth to an infant or rather the infant was taken from her by Doct. Lake & she died in two hours after. She was the last of four daughters of Col. [Eldred] Simkins, all of whom died before they attained thirty years of age. It is melancholy to see so amiable a family, prematurely cut off in the very Spring time of life & with every thing around them to attach them to life[18]....I planted a lot of cotton of something like three acres. This closes my cotton crop both here & at Roselands. I have planted here about 15 acres in

[18] Mariah Simkins (1816–1844) was the wife of James Edward Calhoun, brother-in-law of John C. Calhoun.

cotton & about 70 in corn & 30 in oats. At Roselands I have planted something like 275 acres in cotton, 200 in corn & 150 in small grain....

Thursday 18th....Mrs. Calhoun was buried this afternoon at 4 ocl. in the family burying ground. Mr. Abney performed the funeral ceremonies by singing, prayer & a short address on the subject of the resurrection of the body. I acted as one of the pall bearers. She is the last of the four daughters of my much esteemed & valued friend Col. E. Simkins & the Sixth person, who has died in the house of Col. Pickens within the last six years. Mrs. John C. Calhoun & Mrs. Clemson[19] were with her in her illness & did much to alleviate her sufferings. She was a lovely woman.

....

Saturday 20th....A good deal of rain fell during the night & the earth seems thoroughly wet. I was engaged in reading Arthur by Eugene Sue.[20] His works show genius & originality and delineate the passions with a masterly hand but his characters are always extravagant & paradoxical. I presume however that they are drawn in harmony with the manners & customs of the Society of Paris. I read his works with great interest although they abound in improbable incidents & the exhibition of extravagant & contradictory passions, capriciously indulged and often displayed without any regard to decency or decorum.

Sunday 21....We attended service in the Baptist church & heard a sensible sermon from Mr. Parmly, who is itenerating through the Country for the purpose of promoting a plan for religious instruction & for the dissemination of the bible & religious tracts among the entire community by means of agents, called Col Porters [colporteurs]. The plan is a benevolent one & calculated to do good.

Monday 22....I felt in the morning unusually well & rode to my farm & then to the Village, where I met a committee, appointed to make collections to establish the Col Porter agency. I gave them $5. About 12 ocl. I returned home considerably indisposed & it was soon forced to take my bed. From that moment until 9 ocl at night I was in a state of suffering & agony, defying all the powers of language to describe. If all the suffering of my past life (apart from the same cause) could be concentrated for a few hours, upon my poor head & stomach, I could not have suffered greater agony. I pray God, in his mercy to relieve me from this terrible suffering. Genl. [Waddy] Thompson on his return home called for a moment to see us.

---

19 Anna Maria Calhoun Clemson (1817–1875), daughter of John C. Calhoun; wife of Thomas Green Clemson (1807–1888). Educated in part in Edgefield, she became her father's right arm in Washington until her marriage. Clemson was born in Philadelphia, studied chemistry in France, and was a diplomat in Belgium. He owned "Cane Break" plantation in Edgefield Dist. Helped found Maryland Agri. Col. CSA army. Willed the plantation he inherited from Calhoun to create what is now Clemson University.

20 Marie-Joseph "Eugene" Sue (1804–1857), French novelist who helped to popularize the serialized novel. His melodramatic works aroused concern about the effects of the Industrial Revolution.

He was in fine health & spirits but looked a little more advanced in years, than when he left us. His gray hairs begin to tell of age. His mission to Mexico has been successful, decidedly advantageous to this Country, gratifying to his friends & eminently honorable to himself as a public Minister. I was gratified again to meet with my old friend with whom I have been acquainted upwards of 30 years & on terms of intimacy & friendship.

Tuesday 23....I am free from pain this morning but pretty much infeebled. This is Mrs. Brooks birthday & I thank God that she is in as fine health & looks as well as I have seen her for years. None know the true value of health but those, who have lost it. The loss of it in my case abates very greatly my enjoyment of happiness and my ability to be useful. I have great pride & ambition to be active & useful but my energies are crushed by this afflicted malady under which I suffer & all my efforts only tend to increase my suffering. I try to say in sincerity I submit with assignation, "the will of God be done". I was well enough to spend the evening with Mrs. Carroll, in company with Col. Carroll & his Wife....

Wednesday 24th....Major Blocker and Wife with Mrs. Holden arrived to pass the night with us, on their way to Grahamville to visit their daughter Mrs. Reed. I am plowing & hoeing corn.

Thursday 25....Major Blocker & Company left us at 6 ocl, by whom Mrs. Brooks sent some garden plants & flowers to our niece Mary Gillison. In the afternoon we paid a visit to our Son Preston, whom we found in good spirits & and fine health. His place looked cool & inviting & his crop of young corn promising. In the evening we took a walk by moonshine to Col. Carroll's.

....

Saturday 27th..... For the last two nights, the temperature has been so high as to render it uncomfortable to sleep under any other covering than a light sheet. Its effect upon vegetation was most obvious & far exceeding my previous observations of any former season.

Sunday 28th....I heard a sermon in the Baptist church by the Revd. Mr. Chiles.[21] His manner is persuasive & conciliating and his matter sensible but very commonplace. There is nothing striking, novel or original and the sermons of this gentleman. His benevolence & persuasiveness of manner always prepares the hearer to make allowances for all other defects while the purity of his character always inspires confidence in the sincerity & force of his piety....

Monday 29th....I am still plowing & hoeing corn. I shall finish replanting all my corn to day & get over my crop with both plows & hoes this week. On thursday I expect to commence plowing & chopping out cotton.

Tuesday 30th....I have never seen vegetation grow faster. I observed a young oak

[21] James M. Chiles was pastor of Bethany Baptist Church, 1832–1844. He pastored Edgefield Baptist in 1851.

sprout of the growth of this Spring at least 4 feet in length. I have some corn near knee high & with seven & eight leaves. On Monday I observed cotton with three leaves. In the absence of all my male servants, my bees thought proper to swarm & I was forced to hive them, which I executed with great success. It was my first effort in this line of business & in fact it was the first swarm that I had seen hived for the last twenty years....The cotton market has continued to decline since February until this date. It is now down to the lowest point of depression. I have very sagaciously kept 50 bales to get a high price & my reward will be a loss of near one half the lot. I feel that I deserve it & therefore it chafes me a little. Men ought to pay either for their folly or cupidity and I ought to have taken the fair market price for my cotton when I carried it to market. My loss is nothing more than a deserved punishment.

May 1, 1844

Wednesday 1st. A clear, bright & sweet morning....There was a performance of guglery[?] in the Village last night. It is reported to have been good of its kind. It made everyone laugh most uproariously & it was for this they paid their money. Hampden was delighted & gives an animated account of the various feats, such as frying eggs in a hat, shooting a watch from a pistol, &C &C. We left home for Roselands at 12 ocl & arrived at 6 ocl. Where we found all well except Liddy, the cook –

Thursday 2....I rode over my plantation. The stand of cotton is very good & the corn looks well. The corn was plowed & about one half of it howed.

Friday 3....The agricultural Society met on its anniversary. Col. Pickens delivered an address, interesting, sensible & practicable. It gave great satisfaction to the entire auditory. I rode with him over my crop the previous evening & accompanied him to Cambridge this morning. We had a very excellently dressed barbacue, of which about 300 partook in great harmony.

Saturday 4....I left my Wife & Hampden at the plantation & went down to my fathers, who had only a few minutes returned from the Village, to which he had gone on a visit but finding that my family were at the plantation, he returned home. He is very feeble but enjoys tolerable health & good spirits....

Sunday 5. I returned to my plantation, accompanied by my father as far as Doct. Reidy's.....

Monday 6th. We left Roselands at an early hour on our return home....I visited the Village & remained about two hours. Some property was sold at very fair prices, particularly horses. I heard no local or District news. The earth is very dry & small grain suffering for the want of rain. I rode over my farm in the evening. The crop is pretty good. I began to plow & chop out cotton at the farm this morning. At my plantation the overseer was employed in planting his newly cleared land in corn. He had plowed over the whole of his corn, & howed about one half, which was growing rapidly. He had run the iron tooth harrows over the cotton & would probably commence plowing & chopping out this evening. I saw at my farm cotton with 6 leaves. My small grain at Roselands looks well tho is wanting rain. My sheep are sheared of which I have upwards of 90. I have fewer calves at the plantation than I have ever known in the Spring. I have heard a general complaint on this subject. One of my female neighbors complained to me that they had no young calves & the reason was, their bull had died the previous year.

Tuesday 7....I went this morning to Mrs. Elizabeth Mims, better known as Mrs. Howard & drew her will & attended to its execution. She expressed great gratitude for this act of kindness as I made no charge for it. I saw in this evenings paper the announcement of Mr. B[enjamin] C. Yan[e]cy as a candidate for the Legislature. I think that he has become a candidate for popular favour at too early a period after becoming a citizen of the District & with two [too] limited an acquaintance with the people to calculate on success. He is a clever gentleman, for whom I entertain a favourable opinion & shall not oppose if I do not support him.

....

Friday 10th....Deas was executed to day for the murder of Barefoot. A large assemblage of persons of all ages & conditions were collected in the Village to witness the execution, including old men & boys, women & negroes, cake sellers & jugglers. I was confined to my bed by headache & saw but little of the busy & anxious crowd. In the afternoon I had the evidence of a good deal of drunkenness through the sense of hearing as many noisy & drunken men passed my house. I was informed that a negro of Capt. Bettis[22] was whipped to death by his overseer under the sanction & assistance of his Son in law [Robert?] Hughes. A jury of inquest was held over the body, who rendered the finding, that he came to his death by whipping.

Saturday 11th....The battalion of Cavalry commanded by Major Jas. Smyley[23] are ordered to parade here to day. The officers met for drill yesterday....The cavalry turned out badly, in the Edgefield company about 40 rank & file[,] in the Liberty Hill troop not more than 18 & in the Meeting Street troop not a dozen. They made but an indifferent show....Capt. Lipscomb & Doct. Mays with their families returned from Florida this afternoon. I recd. a letter from my overseer that he had chopped out & worked over about 70 acres of my cotton. The small grain was suffering for rain & my wheat ripening rapidly. I went with Mrs. B. & Preston & Hamden to Hawthorn Glen to get mulberries in the afternoon, where I observed a good deal of cotton, which seemed to be dying in the rows for the want of rain. Oats have apparently stopped growing & vegitables are suffering greatly.

Sunday 12th....I read yesterday a paper of Mr. Ingersoll[24] of the house of representa-

---

[22] Benjamin Warren Bettis (c. 1812–1893), owner of the Pine House, a landmark six miles southeast of ECH; 1850 census: $15,000 real estate, 32 slaves.

[23] James Caldwell Smyley (1820–1872), planter on Meeting Street Road north of ECH. Militia officer; signer of Ordinance of Secession.

[24] Congressman Charles Ingersoll, Dem. of PA, favored annexation. His brother, Congressman Joseph Ingersoll of PA, a Whig, was opposed.

tives in the form of a report from the committee, of which he is chairman on the subject of the annexation of Texas to the United States. It is an able & almost unanswerable argument in favour of annexation. It bears internal evidence of its having proceeded from a vigorous mind & and able statesman.

Monday 13th....The intelligence from Washington represents the Democratic party in a state of great excitement on the subject of the Presidency and very great doubts are entertained whether any nomination will take place at the approaching convention. A large division of the party has abandoned Van Buren & are disposed to run either Commodore [Charles] Stewart [of Pennsylvania] or Genl. [Lewis] Cass [of Michigan]. The question of annexation of Texas is becoming an absorbing & exciting one not only among Politicians but among all ranks of people throughout the Union. It is a grave & momentous question in every aspect, in which it is presented & may exert an important influence over the future destinies of this Country. The silence of the Whigs upon this subject since the letter of Mr. Clay [an equivocal endorsement of annexation if done without war] & their apparent servile subjection to the will of their chief, has done more to cause me to distrust the party than any other fact or occurence that has taken place for some time. If his will is to be the law of his party, he is to all purposes a political Dictator. Can the entire party approve his letter? I cannot believe this, then why such silence?

Tuesday 14th....H. Bleas[e][25] commenced repainting my house this morning & certainly not before it wanted it. I went with Mrs. Brooks to spend the day with Major Blocker & family, whom we found in good health & greatly delighted with their visit to Grahamville, to see their daughter. I was unwell & suffered some nausea & head ache the greater part of the time, I was with them. But for this I should have passed a pleasant day.

Wednesday 15. This was another warm & oppressive day. Such a season of drought & heat I have never witnessed so early in the Spring. Cabbage plants & beets in the garden appear to be drying up. Corn & cotton . . . are too young to sustain any serious injury yet.

Thursday 16th....I rode with Col. Pickens over his plantation & and inspected his crop of corn, cotton & small grains. It was very good & in pretty fair order & a portion of it was much revived by the shower of rain. He has opened a large & fertile field on the Creek & was preparing to plant corn in it. I was pleased with his crop & every thing, I saw except his plow horses. They are too weak for the size of his crop & especially for the quantity of new ground, which he is bringing into cultivation....Danl. Bird Jr. came from Cokesbury on a visit to us.

Friday 17th....I rode as far as E[dmund] Bacons & then through the Village. Corn & vegetables exhibit the strongest marks, for how much they are suffering for the want

---

[25] Henry Horatio Blease (1832–1892) was a private in Capt. Preston Brooks' Company D, Palmetto Regiment, Mexican War. He was the father of governor and senator Coleman Livingston Blease.

of rain. The roads are a little better than a bed of dust, with which the atmosphere is filled & the surface of the earth resembles a bank of arid ashes. The very sky has a settled & fiery appearance & looks like a canopy of brass. The grass in the old fields is parched & withered as tho a volume of fire had gently passed over it. Oats will soon be beyond recovery.

Saturday 18th....The Methodists are holding a quarterly meeting in their church at this place. Information was received at this place of the death of Mr. George Pope, in Columbia, Clerk of the Court of Common Pleas. He had visited Columbia, to obtain medical advice & treatment -- & after submitting to a painful opperation, he sunk under a general diseased state of the system & principally from an affliction of the liver. He was an honest & just man & an excellent officer of the Court. Thos. Bacon[26] has been appointed to the vacant office & I hope that he will make a faithful Clerk. I finished chopping out & working my cotton at Hawthorne Glen this afternoon. Also plowed & howed the potatoes both sweet & irish & my watermellon lot....

Sunday 19th....For the last 10 days the Therm.t has ranged from 88° to 90°. We attended divine service in the Methodist Church. An incoherent sermon was delivered by Mr. Tall[e]y & a very good prayer by Mr. Kennerly. A collection was taken & the sacrament administered. Col. Yanc[e]y & Preston passed the night with me.

Monday 20th....Corn & cotton look well, notwithstanding the dry weather & continue to grow but the oats are partly ruined. They are heading & not above a span high [distance between the thumb and little finger of a splayed hand].

Tuesday 21....I am plowing my crop the second time, painting my house & have my carpenters building a thresher & threshing room at my plantation to get out wheat, also in repairing waggons, carts, gin &C. I take delight in an active life but my efforts are greatly marred by ill health. High wind in the afternoon with several showers of rain. Mrs. Carroll returned from Columbia bringing our dear daughter with her. Ellen is in excellent health, has grown some during her absence & we flatter ourselves that she has greatly improved under the tuition of the Misses Stark. Rain continued to fall gently during the night.

Wednesday 22....My negro man George is very sick. Fire necessary to comfort.

....

Friday 24th....The rain has been abundant for corn & cotton but not for oats nor the gardens of vegetables. It wet the earth to the ordinary depth of the plow. We took Ellen & Hampden in the afternoon to Hawthorn Glen to get fruit &C. At 3 ocl at night I was roused from sleep by one of the Servants informing me that George was in great agony. I [ink stain covers a word] & went to see him & finding his suffering

[26] Thomas Glasscock Bacon (1812–1876), son of Edmund Bacon; brother of Edmund Burke Bacon. Lawyer, Clerk of Dist. Court 1844–1860; 1850 census: $3,000 real estate, 43 slaves. Colonel, CSA army.

to be very severe I went for Doct. [John G.?] Williams.[27]

Saturday 25th. A light fog at early morn & some clouds by 7 ocl. but generally clear through the day....

Sunday 26th....[T]his has been a remarkable Spring. Not one shower of rain fell in the month of April, of the kind called April showers, in which sunshine rapidly succeeds to clouds & clouds to sunshine & where the heavens seem to weep & smile at the same time. Nor has there been a day since the 1 of April, when the earth was too wet to be worked. I have not lost one hour by rain. We attended service in the Babtist Church & heard a sermon from the Revd. Mr. Johnson.

Monday 27th....A convention of the Democratic Party of the United States is appointed to take place at Baltimore this day for the purpose of selecting a candidate for the Presidency. If the weather be consulted, the omens are not favorable either to the harmony or success of the party. The day dawned with heavy peals of thunder & lightning, which may be ominous of a boistrous meeting & violent disruption of the party and the dark clouds & continued rain from 12 ocl. significant of the gloomy prospects of its leaders. Want of harmony in principles & unity in action will be the official cause of the defeat of this party, for I think they compose the majority of the people of the U. States. A difference of opinion on the subject of the Tariff and the annexation of Texas has produced a well-founded distrust of the honesty & fidelity of some of the most distinguished men of the party & thousands who two months ago were willing to support Van Buren have abandoned him. So. Carolina is likely to be placed in such a situation as to be forced to throw away her vote in order to preserve her principles.[28]

Tuesday 28....I left home for my plantation, taking Daniel Bird with me on his return to Cokesbury. I reached the plantation at 3 oclock & found the negroes well.

Wednesday 27th....I rode over plantation & examined my crop in the morning. My corn is very good, a large portion of it from breast to head high & perfectly free from grass. In fact I never saw so little grass in the fields generally at this period of the year. The cotton was in good order but rather small, owing to the dry weather. A copious shower of rain fell on Monday, which revived the crops & caused the cotton to take a new growth. The wheat was cut & stacked & bids far to yield a good crop. The oats are small & some spots, had commenced dying but the rain had already produced a favourable change. My cotton was brought nearly to a stand & only required rain & a plowing to cause it to grow apace. About 10 ocl at night, rain began to fall & continued for three or four hours.

Thursday the 30th....I discovered upon setting out for home that the earth was pretty thoroughly wet on the surface & water was standing in the road. This rain will, I

---

[27] A highly respected citizen. Died in early June 1866 by his own hand.

[28] The state legislature did just that in 1832 and 1836. Antebellum SC was the only state without a popular vote for president.

hope, save my oat crop & make it of sufficient size, to admit of cutting. I may make 2/3 of a crop. The rain was sufficient for corn & cotton on my plantation. I arrived at home at 12 ocl & found the family well. In the afternoon I rode to my farm. My crop promises well & is in good order. I regret to hear of several cases of sickness. Scarlet fever, measles & diarrhea are prevailing in the families of three of our neighbours, only one disease however in each house....

Friday 31. Mild & pleasant day with fresh breezes from the So.West. I rode over Preston's crop, which I found in good order & --- [illegible] growing condition. The crops of corn & cotton in the vicinity of the Village are as promising as they usually are at this period of the year but the oat crop is inferior to any that I have a recollection for the the last 15 years. My corn at the farm is from knee to breast high & looks exceedingly well. A lot of cotton, near the stable about two acres, averages in height to the knee & is altogether the most luxuriant growth of cotton that I have seen. The month of May has been unusually warm & dry. The Therm.t has ranged from 88° to 90°. At no period has the earth been too wet to admit of being worked & scarcely one hour's work has been lost by reason of rain. I recollect no period when at this season of the year so much disease of various kinds was prevailing & with such mortality. Scarlet fever, measles, & diarrhea prevail over the District & cause many deaths. It is reported that Gov.r Hammond has lost about 40 negroes this Spring but I hope the account is greatly exaggerated.[29] Thos. Bacon has received from the Governor, the appointment of Clerk in place of Mr. Geo. Pope decd.

June 1. 1844

Saturday 1st....I paid a visit to the Revd. Mr. Johnson. Mrs. Bacon called to see the newly arrived minister Reverend Mr. Walker[30] of the Epis. Church. I made some purchases for the negroes & saw & conversed with sundry Villagers. I find them much excited upon the subject of the annexation of Texas to the United States & prepared to recommend & demand the meassure, regardless of consequences. Very few of them have reflected upon the question & still fewer have any knowledge of its true merits or of the consequences, which it is destined to have upon the fortunes of this Government and more especially upon the destinies of this State in regard to the great staple, cotton, & to the value of the negroes & lands of our people. I believe it will be to the interests of the Union to ratify the treaty now before the Senate of the United States, & a great importance to the North & West in a Commercial point of view but eminently injurious to this State in the effect, which it must have upon the Value of our property. It is presented to us both as a Southern & National question in the fact that all the Northern Abolitionists & the Government

[29] Mortality among Hammond's slaves was unusually high. In 1841 he noted that in the 10 years since he took possession of Silver Bluff, there had been 73 births and 82 deaths.

[30] Edward Tabb Walker (1818–1896) was a "missioner" at Trinity in 1844.

of Great Britain are opposed to annexation upon the avowed ground that it will favour the extension & duration of Slavery. The ultimate security of our domestic institution may depend in a great measure upon the ratification of the treaty & also the preservation of our rights even in their depreciated Value. I am therefore in favour of annexation upon the principle contained in the maxim "partial evil, universal good" or in other words, that the interests of the few must be subsidiary to the good of the whole.

Sunday 2nd....Service was performed in the Epis. Church by the Revd. Mr. Walker, a young divine who has lately arrived in our Village. He seems to be a sensible gentleman but as a preacher he wants animation & force. He reads the service very well, in a distinct voice & with solemn manner yet in the delivery of his sermon, he is monotinous & unanimated. In the afternoon I rode to Judge Butler's to meet Judge Harper, whom I met there & accompanied to my house to remain with me at least until the return of Judge B. from Columbia. Harper is in feeble health. Preston returned from Columbia in the Stage & is now with me.

Monday 3....The Court did not sit to day by request of the members of the bar. At 12 ocl. a public meeting was called & upon the assembling of the people in the Courthouse, Mr. Griffin, Intendant of the Town was placed in the chair & Mr. [James] Terry appointed Secty. A committee of 32 was on motion of Mr. Wardlaw appointed to prepare resolutions for the consideration of the meeting. A series of resolutions were submitted by him as chairman of the Committee in favour of the annexation of Texas to the Government of the United States. Mr. Wardlaw[,] Col. Pickens & Mr. Yancy addressed the meeting. Another resolution was offered by Wigfall approving of the nomination of Mr. Polk of Tenessee for the Presidency & pledging the support of the District. At the close of the meeting it was announced by the chair that Major Jeter had resigned his office as Senator & Col. Pickens announced as a candidate to fill the vacancy. Every thing seemed to have been settled by previous arrangement so as to forestall public opinion & prevent easy opposition to the Major's nominee. Thus we practice at home, the same conduct, which we denounce abroad. The meeting adjourned in good order.

[written vertically on the left side of this page, over the text above:] Col. Pickens assures me that there was no understanding between himself & Major Jeter & that his name was announced as a candidate by the importuning of friends & not at his insistance.

Tuesday 4th....The Court was in session from 10 ocl. A.M. till 6 P.M. I was unwell & suffering from headache....

Wednesday 5th....I dined by invitation with my neighbour County [Compty] in the Village & in the evening spent a few hours at Doct. Mays, at a small party of young people.

Thursday 6th....I dined with Col. Pickens. The party consisted of Judge Harper & Butler, myself, Genl. Bonham, Mr. Yancy, Mr. Maragnie [Maragne] & Col. P. S.

Brooks. Our host was agreeable and gave us a sumptuous dinner and seven or eight varieties of excellent wine. I will note the courses at dinner as a matter of some curiosity to after times. The first course was soup & a slice of loaf bread, folded in a napkin & placed on your plate. The Second was boiled Salmon & potatoes with bread alone. The third was a course of meats, consisting of lamb, (boiled, roasted & made into chops) ham and a variety of vegetables. The next was a pair of ducks & macarone. And the last consisted of curd & custard & various sweetmeats by way of dessert. A bowl was then placed before each guest with fresh water, & two orange or lemon leaves floating on the surface, in which he could wash his hands & face, if he so desired. The afternoon was then brought to a close in tasting the fine wines of our hospitable host & making comments upon their comparative goodness & age. Some of the gentlemen talked most learnedly about the different importations of wine, their particular merits, cost &C. In this part of the art of gastronomy, I am a novice & I therefore sat in silence. Col. Pickens makes an agreeable host & entertains his company in a style of munificent hospitality and splendor, exceeding any gentleman in the up country. I have no taste for show & parade but do not condemn it in others, who have the means & inclination to indulge in them. The company was agreeable & in good spirits & made the afternoon pass away very pleasantly.

Friday 7th....In the evening we invited a few of our friends to tea. It was a small party, given to our neighbours Mr. Lipscomb & Doct. Mays & families. I passed an agreeable afternoon & the company seemed at ease & social & talkative.

Saturday 8th....We attended a party at Mr. Bausketts, given in complement to Mr. Wadlington, who is a nephew to Mr. B, & his bride, who were all in their first visit to this place. The supper was sumptuous & tasteful. The company was however rather dull and talked with but little or no animation. Our host & hostess were very civil & attentive. A barbacue was given at the Spring near the Village by subscription, and which I am very sorry to learn there was great excess and drinking & many of our Young men were intoxicated.

Sunday 9th....We attended service at the Epis. Church, and heard a sensible sermon by Mr. Walker. He seems to have made a favourable impression on his congregation & to give satisfaction....

....

Tuesday 11....On walking over my fields, I discovered that [yesterday's] rain had pretty thoroughly wet the earth & had greatly revived both corn & all vegetables. It is the best season, that has fallen in a month, in fact Since the month of March. At my farm the land was washed in places & too wet to admit the plough. Cool & cloudy in the afternoon & at night fire was necessary to comfort. Preston & I paid a visit to Judge Butler, whom we found walking over his farm & enjoying the prospect of his crop.

Wednesday 12th....I rode over my crop in the morning. Cotton at Hawthorn Glen is from half leg to half thigh high. I saw several blooms & as many as two on one stalk of cotton. On another stalk I counted 25 forms. The corn looks pretty well & about half of it is as high as my horse & some portion at the old farm is in tassel. I saw the first tassel in my fields on the 8th. Judge Butler dined with me. I began to plow over my corn the third time on Monday & finished plowing my cotton this morning the second time. Oats are ripening.

Thursday 13th....I set out to my plantation by the way of Major Blockers, where I dined & then took Wm. Blocker & went through the Clegg Settlement by blind paths & part of the time through the woods. On arriving at the plantation I was forced by headache to take a bed.

Friday 14....I rode over my crop, which I found in very clean order but growing slowly for the want of rain. The corn crop is superior to any I have ever had at this period of the year & the cotton crop is very promising & and fine condition. The wheat is cut & put under cover. The rye is cut & shocked & they are cutting the oats. The entire crop is suffering for rain. I set out for home at 9 ocl. & arrived at 2, meeting my waggon with planks on the road, which had come down the day previous to bring a load of corn to my friend Carroll as a present & take back a load of lumber. A refreshing shower of rain fell about 5 ocl and another in the night. I heard at Smyley,[31] that Preston S. Brooks was appointed to deliver an address on the 4 of July at Smyley's.

Saturday 15th....My ploughmen report that the earth is too wet for the plough, which is the first instance of the kind since March. In the afternoon I paid a visit to Col. Pickens in company with Mrs. B. & Ellen. The Col. seems somewhat annoyed at the signs of opposition to his election to the Senate of the State, which are developing themselves in the Village & in Hamburg. The Hamburg Journal contains a severe article in opposition to him. I fear that in the end, he will discover that his friends were indiscreet in urging him to be a candidate & that it was short sighted policy in him to give his consent. Success cannot benefit him in any material degree, while on the other hand had a strong vote in favour of his opponent will greatly impair the strength of his position in the State & a defeat will be totally disastrous to all his hopes to a seat in the Senate of the U. N. States. To desire too much is to court defeat. We called on the Revd. Mr. Johnson.

Sunday 16th....Mrs. B. directed all our little negroes to be dressed this morning & to attend at Sunday school. It was no unpleasant sight to a benevolent mind to see them with clean dresses & newly combed heads marching towards the Church, to meet the Pastor & his assistants, their faces beaming with smiles & gratification. It is a difficult task to perform our duties towards this class of our household with reference to their proper & necessary government & to our sense of humanity. Without the enforcement of perfect subordination the slave becomes unruly & troublesome & the rigid enforcement of discipline is painful & distasteful to the owner so

[31] Col. James C. Smyley (1820–1872), home on Meeting Street road.

that upon the whole it is often a conflict between duty & feeling. This is the anniversary of our marriage. Twenty six years ago Mrs. B. & I united our destinies & I truly thank God that I am not in the condition of a worthy female friend of ours, who unthoughtedly said, that she had been married so long, "that she was tired of it." I believe that neither Mrs. B or myself are tired of our bonds but on the contrary that every day that is added to our married state only makes us dearer & more necessary to each other & I humbly pray God to grant us a new lease. We & our household are in health & enjoying a reasonable share of success & prosperity in whatever appertains to this life. I humbly pray unto God, that he would keep us in such a subdued & thankful frame of mind, so that we may never be unmindful or insensible to his great blessings & of our utter & total dependence upon his munificent hand.

Monday 17th....I began to cut oats at my farm. On going to the Village I was informed that Mr. F[rancis] H. Wardlaw had announced himself as a candidate for the [SC] Senate in opposition to Col. Pickens. I am not informed of the grounds upon which this opposition has been originated nor the principles upon which his Supporters intend to rely for success. I shall vote for Pickens under the persuasion that he is much the ablest & most efficient man, of much more promise & influence in the State & qualified to render greater services to the District. Wardlaw is nevertheless a gentleman of intelligence, of sound judgment and of an unexceptionable moral character & would make a useful & respectable Senator. Mrs. Brooks has been much indisposed throughout the day but is better this evening. Our Servant Betsy had a daughter about 12 ocl & is doing well. Heavy cloud at 9 ocl & much thunder and lightning. Rain is greatly wanted in various quarters of the District & particularly about Cambridge. A heavy rain fell about 11 ocl at night, accompanied with wind, thunder & lightning.

Tuesday 18th....I rode to Preston's & over his crop and returned by Col. [William H.?] Moss Mill. The rain at night was heavy & washing in many places. Preston's crop is pretty good & in clean order. His neighbour's crops are in good order but small. In returning I learned in the Village that the election for a Senator is exciting considerable interest & confident expectations are entertained by Wardlaws friends that he will beat Pickens with ease. I am satisfied that in the end Pickens will discover that his candidacy for this office will prove the most short sighted & impolitic of all other acts in the whole history of his political life. Success can confer no benefit while defeat will blight his prospects for promotion for many years, if not for life....[32]

....

Thursday 20th....I recd. a letter from Hamburg, advising me to sell my cotton as there was some demand for the article. A heavy rain fell in the afternoon & night, attended with hail in different places. Doct. [Guiger's] corn was much injured.

[32] F. W. Pickens was elected.

Friday 21....I left home for Hamburg, taking Hampden with me, where I arrived to dinner....I sold 46 bags of my own cotton at 5 ¼ cts & 50 of my fathers at 6 ¼ to Mr. Wray....I had a headache, which forced me to take my bed at 6 ocl & from which I suffered great pain. Hunter gave me a comfortable room & a clean & pleasant bed. The election for a Senator to the State Legislature is the topic of general conversation in Hamburg.

Saturday 22....I left Hamburg & returned by Kelly's where a militia company was to muster, & at which I found some ten or fifteen candidates for different offices. The crops of corn between Edgefield & Hamburg are inferior, greatly inferior to the two last crops but the cotton looks well & most of it is in blossom. This part of the District has suffered for the want of rain....

Sunday 23rd....Divine service at the Epis. Church by the Revd. Mr. Walker. Whitfield arrived from Columbia in good health.

....

Wednesday 26....I rode to Preston's, whom I found engaged in writing his 4th of July speech....

Thursday 27....I rode of over my farm with Doct. Mays.

....

Saturday 29th....I had a violent attack of headache, which deprived me of the pleasure of seeing and conversing with a few friends, whom we had invited to tea. Doct. Laborde & family arrived from Columbia to pass the summer with his friends in this place.

Sunday 30th....I was rendered so feeble by the attack yesterday as to be unable to attend church. My sister Mrs. Blocker spent the day with us – the entire month has been favourable to the agriculturalist & the present prospect of corn & cotton is equal to the best crop since 1829. The wheat crop is good but the oat crop is light & inferior. I never had a better crop at my farm. A small lot of cotton is waist high.

July 1, 1844

Monday 1. Very warm & oppressive. This was sale day but the assemblage of persons at the Village unusually small. The real estate of Col. Benj Frazier was sold & I purchased a pine land tract of 173 acres for $235. The candidates for the Legislature very active &C.

....

Wednesday 3....I went in company with the boys to look at a tract of land, which I purchased on Monday. It is well timbered but the soil is thin. It will furnish me & all my children with timber for 20 years....James and his wife arrived on a visit, to remain the balance of the summer. They are both in good health –

Thursday 4th. Pleasant morning with brisk breezes from the north & partially cloudy. I attended the celebration of this day at [James] Smyley's. The declaration of Independence was read by Doct.[John] Landrum & an oration by P. S. Brooks, which was received with enthusiastic applause. The oration was well written and delivered in a pleasing and animated style. The assemblage of persons was from 300 to 400, consisting of men, women & boys & even children & altho there was a large quantity of ardent spirits drank, the crowd behaved well & separated without any personal collisions or violence. Upon the whole it was a spirited celebration. There were several short addresses in reply to complimentary toasts, one from the reader of the declaration of Independence Doct. Landrum, one from the Orator of the day, one from Genl. Bonham in reply to a sentiment offered to the memory of his brother [James Butler] & Col. Traverse,[33] who were slain in the Alamo in Texas by the Mexican's. Col. Bauskett prefaced his toast by a speech of some 15 minutes on the oppressions of the Tariff & the present attitude of the State in reference to the resolutions of the Legislature in 1842, on that subject. A toast was offered by the committee of arrangements to my father, to which Preston responded in a few remarks. I left the ground at 5 ocl & reached home before Sunset. At night we attended a display of fire works, which was gotten up by subscription.

....

Saturday 6th....Mrs. B. & I paid a visit to Major Blockers where we met my father. I called to see Mr. Ioor who is in a rapid decline & cannot live much longer.

Sunday 7th. This was an exceedingly oppressive day. The Ther stood at 93 ½° at my house....

Monday 8th. Still warm & clear in the morning but heavy clouds in the afternoon and very light showers of rain. I was employed in setting some _____ Major Blocker at the request of my father

Tuesday 9th....I went to my plantation taking Whitfield & Hampden with me where we arrived at 1 ocl, finding the crop, suffering for the want of rain. In the afternoon I rode over my crop. The corn is very good & altogether forms the best crop that I have ever made. About 200 acres of cotton is very promising & the balance of 75 acres is rather small, being on old & worn land. The negroes were all well.

Wednesday 10th....I rode through a part of the neighbourhood, & took a view of the crops. They are not very promising.

Thursday 11....I paid a visit to Col. [Oliver] Towles & transacted some business with him. He is an agreeable companion & clever gentleman. In the afternoon I

---

[33] William Barret Travis (1809–1836), born in NE Edgefield Dist. Family moved to AL in 1818, where he studied law, published a newspaper, married, and had a son. In 1831 he abandoned his family and creditors for Texas, where he joined the resistance against Mexican rule. He was commissioned in the rebellion force in 1835. In Feb. 1836 he commanded the rebel force in San Antonio, which he moved to the nearby Alamo. He died there on March 6 as Santa Anna's forces overran the Alamo.

called to see old Mr. Bean, who was very sick. I prepared a deed of settlement for the benefit of his daughter, Mrs. Saunders, to whom he secured a portion of his estate –

Friday 12th....I returned home & was sorry to find our daughter Sarah [Ann Means, b.1824?] very sick & under medical treatment. I had a paroxysm of head ache, which confined me to the bed the entire afternoon. I learned from Preston that the Citizens had determined to give a barbacue to the Honble Geo. McDuffie on Saturday the 27th instant.

Saturday 13th....I rode over my crop, which is very good, the best in fact that I have ever made at this place. I called on Mr. Clempson [Clemson] & Mr. Jas. E. Calhoun at Col. Pickens where I met Mrs. John C. Calhoun, who had come down to meet her daughter [Anna Maria], who is about to take her departure to accompany her husband Mr. Clempson to Belgium, as minister at the Court of that Government. They were all in good spirits & appear to be much pleased at the appointment of Mr. Clempson to this mission. Mr. Clempson appears to be an educated clever gentleman but I have taken up the impression that he wants judgment & is deficient in energy of character & firmness of purpose. I declined to serve as one of the committee of arrangements, to get up a dinner to Mr. McDuffie. My health forbids me to undertake the fatigue, if I had no other objection but the time is too short.

Sunday 14th....We attended church & heard a sermon by Mr. Walker.

Monday 15th....I rode through a portion of the neighbourhood, looking for a cow & calf, which I desire to purchase.

....

Wednesday 17th....Corn is suffering for the want of rain. I learned that my old neighbour James Bean died on Monday last. He was an honest and good citizen.

Thursday 18th....I am running the sweep through my corn, followed by the hoes, cutting away the grass & putting a little earth to the corn.

Friday 19th....I went to my neighbour [Daniel?] Hollands, to get a cow & calf from his house[.] I paid a visit to Judge Butler who recd. me with more marks of affection, than usual.

Saturday 20th ....A letter was recd. from Mr. McDuffie, stating that his health would prevent his attendance at the dinner, which was proposed to be given to him by his friends at this place on the 27th instant. There was a barbaque in the dark corner [modern McCormick County], at which all of the candidates are expected to be present.

Sunday 21....Judge Butler & Col. Carroll dined with me.

Monday 22nd....I had yesterday a good rain at the farm and a wetting rain this afternoon according to the report of my servants. This last rain will bring my corn crop to maturity, which will now, I think, be a good one.

Tuesday 23rd....We are preparing to pay a short visit to Roselands. The election for Clerk of the Court of common Pleas is now being held. About 175 votes were given to the managers yesterday, of which [Edmund] Bacon recd. more than three fourths. His election is beyond dispute. I invited a large number of friends to a water mellon party yesterday evening but the rain prevented the larger portion from attending. It is our usual luck, for the last three years we have never failed to have rain or a storm at the very moment, when our friends were expected. We took our departure for the plantation about 8 ocl & arrived to dinner where we met James & his Wife, who had gone up on Monday....My crop is suffering greatly for the want of rain.

Wedneday 24th. This was a day of rest & frolick to my negroes. I gave them a barbaque dinner at which all were present, men, women & children, together with the wives of several from the adjoining plantations. They were all, dressed in clean clothes & looked exceedingly gratified. After they had concluded dinner, they formed in line & each took a drink of spirits in my presence, drinking toasts, as they proceeded. I recollect the toast of my man Henry. It was – "the Lord give us grace, to run our race & heaven be our resting place." Their conduct was decorous & becoming. After the toast drinking, I left them to close the evening, agreeably to their own tastes & to divide the remains of the barbaque. The manner in which they enjoyed the dinner, did not fail to give me pleasure & gratification, that I had given them this day of rest & merriment....

Thursday 25th....I rode to Cambridge, where I met a few friends from whom I heard no news. The crops in this section are unpromising. The planters have suffered greatly for the want of rain. On my return I rode through my plantation & was pained to see the parched state of the earth & the suffering condition of my crop. I have 175 acres of good corn & about 200 acres of fair cotton. Thirty acres of highland corn & 75 of cotton on old land will not yield more than half a crop. If I could have had seasonable weather from 1 July to this time, I should have the best crop, that ever grew on my plantation. Several of my neighbours will scarcely make a support.

Friday 26th. We left the plantation at an early hour & arrived at home at half past 12 ocl. where we found all well. A very sad occurrence had taken place during our absence. A young man by the name of McDowell, a school master of the Ridge, cut his throat, near the road in the vicinity of Jas. Murrells. It is supposed that a morbid sensibility connected with the chagrin & mortification at the past [irregular ?] habits of his, preyed with such power on his feelings as to bring him to the dreadful resolution of terminating his existence. Mortified pride at the remembrance of former respectability & shame for present degradation, will unsettle the judgment of the most resolute & firm. I rode in the afternoon to my farm, which was visited during my absence with a storm of wind & rain, which has blown down my corn & washed my land. Judge Butler took tea with us & left us after 9 ocl. to return home by the light of a clear & bright moon....

Saturday 27th....I have given my negroes holiday, having finished my crop last night. About 5. Ocl. there fell a heavy rain, which continued until near 9 ocl. at night. I presume from the appearance of the cloud that the rain has been extensive.

Sunday 28th....Attended at the Epis. church services by Mr. Walker, a poor preacher tho a very good man.

Monday 29th....Recd. a letter from my overseer, informing me that a good shower of rain had fallen on my plantation on Saturday evening which was greatly needed.

Tuesday 30th....I was indisposed & unable to leave my room. The delegates to the [state] temperance convention arrived this afternoon in considerable numbers.

Wednesday 31....At 10 ocl the convention met & the meeting was organized by Judge O'Neal as the presiding officer, who delivered an interesting address. Committees were appointed to prepare business for the convention, on which a recess was taken until 3 o'clock. At this hour Mr. M. Willi[ams] from Camden addressed the convention for upwards of an hour in a sensible, forcible & efficacious speech. Some debating among the members also took place tho not very able or exciting yet it afforded entertainment & instruction. I was much entertained by the Revd. Mr. [Benjamin?] Culpepper, who combines, wit, drollery & sound sense to a rather awkward but facetious manner. He makes a pretty good speech, tells a good story & sings pleasing Song. On the whole he is a very happy & clever fellow.

August 1, 1844

Thursday 1. The convention again convened and transacted a good deal of business. There was a good deal of interesting discussion during the morning & afternoon session. At night the Revd. Mr. Turner delivered an able address in the general cause of temperance & again occupied the attention of the convention by reading one of the most lucid & able reports, that it has been my good fortune to hear. He is an able & promising young man. The addresses of Mr. Garlington & [Revd.] Dubose are spoken of in terms of approbation – after 10 ocl. at night the convention adjourned in great harmony & good feelings. I opened my doors & extended what hospitality was in my power to the delegates during the meeting. I had from 3 to 5 constantly in my house & in the evening from 10 to 12 persons to tea. Among the number was Judge ONeal[,] Col. McWillie, Mr. Dubose Mr. Jno. Brice Mr. Pope, Doct. Simpson, Mr. Aire, Aldrige Summers & others. I was much entertained & gratified with the proceedings of the convention & here record my approbation of their principles & purposes. I was an attentive observer & listener & really at last was very much in the condition of Agrippa before Paul – "I was almost persuaded to give my signature to the pledge--"

Friday 2....The delegates took their departure at an early hour for their respective homes. In the afternoon a very heavy rain fell....

Saturday 3....In the forenoon and I rode over my farm in company with Doct. Laborde & examined my crop, which [they?] pronounced an excellent one. We invited several of our friends & most of the young people to a watermellon party at my farm in the afternoon. The party was numerous, gay & cheerful & enjoyed a repast of good melons with great zest.

Sunday 4th....We attended service and the Episc. Church, where the congregation was small but attentive.

Monday 5th....I have rarely seen so few persons and the Village on Sale day there not being over 100. No news local or foreign. The Charleston Courier contains some account of the great Whig mass meeting, which took place in Georgia on Wednesday the 31st.

It is computed that 15,000 persons were on the grounds – the only new development of parties at this meeting, was the open adhesion of the Whig party to the tariff policy with [J. M.] Berrien[,] [W. C.] Preston & [Waddy] Thompson as the prominent actors & Speakers on the occasion. With what beautiful harmony & consistency does the conduct of my friends compare with their fiery nullification doctrines in 1832. They were then armed to the teeth in opposition to the tariff, ready to peril not only the Union but life & property in the then supposed glorious contest for right & principle. They are now singing hosannas to the Union under the operations of a tariff avowedly for protection & more oppressive to the planting States than that of 1828. Political consistency is the rarest of all virtues in the life of a public man. The game of politics like games of hazard, gradually undermines and saps the moral principle and reconciles in the end any course however questionable in the pursuit of a great party object. In the short space of five years [a] man may become the antipode of himself in his political opinions, principles & conduct & yet can look at the change without a blush or a feeling of shame. To preserve the Soul's whiteness is one of the first dictates of Sound wisdom, if we wish a peaceful conscience.

Tuesday 6th....I went to the Village to complete the purchase of the Youngblood tract of land, which I purchased yesterday for $450 at Shff sale under an order from the Ordinary for the purpose of partition. I made some arrangements preparatory to my departure for the [Glenn] Springs in Spartanburg. This is Preston's birthday, being 25 years of age. He spent the day & night with us in good health & spirits.

Wednesday 7th....I sent Whitfield to my father's to learn the state of his health & to meet me at my plantation to furnish me with the desired information.

Thursday 8. I left home at 12 ocl for my plantation on my way to the Glenn Spring....Friday 9th. I rode over my plantation & examined the State of the crop, which I found greatly injured by the dry weather. Whitfield arrived from my fathers, giving me the pleasing information, that my father's health is pretty good. I set off after dinner for Genl. Gilliam's where I arrived at sunset but found the Genl. & his lady from home but his son Robert was at home by whom I was hospitably entertained. I met with Mr. Key & Shear on their way to Glen Spring. In referring to dates I discover that I went to the plantation on Wednesday & to Genl. Gilliam's on Thursday – on friday morning I rode over a portion of General Gilliam's crop, which I found to be good. On my way I paid a visit to R[ichard] Watts but an attack of headache deprived me of the pleasure of enjoying his & his family's society. I here met my old associate B. Watts Esq. who came to see me. We were both unwell he with fever & I with headache. In the afternoon I went as far as Doct. [Abner] Teag[ue]'s, suffering a good deal of pain on the road. This is a kind & attentive family to their guests & keep a good table.

Saturday 10th. I passed through Lauren's District into Spartanburg & arrived at the Glen Spring in the afternoon. The day was exceedingly hot & clear. The Therm.t up to 97°. On this road the crops have suffered great injury from the drought. I saw many plantations, on which not more than 2 bushels of corn on average can be gathered from an acre. I saw as much as 100 acres that cannot make anything but fodder. The cotton was not more than from half leg to knee high & the greater part of it open. After passing Enoree River the crops began to improve & those in the neighbourhood of the springs were average crops. I found at the Springs from 50 to 60 persons in the public House & from 300 to 400 in the cabbins.

Sunday 11th....We had a sermon from a Mr. Hope, a Lutheran clergyman. He was sensible & very liberal.

Monday 12th. I began the use of the Waters & divided my time as to spend it pleasantly and profitably. I took two glasses of water early in the morning before rising from bed, rose at 5, dressed & visited the Spring at 6. & took two more glasses of Water. At 7 partook of a well dressed breakfast[,] rode at 8, read till 12 & then began again to drink Water, dined at 1. talked read or rested until 4. then rode, returned & took tea at 6. After tea passed an hour either in the drawing room with the ladies or in the dancing room, looking on the merry dance, then returned to my room, read until nine, drank Water & went to Bed. I occasionally passed an hour in playing a game of Whist.[34] I was particular and abstemious in my diet. The company at this spring was composed of respectable & well educated families & young men of good & moral character with a number of accomplished young ladies. They formed an agreeable society, with which I passed many pleasant hours during my stay at this Watering place.

Tuesday 13th. The same routine of occupations. In riding out in the afternoon I was caught in a light rain.

Wednesday 14. The same mode of passing the time.

Thursday 15. No change.

Friday 16. I rode to the gold mine of Black & Co. but I was not taken with the golden mania.

Saturday 17th. The old routine.

---

[34] An English card game, which evolved into contract bridge.

Sunday 18th. No change. We had no preaching.

Monday 19th. Idem –

Tuesday 20th. No change & news. A rather singular occurrence took place about this time. A gentleman labouring under mania a potes, conceived that, evil spirits or the Devil were endeavoring to carry him off & in the alarm of his feelings, he jumped out of a second story Window. He was bruised but not seriously injured.

Wednesday 21....Again the regular routine of drinking water &C &C.

Thursday 22. A continuation of the same life.

Friday 23rd. The Same.

Saturday 24th. Another warm & dry day. Governor Hammond arrived at the Hotel on his way to the Limestone incampment of officers. He was in excellent health & spirits.

Sunday 25th....a little cooler. Preaching in the morning by Mr. Philips of the Epis. church, in the afternoon by Doct. Johnson of the Babtist church & at night again by Mr. Philips.

Monday 26th....After breakfast I took my departure for home by the way of Laurens Ct. Ho[use] where I stopped for a short time & called to see B. Watts, who was confined to his room by fever. I arrived at night at Mrs. Boyds.

Tuesday 27th....I set off after early breakfast, stopped for a short time to see Capt. Cunningham & family, passed through Cambridge & stopped at the plantation of N[athan]. L. Griffin Esq. to get dinner & feed my horses. After dinner I passed by Reeves Martin's, into my plantation & rode over the greater part of my crop. The corn crop is very good one, having been early planted on my low land & well cultivated, but my cotton crop is very inferior. The cotton has grown but little since the middle of July and now exhibits in its brown leaf & faded appearance the very matured & decaying state of the Middle of October in the ordinary seasons. I cannot make more than 2/3 of a crop. The peas look well but are suffering for rain. My overseer had out about 20,000 lb of cotton and from 40 to 50 hogs in a separate lot, intended for pork for the use of the plantation. My negroes were well & the mules & horses in good order.

Wednesday 28th....I left the plantation after early breakfast & reached home by 12 ocl. & met my family in fine health, for which I desire in all sincerity to return thanks to God.

Thursday 29....I paid a visit to the Village but heard no news. I also rode over my crop at my farm. Both corn & cotton exceed my expectations.

Friday 30th. I again rode & examined my crop at the farm. The corn crop will be good & the cotton looks well and in a growing state. The pea & potatoe crops exhibit luxuriant vines but not much fruit yet. By an imprudent mixture of food at dinner I brought on a violent attack of headache, from which I suffered until 1 ocl at night without sleep.

Saturday 31....It is now warm & dry. The entire month has been warm & dry with the exception of three or four days of last week, when fire was necessary to comfort & but little rain has fallen except a perfect flud, which fell on tuesday the 13th. which caused the water courses about the Village to be higher than they were ever known to be before. I am inclined to think from what I have seen & heard that the cotton crop in this State will fall below the crop of last year from 25 to 50.000 bales. Corn in the upper Districts will be high & if the winter should be long & cold, it certainly will fall short of the necessary supply. The seasons in this District have been more favourable than in any other quarter of the State from which I have recd. positive information. The supply of corn in this District will be sufficient for the support of the inhabitants. Many planters however will be compelled to purchase but what may be wanted in one neighbourhood will be supplied by another –

September 1, 1844.

Sunday 1st....It is exceedingly dry & the wells are beginning to fail. We attended divine service in the Epis. church....

Monday 2. Another dry, warm & oppressive day. Ther. 92°. & in exposed situations up to 94°. This being sale day about 200 persons were collected in the Village & while the officers were selling the property on the Steps of the Courthouse Jos. Glover[35] came up & calling upon L. Gomillion[36] to defend himself[,] drew a pistol & fired at Gomillion. The ball passed through the coat of Gomillion in 2 or 3 places but did not touch his body. Gomillion also fired his pistol charged with buckshot & put the greater part of the load into the arm & neck of Col. Moss,[37] who was badly wounded. He also discharged another pistol at Glover, which entered Glover's side near the right [breast?] which killed him instantly. Several other persons were in eminent danger & one gentleman is reported to have had his hair, singed by a shot from Gomillion's pistol. I have seen no one, who condemn's Gomillion as he was forced in self-defense to shoot Glover or be run out of the Village. Glover had sworn to kill him & the attack was deliberate & premeditated. This spot of ground has been the theatre of two bloody rencounters with firearms in each of which life was taken. Is there no method by legislative enactment to punish offenders, who carry about them deadly weapons in such manner as to prevent a pernicious & sav-

[35] Joseph W. Glover dueled with Samuel Bacon in 1839. In the first exchange, Bacon hit Glover. When Glover drew another pistol, Lewis Wigfall, Bacon's second, passed him a pistol. Further bloodshed was averted when Glover charged Bacon, they dropped their weapons, and wrestled until separated.

[36] This affair elicited a strongly worded plea from the editor of the *Adv.*, Sept. 4, 1844. Lovett Gomillion, born c. 1821; 1850 census: $2,000, real estate, 10 slaves, turned himself in after this affray. He was indicted for murder, but was found not guilty. See also WB's entry for April 7, 1845.

[37] W. H. Moss, born c. 1800, had been sheriff, 1836–1840; 1850 census: $10,000 real estate; 40 slaves.

age practice, now too much in vogue among riotous & quarrelsome men? It is much to be desired that some remedy be devised to put this practice down.

Tuesday 3rd....I rode over my farm & examined my crop. My corn crop is very good & the pea crop in the size & luxurience of vine is superior to any crop for many years past ~~past~~ but there is yet but little fruit on them & they are now suffering daily injury for the want of rain. I also visited Mr. Presley & engaged him to gin my small cotton crop, which he is to do at the 13th. Col. Moss is reported to be doing well, with not much fever.

....

Thursday 5th....I am preparing to leave home for Greenville.

Friday 6th. I went to my plantation, where I found some of the negroes unwell. No change in the crop. I have out about 50,000 lb. of cotton –

The overseer was engaged in repairing the gin.

Saturday 7. I left the plantation about 12 ocl. for Capt. Cunningham's,[38] at whose hospitable house I arrived in the evening & recd. a cordial welcome. His negroes were suffering from fever.

Sunday 8th. I set out for Greenville, passing through Laurens District & arrived at night at Mr. Goldsmith's. The crops on the road indifferent.

Monday 9th....I arrived in Greenville Village in the morning & took lodgings at Col. Coleman's. I met here Mr. Seabrook, Doct. Davis, & several other gentlemen from the low country, who had met in Greenville to attend the agricultural society. In the afternoon I called on Judge Thompson & [John] Wesley Brooks. I found the people of the Village & District much excited on the Presidential election. In the evening I was attacked by nausea & headache, from which I suffered great pain until 9 ocl next morning. At this hour I dressed & attended a meeting of the Agri Society, altho very feeble[,] & assisted in the business so far [as] my health would admit. The day was inclement & rain continued to fall gently until night.

Tuesday 10. As above stated the agricultural Society was organized & did some business. A respectable number of members were in attendance.

Wednesday 11....The concourse of persons was large & respectable & the exhibitions of stock consisting of horses, cattle, hogs, sheep and & mules, numerous & highly creditable to the District. Some fine specimens of fruit were presented to the Society by Mrs. Poinsett,[39] which were distributed among the ladies. At 1 ocl. The Honorable Jno. B. ONeal delivered a small & eminently practical address to the Society & to a very large large auditory. The Society closed its labours about 3 ocl.

---

[38] Capt. Robert Cunningham?, Laurens Dist., died 1846. Father of Ann Pamela Cunningham who led the campaign to save Mt. Vernon.

[39] Mary Izard Pringle, Santee River planter's widow, married Joel Roberts Poinsett (1779–1851) in 1833. He was a Unionist, ambassador to Mexico 1825–1830, Sec. of War, and was now living in retirement in Greenville.

in great harmony & under the most favourable auspices in regard to its future prospects for usefulness.

Thursday 12th. I left Greenville at an early hour for the Glen Spring, in conformity with my determination when I left home altho I greatly regretted to decline an invitation of Mr. Poinsett to spend the day with him. I arrived at night at the Walker house[40] in the Village of Spartanburgh, one of the most comfortable public houses in the upcountry, in every respect. I passed a night with my friend & relation Wesley Brooks, who is a kind & warmhearted friend & who has an exceedingly interesting family of daughters. He lives about a mile from the Village of Greenville.

Friday 13th..... I left Spartanburgh for the Glenn Spring after breakfast & reached the latter place at 11 ocl. where I met a large company of Visitors, among whom was Mrs. Jno. C. Calhoun & her party.[41] I soon commenced my usual routine of using the Water[,] exercise &C.

Saturday 14th. I joined a party to the Knot mine, distant from the Springs some 3 or 4 miles. We saw the process of diging, the gold oar & then crushing it under iron wheels & washing it. The steam engine, which propelled the machinery, was a fine specimen of art, manufactured at Philadelphia & cost about $2000. The owner of the machine was working it upon shares.

Sunday 15th. The Revd. Mr. Hoke delivered a sermon in the reception room of the tavern....

....

Wednesday 18th. No change in the weather. A noble & eloquent letter of Judge Chevis[42] on the political condition of the Country & in reference to the proper course of this State appeared in the Mercury. It created considerable sensation at the Springs & must produce great effect over public opinion at the South.

....

Saturday 21. Drinking water & riding morning and evening again the order of the day.

Sunday 22. This was a mild & pleasant day. I went in company with Mr. Seabrook to a babtist protracted meeting in the District of Union and about 10 miles from the Springs. There was a very large concourse of persons of all ages, sizes, sexes & con-

---

[40] Rev. Newton Pinckney Walker opened a school for deaf children in his family's former hotel in 1849. Today it serves the blind also. Its main building is named Walker Hall.

[41] Floride Bonneau Colhoun (1792–1866), the senator's second cousin.

[42] Langdon Cheves (1776–1857), Abbeville native, lawyer, legislator, speaker of the U.S. House, state appeals court judge, president of the 2nd Bank of the U.S., power broker in SC politics. His letter appeared Sept. 11, 1844, and was published separately soon after. It lamented the protective Tariff Law of 1842 and called for southern states to respond by forming associations that would, if sufficiently alarmed, coordinate in planning a defense against it.

ditions, supposed to be from 2 to 3000. I heard a sensible sermon by the Revd. Mr. Rice of Pendleton Dist. with whom I served in the Legislature in 1833 to 34. He was then a nullifier & made a good member of the Legislature but he was particularly distinguished for the humor & ready wit, which he displayed as chairman of the mock sessions at the close of each Legislature – I also met the Revd. Dr. W. B. Johnson from Edgefield, who is an intelligent gentleman & very agreeable companion. He preached in the afternoon. We dined with Capt. Gist –

....

Tuesday 24....About this time the Newberry people left the Springs. It required 10 waggons besides many carriages & conveyances of different kinds to accommodate the party for removal –

Wednesday 25. I left the Springs after breakfast for home & arrived at night at Mr. Nance's in Lauren's, who is a most excellent host & keeps the best table, that I have set down to for many a day in the Country.

Thursday 26. I left Mr. Nance after breakfast & arrived at my plantation to dinner, where I found some of my negroes sick. The overseer had gathered the Burns field of corn of 50 acres, which will yield at least 1200 bushels. I had about 40 acres of rye sowed & up for pastures & about 60 bales of cotton picked out. In the afternoon I reached home and joined my family at Mrs. Labordes, where they were spending the evening. All well.

Friday 28th....I rode over my crop at the farm & found it improved, particularly the peas & cotton. I also heard the particulars of the loss sustained by Doct. Nicholson by the washing away of his newly erected Merchant Mill & of the death of Capt. Cunningham's servant Mike by a sudden rise in Turkey Creek –

Saturday 28....I visited the Village & recd. some account of the dinner to Mr. McDuffie & of his & Burt's speech.

Sunday 29. Attended service at the Epis. church. In the afternoon my father & Mrs. N[ancy]. Blocker arrived home on a visit to us. His health is pretty good but his strength is failing.

Monday 30. A light hoar frost this morning. I accompanied my father to the Village & assisted him in the purchase of sundry articles &C – I heard nothing in the way of news – this has been a peculiar month in many respects. There have fallen but three rains & they at regular intervals & they did not last exceeding 12 hours at each rain & then the weather became clear & pleasant. It has been altogether a dry month & in consequence all late corn suffered greatly & cannot yield above half a crop. The streams & water courses are low & in some places it has become inconvenient to get corn ground. The State generally has been unusually healthy tho in certain localities fever has prevailed to some extent & in many instances has proven fatal. Cotton in the beginning of the season sold low at from $5 ½ to 6 & as high as 6 1/8. Corn is 50 cts. & flour from $4.50 to 5 per barrel.

A catalogue of negroes, owned by me in 1843, at home & at the plantation.

Moses	Toney	Clarissa
Nancy	Rachel	Louis (checked and circled)
Berry	Wiley	Adrene
Henry	Nancy	Harrison
Frank	Cloe	Elizabeth
Albert	Allston	Madison
Garland	~~Louanna~~ dead	Bryant
Laura	Louiza	8 Sampson
George	~~Cealy~~ dead	Cicero (9
Betsy		Jane
L. Moses	Kitt	
Phill	Sally	Daniel C
Clarissa	Lewis (checked & circled)	C. George
Letty 14	Rose	Dianna
Child Jincy	Adam	Lanah
Charles	Peter	Ambrose
Crecy	Patty	Willis
Mariah	~~Eliza~~ 8 Dead	Chaney (checked & circled)
Eliza 4 Ned Nelson		
Child (blank)	Cain	Joe 9 (checked & circled)
	Jacob	
Old George	Hester	Frankie
Lyddy	Sidney	Hagar
John	Washington	Amelia
Allen	Centena	
Henry 5	Daphney 5	
Primus	Barnett	
Lewis	Sue 2	Nancy
Mary	Child L.	Barnett
Alartha	Joshua	Emma
Lucy	Louiza	Sam
Tom	Bella	James

Lyddy	Lilah 4	Judy
Edmund	Willis	(8 Morris
Daniel 8		B. Joe
[rest of column		Ebbin
"Given to James"]		
Jack	Joseph	Harry
Betsy	Paul	(2 Eliza
Julia	Ellick	child Mariah
Critty	Shelton	
William 6	Simon [checked	Hannah
Child John and Minerva		
In No. 15	Surry 7 circled]	L. Sue
	[last 3 checked & circled]	

The following partial index of this journal volume suggests that Brooks assumed that family members would want to read parts of his journal. Page numbers refer to his numbered pages, which have been deleted.

Difficulty between Carroll & Wigfall (page)	1
The same between Preston & W	3 to 10
Col, M. Fraziers marriage	6
Reflection on the past & a record of motive	8
Estimate expressed of the kindness of Inhabitants of Ham.	9
John P. Richardson elected Gor. By 104 to 47	10
Resignation of my trusteeship to academy	11
Visit of David L. Harper to Preston	12
Death of Mrs. G. Nicholson	15
Marriage of E. Mims to E. Addison	17
Unusually cold & gloomy weather	18
Great pressure in the money market	22
The Revd. Mr. Pinckney	24
Meeting at Camb[ridge] to form agricultural society	26
Stagnation of trade & depression of the market	28
Illness of Dr. Nicholson	30
Delay & mishaps to my waggon	31

(Remainder of the volume not indexed)

End of the first surviving volume

VOLUME II

NOTES:

WB's lower case a, meaning and, was changed to &. Raised letters, as with Co. (for Colonel; the l raised) are retained, but interlined additions are brought down.

SCHS Transcriber's Note: "The handwriting for [11/5/44] was cramped, covered with ink spots, and was difficult to read, possibly due to the spirits consumed at Col. Pickens' as the handwriting improved drastically on the 7th. Mr. Brooks does, however, suffer from headaches and other illnesses on a regular basis which also affect his handwriting."

Also, the transcriber has elected to reflect the original spelling, spacing, and punctuation of the diary except where necessary for clarity. I have generally gone along with this practice.

J.F.

November

Tuesday. [Nov] [5th] [1844]

. . . I walked through the Village at sunrise and saw no one in the streets except Mr. County [Compty]. Our daughter Ellen left us this morning for the Misses Stark in Columbia, for the Winters schooling. Miss Julia Lipscomb was in the carriage with her — & Mr. Jas. Mims[1] & his sister in company — They all departed with cheerful spirits and pleasing anticipations. I spent the afternoon with Col. Pickens, who had a large dinner party in compliment to Mr. Calhoun, who was on his return to Washington City with his family. Col. Pickens was agreeable and entertaining & played the part of host with great courtesy and hospitality. His dinner was excellent & his wines various & choice. We did not rise from table until after 7.Ocl. Mr. C– was both communicate & instructive as he always is but scarcely so cheerful and sanguine as when he passed a month since on his way to Pendleton — He appeared to be a little care worn & not as confident in regard to the future prospects ... South as to the results of the Presidenti...

[TORN]

...n glasses of wine at the dinner of my friend, produced a paroxism of headache from which I suffered through the entire day. I notwithstanding attended to planting out some peach nuts, which were sent to us by Mr. [Pea?] & to covering my potatoe banks — It is a great drawback upon my happiness that I cannot participate in the social pleasures of the festive board without paying a heavy penalty in suffering the succeeding day, be my indulgence ever so temperate & cautious.

Thursday 7th. I rose early & dressed by firelight for the purpose of making preparations for setting out for the plantation with Mrs. B & Hampden, the only members of the family now with me. The morning was clear & mild. In fact this has been an extraordinary fall for the mildness of the weather and the small quantity of rain, which has fallen. Occasional showers have fallen, which injured the cotton in the fields, more on account of the dry & porous condition of the earth than from the heaviness of the showers — Mr. Scarborough[2] a portrait painter has this moment called, to commence taking the likeness of Mrs. Brooks. I examined last evening an unfinished sketch of our mother Mrs. Carroll, by Mr. Scarb[orough] which promis-

---

[1] Julia Lipscomb Randall? (1829–1872); see entry of Nov. 18, 1845. She may have been a daughter of John and Sally Lipscomb. James H. Mims (c. 1818–), 1850 census: $8,000 real estate; 42 slaves.

[2] William Harrison Scarborough (1812–1871), itinerate portrait painter. Native of TN. Came to Charleston in 1835 and began getting commissions. Later worked in Cheraw before settling in Columbia. His portrait of Calhoun opened many doors to him, including Wade Hampton II and James Chesnut. Painted over 200 portraits, most of prominent antebellum South Carolinians. Also worked in GA, AL, and TN.

es to be an admirable likeness. We set off for the plantation at 9 ocl & arrived at 3. Ocl. where we found all well & the negroes gathering corn.

Friday 8th....I attended Mr. Coleman a surveyor, in running a line between the land of W. Kemp[3] and myself, which had remained an open line up to this time. In the afternoon I rode over my fields.

Saturday 9th. I rose early & inspected my hogs & cattle. The overseer reported that the number of stock hogs was about 90, pigs about 100 & fattening hogs 45. I counted 78 head of cattle, including milk cows & oxen & 12 calves — They were all in good order & looking in thriving condition.

Sunday 10th....I read to Mrs. Brooks the [Episcopal] services of the day, took some exercise & in the evening paid a visit to our neighbour Mr. King, whose lady had but a few days before given him a large, healthy looking boy. Both mother & infant were doing well.

Monday 11....I rode to Mr. Churchhills[4] to hear the political news but. . .

[TORN]

[After?] gathering the corn from the Corley & Creek fields, I got up a corn shucking & supper for my negroes, which I attended for a few hours & was greatly amused with their crude [improvized] songs ....[T]o cheer their hearts (as an Irishman would say) I gave them a moderate allowance of whiskey. A few of my neighbours negroes came to their assistance & they all appeared very joyous. In the pile of corn there was upwards of 1000 bushels & they shucked out about 400 by 11ocl when they partook of their supper.

Tuesday 12....I was not well & took but little exercise. I hired to Mr. Riley two small boys for 1845. Sold a barrel of flour to Mrs. Strom at $5.

Wednesday 13h....We left the plantation on our return home, which we reached at 2 ocl....We found all well at home & received the welcome intelligence of the election of Mr. Polk President of the Unit. States.

Thursday 14....The papers by this mornings mail confirm the report of Polk's election. The result of this election will confound the Southern whigs & utterly demolish their leaders. I trust that the whig cause has received its death blow at the South & that the advocates of the tariff policy may receive that sentence of condemnation, which their treachery so richly merits[5] — I visited the Village in the morning, purchased a few articles & in the afternoon sat for a portrait likeness by Mr. Scarborough. Rec.d letters from our Sons James & Whitfield[,] the latter of whom was not well.

Friday 15th....I finished gathering my pea crop at my farm & had my hands

3 Wiley Kemp (c. 1804–?); 1850 census: $150 real estate, 43 slaves.

4 Charles or Levi Churchill.

5 Probably a reference to Henry Clay's hedging on the Texas annexation issue.

breaking up stubble land & picking out cotton. There was a strolling company of circus players in the Village, who performed in the afternoon & night. They recived but little patronage, an evidence of the good sense & taste of our Villagers at a period of such depression in all the staple commodities of the Country & consequent scarcity of money. When labour is so poorly rewarded, idle vagrants should be discouraged & discountenanced. The fee for entrance into one of these places of harlequin exhibition would cost a poor man the profits of a week's labour while cotton continues at 5^{cs}. p^{r} lb.

. . . M^{rs}. Brooks sat to M^{r}. Scarborough for her portrait, which for the first sitt[ing] .... [TORN]......likeness.

Saturday 16. ....[TORN].... Morning....The Villagers had a glorification celebration in honor of Polk's election to the Presidency of the Unit. States, in which they had flags hoisted & five barrels of tar burnt -. I did not participate in this [saternalia?] tho I was gratified at the success of the democratic party. I gave M^{r}. Scarborough a second sitting for my portrait, which engaged me till 1. Ocl....M^{rs}. Lipscomb[6] was exceedingly ill during the day & night & fears were entertained for her life. She is reported to be much better & her babe is doing well. What bitter suffering and even danger mothers have to pass through in giving birth to children? & yet with surpassing fortitude most of them bear the trial. She is a good woman & I hope, she will be spared to bless & comfort my neighbour for many years.

Sunday 17th....The Revd Doct^{r}. Johnson is on a visit to the church at Hamburg & the Rev^{d}. M^{r}. Abney is to officiate in his church. I divided last night among my male servants the proceeds of 33 bushels of corn which I had appropriated to their use. It was sold to M^{r}. Wardlaw at 50.^{cs} p^{r} bushel. In the place of going to church I read two sermons by Bishop Dehon.[7]

Monday 18th....I waited on M^{r}. Scarborough & sat for my portrait....

Tuesday 19th....I was prevented by the rain from going to the plantation – More water has fallen since yesterday morning than I have seen since the month of July – M^{r}. Scarborough worked upon M^{rs}. B.^{s} portrait & remained to dinner with us. He is a very agreeable & good tempered gentleman & appears to be obliging in his disposition. My negros were engaged in saving manure but the rain did not admit of much work.

Wednesday 20th....I set out for my plantation at 10 ocl. taking Hampden with me. It is a gloomy day to travel but business calls me to my plantation & it - is a rule of mine, not to neglect the calls of duty or business on account of a little bad weather.

6 Could this be Sarah Lipscomb, wife of John Lipscomb (1790–), who had real estate worth $6,000 and 21 slaves in 1850? She was almost certainly too old to bear a child.

7 Theodore Dehon (1776–1817), Boston native, Harvard 1795, rector of St. Michael's Charleston, Episcopal Bishop of South Carolina.

In order to go ahead, it - is necessary to disregard trifles. Success depends upon enterprise & perserverence & without them, man acts too much in the character of a..........I d...............................in all things.

[TORN]

Thursday 21....I attended the sale of the estate of Ja^{s} Bean dec^{d}.[8] at which I saw a larger concourse of persons, than I ever saw at the sale of so small an estate. I

purchased a tract of land of 230 [acres] for $265. The portions of land were sold in tracts of various sizes at the price of about $1.50 p^{r}. acre – I left the place at an early hour & after my departure a fight took place between Stanford May and James Attoway,[9] in which $_{v}^{May}$ is said to have got the better of his antagonist....rain . . . through the entire night –

Friday 22nd....I . . . set out for home at which I arrived about dark & found all well. The roads are in a very miry & wet condition & all the streams filled with water. I was forced to travel in a walk nearly the whole distance. After tea Co^{l}. Carroll called to see me but had no news to communicate. The calm which has succeeded the presidential election, has left the newspapers without news & they begin already to abound with old

Stories of love & wonder & particularly with advertisements of patent medicines & other quackery. A period of peace & plenty is always destitute of stiring incidents & the lover of the marvelous is deprived of his daily entertainments.

Saturday 23^{r}....In the afternoon a deputy sheriff, arrived [in the village] with three wagons & teams, & 108 negroes, belonging to a family of Byne's in Burke County G^{eo}. In order to secure their property against the just claims of their creditors, they had secretly removed it from Georgia to this State & were on their way to the Rail road to take passage to Charleston, where a vessel was in readiness to convey them to Texas. Upon hearing of the removal of the negroes across the River, the different creditors took out attachments to the number - it is said of 60 or 70 & for an amount of debt not less than 50.000. These were fortunately served by the Dep^{ty}. Sheriff M^{r}. Lindsey, while they were passing with the property through Beach [Beech] Island.[10]

Sunday 24^{h}....We attended at the Epis. Church & heard a sermon by a young divine named Hyat from Charleston. It was sensible but common place. He read the service very well & with a clear & distinct voice.

[TORN]

Monday 25....We went in the afternoon to pass the night at Major Blocker's. We

---

[8] A former neighbor who died on July 15, 1844.

[9] Stanford May (1813–); 1850 census: $800 real estate, 42 slaves. James Attaway (1796–); 1850 census: $5,000 real estate, 22 slaves.

[10] A small community (not an island) on the SC side of the Savannah River downstream from Augusta.

found the family well & enjoyed ourselves much to our satisfaction.

Tuesday 26. We returned home, Mary Blocker[11] in company with us to spend a few days – I visited the Village & purchased about 1200^{lb}. of pork at $^{\$}$2.25^{cs} \$2¼. p^{r}. 100^{lb}.

Wednesday 27....I attended for a short time the sale of M^{r}. Raifords estate but

in consequence of increasing head ache, I was forced to leave the Sale & return to Judge Butler's, where I had left M^{rs}. Brooks & Miss Mary Blocker on a visit to our much valued Aunt Butler. I took to a bed, on which I remained in great agony until the hour for setting out for home.

Thursday 28....Rec^{d}. the message of Governor Hammond to the Legislature now sitting in Columbia. It is a clear, direct, able & bold public document & in point of

style & matter inferior to no message, which it has been our fortune to read for the last ten years. The Governor is clear in his views, bold in thought, fearless in expression & comprehensive in conception. The tone & temper of the Message is firm & dignified & in the true spirit of a Carolina patriot. He treats the tariff & abolition questions with the boldness of a Southern patriot, who feels our wrongs & dares to express them.

Friday 29th....I called at Goodman's [Hotel] to see Bishop Gadsden, who was on his return from Abbeville, where he had been to consicrate a church. I found him in good health & endeavoured to induce him to remain a short time with us but his engagement in Columbia, would not allow of his stopping.

Saturday 30th....My waggons returned this morning to the plantation, having brought down 20 bales of cotton, which in consequence of the low price, I declined to send on to market. Major Blocker returned from Hamburg & informed me that the market was dull. Cotton selling from 3-5¼^{cs}. I devoted the day to looking for a cow, that strayed off about the 1. Novr. and in making preparations for killing hogs. In the Charleston Mercury, I read a series of resolutions introduced into the [SC] Senate by Co^{l}. Pickens, somewhat at varience with the bold tone & spirit of the Message of his Excellency. I do not forsee any evil consequences, that can result from them, tho I cannot discover any necessity or utility in their introduction at this time. The message & the resolutions were made the order of the day for thursday last in committee of the whole.[12]

December 1, 1844

---

[11] Mary (1832–), a daughter of Bartley Blocker and his wife Nancy, WB's sister.

[12] Hammond's message, his last (Nov. 26, 1844), urged unilateral disunion based on Congress' failure to lower the tariff and ratify the Texas annexation treaty. Pickens, in his first act as a state senator, urged the body not to endorse the message since the Polk administration was expected to accomplish both measures. The Senate, choosing practicality over principle, unanimously supported Pickens (Edmunds, *Pickens,* 85–86).

Sunday 1st....We attended at the Episcopal Church & heard the services performed & a sermon delivered by the Revd. Mr. Page,[13] a minister lately employed by the Vestry to officiate in our church. He seems to be a modest & unassuming gentleman, plain in his manners, & courteous in his bearing, but not talented I should think. His sermon was sensible but rather on the common order in point of matter & argument tho delivered in good language. He reads with distinctness but not without hesitation. I recd. a letter from Preston[14] . . . giving some account of a debate of interest, which occurred in the [SC] house on the resolutions introduced by Mr. Memminger,[15] in reference to the Governor's message & to the effect, which the election of a Democratic President of the United States is likely to have upon the questions of the tariff & abolition, in affording relief to the South. The members of the Legislature seem to be much divided as to the position, which the state should at this session assume. A large portion are for trusting for relief to the new administration, which will go into power on the 4 of March next, while a respectable portion are for instituting at this time incipient measures to obtain a redress of our complaints, provided the administration of Mr. Polk, should fail to meet the expectations, of the democratic party. I am not sufficiently informed of the reasons & arguments of either party to pronounce a definitive judgement upon the merits of their line of action[,] yet if I were a member of the Legislature I should oppose any measure that was calculated to lower the tone of the message or to express too strong a reliance upon any other power, than the Sovereign action of our own State.

Monday 2....The Charleston papers contain no news. The demand for cotton has increased & the Sales large since the last arrival from Europe with little or no change in the price. The Manufactories in Europe are represented to be in a flourishing condition. I went to the Village in the afternoon & learned that sales of several tracts of land had been made by the Sheriff & Commr. in Equity at fair prices. I met Capn. Cunningham at the tavern on his return from Hamburg wet & cold by exposure to the rain. There has been no sessation of rain from daylight to 9 Ocl. at night & the earth is thoroughly wet....

Tuesday 3rd....Mary Blocker with Danl. Bird left us at 12 ocl. for Major Blocker's, taking Hampden with them....

---

[13] Rev. Carter Page pastored the church for less than one year.

[14] Preston Brooks was elected to the state House of Representatives in 1844, and served one term. WB's failure to mention his son's election seems odd, but is not inconsistent with his journal-keeping generally.

[15] Christopher Gustavus Memminger (1803–1888): German-born; orphaned in 1807; graduated SC College at 16; lawyer; state legislator 1836–1852, 1854–1860. Unionist in Nullification era, father of Charleston public schools, Confederate Sec. of Treasury.

Wednesday 4th....If nature had designed to present a contrast in the elements, one more striking and marked could not have been produced than by the comparison of yesterday & this morning. Yesterday was one of clouds, rain & blasts of wind, this day of bright sunshine, mild temperature & of quiet repose. External nature seems all in harmony & to be decked in smiles & winning expression & invites the eye of taste to look forth & enjoy the varied beauties, spread out in rich luxuriance before it under a bright autumnal sky. I killed & salted 5 hogs.

....

Friday 6th....I made another killing of hogs. The first five I raised & they weighed about 950lb. The last five were of Kentucky growth & they weighed 947lb. (net weight). I recd. sundry letters from Columbia, [Pickens and/or son Preston likely] in all of which mention is made of the animated debate on the question of the reference of the Governors message & on the various resolutions, which had been offered in regard to the message in the house of representatives. I am pleased with [Colcock's?] as they offer a middle ground, on which both wings of the democratic party may unite, without lowering the tone & position of the State on the Subject of the tariff & at the same time avoiding any expression of opinion injurious to or disrespectful of the great democratic party of the Union or of the approaching administration of Polk, the President elect. The papers also contain the official notification of a Mr. Hoar[16] to the Governor, announcing his arrival in Charleston as the agent of the State of Massachusetts, to enquire into & protect her coloured seamen from the operation of a law of this State, passed some years since as a police regulation. This discourteous act of the State of Massachusetts is both impertenant & insulting to our pride, injurious to our peace & quiet & if permitted or acquiesced in, distructive to our safety. It should [be] rebuked & resisted at all hazards. The election of a Governor is also exciting much interest. There are four Candidates [Whitemarsh] Seabrook, [William] Aiken, Buckhanan & [RFW] Allston. Seabrook deserves to be elected, in consideration of his past services. I am not aware of a single qualification or claim, which Mr. Aiken[17] can set up for this office. I cer-

---

16 Samuel Hoar (1778–1856), lawyer, one-term Whig congressman from Mass. Brooks accurately describes his assignment, but omits the requirement of the "Negro Seaman Act" that they be held in Charleston jails while their ships were in port, and Hoar's intention to bring federal suits against the state. The law was enacted in the wake of the Denmark Vesey slave conspiracy of 1822, in hopes of keeping free black crew members away from local slaves. Governor Hammond ordered Hoar expelled by his aide-de-camp, Preston Brooks, but before Brooks arrived he was forced to leave by local citizens who worried about mob action (Faust, *James Henry Hammond*, 251–52). See also, Journal, Thursday 12th.

17 William Aiken, Jr. (1806–1887), son of a founder and president of the SC Railroad Co. A rice and cotton planter, he owned over 800 slaves and amassed great wealth. He served in both houses of the general assembly, and won the governorship in 1844 as a Unionist opponent of the Bluffton [secession] Movement. He would represent the Charleston area in the U.S. House for three terms in the 1850s, and was almost elected Speaker in 1856. Outgoing

tainly never should have thought of him for this office.

Saturday 7th....I read a very able & argumentative letter from Govr. Hammond, in reply to a letter of remonstrace from a Presbiterian Congregation in Scotland, protesting against the execution of a man by the name of Brown, who had been convicted of inveigling a slave from her owner.[18] The world is growing officious & impertenant, thus to presume to interfere with the municipal regulations of a Sovereign State & to arrest the arm of punishment, in executing the penalty of the law upon a guilty culprit. Verily if this pragmatical interference is tolerated either from abroad or from our northern confederates, the State will be robbed of her Sovereignity & become a petty dependency without power, dignity or character.

Sunday 8th....We attended service in the Epis. church. The Rev.d M.r Page gives us sensible sermons but he is greatly deficient in force & animation of delivery. His manner is modest but stiff & constrained. He is also deficient in that intensity of feeling, which is indespensible to excite a warm & lively interest in the Congregation. A passenger in the Stage brought intelligence of the election of Mr. Aiken as Governor of the State. I cannot account for the election of this gentleman. He is a modest, amiable & worthy gentleman as a man & private citizen, of pleasing manners & of irrepproachable character[,] but I am not aware of a single qualification or claim, which he possesses for this office except that of wealth. I am not sure that he has given any public evidence of his ability of writing the english language for I have no recollection of any production of his, having ever been placed in type for the benefit or entertainment of his fellow citizens. I have no doubt however, he will sustain the new pomp & pageantry of office with a munificent liberality & perform the courtesies & hospitalies, belonging to the station, with the most winning amenity of Manner. I do not approve the principle, involved in this election for disguise it - as his supporters may attempt, it is nothing but a naked homage to wealth. Age, experience & long public service, with acknowledged ability and patriotism were disregarded and made to give way to the power of money. I fear the members of the Legislature, paid homage to their stomachs instead of their heads in making the selection. How will my friend Holland[19] be able to go through the conventional

---

Governor Hammond noted that open electioneering occurred for the first time in this campaign, no doubt adding to WB's dismay at Aiken's victory. See *Journal,* Sunday 8th.

[18] Hammond's "Letter to the Free Church of Glasgow" was published in the Charleston *Mercury* and *Courier* in Dec. 1844, and became "a pro-slavery classic." It argued for the biblical sanction of slavery and compared southern slavery favorably with the "squalid misery" of laborers he had seen in England and Ireland. John Brown was not executed because Hammond, having concluded that he was stealing his lover, commuted his sentence to 39 lashes (Faust, *Hammond*, 246).

[19] Daniel Holland? He owned a plantation near that of Andrew Pickens Butler, including a spring later dubbed Center Spring. He was elected to the state House at some point; however, WB seems to be referring to a butler or other government employee whom he had met while in the legislature.

ceremonies of a fashionable dinner party and what grace & composure he will be able to command, if he should unluckily be called on to cut up & serve a Stratsburg [sic] pie,[20] I leave to the judgement of those skilled in such matters. I should be pleased to witness the exhibition & his performance in this new line of acting.

Monday 9th....I went to my plantation taking Hampden with me. The road was rough & muddy. All well at the plantation.

Tuesday 10....I rode over a small tract of land, which I purchased from the estate of James Bean decd.

Wednesday 11. The earth was frozen this morning. I went this morning to the late residence of Mrs. Scurry to obtain some information in regard to the disposal of the real estate & ascertained from the Esqr. that it was to be rented for the ensuing year. I returned by Col. Pickens plantation & saw the house, which he has lately caused to be erected for his personal accommodation.

Thursday 12th. I called to see Col. [Oliver] Towles on business & also went with Ja.s Bean to agree upon a line of division of a part of the land, which I purchased of the estate of his father & which I finally consented for him to take back except about 10 acres, embracing the Creek & swamp land, which I reserved [21]....My overseer killed 24 hogs, averaging 165lb. About the same number remain for a second killing. The only news, furnished by the papers, relate[s] to a series of resolutions, passed by the Legislature, directing the Governor to expel from the State, the Massachewsetts [sic] agent Mr. Hoar & the fact that the Governor had sent my Son Preston to Charleston to carry the will of the Legislature into effect.

Friday 13....I returned home where I met my Son James from Barnwell, who came up on a visit of business. I rode to my farm to inspect the work of my negroes....

Saturday 14....I walked to the Village but heard no news, except that a young man, by the name of [Swearingin?] had committed suicide. Rode over & inspected my farm. I began on tuesday last to sow oats & will by night have put in the earth about ten bushels, which cover about 10 acres. I paid a visit in the evening to the Revd. Mr. Page.

Sunday 15. James left us this morning on his return to Barnwell. We attended church & heard a sermon by Mr. Page. Col. Carroll returned in the stage from Columbia but brought no news — My old friend [Henry] McClintock called up & passed a few hours in social conservation. Time has produced but small alteration in my old age acquaintance. He looks a little older, but retains the same warm, generous & ardent nature that distinguished him twenty years ago. In his old age he fell in love with a clever lady, living in Walterborough & succeeded in persuading her that it was not good to live alone, so she consented to a union & about 9 months

---

20 Strasburg Pie: Fois gras, wrapped in bacon, surrounded by puff pastry.

21 WB's silence as to money seems to indicate that he did this without requiring that Bean Jr. pay him.

past they were joined in the bands of wedlock. He arrived in our Village on Wednesday last by virtue of an invitation from the trustees of the Male academy, to take charge of that institution for the ensuing year. The second morning after his arrival his lady was confined & delivered of a very large & well proportioned boy child. In this son of his matured age & issue of his loins, is realized his proudest, fondest anticipations. His happiness is so exuberant & irrepressable that it almost intoxicates him. May he be blessed in this child, & may the child imbibe the manly frankness, honesty & independence of his worthy sire.

Monday 16^{h}....I killed eight hogs this morning, weighing 1000^{lb}. for domestic use. On examining the meat first killed, I found the joints of five hogs, a little injured, which I caused to be separated & resalted. The taint was immediately in the joints & seemed to result from bruised blood, which had been produced by driving them from Kentucky. The entire day was cold & windy & the night very severe.

....

Wednesday 18. Very cold ....I rode to Prestons to attend to a little business & then over the pine tract of land, which I purchased at the Sale of the estate of Co^{l}. [Benjamin] Frazier. Old M^{r}. Nipper went round the land with me & showed me the corners & lines. I was much gratified with my purchase. The land abounds in oak, pine, hickory & poplar. There is a good proportion of board & shingle timber & the rail timber will last me & my children 100 years, if none of the land should be cleared. Lightwood & timber for posts are in great abundance & 100 acres of the tract lies level & seems well adapted to cultivation. I would not take $500. for it. In the afternoon I rode to my farm. I have my hands employed in breaking up stubble land, which has rested since last year, clearing & splitting rails.

Thursday 19th....I purchased this morning a few bushels of mountain oats for seed at 50^{cs} p^{r}. bushel.

Friday 20th....I suffered all day from headache. My father & M^{rs}. [Nancy] Blocker arrived on a visit. He was in tolerable health but very feeble. My sister Mrs B. was in fine health —

Saturday 21....I attended to the settlement of some of my store a/c & to hiring out some negroes — Our Son Preston arrived from Columbia in excellent health & spent the night with us together with his Grandfather & Aunt.[22]

Sunday 22....My father returned home this morning & M^{rs}. Blocker in the afternoon. I was indisposed by headache. In the afternoon M^{rs}. Page, wife of our Minister[,] was very ill & called in two physicians. During the night, she was attacked by spasms & her life was in eminent danger – M^{rs}. Brooks sat by her side & waited upon her during the whole night. I remained at home entirely alone, Hampden having gone with his brother to his house —

---

[22] Surely they talked about the Hoar incident, even though Preston arrived too late to perform his duty.

Monday 23....I visited the Village & paid some accounts. On my return I called at Mrs. Carrolls [WB's mother-in-law] & saw Mrs. Page for a moment – I think she was in a dieing state. Hers is a mournful example of the uncertanity of human hopes & expectations. She arrived here four or five weeks since from Kentucky with her husband, who had been invited to take charge of the Epis. Church. She had formed a circle of acquaintances among the members of the church principally[,] with whom she was much pleased & by whom she was highly appreciated & was flattering herself with the prospect of quiet & sunny days ahead, when she was seized by disease, which confines her (I fear) to the bed of death. She remained in a State of unconsiousness for near 24 hours with severe spasms at intervals.

Tuesday 24....I sent at day light to hear how Mrs. Page was, & to my great surprise & gratification I was informed that she was better, that the spasms had not returned during the night & that she was comparitively easy. I anticipated that the answer to my message would be, that she was dead but to our great delight, she was reported to be better. I do most fervently pray, that she may recover & be again restored to health. I attended to my daily duties in playing overseer & riding to my farm. My servants will have nearly finished cutting & cleaning up what land I propose to clear this winter[,] being from 4 to 5 acres, also breaking up the stubble land, except a few acres & sowing from 10 to 12 acres in Oats —

Wednesday 25....I have rarely witnessed a more cheering day....We dined with our Mother Mrs. Carroll & passed a pleasant day. I have heard of but little [Christmas] merry making among the old or young. At the Pine house they had a course race among the neighbours but I did not think proper to attend —

Thursday 26h....I devoted the day to running round & reblazing the lines of a pine tract of land, which I purchased of Frazier. Mrs. Page is represented to be no better but gradually growing weaker & occasionally suffering great pain....

Friday 27th....Mrs. Page was delivered during the past night of a still born child. She is represented to be better & the chances are now in favour of her living....I paid a visit to Judge [A. P.] Butler & to Col. Pickens & passed a pleasant time. My venerable and respected Aunt Butler was in excellent health and spirits. She is an extraordinary woman, for her age, having more firmness of character, true philosophy & cheerfulness of disposition, than any lady of her age in the whole range of my acquaintance.

Saturday 28th....I walked to the Village before breakfast but found very few persons out of their beds. I started the plantation negroes, of whom my yard has been full during the holidays, back to the plantation. I learned that Thos. Bacon had two fights with a Kentuckian about an unsound horse & that Tom gave him a thrashing, for which he deserves the thanks of the public. The people of that State first burthen us with taxation through the tariffs & then drain us of the little money, that is left by the sale of their horses, hogs & cattle, many of which are unsound & die in the hands of the purchaser. It is however the fault & folly of our own Citizens voluntarily to remain in a State of dependence upon other portions of the Union for a supply of these indispensible articles & we deserve to be cheated, if we any longer submit to this slavish condition. We must change the whole system of living & reform our habits or otherwise debt & bankrupcy will be visited upon our people to the ruin of thousands. It would be well for the State if a perpetual barrier was erected on the Point mountain, cutting off all intercourse between us & the West & putting a stop to the present trafic in stock of every discription.[23]

Sunday 29th....Thermt 42$^{\theta}$ at sunrise and above 50 at 8 Ocl. at night. Col. Carroll & lady, Mr. [Francis] Wardlaw,[24] Mr. McClintock & Col. P. S. Brooks dined with us. They formed an agreeable and intelligent party, with whom we passed a few pleasant hours in social conversation. We attended in the Epis. church in the morning & heard a good sermon read by Mr. Page. The manner of reading however, greatly mared the beauty & effect of the sermon. Our Son Hampden is suffering from an injury sustained by climbing a tree. The inflamation of the bruised part is so great as to prevent his walking or taking the least exercise. I much fear that he will be unable to accompany us to Fairfield. His disappointment will be severe & grivous to him on many accounts —

Monday 30th....I rode this morning to the sale of the estate of old Mrs. Cloud & remained a short time. The land sold for $3100, a fair price & higher than I would give. The tract is ordinary pine land. The papers report another decline in the price of cotton in Europe. The highest price now in Hamburg is represented to be 4cs. The present price of cotton will produce the most disastrous affects upon the people of the Southern states & must reduce thousands to penury, who considered themselves in easy & comfortable circumstances — It will require the greatest industry & economy to pay for the indispensible articles of living & no man can hope to pay more than the interest of his debts, if [they?] amount even to his ordinary income three years back — I have never seen or even imagined the possibility of so hopeless a prospect. I actually feel poor in the possession of a good estate & find it difficult to pay the necessary accounts for groceries & plantation supplies — We are preparing to leave home for Fairfield, to witness the marriage of our Son Preston, to Miss Martha Means, a daughter of the late Revd. Robt. Means —[25]

---

[23] The location of "Point Mountain" is unclear, but KY livestock traders brought their stock through the Cumberland and Saluda Gaps into SC through Greenville or Spartanburg Districts. At one point before 1832, public resolutions in favor of boycotting KY stock were adopted, as WB suggests, but to little avail (Colton, *Life and Times of Henry Clay*, vol. 1, 110).

[24] Francis Hugh Wardlaw, a former law partner of WB, had become a political enemy of the "Edgefield Junto" of which WB was a member, as described in Edmunds, *Francis Pickens,* 101–102. Thus, his presence at the Brooks home shows that WB lived his maxim that political adversaries should not be unfriendly.

[25] Rev. Robert Means (1796–1836), Presbyterian minister.

Tuesday 31st....The air is as mild & balmy as an April morning & the birds car~~r~~olling their merry notes as on a vernal day. Poor Hampden was greatly grieved by a hawk striking one of his pet pigeons but he was consoled by the State of his bruises, admitting his going with us to Fairfield for which place we are preparing to take our departure. We went to my Fathers, whom we found in tolerable health & very glad to see us. Preston & Col. Carroll passed the night with us....There could not have been a lovelier day, for the past year to close her cycle of time nor could she have presented a more cheering or more inspiring look upon the millions of human beings, whom she was bidding farewell forever. The season of the year was unusually mild, the health of the District generally good & the supply of the great necessaries of life from the past crop very abundant. As a people & as a nation we have great cause of thankfulness & praise for the many signal blessings, which Providence has vouchsafed to us during & up to the last period of the year. There is no cause of complaint except the low price of cotton. The market of this great staple is depressed below the expectation of even the most desponding. It commands only 4½cs for the best quality. Without some change or a radical reform in the habits of the people, the Country will be reduced to bankruptcy & ruin.

VI

January 1st. 1845.

Wednesday 1...We left my fathers at 10 ocl. passed the Village of Newberry and dined at the Presbiterian church near the Village. We stopped at Glimps for the night within a mile of Ashfords ferry across the Broad River.[1] Some negroes were hired at Glimps during the day & I was informed that prime young women did not command more than $38. Per month. $1 per day seemed to be normal for slave labor.

Thursday 2....We left Glimps after breakfast & crossed the Broad River under as bright a sun as ever shone. The dazling light of the sun as it was reflected on the silvery bosom of the River, occasionally varied by the rocks & riffles in the bed of the stream, presented a charming picture for the eye of taste & imagination. At 12 ocl. we arrived at Mrs. Means & received a cordial reception. I was soon attacked with head ache & was forced to retire. The paroxism was violent & deprived me of all pleasure for the evening. I was forced to decline an invitation to dine with Major Thos. Means[2] & to forgo all society. I did summon resolution enough to rise from the bed & walk to the door to see our Son married. The bridal party presented a very interresting group of young & handsome persons. The Groom & bride stood at the head of two lines formed by six groomsmen & as many brides maids on each side & the minister at the foot. Our Son appeared to great advantage & compared well with his attendants & his bride presented a face radiant with health, youth & beauty. It was truly a lovely sight to look upon, which I enjoyed notwithstanding my great suffering. The marriage of these young people ought to be a happy & fortunate one, for every circumstance even the most triffling was propitious. They are equals in point of age, character, fortune & family. The friends & relations on each side were gratified & gave their cheering assent & approbation.

In appearance she is all that we could expect in a daughter in law – fair, young, & beautiful, with a face radiant with smiles & full of playful & innocent joyfulness. May the whole horoscope of their lives be as auspicious as on their bridal night. We met at Mrs. Means, our children Whitfield & Ellen. They were in fine health & spirits. Ellen was one of the bridesmaids —

Friday 3....We paid a visit to Judge [William] Harper & family & Mrs. Fanny Means.[3] Dined at Mrs. Sarah Means with the bridal party & spent the afternoon at Major Thos. Means at a dancing party. Altho feeble & considerably used up by head

---

[1] The James Ashford Ferry on Broad River is marked on Mills' 1825 map of Fairfield District. It is due west of Winnsboro (near modern SC Hwy. 34).

[2] Thomas Jefferson Means (1801?–1846) was the brother of Dr. David (1794–1840), Rev. Robert (1796–1836), and future governor John H. Means.

[3] Sarah Anne Frances Means (1818–1883).

ache, I enjoyed a good share of pleasure —

Saturday 4. We left Mrs. Means on our return....We reached my fathers at dark & passed the night with him. All well.

Sunday 5....We left my fathers after breakfast for home. My father came in company to Mr. Clempson's [Clemson]. We dined at Judge Butlers Spring & reached home about 4 Ocl. where we found three negroes indisposed tho not seriously ill. Our friends were well. We learned that little Wm. Butler died of measles, during our absence. The negroes of Byne[4] under attachment – & confined in the jail are breeding a sort of Pestilence in the Village. We met [WB's son] James & Danl. Bird on our return.

Monday 6th. This was a busy day in the Village. A large portion of property was sold at public outcry both by the Sheriff & private individuals. S. Kennerly sold a lot of negroes, horses etc. I went in the morning to my farm & laid out the worm [path] of a fence & then went to the Village. The throng of people was very numerous. I called to see Col. [William C.] Preston at Mr. [John] Bausketts. He is in good health but Mrs. Preston is ailing & Miss S[ally Campbell] Preston in a rapid decline. I did not see her.

Tuesday 7th. James left us this morning on his return to Barnwell. Cols. Preston, Carroll & Bauskett – dined with me & also the Revd. Mr. Page & did not leave until 9 ocl at night. We passed a very agreeable afternoon & heard from Col. Preston many interresting anecdotes.

Wednesday 8th....I went to the Village before breakfast to see Col. Towles on business. Mrs. Brooks & I dined with Col. Carroll where we met Col. Preston, Bauskett Wardlaw & the Revd. Mr. Page. We had a good dinner & spent a pleasant afternoon.

Tuesday 9th....considerable frost. I went to my plantation & found the negroes generally well.

Friday 10th....I rode over my plantation & directed the Overseer, how to run two crop fences, inspected the new grounds, small grain, stock etc. Marshall Thompson[5] came down & took breakfast & dinner with me. I returned home in the afternoon.

Saturday 11. I walked to the Village in the afternoon & heard that both measles & scarlet fever were prevailing in different families. Col. Pickens passed with his bride[6] on his way home from Charleston about 1. Ocl. Our Son Preston arrived from Fairfield about dark with his young bride. It is a [novel?] event for two brides to arrive in our neighbourhood on the same day, to become members of our Society.

---

4 See Nov. 23, 1844.

5 Marshall Thompson (1799–); 1850 census: $3,600 real estate, 43 slaves.

6 Francis Pickens married Marion Antoinette Dearing of Charleston on January 9, 1845. His first wife, Margaret Eliza Simkins, died in 1842.

Sunday 12h....We attended service at the Epis. Church. Col. Carroll returned & took a family dinner with us. Preston & his lady rode out to Sweetbrier in the afternoon. This is the first visit of his Wife to this District & of course her first to her future residence.[7]

Monday 13th....We called upon Col. Pickens & his bridge [sic]. He was in most excellent spirits & seemed perfectly happy. His lady has modest, affable & good manners, rather handsome, certainly very good looking and altogether an interresting woman —

Tuesday 14th....I went to my farm, thence to old Mr. Lofton,[8] to get a few tobacco seed, thence to Mrs. Hollisters to engage fiddler Jim for thursday night & thence to Major Blockers to dinner. I returned in the afternoon by my farm, & superintended the running of a fence.

Wednesday 15th....At 2 ocl. I was attacked with headache & suffered great pain for 8 or 10 hours, during which I was confined to my bed.

Thursday 16th....I felt greatly enfeebled by the attack of head ache. Every member of the family busily engaged in making preparations for an evening party to our Son Preston & his bride....Our invited guests began to arrive at half after six & by seven our rooms were filled. Among the number were Col. Pickens & his bride. It was a happiness to have the Company of my father, now in his 80th year, who was in his usual health and enjoyed the passing hour with some jest. The company was large, talkative & hilarious & seemed to enjoy much pleasure. The young people, danced & sung & talked without restraint while the old looked on with approving smiles. We had little to regret but the absence of a part of our children, of Whitfield & Ellen in Columbia and James in Barnwell. The company dispersed about 1. Ocl merry & content to all appearance with their entertainment. Our new daughter was the fairest & gayest in the assembly. I did not succeed in inviting slumber & rest till 2 ocl, for after the company had taken their parting salutations, & I had retired to bed & was wooing Morpheus to take me in his embrace, the pet dog Trip of our little nephew Oscar Laborde, set up a most mournful howling in the house. I was reluctantly forced to come down stairs & release him from his state of incarceration in the supper room, in which he had inadvertantly been locked up. I was much fatigued & got but a small portion of sleep & very little refreshment. A gentleman from the North died at Goodmans & was buried yesterday evening & this morning his brother William Goodman was married & took his departure for Augusta by sunrise....Such . . . is the life of man, presenting perpetually a succession of incidents

---

[7] Sweetbriar, 176 Cantelou Road, stands today about a mile south-southwest of ECH. The original structure was erected in the late 1700s by John Mims. Preston Brooks acquired the house and lived there with Martha, starting a new family. When he volunteered for service in the Palmetto Regiment in 1846, he sold the house to James Rainsford, who enlarged it.

[8] Robert Lofton (1770–); 1850 census: $2,000 real estate, 20 slaves.

in direct contrast with each other. A birth, a marriage & a death follow in perpetual succession but it[s] - rarely the case that they take place so quickly in a small Village. Among the other singular incidents of the week I was informed that M^{rs}. [Reemer?] paid a visit to a near neighbour & was suddenly taken in labour & was delivered of an infant in her neighbours house. This may be called "quick work" or a speedy delivery.

Friday 17....My father & Sister M^{rs}. Blocker left us this morning. Co^{l}. Pickens & lady paid us a visit. Our friend [John] Jeter has a party to night but fatigue & the inclemency of the night prevented M^{rs}. Brooks & myself from attending.

Saturday 18th....The night windy and boisterous. There was a dancing party at Cap^{n}. Weavers, gotten up by the young men but it was badly attended by ladies....

Sunday 19th....rain from morning till night. We read the church service & a sermon of the Rev^{d}. M^{r}. Means[9] at home.

Monday 20....By 12 Oct. the Sleet began to fall & at night it became clear....A lot of hogs arrived in the Village & were sold at \$3.25 ^{cs} p^{r}. 100^{lb}. In Decr. they sold at \$2.25 to 2.50.

Tuesday 21....I suffered another violent attack of headache, which lasted until 10 ocl. at night.

Wednesday 22....a bright & lovely day but I am too indisposed to enjoy it — Chas. Glover returned from Hamburg & paid me over \$565. the proceeds of 38 bales of cotton, which he sold at 4¼ & the storage[10] for me.

Thursday 23^{d}....I went to the Village by Sunrise & found few persons out of their beds. After breakfast I went to my farm, superintended the running a fence, putting up a gate & clearing a small portion of land. I returned to dinner both wet & exhausted.

....The Rain & great horseness prevented me & M^{rs}. B. from attending a party at Co^{l}. Bausketts. Preston & his lady attended & report the preparations to have been handsome & the supper munificent....

Friday 24th....Preston left for Hamburg at sun rise to meet his waggon....I rec^{d}. a sweet letter from Ellen, who is in Columbia. I was again engaged in running a fence & clearing —

Saturday 25....I walked to the Village before breakfast & delivered a box of cake to the stage office for our daughter Ellen. There was a failure of the mail this morning both from Augusta & Abbeville —

Sunday 26th. I heard in the forenoon a excellent & sensible sermon by M^{r}. Page

---

[9] Means, *Sermons and an Essay on the Pentateuch* (1836).

[10] Possibly the stone warehouse to which black militiamen retreated as racial tensions escalated in early July 1876. Whites prevailed in the ensuing gun battle, which climaxed in the "Hamburg Massacre" of July 8, 1876.

from the portion of scripture, where the Thief besought Christ to remember him in his Kingdom and Christ's answer.

Monday 27....There was a light frost but no ice. In fact until now there has been but five or six freezing days, during the winter. There has as yet fallen no snow and but one light sleet, which continued but for a few hours. Preston & his Wife left us this morning & entered upon the business of housekeeping at their own residence. M[rs]. Brooks went with them & passed the day in assisting Martha in arranging matters. I visited them after dinner & brought M[rs]. B. home. The young folk appeared to be very content & happy. Our daughter[in-law] is a dear & interresting young creature. I feel that I shall love her with true paternal affection even beyound, what I had ventured to hope. It is a great happiness to love our children & their wives & to adopt them as members of our family –

Tuesday 28th....In the afternoon we rode to Preston's —

Wednesday 29th....I am making an experiment on a piece of old land, in the mode of plowing, first running a shovel & then in the same furrow a sort of subsoil plow, constructed at the plantation. It breaks the ground thoroughly but turns up more of the clay, than I could desire. I design also to make an experiment by putting pine straw in a few rows & bedding upon it, to test its value as a manure & improver of the soil. We spent a pleasant evening with our relation W[m]. Butler.[11] He & his excellent little Wife gave a party to Preston & his lady, at which most of the gay & fashionable portion of our citizens were present. It was one of the most sumptuous & beautiful entertainments, that has ever been given in our Village & in a style of elegance, taste and liberality rarely witnessed in any place. Our relations have considerable taste & the whole was brought into requisition on this occasion. Three rooms were thrown open for the reception of company, a fourth was appropriated to the supper tables sumptuously & splendidly furnished with all the delicacies of the Tropics & the substantials of our own land & the piazza was canvassed & appropriated to dancing. It is not often that old Edgefield sees such a display.

Thursday 30th....It was on this evening that Butler's entertainment was given.

Friday 31....A heavy hoar frost....The day was windy & disagreeable. I passed the day at my farm, preparing to put up a house. The papers report the proceeding of Congress on the proposition to admit Texas into the Union. The Vote is reported to be 120 to 98. The resolution has been sent to the Senate for concurrence, in which body it will meet strong opposition but hopes are entertained that it will pass. I regard this measure as one of vast importance to the american government & destined to exert great influence upon our future fortune as a united & happy people. It[s] passage will give peace & security to the South on the subject of Slavery for the next half century. Its defeat may involve us in difficulties & even a war in less than

[11] Dr. William Butler (1790–1850) had recently retired from his one term in the U.S. House of Representatives.

twenty years.[12] The market for cotton has improved. It is now selling from 4 to 5½ ^{cs} p^{r}. lb. & the merchants are eager to purchase. The Edgefield Advertiser contains a long list of cautions from creditors & threats of the law if their demands are not paid up promptly. I fear that this part furnishes proof that money is scarce & that many are in debt beyond their means of payment. And yet there is a greater show of improvement in our Village than I have seen for many years.

February 1. 1845

Saturday 1....I was busily employed in erecting a negro house at the farm. M^{rs}. B. & Hampden went with Preston & his lady to spend the day with Aunt Butler. I dined alone for the first time in many months if not years at home. The waggon arrived in the evening with beef, peas, geese & four bales of cotton. I sold three quarters of the beef for $18.48 and the peas for $7.50. The beef was sold at 4 & 5.^{cs} per ^{lb}. & the peas at 0.75^{cs} per bushel. The overseer reports that he has sowed the rye, barley and about two thirds of the oat crop. He has cleared up and fenced about 8 acres of new ground & partly finished another piece of new ground of about 10 acres. The negroes are well....

Sunday 2nd....In the morning I heard a sensible & well composed sermon by M^{r}. Page. His reading is very faulty & his manner artificial, which detract from the merit of his sermons.

Monday 3rd....rain began to fall about 12 ocl. and continued through the afternoon & night. The concourse of persons in the Village was large. From 20 to 30 of Bines [Bynes? See Jan. 5] negroes were sold by the sheriff at very low prices —

Tuesday 4th....Co^{l}. Carroll gave a party this evening to the newly married folk. It was attended by the gay & pleasure seeking portion of our good people & passed off exceedingly well. Our host & his lady were affable & courteous, the entertainment was bountiful & very handsome and the whole company seemed delighted with themselves and each other. As proof of the manner in which every one entered into the spirit of a frolic, it may be stated, that the dancing portion of the company did not leave the house until half after one Ocl. I did not get to sleep until near 2 ocl. The night was cold & boisterous. Preston & lady, the Misses Blocker & Will[13] staid with us —

Wednesday 5th....I reached this day my fifty fifth year, in better health, than I have been for fifteen years and in the possession & enjoyment of as many blessings & comforts, as fall to the lot of most men, for which I humbly thank God, and beseech him in his mercy to continue & prolong them. Among the many causes for

---

[12] WB expressed the popular view of Texas annexation among southerners, and was in step with the policy of Secretary of State Calhoun. His predictions, however, would prove to be backwards.

[13] William Butler Blocker, nephew of WB, would die in the Mexican War.

contentment – & gratitude, not the least important is the health of my Wife & children & that of my Servants & the prosperous condition of my temporal affairs. My children are respectable & honorable and in circumstances of comfort & independence, only requiring industry and perseverence to improve their condition to one of comparative wealth. I beseech the Sovereign Dispenser of these undeserved favours to impress me with gratitude & adoration & always to preserve in my affections a lively sense & just appreciation of all his mercies. The Rev^{d}. M^{r}. Purifoy & his Wife reached this place yesterday about 11. Ocl. on a visit to his Wife's relatives [the Birds] & paid us the compliment of first stopping with us.

Thursday 6th....The Rev^{d}. M^{r}. Purifoy left us after breakfast for Major Blocker's. He is a gentleman of good appearance, of pleasing manners & of respectable intelligence. He is greatly superior to the majority of the Preachers of the Methodist church and in his dress and bearing much more genteel & gentlemanly. My niece was in good health & presented us with two very smart and interresting children. She is mild & unpretending in her manners & modest & reserved in her beheavour, being more a woman of the heart than of the understanding, tho by no means deficient in practical & sound sense. It has been several years since we last saw them. I was engaged in enclosing a lot at my farm, for some negro houses, stables, etc....M^{r}. James Hill[14] is to be married to night to Miss Holden a nice [sic] of M^{r}. John Bones[15] of Augusta. We rec^{d}. an invitation but declined to attend on account of the distance & the necessary exposure in returning at night. Preston & his lady have gone.

Friday 7th....We paid a visit to Major Hughes,[16] to call on the Groom & bride, whom we found in gay spirits & fine health. We then went to Major Blockers & spent the day. I was deprived of all pleasure by an attack of headache, which disqualified me for social enjoyment. We met a gay party of young people at the Majors, who appeared a little faged from the late hours of frolic the night before....

Saturday 8^{h}....I took Hampden & went to the plantation In the afternoon I rode over a part of my plantation.

Sunday 9th....After breakfast I rode over my plantation, then returned & inspected my stock of cattle, sheep & horses, all of which were in good condition. The Overseer had broke up about 150 acres of land, had his oats sowed except about 20 acres & about 20 acres cleared, cleaned up & fenced. These clearings have greatly improved the appearance & convenience of my plantation[.] I regard it as one of the most sightly & valuable plantations in the State, having a fertile soil, an abundant supply of water for every field & the most extensive pasturage for the different kind

---

[14] James L. Hill (1824–1867); 1850 census: $3,000 real estate, 42 slaves.

[15] A leading merchant of Augusta, a Whig, member of the city's canal commission formed in 1845, and an organizer of the Augusta Manufacturing Co. in 1847.

[16] John Halhead Hughes (1801–1871) of Cedar Grove plantation; m. Martha Bones 1831.

of stock. I returned home in the afternoon, witnessing on the road several exhibitions of drunkenness and immorality, [shocking?] to the feelings of every friend of good order and social reform & improvement. On returning I found the Rev^{d}. M^{r}. Purifoy at my house on his Way home.

Monday 10th....The Rev^{d}. M^{r}. Purifoy left us after breakfast. He gave us at night & morning an excellent, sensible & appropriate prayer, without any methodistic extravagance or rant –. In fact the invocations were such as suited the conditions & wants of sinful & dependent beings, who felt a deep & abiding sense of their utter inability to do any good act, without devine assistance, and of the necessity of this aid. We rode to Preston's.

Tuesday 11th....I shall finish this afternoon sowing oats both here & at my plantation. Having omitted to insert a statement of my crop last year at the proper time & wishing to preserve a record of it, I insert it now in connection with the crop of the present year. The fields have not been accurately measured & the number of acres in each field has been ascertained by the eye & the time required in working & also by tasks. I think there is a near approximation to the true number in the following statement.

Vide [see] following page —

Crop of 1844 §		Crop of 1845	
Corn		Corn	
Corley Field & Low ground	75	Burne's field	50
Burnes field —	50	Williams D[itto]^{o} ——	100
Part of Harvey & new gro.	25	Spring D^{o} ———	70
Selection in Spots —	20	Low Grounds & small lot.	20
Prospect field ——	30	acres =	240
acres =	200		

I gathered about 3500 bushels —

Cotton		Cotton	
Williams field —	100	Harvey & branch field	75
Part of Harvey —	50	Goode or Ditch D°	140
Ginhouse field	30	Lot below the stables	15
Part of Evily D° [*] —	90	Part of Corley field —	10
acres =	270	acres =	240

I only made 120 bales, weighing on an average 350^{lb}.
My cotton crop sustained great injury from draught & about 50 acres were killed by rust —

Wheat		Wheat	
Branch lot & part of Harvey	30	Ginhouse field —	33
The crop was an average one in quantity but rather light.		Grape Vine Corner –	3
		acres =	36

Oats		Oats	
Goode or Ditch field	125.	Everly field	— 80
Rather short crop from drought		Corley field	— 40
		Prospect D°	— 20
			140

Rye .		Rye	
Selection (acres)	10.	Selected spots —	15
A good crop. —			

To cultivate the crop of 1845. the Overseer has, 20 young fellows, 10 young women, all of whom are breeders & four now pregnant – 5 boys & 5 girls, in all 40 hands equal to 33 taskable hands — He has 20 mules & horses of superior size & order & two brood mares besides the horse he rides. Also 3 p^{r}. [pair] of oxen —

Wednesday 12th. I began this morning to run a new fence for the purpose of enlarging my garden. I wrote a letter of sympathy & condolence to Co^{l}. Preston for the loss of his daughter [Sally]. She died on the 8^{h}. instant in Columbia of consumption, at an early age. She was an excellent woman & superior in intellegence & those qualities of both heart & mind, which impart consideration & influence to the sex, than most of her associates & contemporarries. She was the only child of her parents —

Thursday 13th....I again worked on the garden fence, until the fatigue became painful — My father arrived in the evening. Night warm as summer & cloudy. I purchased sundry articles for my negroes.

Friday 14th....In the afternoon went with father to pay a visit to Preston. At night our mother Mrs. Carroll was very sick and a Physician was sent for.

Saturday 15th....Our father left us after breakfast on his return home. He is in his usual health but feeble....Rec^{d}. 4 quarters of beef from the plantation & a letter from the Overseer that the negroes were in pretty good healt. He was breaking up land, of which he has already broken up about 200 acres — He reports that there are 20 lambs —

Sunday 16th. I was too indisposed to attend church. M^{rs}. Julia Reed & the two [Blocker?] girls came down to Church and took dinner with us.

Monday 17th....Our mother M^{rs}. Carroll is much better and in fair way of being well in a few days — The reported capture and imprisonment of Santa Anna is confirmed by recent intelligence from Mexico. He is confined in the castle of Perote, the same prison in which he incarcerated the unfortunate Texians. Fortune has been fickle to this ambitious chieftain & has marked his career with most extraordinary contrasts, elevating him at one time to the head of an exterminating & conquering army, & in a few hours reducing him to the condition of a helpless prisoner in the custody of an exasperated enemy –. In a brief space of time after his return to his own Country, again advancing him to the Presidency of an Empire, from which situation he has been removed by revolution & cast by his enraged Countrymen into a loathsome dungeon. Siċ transit – gloria mundi. An earthly crown is rarely a pillow of ease to the head of the wearer & yet how ambitious are men to put it on.[17]

Tuesday 18th....We paid a visit to Preston & remained until 10 ocl at night. Several of the young gentlemen came out to tea & spent the evening in dancing & froliking with the Misses Blocker and the sprightly mistress of Sweetbrier....

Wednesday 19th....I completed ploughing a piece of land by first running a shovel and in the same furrow a subsoil plow. It is tedious but thoroughly done. M^{rs}. Mean's & her daughter Sally[18] arrived on a visit – to Preston & her daughter Mar-

---

[17] This synopsis of a portion of Santa Anna's career typified the political turmoil that affected Mexico during this era. His star would rise again, only to fall the last time.

[18] Sarah Anne Means (1824–1896), daughter of Rev. Robert and Sarah Means. Died unmarried.

tha. I rode to direct them the Way. On my return, I came by Saml. Goode's,[19] William Burts & Co^{l}. Fraziers farms, all of which are in a state of progressive improvement. In [fact?] there is a better spirit – for improving lots and attending to the comforts & conveniences of life than I have ever known to prevail in this place before. There is no part of the Village but what exhibits signs of improvement.

Thursday 20th. Therm^{r}. is up to 50$^{\theta}$. I have no recollection of so mild a winter altogether. There have been three or four cold days, when the ground was frozen very hard & ice prevailed on all still water but with the exception of these cold days, the winter has been as mild as that of 1828. There has been but one sleet, no snow and only 3 or 4 days of sufficient cold, to freeze the earth & water. It is this morning as warm as May. We called on Mrs. Means —

Friday 21....I learned in the Village that a duel had been fought below Augusta between a M^{r}. Portlow from Abbe. and a M^{r}. Burton[20] of Newberry District. Burton was shot in the hip & died that night. It was a family quarrel, which grew out of the ill treatment of Burton's Wife, who was Portlows Sister. They fought with musketts at 10 paces. Preston came from my plantation & reports the negroes to be well. M^{rs}. Means Miss S. Means & Preston & Wife took tea with us. The temperature up to summer heat.

Saturday 22nd....The week has been . . . the warmest week, I recollect ever to have seen in February. I have heard of several persons who have planted corn. We took tea with Preston & returned about 8 ocl....

Sunday 23....The inclement weather, prevented us from attending church. We read the Bible & a sermon from Chillingworth,[21] a writer of the 17th Century of great learning and ingenuity. His style is a little tedious & quaint - but his reasoning is logical & convincing. He seems to have been a most consciencious churchman & greatly opposed to Romanism. Our friends from Sweet Brier, disappointed us in not coming to Church & dining with us – I am prepared to scold them.

Monday 24....Preston & his lady, M^{rs}. Means & Miss Sally & the Rev^{d}. M^{r}. Page dined & took tea with us. M^{rs}. Purifoy & children are with us.

Tuesday 25....Genl. [James] Hammond, M^{r}. Purifoy & Wife & M^{r}. & M^{rs}. Page

---

[19] Samuel Goode (1812–); 1850 census: $8,000 real estate, 42 slaves. As of 1853, had a blacksmith shop in ECH.

[20] John G. Burton killed John Portlow. A local paper informed readers that "the difficulty which led to this fatal result is said to have originated in private affairs, of which the public should know nothing."

[21] William Chillingworth (1602–1644), Fellow of Trinity College, Oxford. Author of *The Religion of Protestants, a Safe Way to Salvation, Together with His Sermons, Letters, Discourses, and Controversies*, 12th ed., 1836. Incidently, Nathaniel Hawthorne chose this surname for Hester's husband in *The Scarlet Letter*.

spent the evening with us.[22]

Wednesday 26th....M^{r}. & M^{rs}. P. left us on their return to Georgia. Spent the evening at Co^{l}. Carroll's. I was deprived of much of my enjoyment by the thoughtless beheavour of one of the Company.[23]

Thursday 27th....We dined with our Son Preston in company with M^{rs}. Means & Sally,Co^{l}. Carroll & D. Adams.[24] Our daughter [Martha] gave us a very good dinner, which seemed to be well relished by all present & the afternoon passed off pleasantly in free & social conversation. I was much pleased with the deportment of our daughter in performing the offices of hostess, uniting on this occasion, the requisite proportion of gravity and dignity with cheerfulness & good temper, necessary to impart the highest interest & loveliness to the female character. It pains me to witness levity of manner or frivolity of beheavour in a married woman[,] however young, for they both indicate bad breeding or a weak head or badly regulated passions.

Friday 28....I visited M^{c}.Clintocks school & heard several of his classes recite. I was pleased with the general promptness & correctness with which they answered the questions given them. There is a striking improvement in his mode of teaching over that pursued here for the last fifteen years, & the progress of his pupils afford the best proof of its superiority. He has succeeded in inspiring the boys with emulation by offering to their young minds proper & wholesome incentives. One class was examined on the whole of South America and a part of the table of numbers; and several of the boys did not miss a question. Among this number was our Son Hampden. The house was clean & neat, & the benches, desks & books well arranged & in good order. The boys demeaned themselves with great decorum & manifested the requisite defference for their teacher, to insure respect and obedience — In short there were evidences of an entire reformation in the mode of teaching, in the progress and beheavour of the boys, in their habits of study & attention to cleanliness and in the whole appearance of things. My old friend talks in school to the boys, precisely as he does every where else & to every body. He has an ardent temperament & takes a deep interest in all he does or says, consequently he talks much & fluently & gives utterance to his ideas & opinions & feelings as they arise

---

[22] WB hosted Hammond either through ignorance of a scandal that had broken two months earlier, resulting in the legislature's selection of A. P. Butler over Hammond for the U.S. Senate, or in spite of it (Faust, *Hammond,* 288–89). Considering the presence of two clergymen and their wives, it must have been the former.

[23] This comment suggests the possibility that the guest mentioned the Hammond matter.

[24] David L. Adams (1797–185?); had a home in the Augusta GA suburb of Summerville. WB spent the night there after the funeral of Lt. David Adams of the Palmetto Regiment, who was killed while carrying the regimental banner in battle at Churubusco. The SC legislature rejected Adams' request to be allowed to free his slave Charles for his attendance of his son's body from the battlefield.

without disguise or equivocation, & without correction in nine cases out of ten. He puts all rules of logic & sologistic reasoning at defiance & follows the loose associations of his rambling mind, whethersoever they lead him. He is nevertheless an admirable teacher & as a gentleman is characterised by frankness, independence & great integrity.

March. 1. 1845

Saturday 1. March has truly made her appearance as mild as a lamb....The last month was generally warm, dry & clear. There was not more than three days of cold weather and only two or three rains fell. I have never seen a month better adapted to the purposes of the planter as neither rain nor cold retarded his operations for more than twelve hours in the entire month ....

Sunday 2....Vegitation is gradually advancing. The fruit trees are in bloom, most of the bulbous roots are in flower and many of the forest trees are budding. All small grain looks exceedingly promising & if this month should prove to be mild, the spring will be forward & propitious. James and his Wife arrived about dark & took us agreeably by surprise.

Monday 3rd....The concourse of persons in the Village was large and all busily engaged in their business & various interests — A large gang of negroes, belonging to the Bynes, were sold under mortgages and executions. Under all the circumstances they brought fair prices — In the afternoon a paper reached the Village, containing intelligence of the passage of the resolutions, for the annexation of Texas in the Senate of the United States. The Vote was 27 to 25. Our acquaintance Mr. Berrien voted against them. I hope this existing question is now forever settled & that quiet may be restored to the Country. It is the crowning measure of Mr. Tyler's administration & for which I am disposed to think, millions yet unborn will laud & magnify his name. It will certainly exert great influence over the destinies of this Country & settle & consolidate the foundations of our Union in peace for the next fifty years. The Slave holding portion of the confederacy [the U.S.] will hold their property by a safer tenure altho the measure of annexation may reduce its value, of which I am by no means certain. I was very sick at night. Preston & Wife, Mrs. Means & Sally paid us an unexpected but pleasant visit about dark & returned after tea. The night was warm & sultry.

Tuesday 4th....The Sale of Byne's property was continued by the Sheriff, consisting of mules, horses, wagons, etc. This is [a] beautiful day for the installation of the new President and every thing looks at present, propritious to his successful administration. God grant that all his measures may be dictated by wisdom & patriotism & that they may redound to the peace, glory & prosperity of this great & growing nation. Mules sold unusually high, from 40 to $100. The anxiety to purchase & the liberal manner of bidding, afford indications either of great demand for plough animals or an abundance of cash in the hands of the planters....

Wednesday 5th....The plants, & flowers and shrubbery in the gardens look refreshed by the rain which fell last night, and the birds are singing their gay spring notes in gratitude to the great Creator of light & life – I have seldom seen a clearer, brighter or more lovely day or one more animating. What a source of pure delight & sweet contemplation is the bright aspect of external nature when man's internal feelings & passions can be brought in harmony with the scene before him? It is now about the hour of sunset and the temperature is mild & balmy as an April evening and the air calm & tranquil as if only breathing in gentle zephyrs.

Thursday 6th....James & [wife] Sarah left us after breakfast on their return home with a full freight in their carriage of flowers, shrubbery, sundry articles of domestic use & a large family bible, the precious gift of a fond mother. May God bless our children & prosper them in the good things of this life & so govern & regulate their affections by his Sovereign grace as to qualify them for the important duties of the social state & for the fruition of happiness in their last & final state of existence — At 1. Ocl. I set out for my plantation with D[avid] L. Adams in company with us. We arrived before sunset.

Friday 7th. After breakfast I rode over my plantation & returned to dinner. In the afternoon I rode alone over my fields & inspected their condition, the state of preparation for a crop, the ditches, new grounds & small grain & also my stock, stable, cribs, well of water, negro houses etc. They were in good, even excellent order. My Overseer discharges his duty with great fidelity. He relieves me of all care & anxiety except what are incident to all plantations from accident & the dispensations of God....He has both the cotton & corn land principally broken up & is ready to plant. Vegitation was very visible & many of the forest trees in bloom — The wheat is jointing & looks exceedingly promising — The Overseer has cleared, ditched & broken up about 25 acres of new ground. He has hauled out all his manure sufficient for about fifty acres of land, & principally on the cotton land. I have 31 lambs, 3 young calves & one colt by Agile —

Saturday 8h....We set out for home at 8 ocl. & arrived at one. I left all well at the plantation & found all well at home. Partly clear at 12 ocl & very warm. After dinner I rode out to my farm & at night called to see our Mother. Col. Carroll called for a few minutes but had no news to communicate.

Sunday 9th....At an early hour the garden was vocal with music by sundry kinds of birds & especially by two mocking birds, who vied with each other in their powers of memory. We attended divine service in the Epis. church by the Revd. Mr. Page. He gave us a good sermon & read the service with more distinctness than usual.

Monday 10th....The Court of Com. Pleas commences its Spring session this morning, Judge Frost to preside. He & the Solicitor Edwards have arrived. The Court met at 10 ocl, was organised & proceeded to business. I was made foreman of one of the Juries....

Tuseday 11....The Court opened at 10. ocl & was engaged in disposing of the Sum pro. docket until dinner. This & the Enquiry docket occupied the balance of the day.

Wednesday 12th....I was forced by indisposition to leave the jury box at an early hour & was very sick from headache the whole afternoon ——

Thursday 13th....My father left us on his return home, notwithstanding the inclemency of the day....I sat on the jury & found two verdicts, one guilty & the other not guilty. The jury was discharged about 6 ocl. An aggravated case of assault & battery was tried before Jury N°.1. in which [J. P.]Carroll & [Nathan] Griffin appeared for the Def[endants] & in which Mr.[John?] Edwards made one of the poorest arguments I ever heard from him. Carroll made an ingenious speech and the Judge an exceedingly favourable charge for the Defendants –

Friday 14th....Vegitation is rapidly advancing....Several of my neighbours have planted corn and if the wet weather continues much longer, the grain must rot. I have a lot in the garden above the ground & growing finely. I was discharged as a juryman about half after four ocl. in the afternoon....The jury to which I belonged only tried four cases, two on the criminal & two on the civil docket — A case of quare clausum fregit[25] was tried between Mrs. Riley & Col. Denny, which occupied the whole afternoon & was suspended until tomorrow.

Saturday 15....The jury returned a verdict in favour of Col. Denny. I am pleased with Judge Frost[26] as one of the magistrates of the law. He is courteous, patient & attentive in hearing the arguments and statements of counsel and if there be any fault, it exsists in his indulgence & patient waiting on the bar. When he is required to decide he is prompt, & clear in his perception of the points at issue & equally ready in expounding the legal principles involved, manifesting a familiar acquaintance with the law and the rules of practice. He will make a safe, honest and conscientious Judge and in the enforcement of the law a meritorious & useful judicial Magistrate. My waggon brought a load of provisions from the plantation & passed on to Hamburg with 9 bales of cotton. I rode to Preston's in the afternoon & on my return was attacked with headache, from which I suffered all night....

Sunday 16th....I was exceedingly sick all day & did not leave the house. About 10 ocl. at night we heard the alarm of fire in the Village & learned that it – originated in the stable of Mr. Tibbets.[27] The corn crib & stable were consumed & some of the fencing.

---

25 Unlawful entry to another's property.

26 Edward Frost (1801–1868), Charleston native, Yale 1820, U.S. District Attorney, SC House. Elected Judge of Court of Common Pleas and trustee of SC College, both in 1843. Later president of the Blue Ridge RR.

27 J. D. Tibbetts (1809– ?), shoemaker and stable owner whose business failed in late 1851; 1850 census: $1,000 real estate, 22 slaves.

Monday 17th....I began this morning to plant corn in the Durham field. My Overseer has planted from 50 to 75 acres at my plantation & will finish planting his corn crop in all probability this week....Harvey's[28] negroes, suffered fire to be communicated to the woods, near a small piece of land, which they were clearing and I am informed that the fire spread with great rapidity & violence & consumed a portion of Co^{l}. Pickens fence & in even endangered his dwelling house etc. For such acts of carelessness a party deserves to be indicted & punished. I was feeble & in a state of suffering all day & at night fell really ill.

Tuesday 18th....somewhat smoky, as is very usual in the Month of March....I was engaged in manuring and planting corn in the drill[29] & covering by running two furrows with a small bull tongue plow. I planted the Durham field in different ways by way of experiment. In part the corn was planted in the centre of the ridge & another portion in the Water furrow, in each of which the manure was placed on each side of the corn, as dropped in the furrow.

Wednesday 19th....The servants inform me that they saw Water frozen in several places & but for the prevalence of clouds, during the night, there must have fallen a considerable frost. I rode to the Village & paid a few bills of articles, purchased by M^{rs}. B.

Thursday 20th....Ice & a light frost were visible but I trust that in consequence of the very dry state of the atmosphere not much injury will be done to vegitation. Very tender & succulent plants were partially killed, not by frost but by freezing, such as irish potatoes young corn etc. Such as I saw, seemed to be killed by the freezing of the sap & not by frost. I planted a lot of corn with seed of a new Variety, the colour being entirely red, which I soaked for 24 hours in a Solution of Salt petre.

Friday 21....Frost was quite visible over the fields & the Therm^{r}. was 34$^{\theta}$. At sun rise I observed that his broad face was in a line with [the] Elm tree and the first bar of the sash towards the North of the east window. Sitting at the fire & looking at the scene, the three objects, the bar of the sash, the elm tree, & the sun, appear to be in an exact line. I rode to the farm, inspected the work of the few hands there, returned by the Pottery & had my horse shod — Heard a good deal of gossip in regard to a portion of the people of Pottersville & returned home to dinner. In the afternoon I paid a visit to Preston. On my return I saw old father Moore,[30] who said that Preston had planted all his crop of corn & he had not yet commenced to plant. One had finished & the other had not began....

---

[28] Thomas Harvey? (1786–?); 1850 census: $2,000 real estate, 20 slaves.

[29] Drill: a trench or furrow.

[30] Rev. Joseph Moore (c. 1766–1851), a Methodist pastor for 65 years, was known for his doctrinal sermons. He deeded the land on which the Edgefield Methodist Church stands in 1841. His portrait hangs in its parsonage.

Saturday 22....I am afraid that most of the fruit has been killed. Upon a slight examination, I find that the peaches, figs & all tender and succulent plants in exposed situations, are much injured or killed. I finished yesterday, planting the Durham field of 30 acres in corn. I am informed by a gentleman from the neighbourhood that ice was abundant in the ponds & branches on thursday morning, from which I infer, that the cold was even severer than I supposed & have noted in this book. It must have been below 33$^{\theta}$. In examining the forest trees, I find that the young leaves are mostly killed & will crumble in the hand, like dry fodder....The Spring has been put back at least two weeks by the cold & frost. I enclosed and cleaned up a pond of 2 acres, ready for the plough, in which I design to plant rice.

Sunday 23^{r}....We attended service in the Epis. Church. The music was excellent & the hymns well selected for the occasion....Preston & Martha dined with us.

Monday 24....The mild temperature of the air (50$^{\theta}$) and the gentle showers of rain will soon revive vegitation and restore the fields, the forests & gardens to the green & growing condition....I devoted the afternoon to raising a log house at the farm, intended for the use of the negroes — Price was brought to jail for killing Jones.[31]

Tuesday 25th....I began to plant corn at Hawthorn Glen at the distance of 5 by 3 in the [check?] & covering with the hoe. In the afternoon we rode to Preston, to accompany M^{r}. & M^{rs}. Page. I was informed at night by my servant that fire was communicated to a pile of boards at the M^{t}. Parsons farm & consumed about 1500 [acres?] & also from 100 to 200 rails. I cannot account for the fire. It had been used the previous afternoon in burning a brush heap and as I supposed had become extinguished before I left the place. I passed by the spot at 10 ocl & again at 1. next day & saw no sign of fire yet I cannot suspect any person of wilfully communicating fire. It must have taken from the old embers, which I supposed to be extinguished.[32] There is a small rise in the price of – cotton as reported by the last packet from England.

Wednesday 26....For the last 10 days the cold has been greater than for the same space of time at any period of the Winter although in December & January there were two or three days of greater cold. Fruit is greatly injured but I hope there will be enough for edible purposes or as the politicians say, for the home consumption.

Thursday 27....Hampden set up to day for the first time since Sunday, when he was attacked with measles. I was engaged in planting corn at Hawthorn Glen. Preston & Martha dined with us. The last arrival from Europe represents the State of trade as very flourishing with an increased price & demand for cotton. In conversing with the Villagers, I discovered that much sympathy is felt for Price & every one seems

---

[31] Charles Price shot and killed Benjamin F. Jones in a family-related dispute, and presented himself to the authorities (*Adv.*, March 26, 1845).

[32] Although in this instance the fire might have reignited, slaves were often suspected in such cases. WB's comments suggest that in his mind he was a benevolent master whose servants, in the absence of clear evidence, should not be suspected.

disposed to palliate his offense. It is alledged that he killed Jones for seducing his daughters.[33]

Friday 28th....Two of my servants report themselves sick this morning[,] one of headache & the other of backache[,] and their inability to work will derange my plans for the day. I killed at the farm two very large black snakes, called the adder. The heat of the day had tempted them to leave their den, to bask in the Sun....

Saturday 29th....It is a sweet morning and has inspired all the birds in the garden to strike their sweetest tones in general chorus. I purchased a large bill of articles for my negroes, drapes, shoes, etc. to the value of $30. I finished this morning, planting a field of 16 acres of corn, adjoining a field of old M^{r}. Clark, & commensed another field, called the ditch field. In the afternoon we paid a visit to Co^{l}. Pickens & lady, who had just returned from Alabama.

Sunday 30th....The Rev^{d}. M^{r}. Ford from Augusta performed divine Services in the Epis. church. He delivered an excellent sermon both in the morning & afternoon & also administered the sacrament - in the morning. There is no system of morals and piety so beautiful and attractive as the Christian religion, when it is set forth & displayed by an eloquent Divine in all its purity & simplicity[,] nor is there any character so interresting as the meek, gentle forgiving & self sacrifising follower of Christ. M^{rs}. Julia Reed[34] & her Sisters came down to Church & dined with us & also Preston & Martha.

Monday 31....The termination of this month has not verified the old adage, that when it comes in like a lamb, it goes out like a lyon. The entire day was mild & pleasant altho cloudy....I planted in the afternoon a small bed of the red potatoe & examined my seed potatoes, which I found in excellent order. The general condition of the Country is more prosperous than at the same period last year although produce is not higher. — At that time the market for cotton had sustained an unexpected and most alarming reduction & thousands felt that they were ruined by it unless there should be a reaction, of which there was but little hope. Cotton is now selling from 4 to 6^{cs} p^{r}. ^{lb}. Corn at 60 ^{cs}. per bushel – Peas at from 60 to 75 ^{cs}. Fodder at $1. Turkey p^{r}. pair $1. & chickens at 8 for a dollar. Beef sells from 5 to 6^{cs}. Money is scarce but provisions & the means of living are abundant. I regard the Country as in a good & safe condition. No political news —— .

---

33 Here an honor culture sympathizes with a family member's physical response against dishonorable behavior.

34 Julia Blocker Reed, wife of Rev. Edward Reed.

April 1. 1845

Tuesday 1....Vegitation is progressing with a quick pace....In the morning I sent the Misses Blocker home, passed the fore part of the day at the farm, planting potatoes & Watermellons and in the evening paid a social visit to our neighbour Genl. [Allen] Addison....

Wednesday 2....I am busily engaged in planting corn & hope to finish this week. I left home for the plantation at 1. ocl. & arrived before Sunset –. Negroes in pretty good health.

Thursday 3....After breakfast I rode over the greater part of my plantation, which I found in superior order. The crop of corn was planted & the land for cotton in a state of preparation for the seed, but the Overseer was waiting for rain before planting cotton. I saw two ditches, which he had caused to be cut, changing the current of two branches & filling up the old channels, which were highly creditable to his skill & industry. He spayed 52 young sows & castrated four boars during the day and the day previous he had castrated 36 young boars. The hogs were in very good order but the cattle were considerably reduced. The horses & mules were in excellent condition, so also the sheep & goats. The Overseer reported that he had about 100 young hogs or shoats, about 80 [one] year olds, beside the sows. 33 lambs & 8 or 9. young calves & a mule colt. The colt is a very fine one, out of the old Blond mare....I rode through a part of the neighbourhood & saw several of my neighbours planting cotton. One was dropping the seed and leaving them uncovered & the other was covering with a small bull tongue plow. The wheat crops are unusully promising tho they are suffering for the want of rain. I never saw my plantation look prettier or more interresting. The trees were getting in leaf many of them covered with flowers, such as the wild crab, the haw, the plumb & the dogwood[.] [T]he fields around the house were green with a growth of luxurient wheat & other small grain & the lawn in front of the house, becoming verdant with a young growth of grass.

Friday 4th....I left the plantation at 7...& arrived at 1. ocl. On my return I found the Rev^{d}. M^{r}. Reid & lady[,] M^{r}. Page & lady, M^{rs}. Blocker & M^{rs}. Carroll with Preston & his Wife at my house. Soon after my return the family of Mr. Mims, passed with the corpse of Sarah Mims who had died in Columbia the day before. It was a melancholy spectacle, which deeply affected the whole Village. Here was seen a fond mother returning in mournful procession, with the inanimate body of an only daughter, who had been sent to Columbia to complete her education, & who promised by her amiable qualities & sweet temper to impart great happiness to her parents & friends. To see this young & beautious flower cut down & nipped just as it[35] was expanding into maturity, was well calculated to awaken the strongest feelings of regret & sorrow. At 5 ocl. the Rev^{d}. M^{r}. Johnson delivered a sermon in the Baptist Church on the mournful occasion, from which place the body was removed to the family burial ground, now the property of Doct^{r}. Richard Mims, & committed to the earth. Thus has prematurely fallen this amiable & interresting girl, at a very tender and attractive age....Co^{l}. Carroll & lady returned from a visit - to Savannah of two weeks in fine health.

Saturday 5. I purchased a load of oats, for which I paid $15.62. The Overseer sent me down 4 quarters of very excellent beef, two of which I sold & the remainder was kept for the use of the family. I packed in sand two boxes of sweet potatoes for eating uses, as a means of preserving them through the Summer —

Sunday 6th....The Rev^{d}. M^{r}. Reed performed service in the Epis. Church both morning & evening. As usual he preached two sensible & orthodox sermons. Preston & wife, M^{r}. Yancy, M^{r}. D. Adams & the two Misses Blocker returned with us from Church to dinner.

Monday 7....This being sale day, brought a good number of persons to the Village, either on business or from a motive of idle curiosity. Some property was sold & at very fair prices, including land[,] negroes, horses & mules – I purchased a plow horse at $50. In the afternoon there occurred a shocking riot or fracus between Murrel & Loue Gomillion, in which a M^{r}. Watley was shot by Murrel, whose purpose was to shoot Gomillion.[36] There were several other frays, in which not much injury was done. I understood that there was an exhibition of beastly drunkeness, discreditable to the District & offensive to the eye of decency. The temperance societies have reformed a portion of the drinking community but the other portion now drink to greater excess, than formerly & in their drunken debaucheries have less regard for decency & public opinion than they ever had. There is also prevailing in the District a sanguinary spirit of revenge, that has made violence & bloodshed common occurrences in our Village on public occasions. Whenever a dispute arises & proceeds to violence, the use of deadly weapons is constantly resorted to and the spilling of human blood or taking human life is regarded with very little more repugnance or abhorence than killing a wild beast. In fact there is no portion of the United States, where life is regarded at so cheap a rate & I regret to say that public opinion in this District is greatly at fault in this matter. Death by violence has become so common, that it - has ceased to shock public sentiment, – the consequence

---

[35] Sarah Manly Mims, age 16, only daughter of Mathew Mims (1780–1848) and Elizabeth Tutt Mims (1790–1874).

[36] B. L. Murrel (1807–); 1850 census: $5,600 real estate, 22 slaves. If WB's spelling is correct, the wounded man was Asha Watley (1800–). However, on April 11 he writes the name as Whatley. On Gomilion, see Sept. 2, 1844, entry on a sheriff's day exchange of gunshots in which Lovett Gomillion killed Joseph W. Glover.

is, that the law is disregarded & the offender escapes punishment. I was informed that a servant boy of Major Talbot about 16 years of age, made an attempt upon the life of his master who was sick in bed, during the tempory absense of the family from the room, in which he lay. He injured his master very severely & would have taken his life, if he had not been prevented by some of the other servants.

Tuesday 8th....We made a call on Mr. & Mrs. Dearing [of Charleston] at Col. Pickens, who were on a short visit to their daughter. I finished planting corn & commenced bedding for cotton this afternoon. I am more backward than my neighbours from the fact that two of my work horses had foals, which deprived me of the use of their labour for several days. In the afternoon I was attacked with head ache & was forced to lie down. Doctr. & Mrs. Barrett passed the night with us on their way to Hamburg. He is a very agreeable gentleman & abounds in information on almost every subject. In the natural sciences he is a great enthusiast and in chemistry, botany and zoology he has some reputation, I regard him among the most successful physicians in the upper Country & altogether an excellent & useful member of Society. His lady is an industrious, hospitable & kind hearted woman & fills her station in life with great fidelity....

Wednesday 9....There was a light frost yesterday morning & I presume another this morning. Doctr. Barrett & lady left us after breakfast. I was prevented by severe suffering from rising from bed until near 7. ocl. I devoted the day in preparing a piece of land for cotton.

Thursday 10th....I began this morning to plant cotton at the farm. My Overseer delayed planting during the whole of last week, waiting for rain. He was forced to begin on last monday, when the earth was much drier than the week previous. It is more exceedingly dry & dusty & the earth is becoming too hard to plow in places. It proved to be a fatal error.

Crop for 1845 at home.

Corn		Cotton	
Mc.Neil field	16	House field	5
Pond Do.	12	Part of [Stoney?] field.	8
[Grave?] yard	12	Lot at house —	2
Durham field	30		acres 15
	acres 70	§ Lot of potatoes & §	
		§ rice 1½ acres §	

Friday 11th....I finished planting a lot of cotton about 5 acres, also a small lot of potatoes & one of water mellons. In the afternoon we paid a visit to Preston & lady. Heard that Whatley, who was shot on Monday last by Murrell, was in eminent danger of loosing his life.

Saturday 12. Went to my farm morning and evening & caused to be beded about 8 acres for cotton & planted a small lot of sweet potatoes.

Sunday 13h....exceedingly dry & dusty. Corn & cotton comes up very slowly & irregularly and vegitation advances tardily. Mr. Reed officiated in the Epis. church morning & evening. He is an able & interresting preacher notwithstanding his manner & voice, which are faulty. I regard him as one of the most promising, able & improving Ministers in the State & destined to some distinction, if his health does not fail.

Monday 14th....My waggon arrived from my plantation with a load of corn for Preston. The overseer writes that the negroes are well & that he had planted about 200 acres of the cotton crop. I received a pamphlet by mail, containing a statement of some of the particulars of a personal difficulty between Col. P.M. Butler[,] Indian Agent[,] & the Officers at Fort Gibson, [Oklahoma] originating from the report of the agent to the Government. I exceedingly regret that this misunderstanding should have occurred on many accounts, for even if Col. Butler be in the right it – will place him in a very disagreeable & embarrassing relation with the officers, with whom he must hold official intercourse; but my principal regret arises from the apprehension that this quarrel with the officers may induce the President, to decline, to continue him in office. I have no relation, whom I hold in higher estimation & no one to whom, I owe higher obligations for his generous services to my Son [Preston]; it is therefore natural that I should feel a deep interest in whatever affects the character or success of my friend. Mrs. C[arroll]. left for Colum[bia].

Tuesday 15....My waggon left this morning for Hamburg & I & Mrs. Brooks are preparing to follow. I have just heard from a Waggoner that the Village of Anderson has been partially distroyed by fire. But our store[37] escaped the conflagration. We reached Hamburg at 3 ocl. I purchased a few articles & sold my cotton to Mr. Garmany[38] at the following prices (to wit) 9 bags at 6¼.cs 5 bags at 5½ & 4 bags at 5. At night we took lodgings at Mrs. Campfields[39] in Augusta.

Wednesday 16h....I returned to Hamburg, purchased a bill of articles, settled for my cotton & prepared my waggon for its return home....After dinner we left Augusta, passed the River at the Sandbar ferry[40] & reached our Son Jame's in Barnwell Dist

[37] No information has been found regarding this store.

[38] George W. Garmany (c. 1813–).

[39] Capt. Edward Campfield and his wife [name not found] were founders of Augusta's First Christian Church in 1835. It is not known whether she also ran an inn there.

[40] Ferry on the Savannah River about four miles downstream from Augusta. The nearby sand bar was a popular dueling ground due to its location on the line between South Carolina and Georgia.

about Sunset. We found our children in good health and anxiously expecting our arrival.

Thursday 17....After breakfast I rode with James to inspect his land & crop. His corn looked very well & his cotton had not come up. The land is free pine land & susceptable of great improvement but as a tract, it is too small & too much surrounded by other plantations. It will not answer for a permanent settlement – unless he can purchase lands, adjoining his. His house is small but convenient & very comfortable. It has a clean & neat appearance and does credit to the taste & industry of our daughter in law. They appear very happy & contented, which is better than riches. In the afternoon Genl. Hammond & lady & his mother came down & took tea with us. He is a gentleman of more than ordinary intelligence, of correct judgement & remarkable discrimination. As a writer he is logical & cogent & has attained an enviable reputation by the force and ability of his messages to the Legislature while Governor of the State & some miscellanious articles on the subject of slavery. His lady is remarkable for her gentle manners, mild & benevolent disposition & for her winning & enlarged hospitality.

Friday 18th. Immediately after breakfast I and James joined the Genl. at his house, for the purpose of riding over his plantation. We set out at 8 ocl & returned at 1. ocl. We passed through his entire plantation & I had an opportunity of seeing the arrangement & order of his fields, the condition of his houses, and every thing appertaining to a plantation. He has about 2000 acres cleared, the greater part of which was planted in corn & cotton, & the whole has been manured with marl, within the last three years.[41] The Genl. is engaged in making & spreading manure on his fields on a more extensive scale than any man in the State & I presume there is no one more enthusiastically occupied in making experiments, both in the different modes of application and the different kinds of manure. His fields were in good order & his crop well planted, but I saw no great evidence of attention to neatness. His houses and fixtures were large, convenient & well erected, for the accommodation of his negroes & stock of all kinds. Water & shade were abundant & convenient to his stables & lots. A portion of his effective force, is employed in boating marl, making manure & ditching & draining throughout the year. I saw large piles of manure, made of peat, or swamp mud, mixed with contributions from the stable, the cow yard & the hog sty. Every animal that dies, is added to the manure pile & even the excrement & urine from his negroes are not lost, but are made to enrich his turnip fields. He has already reclaimed & is in the process of reclaiming some swamp & low lands which appear to be very rich, on portions of which he has made very large crops & if they equal their appearance, they will be very valuable. We also

[41] Hammond had concluded that if he were not to move West, he would need to apply scientific ideas to his farming. After reading Edmund Ruffin's *Essay on Calcareous Manures* in 1841, he became a disciple and began to apply marl to some of his fields. He found and rented a bluff 12 miles down the Savannah very rich in marl, and assigned 11 slaves to dig and boat it to his plantation (Faust, *Hammond*, 113–17).

visited his mills, saw & grist, which are very valuable. At his grist mill he has a pair of stones prepared for grinding corn in the rear with the shucks on. I saw a few bushels ground, & a better mixture of corn, cob & shuck, all reduced to the proper fineness, no one could desire. It is done very rapidly & with not much trouble. The only trouble is in feeding the Mill. I think the Genl. told me, that he gained eight (8) quarts in each bushel by the process of grinding, corn, cob & shuck together. He also exhibited to me an experiment of grinding bones for manure. The mill ground 3 pecks of bone dust in 12 minutes, reducing the bones to the fineness of grist for homony. He is collecting all the bones, within his reach for the purpose of reducing to manure. I saw several spots of land, arranged for making experiments with various kinds of manure, such as guano, marl, plaster of Paris, & compost, saturated with human urine. From what came under my eye, the General is a practical, ardent & enterprising, planter, who is pursuing a judicious system of enriching his lands by the process of manuring which must result in great benefit to himself and prove of signal service to his neighbours, if by his example he can rouse them to the importance of the great work. Hammond has a clear head, sound judgement & the most discriminating mind of any man, with whom I am acquainted.

Saturday 19th....At 8 ocl. we parted with our children at Genl. Hammonds & took our departure for home. We passed a day & night with the Genl. & his lady in all the enjoyment, which unaffected hospitality & free & friendly intercourse can under any circumstances impart.[42] We reached home about Sunset & found all well. The day was warm & dry, the road dusty & heavy & our ride fatiguing. On our arrival we rec^{d}. a letter from Whitfield. He & our daughter were well, altho he had been indisposed.

Sunday 20th....Service in the Epis. church by the Rev^{d}. M^{r}. Page. In the afternoon I rode to the Pottery to enquire after the girl Elizabeth, who was reported to be sick. — Preston & Martha dined & passed the night with us —

Monday 21....All small grain is suffering very much & it is reported that the crops of wheat are expected to be short. Lately planted seed cannot germinate & the

---

[42] Some might read "under any circumstances" as a veiled reference to the Hammond scandal. If WB's journal-keeping was ever to prompt him to comment on Hammond's recent political isolation, and allude to the reason for it, this page would seem the place. Obviously the subject would not have come up while Mary Brooks and Catherine Hammond were present, and a man as proper as WB would have been unlikely to raise it during the tour. Clearly he thought very highly of Hammond's intellect, as did many. In July 1845, after publication of Hammond's *Clarkson* (pro-slavery*) Letters,* he would write him a letter of effusive praise (Bleser, *Secret and Sacred,* 151). He also still felt obliged to Hammond for his efforts toward settling the Brooks-Wigfall affair. As to what Hammond thought of Brooks, the one comment found in his published diaries, in Dec. 1844, dismisses Preston, then his aide-de-camp, as "fidgety to be doing, and always moving in the wrong time and place," and adds, "just like his father" (Bleser, 140). But Hammond was almost habitually dismissive about his associates.

stands of corn & cotton will be very deficient if rain should not fall in a few days. Peas & vegitables in the garden are suffering & the cabbage plants seem to be withering & dieing in the beds, where they were planted, there not yet having been rain enough to admit of their being transplanted. It is the most extraordinary drought, that I have ever seen in the month of april. We have not yet been blessed with an april shower & but one gust of rain has fallen in this month. I witnessed an exhibition of ill temper and perverseness on the part of a fair one to her husband, in which, as usual, passion dethroned judgement, prudence & discretion & run riot in extravagance & folly. How unfortunate it is, that man should ever forget to exercise the attributes of a moral, rational & responsible being and surrender himself to the sway of mere animal impulse & blind passion. It is the part of wisdom to bear with phylosophic resignation those circumstances & events in life, which we can neither prevent nor guard against.

Tuesday 22....Co^{l}. Pickens gave [illegible] a large party, at which all the fashionables of the Village were present, together with some persons from Augusta, Hamburg & Charleston and also a Major Hamilton & daughter from Columbia County G^{eo}. It was a sumptuous & elegant entertainment. Our host was exceedingly hospitable and attentive & his young Wife all kindness & smiles. There was dancing & the company did not disperse until 1. Ocl.

....

Thursday 24. I set out for my plantation & in getting out of my buggy on the Way, I spained my left foot very badly. After resting at the plantation for a few hours, I rode into my fields in my buggy, not being able to ride on horse back. The corn looked pretty well, having been enlivened by a shower of rain on the preceeding afternoon. The cotton was coming up & on the fresh land, there was nearly enough for a stand. The wheat will be better than I expected altho the heads are small. The oats looked pretty good. I had no time to examine any thing else & I was incapable of walking.

Friday 25. After early breakfast I set out for my fathers, where I arrived at 12 ocl. I found him in exceeding feeble health, tho better than he had been a few days before. Major Blocker & my sister arrived in the evening on a visit to father.

Saturday 26. I left my fathers at 6 ocl. on my return home. I called at the Judge Butlers for a short time & arrived at home about 12 ocl. where I found all well. I met Preston & Martha, he having only a short time, returned from hunting his runaway mules. In the afternoon I rode over my crop at the farm. All that is up looks well but I have from 15 to 20 acres of corn, that I fear will not come up. I have no recollection of so dry an April....Even the grass looks parched & withered. The therm^{r}. stood at 80$^{\theta}$. at 8 ocl at night.

Sunday 27th....I attended at the Epis. church and heard as dull & sleepy a sermon as even stupidity could desire. The composition & ideas were as correct & orthodox as most sermons are but the delivery was abominable. Our minister seems to be too inert to make the necessary effort to read audibly & distinctly....

Monday 28....The dust in the roads is from one to two inches deep & so dry & impalpable as to render it – unpleasant to travel over them either on horse back or in a vehicle.

Tuesday 29th. I purchased a set of waggon gear for which I paid $20. to Carpenter, a Tenessee trader. An infant child of Mr. Goodman, was buried this afternoon in the Epis. church yard. The children are suffering from the measles & various other complaints both

in the Village & neighbourhood —

Wednesday 30th....I rode over my farm & inspected the State of the crop. The corn & cotton, that had come up, looks very well & is growing but all seed that are now in the ground, must remain there, as there is not moisture enough to produce germination. I examined my oats & they are greatly damaged. They do not appear to have grown any for the last three weeks & portions are turning yellow. The drought is doing great injury to the small grain crops, to the gardens & retarding the coming up of late planted corn & cotton to a late period. I observed that a cloud of dust followed the tract of the ploughman in the fields & that the plough turned up but little moist earth. We rode to Prestons in the afternoon & found all well....The temperature is mild & pleasant & but for the drought the weather would be delightful....This month very much resembles the month of May of last year, hot, dry & generally clear.

May 1. 1845.

Thursday 1....On examining a field in corn this morning, I discovered that not more than one third had come up or it had been distroyed by birds, worms or dry weather, so that not more than two thirds of the hills of corn were standing. In fact I never had a crop of corn to come up so indifferently & I see no remedy if the dry weather continues.

Friday 2....I called on the Revd. Mr. Page at his lodgings & had a long conversation with him in relation to some unpleasant disagreement between him & the Vestry of the Epis. church, which had caused him great mortification. I could not under the circumstances censure the Vestry yet my sympathies were strongly excited in behalf of Mr. Page. I believe him to be a good & virtuous man, very conscientious & strictly pious but he has been unlucky in the formation of his domestic relations. His Wife is (I fear) weak & imprudent both in speech & behaviour. Mr. E[dmund] Bacon lost his youngest child at night, being an only daughter.

Saturday 3rd....At 6 ocl. the ceremony for the burial of Mr. Bacon's little daughter commenced in the Epis. Church, thence we proceeded to the family burying ground & the body was committed to the earth. The Revd. Mr. Page conducted the services.

The Babtist denomination of Christians are holding a convention at this place to consider the course, which it may become the Southern branch of this Church to take in relation to some resolutions, passed by the board of Missions on the subject of the nonemployment of Slave holders in that line of duty. I understand that the convention is not large. I believe the convention here was intended to be preliminary to the convention which is intended to be held in Augusta, during the ensuing week, at which delegates are expected from all the Slaveholding States. [43]

Sunday 4....There was preaching in the Babtist church morning, afternoon and at night. The Revd. Mr. Page dined with us, & after tea, he took leave of us, expecting to leave the Village in the morning, to find an engagement elsewhere. I am fully impressed with the belief that he is an excellent man, tho not strong minded and that he merits the good opinion & kind sympathies of his late congregation. He has physical defects, which will always prevent him from being an interresting Preacher yet he is sensible & well educated.

Monday 5....The assemblage of persons in the Village was not large. They were very orderly & left the Village at an early hour in the afternoon. The Convention of Babtists adjourned this morning, after adopting a report & choosing some 20 delegates to the Convention, which is to assemble in Augusta on thursday next — Mr. C. Pinckney & daughter came over in the evening & took tea with us. He is a pious, worthy man, of high character.[44]

Tuesday 6th....About 4. ocl a light shower fell, which wet the earth from ½ half to an inch in depth....

Wednesday 7th....Vegitation looks refreshed but the heat of the Sun will soon evaporate the moisture imparted by the light rain, & vegitation will soon again suffer....After waiting for three weeks for rain to enable me to break up & plant a small field, called the pasture, I caused it to be plowed & planted in cotton today. The earth was very hard & broke badly.

Thursday 8h....Mrs. Brooks recd. a letter from Mrs. Carroll informing her that her Sister Mrs. [Elizabeth] Laborde had a daughter, some time last week. Both mother & child are doing well.[45] I began to day to plant over a field of corn of something like 10 acres, in which not more than one hill in fifty had come up. In the afternoon we paid a visit to Preston, taking Mr. & Mrs. McClintock with us....

---

[43] A crisis over slavery reached its climax when the national Baptist Triennial Convention's mission board refused to appoint slaveholders as missionaries. In response, southern delegates met in Augusta May 8–12, 1845, and formed the Southern Baptist Convention. Rev. William B. Johnson of Edgefield was its organizer and first president.

[44] Rev. Charles Cotesworth Pinckney (1812–1898), Beaufort native. Rector of St. James, Santee, and then Christ Church, Greenville 1835–1845. Afterward he served Christ Church, Charleston, of which he was Rector 1854–1898.

[45] Online sources do not include a child born to the Labordes in May 1845.

Friday 9th....Finished the field of corn, which I began to replant on yesterday & commenced, plowing & working the cotton, of which I have planted a small crop but not ¼ of which has come up — Our daughter Ellen arrived from Columbia very unexpectedly about dark — We did not expect her until next day. She is in good health but has grown much since she left us last November.

Saturday 10th....On riding to my farm in the afternoon I observed that the branch in the old field had ceased to run & that the two small streams at the farm had also failed. I certainly have never witnessed so dry a period in the Spring of the year or one, so injurious to all kinds of small grain.

....

Monday 12. Rain began to fall a short time before daylight in light showers. On rising, I saw that the wind was blowing from the east & that the morning was dark & cool, resembling a rainy morning in September. The rain ceased about 11. ocl. wetting the earth to the depth of 3 or 4 inches. Cloudy throug [sic] the day & light mist occasionally but rain after 11 ocl....It was the first rain since March Court [?] that wet the ground, sufficiently for transplanting. This rain was on thursday the 13th.

Tuesday 13th....I planted two lots of corn, which had been delayed by the dry weather, one for the negroes crop & the other for fodder & mutton[46] corn....

Wednesday 14h....About 10 ocl. a cloud formed in the North & rain began to fall & continued moderately until 12 ocl. at night, when a very heavy shower fell. We spent the evening with our neighbour Mr. Mc.Clintock where we met a talkative & cheerful widow (Mrs. Glover), from near Walterborough.

Thursday 15....Rain began to fall about 7. ocl. in the morning & continued in one uninterrupted shower until about 12 ocl. Notwithstanding the inclemency of the day our children Preston & Martha set out for Fairfield. Rain constitutes only a trifling obstacle in the Way, when a visit from a child to parents is contemplated. Light Showers from 4 ocl until night. The earth thoroughly wet & the vegitable Kingdom greatly revived.

Friday 16....Every thing in the gardens, fields & forests look refreshed & enlivened. I have rarely ever seen a more favourable season of rain. It fell in copious yet gentle showers....I set out for my plantation at 1. ocl & arrived at 6 ocl. I found all well. I walked to the fields & saw the negroes cutting wheat. They began two days before on the 14th.

Saturday 17....After breakfast I rode over my plantation & examined my crop with some care. The corn is good & about 100 acres very superior. The wheat is as good as I expected & the oats will make a tolerable crop, if we can get a few more rains. But I have not had such a prospect of a cotton crop in 20 years. Not more than half the cotton has come up. Altho the balance seems now to be in a germinating State,

---

[46] Sweet corn, just ripe enough for eating.

It will be too late to make a full crop.

Sunday 18th....After breakfast I set out for home & arrived at 12 ocl. I was attacked with headache & suffered greatly until 2 ocl at night, when I felt partial relief.

Monday 19th....I set out for Augusta with Mrs. Brooks & Ellen & arrived at 4 ocl.

Tuesday 20th....I devoted the day in looking for & selecting a carriage, buggy & Sundry things for the children. I also went to Hamburg & sold a lot of 27 bales of cotton for my father to [Josiah] Sibley & Co. at $5\frac{7}{8}$ pr. 100 lb. I heard neither in Augusta or Hamburg of any news of the slightest interest except of a local or personal character. It was in Augusta a subject of much interest that the Contractors had commenced operations in opening the new canal, on which the Town had lately resolved & for which contracts had been formed.[47] The only item of news in Hamburg was the marriage of Hubbard's daughter to a young man from Mobile. We passed the evening with the Revd. Mr. Ford. Began to plow over corn the 2nd time & to plant peas at the Mt. Parsons farm.[48]

Wednesday....We left Augusta after early breakfast and reached home at 2 ocl. All well. In the afternoon I rode over my crop at the farm. It grows finely & looks well & is in pretty good order.

Thursday 22. In looking over and arranging my papers, I ascertained that I had expended in Augusta about $725. & paid in Hamburg two or three bills, amounting to about $31. My kind, liberal, affectionate & venerable father gave me the means of making these purchases, to whom I am indebted for as many favours as ever Son received from a father, from my infancy up to the present time. This record can never meet his eye nor is it likely that it will reach his knowledge, yet I take pleasure in bearing my testimony to the fact, that for his circumstances in life & for his opportunities he has been one of the Kindest & best of fathers. Few men have submitted to such privations & exercised so much self denial for the benefit of his children, whose welfare & happiness has always been the nearest wish to his heart.

Friday 23....I began to plow over corn the second time & to plant peas at Hawthorn Glenn. On riding over my fields I was struck with a fact in regard to the germination of cotton seed, that is (in my opinion) worthy of record. The seed, which was planted in or about the 10 of April, in consequence of the dry weather, failed to come up except in damp places and even partially in those places. They lay in the ground from the 10 of April until after the rain, which fell on the 15 of May without the slightest appearance of coming up & even after the rain, it germinated more tardily & came up a few days later than a small lot, that I had planted on the 7 & 8 of May. This seed, which had lain in the ground about 35 days, came up slower by two or three days, than seed which had been planted only about 10 days. I observed the same fact in a field, where corn had been manured with cotton seed about the 1st

[47] See introduction, xxxviii.

[48] Probably inserted later.

of april. About 6 ocl. a cloud formed rather suddenly in the N°.West &...three plenteous showers before 9 ocl, wetting the surface of the earth thoroughly and not washing it injureously.

Saturday 24th....There is a freshness & green & growing appearance in the whole vegitable kingdom, which has not before been exhibited during the present year....About 9. ocl. we set out on a visit to Major Blocker but were forced to return by a very threatening cloud & mist of rain. By 12 ocl. it - became clear & at 4 ocl. we again left home for Major Blocker's, where we arrived early in the afternoon & found the family well. I rode with the Major to look at his flocks of sheep and purchased 4 lambs for which I agreed to pay him $6.00 upon delivery.

Sunday 25....I rose in a state of indisposition & immediately after breakfast, we returned home – Mrs. Brooks, Ellen & Hampden were in company, for the purpose of attending church. I felt too much indisposed to leave the house & remained the greater part of the day in bed, the rest of the family going to Church. Fire was comfortable from morning till night.

Monday 26th....I paid a visit to the Village & called on the Revd. Mr. Pinckney & his mother at County's [Compty's] who were on their way to Pendleton. I sent Shelton this morning after my old carriage & a new Buggy to Hamburg, from which he returned about dark, going & coming in the day....

Tuesday 27....Fire indispensible to comfort. At 1 ocl. I left home for the plantation, taking Ellen with me, at which we arrived about 6. ocl. finding all well.

Wednesday 28th....I rode through my fields & then to William Griffins, to attend the sale of a portion of his personal property, which had been advertised for sale under FiFa,[49] but the Depty. Shff postponed the sale. I returned to dinner and in the afternoon, rode over my crop & inspected the greater part of it. The corn crop is good but I never have had so bad a prospect for a cotton crop. Since the last rain the cotton has come up in great abundance but it - is too late, to yield an average crop. There are 175 acres, which the hoe has not yet touched, & most of what was first chopped out, now looks as tho it - had never been worked from the quantity of cotton, which has come up since the rain. The corn has been plowed over twice, peas planted & this part of the crop is in good order. There are 200 acres of first rate corn. The wheat crop is principally cut & packed in the ginhouse, ready for the threshing machine. The oats & rye only tolerable & the barley almost a failure. I have an abundance of old corn & have sold about 100 bushels at 50. & 56¼cs pr. bushel. The mules & horses were in good order but the cattle are thin. Sheep & hogs were in a thriving condition. I saw no cause of dissatisfaction except with the cotton.

---

[49] Fieri Facias: a court document ordering a sheriff to seize an amount of property equal to the amount due on debts.

Thursday 29th....We reached home at 11. Ocl. & found all well. A convention of the Southern babptists at Augusta Ge°. and another of Methodists at LouisVille, Kentucky, have recommended a separation of their respective churches from their Northern brethren.[50] This step became enevitable in consequence of the conduct of the Northern durision [division] of these two churches towards their Southern brethren in regard to the matter of slavery. I do not regret the separation for it will remove one cause of agitation from the fanatics of emancipation. Mr. Hiram Hutchinson called over after dinner & sat with us a short time. The last accounts from Europe caused the cotton market to advance about ¼. pr. lb....

Friday 30th....I saw in the Abbeville paper a confirmation of the rumour that Mr. Mc.Duffy had suffered an alarming stroke of paralysis, which threatened to terminate his life. This attack does not supprise me as the infirm state of his health for the last 15 years, rendered such an event more than probable. The methodists are holding a protracted meeting in the Village and I understand that it – is poorly attended.

Saturday 31. This is the last day of May & it is cold enough for the first of April....The entire month of May has been colder than that of April and more unfavourable to the growth of the crops. Two rains only have fallen & one or two very light showers & each of these was succeeded by high winds and cold weather. I have never known the streams of water in the Spring so low....During the continuance of this cold & dry weather it is impossible for the crops to grow much & young cotton must die for want of the necessary heat & moisture. Preston & his Wife passed by in the afternoon on their return home, having Miss Bratton & Miss J. Means in company.[51]

June 1. 1845.

Sunday 1st. This morning presents a bright sun and clear sky but it - is cold enough for the 1. of April....We attended at the methodist church & heard a sensible sermon from Doctr. Holliman, a surgeon Dentist & preacher & a very appropriate exhortation from Mr. Mc.Corkindale[?]. The communion was administered to 7 males & about 30 females — I suffered during the whole service by reason of sick stomach & great nausea. Mrs. Blocker & part of her children, Preston & his Wife & her Sister Belle & also Miss Bratton dined with us. I suffered the greatest agony until after 1. ocl. at night & until I was almost exhausted from an attack of head-

[50] The Methodist situation resembled the Baptists' (n. 225), with two exceptions. It focused on one slaveowning clergyman, Bishop James O. Andrew of Georgia, and the Methodists had a history of opposition to slavery especially around the turn of the 19th century.

[51] The Bratton family was prominent in York District.

ache. I have never experienced greater pain during the paroxism, nor greater debility from its affects upon my nervous system.

Monday 2....The Court of Equity was opened this morning at 10 ocl, Chancellor David Johnson presiding. I was feeble and indisposed during the day & was only able to ride to the Village & remain for a few minutes. In the after noon we rode to Preston's & he & his family returned & remained until after tea. We had also the company of Mr. Yancy. I was able to sit up, tho not free from suffering.

Tuesday 3d....The crop of this grain must be light. In the afternoon we paid a visit to Col. Pickens. I met Judge Johnson & Genl. [Waddy] Thompson & rode in the carriage with them to Col. Pickens. I was gratified to see that the health of these gentlemen was as good as I have ever seen it.

Wednesday 4th. I held a long and agreeable conversation with Genl. Thompson in the morning, during which he narrated a number of interresting facts in regard to the two great political parties of the Country, interspersed with ludicrous anecdotes. This gentleman is peculiarly gifted with conversational talent, & his mind is well stored with all sorts of knowledge, which imparts unusual interest to his conversation. In riding over my fields this evening, it was apparent to the sight that the corn had grown rapidly for the last two days & the cotton has improved....There is a party of young people at Mr. Wardlaws, this evening, to which our daughter has gone —

Thursday 5th....The Court of Equity still in session but not doing much business as few of the parties are ready for trial. I began to cut oats at my farm this morning, from three to four acres being ripe enough for the sythe.

Friday 6th....Mr. Mc.Clintock, the teacher in our Male Academy had an examination of his pupils this morning. They were examined in English, Geography, Latin & Greek and exhibited a highly creditable accuracy of Knowledge in each department for the length of time they have been at School to him. It is but common justice to this gentleman, to say that he discharges his duties with ardour & fidelity & that he is a successful & eminently useful teacher. There was a small audience of both gentlemen & ladies, all of whom seemed pleased with the performance. Several of the young gentlemen exhibited in Oratory & two, John Simkins & Jos. Terry, delivered addresses of their own composition, which were very well written & spoken — The exercises closed at 1. Ocl. Our Son Hampden acquitted himself very well, not missing a question. I passed the afternoon at Col. Carrolls with the Judge & members of the bar in discussing the merits of a good dinner & partaking with the Col. some of his good wine. It was a pleasant party. Judges Johnson & Butler & Col. Pickens were of the company. We had a few songs from Mr. Arthur Simkins, who sings with exquisite taste.

Saturday 7th....I & Ellen paid a visit to Judge Butler & his family & on our return called at Col. Pickens..... The crops on fresh land are growing & doing well but on old land the growth is slow. I observed a lot of [illegible] corn in my garden was in tassel on the 5th. of this month, nearly as soon as the early varieties. No new feature in the political news but a slight fall in the price of cotton....

Sunday 8th....I attended at the Baptist church & heard a common place sermon from the Revd. Mr. [James] Chiles. The manner of this gentleman is good & his matter sensible but he is totally destitute of genius and imagination. He will always preach with good sense but he can never stir the feelings of his audience for he has none of the elements of eloquence. Preston & his family took tea with us.

Monday 9th....The papers of this morning are utterly barren of all news ....There was a party of young people at Doctr. Mays at which our daughter was invited & attended.

Tuesday 10th....After breakfast I rode through the Village & thence along the road by Col. Fraziers & Burts farms, thence by Saml. Goode', [J] Lyon, R. Mim's, [J] Terry', John Hollingworths, James Griffins[52] & thence by the Hawthorn Glen farm home. My object was to see the state of crops as compared with my own. The corn looks pretty well & is in a green & growing state. It is from knee to head high. Cotton is also of all sizes from that which has four & six leaves & is not more than four inches high, up to that which is knee high & full of limbs & squares, some of which will exhibit – blooms in a few days. The corn would be greatly benefitted by rain as I saw some portions of it beginning to wilt by 10 ocl. About 11. ocl. there was a formation of light clouds in the SoWest, which discharged a light shower of rain. It is the only shower that I have seen this year, that resembled at all the half crying half laughing showers, which usually fall in April, where sunshine & clouds succeed each other in rapid succession & where the face of nature exhibits tears & smiles in harmonious union....

Wednesday 11....In the evening we had a dancing party at our house. The young people were merry & gay & kept up the frolick till after one Ocl. I retired at 2 ocl....

Thursday 12th....Preston & his family with Mary & B.M. Blocker spent the night & day with us after the dance.

Friday 13th....Vegitation has been seriously affected by the dry winds & hot sun of the two last days. I made an effort this morning to settle an angry dispute between Mr. [Henry?]Spann & the Revd. Mr. Mc.Corkadale, which has already & is likely to involve several families. Spann exhibited a good temper & willingness to compro-

---

[52] James Griffin (1782–1855), a "wealthy" planter who owned a plantation north of ECH on Long Cane Road. A charter member and deacon of Antioch Baptist Church. His son James B. Griffin's Civil War-era letters were published in McArthur and Burton, eds., *A Gentleman and an Officer.*

mise the dispute but Mr. Mc. was not very lamblike altho he professed a wish to settle the matter — I hope that I may succeed. I also attended at 1. Ocl. at Pottersville, as one of a Court to try a negro of Mrs. [Fanny?]Landrum's for insolence & threats of violence to Caleb Mitchell. The proof was clear & positive as to the charges yet the Court entertained no doubt, that Mitchell was alarmed without reason & that altho the negro was a muttering, insolent rascal yet there was no danger to be apprehended from his violence. They sentenced him to a light flogging. Mitchell must be an arrant coward for he swore that he did not feel that he & his family were safe if the negro was allowed to go at large & remain on the plantation with them — I cannot pass over this trial, without recording the fact, that Mr. [John?] Kirksey is the most ignorant and inefficient magistrate, that I have seen attempt to dispense justice or to execute the laws.

Saturday 14th....The squadron of cavalry paraded in the Village under the command of Col. Smyley[53] & reviewed by Col. Nichols. I was too unwell to witness their performance, & in fact was confined to the bed the greater part of the afternoon —

Sunday 15....The vegitable kingdom is somewhat revived by the rain & the earth relieved from its arid & parched appearance — The Revd. Mr. Walker[54] preached his first sermon in the Epis. Church to a very large audience. There was no preaching either in the Baptist or Methodist churches, & the greater part of the church going people attended at the Epis. & filled the house. There were not less than 150 persons. I was pleased with Mr. Walker. His manner is good & his style of reading clear, audible & distinct. His sermon would compare very favourably with those young preachers of intelligence & education in any part of the Union. I suffered another paroxism of head ache in the afternoon & night — Monday 16th....I am engaged in saving my crop of oats which is turning out beyond my expectations. Our daughter Ellen attended a party of young people at Col. Pickens, at which they had dancing. A letter was recd. by Major Jeter from Capn. Bird informing him of the death of Col. E[ldred] Simkins in Florida.

Tuesday 17th....The Hughes family performed in the Village, to a crowded house. These children perform admirably on the Violin and harp. Ellen & Hampden attended. I was too unwell to venture out. Wednesday 18th....I called on the Revd. Mr. Walker at Goodman's hotel. I found him a gentleman of agreeable manners & of liberal education & I was altogether pleased with him. I saw our daughter Martha at Mr. Scarborough[s] painting room, sitting for a likeness – In the afternoon Preston & Martha, Mrs. Brooks & Ellen paid a visit to Judge Butlers, to call on Mrs. P[ierce] Butler & daughters. At half past four Ocl. a dark cloud began to form in the South & SoWest & in a short time discharged . . . the most copious rain, that I

---

53 James Caldwell Smyley (1820–1872), Colonel of an Edgefield militia company. Cousin of John C. Calhoun; signer of the Ordinance of Secession.

54 Rev. Charles Bruce Walker (1817–1875) became Rector of Trinity Church June 15, 1845. He married Caroline Simkins Jeter, daughter of John S. Jeter.

recollect since Christmas....It is the only washing rain that has fallen since the planting of the crops — I learned that the Creeks & branches in this vicinity were considerably swollen & Beaver Dam [Creek] was impassable between M^rs^. Carroll & M^r^. Terry's – M^rs^. Brooks returned after the rain & reports, that it - was not so abundant at Judge Butler's as here .... Thursday 19th....Every leaf & sprig of bush or vine and the entire herbage are gemed with glistening drops of rain. To a man of unadulterated taste and pure heart, the visible world presents this morning one of the most beautiful and interresting objects for contemplation. In the afternoon I rode to Prestons in the carriage & returned in great suffering. I have rarely suffered a more excruciating attack of headache. It lasted through the night. Friday 20th....I rose still under the influence of headache & took a dose of Magnesia rheubarb. This dose was very slow in affecting the bowels, which were in a torpid state and I caused two enemas to be administered. These threw me into violent pain & I sent for [Dr. John?] Williams. He applied a mustard plaster to the abdomen, which I wore all day & reduced me to gruel. I was exceedingly feeble and confined to the bed throughout the day. Whitfield returned from Colledge in the stage at 12 ocl. His health is now good but he is rather thin in flesh. We learned through the papers yesterday that Genl. Jackson was dead & to day through M^rs^. F.[rancis] Wardlaw that M^rs^. Sarah Wardlaw, wife of Judge [David] Wardlaw died on monday last.... Saturday 21....I rode to my farm in the buggy & saw the larger part of my crop. It has improved, much since the rain — I was very sick in the afternoon & during the entire night.... Sunday 22....I was very sick in the morning & continued to suffer great agony until I caused an emema to be administered, which gave almost instant relief. I am now exceedingly feeble and ^was^ prevented from attending church — Our children were at dinner except James, who is in Barnwell. It was a source of great gratification to have them again collected under the paternal roof. Monday 23^r^....I rode to my farm in my buggy. The corn looks green & thriving altho very low. Cotton is small, except the portion, which was planted in fresh land & this looks well & sufficiently large. Tuesday 24th....There was a procession of Maysons in the Village & an address delivered by a Doct^r^. Mackey from Charleston in illustration of the principles & purposes of this ancient institution. I was too feeble to attend. On removing the Therm^r^. about 4 ocl. & placing it on a bench near the door, leading from the Portico, it - rose to 100^{θ}. I presume this was about the true temperature in the shade.... Wednesday 25....Whitfield had a dancing party, composed entirely of the young people. To make our children cheerful & happy and contented with home is one of the richest sources of enjoyment to me. .... Friday 27....I feel better this morning than I have done for a week. In the afternoon I met M^r^. Ja^s^. Blocker & daughter from Alabama on their way to Major Blockers. M^r^. Blocker left this District about 17 years ago, before he was of age and settled in Mobile. He is now a gentleman of fine appearance & good address & is reputed to be a successful lawyer. His daughter is rather handsome.... Saturday 28....I rode to Hawthorn Glen & found the earth too wet, to admit – the plow. From appearances double the rain fell there, to what we had here. I never saw corn more improved by a rain. Cicero returned from my plantation with butter, poultry etc. & bringing me a letter from my overseer M^r^. Lowry, informing me that I have the most inferior crop, that he has seen grow on my plantation. The drought has been so protracted and severe, that the grass became parched & the water courses failed, so as scarcly to afford food & water sufficient to keep the cattle alive. The greater part of the cotton in a field of 150 acres may be covered by a pint cup. Whitfield returned to dinner from my fathers, whom I requested him to visit from the plantation to ascertain the state of his health. He reports that the old gentleman is exceedingly feeble and greatly annoyed by the misconduct of the negroes, who are constantly stealing from him.... Sunday 29th....I was well enough to attend Church. Our new minister reads the services of the church exceedingly well and delivers a sensible sermon. He is a well educated & well bred gentleman & rather an interresting man in or out of the pulpit .... Monday 30th....It is impossible to conceive of a lovelier sky or of a more refreshing atmosphere — On riding to my farm I discovered for the first time since March that the earth was too wet for the plow....The last day of the month was the most temperate, clear & bright & the night the most tempting to sleep of the whole thirty. There is a fair prospect now of good crops in this neighbourhood.

July 1st. 1845.

Tuesday 1st....[Today] is the counterpart of yesterday in brilliancy of the Sun and in the clear cerulian blue of the firmament. Italy never presented a lovelier sky. There was a party at Mr. Lipscombs to which the grown children of Major Blocker came down & returned home after 12 ocl. at night. They should have remained here till next morning or not attended the party. Wednesday 2....I again rode to my farm where the corn & cotton look green & growing. So does the grass also. I visited the Village & purchased some clothes for Whitfield, of Colgan, the Taylor.[55] Mr. Harris accompanied me to the farm, with which he expressed himself much pleased. In the afternoon we rode to Prestons & remained to tea. .... Friday 4th....There was no celebration of the day in the Village. Mr. Francis Johnson delivered in the Babtist church a kind of speech, being half sermon, half oration & interspersed with a good deal of the alloy of nonsense. The Ladies of the Methodist church held a fare in the afternoon, to which my family went & to whom I gave $5. to be expended or given away for the occasion – About 1. ocl. at night there was a riotous & singing assemblage of negroes in the street between my lot & Mr. Wardlaw, that disturbed the whole neighbourhood.

Saturday 5th....I rode to my farm with Doctr. Laborde & inspected the crop. He was delighted with the prospect. At 11. ocl. I attended at [Nathan] Griffins office, where the riotous negroes were on trial for their conduct. They were sentenced to

[55] John Colgan (c. 1813–); no real estate, no slaves. 1850 census.

receive 25 lashes each.[56]

Sunday 6h....Service in the Epis. church by the Revd. Mr. Walker & in the administration of the sacrament....

Monday 7....I went to the Village & remained but a short time. I have seldom seen as few persons, in the Village on Sale day. There did not appear to be over thirty persons, from the Country. The Washington Union published by Mr. Ritchie announces the passage of joint resolutions by the Congress of Texas, accepting the terms of Union, offered by the government of the United States. Official information had been communicated to the President, of this important measure. The joint resolutions were passed unanimously by the Texas Congress ....

Tuesday 8....Govr. Aiken arrived in our Village on his tour through the State, attending reviews & encampments — We all passed the evening at Mrs. Carroll' where we met Preston & his family, Col. Carroll & his family[,] & Doctr. Laborde & his entire family — Preston & his Wife spent the night with us —

Wednesday 9th....At an early hour I rode over my crop & gave general directions to be observed during my absence to the Glenn Spring to which I propose to set out in the morning.

Thursday 10th. I set off for my plantation on my way to Glenn Spring....In the afternoon I rode over a part of my fields but was forced to return by a fall of rain....

The crop was rather unpromising & the drought severe & injurious.

Friday 11....I set out at an early hour for the Glenn Spring & reached the widow Godfreys about sunset in the midst of a heavy gust of rain & wind. I had rather bad cooked food for supper & breakfast but a good bed.

Saturday 12h....I set out after breakfast & reached the Glenn Spring about 6. ocl. much exhausted. I took lodgings in one of the cabbins, which my man Joseph furnished & prepared with considerable care and judgment....

Sunday 13h....I felt feeble and only left my cabbin to go to the table at eating time. The company was small & uninterresting. Not more than forty persons & they not remarkable for either manners or intelligence.

Monday 14th. I suffered much from headache & nausea at the stomach....The drought in this Vicinity & through the District of Laurens was ruinous to the crops at this time & the rains were too light & partial to benefit them much. I saw (100) hundreds of acres that would make literally no corn & the cotton was little better —

....

I never saw such prospects of crops and such appalling appearances of want & suf-

[56] Courts of (2) Magistrates and (3) Freeholders (real estate owners), which tried all cases involving slaves and free people of color. Punishments usually involved a prescribed number of lashes, although death sentences were not excluded.

fering during the ensuing year.

Tuesday 15th....I was still feeble & indisposed. The waters of the spring were strongly impregnated with the different minerals & had a powerful & active effect upon my system & by no means favourable to my head.

....

Thursday 17....I felt in better health & rode out. Nothing new at the Springs.

....

Sunday 20th....I attended preaching in the drawing room of the public house & heard a medley sort of sermon from a methodist minister.

Monday 21. The too free use of the water produced an unfavourable effect upon my health & I began to suffer considerable pain.

Tuesday 22....I was prostrate on the bed from 11. ocl. A.M. till 9 ocl. at night with violent headache. My suffering was very severe.

Wednesday 23....I passed another day of suffering, being confined to bed from 10 ocl. till late at night before I felt any relief—

Thursday 24....I applied a mustard plaster to my abdomen & took about half tea spoon full of N°. 6. internally. They gave me partial relief in the afternoon when I eat a little milk & rice.

Friday 25. I felt better this morning & determined to set out for home. At half past 3 oclock I left the Springs and reached a Mr. Braggs about sunset. He keeps a most excellent table & is a kind host. His wife makes the best kind of bread & butter....

Saturday 26h. I left Mr. Braggs after early breakfast & reached my plantation at 9. Ocl. at night, very much fatigued. In passing through Laurens, I discovered that the drought was even more ruinous to the prospects of the planter than when I passed to the Springs – The streams had nearly stopped running, the mills had ceased grinding & even the cattle of the fields found it difficult in places to get water – Many persons were cutting down their corn to make fodder of it as they dispaired of any grain. My overseer reported my crop to be inferior, to any that I had ever made on the place. I did not see it, being too unwell to ride over it—

Sunday 27....I left the plantation at half past 6 ocl. & reached home at a quarter after 10. ocl before the family had gone to Church. I was soon forced to take my bed, from which I did not rise till next morning. All well at the plantation & at home.

Monday 28....I rode out in the afternoon but at an early hour in the night I felt very unwell—

Tuesday 29th. I was confined to my bed & suffered a good deal of pain—

Wednesday 30th. I became very ill & sent for Doctr. Laborde. For 4 weeks I was confined to my bed and unable to set up. At one time my life was dispaired of and I thought I should certainly die but I felt not the slightest alarm. I had endeavoured to come to God through Christ, humbly & deeply repenting the commissions of my manefold sins and putting my trust for salvation in Christ and not in any merit of my own. My mind was prepared for the great and eventful change & I felt no apprehension for the future. I humbly pray God that I may be as well prepared, when it shall be his pleasure to summon me to leave this life. The entire month of August was a dry one, only two moderate rains falling during the whole month. The water courses were nearly dried up & few of them afforded running water. The entire month of September was dry, warm & clear. In the early part of the Month the rains about the Village of Edgefield were frequent & heavy, & but for two weeks of unexampled heat & drought would have made the crops of corn abundant. The rains benefitted greatly the cotton, peas & potatoes & caused grass & other vegetation to become abundant & luxurious.

October — [1845]

This was rather an unusual month both for the coolness & inclemancy of the weather. For the first 20 days, it was cold & disagreeable & two of the heaviest rains fell in this time, that I ever saw. The creeks & rivers became very full & more damage was done to Mill, bridges & crops. I think that more rain fell in October than had fallen since January last — The last week in October was mild & clear & admirably favourable to the gathering of crops of either corn, cotton, or peas. On the last day of this month my father was with me but in a feeble State of health. He came out to give & deliver a few negroes to his grand children, M^rs^. P[e]urifoy, M^rs^. Gillison & M^rs^. Cross,[57] which he did at my house, where they met him to receive them – Purifoy & Wife and Gillison & Wife paid us a visit - of several days. There were three or four light frosts during the month.

November 1. 1845.

Saturday 1....My father left us on his return home. His parting with me was affecting as he had conceived the idea that we should never meet again in this life —

Sunday 2....We attended church & heard a good sermon from our young Minister M^r^. Walker. He administered the sacrament, of which I partook under a deep feeling of unworthiness but encouraged to do so by the promises of Christ. I have omitted to mention in the proper place that Bishop Gadsden paid us a visit during the last month at which time he confered upon me the solemn right of confirmation laying on of hands etc. I have thus united myself to the Visible Church of Christ

[57] Louisa Ann Bird Peurifoy (1816–1878), Mary Simpson Bird Gillison (c. 1821–), and Cornelia Lucinda Bird Cross (1825–1902) were daughters of Daniel Bird and Lucinda Brooks Bird. Cornelia was the niece whose elopement so distressed WB.

and I humbly implore the great head of the church that I may have grace always to live in the daily & habitual performance of every duty towards God & man – That I may progress in christian charity & holiness always depending upon the spirit - of God to impart strength and ability to do the will of our heavenly father & not upon any strength, power or will of my own —

Monday 3rd....It being sale day there was a respectable assemblage of persons in the Village & some property was sold at fair prices. During the past week I visited Hamburg & sold 40 bales of cotton to Dunbar & Burnside[58] at $7.37½ a lucky sale as things have turned out — I began to day to hawl rails from the pine woods in two waggons & an oxcart to make a fence around my land near the Village — The waggon & oxcart from the plantation —

Tuesday 4th....My hands are engaged in picking out cotton, hawling rails & making fence ....

Thursday 6th. We spent the day with Preston. Our daughter gave us an excellent dinner & our time passed pleasantly in company of our Son & his Wife & Mr. & Mrs. Gillison —

Friday 7th....I dug a small field of potatoes on this day. Doctr. & Mrs. Gillison left us for Mr. Purifoys in Georgia on a short visit – In the afternoon Mrs. B & I took a pleasant ride in the Buggy to my pine tract of land where my hands are getting rails.

Saturday 8th....The last two weeks have exhibited a temperature in the weather as mild as april, and most delightful to the senses..... I have observed one remarkable feature in the season this fall. Fall has advanced for the last three weeks with unusual rapidity & the forest trees & all vegitation exhibit rapid decay and falling of their leaves without any frost, sufficiently to kill vegitation. Cotton & pea Vines have cast their leaves & the stalks are drying up. The last papers report a fall in the price of cotton in Europe and a decline of half a cent in the markets of the United States. It will now not bring more than from $7. to $7.¼.cs Breadstuffs are advancing in Europe in consequence of the partial failure in the crop of wheat & potatoes. There is prevailing in England a mania for rail road stock and serious apprehensions are entertained of ruinous losses & great individual ruin —

Sunday 9th....We had no service in the Episcopal church in consequence of the absence of Mr. Walker. Preston & his lady passed the day with us. Mr. Gillison & wife returned from Georgia about 8 ocl. at night.

Monday 10th....I was employed in digging potatoes at Hawthorn Glenn, the crop of which is rather poor, not many potatoes & they small.

---

[58] B. S. Dunbar came to Hamburg to enter the grocery business but soon shifted to cotton. He was a "wild speculator," making and losing fortunes over a twenty-year period. Andrew Burnside was a Hamburg agent for the Bank of Charleston who "Speculate[d] largely in cotton" (Downey, *Planting a Capitolist South,* 81).

Wednesday 12th....I rode to my farm & gave general directions to my servants in regard to their work, during my absence. Preston & Martha were with us at night.

Thursday 13th....I was engaged in making preparations for my departure for Florida.

Friday 14th. About 11. ocl. I took leave of my family & left home for Charleston with my daughter Ellen in company, whom I was taking with me to place her at school with Mrs. Dupre.[59] We reached Aiken before sunset & took lodgings at Mrs. Swartz,[60] where we passed a pleasant evening in company with several persons, who were boarding with her for the benefit of the air of Aiken.

Saturday 15th....At an early hour we took the [railroad] car for Charleston & without accident or delay, arrived in the City at 2 ocl. My old friend John Beckley[61] and Charles Carroll[62] got into the car on the Way, with whom I had some conversation. Beckley promised to call next day in his carriage & take me to Church. At the rail road depot, I procured an omnibus & taking Ellen to Mrs. Dupre's, I then went to the Pavillion hotel[63] & took up my quarters.

Sunday 16th....Early in the morning Mr. Beckley called at the tavern, where I joined him & then going to Mrs. Dupre's for Ellen, we all repaired to St. Pauls Church. I heard a sensible sermon from the Revd. C. Hankle.[64] I enjoyed a high gratification in visiting this Church, to which my Wife & family in her young day was accustomed to worship the Father of spirits & where a part of our children were baptised. I returned with Mr. Beckley to his house & partook of an excellent dinner, prepared in superior Style. His lady was kind, courteous & attentive [to] both to Ellen & myself[,] also his daughter, who was a few months older than Ellen — We also in the afternoon paid a visit to Mrs. Wilson, whom we found very courteous but as artificial in manner as in her younger day. About 5 ocl. we returned to our respective quarters —

Monday 17th....I devoted the day to the purchase of a few articles, necessary to my

---

[59] Abigail Dupre ran one of several Charleston private schools for daughters of the elite. It was not up to the standards of some, including the Allstons of Georgetown, whose disappointment with the language course led them to remove their daughter Della in 1851 (Pease and Pease, *A Family of Women,* 45).

[60] Mrs. Schwartz's hotel and boarding house were said to feature a 200-foot double piazza that was a popular promenade. In a separate travel diary (p. 2) WB called it "an excellent house." See note 96. In the 1840s Aiken was a summer resort for Low Country residents who could reach it by the railroad. After the Civil War most of its visitors were Northerners seeking a healthier winter climate.

[61] Planter, Radcliffeborough, Charleston Neck.

[62] Charles Rivers Carroll? Barnwell District, SC House of Representatives 1840–1842.

[63] At the corner of Meeting and Hasell Streets. Hosted Edgar Allen Poe while he was stationed at Ft. Moultrie. Now the site of the King Charles Hotel.

[64] WB and Mary were presumably married in the Carroll home, which he showed to Ellen (Florida diary, 3). Rev. Christian Hanckel, a Pennsylvania native, was the pastor of St. Paul's.

comfort in going to Florida & in the afternoon in walking to M^{rs}. Dupre's to bid farewell to my daughter. I met during the day a few of my old acquaintances but in the City I felt that in truth I was almost a stranger where 25. years ago, it seemed as if I knew half the people, who were worth knowing, who lived in the Town. Some few friends called to see me, who learned that I was in the City.[65] I was very feeble & could not walk more than a few hundred yards at a time & rarely left the hotel.

Tuesday 18th. At the hour of 9. Ocl. I left the hotel for the warf to go on board the Steamboat Charleston for Savannah. The day was mild & calm. In a short time the boat left the warf & took her departure for Savannah. I was feeble & after remaining on deck until we approached the bar I retired to my birth, on which I lay the greater part of the day in order to avoid sea sickness. By adopting this course I was saved from the almost invariable attack of nausea at the Stomach and was even in condition to partake of dinner. The boat reached Savannah at 9 ocl. & I repaired to the Pulaski house.[66] I remained in Savannah three days, passing my time most pleasantly in visiting Judge [John] Berrien & Doct^{r}. Bartow[67] & their families. At 4 ocl. on Saturday I went on board the S^{t}. Matthews for Jacksonville in East Florida where I arrived on monday following & took lodgings at M^{rs}. Maxey.[68] I remained here one week & then left in the steam boat S^{t}. Matthews for Picolatta [Picolata],[69] at which place we arrived about 9 ocl at night & where I remained until 3 ocl. on tuesday & then left in the Stage for S^{t}. Augustine. I remained in S^{t}. Augustine one week & returned to Picolatta. From thence I went in the Steam boat Sarah Spalding to Enterprise[70] on Lake Monroe. I passed a week at this place & then returned in the same boat to Jacksonville on the S^{t}. Johns River. I passed another week with my landlady M^{rs}. Maxey and at the end of the week, I took leave of this little Town and went on board the Gaston for S^{t}. Mary's. I arrived safely at S^{t}. Marys not however without suffering a good deal of sea sickness in crossing the bar of the S^{t}. Johns river. I remained in S^{t}. Marys three days & left for Savannah in the steamboat S^{t}. Matthews. I passed Christmas at Jacksonville & on New year day I was partly at sea & partly in Savannah. I did not stop in Savannah but a few hours but took my departure for Charleston on board the Genl. Clinch. We reached the City on Saturday

---

[65] In his Florida travel diary, WB mentioned William Gilmore Simms (1806–1870), the Old South's leading man of letters, as among these.

[66] Hotel on Johnson Square, named for Count Casimir Pulaski (1745–1779), Polish patriot and general who provided professional expertise to the American cause in the Revolution and died in the Battle of Savannah.

[67] His Florida travel diary heaps praise on the Berrien family. Theodosius Bartow (1770–1857), New York-born physician. His son Francis, a leading secessionist, married Louisa, daughter of John Macpherson Berrien.

[68] Ran a boarding house at the corner of Bay and Market Streets, owned by I. D. Hart.

[69] On the St. Johns River, west of St. Augustine.

[70] About 90 miles south of Picolata. Named and being developed by a Major Taylor, an impressive figure. WB visited to evaluate it as a possible place to settle, but saw "little inducement."

the 3rd of January 1846 about 9. Ocl. in the morning, having been delayed by bad weather & stopages for 24 hours — As my daughter was in the City at School with Mrs. Dupre, I remained here until tuesday morning the 6 of Jany. and at 9 ocl. took my passage in the Steam car for Aiken on my way home.

About 4 ocl. on Wednesday evening I reached home after an absence of some two months, greatly improved in health and found all my family in the enjoyment of the same blessing. Oh, What a weight of Gratitude is due from me & mine to the divine disposer of all things for the great & inestimable favours and blessings which he has bestowed on us. It will be seen that I left home on friday the 14th of November 1845 and returned on Wednesday the 7 of January 1846. I was absent nearly two months and continued to improve in health from the day, on which I left home to the day of my return. Every thing seemed to act in concert & harmony to make my time pass pleasantly and profitably so far as regards my health — Whatever incidents occurred, affecting me personally or that came under my observation will be found in a book of record in the form of a diary, which I kept during my absence & in which is minutely mentioned, every thing, which was esteemed of sufficient interest.[71]

I was informed on all hands that the present has been the coldest & most inclement winter that has occurred Since 1835. For a week the whole surface of the earth was frozen and ice abounded in great quantities. The Thermr. fell to 10^{θ}. Notwithstanding the extreme cold, the injury to plants and shrubbery was not as great as I expected to see. The oats sowed in the fall are considerably injured & in some places almost entirely killed. During the time of my absence two weddings occurred in the Village, Miss Julia Lipscomb to Mr. Randal & Miss Kennerly to Mr. W[i?]ghtman.[72] It is with regret that I must also record an incident of no small consequence that befell my neighbour Mr. Wardlaw. He had his dwelling burned down and a great part of his furniture consumed. No evil or misfortune befell my family but I found as I had left them in health & in the enjoyment of much entertainment & happiness — Several deaths had also occurred, among the number was that of Mrs. Susan Griffin, Wife of Doctr. Griffin, whose maiden name was Allen — She was a lady of some strong points of character & when a girl exceedingly pretty. The wheel of time seemed to turn in its accustomed course bringing to pass the ordinary incidents, which mark its progress from point to point in its diurnal course, but nothing of great import or startling interest took place except what I have recorded. An absence from home for a few months prepares the mind to expect considerable

[71] This 97-page manuscript diary is at the South Carolina Historical Society in Charleston, and has been transcribed. The Florida excursion was primarily for his health, but WB took more than ordinary interest in the environment. Although he never says so, he was considering moving there. Mary did not accompany WB; he took "my man Cicero" with him (49).

[72] Sarah N. Kennerly, daughter of Rev. S. W. Kennerly, married Rev. J. W. Wightman, Nov. 18, 1845.

changes during our absence, altho reason argues that there is no ground for such expectation beyond what transpires weekly & even daily while we are at home. I realize but little change in any thing & now return to Almighty God, my profound gratitude for his great mercy and goodness in restoring me to my family in improved and improving health and I humbly pray that he would aid me by his holy spirit, in preserving a deep sense of my weakness & unworthiness and of the great & absolute necessity of dependance upon him for power & ability to do his holy will and pleasure, so as ultimately to meet his forgiveness & approbation in the great day of final accounts –

VII

January, 1846.

Wednesday 7th....I left Aiken about 11. ocl. and reached home about 4 ocl where I met my family and James & his Wife & child in excellent health. All my friends seemed delighted to see me yet each and every one condemned me for returning so soon. My negroes appeared to rejoice at my safe return.

Thursday 8th....I rode to my farm to examine a pasture fence, which the negroes had run during my absence. It was well done & met my entire approbation. My servants had conducted themselves well and even worked faithfully during my absence & it afforded me great pleasure to praise them for their good conduct.

....

Saturday 10th....I again rode to the farm & gave some direction in regard to clearing land. The cold weather was rather oppressive to my lungs but I avoided exposure.

Sunday 11th....I attended church in the forenoon & heard a sermon by our minister Mr. Walker. It was so cold that I did not venture out in the afternoon.

Monday 12th....I rode to the Village for a short time in the morning & saw many of my kind neighbours, who appeared gratified at my return. I transacted a little business with Mr. Butler and returned home....

Tuesday 13th....I rode out with Mrs. Brooks to our Son Preston & passed the forenoon with his Wife — There is no news of any interest either public or private. There were established in the Village, during my absence three new fancy good stores & sundry changes in the occupants of different houses took place.

Wednesday 14th. This was the last of a period of eight days of clear, cold, bright & most invigorating weather....Mrs. Brooks called on Mrs. & Sally Means at Preston Brooks. I paid a friendly visit to Mr. Walker & also one of business with Mr. Boleware[1] – The Sheriff has advertised more property for sale on the first monday in next month, than I have known for years — And unfortunately for me I am concerned in a portion of it as trustee for my sister Mrs. Blocker —

Thursday 15th....No news in the papers except a continuation of War speeches in the house of representatives, on the Oregon question[2] — Mr. Wardlaw & Col. Carroll sat with me until near 10 ocl at night.

Friday 16th....The weather is inclement & unfavourable to invalids & yet I feel very

---

[1] Humphrey [also Humphreys] Boulware (1808–), son of Spencer Boulware. Edgefield merchant born in the Big Creek section. He was Clerk of Court 1834–1836 and Sheriff 1844–1848; 1850 census: $2,400 real estate, 22 slaves.

[2] Boundary dispute between the U.S. and Canada, then a part of the British empire. James Polk famously campaigned for president calling for "54° 40" or Fight," a border well above the eventually agreed-upon 49° north latitude.

little inconvenience from it. I trust that my health is about to be established upon a firmer basis than it has been for years & that I may entirely escape those excrutiating headaches, with which for the last sixteen years I have been so sorely afflicted....

Saturday 17th....I set out for the plantation (Roselands) about 10 oclock, accompanied by Mrs. Brooks & Whitfield and arrived at 3 ocl. finding the negroes in good health & in excellent condition —

Sunday 18th....We passed the day at home, the roads being in such bad condition, as to prevent us from attending church — Most of the negroes came up to the house to see me & seemed greatly rejoiced that I had returned home in an improved state of health.

Monday 19th....I rode with Wiley Kemp[3] over a tract of land, adjoining him for sale but concluded not to purchase....

Tuesday 20th. Sleet was falling at day light and continued to fall during the entire day, so that the whole surface of the earth, became covered before night. I have never seen a more inclement day. The trees were covered by the sleet & icecles [sic] were formed from 6 to 10 inches in length. It was a severe and trying day for all domestic animals. I lost nothing but a calf, which strayed off and perished in the cold.

Wednesday 21....The men were employed in the new ground & the women at spinning — There was in the afternoon a partial thaw of the ice & sleet. I was attacked with headache & was forced to take my bed, upon which the pain subsided.

Thursday 22....I rode over my plantation, examined the condition of the small grain, of the fences & of the new ground which I am opening. Also the condition of the stock of cattle, sheep, etc. and the quantity of corn and provisions. My plantation is in very good order, a great portion of the fences, having been repaired; & several new gates made. There were about 15 acres of land, cleared ready for the plough & about 10 more cut down. The wheat & rye looked tolerably well but I fear that I shall loose at least one half of a 50 acre field of oats. My stock appeared to be in living order & will be able I trust, to get through the winter. I have an abundance of coarse food for them — On an examination of the cribs, I estimated the corn at 1600 to 1700 bushels, sufficient to serve the plantation until the new crop shall be matured — I was informed that there was an alarming scarcity of corn in the neighbourhood and that not more than four or five persons had made a supply & many not half of what would be required for their support. The hogs & cattle were suffering & dieing for the want of food. The severe winter is adding to the suffering, incident upon a failure of crop of provisions & want & misery will follow in the train in a large portion of the up Country. At a sale near the Abbeville line, corn was sold at $1.37½ pr. bushel & it - cannot at this time be purchased for less than $1. in cash.

---

[3] A neighbor of WB, he apparently died before the 1850 census was taken. His son, also Wiley (1828–), is listed there with 42 slaves.

Provisions are dearer than they have been since 1819 & money exceedingly scarce. Cotton is selling from \$5½ to 7¼ p^{r}. hundred & flour from \$6½ to 7½ per barrel. Oats at 62½ to 75.^{cs} & rye from 1.25 to 1.50. p^{r}. bushel.

Friday 23^{r}....I left the plantation at 10 ocl. for my fathers, where we arrived at 4 ocl. & found my father in his usual health tho very feeble. His negro woman Ginny was very ill but his other negroes were well.

Saturday 24....About 10 ocl. I rode over to the plantation of Aunt Butler but now in the possession & cultivated by Judge Butler for the purpose of seeing my old acquaintance M^{rs}. Yarborough & her daughter M^{rs}. Culbreath, whom I found in good health.[4] From fifteen to 20 years have passed since I was at the old residence of my Uncle Genl. [William] Butler & great changes had taken place in that time in both the appearance of fields & houses. I looked on this old residence with peculiar interest and with feelings of melancholy as it - was the playground of my boyhood, whenever I visited my friend & contemporary the present Doct^{r}. W^{m}. Butler, with whom I have passed many pleasant hours. We passed a happy day with our aged father & partook of an excellent dinner.

Sunday 25....We left my paternal residence at 9. ocl. for home, my father returning with us. We were prevented from returning yesterday from the fact that his carriage was at the shop for repair. We stopped at Judge Butlers to see my old & much respected Aunt Butler, whom we found in cheerful spirits & in excellent health. We arrived at home at 4 ocl. & found all well.

Monday 26th....Several flocks of pigeons were seen to fly over the Village — I attended my father to the Village....In the afternoon I visited my farm . . . & purchased of E. Kirksey four stacks of fodder at \$12. and also agreed upon a dividing line between Ja^{s}. Hollingsworth[5] & myself —

Tuesday 27....I accompanied my father to Major Blockers, where we passed the day with my Sister — In the afternoon I returned home on horseback, making 14 miles, that I had rode that day. I was considerably fatigued by the ride —

Wednesday 28th....I passed the greater part of [the day] at the farm, running the dividing fence between me & Hollingworth, which occupied me until after sunset. Upon reaching home I was exceedingly weary & recovered after resting.

Thursday 29th....I was engaged in removing a gate & pair of bars at the farm & in cleaning up a field, to be ready for the plow.

Friday 30th....I commenced this morning, breaking up the remainder of the stubble land with three ploughs, about 15 acres, having been broken up in the fall. We are engaged to dine with Preston....

Saturday 31....The rain forced me to stop my ploughs & I employed my hands in

---

[4] Elizabeth Yarborough (1782–)? Dr. George M. Yarborough, born on Big Creek, was a relative of WB's Butler kin. She may have been his widow.

[5] James Hollingsworth (1804–); 1850 census: \$400 real estate, 22 slaves.

collecting & carrying out manure....Our daughter Martha Brooks was delivered of a sweet daughter about 3 Ocl. M[rs]. Brooks rode out to see her & on her return reported the mother to be doing well and the babe to be not only of good size & perfect shape but very pretty — I thank God, that the child has no physical deformity or defect, which is of much greater importance than beauty altho this quality in a daughter is very desirable — M[rs]. Means & Miss Sally Means, the mother & sister of Martha, were with her & Doc[t]. [Edward J.] Mims as officiating physician. Her sufferings were not great nor protracted, which also should inspire her family with emotions of gratitude to God. The child is named Mary Carroll Brooks, after Grandmother & Great Grandmother.

February. 1, 1846

Sunday 1....After breakfast I rode out to Prestons to see my daughter and my first Grand daughter. I visited her in her room & saw a most interresting sight, the sweet babe lying in the arms of its mother. I was greatly gratified to find the mother in a comfortable state and without pain or fever. The infant is a sweet & beautiful child. I placed a necklace around its neck, kissed & blessed it and returned to church after taking leave of the family — M[r]. Walker delivered a sermon upon this text – "This is my body, which is broken for you", and also administered the sacrament, at which there were about 15 communicants — In the afternoon I was too indisposed to attend church —

Monday 2....I began to sow oats at my Durham Farm with four ploughs running.

About 11. Ocl. I went to the Village & remained a Spectator for 1 or 2 hours – The Sheriff seemed busily engaged in selling negroes & horses etc. They brought fair prices, I am informed. The crowd was large & well dressed & very orderly while I remained — I delivered to Durisoe an Obituary notice of the life & death of the late lamented Major John Middleton.[6] I had headache in the afternoon —

Tuesday 3....In consequence of bad weather & indisposition, I declined to go to Hamburg & sent my son Whitfield to make Some purchases for me — He set out about 11. Ocl.

Wednesday 4th....I rode over my farm & inspected the work — The Rev[d]. M[r]. Walker took tea with us with whom I passed an agreeable evening in social conversation.

[6] John Middleton (c. 1780–1846); obit. in *Adv.*, Feb. 4, 1846. Planter near Savannah River above Stevens Creek. As a young man he went to Africa and brought back a number of natives. His ship was wrecked on the return voyage and he survived by eating rice, which he never ate again. Served in the legislature 1818–1821. In 1830 he owned 55 slaves. In 1850 John M. Middleton owned 80 slaves, and John Middleton owned 91. John Sr.'s wife Elizabeth's family owned Scott's Ferry.

Thursday 5....I am this day fifty six years of age — My health is not robust but on the contrary it is feeble, yet I have cause of praise & thankfulness to God for the portion, which I enjoy. I have been somewhat indisposed for several days but I am better this morning & nearly free from pain. My wife & children are all in excellent health, also my relations & friends so far as I know and also my servants. What great cause of gratitude for this inestimable blessing & for many other favours, with which my family are favoured May I never be wanting in gratitude to the bestower of every good gift.[7] We rode out in the afternoon to my Son Preston's to see Martha & the babe. They were both well. Whitfield returned from Hamburg bringing me a beautifully worked pair of shoes & a present from my young friend David Adams.

Friday 6th....We rec^{d}. a sweet letter from our daughter, addressed to Whitfield. From 12 ocl. till night the rain was heavy & constant.

Saturday 7th....I was engaged in collecting & carrying out manure & in repairing the fence round the field next to M^{rs}. Carrolls — Joseph came down from Roselands with a note from the Overseer, that all were well & that he had sowed his oats. He reports that I have 24 lambs —

Sunday 8th....In the afternoon I had some fever & rode on horse back some five or six miles for exercise, which caused me to feel better ....

Monday 9th....I sent this morning in the stage to Columbia a poor dissipated Son of my old acquaintance Jeptha Dyson, who reached the Village yesterday in a state of destitution & made application to my Son Whitfield for assistance — I trust he will return to his father & reform his habits.

Tuesday 10th. Very heavy hoar frost this morning. Therm down to 28$^{\theta}$. & a good deal of ice....I was engaged in repairing fences & cleaning up land. Joseph came from the plantation with butter, cotton, chickens & a turkey & also some seed corn for M^{rs}. Carroll....

....

Thursday 12th. Clear & mild day — I was engaged in resetting a fence & hawling rails.

Friday 13th. I recommensed to sow oats from which the wet weather stopped me about a week past....We rode to Preston's, where we found all well, except the babe, who had sore eyes....

Saturday 14th....Rain…continued with but short intervals, during the day. M^{r}. Morris was engaged to putting up a forge to a new blacksmith shop.

---

7 Thomas Jeptha Dyson (1812–); 1850 census: $13,000 real estate, 42 slaves. Son not listed.

Sunday 15th....It was too inclement – & windy for me to venture to church, so I remained at home by myself. At sunrise the Therm^{r}. was about 39$^{\theta}$. The afternoon was clear & sufficiently mild, to admit of my attending church.

Monday 16th....I had my hands hawling wood, scattering manure & repairing the road to the farm. Co^{l}. Pickens & lady called to see us. I always find this gentleman social, agreeable & communicative & his lady courteous & affable. Our neighbour W^{m}. Mays[8] was buried to day at 11. ocl. He had been to Hamburg & returned home on Saturday afternoon, got out of his buggy and walked to the house in his usual gate but fell just as he entered the house & was dead by the time, they got him on a bed. He died of apoplexy. What a sudden unwarned & lamentable death. He was an industrious & enterprising citizen. His death will produce a great change in his family. I heard to day of the death of Ja^{s}. [Misiyard?] of Saluda, after a protracted and painful illness. Both of these gentlemen were men of property & $_{v}^{had}$ several children. It is understood that each left a will, disposing of their property....

....

Wednesday 18th....I rode by Ja^{s}. Griffins & then by my farm, in order to see the preparation of my neighbors for a crop. Very little has been done except repairing fences & hawling out manure. We have invited a few friends to spend the evening with us — Our neighbour M^{rs}. McClintock had a daughter about 1. ocl. on yesterday. Both mother & child are doing well....We had the company of our friends, consisting principally of the families in <u>Buncomb</u>, They all appeared cheerful & in good spirits.

Thursday 19th....I have not seen a more inclement day this winter nor a more constant day of rain up to 12 ocl. I heard this morning of the death of M^{r}. Saml. Marsh at the house of M^{r}. A.[llen] B. Addison. He was attacked with paralysis several years past & has been literally dragging a miserable existence ever since, not having the use of his limbs or tongue. I saw him once but he did no more than nod his head while I spoke to him & utter an unintelligible sound. His death is a relief to him & his friends....

....

Saturday 21....I rode to my farm & inspected the work of my negroes — In the afternoon I was too unwell to leave the house....I received a letter from my Overseer M^{r}. Lowry, informing me that two of my negro men had rebelled & ran away — The rest are well —

Sunday 22....We attended Church & heard a sensible sermon by M^{r}. Walker from the text, "If I be a father, where is my honor." Major Blocker, Miss S[arah] Means & Preston Brooks dined with us — In the afternoon I rode as far as Hollingsworth for exercise, in company with Blocker & Preston —

---

[8] William Baker Mays (1793–1846). In the 1840–1841 season the racehorse Argyle stood at stud at his farm.

Monday 23rd....Whitfield returned last evening from my fathers, to whom I had sent him, to ascertain the state of his health before I set out for Florida, for which

I am now making preparations — The health of my father is about as good as it – has been for the last six months —

Editor's note: Brooks embarked on his second trip to Florida, traveling in his carriage and taking Mary and a slave, likely his usual traveling companion Cicero. A second trip so soon after the first suggests that, despite the less-than-enthusiastic comments he made in his Florida diary, northern Florida held considerable appeal for him. His improved health while on his first visit may have been the main reason, but now that Florida was a state and the Seminole Wars were receding into the past, he and Mary must have foreseen a better future on that frontier. Also, he wanted to explore the environment to the west of the area he had visited before, where he could be escorted by men he knew and see the results they had achieved in turning that wilderness into productive farms. Thus he chose to follow a southwesterly route across Georgia and toward Jefferson County, Florida, home of the Birds and other Edgefield families who had made the move. Preston also considered moving to Florida, likely influenced by his father's impressions, but decided against it.

Tuesday 24th....We set out for Florida, made a short stay in Hamburg & took up quarters for the night at Fraziers in Augusta.

Wednesday 25....We arrived at night at Mr. Jordons about 40 miles from Augusta where we were comfortably entertained. Thursday 26....We passed the Ogechee....

Friday 27....We crossed the Oconee River....

Saturday 28th....We crossed the Oakmulgee [Ocmulgee] near Hawkins Ville, passed through that Village & arrived at night at Mr. Watson's....Between Augusta & Hawkins Ville the Country is generally settled & many of the inhabitants are independent planters. The land is generally free pine land with occasional strips of oak & hickory, on which are cultivated corn cotton & small grain. I observed with pleasure large fields of wheat, rye & oats on the entire rout & more attention paid to manuring than I was prepared to expect.

March 1846.

....

Monday 2nd....This was the first day, on which we encountered any difficulty. We soon after setting out, came to a creek that was impassible at the usual crossing place but we succeeded in getting over it on a pole bridge, which had been made by the neighbours about a mile below the ford. In a few miles we came to another creek that was 100 yards wide at least & over which, there was no possibility of passing or heading. We were advised to turn back, cross the Flint river & pass by StarkVille & Albany, by which rout we should find bridges over the Creeks. I pursued this advice

& took the road back…within three miles of our previous nights sojourn ….

Tuesday 3rd….We crossed the Flint river into Lee County, in which I saw some fine lands & passing through StarkVille & Palmyra arrived in the afternoon at Albany in Baker County. This is a new Town at the head of navigation on the Flint river & is already a place of some trade. It is yet a dirty place & in a rude state.

Wednesday 4th….We recrossed the Flint river & arrived at night at a Mr. Crawfords ….

His house is open & uncomfortable but his Wife is obliging & keeps a good table.

Thursday 5th….We crossed the two Ocklockney's [Ochlockonees] & arrived at night at…Thomas Ville….

Friday 6th. We…reached Capt.[Daniel] Bird's in the afternoon. The family were expecting us & gave us a most affectionate reception. They were all in good health & seemed to be rendered happy by our visit.[9]

Saturday 7th. I rode during the day over Capn. Birds plantation & inspected his fields & the character of the soil. He has a valuable plantation but the land is not the richest. I saw several tracts more fertile but none, equal to it in point of location, health & Water. He had planted his corn & was preparing his cotton land. The Sugar crop was also planted.

….

Tuesday 10th. In the morning we paid a visit to Mr. Bellamy, Capn. Bird & Sister accompanying us. Smith Simkins[10] & Wife & Miss Ware dined at Bellamy's & we all passed a pleasant day.

Wednesday 11th. I went this morning in company with Bellamy, Bird & Simkins, to look at the Hollingsworth tract of land, of the fertility of which I had heard such extravagant representations. It lies on the West side of the Ocilla [Aucilla] river & is certainly one of the richest tracts of land, that I have ever seen. It has however a bad reputation for health, which detracts greatly from its Value. We dined on our return with Smith Simkins & passed the night with him. I rode over his farm & found it to be a free & generous soil, on which he makes good crops.

….

Saturday 14th. I went to Monticello [the county seat] to look out for a purchaser of

---

[9] Daniel Bird, Jr. (1784–1865), married two sisters of WB. In 1814, following the death of his first wife Sarah, he married Lucinda Brooks. After Lucinda's death in 1826 he married Behethland, widow of Jesse Simkins, in 1827 (see introduction). An "Indenture Tripartite" between Bird, Behethland Simkins, and Whitfield Brooks gave Behethland ownership of her estate, which was to be managed by WB. Although he did not move permanently to Florida until the late 1840s, Bird began buying land there in the late 1820s. Behethland Brooks Simkins Bird (1893–1864) was presumably present to welcome her brother, although WB did not mention her.

[10] Zachariah Smith Simkins, son of Behethland and Jesse Simkins.

the boy Sandy, whom I had taken out for Sale at the request of his owner. The Village of Monticello is situated upon a hill of gentle elevation & moderately undulating on all sides. It is improving & now offers an agreeable residence. The surrounding Country varies in the character of the land, & fertility of soil but all is well adapted to planting & yields good crops of corn, cotton, sugar cane, peas, pumkins & potatoes. I regard it at present as the most thriving portion of the State, that I saw — The land sells from $3 to $8 pr acre & some on the Lake is held higher.

....

Monday 16th....I sold Sandy to a Mr. Braden for $650, of which he paid in cash $460 & gave his note for the residue.

Tuesday 17th. In the afternoon we left Capn. Bird's taking with us our niece Sally Bird, on a proposed visit to our friends in Madison County & stoped for the night with Mr. Bellamy, whom I find to be a kind, hospitable & courteous gentleman. He is a man of wealth & lives in great plenty & comfort[.] He has a good Wife & very interesting family of children. I was also pleased with my nephew Smith Simkins & his Wife is an intelligent & exceedingly clever lady....Doctr. Taylor stands well as a gentleman and as a physician & commands a good practice. His style of living is equal to any I saw in the State. In short my relations in Jefferson County are in easy circumstances & generally esteemed. I was gratified at their respectable position in Society & with their favourable temporal circumstances —

Wednesday 18th. We left Mr. Bellamy's for Richard Mays....[11]

Thursday 19....In the morning I rode over the plantation of my friend Mays & I saw his hands preparing for & planting cotton. Col. Butler & lady dined with us, with whom we returned in the afternoon.

Friday 20th....Col. Butler & I rode over a part of his plantation in the morning. He has a large tract of land & some very good land, but the larger portion is pine land. His lady is a cheerful, affectionate & kindhearted woman, with good manners & good breeding....Saturday 21. We left our friends after breakfast on our way to Capn. [John] Lipscomb's,[12] where we arrived in the afternoon. We received a cordial & warm reception from my old friend & his very kind lady.

Sunday 22nd....He has a large & valuable body of land, on & near to Lake Sampala, on which he makes abundant crops. Doctr. Mays & family called to see us in the afternoon by whom we were invited to dine with them the next day. Also Mr. & Mrs. McGehee called to see us.

---

[11] Dr. Rhydon G. Mays, son of Gen. Samuel Mays, was clerk of Sardis Baptist Church, Edgefield District, in 1835. See Monday 23rd for his title.

[12] John Lipscomb (1789–1856): His younger sister, Ann, married WB's cousin John Wesley Brooks. John L. sold his Abbeville District plantation and moved his family to Jefferson County FL in the late 1830s, but retained Halcyon Grove, his house in ECH, and business interests there.

Monday 23rd....We dined with Doct^{r}. Mays in company with Cap^{n}. Lipscomb & Wife, M^{r}. & M^{rs}. McGehee & Miss Freshwater....

Tuesday 24....we went to M^{r}. McGehees to dinner ....McGehee has a good garden & a collection of fruit among which are 500 young orange trees besides a few now bearing fruit.

Wednesday 25....having rec^{d}. an invitation to join a party of pleasure down the Suwanne [Suwannee] River to the Ceadar [sic] Keys at its Mouth, we set out from M^{r}. Lipscombs after breakfast in company with M^{r}. & M^{rs}. Lipscomb & Miss Freshwater. About 2 ocl we arrived at the river at a point called Lipscomb & Mays warehouse & immediately went on board the Steamboat on which we met Doct^{r}. Mays & Wife with his two daughters, Dennet Mays Esqr. M^{r}. & M^{rs}. Pope of Madison County & Co^{l}. Cole, the very polite & hospitable owner of the boat ....The entire company was well bred, well educated & disposed to be kind & affable & constituted the most favourable materials for social entercourse & enjoyment. Every one seemed desirous to please ....At all events it was one of the most agreeable parties, that it has been my fortune to participate in the progress of my life ....

Thursday 26 ....[Traveling on the river]

Friday 27th....We reached Ceadar Key about 9 oclock which is one of a group of small Islands near the Mouth of the River & some 20 miles in [from] the Gulph. It is a barren sandbed & does not contain more than 40 or 50 acres of land, on which reside some three or four families & a few other persons, engaged in trade. To us however it - presented various objects of interest & each one betook himself to a search for pleasure & amusement, agreeably to the taste of the party — M^{rs}. Brooks went on a shell hunting excursion & M^{r}. Pope to fishing while others gratified the sense of seeing whatever attracted the sight. Among the residents on the Island is a Judge Steel, who keeps a kind of private boarding house & holds some office....We all dined at his table & had a very good dinner of fish, oisters & turtle soup, served up in good style. In the afternoon we took an excursion in a small pilot boat to an Island called Seahorse about 4 miles distant from the place of our tempory sojourn. It affords a fine view of the Gulph of Mexico & offers some desireable sites for houses [although] the soil is poor & sandy. I saw nothing remarkable on the Island except a few wells or sources of drinking water which is obtained of good quatity by sinking a barrel a few feet in the ground on the beach....

Saturday 28^{h}....I devoted the morning to writing letters home. At 1 Oclock we took our departure on our return home & passed the night again on the bosom of the river some fifty miles from its mouth.

Sunday 29th....We had a pleasant passage up the river & arrived at night at Charles ferry, where we remained until morning....The lands on this river are generally poor pine barren & afford few objects of interest to the eye. Even the forests are meager & the folliage neither rich nor beautiful except in occasional small hammocks of moderate fertility....

Monday 30th....We arrived about 1 ocl. at Columbus, a small Village on the East side of the Suwannee, opposite its junctions with the Withlacoochy. This point is the head of navigation. The town is small, the houses ordinary & the . . . Water is infamous. We dined for the last time on the boat with our liberal & hospitable host & at two ocl. took our departure for Madison Courthouse....

Tuesday 31....We...left the Village about 9 ocl. on our return to Monticello....We arrived at M^{r}. Bellamy's in the afternoon & passed the night with his family. We had been absent two weeks & our friends did not know, what had become of us. Our time had been most agreeably passed either at the houses of our friends or the Steam boat & we were not very anxious about returning. We found our friends & acquaintances in Madison kind and attentive....I shall always remember this visit with much pleasure —

April 1st. 1846

Wednesday 1st....In the morning we returned to Cap^{n}. Birds. The family were well & had been expecting us for several days. Sally Bird having now returned, almost sated with pleasure, was anxious to resume her studies. I assisted her in getting her lesson in Ceasar's commentaries, which I read [in Latin] with more ease than I expected.

....

Friday 3^{r}....[W]ent to M^{r}. Bellamys plantation, called the Graves tract, for the purpose of examining it....I rode over a portion of the tract & was able to form some general opinion of its quality etc. It is free land[13] but not rich.

Saturday 4th....Cap^{n}. Bird & I went about 8 miles to look at a tract of land, belonging to Co^{l}. Gamble, which we understood was in market. We saw a portion of it of which about 40 acres were in cultivation. It is a good tract & portions very rich. It is deficient in water.

Sunday 5th....a short ride for exercise.

Monday 6th....We paid a visit – to Doct^{r}. Taylor & I availed myself of the oppertunity of riding up to Bellamys plantation again to look over it. I was however attacked with headache & was prevented from taking a minute examination. My second visit only confirmed my first impression, that it was a free & generous tract of land, lying well & having good water & offering every prospect of comparative health. I returned to Taylors in great suffering & went to bed. We returned in the afternoon to Cap^{n}. Birds. I was deadly sick.

Tuesday 7th....We took leave of our dear relations this morning & set out for Doct^{r}.

---

[13] By the Armed Occupation Act of 1842, Congress offered free land as inducement to settle in Florida.

Treadwell's near Talahassee....

Wednesday 8th....we went into Town accompanied by the Doctr. & his lady. I called on Mrs. Gamble & the ladies went shopping for a short time. We also visited a very pretty garden, belonging to Mr. Brown. It was in a neat state & presented a pretty collection of flowers & choice fruit. This is to me a most uninterresting place. The location is bad & the houses, built without order or neatness. There are some good buildings, among the number is a new State house. I did not see much of the Town or of the Country but I was not proposed in favour of what I did see.

Thursday 9th....We left Doctr. Treadwell's after breakfast for Col. Whitner, at whose house we arrived about 11. ocl. I regretted to find that he was absent. In the afternoon I rode over a part of his plantation....I was unacquainted with such land & therefore forbore to make up any judgement, tho I was not pleased with it....

Friday 10th....We left Col. Whitners after breakfast on our way to Doctr. Winns in Thomas County Geo....He & his lady gave us the warmest reception —

Saturday 11th....I rode with Doctr. Winn over his plantation. It lies on the Oklockney & is fertile & well adapted to corn, cotton & small grain, tho too rolling to last.

Sunday 12....We attended preaching . . . & heard a rather rambling & abstract sermon from a Mr. Cooper of the baptist order....

13th - 19th. The return trip was uneventful except for wrong turn by WB'a unnamed "servant" onto a rough road, resulting in a broken carriage tongue.

Saturday 18th ....I was forced to stop at the Ogechee to get it repaired. I never saw a rougher piece of workmanship but it enabled me to get to Hamburg....This short delay & injury to the tongue of the carriage was the only thing in the class of accident or the least unpleasant occurrance, that happened to us on the road —

Sunday 19th....We resumed our journey after a late breakfast & arrived at Mrs. Hubbards in Hamburg about Sunset. Here we heard from home & learned, that our family & friends were well. No local news of any importance.

Monday 20th....I had a new tongue made for the carriage, transacted some business with the bank & with two or three merchants & set out for home about 11. ocl. We arrived at home about dark & met our children & relations in good health. And now I desire to return to Almighty God humble & sincere thanks, that he has in his merciful providence enabled us to reach our home in improved health & to meet our children and relations in the full enjoyment of this greatest of blessings & I humbly implore his mercy, that he will vouch safe so far to restore my health, that I may not be forced again to leave my own firside to preserve it – by removal to any other region.

Tuesday 21....I rode to my farm & found the hands planting corn. The Wet spring has prevented them from getting the crop in the ground as early as I desired. Several of my neighbours called to see me.

Wednesday 22nd....I was engaged in preparing a few acres for cotton at the Youngblood place.

Thursday 23rd. Clear & warm & the earth hard & dry. I finished breaking up about six acres for cotton & began to plant. I omitted to mention that on Wednesday I planted about 6 acres.

Friday 24th....I planted six acres of cotton, a small plot of watermellons & a few rows of the Mastodon cotton[14] the seed of which had been given to me by Mr. Bellamy of Florida. I also began to plow over corn in one field & to run a board over a field in which the corn was beginning to come up —

Saturday 25....I was engaged in plowing corn. My oats are very promising and the most encouraging accounts are received in regard to the small grain crops from every quarter of the State. They never were more promising. The health of the Country is also good. Provisions are exceedingly scarce. Corn sells for $1. pr. bushel and very little can be procured at the price – Fodder for $1 pr. 100lb. Bacon $8 pr. 100lb. Grown chickens at 25cs. each & none to be had.

Sunday 26th....We attended at the Epis. church and heard the services of the church read by a young man by the name of Bland.[15] I was indisposed in the afternoon & did not attend church. Preston & his Wife dined with us. They have a very sweet babe.

Monday 27th....Mrs. Brooks & Whitfield set out this morning for Charleston for our daughter Ellen, whose session at school terminates the last of this month — I plowed up & replanted a piece of low land at the Durham place. Heavy rains at night —

Tuesday 28h....The Earth is very wet & will not allow of the plough. I employed my hands in hawling wood & replanting corn and setting out plants —

Wednesday 29....I rode to my farm & had about two acres broken up for a crop for the negroes. Went to the Village & paid a visit - to my old friend Major Jeter, whose health is good but his eye sight has nearly failed him. I met both his daughters, who are clever ladies in the highest sense of this term.

Thursday 30th....I have seldom seen the shrubbery in the gardens more green and flourishing or the foliage of the forests richer or more luxuriant. It is a most lovely spring and at this time promises rich harvests of fruit of all kinds and the most abundant crops of all sorts of grain, which to the entire community, in its present State of scarcity & almost destitution is a source of relief & gratification & thanks. Wm. Blocker left me after breakfast on his way to Columbia, to convey a man by the

---

[14] A long-staple (fiber) cotton, said to be equal to the highest quality of Sea Island cotton.

[15] Rev. Charles T. Bland was a missionary to six stations in Barnwell and Edgefield Districts.

name of Harden, to the jail of that District, who had been tried at the last court of Com Pleas for this District for the murder of his slave & found guilty. He has appealed for a new trial....[16] The prospect of crops & of fruit is at present very promising & if no disaster takes place, they will be abundant. Some apprehentions are entertained of rust in the wheat. I have heard that it has made its appearance in some places.

May 1. 1846.

Friday 1st....I left home in company with my Son Preston for my plantation at which we arrived at 12 ocl. In the afternoon I rode over my plantation & took a general inspection of the crop. The small grain is very good, to wit, wheat, oats & rye; the corn is small but looked well; The cotton was generally up & presented a fine stand — The negroes were all in health & looked well. I thank God that I shall have a supply of provisions for all purposes until the growing crop shall mature & be ready for use —

Saturday 2nd....I attended the battalion parade at Lewis Towles, where I saw most of my neighbours. In the afternoon I returned to the Village. At 12 ocl at night Mrs. Brooks, Whitf. & Ellen returned from Charleston, at which place our daughter had been at school for the last six months. I was up to receive them & was gratified to see my daughter again at home.

Sunday 3rd....We were too dull & sleepy to attend church, so we read the service at home. Preston & Martha dined with us & we had all our children under our roof except James....My father arrived about 3 ocl. His health is infirm.

Monday 4th....This being sale day, brought together a large number of persons from different parts of the District. Not much property sold. I heard no District news. The crops are reported to be promising over the whole District.

Tuesday 5th....We spent an agreeable day with Preston & family & returned home by moon light.

---

16 Russel (sic) Harden of Beech Island in Edgefield Dist. fled, probably to Georgia, after allegedly killing his unnamed slave. Gov. Aiken, calling the act "atrocious," offered $200 for his capture. In March 1846, an Edgefield jury convicted Harden of murder but recommended mercy. (The normal penalty was a substantial fine.) The SC Court of Appeals reversed the ruling because the court session had not been extended. On retrial in Edgefield that October, the jury found Harden guilty of manslaughter. Judge A. P. Butler sentenced him to pay $500 and serve six months in jail. Later some of Harden's property was auctioned by the sheriff, two slaves included (Fede, *Homicide Justified,* 184). In 1849 Martin Posey of Edgefield became the first person in South Carolina to be executed for the killing of a slave, but he had also hired the killing of his own wife (offering freedom) by the slave he then killed (Fede, 184–85). Almost all slave-killing cases were decided in favor of the defendant based on a plea of self-defense.

Wednesday 6[h]....I planted a small field for the negroes at the Youngblood place. I also finished plowing over the first time a field of 30 acres of corn, next to Hollingsworth on the Beaver Dam and commenced at the Youngblood place; where the corn looks very well. M[rs]. Carroll returned from Columbia this evening, accompanied by our Sister M[rs]. Laborde, who is in very feeble health and is very much reduced. Her general health is very indifferent & requires change of air climate, etc. A visit to Saratoga & the White Sulpher Spring might be of great benefit. I made a trade with Preston, exchanging two fellows for a woman & child & receiving in notes $650 in boot. As usual I let him cheat me out of something like from $100 to 150. The fellows are young and likely but somewhat insubbordinate....[17]

....

Friday 8th....I sent a servant to Roselands with directions to my Overseer to send me a load of oats & fodder and also another to Aiken to bring up some articles, which had been sent by the Railroad from Charleston. The Rev[d]. M[r]. Reed & family and Elizabeth Blocker passed on their way to Major Blockers — They appeared in excellent health. Information has been received that hostilities had commenced between the Mexican & United States armies & that a company of U.S. troops had been surrounded & either killed or taken — Gen[l]. Taylors situation is regarded as somewhat perilous and as demanding immediate reinforcements. The post at Point Isabel is in danger. Requisitions have been made on the Governors of Mississippi, Louisianna & Texas for troops — It is thought that 20.000 will be required to oppose with success the forces of Mexico, now being concentrated at & near Matamoras. The Sun shone out in the afternoon & I rode through the Village for exercise but the appearances of clear weather were deceptive for on my return, clouds began to form in the Southwest & the most extraordinary thunder or rumbling noise in the heavens succeeded, that I have heard for many a long day. The cloud discharged a heavy shower of rain about sunset — I met our Minister M[r]. B[ruce] Walker, riding out in his buggy, whom I had not seen for three months, owing to his & my absence from the Village. He returned this morning in the Columbia stage & looked in fine health. I entertain for this gentleman great respect on account of his consistent piety, gentlemanly deportment, amenity of manners & integrity of character, to which may be added the qualities of a cultivated mind & sound good sense.

Saturday 9th....The Rev[d]. M[r]. Reed & his lady arrived & spent the night with us.

Sunday 10th....M[r]. Reed preached in the Episcopal church & the sacrament was administered by M[r]. Walker. In the afternoon M[r]. R. again preached & also at night. His manner has improved since he left this place for Grahamville, being milder, more persuasive & less hurried. His morning sermon abounded in passages of eloquence, not often heard in our pulpits & the matter was such as to rivet the

[17] Presumably PSB got the "fellows" and WB the woman and child. This suggests that his sense of PSB's capability as a planter was more positive than other comments have suggested.

attention of the audience. He is an able & interresting preacher. Major Blocker & his Wife, Preston & Wife & Mrs. Reed passed the day & dined with us....

Monday 11th....I began to plow & chop out my cotton at the farm. Mr. & Mrs. Reed left us this morning on their return to Log Creek.[18] I visited the Village in the afternoon & transacted a little business....

Tuesday 12th....On riding through my fields, I found the earth still wet & barely admitting the plough. I set out to pay a visit to my Aunt Butler & met her at the present residence of Col. Butler, she having come to the Village this morning. I was pleased to find her in pretty good health. I then went to the Village & paid a visit to Mrs. [Eliza?] Bacon[19] & Mr. Walker.

Wednesday 13th....We paid a visit to Mr. & Mrs. Terry. They have a commodious & comfortable house & a well arranged and handsome lot. Upon a close examination of a field of corn, I found it - greatly missing & requiring more time in replanting it - than was required at the first planting. The cold nights are causing the cotton to die and most of it looks drawn up & sickly. Our sister Mrs. Laborde & Ellen spent the day with us. Her health is delicate.

Thursday 14th....I rode through the Village & thence by Mr. [James] Terry's & Mr. Jas. Griffins, across Log Creek to my farm. Griffins plantation reminded me of the discription given by John Blackburn of his own farm some years since. He said it - was composed of gully warp & broom straw filling, on which he would starve, unless he removed from it. Griffins is a large plantation, for the improvement of which he takes great pains by manuring, resting & changing the culture. I saw several lots of excellent wheat near his house....My corn looks well but is in want of work. The mail brings no news from the army & the foreign accounts in regard to the settlement of the Oregon controversy are not so favourable. The Peel Ministry is about to retire to be succeeded by Lords John Russel & Palmeston.[20] About 5. Ocl. till dark, heavy & successive showers of rain fell until the surface of the whole earth was flooded. I shall not be able to run a plough until monday.

Friday 15th....My negroes are engaged in planting out potatoe drawings & thinning corn. We paid a visit - to Major Blocker, & passed the day in company with Mr. and Mrs. Harris & Miss Jeter.[21] On our return we were overtaken by rain, near Hollingsworths about 6 ocl. & it continued to fall for an hour by which the earth is again rendered very wet.

---

[18] Blocker home.

[19] Likely Eliza Fox Bacon (1782–), widow of Edmund Bacon (1776–1826).

[20] Lord John Russell (1796–1878), a reform-minded Whig and free-trader, was Prime Minister 1846–1852. Henry John Temple, Viscount Palmerston (1784–1865), was Foreign Minister in the Russell cabinet.

[21] William A. Harris (1815–) married Sara Jeter, daughter of John Speed Jeter of Edgefield. They lived in Columbia for some part of their married life. This "Miss Jeter" could be her sister.

Saturday 16th....I saw an Extra slip from the Chronicle office in Augusta, in which it – is stated that an engagement had taken place between the United States & Mexican forces near Matamoras, in which the U.S. Army was victorious, killing about 700 of the enemy and distroying the Town of Matamoras with trifling loss on our Side. Genl. Taylor was not present at the engagement, having marched with a part of his army to open his communication with Point Isabell & leaving Col. Ringold in command of the Fort with some 800 men. It was this force that achieved the Victory. The President has sent a message to Congress, in which he announces a state of war to exist with Mexico & calling for men & money to prosecute it. The house of Rep. passed a bill, appropriating $10.000.000 & authorising the President to call into service 50.000 Volunteers. The bill was before the Senate when the paper was issued, which contained the account – (ie) the [Washington] Union —

Sunday 17th....I felt rather indisposed & did not attend church. Doctr. Laborde arrived in the stage from Columbia, looking to be in fine health & spirits. He brings no additional news from the army or from Congress.

Monday 18th....The papers of this morning contain the proceedings of the house of Representatives & of the Senate upon the Presidents message in relation to our difficulties with Mexico & of the passage by the Senate of the bill declaring a state of war to exist between the two Countries & making an appropriation of 10.000.000 to carry on the war. The Vote in the house was 174 in the affirmative & only 14 in the negative — In the Senate 40 in favour & 2 against the bill & 3 Senators refused to Vote, to wit Calhoun, Berrien & Evans. The President has issued his proclamation, declaring the existence of hostilities between the two governments & calling upon the citizens of the United States to aid the government in bringing the War to a speedy and successful termination. Volunteer companies are forming in all parts of the Union and tendering their services to the Government from New York to Louisianna. My Son Preston is endeavouring to form a company & the young men of the District are invited to attend a meeting on Saturday next to consider of the matter. Great unanimity & enthusism prevail in every quarter from which we have received any accounts among old & young; a most gratifying evidence of the patriotism & spirit of our people. This is the time to test the mettle of men —

Tuesday 19....My corn at the farm is suffering greatly by the wet weather, much of it having turned red & stopped growing & the land is now barely dry enough to admit the plow....

Wednesday 20th....Mrs. Brooks & Ellen are preparing to set out on a visit to our Son James in Barnwell & I & Whitfield to Roselands. We all left between 7 & 8 ocl. ocl. I & Whitfield arrived at the plantation about 1. ocl. In the afternoon I rode through my plantation & made a cursory examination of the State of the crop.

Thursday 21....I rode over my plantation and examined the condition of my crop. The wheat & oat crop is excellent & promises a large product. The rye is only moderately good. The corn & cotton are young but are in a growing state & in pretty good order. Altogether my plantation is in as good if not better order than I have ever seen it – & the entire crop is promising. The negroes were in good health. My mules and horses were in good condition for the season & a horse & mule colt . . . equal to any in the State. In fact I saw nothing to dissatisfy me but the condition of my cattle & hogs. They are poor & look badly. Many of each kind died during the Winter & Spring of a kind of disease. I sent a message to my overseer that I was apprehensive that he would get out of the breed of cattle in a few more winters. In the afternoon I paid a visit to M^{r}. King[22] & sat an hour with him in social converse....

Friday 22....I left the plantation before 7 ocl & arrived at home at 12 ocl. where I learned from Hampden that a second engagement had been fought between the Americans & Mexicans in which the American army was again Victorious. On getting a paper containing the account, I read a confirmation of his report. There were from 7 to 9000 mexicans & about 18 or 1900 of the American army, & yet the former were routed with great loss of men & stores. Genl.[Romulo Diaz] De La Vega taken prisoner, etc.[23] In the afternoon I rode to my farm & found the corn still suffering from excess of rain. In many places in the fields, the young corn has turned red & ceased to grow. The cotton is small & rather unpromising....

Saturday 23rd....It is now & has been for a few days past summer weather, which causes the crops to grow with rapidity. The growth of the entire vegitable kingdom has been unusually vigirous & luxurient this Spring and the umbrageous covering of the trees never was more dense. I shall finish during the day plowing over my corn the first time and chopping out the cotton[.] In a letter received yesterday, from Cap^{n}. Bird [in northern Florida], he States that his corn is from waist to head high and that he was plowing it - over the third time. I suffered at night from a paroxism of headache.

Sunday 24th....I prepared to go to my fathers but was too unwell & postponed the trip until next day. I attended service in the afternoon at the Epis. church & heard a very able & philosophical sermon by the Rev^{d}. M^{r}. Reed. He is among the ablest preachers in the State. Service in the church at night but I could not attend. M^{r}. Reed returned with M^{rs}. Brooks & remained with us.

Monday 25....I left home for my fathers, with my daughter for a companion at half after 8 ocl., having waited for the Southern mail from Augusta, which however brought no late intelligence. We reached my fathers about 4 ocl. & found him in better health than I expected & in very good spirits....

Tuesday 26th....Our father being still cheerful & free from any oppressive suffering & consenting to our return, we set off at half after one oclock & arrived at home at 7 ocl....The crops of small grain from this to Saluda are abundant & promise a

---

22 Possibly William King (1797–); 1850 census: $1,200 real estate, 22 slaves.

23 Battle of Resaca de la Palma, May 5, 1846.

heavy harvest. I heard of no rust in the wheat & but little on the leaves of the rye. The Country will soon pass from a state of scarcity almost amounting to suffering both to man & beast, to one of plenteous abundance. The crops of corn & cotton are small but look well & in a growing condition. What abundant cause of thankfulness to God for this manifestation of his kind Providence, in blessing the State with rich harvests in the midst of our greatest want? His blessing is thus made to follow his chastisement, each of which, I trust, will make a wholsome & lasting impression upon the hearts of our people & draw them to a greater dependence & grateful reliance upon him. I found all well at home & no news from the seat of war....

Wednesday 27th....Intelligence was received that a part of our troops had crossed the Rio Grande & taken possession of a small Town, called Barita in Mexico & that Genl. Taylor was preparing to take Matamoras. Govr. Aiken has issued his proclamation, calling for a regiment of Volunteers (ie) 777 men, to be in a state of readiness, whenever their services may be required by the Government....The four last days have been exceedingly warm & Sultry. It has been very drying to the earth & . . . hard & difficult for the ploughman.

Thursday 28th....Planters are cutting wheat in various parts of the District, for which the week has been favourable. No additional news by the papers of this morning —

Friday 29th....In the afternoon I met several gentlemen at [Nathan] Griffin's Office, to prepare some resolutions to be offered at a public meeting to be held on Monday next in regard to our relations with Mexico. My friend Doct^{r}. Laborde came over & sat with me until 9 ocl. in social conversation, the family absent at church —

Saturday 30th....M^{r}. Reed & lady, M^{r}. Walker & E[lizabeth] Blocker dined with us, with whom we passed a pleasant day. There was a battalion muster at the Pine house[.] Nothing unusual occurred. The Rev^{d}. Mr. Reed again preached in the Epis. church. He is a great favorite with the people of Edgefield both as a gentleman & Preacher.

Sunday 31st....We had a sermon from the Rev^{d}. Mr. Reed on a very interresting subject, – "The glory of Christ in his priestly & kingly character." I was unwell during the service & in the afternoon too indisposed to attend Church. Sister [Nancy] Blocker came down & passed the day with us, with whom M^{r}. & M^{rs}. Reed & Betty [Elizabeth] Blocker returned in the afternoon....My crop at my farm has suffered by the wet weather but is now fairly beginning to grow, tho wanting work. I have more grass than I have had for several years & the hands seem to get on slower.

June 1. 1846.

Monday 1st....I rode over my entire farm before 8 ocl. My crop is growing but a portion of it is, as the farmers say, "very foul." ....A public meeting was held in the Courthouse, to take into consideration, our relations with Mexico, at which M^{r}. [Frank] Wardlaw was called to act as chairman & M^{r}. George Addison as secty. A series of resolutions were offered by Co[l]. Pickins & supported by one of the most sensible speeches, that I have ever heard from that gentleman.[24] It was somewhat too violent & denunciatory. Addresses were also made by M[r]. Bauskett, Wigfall, Yancy, P.S. Brooks, Griffin, & Bonham. The meeting was unaminous on the subject of our relations with Mexico & adjourned in good order after passing the resolutions with unaminity....

Tuesday 2....The negroes of L.T. Wigfall were sold at the Courthouse at very high prices – a fellow sold for over $800 & a woman for $705. No news by the papers. I was very sick in the afternoon & was prevented from attending the burial of E.[dmund] Bacons child which died on the preceeding afternoon about one month old.

Wednesday 3....I paid a visit to Rev[d]. M[r]. Walker & saw E. Bacon, whom I invited to take his Wife & spend a week at my plantation. She is in very feeble health. While in the Village I learned that the personal property of M[r]. Wigfall was then being sold by the Sheriff. I saw a late New York paper, which gives the advices by the last Steamer from England. The tone of the public prints from that Country is pacific on the subject of Oregon and hope may be now entertained of the peaceable settlement of that question. I began to day to plough over my corn at the Youngblood farm the second time & to plant peas ....

Thursday 4th....I accompanied a party of gentlemen in the afternoon to arrest a parcel of negroes, lying as runaways in a dense thicket of woods within my enclosure. We ran down & caught three with a couple of hounds, belonging to young Matthews, two men & one woman....[25]

....

Sunday 7th....I felt indisposed & unable with any comfort to attend church in the afternoon. Rec[d]. a letter from my Overseer, informing me that he had cut both the wheat & rye & that he had planted peas.

Monday 8th....The earth is now wet for several inches in depth & admirably fitted for transplanting all kinds of plants or vines. There was scarcly a moment during the day, when it was not raining & also through the greater part of the night. The Volunteers, who are forming a company for the war with Mexico, met in the Courthouse & held an election for officers — P.S. Brooks was elected Captain without opposition, M[r]. Maragine[26] first Lieutenant & M[r]. Jones,[27] second Lieut.

---

[24] *Adv.*, June 3, 1846, noted some uneasiness with Pickens' remarks since Senators Calhoun and McDuffie had opposed war (Edmunds, *Pickens*, 101–102).

[25] Did the hounds, or the slaves, belong to Matthews? Were any of them WB's? Women runaways were rare.

[26] William Caine Moragne (1818–1862); Huguenot ancestors settled in Abbeville Dist. Honor graduate SC College 1837, Univ. Gottingen, Germany. Student of history and literature, lawyer. Resigned from Pal. Reg. 1848. State legislator 1850s, *Adv.* staff; m. Emma Butler, daughter of Stanmore and Anne Patience Butler (Chapman, *Edgefield*, 268–71).

Tuesday 9th....I had a violent attack of headache which lasted until near 1. Ocl.

Wednesday 10th ....I have at no time seen the earth more thoroughly saturated with water. It will put a stop to ploughing until monday, which will cause the loss of one week in the cultivation of the crops.

Thursday 11th....This is the fifth day that rain has fallen almost without cessation & there is now no appearance of clear weather....There was an examination of Mr. McClintocks school, which I attended for a short time & heard one or two classes — The boys acquitted themselves very well. I learned that the wheat was sprouting in the fields & that great damage would be sustained unless the weather became clear....

Friday 12th....The boys had an exhibition in the Courthouse & performed a farce & comedy, in both of which they acted very well. The different parts were naturally performed & with spirit. The scenery & music were not very good. The house was exceedingly crowded, & so great was the anxiety to see & hear, that a mass of all classes both black & white filled the portico & entrance, as compact as they could stand.

Saturday 13th....I rode to my farm & found the earth still too wet for the plough & also to the Village, to make some purchases for my negroes at the plantation. At night the young gentlemen again had an exhibition in the Courthouse. The house was again crowded by a jam of all ages, sexes, sizes & conditions, all of whom appeared much delighted with the performance. In truth the young gentlemen deserve much praise for the spirit & taste manifested, in getting up such a creditable exhibition & for the correctness and animation, with which they performed their several parts —

Sunday 14th....We attended church as usual.

Monday 15th....About Six Ocl. there occurred a vivid flash of lightning, followed by heavy thunder, in a north direction, when to the West & So.West it was nearly clear. It was one of those sudden & unexpected claps of thunder that sometimes occur, when the appearance of the elements do not indicate it. I rode to my farm & was caught in a light rain. After ten days suspension, I began this morning to plough my corn, which is now suffering from grass & the want of work. In the greater part of my fields at the Youngblood place, I found the earth still too wet for the plough & was therefore forced to select the drier spots.

Tuesday 16th....I rode to Preston, roused him & Martha from their late slumber & then back home to breakfast.[28] Very clear & pleasant – at 9 ocl. There was a party of young people at Mr. Addison's in the evening , to which the young members of our

---

[27] William P. Jones (1820–) resigned in 1847.

[28] Here WB showed awareness of and concern about PSB's lack of energy or maturity. Perhaps Preston's anticipation of military glory had detracted from more mundane responsibilities. However, see WB's comment on the 18th.

family were invited.

Wednesday 17th....I rode to Major Blockers after early breakfast & spent the day with the family. On my return in the afternoon I found M^{rs}. Cunningham at our house on her way from Hamburg. She is a sensible & agreeable lady & we were gratified to have her company for the night. We received intellegence through Judge Butler of the settlement of the boundary in Oregon with the British nation at 49$^{\theta}$ of latitude from the Rocky mountains to the Pacific Ocean.

Thursday 18th....M^{rs}. Cunningham left us after early breakfast. I took Ellen in the buggy & went out to breakfast with Preston – After taking breakfast I rode with him over his crop of corn, which I found, to be very good & in excellent order. Take it altogether it is the best & cleanest crop, that I have seen this summer. I saw only a small part of his cotton crop & can therefore give no opinion in regard to it.

Friday 19th....I began yesterday to cut oats & to day had five cradles in use. My oat crop is very good....

Saturday 20th....a light shower of rain. It was copious enough to stop my reapers, by reason of which, I failed to finish my oat crop as I had designed & expected. M^{r}. Toomy [Tuomey][29] the agricultural & geological surveyor for the State, called for a short time at my house. He was on his way to Log Creek to examine a quarry of rock, which is reputed to be adapted to the purposes of Whetstones. M^{r}. Walker took tea with us.

Sunday 21....I called to see M^{r}. Toomy at Goodman's hotel & invited him to my house. I am anxious that he should visit my plantation with me & give me the benefit of his knowledge in regard to soils & their improvement. I was indisposed in the afternoon.

Monday 22^{n}....I employed this morning Six ploughs & I trust, I will by these means save my corn from the grass. Many planters have been compelled to abandon a portion of their crops in order to Save the balance. Judge Butler, M^{r}. Toomy & Preston & his Wife dined with us. The mild temperature of the air invigorated me & I got through the day without discomfort or much pain. No news.

Tuesday 23....I took our daughter in the buggy & went to Jo^{s}. Ferguson's[30] to look at a cow & calf, which I agreed to purchase at $15. We returned by Ja^{s}. Griffins & saw the crops on this road. They looked well & were generally in good order, much better than on the Pottersville road. I began this afternoon to plough over corn the third time, later than usual with me. The wet seasons which prevailed early & late

[29] Michael Tuomey (1805–1857), born in Ireland, studied geology at Rensselaer Inst. in Troy NY. Recommended by Sir Charles Lyell to succeed Edmund Ruffin as state geologist, he was employed 1844–1847. He then joined the faculty at Univ. of Alabama and was state geologist there. His *Report on the Geology of South Carolina* (1848) included a description of Edgefield District's geology.

[30] Joseph Ferguson (1781–); 1850 census: $1,350 real estate, 52 slaves.

in the Spring at these different times were the cause of my being so far behind in working my crop.

Wednesday 24....fire necessary to comfort. After breakfast I rode to the Village, to purchase a few articles for the negroes at the plantation. On my return I met Co^{l}. Pickens, with whom I had a long conversation on the Edgefield meeting & other matters. I agreed to meet him at his plantation on Friday next & spend the day. About 11. Ocl. I set out for my plantation & had a warm ride. Having a light attack of headache, I retired to bed about twilight & saw neither the overseer nor any of the negroes.

Thursday 25th. After breakfast I rode over my crop. The wheat, rye & oat crop principally cut & in shocks. It is the most abundant grain crop that I have ever made.... Doct^{r}. Barrett & M^{r}. Toomy arrived to dinner & spent the afternoon with me. Towards evening we rode over a portion of my crop with which the gentlemen expressed themselves well pleased. M^{r}. Toomy remained with me. Doct^{r}. Barrett prescribed for some of my servants, who were unwell....

Friday 26th. After early breakfast M^{r}. Toomy & I went to Col. Pickens plantation on Saluda river, where we met Co^{l}. P. & M^{r}. Harris. We rode over & inspected his crop of corn & cotton, which is principally planted on the low grounds on the North side of the river & in the District of Newberry. The crop of corn & cotton was excellent & in good order. This is a very valuable plantation, is both level & productive & at present is protected from inundation by embankments. A great disadvantage & drawback from its value, is the fact, that the settlement or residence for Overseer & negroes, is on one side of the river & the body of arable land on the other, in consequence of which his negroes are under the necessity of crossing the river both morning & evening, producing delay & some risk in times of high water. It is however a very valuable tract of land. Our host as usual was hospitable & entertaining. In the afternoon we all returned to my plantation & passed the night.

Saturday 27th....After early breakfast, we parted with M^{r}. Toomy, & Co^{l}. P. & M^{r}. Harris rode with me over my crop. They pronounced it good & paid a high compliment to the productiveness, beauty & arrangement of my plantation. We set out for the Village at 9. ocl. & arrived at our respective homes about 2 ocl, finding all well. The only news furnished by the papers was the ratification by the Senate of the Oregon treaty and the debate in the house on the new tariff bill. No late intelligence from the army. I cannot close my remarks, without noting the fact, that this excursion was one of the most instructive and agreeable in which I have participated for many a day. The weather was clear & mild & the the company intellegent – & entertaining. They ought to occur more frequently as a means of social emprovement and as a stimulus to our agents & negroes, who are made to take pride in the exhibition of a good crop & well ordered plantation. In the afternoon I rode over my crop at the farm & feel warranted in pronouncing it - the most inferior one, that I have ever had at this period of the year. It wants both rain & work.

Sunday 28th....We attended church both in the morning & afternoon & heard two sensible sermons by Mr. Walker. I called to see Chancellor Dunkin[31] at County's [Compty's], who is here to hold an extra Court of Equity. He accompanied me home & spent the evening with my family. He is an urbane & agreeable gentleman & a faithful & highly intelligent public officer.

Monday 29th....Judge Dunkin is now holding the Court of Equity for this District & I observed Mr. Dessasure from Columbia, Martin & Wilson from Abbeville[,] Gray of Augusta and Messs. Pope & Fair from Newberry. The Volunteer company called "Old Cambridge boys", commanded by Preston S. Brooks, were assembled in the Village to day & were inspected by Genl. [M. L.] Bonham. There were about 60 in attendance & exhibited a fine appearance. They went into an election of Col., Lt. Col., & Major, & they are reported to have voted for Col. P.M. Butler, Col. Dickerson & Thos. Butler for the different offices, in the order in which they stand.

Tuesday 30th....This month has exhibited a succession of contrasts. In the early part of it, rain fell for five successive days, & so thoroughly wet the earth as not only to do great injury to the growing crops of corn & cotton but to impart such a rapid growth to the grass, that rendered it necessary for any planters to abandon a portion of their crops, from inability to work them. My crop of corn became much infested with grass & in order to subdue it -, I ran a twisted shovel,[32] breaking up the earth to a great depth & covering the grass. I run the risk of ruining my corn & if I do not get rain in a few days, it will yield but little. Since the heavy rain above mentioned, it has been clear & warm in the day time (except for five or six days when fire was comfortable) & no rain fell until the light shower stated above. It is now dry & the earth in the fields, hard to the plough. The general feature of the weather has been warm days & cool nights, cool enough for blankets. There are more cases of sickness through the Country, than is usual at this early period of the summer. A peculiar disease has been observed among the flies, which results in their death. They resort to water, drink & then burst open, & drag their entrails until they die.

July 1. 1846

Wednesday 1st....The case of Hill vs Hill was heard to day by Chancellor Dunkin. It is a case of great interest – in the neighbourhood of the parties, as the amount involved is large & it has already produced a family feud....Chancellor Dunkin called & took tea with us, with whom I passed a very pleasant evening.

....

[31] Benjamin Faneuil Dunkin (1792–1874), Philadelphia native, Harvard graduate. Moved to SC 1811. Attorney, Speaker of the SC House, 1828–1830, and Chancellor of the Court of Equity 1837–1860.

[32] A cultivator with a curved and twisted blade.

Friday 3rd....Rain is now much needed for the gardens & cornfields....The Stalk is unusually Small & the fields exhibit great irregularity in the the size of the growing corn. This is owing to the long & heavy rains, which not only run the earth together but kept it – too cool & prevented the decay of the nutritive properties by which the plant is fed. In fact in low flat land, the rain seems to have rendered the earth inert & to have locked up its nutritive qualities. On high red land the corn is very good as it suffered less from the rain....The Court of Equity adjourned & Chancellor Dunkin went as far as Aiken on his return to Charleston. An extra Court ordered in August.

Saturday 4th....This is the anniversary of American Independence & should be celebrated & observed as a political Sabbath in every quarter of this wide spread republic & yet I hear of no preparation for its observance in the Village & only in one or two places in the District. This apathy should not exist in the minds of the people, if they put any value on their liberties — There was a barbacue, at Horn's Creek church, where Doctr. Burt delivered an address on the subject of education & the young men of the neighbourhood performed a piece on a temporary stage. At night the young folk had a dance at Samp. Mays. Mr. Jos. Abney delivered a temperance address in the Courthouse, to which succeeded some fine instrumental music by the young men of the Village. Our Village has lost its former spirit & liberality, for 20 years ago neither the young or the old would have allowed this anniversary to pass with so meagre a demonstration of public gratitude and joy —

Sunday 5th....At ten Ocl last night the firmament had the appearance of light coloured marble with a bright light around the moon, something like a halo, from which I augured a change of weather. It continued to drop rain, during the day except at short intervals & . . . rain. . . continued through the entire night....

Monday 6th....The earth is now thoroughly wet & I am setting out potatoe slips[33] & cabbage plants....This was sale day but few persons were in attendance & only one-tract of land & no personal property was sold. I heard of no local news. The general opinion seemed to be that the crops in ten miles of the Village are not as good as they were last year. My own at present is not equal to that of last year. It has suffered both by wet weather & the want of work at the proper time. The rain on Sunday night has improved it – greatly & I may yet make an average crop. I suffered a good deal from headache. James & his family arrived on a visit. He has a fine child near one year old & is named after me.

Tuesday 7th....I paid a visit to Judge Butler & my venerable Aunt Butler in company with my Son James. Preston & his Wife dined with us & I again had all our children, with their wives & two grandchildren under our roof at the same time, being 9 in number. Our two grandchildren will favourably compare with any two children in the District for soundness of health & beauty of appearance.

---

[33] Shoots from a mature sweet potato plant.

Wednesday 8th....I rode over my crop & the improvement is most obvious since Saturday last....A brighter and lovelier moon light cannot be imagined or one more inviting to exercise and Social visiting. It tempted me from home for the first time after dark, for about twelve months. We visited our neighbours Harris, Mayes and M^{c}. Clintock.

Thursday 9th....We passed the day with our Son Preston & had at dinner Mrs. Carroll, John & Ellen Laborde,[34] James Brooks & Wife, Myself, Wife, Whitfield & Ellen. My entire family were collected together except Hampden, whom we left at home, to attend school. We remained to tea & returned by moon light....

Friday 10th....I breakfasted with Co^{l}. Pickens, having gone to his house in company with my neighbour M^{r}. Harris, to look at his crop. After breakfast, we rode over a portion of his corn & cotton crop & had a view of its general character. The corn is a fair crop, & the cotton, exceedingly likely & promises well. It is full of blooms & forms — I was attacked with acidity & so great was my suffering, that I was forced to stop at his [grove?] spring & await the return of the gentlemen. I saw a pretty flag, which Miss Susan Pickens was working for the Volunteer company, called old 96 boys, which is commanded by my Son Preston. It is stated in the papers that McKays[35] revenue bill has passed the house of Repres. by a magority of 19 Votes & it [is] thought, it will pass the Senate. A M^{rs}. Doby died yesterday in the Village by inflammation of the bowels....

Saturday 11th....We learned with great regret of the death of Major Thomas Means of dropsy in the chest. He was a most worthy & amiable gentleman & for the last 6 or 8 years has performed the offices of a father to the children of his two deceased brothers, Doct^{r}. Dav. Means & of the Rev^{d}. R[obert] Means. To them his loss is irreparable as well as afflictive. He was never married but lived & died a bachelor. I entertained great respect for him....

Sunday 12th....Having no service in our church, in consequence of the absence of Mr. Walker, we attended at the Baptist church & heard a long, sensible but rather dull sermon by the Rev^{d}. Doct^{r}. Johnson, in which he undertook to prove the perfect Sovereignty of God & the free agency of man and their compatibility with each other. I was very attentive but I regret to say, that I derived no instruction from the sermon. I receive them as evident propositions, which cannot be explained, enforced or reconciled by reason, as truths which must be received upon faith, the best evidence of which is furnished by our own internal convictions. The sermon had been prepared with care & written out yet it failed to produce much interest....

---

[34] Ellen Carroll Laborde (1832–1902) was a daughter of Maximilian and Elizabeth Carroll Laborde.

[35] James Iver McKay (1793–1853), Dem., NC, was chief House sponsor of the Walker Tariff bill, which returned to the ad valorem approach (tax based on the value of the item, as opposed to rates varying by commodity). Its passage was a victory for southern interests.

Monday 13th....Went to the Village, transacted some business with Col. Carroll, purchased a few articles for the negroes and returned to read the papers. No news.

Tuesday 14th....I rode to my farm & returned after examining my crop, considerably fatigued. I had a tooth drawn by Mr. Halleman, which gave me great pain, and was succeeded by a violent attack of headache & confined to bed during the entire day. I was disappointed in passing the evening with Mrs. Carroll, to whose house, we were all invited. The paroxism passed off about 10 ocl. at night —

Wednesday 15th....showers until 10. ocl. The earth wet about 2 inches. I finished plowing my corn at the Youngblood place the third time & directed my hands to hoe over the grassiest parts of the crop....Preston & his Wife came & passed the night with us on their way to Fairfield – James & his Wife went to my fathers —

Thursday 16th....After breakfast I left home with Ellen for the plantation, accompanied by Preston & Wife, at which we arrived about 12 ocl. In the afternoon we rode over my crop. The corn is very good & about 200 acres of cotton pretty good and about 50 acres indifferent, being either on old land or portions of fields on the creek, where it was drowned by rain. Just as we sat down to supper Major Hibler[36] & Yancy with a youth by the name of Garmany[37] arrived & staid all night....

Friday 17th....After breakfast we all set out for our respective points of destination & I reached home at 2 ocl. All well & no news except that Miss [blank space] had most heartlessly & cruelly rejected the Revd. Mr. Walker in one short month after their solemn engagement & while he was on his first visit to her in New York. I can find no excuse for the shameful conduct of this young lady if the representation of her beheavour be true....

Saturday 18th....I set out to my farm but was forced by the rain to return & dry myself by fire. James & his Wife left us at 9 ocl. at which time there was some appearance of clear weather. They proposed to go to Beach Island on their way home....The sun went down clear, forming a beautiful rainbeau in the So.East. A man by the name of Price was taken to jail for the murder of a Mr. Bailey, an Irishman —

Sunday 19th....We attended church morning & evening & listened to sensible sermons by Mr. Walker, our minister who had been absent for the last two sabbaths....

Monday 20th....The death of Mr. Bellamy is announced in a Talahassee paper, caused by inflamation of the lungs. I greatly regret the death of this estimable man,

---

[36] Thomas Jefferson Hibler, Captain of a militia company in one of the Seminole Wars.

[37] Likely a son of a Hamburg cotton merchant named Garmany. He and his partner, Howard, had helped close the loop of southern agriculture, commerce, and manufacturing in Sept. 1841 when they bought the season's first bale of cotton from Edgefieldian John Mosely with money from a SC bank. They sent it to the Vaucluse factory and the next day John Bauskett returned it as a bolt of woven cloth, which was then displayed on a shelf in their store (Downey, *Planting a Capitalist South,* 144).

on many accounts, particularly as he was the last male member of his family & upon whom devolved the care & management of his fathers estate, the estate of his brothers children & his own family, consisting of a Wife & young female children. The ways of Providence are inscrutible yet they originate in wisdom & end in good to his creatures.

Tuesday 21....I heard from the Plantation, where no rain has fallen during the whole of this cloudy weather....Whitfield & Ellen left home on a visit to our relations in Abbeville [Wesley Brooks & family?] — In the afternoon I rode over a part of my crop with Col. Bauskett & then over his crop on the Beaver Dam Creek. It is really a fine crop of corn & exhibits evidence of good management. He has opened a valuable grain plantation on this creek & adjoining his residence....

Wednesday 22nd....I rode over my crop and saw that it was suffering for rain. I have at last succeeded in overcoming the grass but too late to make a full crop.

Thursday 23d....I rode to a pine tract of land about four miles from this place & discovered a new & shorter rout – by which I can hawl rails & timber to my farm. No news by the papers — Rode to my farm in the afternoon. The corn is improving but wants rain.

Friday 24th....My waggoner returned with a new Piano for Ellen. It is a handsome & sweet toned instrument for which I gave a negro fellow that cost me two years ago $650. rather a costly present to my daughter.

Saturday 25th....I rode by the cotton fields of P.S. Brooks, a part of which was good but the stand bad. I also rode to the house & ascertained that the Overseer & negroes were well. On my return I passed by Col. Christies[38] & saw portions of his corn & cotton crop, which were very good. The papers of this morning announced the resignation of the Peel Ministry & the appointment of Sir John Russell at the head of a new ministry. The closing speech of Mr. Peel was able, mild & patriotic. He is one of the leading spirits of the age, the impress and influence of whose mind will be felt for half a century yet to come....

Sunday 26th....My feelings and the difficulty of breathing, indicate a change in the State of the atmosphere & I hope, it will prove the harbinger of rain. Our worthy neighbour Mr. Harris was attacked yesterday with a severe chill, which was followed by high fever & very sick stomach. He is very sick this morning....rain prevented us from attending church in the morning. The afternoon was mild & partly clear & our church was well attended....

---

[38] Simeon Christie (1800–1860), Sheriff 1840–1844 and 1848–1852, lived on outskirts of ECH. His father Robert Christie believed to have been 1st Lt. in Capt. Zachariah Smith Brooks' militia company.

Monday 27th....I heard from my plantation that on Sunday night an abundant rain fell at that place, which reached as high up as Cokesbury & as low down as Dorns. The light rain on Sunday has revived my corn.

Tuesday 28th....My father arrived at 12 ocl. in very feeble health. He is becoming very infirm. [L]ightning struck the house on which Mr. Cohn[39] keeps goods & did some damage to the house but without injury to any person. In the evening Mrs. Brooks had a few young persons to meet Mr. Walker & his Sister, who is at present on a visit to her brother. The party was small but sociable & agreeable.

Wednesday 29th....I rode to the Village with my father [and] called on my neighbour Harris, who is sick at Major Jeters & returned without hearing an item of news.

Wednesday 30th....The corn at my Youngblood place is suffering very much for rain. I am feeding my hogs morning & evening with peaches, upon which they seem to improve, in appearance at least. I give this food as a substitute for corn, of which I have none to spare. Preston returned from Fairfield & reports that his friends are well....

Friday 31st....In riding to my farm, I came upon two boys of L. Corley[40] in my pasture under suspicious circumstances, from which I was induced to take them home & ascertained that they had run away the day before. They tried to deceive me by asserting that they were looking for the cows, which had strayed away the night before — Dark clouds & heavy rain in the evening to the South & good rain in the Village with severe thunder.

August 1. 1846.

Saturday 1....It is surprising that while to the South & East of the Village, the rains were heavy during the week & the creeks overflowing their banks, I have not had enough at my farm even to run in the road....The [D]emocratic papers are filled this morning with denunciations of Senator Heyward[41] of No.Ca. for his resignation of his seat in the Senate at the moment when the Vote upon the tariff bill was expected to be taken — His defection at such a juncture has excited great surprise & indignation from all quarters. It is an act of treason to his party for which he is visited with scorn & contempt. His fall is compared to that of Lucifer, never to rise.

---

39 Jacob Cohn (1812–); 1850 census: 22 slaves.

40 Lemuel Corley (1823–); 1850 census: $2,450 real estate, 42 slaves.

41 William H. Haywood, Jr. (1801–1852), U.S. Senator 1843–1846. He resigned rather than follow the NC legislature's instructions on the tariff bill vote. He supported the Free Soil Party and Martin Van Buren in 1848.

Sunday 2....We attended morning & afternoon preaching at the Epis. church. Sacrament administered in the afternoon.

Monday 3[r]....I rode in the morning to my pine land to show Paul, where to get shingles & returned by Goode's farm to see his crop of corn. It is good but not equal to the representations, which I had received. Not many persons in the Village & no property sold. I heard no news either local or foreign except the passage of M[c]Kays tariff bill in the Senate by a majority of one. The Whigs made a last struggle to defeat the measure, resorting to motions, denunciations, arguments and lastly prophetic predictions of evil, but all in vain. The Democratic party stood firm & unawed & passed the bill, independent of the desertion of one or two of its members beside the Senators from Pennsylvania, who voted against it. A refreshing shower of rain fell about Sunset, which extended to my farm. My Overseer came down from my plantation & reported that my crop is very good & that some of the negroes were & had been very sick. He had thrashed out & measured 625 bushels of wheat a portion of which I have grounded into flour & I find it – very white & good —

Tuesday 4th....I rode to my farm & found my crop greatly enlivened by the rain. Another such rain this evening would be of infinite benefit to my corn. The cotton looks well & is full of bolls, blooms & forms & promises to yield a good crop....

Wednesday 5th....I am now endeavouring to get ready to set off on a short excursion to the Mountains. We left home at 7 Ocl. & reached M[rs]. Frazier's in AbbeVille about sunset....On red land the crops were generally pretty good but on grey land they were small & indifferent....

Thursday 6th. We left M[rs]. Fraziers after breakfast & passed by Calhouns mill, thence to Petersburg in Georgia & at night obtained quarters with a M[r]. Wall. A light shower of rain fell as we crossed the river & after travelling about two miles, two of the heaviest rains, descended in torrents upon us. The crops on the entire rout this day were very unequal. On the plantations of M[r]. Belcher & Co[l]. Elmore they were excellent with one exception, the cotton was growing too fast & was too full of sap to bear abundant fruit.— On other plantations they were merely up to mediocraty & on others exceedingly indifferent. I saw fields of both corn & cotton abandoned to the grass — In passing through Vienna in Carolina & Petersburg in Georgia I was forcibly impressed with the mutability of all human things — These once flourishing Villages, which boasted of their wealth, intellegence & refinement are now deserted & in a state of utter dilapidations — The sight of them produced a feeling of melancholy, which I could with difficulty cast off.

Friday 7....We left M[r]. Wall & passed through Elberton & reached the Franklin Spring at night. Finding that I could not reach the Madison Springs until a late hour & hearing that I could get to the Franklin Spring at an early hour, I determined to make it - a stage for the night. On arriving at the place, I was at a loss to determine, whether the landlord or myself was the most surprised, he at such an arrival & I at the plain Country appearance of my expected host — We made out to stay until after breakfast next day but Saturday 8th....We reached the Madison Springs[42] at 11. ocl. & were assigned to a very comfortable cabin, within convenient distance of the boarding house — I was informed that there were near 200 persons at this watering place, with many of whom I was acquainted. I was forced to retire to my cabbin on my arrival by an attack of headache & saw very few persons on this day – I was not able to leave my room until Sunday morning —

Sunday 9th....The Revd. Mr. Stephens preached morning & evening. I heard his morning sermon, which was the most eloquent, that I have heard for many years. It was characterized by profound thought and chaste & figurative language. I have omitted to mention that on Saturday last, as we passed to the hotel we saw the preparations on the road for the old, disused & cruel sport of "pulling the gander"[43] which I learned the company enjoyed or witnessed in the afternoon. This is the only instance of the indulgence of this species of sport, that I have heard of for the last thirty years. I met my friend Genl. Harris & a part of his family & several other acquaintances.

Monday 10th....I met Mr. Gourdine[44] from Charleston, with whom I held a long & interresting conversation on the measures of the General Government & particularly the late tariff bill. He gave me an interresting history of this measure from the date of the Presidents message up to the report of Mr. Walker. He is a very sensible & well informed gentleman and enjoys a high character in Charleston.

Tuesday 11th. No change in the weather or in the routine of passing the time at this watering place. First breakfast then music on the piano, then a game on the nine pin alley, when the fashionable bells [sic] would retire to their rooms either to sleep, read or dress as suited their several tastes — Dinner at 2 ocl., & short conversation in the parlour, & then each would retire to their rooms to prepare for an evening ride or to sleep & prepare for a night of frolick. Dancing usually commenced at candle light & was kept up until 10. 11. & sometimes 12 ocl. I have been to many watering places from Saratoga in New York, through Virginia, North & So. Carolina and I have never met a more intelligent, wellbred & respectable company of both ladies & gentlemen. There was not a blackleg, blackguard or dandy at the place; but every visitor belonged to that class in society, which removed all objection to a general acquaintance. I heard a highly respectable gentleman say, that he would not hesitate to introduce to his family any gentleman, whom he had met, for that all

[42] A well-known mineral spring about 20 miles NE of Athens GA.

[43] The gander was plucked, the body greased (esp. the neck), and suspended head down with his feet tied to a tree limb. The object was to ride a galloping horse, grab and hold on to the goose.

[44] Henry Gourdin (1804–1879), or his brother Robert N. (1812–1894). They were partners in a prosperous merchant house in Charleston. After the closing of the 2nd Bank of the United States, which had a branch in Charleston, Henry Gourdin led a group of investors in obtaining a charter for the Bank of Charleston in 1834. Robert was a signer of the Ordinance of Secession.

were wellbred & of good character.

Wednesday 12th. This was an inclement & rainy day & the ladies in the cabbins were deprived of dining at the public tables & partook of this meal in their rooms.

Thursday 13th....I formed acquaintance with a Judge Andrews[45] from Washington Ge°. of whom I formed a very favourable opinion. He is a gentleman of plain manners, sound understanding and of upright & virtuous instincts & sentiments. Between him & myself there was a marked harmony of thought & action in relation to the duties & obligations of the social & responsible man. We agreed in morals, politicks and even in agriculture & particularly in the proper education & training of children. Genl. Saunders has a strong mind but it is not well trained & in his manners, he belongs to a bygone age. His Lady & niece Miss Jordon may challenge comparison, with the first ladies in Georgia for good breeding & easy manners —

Friday 14th....We had departures & arrivals every day which would occasionally relieve the monotony of the passing scene — Judge Berrien passed on his way from Washington to join his family at Clarskville, where they were spending the summer. He gave us the information of the loss in the Senate of the joint resolution appropriating 2.000.000 to be at the disposal of the President in negociating a treaty of peace & boundary with Mexico —

Saturday 15....We set out after breakfast for Clarksville & reached a house near the Currahee mountain at night just in time to escape a heavy shower of rain. We were here joined by a Mr. Lumpkin[46] & Wife & a Miss Jemmason & a young gentleman from Charleston by the name of Gunning. They were exceedingly clever people & made an agreeable addition to our company. The house was tolerable & we passed a pleasant night, without the "forewarned" annoyance of the bedbug. This house is situated at the foot of the Currahee Mountain in a valley, which seemed to be adapted to garin [sic] & on which a good crop of corn was growing. We did not ascend the Mountain as we learned that it was difficult of ascent & fatiguing.

Sunday 16th....We set out after breakfast to Clarksville by the way of the Tuckoah [Toccoa] falls, at which we arrived about 11. ocl. This fall is stated to be 150 feet high & is formed by the passage of the water of a Creek, over the brow of a solid rock presenting a perpendicular surface the whole distance of the fall. The width of the volume of water as it – passes over the brow of the rock is from 10 to 15 feet but extends to something like 20 feet & terminates in spray, not unlike a white veil spread out & flowing down. The water in the basin below is always turpid, occasioned by the fall and a brisk wind constantly prevails. The rock extends some 50

[45] Garnett Andrews (1798–1873), lawyer in Wilkes County. Appointed Judge of the Northern Circuit of the Superior Court of Georgia in 1834. Agricultural reformer, American ("Know-Nothing") Party candidate for governor 1855. Unionist in 1861.

[46] Not likely Wilson Lumpkin (1783–1870), U.S. Congressman, Georgia Governor 1831–1835, U.S. Senator 1837–1841. WB would have known of him. Possibly his brother Joseph, a state Supreme Court justice.

yards on each side of the fall, gradually growing smaller until it – is merged in the hills, or mountainous ridge on the right & left of it. On leaving this fall, we had to pass over a range of hills, almost equal to Mountains, where the road was rough & precipitous. A light rain began to fall as we crossed this range of hills, & continued to fall until we reached ClarksVille, which was about 6 ocl. in the midst of a heavy shower.

Monday 17....Judge Berrien & his lady called to see us. We left Clarksville with a party to visit Nacoochee Valley and the Eony [Yonah] mountain & arrived in the afternoon at Williamsons. This Valley with its associated objects constitutes the very gem of Mountain scenery in this neighbourhood....It was covered with a luxurient crop of corn. The Eony Mountain is a regular cone, of regular proportions & stands somewhat detached from any other mountains. It is easy of ascent & presents from its summit some handsome views.

Tuesday 18th....The party set out for the Eony Mountain after breakfast & returned to dinner much pleased with their excursion. We met at Williams, M^{rs}. Ge^{o}. E. Calhoun & her daughter, awaiting the return of Co^{l}. Calhoun from Delonaga. This section of Georgia is interesting from its scenery & is much prized for its climate & health. The lands are very poor except in its vallies & on the water courses, which is limited in quantity. Its mild climate & reputed health are attracting many gentlemen of talent & wealth for summer residences from Savannah & the seaboard in Georgia & also several from this State [SC]. Our stay in the Village was too short to see any of them. We returned to Clarksville after dinner.

Wednesday 19th....After breakfast the same party of the previous day set out for Taloleh [Tallulah] falls, at which we arrived at 12. ocl. We found a party of 15 to 20 from Augusta on a visit to the falls, who were preparing for their return to the Village. As they took their departure the carriage of M^{rs}. Adams was upset by too suddenly making a turn on the side of the hill but no injury was sustained. Our party devoted the afternoon in viewing different points of the fall, while I was tossing on a hard bed with violent headache. The charm in the mountain & the fall of water with their adjuncts inspire the mind with awe & a feeling of sublimity.

Thursday 20th. After breakfast we took leave of our friends & set out for Jarret's on our return home. we passed over a mountainous road & reached the Tuckoah [Toccoa] fall about 2 ocl. We dined at this place & again saw & examined the falls. The sun had passed over the Mountain & did not shine on the water, so we were a second time deprived of seeing the rainbow colors, which are observable when the sun shines upon the spray. We reached Jarrets at sunset, who lives on Tugulo [Tugaloo] river.

Friday 21....We passed over a poor Country & reached old Pendleton about dark. No incident on the road, except – that of meeting a poor, degraded creature in the form of a woman, who was a begger with two children, all of whom were half clothed & half starved.

Saturday 22....We set out after breakfast, passed Anderson Courthouse, when I saw my old friend Whitner[47] & arrived near night at Mr. Fair's in Abbeville District. We were hospitably entertained by this gentleman, who lives in a plain but abundant Way or style ....

Sunday 23^r^....We left for my plantation after breakfast & after passing through Greenwood & old Cambridge, reached my plantation before night. Here I learned that some of my negroes were sick tho not seriously ill....

Monday 24....After breakfast I rode over or rather through my crop & saw a considerable portion of it. The corn is tolerable & the entire crop of cotton unusually promising both in the size of the plant & the abundance of fruit. My wheat crop is thrashed out & the overseer measured over 600 bushels. He made about 100 bushels of rye & a very large oat crop. Rain began to fall about 10 ocl. & continued through the day — One of my neighbours Wiley Thompson died today of consumption. I truly regretted to hear of the death of Major T.J. Hibler & of old M^r^. R. Martin, which had occurred, during my absence. Hibler was a good citizen and a useful member of the community in which he resided. His death will be felt as a serious loss by his neighbours.

....

Wednesday 26....After breakfast we set out for home at which we arrived about 1 ocl. finding all well. On our return I learned very little that was either new or interesting in regard to our neighbours or the District, that had occurred during our absence. After dinner I rode to my farm, & found the State of the crop equal to my expectations.

Thursday 27....I again visited my farm, where I am busily employed in pulling & saving fodder. There has been scarcely a day without a shower of rain, since the 22^n^. & consequently most of my fodder has been more or less wet.

....

Saturday 29th. Warm & clear. I rode to Prestons & saw a part of his cotton crop. It appeared to be good. In the afternoon I was rather feeble & did not go out to my farm as is my custom. Heard that young Lundy[48] had shot himself accidentally.

Sunday 30th....I attended Church morning & evening but felt dull & heavy & did not enjoy myself.

---

[47] Probably Judge Joseph N. Whitner (1799–1864).

[48] Theo N. Lunday (1825–); 1850 census: 21 slaves. Family lived near Horn's Creek, south of ECH.

Monday 31^{r}....An extra Court of Equity was begun to be held on this day by Chancellor Dunkin. Preston & his family spent the day & night with us, also Miss B[ell] Means — There was a meeting of the temperance Society held in the Courthouse, at which the young folk of our part of the Village attended & which turned out a very dull affair — They returned to my house & closed the evening by music, & frolick & song after 12 ocl at night. The month of August was warm & showery & unfavourable to fodder saving, a great part of which must have received more or less rain after it was pulled & before it was tied into bundles & stacked or put under cover. The rains have caused vegitation of all kinds to be rank & luxurient & the fields are clothed with a rich carpet of grass — The entire face of nature & all its productions present this fall a total contrast to that of last year. There is an abundance of all the articles of human or animal sustanance & the fountains of Water are full.

<u>September 1. 1846</u>

Tuesday 1st....In the afternoon I took the Chancellor in my carriage to pay a visit to Aunt Butler & the Judge....

....

Thursday 3^{r}....I was indisposed & prevented from dining at Judge Butlers with the members of the bar & the Chancellor.

Friday 4th....I dined at Co^{l}. Carroll's with Dunkin, Butler & a few gentlemen of the bar....Doctor Laborde returned from a three months excursion in the Mountain & to the Springs for the health of his Wife & Child. They were partially relieved but still in feeble health.

Saturday 5th....The squadron of [militia] Cavalry paraded in the Village. They made a poor show. The Court adjourned between 12 & 1 ocl.

Sunday 6th....We had preaching morning & evening in the Epis church. Chancellor Duncan, Laborde & Carroll took dinner with me....there has not past a day for the last fortnight without – showers of rain in some part of the District & neighbourhood. I have never seen the earth covered with a more luxurient crop of weeds or richer growth of grass. The pea Vines are very promising.

Monday 7....I saved about 8 acres of fodder that has been hanging on the stalk since friday. This is Sale day & on riding to the Village for my papers I mixed with the croud for a short time but heard nothing new — I called on the Chancellor at Comptys, who expects to go in the Stage at 1 ocl.

Tuesday 8....A protracted meeting is now being held at pleasant Grove, with what sucess, I have not heard. I do not approve of these artificial means of making christians. They are made in a moment of excitement & last but for a season & the last state is worse than the first–

Wednesday 9th....A load of flour arrived from the plantation, which was ground at Doctr. [John] Nicholson's Mill & which I sold in the Village at $2. pr. 100lb. and could have sold as much more. I was gratified to learn that my sick negroes were convalescent. They had chills & fever but were relieved by light medicine & quinine....I learned from a servant of Col. Pierce Butler that his Master arrived at Judge Butlers last night from Washington City Via Aiken in an improved State of health.

Thursday 10th....In the afternoon I rode to Judge Butlers to call on Col. P.M. Butler. I found him cheerful but in feeble health & greatly reduced in flesh — my respected & venerable Aunt was free of fever & much better than she had been two days before, when Doctor Laborde & I paid a visit to see her.

Friday 11. The weather this morning was mild & ....refreshing & strengthening both to the feelings & body. I was engaged in sowing small grain as winter pasturage for my milk cows. Our daughter & Bell Means dined with us —

Saturday 12th....I dined with several friends at Major Jeters & partook of an excellent repast. It was a dinner in compliment to Col. P. M. Butler....I sold another load of flour in the Village for upwards of $43.00. It is the fourth load, that I have sold from this crop & expect to have two more.

Sunday 13th. This is . . .the only clear & cloudless day, that I have seen for the last month....in the church both morning and evening the heat was oppressive —

Monday 14th....At 1. ocl. I set out for my plantation, taking young Barnet with me to pick out cotton. The clear & warm weather is admirably adapted to maturing the growing cotton. I reached my plantation about dark & was informed that my negroes were all convalescent & at work except Harry....

Tuesday 15th....I rode over a part of my crop & returned to witness the starting of a new gin by Mr. Chapman.[49] It performed well & ran with great ease & regularity....The corn & peas looked well & I think will yield well. The cotton is of fine size, in fact of more luxuriant growth, than it has had for several years past but I do not think it - is heavily laden with bolls my crop cannot exceed an average one....

Wednesday 16. Cloudy with high wind from the North. I set out for home at 7 ocl & arrived at 1 ocl.

....

Thursday 17th....I rode to Preston's & on my return stoped at the Village for a short time, to get my papers, etc....I sent Shelton with the carriage to Aiken for Mrs. Wilson,[50] who is coming to this place on a visit to Mrs. Brooks —

Friday 18 h....In the afternoon Mrs. Wilson, with her two daughters & Sons arrived

---

[49] John Chapman, father of John A. Chapman, author of *History of Edgefield County*, 1897.

[50] Sophia Frances Sheppard Wilson (Mrs. Alexander Wilson); "our friend" WB wrote while in Charleston. See Dec. 16, 1845. If so, she was widowed in 1840 and now owned Cockfield Plantation.

from Charleston on a visit to us. She was the early acquaintance & friend of Mrs. Brooks, between whom a strong attachment still continues.

Saturday 19th....I gathered to day a lot of corn, which turned out well. The warm weather has the effect of hastening the maturity of cotton & I have never seen it open more rapidly. At night our house was crouded with young people of both sexes, which is to me an interresting sight.

Sunday 20th....Our Son Preston returned from his Grandfathers & gave us the pleasing information that his health had improved and that his spirits were cheerful. I felt too much indisposed to attend church in the afternoon but was relieved from pain after sleeping a short time.

Monday 21....I read in the papers of this morning, the proclamation of Santa Anna[51] on his arrival at Vera Crux. It professes republican principles & great devotion to Mexico, while it lavishes unsparing abuse on Paredes[52] for his supposed preferance of a Monarchy — We took tea at Mrs. Carrolls —

....

Wednesday 23....The woman Betsy had a child at my farm. In the evening had a dancing party at my house, at which most of the young people were present — They continued the dance till 1. ocl.

Thursday 24....Nothing interesting in the papers except accounts of the ravages

of the worm in the cotton crop in three of the Southern States & a rise in the price of cotton —

Friday 25....I gave a dinner in compliment to Col. Butler & my friend Doctr. Laborde at which Mrs. Wilson & family, Col. Butler, Judge Butler, Col. Pickens, Doctr. Laborde, Col. Carroll, Mr. Mc.Clintock, Genl. Bonham, Doctr. Mays, Mr. [William?] Butler & my own family were seated at table, 17 in No. It passed off well & all appeared to enjoy themselves very well. I never was in better spirits or enjoyed company with a higher relish. I thank God for the portion of health, which he allows me now to enjoy & for the large share of happiness which I participate with my dear family.

Saturday 26th....I had headache & was confined to the house, the greater part of the day.

Sunday 27....I visited Eliz. Blocker at Mrs. Carrolls & found her very sick with fever. I did not attend church, in consequence of the inclemency of the weather. It became

---

[51] Antonio Lopez de Santa Anna (1794–1876) imposed the centralist policies that contributed to the Texan revolution in 1836 (in which Edgefieldians William Barrett Travis and James Butler Bonham played major roles). During the U.S.-Mexican War, he symbolized for Americans the corruption of their enemy. Exiled by his chief rival, Paredes, he returned in August 1846 and overthrew the monarchist president.

[52] Mariano Paredes y Arrillaga (1797–1849) led the overthrow of his predecessor, Jose Herrera, in late 1845, and was himself ousted less than a year later.

gradually cooler until fire was necessary to comfort ....

Monday 28^{h}....At one I set out for my plantation, having first set my negroes to gathering corn from the Clark field. I arrived at my plantation at 6 ocl. & went immediately to the settlement of my negroes, to learn how they were. I was pained to learn that some dozen were still sick of chill & fever & my boy Berry the blacksmith ill from inflamation of the bowels.

Tuesday 28th....After breakfast I rode over my crop which exhibited an interresting appearance. The ripe corn, the white cotton fields and the matured peas on their luxurient vines, with the rich grass & herbage presented a pleasing group of objects in passing through the plantation. At 11 ocl. I returned & visited & examined all my sick negroes & gave directions as to their treatment, & At 2 ocl. I took my departure for home, at which I arrived at dark finding my house, crouded with company — For the last two weeks my house has been like a public inn & I have had command neither of my time, servants or any thing else while M^{rs}. B. seems delighted to toil & cook for the pleasure of seeing others eat – – I confess I am worn out & tired of this waste of time —

Wednesday 30th....I am gathering corn at my farm. The entire month has been peculiar in its character. From the first day to the seventh there was a constant prevalence of cloudy weather with showers of rain more or less every day; from the seventh until the last there has been a continuation of the finest weather, that I have ever seen at this season of the year. It has been very warm & clear for the greater part of the time. On Saturday morning . . . a light fall of rain . . . & brisk wind, . . . produced a decided change in the temperature of the weather. Nights & mornings now cool & fire comfortable — Two loads of cotton arrived at night from the plantation, each with 10 bales on their way to market. I am informed by my overseer that my negroes are better & all of them, I hope, on the recovery. Cotton is reported to be worth 8/..75 8$^{6}/_{8}$ in the Hamburg market & even 9^{cs}. is anticipated in a few days — Corn has fallen to 50 ^{cs} p^{r}. bushel. The crop will be abundant for consumption if taken care of but it is not a heavy one. Peas & cotton have improved much within the last twenty days —

[Written vertically in the left margin:]

M^{rs}. Wilson & her four children left us after a visit of two weeks on their return to Town [Charleston].

<u>October 1. 1846 —</u>

Thursday 1st....It was on this day that M^{rs}. Wilson & her family left us on their return to Charleston. I sent them in my carriage to Aiken. I was engaged in gathering corn, pulling pea Vines & picking peas. The papers report the advance of Genl.

Worth[53] with a part of the army towards Monterey & a battle was daily expected near the little Town of [Blank Space] between him & the Mexicans under the command of Ampudia.[54] Some apprehensions were entertained for the safety of our army as the enemy were reported to be concentrating their forces from all quarters of the Nation for the purpose of stopping the further progress of our arms —

Friday 2nd....Young Mr. Huger[55] left us to day after a two weeks visit to Whitfield.

Saturday 3rd....I heard yesterday of the death of Revd. Mr. [Mark] Abney. He was a pious, good man, whose loss will be seriously felt by his church. I was engaged in erecting a crib at my farm. My waggon returned from Hamburg, bringing the articles for which I wrote & having deposited my cotton with Walker....the night was illuminated by a refulgent new moon ....Whitfield returned from Hamburg about 10 ocl. having sold my cotton at 9cts. The 20 bales brought $699.93.

Sunday 4th....We had the usual services in the Epis. Church & also the administration of the sacrament. Preston & Wife, Mrs. Means & Miss Bell Means dined with us —

Monday 5th....The court of common Pleas, commenced its fall session, Judge Butler presiding. I was in the Village for a very short time but heard no news.

Tuesday 6th....I was engaged in gathering the crop of corn at the Youngblood place & putting it - up in the shuck —

Wednesday 7h....We paid a visit to Major Blockers & spent the day with his family.

Thursday 8th....Price was tried to day for the murder of Bailey. Verdict – Manslaughter.[56] The news from Europe very favourable in regard to the market for all kinds of grain & breadstuffs and also for cotton. [A British passenger ship bound for New York] The Great Western was nigh being lost in a terrible storm.

Friday 9th....Intelligence was received of the capture of Monterey by Genl. Taylor after three days of hard fighting. On the fourth day Genl. Ampudia agreed to capitulate & surrender the Town upon terms highly favourable to the Mexicans. Our loss

---

53 William Jenkins Worth (1794–1849), New York native, veteran of the War of 1812 and 2nd Seminole War. Led a division (2,000 men) under Gen. Winfield Scott in the Mexican War and was promoted twice during that conflict. Ft. Worth TX is named for him.

54 General Pedro Ambudia led Mexican forces defending Monterey and vicinity.

55 William Harleston Huger ? (1826–1906) South Carolina College 1846. A close friend of WB.

56 In the death of William Bailey, Thomas Price was charged with murder and convicted of manslaughter. He was defended by Lewis Wigfall, James P. Carroll, and John Bauskett. Judge A. P. Butler sentenced him to five years in jail and a $100 fine, and rebuked him in "very appropriate remarks" (*Adv.*, Oct. 14, 1846). The pairing of Wigfall and Carroll illustrates how a duel could clear the air between "honorable" men, perhaps aided by the passing of time.

is reported to be 500 in killed, wounded & missing. Genl. Taylor had under his command about 6000 effective soldiers composed of regulars & Volunteers & the Mexican Genl. about 1200. Genl. Worth distinguished himself as a skillful & brave Soldier.

Saturday 10th....I finished gathering my grain & pea crop at the Youngblood place & hawling home the fodder & hay, of the latter of which I saved a large quantity of superior quality. In the afternoon I went to Co^{l}. Pickens to dine with him but in consequence of indisposition I returned before sitting down to dinner. I left a large and agreeable company at his house, from whom I was loth[e] to separate....

Sunday 11....& high wind from the N^{o}.East at 12 ocl. there was every appearance of a continuation of clear weather. I have never seen the dust more disagreeable & annoying. It is from 1 to 2 inches thick in the roads & the whole atmosphere is filled with it....

Monday 12th....This is the day for holding the election over the State for members to the Legislature. There are ten Candidates in this District of whom six are to be chosen. About 10 ocl. it began to drop rain and by 1. ocl to fall in wetting showers, which continued to encrease in quantity until 4 ocl, at which time this entry was made ....

It has been 35 days since the surface of the earth has been as wet as at this moment, in fact there has fallen but one light rain since the 10 September, which fell on Sunday the 27. & barely enough to lay the dust....About 8 ocl. my waggons arrived from the plantation with twenty bales of cotton on their way to market in a heavy shower of rain. Rain continued to fall throughout the entire night . . . & the wind to blow with some violence from the N^{o}.East....

Wednesday 14^{h}....The votes [for] Senator & representatives were counted to day & resulted in the elevation of N.[athan] L. Griffin to the Senate and Co^{l}. Oliver Towles, B[enjamin] Yancy, Arthur Simkins, Danl. Holland, John Holmes[57] & James Pope to the house of representatives.[58] I was busily engaged in enclosing a lot & putting up shed for stables at the farm. M^{rs}. Means & Bell, Preston & Wife spent the day & evening with us —

Thursday 15....The papers gave an account of a heavy gale of wind on the coast on monday last & some of the damage. No further news from the army.

Friday 16th....I was engaged in building some sheds for stables at my farm & in repairing the road in front of the house.

Saturday 17th....My engagements the same as yesterday. The court adjourned after a

---

[57] John B. Holmes (1811–); 1850 census: $3,000 real estate, 32 slaves.

[58] Also in the field for state House were John Wever, P. S. Brooks, Richard Ward, and John Doby, whose vote totals were in that order. For complete totals, see *Adv.*, Oct. 28, 1846. Preston Brooks had held a seat for the previous term. WB's lack of comment on his son's loss is difficult to assess. Griffin defeated John Bauskett by roughly 100 votes.

labour of two weeks without getting through the business.

Sunday 18th....In the afternoon I called to see Doct^{r}. Butler at his brother's in company with Co^{l}. Carroll & P. S. Brooks, where we found Co^{l}. P. M. Butler somewhat indisposed from an attack of cholic. The sky in the West at sunset exhibited a beautiful appearance in the variegated tints, in the light, floating clouds, which being in fanciful shapes on the Western horizon.

Monday 19th....I observed this morning that two lots which had been sowed in rye early in September, exhibited the young rye, coming up finely. It had lain in the ground near forty days, without germination on account of the dry weather & I was apprehensive that the seed had rotted. My hands at the farm picked out over 500^{lbs}. of cotton.

Tuesday 20th....& light frost. I attended a sale of Doct^{r}. Mays disposible furniture & purchased two bedsteads. I had over 500^{lb}. of cotton again picked out.

Wednesday 21....I was exceedingly sick during the night and continued so until about 9. Ocl. from violent pain in my right eye & nausia of the stomach. Cotton has fallen from $9^3/_8$ to $9^1/_8$—

Thursday 22....Doct^{r}. Mays & family left this place this morning for Florida, to which he has now finally removed. M^{r}. Wardlaw has purchased the house & lot of the Doctor but leaves his own lot unoccupied & unimproved, so that we loose one family from our Society and an interresting family. For intelligence, refinement & social intercourse the family of Doct^{r}. Mays would compare favourably with any other in the Village. His removal is a loss to our part of the Village & I sincerely wish, it may eventuate to his own profit and advantage & to the advancement of the true interests of his family.

Friday 23rd....We are making preparations for a short visit to the plantation, for which place we shall set out after breakfast. We arrived at the plantation about 4 Ocl. The negroes were in better health & principally engaged in gathering corn, from the Williams field which must have yielded from 1500 to 2000 bushels — 100 acres in the field Saturday 24....I rode over my plantation & examined the cotton fields, which are yielding less than I anticipated one month ago. I have now sixty bales packed, weighing from 380 to 400^{lbs}.

Sunday 25....I passed the day quietly at home. M^{r}. & M^{rs}. King [neighbors] called in the afternoon.

Monday 26....I gave out to all the women & girls, frocks of the striped Gingia osnaburgs.[59] I also gave Blankets to Hester, Mary, Franky, Louiza, Rachel, Eliza & Crecy. also to Joshua, Toney & Little Joe. I attended a sale of the estate of John

[59] Osnaburg was a coarse fabric made from low-grade cotton.

Dorn[60] decd. & purchased two cows & calves —

Tuesday 27. Still cool & a little cloudy. I again went to the sale of Dorn's estate but did not purchase any thing. I left the place at an early hour & the negroes were sold after my departure at very high prices — Negro men from $750 to 1000. Thirty two negroes sold for upwards of $16000. Corn was sold from 39 to 41cts fodder for 40cts . Cows & calves from $11 to 14. Cloudy in the afternoon & night & about 1. ocl. a very high wind, which dissipated the clouds —

Wednesday 28th....My waggons set out for Hamburg with 20 bales of cotton. Whitfield also went down to sell it. I rode to Hamiltons[61] & purchased a cow & also to Wilson Kemps[62] & bought six turkeys.

Thursday 29. Clear & cold with considerable frost. I rode through the neighbourhood as far as Doctr. Lakes & by Col. Griffins on my return. The cotton crops about Cambridge will turn out much lighter than was expected. Crops of grain are abundant – —

Friday 30....After breakfast we set out for our home at the Village at which we arrived about 2 ocl. hearing of the present indispositions of Miss Leslie[63] & of the deaths of Mrs. [Geiger?] & old Mrs. Harden.[64] We also learned that during our absence Mrs. Col. Carroll & Mrs. Bauskett[65] had been confined & each had a daughter. — No news in the papers of any interest –.

Saturday 31....Whitfield arrived late last night from Hamburg & this morning informed me that he had sold my two loads of cotton as follows 12 bales at 9cts. & 8 bales at 8$^{6}/_{8}$. The waggons got back about 10 ocl on their way to the plantation. On thursday & Friday I dug my potatoes. The crop only moderately good. The first 20 bales of cotton brought $699.90cts. & the last 20 bales $696.90cts. = $1396.80. Copious showers of rain in the afternoon ....The entire month of October has been dry & mild, with only one rain & a few days of cold weather & three light frosts. Sickness by chill & fever has prevailed over the entire district but I have heard of few deaths.

November 1. 1846 ——

Sunday 1st....one or two light showers of rain but not enough to keep the family from Church. At 3 ocl. my father arrived on a visit to us. He seems in better health

---

[60] John Dorn (1768–1846), father of William Burkhalter Dorn, magistrate, legislator, gold-mine owner, 180 slaves.

[61] Major ____ Hamilton of Columbia County, GA.

[62] Wilson Kemp (1790–); 1850 census: real estate $2,100, 22 slaves.

[63] Possibly a sister of James Leslie, teacher at a school in Currytown, near the Savanah River.

[64] Martha Harden (1789–).

[65] Sophia Creyon (1800–1872), wife of John Bauskett (1794–1867), was a devout Roman Catholic who commented on anti-Catholic prejudice in Edgefield. The Bausketts moved to Columbia and both were buried in the St. Peter's cemetery there.

than I have observed for several years, tho failing in his mind & memory.

Monday 2....There was a large concourse of persons from various parts of the District & some property sold by the Comm[ishioner] in Equity but none by the Sheriff. A public meeting was held to take into consideration the utility of constructing a rail road to Aiken from the Village, at which I presided as chairman. Co^{l}. Pickens offered resolutions & delivered a short sensible & practical address, which was well rec^{d}. Co^{l}. P[reston] S. Brooks also made a few remarks. The afternoon was clear & warm....Violent headache.

....

Wednesday 4th....I witnessed the execution of Miss Leslie's will, making M^{rs}. Carroll her devisee & Ex^{x}. after a few small specific legacies. Rode to my farm to see a sick child. The ride any thing but agreeable but one must expect clouds as well as sunshine.

....

Friday 6th....I was engaged in saving manure, hawling straw for the stables & lots and working on the road....

Saturday 7th....The inclemency of the weather confined me to the house, during the greater part of the day. Among other things I wrote a letter to Co^{l}. Gadsden[66] on the subject of the rail road, which is proposed to be run from this place to Aiken.

Sunday 8th....Preaching as usual by M^{r}. Walker – In the afternoon I rode with Preston to see Co^{l}. P.M. Butler.

Monday 9th....My negroes are gathering corn & putting it - in the cribs unshucked. I went with Co^{l}. Butler to pay a visit to Preston.

Tuesday 10th....I sent Adam to my plantation to change horses — On his return received a letter from my Overseer that all were well & that he had shucked & put in the cribs about 2200 bushels of corn. This is rather more than one half of my crop although not more than half the quantity of land planted, has been gathered. I shall make about 4000 bushels of corn from 220 or 225 acres —

Wednesday 11....Vegitation has taken a second growth. Cotton is blooming as in the month of September & peas & corn coming up in the fields. My Wife & Ellen & Preston & his Wife left home this morning for Augusta, to attend to some shopping.

Thursday 12th....I rode to my farm before breakfast to attend to some business & give directions. I finished in the afternoon hawling & securing under cover my corn crop at the Durham place. I suppose about 350 bushels were gathered from the field

---

[66] James Gadsden (1788–1858), Charleston native. Grandson of Christopber Gadsden. Yale, U.S. Army War of 1812. In charge of Seminole removal, lived in FL and held office there. Returned to SC in 1839. Pres. of Louisville, Cincinnatti, and Charleston RR/SCRR 1840–1850. Minister to Mexico 1853 and author of the Gadsden Purchase.

on the Creek.

Friday 13th....I began this morning to sow in rye & wheat the field next to M^{rs}. Carroll for pasture for the milk cows and calves. Plants and vines are still growing & cotton blooming.

Saturday 14th. Clear & mild day....Vines, plants, tomatoes & even irish potatoes are in green & growing condition. A meeting of the rail road committee was held to day & a communication addressed to the board of directors of the Aiken rail road, on the subject of the union of the contemplated road from this place with the present road at or near Aiken.

Sunday 15....Service morning & evening. in the Epis. church. M^{r}. Walker has improved in his preaching both in manner & matter & I think, he promises to be a very useful & popular preacher.

Monday 16th....I began this morning to sow oats at the Youngblood place, running three ploughs. In the afternoon I rode to my pineland track, to get a sample of iron oar, which is found there, for the use of M^{r}. Toomey, who desires to test its value.

Tuesday 17th ....Our Son Preston called & informed us that he had sold his residence to Ja^{s}. Ransford & that his purpose was to move to Florida. The change may be of advantage to him if he will avail himself of all the elements of sucess, which may be presented to his acceptance. He must however radically change his habits both moral physical & mental. He is deficient in moral energy and decision, in mental activity and is too indulgent in more physical gratifications. The spiritual man must overcome the more corporeal.[67]

Wednesday 18th....I went to my plantation, where I found my negroes again restored to health. After dinner I rode over a part of my plantation & examined my cotton fields. I have about 20 bales in the ginhouse & about 20 bales more in the fields, which with the 60 bales already sold, will give me about 100 bales for the entire crop, each bale weighing from 385 to 400. pounds. The cotton was still growing but most of it was fully matured, & my crop will be increased by the favourable fall. My wheat crop was sowed (about 30 acres). I had 46 hogs for the use of the negroes in a pen, fattening for pork. The cattle, mules, horses & stock hogs were in good condition.

Thursday 19th....Rain began to fall about 10 ocl. & continued in light showers until about two ocl. when the clouds began to disperse & 3 ocl. it – was entirely clear & cooler. I returned from the plantation. After dinner I rode to my farm etc.

Friday 20th....Therm^{r}. 35$^{\theta}$. with considerable frost. We paid a visit to Major Yancy & Lady at Co^{l}. Pickens, who are on their way to Columbia. I made this morning

---

[67] For a suggestion that WB is referring to PSB's weakness for strong drink, see Berry and Welborn, "The Cane of His Existence," 19 n. 4. The article focuses on PSB's indecisiveness, which William Freehling sees as revealing, and Lawrence Keitt's role as instigator prior to the caning of Charles Sumner.

the first killing of hogs, one of which, not more that 18 months old, weighed 200[lb].

Saturday 21....On riding to the Village I learned that the regiment of Volunteers for Mexico had been required by the Government for immediate service. I rode to my Son Preston's & informed him of the requisition. I here met M[r]. Ja[s]. Ransford, to whom my Son sold his stock of cattle, hogs, blacksmith tools, oats, ^part of his^ fodder & corn to the value of $250 to 275. I also traded for two cows & calves & a mule & horse colt. Our daughter Martha was at first considerably distressed by the intelligence that the Volunteers had been called for but she soon rallied & resumed if not her wanted yet an agreeable cheerfulness. I passed the day with them.

Sunday 22....a more fitfull and fantastic day I have rarely seen ....[describing changeable Weather throughout the day]

Monday 23[r]. Clear & cold with heavy hoar frost....Ice was to be seen for the first time this fall & vegitation is now throughly killed. The entire fall up to this date has been mild & pleasant with not more than three or four rains except in the month of October; there was a week of showery weather at that time. The Legislature of the State Convenes to day & I shall look with some interest to see the Governors message as indicating the policy of the democratic party in reference to several important matters both State & federal.

Tuesday 24 [h]....I rec[d]. a note from Co[l]. P.M. Butler informing that M[r]. M[c].Duffie had resigned his seat in the Senate of the United States & Co[l]. [Franklin] Elmore is spoken of as his successor....

Wednesday 25....The entire day was cold & boisterous and exceedingly uncomfortable. My waggons arrived between two & three ocl. with 20 bales of cotton on their way to market The Rev[d]. M[r]. Walker spent the evening with us. He is an agreeable companion & worthy gentleman —

Thursday 26th. The surface of the earth is now thoroughly killed. The Editor of the Edgefield Advertiser issued an extra sheet this evening containing the order of Co[l]. P.M. Butler to the Volunteers for the Mexican War, with a warm & patriotic appeal to their gallantry & State pride to rally under the Palmetto banner, to march to the theatre, where glory & honor invite them — Cap[n]. P.S. Brooks has also issued in the same paper an order to his company to assemble at Edgefield Courthouse on Monday next and an invitation to every man between the ages of 45 & 18 to enroll his name, "who regards personal comfort less that the honor of his Country."

Friday 27th....The two last days have been unprecedentedly cold & uncomfortable & the frost this morning unusually large....My waggons returned from Hamburg, having deposited my cotton in the warehouse unsold. Whitfield went down to sell but not being able to get more than 8 [cts]. he declined to sell.

Saturday 28....I made this morning an entire change of my arrangements at the farm by removing George & family from the Youngblood place & locating him at a newly settled place near Mount Parsons hill....

Sunday 29th....Mr. Walker preached a good but rather long sermon. He improves.

Monday 30th....A meeting of the Volunteers to the war in Mexico took place in the Court house, to take into consideration the new proposition of the Secretary at War, to Volunteer for the entire war. There was a large assemblage of citizens from the neighbourhood who took a deep interest in the proceedings. Capn. P.S. Brooks was called to the chair, who introduced the business of the meeting by a spirit stirring and patriotic address. Addresses were delivered by several gentlemen and much patriotic ardour infused into the meeting — Between 30 & 40 Volunteers enrolled their names before the meeting adjourned. At 4 ocl in the afternoon Miss Susan Pickens presented a beautiful flag to the company, of her own workmanship — The company was formed in line & the spectators on the flanks thus forming the three sides of a square. She advanced on horseback, attended by her Uncle John Simkins in front of the line & making a short address to Capn. Brooks, most gracfully presented him with the stand of colours. Upon receiving the colours, he responded in a manly speech, in which the thoughts were happily conceived & eloquently delivered. Altogether it was one of the most imposing & interresting ceremonies that I have ever witnessed. It was a beautiful pageant or in the language of a spectator it - was a perfect picture. To me the occasion was deeply exciting as two of my Sons were among the Volunteers & taking an active part in making up the company. If high spirit, ardent patriotism and manly bearing are qualities, of which a father should be proud in his offspring, I feel that I have reason to be satisfied with my Sons. They carry with them my blessing & my earnest prayers, that the God of the Universe may protect & guard them from danger and injury in the perils, which lie before them & after they shall have discharged their duty to their Country to restore them safe & unhurt to their homes —

<u>December</u> 1. 1846 —

Tuesday 1....At a meeting held in the Courthouse it - was resolved to give a dinner to the Volunteers during the ensuing week ....

Wednesday 2....I sent Adam to the plantation with a letter to my overseer with directions for my man Joseph, to come down, to be in readiness to accompany his young masters to Mexico, if the company should go.

Thursday 3....I sent to the Village two young pines, for the purpose of erecting a liberty pole for a new flag.

Friday 4th....I met the committee of arrangements for the dinner to the Volunteers and adopted such measures as we considered, necessary for the occasion — The new flag was floating some sixty feet in the air —

Saturday 5....After early breakfast I accompanied Preston to the old Wells,[68] to be present at the mustering of the 7. Regiment which had been called out by order of

[68] A few miles north of Hamburg.

the Governor to procure Volunteers for the Mexican War. About 12 ocl, the drums began to sound the notice of preparation for the formation of the regiment into line, When Cap^{n}. P.S. Brooks suddenly mounted the head of the bass drum & addressed the crowd in animated strains, with the view to stimulate them to Volunteer in sufficient numbers to form his company before going on the field — Major Thos. Bacon followed him in a sensible & appropriate address. After which the roll was presented for Volunteers when some ten or 12 marched up & joined the company — A sufficient number not having volunteered, the regiment was formed into line & was addressed by Doct^{r}. Burt[69] & myself. Again a call was made for Volunteers & some 6 or 7. marched out & enrolled their names.

The Regiment was discharged between 3 & 4 ocl, when it was announced, that seventy two had enrolled their names – It was an exciting & interresting day & passed off in great harmony & unamity of feeling and actions.

Sunday 6th....Service in the Episcopal church by M^{r}. Walker, by whom our Grand daughter Mary Carroll Brooks was baptised.

Monday 7th....There was an immense croud in the Village, attracted to the Courthouse to see the Volunteer company. A meeting took place in the Village, at which Capt Brooks, presided. Several short & animated addresses were made by different persons & the roll was opened for Volunteers, when some three or four came forward & signed their names under the excitement of the occasion — A collection was made for the Volunteers & paid over by myself to Corporal Adams amounting to near $400. The entire audience seemed inspired with patriotic ardour & the day passed off finely & very much to the gratification of every citizen, who felt an interest in the honor & character of the District. The Captain of the Volunteers is exceedingly popular with his men at this time.

Tuesday 8th....The Volunteer company dined with the Citizens at Goodman's Hotel at a public dinner, tendered to them by the District — About 300 partook of dinner[,] The Volunteers & old men seated at two tables & the younger men standing at three other tables. Regular & Volunteer toasts were given of an exciting character, to portions of which, Cap^{n}. Brooks, Genl. Bonham, Lieut. Maragine [Moragne] & Co^{l}. Pickens delivered addresses in reply. One of the happiest addresses, that I ever listened to, was delivered by Cap^{n}. Hammond in response to a toast, given by Major Bacon to his company of cavalry. It was short but spirited & appropriate. It was assigned to me to preside at the dinner and Co^{l}. Pickens acted as Vice President. It was a glorious occasion for Old Edgefield & long to be remembered as a proud day in her annals — At 4 ocl. the Volunteer company was formed in front of Goodman's hotel in presence of an immense croud of spectators both male and female & under the escort of Cap^{n}. Hammond company, took their line of March for Hamburg cheered by music, by the shouts of the assembled multitude & by waving of handkerchiefs from the ladies, who filled every piaza & portico on the public

[69] Three Burt brothers—Augustus, William, and John—were doctors.

square — The occasion was solemn and interresting to all & especially to those, who had children & relatives — The hoary father & the gentle maiden dropped a tear by the side of the agonized mother at parting with those gallant spirits. May the God of battles shield them in the hour of peril, cover them with his egis [aegis] in the day of trial & bring them after they shall have faithfully served their Country, back to their homes and their families.

Wednesday 9th. Clear, warm & lovely day. I rode to the Village & heard that the Volunteers had left their camp at day light on their march to Hamburg. At 5 ocl. our Son Preston took leave of us & joined his company at Camp Bonham at day light - —

Thursday 10th....I heard of the reception of the Volunteers in Hamburg & of the handsome entertainment – given them by the citizens; also of their departure in the cars for Charleston....

Friday 11th. I was very sick at day light & continued so throughout the day, so much so as not to leave the house. Cold & clear —

Saturday 12th....I rode to the Village & learned that the Volunteers had arrived in Charleston. I received the Presidents annual message to Congress, printed in the [Washington] Union. It is a very long & I think, able State paper giving a gratifying account of the State of the Country and our relations with other powers, particularly with Mexico. The attempts to raise a Volunteer company for the Mexican War, has so completely engrossed our feelings in this place, that I have omitted to mention that Judge Butler is elected to the United States Senate in the place of Mr. Mc.Duffie[,] that Judge [David] Johnson is elected Governor of the State & [Patrick?] Caldwell Chancellor in his place[,] and also Withers is elected Judge of the Common Plea bench in place of Judge Butler — At any other time, these elections would have produced a good deal of interest among our people but at this time they have taken place almost unheeded. Senator Cain is elected L.[t] Governor —

Sunday 13th....I felt too unwell to attend Church —

Monday 14th....My waggons arrived with the last of my crop (20 bales) on their way to Hamburg Tuesday 15....I went to Hamburg to sell my cotton & purchase supplies — I reached the Town about 4. ocl & went immediately to bed in consequence of a violent headache.

Wednesday 16th....I rose at a late hour free from pain & after getting a cup of tea, I went into the street – to attend to my business. I sold the two loads of cotton at 8½ before its arrival & soon purchased my supplies — Rain began to fall at 10. ocl & continued until in the night — after dinner I set out for home & reached Doctr. Geiger's about Sunset, somewhat wet & very cold. I remained here for the night.

Thursday 17th....I reached home at 12 ocl. In the afternoon the citizens rode as far as the Pottery to receive & welcome the Company of Volunteers from Abbeville. They were addressed by Genl. Bonham, tendering them the hospitalities of the Village etc. Cap^{n}. Marshall[70] made a short and modest reply — The company was then conducted to Go[o]dman's hotel – where they partook of a neat supper. Doct^{r}. [John] Barrett [Space] El[ijah] Watson came over & passed the night with us —

Friday 18 –...at 10 ocl. very cloudy & indications of approaching snow with high & howling Wind. The Volunteers took up their line of march after breakfast, cheered by the huzza's of the Citizens — Fitful day.

Saturday 19th....I raised a framed negro house to day at my farm & paid a visit to Genl. [Waddy] Thompson at Judge Butler's. I met my old acquaintance & relation Doct^{r}. Butler at the Judge's, who is on a visit to his mother.

Monday 21....I rode to Prestons & gave the necessary directions in regard to the Sale. Rec^{d}. letters from Preston and Whitfield, both of whom seem pleased with a military life[.]

Tuesday 22nd....I am not well this morning nor qualified for the labours of the day. After breakfast I went to Prestons, & sold what property was left by him for Sale & also hired out the negroes. The Sale amounted to upwards of $1500. Mules sold from $100 to 120. Corn sold from 54 to 60^{cts}. per bushel. Negroes hired from $80 to 90 [a year]. I sustained the fatigue better than I expected. We received letters by the Aiken mail, informing us that the Palmetto regiment had been ordered to Mexico, Via Augusta, Mobile & New Orleans & it was supposed, that they would be in Hamburg on Wednesday or thursday —

Wednesday 23....We have suspended our trip to Hamburg, to meet the Volunteers in conformity with instructions from Preston to wait until further advised — I rode out to see to the delivery of the property sold yesterday.

Thursday 24th....No news from our Sons or from the Volunteers — Miss Lesley [Leslie] died about 9 ocl. at night after a protracted illness at M^{rs}. Carrolls. She was a most estimable lady, and for her humble origin & limited education one was of the worthiest and most superior women, that I have ever known & would compare favourably with the first in the Country for lady like manners, intelligence and a uniform & consistent benovolence of disposition.

Friday 25....We attended church in the morning when the sacrament was administered, dined with our mother M^{rs}. Carroll, and in the evening attended the funeral of Miss Lesley.[71]

Saturday 26th....I was in the Village for a short time but heard no news nor intelligence of the Volunteers. At 2 ocl at night Preston arrived on a flying visit from the encampment near Hamburg, at which he had arrived in the cars from Charleston in

[70] Jehu Foster Marshall (1817–1862), lawyer, legislator after the Mexican War, died commanding a regiment at 2nd Manassas.

[71] Chapman, *History of Edgefield County*, 105, mentions a "distinguished teacher" at a male academy at Currytown, but no Lesleys are listed in the 1850 census.

the evening. He is in good health & reports Whitfield to be well, whom he left in Charleston in charge of [tents?] [TORN] baggage etc. He will come up on monday.

Monday 28th....I rode to my farm & engaged a ditcher to run a ditch on the branch between Hollingsworth and myself, for which I agreed to pay him $25 & put two hands with him.

Tuesday 29th....We set out for Hamburg, to see our Sons, who are encamped about four miles from the Town & near the residense of M^{rs}. [Lamar?] — We reached the encampment about 4 ocl, saw & conversed with our Sons and after the evening parade went to Hamburg & took lodgings at M^{rs}. Hubbards —

Wednesday 30th. Cloudy & warm in the morning and several light showers of rain. We went to the encampment after breakfast & remained during the day. In the afternoon I was indisposed yet we remained until after the evening parade & then returned to the Hotel.

Thursday 31....After breakfast we went to the encampment & loitered about until 2 ocl dining with many of the officers & citizens at Prestons tent and enjoying social conversation. At two Ocl. the regiment was formed into a line & was reviewed by Governor Johnson, after which it was formed into close column & the officers ordered to march in front. The Governor then presented to the officers from Co^{l}. Butler down, their commissions, addressing a few words to each company, to the effect that he delivered their commissions as the highest testimonial of the confidence, which the State reposed in their skill & courage. Cap^{n}. Brooks was selected by the officers, at the suggestion of the Co^{l}. to respond to the Governor, which he did in a short & appropriate address, which he delivered on the spur of the occasion without a moments preparation — Co^{l}. Butler made a few remarks taken an affectionate leave of the Governor — The occasion was impressive & affecting & will long be remembered by the Palmetto regiment & the people of this District. Thus closed the year [TORN] [1846]. Who shall see the close of 1847?

[END OF MANUSCRIPT VOLUME 2]

JOURNAL OF WHITFIELD BROOKS, VOLUME III

VIII

January 1st. 1847

Friday 1st....Instead of going to the encampment, Mrs. Carroll, Mrs. Martha Brooks, myself, Wife & daughter went to Augusta to attend to a few purchases & while absent, we availed ourselves of the opportunity of visiting the canal,[1] with its basin, the railroad depository & viewing some of the public buildings. We returned to Hamburg to dinner. About 5 ocl in the afternoon one battalion of the Volunteers passed through Hamburg & across the bridge on their way to the railroad enroute for Mexico. There was an immense concourse of persons collected on both banks of the river & on the bridge to witness the passage of the battalion over the bridge at the South end of which a Volunteer company of the City awaited the arrival to escort the battalion through the town to the depository. The cannon continued to fire from the time the battalion arrived in sight until it had passed the bridge. Twenty six guns were fired – on my return to Hamburg I met Dr. [David] Gillison on the bridge, who had just arrived in the cars & was only his way to join the company from Charleston in which he was volunteering. Our Sons Preston & Whitfield came in & remained at the tavern with us until next morning.

Saturday 2nd....We left Hamburg at 9 ocl on our return home & came by the encampment to take leave of our Sons & acquaintances. Mrs. Carroll, our daughter Martha Brooks & Child, also our two children Ellen & Hampden were with us. When we reached the camp, the left wing of the regiment being five companies, were striking their tents, preparatory to their departure on the rail road, for the seat of war. The scene presented a faint idea of an army, breaking up camp, with the noise, bustle, & apparent confusion, which is attendant upon such a procedure. About 11 ocl. we parted with our Sons & with heavy hearts & moist eyes directed our course homewards. We arrived about 4 ocl. & found all well. Nothing of interest had transpired, during our absence, except the reported death of Jas. Pope, who died suddenly of Pneumonia. He was an honest man & a good citizen but somewhat visionary & impracticable.

Sunday 3rd....It was too inclement to attend church.

---

[1] Begun in 1845 primarily to provide water power for manufacturing, the canal was developed under the leadership of Henry Cumming. It allowed river traffic to avoid the rapids at the fall line and, by bringing it into Augusta, took business, especially cotton buying, away from Hamburg. Water was let into the canal on Nov. 23, 1846. On Feb. 22, 1847, the Augusta Mfg. Co., the canal's first fruit, was organized.

Monday 4th....The concourse of persons in the Village was large. Not much property sold....

Tuesday 5....I rode to the Village & down to the late residence of Mrs. Johnson, whose property was advertised for sale by the Exor. Sale was over before I arrived & I turned back without alighting from my horse. In the afternoon I rode to my farm to see after my business & to give directions in regard to a ditch. Col. P. M. Butler[2] called on his way to the South to bid us farewell –

Wednesday 6th....There was a light hoar frost. I heard with pain that Jacob B. Smith[3] is reported to be dead. If the report be true, his family will be left under very embarrassing circumstances in many points of view. Smith is not dead but extremely ill of inflammation of the lungs –

Thursday 7th....Last evening at Sunset, the entire firmament was perfectly clear & the Sun went down with a gorgeous display of crimson light, which I thought betokened clear weather but which was the harbinger of rain. There was a heavy shower, during the night & . . . the wind . . . blew with great violence....[By 10:00] at night . . . the Therm.t had fallen to 18°. I have rarely seen a more boisterous and disagreeable day. There was a failure of the mail this morning, a link to some change in the mailbags....

Friday 8th....Therm.t at Sunrise was below 15°. The surface of the Earth frozen & hard as rock – at 11 ocl the Therm.t stood at 18° and at 1 ocl at 26. I walked to my shop[4] about 11 ocl. & the air was so cold that I breathed with some difficulty. I feel that I ought to be in a milder atmosphere. A servant returned from my plantation, from whom I learned that all were well. The overseer writes me that he finished his crop on Christmas evening & that every crib was full of corn & a pen in addition. I made about 4000 bushels.

Saturday 9th....Therm. 20°. I rode to Pottersville & then to my farm to attend to some business. It was mild at 12 ocl. & the Therm.t rose to 36°. I received letters from our Sons at Atlanta in Georgia. They were well but had been wet for two days & nights and subjected to most unpleasant exposure with nothing but a blanket to protect the soldiers from the inclemency of the weather – this is but the beginning of their sufferings. Mrs. Genl. Bonham had a daughter to day.

Sunday 10th....It was so gloomy & disagreeable that I did not go out of my yard. I learned in the afternoon that a Volunteer company was formed & organized yesterday at Richardsons for the Mexican War, over which Col. Oliver Towles was elected Captain ....

---

[2] Commander of the Palmetto Regiment.

[3] A resident and grandson of the original settler of Mount Willing, and a member of Sardis Baptist Church. His slave, Miller, was elected a deacon of the church to oversee the black members. Sardis was known for its interest in the souls of slaves.

[4] Location unknown, but presumably near the courthouse.

Monday 11th....The papers from the South contain rumours of the perilous condition of Genl Worth's division of the army from an attack of Santa Anna with a force of near 17,000. It is also supposed that a bloody battle was fought about the 25 ultimo at or near Saltillo.

Tuesday 12th....a portion of a Volunteer company under Col. Towles, numbering some 35 or 40 arrived in our Village in the forenoon. I understand that the arrangement is, that they are to remain in the Village until Friday next, when a call will be made on the District & a last effort made to fill the ranks – I hope that they will succeed tho I have my doubts –

Wednesday 13....the weather is more disagreeable than it was when the Therm.t was below the freezing point....On the return of my man Barnett from Barnwell, where I had sent him for a runaway servant, in passing through the Village his horse became frightened at the poping of crackers by a parcel of mischievous boys & ran off with the buggy in defiance of all the efforts to hold him that he was able to make. The horse ran about 4 miles & was stopped by some waggoners near James Griffins,[5] with the buggy uninjured except the splintering of two spokes & the loss of one cushion & the whip, which I hope to recover tomorrow. My man Barnett was slightly injured by the horse running over him.

Thursday 14. About 5 ocl. this morning I was disturbed by my runaway boy Jacob, whom I had confined in the third story of my house at the time of his arrival last night, who seemed to [be] making efforts to get out of the window. I rang my bell, which brought my man Cicero to me immediately, who upon examination, discovered that Jacob had got out of the Window & then let himself down to the roof of the Pantry, from which he leaped to the ground a distance of some 12 to 14 feet. From the ledge of the window to the roof of the pantry is about 8 feet & I supposed the leap so hazardous, that I did not think, he would attempt it & did not therefore provide against it. He had on his arms a pair of handcuffs & while they were on I did not believe he would attempt to get away

....

Friday 15th....The Volunteer company from Newberry under the command of Capt. Williams arrived in our Village about 11 ocl. They were met opposite Mr. Mims, by the Butler guards, a Volunteer company from the Saluda regiment commanded by Oliver Towles and a large cavalcade of gentlemen on horseback and conducted to the public square, where they were addressed by Major Bacon[6] as Marshall of the day – A meeting was then called in the Courthouse & Mr. Wardlaw appointed chairman, who made a short address, complimentary of the objects of the meeting – Public addresses were also delivered by Capt. Griffin & Col. Carroll, urging the

[5] On Long Cane Road, NW of ECH.

[6] Thomas Glasscock Bacon (1812–1876), son of Edmund Bacon. 1st Seminole War, Clerk of Court 1844–1860, Palmetto Regiment. Horse breeder and cock-fighter. Colonel CSA, SC Senate 1863–1864.

young men to Volunteer & fill the ranks of the company. The meeting then adjourned & partook of a public dinner which was prepared by Mr. Goodman & spread on two long tables, prepared in the public square – after dinner the meeting again was formed & several short addresses made when some 8 or 10 signed their names on the role of Volunteers. The meeting then adjourned in good order. My friend & relation [William] Butler Brooks[7] passed the night with me....

Saturday 16th....I took my bed at 12 ocl & was quite sick until about the same hour at night....Mrs. [Elizabeth] Laborde arrived at [her mother] Mrs. Carroll's in the afternoon from Columbia.

Sunday 17th....I went to Church but felt too unwell to remain & left the house during the singing of the hymn, preceding the sermon ....

Monday 18th....Heard through Mr. Harris that the Palmetto regiment has passed through Montgomery in Alabama & that he saw our Sons Preston & Whitfield ....

Therm.t 54°. The 9th or Dark Corner regiment was called together yesterday for the purpose, of obtaining Volunteers, to complete the company of Capt. Towles, which consisted of some sixty men. The Regiment was addressed by Major Bacon[,] Col.s Carroll & Hill but the call for Volunteers turned out a water hawl, a flash in the pan, for only three persons, felt the war spirit or the impulse of patriotism sufficiently powerful to induce them to enroll their names & two of these were rejected. The efforts to raise Volunteers have been too stringent & oppressive to the people[8] & I fear that the spirit of our young men has been depressed instead of animated by them. It is great error to attempt too much.

....

Wednesday 20th....Rain fell without interruption throughout the day in mist & gentle showers – I went [to Augusta?] with Mrs. B. & Ellen to see Wests[9] celebrated painting of Christ heeling the sick. It is certainly a beautiful & well executed painting and yet it did not come up to my expectations, which had been formed from the lauditory notices of it which I had read in the papers – My father arrived most unexpectedly about 4 ocl. His health is better—

Thursday 21....Col. Towles again made an effort to fill the ranks of his company but upon calling the roll, there were only sixty-four, who answered to their names. A proposition was then made to dispatch a messenger to the Governor, who is in Hamburg, to ascertain whether he would receive the company with its present number, to which the company acceded & a messenger was sent off immediately. A fist fight took place in the Village between two men from Saluda, the only one,

---

[7] 1806–1868; son of Elisha Brooks and Nancy Butler. See introduction.

[8] See Sunday, Jan. 24.

[9] Benjamin West (1738–1820): Born near Philadelphia, he studied in Italy then settled in London. President of the Royal Academy. A favorite of George III, he is best known for "The Death of General Wolfe" (1770), "a milestone in English and American art."

which I have seen for many years.

Friday 22..... Therm.t 20° at sunrise. An answer was received from the Governor, that he had no discretion in the matter & if the company was not full, he could not receive it. It was then determined to disband & in a few hours all the volunteers were on their way home. All the mustering, eating & speaking for ten days thus ended in a flash. I understand that the bill of Goodman for Board of these men is over $400. for which the Village is liable –

Saturday 23rd....I was confined to the house by an attack of head ache & was on the bed the greater part of the day. My father returned from [the] Blockers & then went over to the Village, where he was informed that Thos. Bacon had turned out, for the purpose of using his efforts to make up and complete the company, which had been dismissed the day previous. I wish him success – it will be plucking the drowning honor of the District by the locks if he succeeds. I omitted to mention that I sold my negro man Young Saluda Barnett to Chs. Jones for $650. No news in the papers. I recd. a very friendly letter from Judge Butler, in which he speaks in very kind terms of my Sons, who have gone to Mexico.[10]

Sunday 24th....My father set out for home early this morning, intending to take breakfast with his venerable friend & sister-in-law Mrs. Beh[ethland] Butler, who resides with her Son Judge Butler. The day was too inclement to go to church, so we had church service & a sermon read at home....Col. Carroll called & passed a short time in social conversation. He confirmed the rumor that Thos. Bacon was making efforts to raise a volunteer company, to save the credit of the District & to prevent the disgrace, arising from the sudden & unexpected disbanding of the Butler guards by their vacillating & blustering Captain. [Oliver Towles] Rain from 4 ocl till night. The earth is very wet & the roads in bad order –

Monday 25....fog & clouds....This has been an unpleasant winter from its extremes and contrasts of heat & cold. The Therm.t has gone from 70° to 16° in something like 24 hours – I recd. letters from my Sons dated at Mobile. They were well & in high spirits....

Tuesday 26....Our relations Mrs. Carroll, Mrs. Laborde, Col. Carroll & the children dined with us – in the evening my old friend Col. Watts[11] called and took tea with us. He was in good health and spirits.

....

Thursday 28th....every appearance of snow or sleet....We heard from our Sons at

[10] PSB surely heard about this, and may have read the letter at a later date. If so, it may have added to his sense of obligation in the wake of Senator Sumner's "Crime Against Kansas" speech. See introduction.

[11] Probably Beaufort Taylor Watts (1789–1869) of Laurens District. SC College 1812, held diplomatic posts in Colombia and Russia, SC House, and secretary to the governor 1834–1861.

Mobile through John Blocker in a letter to the Major – An entertainment has been tendered by the Citizens of Mobile to the Regiment & accepted by Col. Butler.

Friday 29th....Our Sister Mrs. Laborde set out on her return to Columbia. I sent by this day's mail a letter to James Brooks, one to Whitfield & also one to Judge Butler all of which have been written since supper last night....I suffered another attack of headache, which afflicted me throughout the night.

Saturday 30th....In the afternoon we paid a visit to Col. Pickens & learned that Mrs. P. had just received intelligence of the death of a brother about 18 or 19 years of age. My kind neighbour Mr. Harris, who had only returned from Alabama after dark last night called to see me – I received a long & interesting & in many respects a gratifying letter from my Son Preston –The Palmetto regiment was to sail from Mobile on the 24th instant for Mexico.

Sunday 31....I attended church in the morning but felt greatly indisposed in the afternoon. On going to bed, I took a warm cup of lightwood tea, which gave me a good deal of relief....I have never seen the roads in worse condition by mud and water. It is reported that the last intelligence from Europe has caused an advance in cotton & great excitement among speculators. It will bring from 11 to 12 cts. in Hamburg –

Editor's note: I inserted here an unnumbered page from Bettis Rainsford's copy of WB's journal (not found in the ms journal) on which Brooks wrote a long quotation about soil nutrients. I think it worth including as evidence of WB's interest in and knowledge of progressive farming, and adds a bit on his renting slaves. I placed it here because he wrote vertically

"Whitfield Brooks 1st Feb. 1847" It reads:

Sam was hired by Morris on Tuesday the 12 of September at $5.00 per month. Returned 12 October. Kitt began to work with Morris at $10.00 per month on Monday 25th Sept. and continued one month = $10.

"It is now well known that the earths silica[,] alumina, lime etc. contribute very little to the growth of plants, & that these derive their subsistence from other sources. The Earth is however, necessary as a depot of nutritive matter & a reservoir of moisture, which in some form is essential to plants; and as these must have something for their roots to penetrate to ensure support, tillage, by rendering the earth permeable, secures this object & also enables the earth more readily & abundantly to absorb from the air, those gaseous matters which all admit are useful to vegitation." Agreeably to the latest theory, plants absorb portions of earthy & saline matter & in fact that they are indispensable to their Vigorous & beautiful growth –

George & Paul commenced work for me on Monday, 11 September 1843. George worked out his time & returned home. [The preceding sentence was Xed through]

Kitt began to work with Mr. Trowbridge on Monday, the 6th of November –

February 1. 1847

Monday 1st....There was a large concourse of persons in the Village, to attend the sales, which had been advertised & an unusual quantity of property sold. Negroe fellows sold from $7 to 800 & boys from $650 to 700. I have never seen greater anxiety [i.e. eagerness] to purchase nor the bidding more liberal & spirited. The rise in cotton has given an impulse to trade & speculation. There was a public meeting in the Village but I have not heard the result ....

Tuesday 2nd....I was again indisposed & went to bed about 6 ocl. in consequence of which I lay a part of the night unable to sleep & listened to the howling wind & rattling of windows. At one time the house shook with the violence of the wind.

Wednesday 3rd....about sunrise . . . a dark cloud formed in the West & came sweeping over with violent wind & a gust of rain with a little hail....The wind was so violent as to blow down fences etc.

Thursday 4th....I had another attack of dyspepsia which lasted until 2 ocl.

Friday 5th....This is my 57th birth day and altho my health is not good, yet in any situation & circumstances in life, I have much to be content with & thankful for. My family are in good health & all my negroes are doing well & behaving well. The only just ground of uneasiness is the absence of our Sons & the perils to which they must be subjected both by sea & land in their expedition to Mexico. I went to the Village for the purpose of purchasing some things for my negroes & laid out upwards of thirty dollars. The day was chilly and disagreeable with every appearance of snow....

Saturday 6th....I rode over my farm & found the day mild & agreeable. We received a letter from Preston on board a ship in the bay of Mobile, by which we learn that he & Whitfield were well & that they would sail for Mexico on the following morning. My servant Josh returned from Hamburg, to which place I had sent him with a load of cotton. My agent was offered $11 ½ but refused it & had not sold when the boy left ....

Sunday 7th....A rain at this time will very much delay the planters in their preparations for a crop as the earth is now exceedingly wet and only fit for the plough on the highest parts of a plantation – I have been able to sow oats but two days since Christmas & at this time have not sown more than half my crop, including 15 acres, sown in Nov. which have been considerably injured by the cold weather. I was confined to the bed the greater part of the day with headache – our Son James arrived in the afternoon on a short visit –

Monday 8....I went to the Village & purchased sundry articles of dress etc. for my negroes at the plantation. Also went to my farm & gave general direction to my overseer, whom I had employed & who arrived at the Youngblood place, the night before – I pay him $12 per month. His name is Pulatti – Too wet for the plough –

Tuesday 9th....I set out for my plantation about 9 ocl. with Mrs. Brooks, Ellen & James in company. Notwithstanding the dreadful state of the roads (a portion of which was almost impassable) we reached the plantation about 3 ocl. At 4 ocl I rode into the plantation & over a portion of it. It is in fine condition for the plough, being thoroughly cleaned but the rain has thrown him back in plowing. My negroes were in good health & looked fat & cheerful. Nearly all of them came to see us. . . soon after dark, there was much thunder & lightning, which ushered in about 12 ocl a storm of rain & wind, of no common violence –

Wednesday 10th....I examined my new cow house with the cattle, also the horses & colts, the state of the corn cribs, stables & the fattening cattle. I found nothing worthy of complaint but of approval – The shuck houses & cow sheds are the most convenient & admirably planned, of any that I have ever seen. I suppose that I have now about 3000 bushels of corn & other provisions in great abundance –

Thursday 11....We set out for home & in consequence of the bad condition of the road, we came by Major Allen's & Judge Butler's. This road was bad enough but not equal to the direct one. We called to see our venerable Aunt Butler, who we found cheerful but exceedingly feeble & emaciated. She is one in a thousand. We reached home at 4 ocl & found all well.....

Friday 12th....Therm at sunrise 24°. The Earth quite hard frozen. Our son James left us this morning on his return home. There is no news of any interest. Upon comparing the present with my notes of last spring, I find the planters not so forward by several days as they then were. My oats both at my farm & plantation were sowed at this time last year. I had also 22 lambs at the plantation & when I left yesterday the overseer reported that there were eight when he examined them on Sunday last. The winter has been inclement & disagreeable from continued rains & the sudden changes in the temperature of the weather. I was sick the greater part of the day –

Saturday 13th....I rode to my farm & examined the work of my negroes during my absence & in the afternoon went to the Village and transacted a little business. We began to day to attend to the business of the garden & to the sowing of seeds among which were peas, cabbage, onions beets and radish & salsify[12]....

Sunday 14th....We attended divine service at the Baptist church and heard a rather singular sermon from a stranger.

Monday 15th....I set out fruit trees & planted garden seeds. I went to the Village & made sundry purchases for my negroes. Met Col. Pickens, who gave me a demajon of water from the White Sulfur Spring in Virginia ....

Tuesday 16th....I expect to leave for my plantation in a short time with the view of attending the sale of Jas. Popes estate ....I have been forced to suspend sowing oats

[12] An herb with purple flowers and a long, edible root, sometimes called an "oyster plant" because of its taste.

to day by the wet condition of my land – I [arrived at __] ocl & found the negroes in health – Col. Frazier arrived about sunset & remained the night with me.

Wednesday 17....Col. Frazier & myself set out for Mr. Popes plantation & arrived there at 10 ocl. From 40 to 45 negroes were sold at high prices. Two negro men without trades brought upwards of $800....There were a number of persons, who seemed anxious to purchase negroes & the bidding was eager & spirited. I returned to my plantation.

Thursday 18....I rode over my plantation in the forenoon & inspected its general condition. I found it an excellent order & more thoroughly cleaned, than at any previous period. The hands were employed and in hawling out manure, preparing the land for corn & cotton, ditching &C. In the afternoon I returned home. All well and not an item of news. At night I had a violent paroxysm of acidity & cructations [belching], which deprived me of sleep for several hours.

Friday 19th....I rode over my farm & ascertained that I should finish sowing oats, during the day, except some very small spots of land, that are too wet for the plough. I went to the Village in the afternoon but heard nothing of any interest. Therm in the day upwards of 70°.

Saturday 20th....The fruit trees began to show the effects of the warm weather by the swelling of the buds but there are yet no flowers. I see a few white hyacinths in bloom in Mrs. Brooks flower garden. From 11 ocl. until late at night I suffered excruciating agony from sick stomach & headache.

Sunday 21....I was too feeble to leave the house.

Monday 22....I felt too feeble & unwell to take much exercise. Nothing of interest in the papers – I sent our Servant girl Rose to the plantation to work under the overseer with the hope of correcting some bad habits.

Tuesday 23rd....I was exceedingly unwell & feeble. Great acidity on the stomach & occasional fits of coughing and cructations – Recd. a letter from Genl. Thompson –

Wednesday 24....I rode over my farm & gave general instructions to Mr. Polatti as to the best mode of planting etc. In consequence of the representation of Genl. Thompson I abandoned all idea of going to Tampico[13] & began to make preparations for a trip to Florida.

Thursday 25....I devoted the day in making arrangements for my departure for Florida.

Friday 26th....I & Mrs. Brooks left home at 9 ocl for Hamburg on our way to Florida. Rain began to fall by 10 ocl & from that time till night there was no cessation – The carriage driver became thoroughly wet. I believe it rained all night. I took lodg-

---

[13] Mexican city about six miles inland from the Gulf of Mexico, north of Vera Cruz. Apparently WB was hoping to see his sons. While minister to Mexico 1842–1844, Thompson had established a good relationship with Santa Anna; WB had reason to trust his advice.

ings with Mr. Ketchum at Mrs. Hubbards old stand.

Saturday 27th....We left the tavern & went to the Steamboat in a shower of rain. We took our passage to Savannah in the steam boat Ivanhoe at 7 ocl & dropped down the river so soon as we got on board. I was feeble & unwell & saw but little on our passage this day. In fact there are but few objects of interest on the banks of this river.

Sunday 28th....I was prevented by high wind from going on deck through the greater part of the day & confined myself principally to reading and conversation – my old acquaintance Major W. Stark joined us at his landing in Scriven [Screven] County & was an agreeable companion. The Captain of the boat is a very accommodating gentleman and is free to communicate all he knows. Our passage to Savannah was rather agreeable although very monotonous. We took lodging, at the Pulaski house, where we were assigned to a good room & comfortable bed. This house is admirably regulated & the table remarkable for neatness & the excellency of the cooking. It is no uncommon thing to see tables supplied with larger supplies of provisions but I know of no one, where the appetite is more tempted by the neatness & well cooked appearance of the viands. The price of board is however high, being two dollars per day & extra charge for fire & in many instances petty charges are made that annoy & provoke a man – you are taxed for every thing you get & the Proprietor or his clerks seem to consider themselves privileged to extort money from you in any form & for every thing except light & air –

March 1, 1847

Monday 1....In the morning I walked a short distance with Mrs. Burress & Mrs. Brooks to see the Ivory crucifix, which was being exhibited in Savannah. It is a remarkable specimen of art & is said to be the work of an untaught monk in his retired cell. In the afternoon Mrs. Talcot called in her carriage & took us to a very pretty and rural place, called Bona Venture, formaily the property of the Tattnall[14] family but now belonging to [Peter] Wiltberger, the Proprietor of the Pulaski house. It is about 4 miles from Town & located on the elevated ground on the margin of a Creek or inlet of the Sea. It abounds in venerable live oaks, ceadars & various other treas & luxuriant shrubbery. On our return we passed through the best portion of the city & saw the largest & most costly buildings both, public & private. The town is laid out in squares, with spacious & convenient streets & with occasional reservation of a lot for a public walk, which catch the eye by its cool & green appearance, most of them abounding in evergreen trees & grass —

Tuesday 2....This was to me a day of suffering & I did not leave the bed until 4 ocl

[14] Later Bonaventure Cemetery. Josiah Tattnall (1795–1871), a career naval officer best remembered for ordering the sinking of the ironclad CSS Virginia as U.S. Naval forces approached Hampton Roads, VA, in 1862.

in the afternoon – we were invited to drive with Mr. Barton & Lady but I was too sick to go. I however prevailed on Mrs. Brooks to go & in the afternoon I called for her, where I saw our friends together.

Wednesday 3....At 10 ocl. we left Savannah on board the Wm. Gaston for Jacksonville in Florida. A paroxism of sick stomach & headache soon forced me to take my birth & I saw a little and noted but little until next day. I never suffered greater agony....we were delayed some 4 or 5 hours by low tide on the way & stopped for a part of the night near Darien –

Thursday 4th....I was exceedingly feeble & confined myself to my birth, forming an acquaintance with only two gentlemen on board. We passed St. Mary's about 10 ocl. & took the outside passage. The Sea was a little rough but it did not make me sick, which I desired. We reached Jacksonville about 6 ocl. and procured lodgings at Mrs. Maxey's – we met some 15 or 20 boarders at this house, from various portions of the Union, some on business but the greater portion in search of health.

Friday 5th....I felt greatly indisposed and took medicine. I also applied a plaster of tartar emetic oitment to my stomach & abdomen. Both were of great benefit & afforded me much relief. In the afternoon & night I was measurably relieved from pain.

Saturday 6th....In the morning I took a walk with Mrs. Brooks of a part of the Town. Doct. & Mrs. Holland called to see us & also Mr. Daniels formerly of Columbia – light diet and rest are producing happy effects on the condition of my health & I passed the evening without suffering. I have not a remark to make in regard to this place, in addition, to what I stated in my notes on my first visit in the fall of 1846. The dilapidation of buildings keeps even pace with the improvement of their houses, so there is little or no visible improvement –

Sunday 7th....We attended divine service at the Episcopal Church & heard the church service read & the Communion administered with becoming pathos & solemnity. We partook of the memorial of Christs suffering & death and I trust not entirely unworthily....Rain prevented our attendance in the afternoon so we did not hear the resident Minister Mr. Young preach, as there was no sermon in the morning.

Monday 8th....We took a walk over a part of the town & called to see Doct. & Mrs. Holland. The mail boat arrived about 12 ocl. but brought neither letters nor papers for us. I felt some nausea at the Stomach but by lying on the bed, I escaped a paroxysm of headache. The news from Washington is that the three million bill had passed the Senate without the Wilmot proviso[15] & had been returned to the house of representatives – Therm.t at 3 ocl. 84°.

---

[15] Congressman David Wilmot's amendment to the appropriations bill would have banned slaves from any territory acquired from Mexico. It passed the House Feb. 15, 1847, for a second time, but was defeated in the Senate as it would be repeatedly down to 1860.

....

Wednesday 10th....So warm at night as not to require covering.....

Thursday 11....We left Jacksonville after dinner in the Wm. Gaston for Picolatte [Picolata], reached Black Creek about dark, stopped from 1/2 to an hour & then dropped down the creek to a landing, took in Wood & arrived at Picolatte about day light. We went to Col. Williams,[16] got breakfast and set out for St. Augustine about 10 in a two horse conveyance with four passengers, leaving our baggage behind. We arrived at St. Augustine near 3 ocl. when by headache I was forced to take my bed, which I did not leave until the next morning.

Friday 12th....Our ride to St. Augustine was slow & uninteresting but not disagreeable as I expected. The road passes over a poor pine barren with stunted growth and wire grass & scarcely an object to relieve the eye. Some ladies called in the afternoon to see Ms. Brooks.

Saturday 13th....I am better to day tho not entirely relieved. Doct. [Sunrious?] called to see me. In the afternoon I took a short walk with Mrs. Brooks & saw a part of the Town. The buildings are in better condition than when I was here last winter.

Sunday 14th. Mild & clear day but I was so indisposed that I did not leave the house – Mrs. B. attended at the Episcopal church in the morning and the Catholic in the afternoon.

Monday 15th. Cold & windy. I indulged in the use of a small quantity of oil during the day but the effect was not favourable. I was again able to walk from one to 200 yards in the afternoon but the effect was to aggravate my cough –

Tuesday 16th....We received a letter from our daughter, which was very gratifying as our family were all well when she wrote. I also recd. the Edgefd. Advertiser & a letter from Judge Butler but no news in either – After breakfast I walked to the post office & saw a late number of the [Charleston] Mercury, which contained the proceedings of a public meeting in Charleston at which Mr. Calhoun was present & addressed the assembly. On my return to the boarding house I took a chill, which lasted some half hour & was followed by a light fever which confined me to the bed the balance of the day. Several ladies called to see Mrs. Brooks & Mrs. Anderson came with her to our room to inquire personally about my health – She & Mrs. Shaw have been very kind in sending things for me to eat & in their efforts to contribute in any way to my comfort. I passed a restless and sleepless day and also an uncomfortable night.

Wednesday 17th....high wind in the morning...kept up a howling noise through the narrow piazzas & passages of our boarding house – I experienced a good deal of

---

[16] John Lee Williams (1775–1856), Massachusetts-born lawyer who moved to Pensacola in 1820, one year after the U.S. acquired Florida from Spain. Later moved to Picolata. Commissioner to select site of the territorial capital. In 1837 he published *The Territory of Florida,* based in part on knowledge gained while searching for the best site.

debility in the morning with some nausea at the stomach & headache. I passed an uncomfortable day with a feeling of great debility –

Thursday 18th....I rode a short distance in the morning & felt much relief from it. Some headache & nausea in the afternoon – The citizens of St. Augustine exceedingly kind & hospitable –

Friday 19th....I again took exercise on horse back, which again resulted in imparting some strength to me. I rode to the old Spanish fort & looked over a portion of it – in the afternoon a party of ladies & gentlemen embarked on a boat on an excursion of pleasure to the Island, on which the lighthouse stands. Mrs. Brooks was one of the party but I was too feeble to join them. They returned about dark giving a flattering account of the agreeable jaunt which they had taken. After tea Several ladies called to see Mrs. Brooks, who uniting with the boarders in the house, formed an agreeable party & enjoyed music & dancing until about 10 ocl. All the ladies that I have seen sing & play well on the piano & dance with very great grace. Music and dancing are natural tastes & they all seem to follow them by instinct. Even the little Minorcan children[17] that run the streets learn to waltz almost as soon as they learn to talk. There is an air of polish, grace and suavity of manners in the young ladies of this old Town, that are rarely seen and which are very captivating to Visitors. Many of them have married officers in the United States army & other northern gentlemen of respectability, who came to the State in pursuit of new homes & employment.

Saturday 20th....I made out to pay two calls in the morning with Mrs. Brooks to Doct. & Mrs. Peck[18] and to Judge Bronson[19] & lady – I also paid a visit in company with Mrs. Brooks & Ms. Peck in the afternoon to Mrs. Worth,[20] who is now residing in the U. States barracks – There being few horses & carriages in town, the usual mode of visiting or taking exercise is by walking. Its tendency is to give colour & health & activity to the ladies & in fact I am not sure but it imparts a large portion of the grace which is habitual in all their movements –

....

Monday 22....I wrote several letters & took some exercise by walking. My health is

[17] Descendants of some 1,400 indentured Greeks and Italians brought to Florida in 1768 under British authority. Many died; others were worked abusively and fled to St. Augustine, where they were set free in 1777.

[18] Dr. Seth Peck and wife had come to St. Augustine in 1837 from Connecticut. He restored the home of a former Spanish official and practiced medicine there.

[19] Judge Isaac H. Bronson, New York congressman 1837–1838, supported Florida statehood. Territorial judge for East Florida, 1840. Indian hostilities led him to support their removal. After statehood he became federal judge for northern Florida.

[20] Mrs. Margaret Stafford Worth, wife of Gen. William J. Worth (1794–1849). During the Mexican War she was quartered in St. Augustine, and she remained there until her death in 1869.

gradually improving.

Tuesday 23....There is a rumour in the papers that Santa Anna has advanced from San Louis Potose with an army of 15 or 20.000 men upon Saltillo & that a battle has been fought between him & Genl. Taylor – That Taylors Army was from 5 to 6000 men & that he was fighting & falling back on Monterey – The American army is in a perilous situation from the number of the enemy & the reported fact that the communications have been cut off between Camargo & Monterey & all supplies intercepted.

Wednesday 24th....The rain at night was very copious as the streets were flooded with water in the morning. We dined with Mrs. Geo. Anderson[21] & passed a very pleasant day. To this kind lady & her family we were indebted for much attention & hospitality. In the afternoon we paid Several visits & recd. several in anticipation of our departure the next day....

Thursday 25th....At 9 ocl we took leave of our polite & attentive hostess Mrs. Reid[22] & her boarders, with several of whom we had held very agreeable social intercourse from the day of our arrival in Augustine & for whom we had . . . formed the most favourable opinions & very kind feelings. Mrs. Reid is a lady of cultivated mind, of pleasing manners & of an obliging disposition and although inclined to be cheerful & even gay yet she is free from frivolity or levity. She is the widow of Judge Reid, formally of Augusta Geo., who married her at an advanced period of his life & left her a widow with one child & poverty to her portion. She seems to be fulfilling her duties with fidelity & cheerfulness. She has some 10 to 15 boarders at present in her house of the most opposite characters & dispositions yet most of them engaged in the same kind of employment. The first in the order of rank & influence is Col. Butler,[23] a gentleman about 65 years of age, of grave & rather dignified deportment, from 6 feet 2 inches to 3 inches in height & weighing (I should think) 250 pounds. His style of conversation is grave, slow & somewhat turgid. When I first entered into conversation with him, I thought him a rare specimen of bombast, egotism and vanity, throwing out his ideas in a pompous manner peculiarly his own & mixing up vigorous thought & strong common sense opinions with a great deal that was trashy

---

[21] Sarah Petty Anderson and her husband George settled in NE Florida in the early 1820s after they inherited 450 acres there from her mother. They later amassed over 2,500 acres. After George's death in 1838, Sarah bought the Ximeniz House and made it "the best boarding house" in St. Augustine.

[22] Mary Martha Reid, widow of Judge Robert Raymond Reid (1789–1841), Beaufort SC native, congressman, mayor of Augusta, who moved to Florida in 1832 to become a territorial judge. Appointed governor in 1839; president of the constitutional convention. Mrs. Reid was very highly regarded.

[23] Robert Butler (1786–1860), PA native, a ward of future president Andrew Jackson. West Point graduate, married Jackson's niece Rachel and was his adjutant at the Battle of New Orleans. Briefly acting governor of East Florida, and later surveyor general of the territory.

& worthless. For example he said in a large company that if the President of the United States had confided the direction of the Mexican war to him he would have ended it in Six months. I thought it required a large share of self love to have fostered such an opinion & that an unusual portion of vanity was necessary to embolden the possessor to give utterance to it. Upon a further acquaintance with the old gentleman, I was pleased with him. To the light & inoffensive qualities above ascribed to him, he unites many excellent properties of both head & heart. He has seen a good deal of life, has much experience & has collected a stock of useful information. In the war of 1812 with Great Britain, also in the wars with the Creek & Seminole Indians, he was with Genl. Jackson & rendered important & efficient services to the Country. His principles are sound, his morals exemplary & his disposition kind & benevolent & altogether I think him an excellent man –

The next in order is Doct. Simms, formerly of Charleston So. Car. but for many years an inhabitant of St. Augustine and attached to the land office Department of which I omitted to mention that Col. Butler is superintendent. He is a gentleman of pleasing & unpretending manners, sensible, well informed affable & communicative but modest & unassuming. Mr. Hawkins, the Son in law of Col. Butler is a young man of education & respectability, who delights to play the part of a humorist & indulges in some levity & extravagance of expression, in which it is difficult to say whether he is jesting, or in earnest. He has a taste for the ridiculous & seldom fails in conversation to say something to produce a laugh – I left him with the opinion that he was a clever fellow with a good deal of talent but without much discipline of mind. There were also two New York young men in the house of totally opposite characters – Bleker was a bluff jolly fellow, whose only aim was to enjoy each moment as it passes & to make out of life all the pleasure, of which it is capable. He would laugh, and joke & dance or comment without any apparent regard, of what tomorrow was to bring forth – Sharp is a man of education & good manners. He has evidently mixed with much good society & improved from the intercourse. In many respects I regard him as a gifted man. He sings, dances & converses exceedingly well & can play upon any instrument. He is a hearty laugher but without levity. It seems to be the excess of good nature, to which he unites a relish for wit & repartee. He was a large contributor to the pleasure of our social circle & a willing contributor but never forward or offensive. We have much cause for being pleased with our visit to St. Augustine, if the courtesy, attention & hospitality of the people should inspire such a feeling & I shall be at all times gratified to have an opportunity of making a return under my own roof – We reached Picolatte [Picolata, earlier Picolati] at 3 ocl. when by headache I was forced to take my bed....

Friday 26th....it blew a gale through the entire day, which confined me to the house. Near 6 ocl. P. M. we left Col. Williams for Jacksonville, at which place we arrived after 10 ocl, at night. About 11 ocl. we reached our lodgings at Mrs. Maxcy's. The night was clear & cold & the moon shown with unusual brightness.

Saturday 27th. Clear & cold morning....The young beans were somewhat injured by the cold and I believe there was no frost. In the afternoon Mrs. Brooks & I walked to the River to see a small boat launched, which would have been a pretty sight but for the breaking of the scaffolding, which in giving way, left the boat not more than half her length in the water – Our morning was occupied in reading a sweet letter from our daughter & some others & also the news papers –

Sunday 28th....In passing down the River or in getting from the steamboat to the boarding house, I took a slight cold, which affected me considerably during the day & kept me from church. I roused myself in the afternoon & took a long walk with Mrs. B. greatly to my benefit. A citizen of the place, died to day of parallysis.

Monday 29th....There are not many visitors in Jacksonville at this time & none of any distinction. We find on our return that the table of our hostess has improved in the quantity and quality of its viands, which it somewhat needed. We received by the mail a letter from our Son Whitfield who was on the Island of Lobos near Mexico, giving us the pleasing intelligence that he & his brother were in good health, although they had suffered greatly by sea sickness on their passage. We also recd. a letter from Ellen & Hampden from home, by which we learned that all were well there. The papers also confirmed the previous reports of a sanguinary battle between Genl. Taylor & Santa Anna at Monterey, in which the loss of men on both sides was great. Santa Anna's force is represented to have been over 20.000 and loss about 4000 while the American force was not above 5000 & the loss above 1000. If it be true as reported, this victory of Genl. Taylor will be the most distinguished in modern times, but a loss of 1/5 of his army is without a parallel & can only have resulted from the smallness of his forces, compared with those of his enemy. Santa Anna was preparing for another battle.

Tuesday 30th....We attended service in the Episcopal church in the morning & paid some visits. In the afternoon took a long walk for exercise. There was a marriage in the Town also the birth of too male twins, so that since our arrival there has been a death, a marriage & a birth, three events which are constantly taking place within human existence.

Wednesday 31st....In the morning I rode into the country about 1 mile for exercise but saw nothing but sterile land, with pine & the low palmetto. I have been in every direction in the vicinity of this town & I hesitate not to say that it is as barren & uninteresting a spot of earth as my eyes ever beheld. It is a mystery to me how the people get the food, sufficient for comfortable subsistence. I went to the Courthouse to hear a trial before a Judge upon the application of a Major Taylor,[24] late of Enterprise, for the possession of his children, now with their mother, from whom he has lately separated. The case was postponed until tomorrow 9 ocl, to allow Mrs. Taylor to make a return to the process of habeas corpus. She had outwitted the old

---

[24] Major Cornelius Taylor, Virginia native, a cousin of Gen. Zachary Taylor, was the first settler of Enterprise in 1841. He operated a steamboat and an inn until the death of a daughter later in 1847 apparently led the family to move away.

Major and secured the custody of the children without his knowledge, while they were at school in Macon Geo.

April 1, 1847

Thursday 1st....I rode for exercise from 2 to 3 miles & on my return stopped at the Courthouse to hear the issue of the case between Major Taylor & his Wife in regard to the custody of their children. The return to the writ of habeas corpus was read, testimony taken on both sides & a short argument made by an attorney on each side, when fatigue caused me to leave the house before any decision was made by the Judge. I learned that the case was suspended until 3 oclock, at which hour the Court ordered the children to be produced. The Court is now sitting. Finally a compromise was effected, by which they agreed to come together again & upon the signing of articles of agreement, the Court dismissed the case. Upon the arrival of the boat, I received Savannah papers, containing an account of the battle between Santa Anna & Genl. Taylor & of the success of the American arms. Also of the landing of the forces under Genl. Scott & of the investment of Vera Cruz –There was a great deal of skirmishing & some fighting in getting possession of the fortified positions of the enemy, in which the Palmetto Regiment participated as Col. Dickerson[25] is reported to have been wounded. Genl. [Winfield] Scott was preparing for an assault upon the Town & Castle, which it was thought, he would soon take –

Friday 2....I again took a ride & on my return recd. a visit from Judge Douglas[26] of this town with whom I held a half hours conversation. In the afternoon I recd. a letter from our daughter, who was in Savannah & also the Edgefield Advertiser but no news from either place.

Saturday 3rd....At 2 ocl it was like summer. On my return from a ride I was attacked with head ache, which confined [me] to the bed the balance of the day & deprived me of the pleasure of taking dinner with Doctor Holland, whom I find to be [a] clever & hospitable gentlemen & his wife a pleasant & estimable lady. I did not get relief until towards 9 ocl at night.

Sunday 4th....I felt too feeble to attend Church, so I occupied my time in reading the life of the Apostle Paul who in every respect was a remarkable man....I took a ride in the afternoon by which I was refreshed.

Monday 5th....I will here give a statement of my expenses to Florida up to this date as it may be desirable at some future period to know the price of traveling to this

---

[25] Lt. Col. James Polk Dickerson (1816–1847) of Camden, second in command of the Pal. Reg., received a chest wound on March 10. He and Col. P. M. Butler were mortally wounded at Churubusco on August 20.

[26] Thomas Douglas, Indiana native. U.S. Attorney for E. FL 1826. Circuit Court Judge 1845. Episcopalian, temperance advocate.

part of the State.

Expenses at Hamburg	$4.00	Board to Mrs. Maxcy for	25.00
Passage to Savannah	15.00	Incidental expenses	2.00
Expenses at Savannah	16.00	Passage to Savannah	20.00
Passage to Jacksonville	20.00	Expences at Savannah	7.00
Expenses at Mrs. Maxeys	12.00	Passage to Charleston	16.00
Passage to Picolatti	6.50	Expenses in Charleston	15.00
Do. To St. Augustine	6.00	Passage to Aiken	21.00
Two weeks at Mrs. Reid's	30.00	Expenses at Aiken	5.50
Incidental expenses	5.00		
			$108.50
Passage to Picolatte	6.00	Add - - -	$131.00
Expenses at Picolatte	3.50	Total =	$239.50
Passage to Jacksonville	6.50	The sum of $239.50 was the	
	$131.00	amount of my expenses to & from	
This was the amount of expenditure		Florida for self, wife and Servant --	
for myself, Wife & servant.			

We received by the mail boat a letter from our Sons Preston & Whitfield, dated 23rd of February. They were still at Lobos but expected to embark in a few days for Vera Cruz. We recd. verbal intelligence that Genl. Scott had taken the town of Vera Cruz & the castle of Ullos by the loss of 900 of his troops. This information leaves us in a state of painful anxiety in regard to the safety of our Sons & also of the relations & young friends in the Palmetto regiment. I rode in the morning & took a walk with Mrs. Brooks in the afternoon & returned some visits....

Tuesday 6th....I rode with a Mr. Chiles about 3 miles into the Country & got some fresh & rich milk at a place called Hunger & Hardship. The people were kind & communicative & offered us breakfast. In the afternoon we returned some visits & again took a walk for exercise near the river & on the warf [wharf]. My health is gradually improving & my head measurably free from that dull & oppressive feeling, which has continued to pursue me for the last five weeks & which imparted to the mind a sluggish & feeble operation, causing me to loose much of the enjoyment of social intercourse, of which I am so fond under other circumstances. The mornings & evenings mild & pleasant but the heat oppressive at midday.

Wednesday 7th....I devoted the morning to writing letters, noon to rest & the afternoon to exercise near the river & on the warf & the evening to reading. Time passes away in a dull & monitinous routine, of which I am becoming exceedingly tired.

Thursday 8th....I rode into the Country on the Panama road about two miles for exercise & saw nothing but pine barren & dwarf Palmetto. In the afternoon had an attack of headache, which though not very severe, confined me to my bed till next morning. No intelligence by the Gaston in addition to what we had previously recd. from the Army, except a rumour that the town of Vera Cruz had capitulated to Genl. Scott & that he was bombarding the castle....

Friday 9th....Mrs. B. recd. flowers & I, little nicknacks with kind messages from several families in Town as tokens of goodwill in anticipation of our departure for home. We are invited to spend the day with Captain [John] L'Engle & Lady [Susan Fazio] & expect to leave our boarding house at 1 ocl. Dined at Captain L'Engles & passed the evening with his hospitable family. At 10 ocl we went on board of the Sarah Spaulding after taking leave of our friends.

Saturday 10....We passed St. Mary's in the day & passed the night partly in motion & partly at rest....

Sunday 11th....We reached Savannah about Sunrise & took quarters at the Pulaski house. I did not go out during the day. In the afternoon I called with Mrs. Brooks on Mrs. Barton.

Monday 12th....We left Savannah at 7 ocl in the Steam boat Santee for Charleston in the midst of a shower of rain. About 10 ocl the wind rose & the dashing of the waves became exceedingly unpleasant. Many of the passengers were made sick....Many pleasing objects were presented to view in different places, such as Islands with their green shrubbery & their well ordered plantations – we also passed the town of Beaufort, which has an imposing appearance as you sail up the Sound. In the afternoon just as we were entering the bay of St. Helena a dark murky cloud arose and discharged its its contents of rain & hail, attended with high wind, rendered our situation for a few minutes exceedingly perilous. The Capt. turned the boat & dropped back under the shelter of a small Island, where we remained all night....

Tuesday 13th ....We had a pleasant passage throughout the day & saw many valuable rice & cotton plantations, among the number was that of Ex-Governor [William] Aiken. We reached Charleston about 7 ocl & passed from the boat to the Charleston Hotel.

Wednesday 14th....I took a walk as far as broad street & then up King street back to the hotel. I saw very few persons with whom I was acquainted. The city has a clean, & thriving appearance, with many good houses of recent construction.

Thursday 15th....I again took a little exercise by walking and purchased some wine of Paul & Brown.[27] At 3 ocl we changed our quarters & went to our friend Mrs. Alex [Sophia] Wilson. The family gave us a kind & hospitable reception....

Friday 16th....Early in the morning I rode with Young Mr. Wilson over a large part of the city & a portion of the neck in the forenoon & rested after dinner.

[27] Grocers at 47 Broad St.

Saturday 17. Still clear & cool. I rode to King Street & made a few purchases of books & also had some Dagaratipe [daguerreotype] likenesses taken. Nothing of interest occurred during the day. I visited the new steamboat Southeron & examined her accommodations for passengers, which are handsome & comfortable –

Sunday 18th....I attended divine service at St. Paul's Church & heard a sermon from a young Mr. Hankle, [Hanckel] who appears to be a young man of some promise – During the day Messrs. Pettigrew, [James Louis Petigru] Gantt,[28] [Christian]Hankel & [Benj. F.] Pepoon[29] called to see me.

Monday 19th....At half past 10 ocl we took leave of our attentive friends & repaired to the depot of the rail road, where we took the cars for Aiken at 11 ocl. I cannot allow the occasion to pass without bearing testimony to the kindness & hospitality of every member of Mrs. Wilson's family while we remained with them. Each member of the family appeared [jealous?] to make themselves agreeable, so that our time might be pleasant, & each succeeded to my entire satisfaction. I am acquainted with but few families, who can be more agreeable than this one & there are but few girls, who possessed the interesting qualities of Miss Sophia. They have my kindest wishes for their prosperity & happiness – on my arrival at the rail road I learned the melancholy death of my old friend & neighbor Major John S. Jeter caused by inflammation of the brain. Major Jeter had many ster[ling?] & high qualities with incorruptible integrity of purpose & conduct with some peculiarities of character. He was a true & steadfast friend but an open and uncompromising opponent. We reached Aiken & took lodgings at Mrs. Swartz,[30] where we met some 15 or 20 persons from the North, on a visit to the South for their health –

Tuesday 20th....We left Aiken at 8 ocl. & reached home to dinner, where we found all well. I also received a long and interesting letter from our Son Whitfield, bearing date the 28 & 29 of March from Vera Cruz -- he & his brother were well. I was much gratified to learn that all our relations, friends & neighbours were in good health. Several of my neighbors called to see me & seemed to be much gratified by my improved health.

Wednesday 21....I rode over my farm & inspected the state of my crop. It is equal to my expectations. The stock of hogs & cattle were in rather low condition & evidently had not been sufficiently fed.

Thursday 22nd....I called to see Mrs. Julia Butler,[31] who had just recd. a letter from the Col. in which he spoke in kind and complimentary terms of Preston & Whitfield. They were at Alvarado in Mexico.

---

[28] Probably either James L. Gantt, a director of the Bank of the State of South Carolina, or Thomas J. Gantt, a Commissioner of Public Buildings and Alderman.

[29] Charleston attorney, member of the South Carolina society.

[30] Margaret Martha Schwarts (died 1891).

[31] Miranda Julia Duval, wife of Col. P. M. Butler. They met while Lt. Butler was stationed at Fort Smith, Arkansas Territory, in the mid-1820s.

Friday 23rd....I again rode over my farm & returned by Pottersville. My sister Mrs. Blocker & her daughters came down & passed the day with us. I heard from my venerable father, whose health is represented to be without change since I last saw him....This was the birthday of my dear wife, who is in most excellent health.

Saturday 24th....Fire was necessary to comfort at night. The cart came down from the plantation with beef & poultry with a letter from my overseer giving us a report of the status of things there.

Sunday 25th....It was too cold for me to attend church so I remained quietly at home. My father arrived on a visit at 2 ocl, in his usual health but more feeble than when I last saw him.

Monday 26th....In the morning I rode to the Village but heard no news. Several persons stated that they saw frost in the morning. In the afternoon I rode over my farm. I have plowed over about 30 acres of corn, which was first replanted, I am running an iron harrow over my cotton....

Tuesday 27th....We went with Father to spend the day with Major Blocker & family. I was attacked with headache & confined to the bed, the greater part of the day & suffered greatly on my return home in the afternoon. We met on our return Doct. Jno. Williams[32] & a very large party, going to his wedding. He is to be married to a Miss Timmerman....

Wednesday 28th..... I feel feeble & spiritless from the attack yesterday & no inclination to leave the house. In the afternoon I went with Mrs. Brooks & Ellen to the farm & examined into the State of the poultry &C. We passed through the fields at the Youngblood place, by the Spring & then returned by the way of the Pottery. My small grain looks greatly superior to any that I have seen, particularly the oats....

Thursday 29th....The intelligence by the papers is that Santa Anna is defending the passage to Mexico [City] & that he has about 15,000 troops at a point called Cerro Gordo, where it is expected that a battle will be fought between Genl. Scott & himself. The Palmetto regiment was at Vera Cruz on the 14th instant but was expected to March towards Jallapa in a few days –

Friday 30th....A large party was given by Mr. and Mrs. Thompkins to Doct. Williams & Wife. The entertainment was very handsome & tasteful & the company numerous & merry. They had dancing, which I regard as the only decent amusement for young people at an evening party –

May 1, 1847

Saturday 1....In looking to the State of vegitation, I find the leaves of the forest trees nearly fully grown, wheat, rye & barley heading, corn about half leg high, oats ra-

[32] Dr. John G. Williams (1820–1866), "one of the most respected citizens of our District, came to his death...the act of his own hand" (*Adv.*, June 6, 1866).

ther small, part of the cotton crop up but looking indifferently and vegitation in the main, growing rapidly. So far the Spring has been favourable but rain is now needed. Early planted cotton has come up well but the later plantings show an indifferent stand as I was informed....No additional news from the army. The only thing in the papers of any moment is the announcement of the preparations by the Citizens of Charleston for the reception of Mr. Webster[33] in all the papers of the City, by which they are rendering themselves ridiculous & socophantic [sycophantic] in an eminent degree in my estimation. Mr. Webster is a distinguished man & has rendered important Services to the Country in his public character, thereby entitling himself to the respect & attention of our people, where ever he meets them & it would afford me pleasure to unite in all reasonable ways of showing our appreciation of his talents & services but I dispise any thing like manworship.

Sunday 2nd....Attended church [in the afternoon] and partook of the solemn ceremony of the sacrament. This was the first day, on which religious services were had in the church since its alteration & repair. The comfort & appearance of the whole building has been improved & particularly the inside.

Monday 3rd....a disagreeable day on account of a bleak east wind, which blew a fresh gale throughout the day. I visited the Village & remained a short time on the hill, speaking to my friends & acquaintances from the Country. I heard no news. There appeared to be a number of negroes, horses & waggons for sale by traders & speculators but I did not ask the price of either. The concourse of persons was not large. There was also a company of Circus riders, preparing to perform at 2 ocl. I began to day to plough over cotton at my farm....

Tuesday 4th....We rode out to see Aunt Butler, who had been indisposed but was now better & free from pain....

Wednesday 5th....I [went to] Hamburg to sell a lot of cotton for my father – Mrs. Brooks went down in company with me & we reached Hamburg at 2 ocl. I sold a lot of 18 bales of cotton, belonging to my father to Jos. Sibley & Co. for $11 ¾ cts & rode to Augusta. Intelligence had been received by the last mail from the South, that a signal victory has been achieved the American forces under Genl. Scott over the Mexican army under the command of Genl. Santa Anna. The loss in killed & wounded was severe in both armies. Five Generals, many other inferior officers & 6000 men surrendered as prisoners of War. The battle was fought at a passage in the mountains called Cero Gordo, not far from Jallapa on 18th April.

Thursday 6th....After getting through my business I set out for home at 11 ocl. & on reaching there at 5 ocl. we found our daughter Martha Brooks, with our little grand

[33] Daniel Webster (1782–1852), Congressman and Senator from Massachusetts beginning in 1812 and concluding in 1850, and Sec. of State under three presidents. His views on tariffs evolved with his state, opposing protection until 1828 and supporting it thereafter. Argued against SC's nullifier Robert Y. Hayne in a famous Senate debate, and supported the Compromise of 1850 in another.

daughter Miss Sally Means, who had arrived the day previous from Fairfield – I rode to my farm to see my overseer but he was sick....

Friday 7th....The five last days of April & the entire month of May to this date has been cold & dry except a light shower of rain on Sunday morning last. I fear the stand of cotton will be bad & that the small grain has been injured by the cold & wind – a good deal of the cotton between this [place] & Augusta has been worked & looks in a growing condition. The corn also looks pretty well & most of it has been plowed over – At 11 ocl. I set out for my plantation, taking Hampden with me, at which we arrived about 4 ocl. but I was so indisposed that I was forced to take a bed, where I remained until next morning.

Saturday 8th....I rode over a good part of my crop & saw every field. The corn is very promising and all of it has been worked with both hoe & plough. The cotton is only tolerable & the stand not good. The Spring has been too cold & dry. About four fifths of the cotton is up & presents a good stand & the balance would soon be up if it had a light rain, to impart moisture to the earth. The hands were engaged in chopping out & working the cotton. My mules & horses were in good working order & the colts in very excellent condition, particularly a young stud by Argile, just two years old, that I regard, among the finest colts in the State – I was too indisposed to examine the stock etc. but the report from the overseer was favourable. My negroes were generally well & in good spirits. They appeared greatly rejoiced to see me as they had heard that I had died in Florida. I was pleased with my trip. The small grain bids far to be an average crop – I was confined to my bed the greater part of the afternoon ....

Sunday 9th....I set out for home after breakfast & arrived at 1 ocl ....All well at home and no news....Good rain in the Village on Saturday night.

Monday 10th....I am planting out potato slips, cabbage, tomatoes & other plants – On riding to my farm at the Youngblood place, I was surprised to find that not more rain had fallen there, than merely to wet the surface of the ground. The small grain would be greatly benefited by rain. We received a letter from our Son Whitfield from Vera Cruz. He writes in good spirits & says his health is good but that his brother has been very sick tho at that time convalescing. His regiment was to march on the 17 of April for Jalappa, to join Genl. Scott. To the great disappointment of my Son's company Genl. Quitmans division was not in the battle of Sero Gordo & therefore gathered none of the laurels, that were won on that hard fought field. This division of the Army had been sent to take Albarado & has not joined the main army but had reached Vera Cruz on its return & took up the line of march for the scene of action on the 17th the very day on which the battle commenced. I greatly regret that the 96 boys were thus deprived of the opportunity of distinguishing themselves on this occasion –

Tuesday 11th....Judge Butler called to see me. He is in excellent health & good spirits. I went this morning to take tea with Col. Carroll, being the first time, that I have ventured out at night for two year....

Wednesday 12th....Mrs. Brooks with our daughter Martha & her infant & Miss Sally Means, set out this morning on a visit to our Son James & his Wife, to be absent 4 or 5 days, and Ellen also leaves home with her grandmother on a visit to her cousin E[llen] Laborde in Colombia, leaving myself & Hampden to keep house during their absence....

....

Thursday 13th....On examination this morning I discovered that the rain was abundant & the earth thoroughly wet. It will be of incalculable advantage to the oat crop, which was suffering for want of rain. In riding to my Youngblood place I was surprised to find that the rain was not general, for at that place, there had very little fallen, not even enough to run in the road....We received from our dear Son Whitfield through Doct. [space] a collection of shells & other specimens of Mexican production, which he had sent as a present to his Mother.

Friday 14th....I do not recollect ever to have seen such a continuation of cold weather in the month of May. It is now cold enough for the last of March or first of April – I made a short excursion into the country after breakfast, as far as James Griffins and then by the Youngblood place home. The cotton looks badly & very small but the corn has a growing appearance. At night I was attacked with tooth ache & suffered greatly until after 12 ocl. The pain was so severe that I got Mr. Lipscomb's William to cut round the gum & to make an effort to pull it out. He made two attempts to draw it but not succeeding, I sent for Doct. Williams but before he arrived the tooth became less painful & in a short time so easy that I fell to sleep.

Saturday 15th....like a March day with high wind from the East. It is difficult to say, what may be the effects of such weather on the growing crops of cotton. I was indisposed & confined to the house the greater part of the day. We rec.d a letter from our Son Whitfield who was in Jalapa. He was in fine health & writes that his brother Preston was rapidly recovering from his attack of fever. In a week they were to take the line of March to Puebla, on the way to the Capital. Mrs. Brooks & the girls returned from a visit to our Son James & his family, whom they found in good health, except our daughter Sarah, who had chill & fever. They speak in high terms of my two grandsons & particularly of my namesake.

Sunday 16th....We attended church & heard a sensible sermon from Mr. Walker. My Sister Mrs. Blocker came down with the girls to attend church & pay us a visit....Monday 17th....At one ocl hour daughter Martha set out for my plantation on her return to Fairfield. In the afternoon I rode to my farm & observed about 5 ocl a dark cloud forming....about [dark] it commenced raining & so continued until I went to sleep between 9 & 10 ocl.

Tuesday 18th....On walking out I was much gratified to find that the rain had been abundant for the present. I rode to the Village & made a number of purchases for my negroes at the plantation & then to my farm. The Earth was in fine order for the plough. I began yesterday to plough over my corn the second time & to plant peas this morning ....

....

Thursday 20th....The warmth of the atmosphere and the white floating clouds make you feel for the first time that we have the genial, growing weather of Summer. No news by the papers except the advance of Genl. Scott towards Puebla en route for Mexico, the Volunteers to march in advance.

Friday 21st....This has been a peculiar spring & a very unfavourable to the growth of corn & cotton & most of the garden plants. The cotton is very little larger than it was on 20th of April, the day on which I arrived from Florida. I have never known the worm so destructive to the corn. In some portions of my fields there is not a fourth standing, although I have replanted it twice. It came up & was then killed by the worm. The stand is good in land which was cultivated in cotton but on stubble land it is almost a failure. The beans in the garden have been also almost destroyed by insects.

Saturday 22....During the last two days the Therm.t has been above 76° & the crops of corn & vegetables in the gardens have grown more in one week than they had done in the previous three....I recd. a letter from my overseer, informing me that my Servant Barnett was thrown by a mule & dragged some 200 yards by the trace chain, in which one of his feet became fastened & that when taken up, he had no sign of life, save a weak pulse. He is however getting well....

Sunday 23rd....I was indisposed during the day, yet I attended church in the morning. The afternoon temperate & clear. (I heard from my neighbour Mr. Harris, that intelligence had reached Augusta that Genl. Scott had taken the City of Mexico without resistance.)

Monday 24th....We saw in a New Orleans paper, the arrival of our Son Preston in that City. His health has been for some time very precarious, having had the typhoid fever for 20 days & we presume that he has left the army to recruit his strength & may be on his way home for a short period. The death of Marshall Smith at Vera Cruz of Vomits is announced in the papers. He was sutler to the Palmetto regiment & was doing well when attacked by that shocking disease, Yellow fever & sunk under it.

Tuesday 25....Our Son Preston arrived about 2 ocl. in rather feeble health. He had been extremely ill for upwards of 20 days & at one time in imminent danger but he is now convalescent. Doctor [John P.?] Barrett came with him, who had gone out to Georgia, to see a young man by the name of Watson, a volunteer with the Abbeville Company, on his way home & who had become so ill as to be unable to travel. Preston brought a letter from our Son Whitfield, who wrote in fine spirits, informing us that his health was never better. He also makes a favourable report of those friends in his company with whom we take a deep interest, & also of my old Servant Joseph, whom I have owned for thirty years. He states that he has been faithful &

attentive & consented to remain with his young Master Whitfield with great cheerfulness because he thought that I would be better satisfied, than for him to return. He has been a faithful servant to me & carries out his fidelity to my children, which is very gratifying to my feelings & for which he shall receive a due reward. We had recd. later news from the army than what our Son brought, for he did not travel as rapidly as the mail –

Wednesday 26th....Most of the gentlemen called to see Preston.

Thursday 27th....a heavy fall of rain up to 10 ocl. [a.m.] The earth is wetter than it has been since the 1 of April. The rain comes at a favourable period for the grain crops & will, I trust, ensure a plentiful harvest....No important news by the last mail. Our daughter Ellen returned from a visit to Colombia, where she reports that she enjoyed much pleasure.

Friday 28th....I rode to my farm & ascertained that the earth was very wet & miry. The crops of grain & cotton have greatly improved within the last three days....

Saturday 29th....Preston has just left us with the expectation of meeting his Wife on the road between this place & Fairfield, taking Hampden with him. Our son James arrived with his family. He has two sweet boys.

Sunday 30th....Recd. a letter from Mr. Lowry my overseer at the plantation, giving me the agreeable information, that a copious rain had fallen in gentle showers, thoroughly wetting the earth & not washing, by which the appearance of the crop, had been greatly improved. He had ploughed over the corn the second time, planted his peas & was engaged in cutting wheat. During the morning Col. Pickens & Genl. McDuffie called and remained for some time in social conversation. Judge Butler dined with us in the afternoon. I rode with him to Col. Pickens. My son James & his wife with their two fine boys arrived the preceding afternoon & we had their company & also my Sister Mrs. Blocker & her two daughters.

Monday 31st....Vegetation is growing rapidly & the crops are improving. I have not worked up over my crop the second time yet & in fact in consequence of the sickness of my overseer, it is rather in the grass. We recd. no intelligence by the papers of this morning from Mexico.

June 1, 1847

Tuesday 1st....I rode to my farm as usual. The oats are in head & promises a good crop. I sold yesterday my horse Dave to Mr. Griffin for $150. & purchased one of John Mays for $145. Dave has many good qualities but his gate did not suit the carriage. By himself he is a hearty and excellent draft horse.

Wednesday 2nd....At 7 ocl. I set out for my plantation with my Son James in company at which we arrived at 12 ocl. In the afternoon and I rode over a portion of my crop & saw a large portion of my corn, cotton & small grain. The entire crop is good as I have a right to expect, although in places the stand of cotton is not good.

My mules & horses are in excellent order & also the colts. The cattle are rather in low order. I did not see either the sheep or hogs. The negroes were in good health & looked in a contented state....Thursday 3rd....Immediately after breakfast I rode over a part of my crop, which I had not seen ....It was better than I expected to see it. At 9 ocl. I left the plantation and reached home at 2 ocl....The crops of corn & cotton on the road were small & not very promising. There was service in the Episcopal Church at night at which time our daughter in law Mrs. Sarah Brooks was baptized & united herself to the church. I was prevented by indisposition & a light drizzle of rain from attending.

Friday 4th....In the afternoon I rode to the Pottery & was struck with the rapid growth of the corn in the vicinity of the Village. Mrs. Mary Gillison arrived with her two children on a visit to her relations.

Saturday 5th....A servant came down from the plantation & brought intelligence that the wheat crop was cut & the negroes were well with the exception of one or two –

Sunday 6th....We attended service morning and evening in the Epis. Church. In the afternoon I observed several arrivals of persons, to attend the Court of Equity which sits tomorrow....

Monday 7th....The Court of Equity began its annual session this morning, Judge Job Johnson presiding. The Village was not crowded although it was sale day & the time for the sitting of the Court of Equity. The house & lot in the Village of Edgefield, belonging to Jabez Ryan was sold by the Sheriff for $2000. The lot is small & inconvenient yet a favourable stand for a public house. His stable lot & some few negroes were sold at the same time. There was no recent intelligence from the army.

Tuesday 8th....I was confined to my bed from 12 ocl until Wednesday morning by a violent paroxysm of headache. My nephew Abner Blocker on his return from Mexico to his fathers, passed through the Village & called to see us. He appeared to be in fine health....

Wednesday 9th....I rode to the Village & paid a visit to Colonel [M. L.] Bonham, who has just returned from New Orleans[34] –

....

Friday 11th....The earth quite wet & the crops of vegitation much enlivened. The case in which I am complainant as trustee for my Sister Mrs. Blocker against the Misses Penns[35] was called for trial at 2 ocl and the examination of testimony entered upon, which occupied the Court until 9 ocl at night at which hour the Court adjourned.

[34] Now a Lt. Col. in U.S. Army, Bonham would return to action in Mexico and be wounded Aug. 20, 1847.

[35] Probably daughters of George Leith Penn (1807–1877) and Louisiana Mims Penn. He opened a drug and grocery store in ECH c. 1845, and later sold it to his son Edmund.

Saturday 12th....My father left us this morning in a feeble condition & evidently declining in health. I was attacked with headache as early as 9 ocl & deprived of the opportunity of attending the argument of the case of myself as trustee of Mrs. Blocker against the Penns. The paroxysm passed off about 4 ocl & I was able to ride to my farm. I learned with pleasure that Mr. McDuffie (whom I had left at Col. Pickens very ill the previous afternoon), was much better. When I parted with him, I verily thought he was dying.

Sunday 13th....In the afternoon I rode to Col. Pickens to see Genl. McDuffie, who had been taken ill on the Wednesday preceding on his way from Columbia home with his daughter. His situation is a peculiar & precarious one. There is an almost total paralysis of the corporeal system, attended with mental and physical torpor. It is a melancholy sight, to look upon a great man in ruins & to contemplate the ravages of disease. I have been acquainted with this gentleman since 1810 & have known him intimately, during the intermediate time and all the relations of life and at particular periods, under the most trying circumstances, & there is no man, who has during this entire time, proved himself more honest, fearless, independent and conscientious in the discharge of all his private duties & whose trusts. (sic) He has often changed his opinions upon certain questions of National policy & subjected himself to the charge of inconsistency but I am sure that he was always a sincere & honest. He never has been a party man in the strict sense of the term but has always professed republican doctrines & has acted with the great democratic party upon the leading measures of policy, pursued by the different administrations of the Government during his long period of service in Congress.

Monday 14th....Our Son James left us this morning after a visit of 18 days with his wife & two sweet children on his return home. I went to the village and got letters & papers. Not a word of intelligence from the army in Mexico. I began this morning to cut oats at the Youngblood place with two cradles, giving special directions not to cut down more than could be saved without hazard....

Tuesday 15th....We are preparing to leave for the plantation at Roselands, where I propose to remain some two or three weeks in the hope, that the change may improve the state of my health. We set out between 8 & 9 ocl & reached the plantation at 2 ocl where we learned that the negroes were generally well. I saw a part of the crop in the afternoon.

Wednesday 16th....I set out at 8 ocl to ride in my fields & very soon encountered a cold west wind followed by a dark cloud from which fell two light showers while I was in the plantation. The corn crop is very good tho a little grassy. The cotton is small and not more than two thirds promises to make a good yield. On the old land the stand is bad & the plant very small. The oat crop is very good & nearly ripe enough for the reaper. The wheat & rye crops have been cut & are pretty good. No part of my crop is suffering much from grass, yet it would be benefitted (as the planters say) by being stirred. I saw my mules, horses & colts & a portion of the hogs. They are in excellent order. In the evening the cattle were driven up & I was in pain to find them in indifferent order. Some of them are even poor. I am at a loss to account for it, unless it be the exhausted state of the range. The calves are in tolerable order....A light soaking rain would now be of advantage as the last rain was heavy & washing & caused the earth to run together.

Thursday, 17th....Clouds began to form at dark, which were attended by thunder & by 10 ocl rain began to fall in gentle showers that continue to the greater part of the night.

Friday 18....The earth is thoroughly wet & rather too wet for the ploughs to run. After breakfast I rode by Thos. Paynes, Mr. Whately, Mr. Mims & Col. Griffin's plantations & had a view of their crops from the road. All pretty good & Col. Griffins the best that I have ever seen grow on his plantation. His corn is very superior for old land & his cotton equal to any that I have seen – I returned through my fields, where corn & cotton looked refreshed....The road was much washed & is so muddy as to be almost unfit for traveling over it even on horse back. I saw but little of Doct. Andrews crop & that was only passable, most of the fields on the road being in small grain....

Saturday 19th....I rode to the Edgefield road to meet the Aiken stage & while waiting for the stage Wiley Adams[36] shot a two year deer near the road. We followed it about 100 yards into the woods & found it dead. By the time that we had drawn the deer to the road, the stage arrived, by which I recd. papers & letters & returned to the plantation. No news of any interest from Mexico....by 9 ocl rain began to fall & continued without slight interruption during the night.

Sunday 20th....occasional showers....It was too wet for me to leave the house & I was too unwell even if the weather would have allowed it. On Saturday I was exceedingly sick & the paroxysm did not leave me until about 12 ocl at night. My suffering was very severe & almost without interruption for 12 hours.

Monday 21....My overseer began to cut oats with ten cradles & the same number of hands to tie & shock – he reported to me at night that he had saved [Blank space. One line may have been erased] I rode through a portion of my fields & found the earth thoroughly wet tho not washed in the least. The corn & cotton looked much revived & in a state of rapid growth. On returning home, while riding near a small ditch in one of the fields my horse mired down & in attempting to recover, he fell prostrate in the ditch with his feet on the bank & his side & part of his back in the ditch. By great presence of mind I was mercifully saved from being crushed beneath him for as he fell into the ditch I made an effort & rolled on the bank, having previously extracted my feet from the stirrups & drawn up my legs – on recovering my feet & rising I discovered that my horse could not get out of the ditch without assistance & I was in the middle of a cotton field with no one near, unable to walk & as I feared, unable to call any one to my assistance. I however raised my voice to the

[36] Wiley F. Adams (1816–); 1850 census: $1,200 real estate, 22 slaves.

highest note & after some time was heard by my man George, who had just come within hearing to put up some wheat shocks in a distant part of the same field. He came to my rescue & soon dispatched a boy after 10 negro men, all of whom soon arrived and by no inconsiderable effort succeeded in extracting my horse from his perilous condition. It was first necessary to dig down the bank to get his feet on a level with his body & then to raise by main force his body from the mud, into which it had partially sunk – I was greatly relieved when I ascertained that no limb was broken or other serious injury sustained by the generous animal. While lying in the ditch he would look at me most earnestly & then [brouge?] the weeds, that grew near him. I sustained no injury not even by standing on the damp earth & straining my voice in calling for help – I have cause for much thankfulness that I escaped so well.

Tuesday 22nd....After breakfast I took an excursion through a portion of the neighbourhood & passed by King's, Mrs. Pope, Holloway, Cresswell & to Griffins plantation & thence by R. Martins up the Creek home. I saw a good deal of corn & some cotton on the plantations of each individual. The corn crops are very good & equal to either of those for the last ten years in this vicinity. The cotton is small especially upon old land. Holloway & Martin each had a field of very pretty cotton, about the best that I have seen. While returning I came by a Mineral Spring on the Creek near to Mr. Martin's, the water of which [is] slightly tinctured with sulfur but it is pleasant to the taste....The overseer caused about one half of my wheat crop to be hauled & put undercover.

Wednesday 23rd....by 10 ocl [rain] descended in wetting & uninterrupted showers & at 12 ocl it became a heavy & constant flood of rain. The earth was wet by previous rains & could only be worked in the highest & driest places. The present rain will put a stop to ploughing for several days. In the meantime the grass will become large & unmanageable on the low lands, which are already suffering from wet & the want of work....

Thursday 24th....A portion of the negroes are engaged in thrashing out wheat, which the overseer luckily caused to be hawled and housed on tuesday....In the afternoon I rode to a mineral spring near the residence of F[reeman] Martin & drank freely of the water. It is sulphur....about 9 ocl [p.m.]...a wetting shower began to fall, under whose gentle music [I] fell to sleep.

Friday 25....About noon a heavy shower prevailed in the lower part of my plantation, which literally inundated the fields and washed the land, where ever it lay rolling or hilly. The creek was higher than it has been this year & overflowed a part of my corn. I have never seen the swamp wetter or in a more boggy condition.

Saturday 26th....I rode this morning by Doct. Andrews plantation, also by S. Whatley, Mr. Thompson, Jas. Matthews, B. Connerly & as far as Wiley Adams to meet the stage, by which I expected to receive both papers & letters but much to my disappointment, I learned from Wiley Adams that the stage had stopped running the

18 route & I had to return home without papers or letters....Preston arrived with his family from Fairfield in good health. One of his Volunteers, who was in the hospital in Charleston, when the regiment departed for Mexico, called to see his Captain & remained until next day. He professed to be on his way to his family in No. Carolina.

Sunday 27....I took a short ride in the morning with Preston. During the day a gentleman by the name of Pass from Augusta called, to make inquiries about the Volunteer, who had remained with us the night before & who was represented as having ran away from Augusta. I gave Mr. Pass his dinner & he left in pursuit of Barrum the Volunteer. Mr. & Mrs. King called in the afternoon.

Monday 28th....Preston & I rode through a part of the neighbourhood as far as Freeman Martin[37] & thence home, inspecting a part of the tract of land on which he is living & which will come into market this fall....

Tuesday 29....In the forenoon I again rode with Preston to F. Martins & returned through my plantation. The rain & warmth have imparted to corn & cotton a rapid growth except on low land, where the accumulation of water is doing great injury to both plants. After seeing more of the Martin land, Preston & I came to the conclusion that $7000 is a full price for it. There are about 300 acres in detached spots of excellent arable land, in woods & nearly in its Virgin State. This portion of the land is worth from 12 to 15 per acre. The balance is either old & worn land or wet Swamp & not worth more than $5 per acre. I have pretty well abandoned all idea of purchasing it.

Wednesday 30th....After breakfast we went with the ladies into the plantation to look at the crop with which they seemed much pleased. On our return we took a ride by Washington Holloway's, to see the place first settled by Preston & passing by his house, returned by the Island ford road, stopping at Mr. Kings, to pay him & his lady a visit....

<u>July 1. 1847</u>

Thursday 1st....After breakfast Mrs. Brooks & Ellen set out for our house at the Village leaving myself & Preston & wife to await the return of the horses. About 10 ocl I was attacked by sick stomach, which continued to afflict me during the entire day without headache & with headache from 7 ocl until day light next morning. The paroxysm lasted 20 hours. Young Mr. [James?] Hill came down & passed the day with us.

Friday 2nd....We left the plantation at 1 ocl on our return home & arrived about sunset.....

Saturday 3rd....I rode over my crop at the farm. It is pretty good but in a grassy con-

[37] Freeman Martin (1820–); 1850 census: 41 slaves.

dition. If I could have cultivated it well, it would have been among the best crops that I have ever made on my present farm. The oat crop is abundant & well saved....

Sunday 4th....I was indisposed in the forenoon but was able to attend Church in the afternoon. Preston received an order by the mail from Columbia, directing him to open a recruiting station at Edgefield, very much to his disappointment as he was preparing to return to Mexico on tuesday next. I observed in the afternoon the arrival of sundry carts & waggons, loaded with provisions for a barbaque dinner, to be given tomorrow. A meeting of the District has been called, to consider the utility of a rail road to Aiken & of procuring subventions for the erection of the same....

Monday 5th. Clear & pleasant morning but cool....The warmest weather that I have felt during the year was in the month of March. The Therm.t on one day was above 90°. This morning it is as low as 61°. There was a large concourse of persons collected at the Village & a public meeting held in the courthouse on the subject of the Rail road from this place to Aiken. I was not present but understood that Colonel Pickens & Major Black[38] of Charleston addressed the meeting. After the adjournment of the meeting in the Courthouse the crowd repaired to the Academy lot, where they were addressed by Judge Butler on the importance & utility of the enterprise, which had brought them together for the purpose of consultation & union – After the address, they partook of a public barbaque & also organized a committee to carry out the objects of the meeting, by procuring subscriptions of stock to the road. Much union, hilarity & public spirit were exhibited on the occasion & in great harmony & good humour the assemblage dispersed after . . . a plentiful & well-prepared barbaque. I learned in the afternoon that subscriptions were obtained over 100.000. Mrs. Johnson[39] wife of the Revd. Doct. Johnson died this afternoon after a protracted & painful illness.

Tuesday 6th....I saw some property of Mr. J[abez] Ryan sold by the Sheriff under various executions. Poor Ryan is said to be broken up & rendered bankrupt. Mrs. Johnson was buried this afternoon. There was a large concourse of persons at the funeral. The family had only a few days previously received intelligence of the death of Chs. K. Johnson, their Son, by drowning.

Wednesday 7th....a light shower about dark. The rain has come in good time to save the corn, that has just been ploughed, especially such as is grassy....

Thursday 8th....Recd. a letter from our Son James informing us of the alarming illness of his Wife.

Friday 9th....about 2 ocl . . . there fell one of the heaviest rains, I ever saw descend from the heavens. The rain poured in torrents for two hours until the whole face of

---

38 John Alexander Black (1810–1875), while representing Charleston in the SC House in 1827, obtained the charter for the South Carolina Canal and Railroad Company. He chose the stops along its route between Charleston and Hamburg, including one that became the town of Blackville.

39 Henrietta Hornby Johnson (1786–1847).

the earth was flooded, swelling every creek & branch to unusual height & washing fences away at almost every crossing place....Preston left us in the morning for the residence of his brother James & I fear was exposed to the rain.

Saturday 10th....Great dampness prevails in the atmosphere, to correct which I caused a fire to be made in our little harbour. My servants are engaged in collecting litter & manure, the only employment, of which the wet weather will admit. After breakfast I rode over my fields & had the mortification of seeing more injury done to my lands by the severe rain than they have sustained and twenty years. In several places the fences had been washed down & cattle & hogs in my corn. This is pregnant proof of what little reliance is to be placed on negroes for out of three negro men at my farm, when the rain fell not one of them thought it worth their attention to examine the State of the fences after the rain....

Sunday 11th....I was indisposed in church & after my return home was confined to my bed for seven hours, which infeebled me very much.

Monday 12th....I rode over my farm & inspected my crop, which is exceedingly grassy in several fields. I have about forty acres of pretty corn & it is in good order, the balance say 30 acres, & the cotton is in bad order.

Tuesday 13th....I left home after breakfast on an excursion to the mountains for my health & came by the way of Major Blocker to see & take leave of my Sister but finding on my arrival at his house, that the family had gone to spend the day with Mr. Felix Lake,[40] I followed them & took a dinner with the family. Mr. and Mrs. Lake gave me a most cordial reception. In the afternoon I came up to my plantation.

Wednesday 14th....After breakfast I rode over & inspected my crop in the different fields. The corn is excellent & the cotton has improved very much. It was not as grassy as I was prepared to see & was beginning to bloom generally. On examining my milk cows, I found that they had improved in flesh for the last two weeks. My mules, colts & hogs were in good order....

Thursday 15th....After breakfast I set out on a visit to my father, at whose I arrived at about 12 ocl. considerably fatigued & not finding him at home I remained on the bed, the greater part of the afternoon. I went by the way of Richardson's & saw the crops on the road, which were more indifferent than usual. Both corn & cotton have suffered by excess of rain. There was more grass in my father's crop than I have seen for years. The venerable old gentleman returned in the evening, looking in better health than I have observed for some time....

Friday 16th....About 6 ocl. Judge Butler came over & sat with me until near 11 ocl at which hour I set out for my plantation. It was at this hour somewhat cloudy & not unpleasant to travel. By the time I reached Col. Pickens plantation I became so sick as to be induced to stop, where very unexpectedly I met the Col. & his lady there.

[40] Felix Lake (1811–); 1850 census: $5,000 real estate, 42 slaves.

They gave me a warm & cordial reception & were both kind & attentive. I remained all night not being able to leave the bed until dark. He spoke of his crop as being good & showed me a cotton bowl that was half grown. The crops on the rode are greatly superior to those on the road by Richardson, especially the cotton....

Saturday 17th....I parted with Col. P. & lady after breakfast & returned to my plantation at which I arrived about 10 ocl not feeling as great fatigue as I expected. The plantation & grounds around & in view of the House never looked more interesting. It is one of the prettiest places in the up country & would make a noble residence for a family, to whose tastes a country life was congenial. In the afternoon I rode over my crop. The cotton was rapidly improving but the corn was firing[41] from the recent plowing. Preston arrived in the evening with Hampden, bringing me intelligence that my family were well.

Sunday 18th....about 1 ocl, there fell one of the most gentle yet thoroughly wetting rains, that has fallen this year. It will greatly benefit the corn & almost mature the crop. Preston & Hampden left me after dinner on their return to the Village.

Monday 19th....I left my plantation for the Glenn Spring & arrived in the afternoon at Richard Watts,[42] with whom I remained until the following morning. My old acquaintance & friend, Col. Watts hearing that I was at his brothers, came down & passed the night with me, making himself agreeable by his affability and politeness. My relations gave me a kind greeting & seemed glad to see me....

Tuesday 20th....I set out after breakfast & reached Mrs. Boyd's at 11 ocl. so deadly sick that I was forced instantly to bed. I remained here in great agony until 6 ocl. & then started for the Village on my arrival at which I immediately retired without eating or drinking since breakfast. I observed that the cotton on the yellow rolling & porous land on Saluda river and towards the Village of Laurens was well grown & larger than the cotton on the red lands in the vicinity of Cambridge. It was not however well limbed, & showed few squares or blooms. From my observation of the crops in Edgefield, part of Abbeville, Laurens & Spartanburg, I am persuaded that about 1/4 of the land planted is destitute of cotton, either from the plant not coming up or dying so that there is a stand of cotton only on about ¾ of the land planted. Heavy rain at Mrs. Boyd's, which extended to the Glenn Spring. The roads in very bad condition, being both rough & miry.

Wednesday 21st....I left Laurens after breakfast & reached Mr. Miles at 11 ocl. Here I was detained until Thursday morning by rain.

Thursday 22....I reached the Glenn Spring early in the day & took a cabin, which I did not leave until the following morning seeing only the few friends, who called to

---

[41] Leaves turning yellow. If this happens before the fruit is mature, it indicates nitrogen deficiency.

[42] Richard Watts (1797–) m. Mary Simpson Brooks (1804–1852). Named a son Pickens Butler Watts (*Adv.,* Jan. 11, 1865).

see me, to wit, Col. R. Griffin, Jas. Treadwell Esq.[,] Mr. Jno. Chappell [of Newberry] and young Daniel Smyley. I understand that there are from 50 to 60 boarders at this place and several families in the log cabbins on the road to the Spring....

Friday 23rd....The present Visitors at the Springs constitute rather a mixed crowd and not remarkable for their intelligence or refinement. I have rarely seen so uninteresting a company at a watering place. Judge Harper & his two daughters arrived to dinner & Treadwell & family left us in the afternoon. I have not heard the least news of any description. The crops of corn through the State are represented as being very promising..... I am encouraged to believe that the Water is salutary to me & that I shall derive benefit from its moderate use. It appears to cool & relieve the feverish symptoms of the Stomach.

Saturday 24th....The water is producing a gentle action on my bowels, very greatly to my comfort & relief. They had been for three or four days in a state of considerable irritation & the state of my system required a mild aspirant.

Sunday 25....I heard a sensible sermon from a young man by the name of Wilson of the Presbyterian Church, in the morning. In the afternoon I felt well enough to take a ride & I drove Miss Netty Harper some two or three miles....

Monday 26th....by 11. ocl....I was forced to take my bed in consequence of an attack of headache. These dreadful paroxysms of pain & suffering come on now every two or three days & keep me greatly reduced in strength. I sent a letter home by John Bland, who departed this morning & I am fearful that the writing of that letter last night was the cause of my headache....

Tuesday 27th....I took medicine yesterday & in consequence, feel much better to day. So much so as to be able to read more than usual. Among other articles I read the life of Genl. Charles Lee by Headley.[43] He was a daring, restless, wreckless and ambitious man who was like a fiery spirit getting constantly into difficulties & doing the most extravagant things. I also read a part of the life of Genl. Green[e], whose principles and character formed a perfect contrast to those of Lee. He was brave & honest & just & patriotic, the model of a great commander & a bright example of a virtuous citizen....[T]he house is now fully occupied. Before night it is said there were between 45 & 50 arrivals, both whites & blacks, old & young. The evening was cool & clear. I was in the dancing room for a few minutes & found it crowded with a heterogeneous assemblage of young & old, among whom were members of all the churches, looking with delight at the dancers.

Wednesday 28th....I felt symptoms of headache after breakfast & that lay on the bed for some hours to avoid a paroxysm..... Col. Preston & his lady with several other

---

[43] Charles Lee was an erratic and controversial officer in the Continental Army during the American Revolution. Early in the war he commanded rebel forces in the southern theater. His dismissive view of Washington's ability, and that general's negative opinion of him, stigmatized him in the eyes of most Americans. The biography by T. J. Headley is long forgotten.

Visitors arrived, during the day. His health looks better than I expected to find it from the reports, which had reached me. That of his lady is exceedingly delicate.

Thursday 29th....I had a long conversation with my old friend Col. Preston at my cabbin & found him as in days gone by, intelligent, affable & communicative. It is refreshing to the feelings to meet an old companion after years of separation & find no abatement of friendship. Doct. Winn Smith called to see me at my cabbin & manifested solicitude for my health. I joined Col. Preston on a ride in the afternoon which imparted strength to me.

Friday 30th....I was principally engaged in writing letters, to be sent home by my servant in the morning. Passed a short time very pleasantly at the 9 pins ally in company of several ladies & witnessed a laughable game between Mrs. Preston & Mrs. Robt. Means-

Saturday 31st....I roused my boy about 4 ocl & started him home....I had another attack of headache & did not leave my cabbin from 8 ocl until next day.

August 1, 1847

Sunday 1st....The rain & some indisposition prevented me from going out in the morning & of attending church. My worthy countryman the Revd. Mr. H. Watkins preached a very acceptable sermon in the boarding house both morning & evening. I was confined to my room until the afternoon, when I went up to supper. The entire month of July has been peculiar both on account of cool temperature of the weather and the quantity of rain, which has fallen in all parts of the State if not over the entire Southern section of the Union....

Monday 2....I received a very sweet letter from my dear Wife this morning, which was a great comfort to me. Among other things I have cause of profound [thankfulness?] to God for the entire exemption from pain, which I am allowed to enjoy at this moment & for the symptoms of improving health, which I feel. I am better at this time than I have been for many weeks, and would be tempted to walk up and look at the dancing but for fear of the humidity of the air. The Violin sounds right merrily & the young folk seem gay & frolicksome, a sight always interesting to me. I have no respect for the ascetic old bigot, while I desire to render implicit obedience to the law of God & to do his holy will & pleasure as far as I am capable of ascertaining them –

Tuesday 3rd....I feel more strength to walk & take exercise, than I have done for some weeks. Cicero returned from home, bringing me letters & the pleasing information that all were well....My overseer writes me that my crop of cotton has greatly improved & that the blossoms are very numerous, tho rain had fallen in too great quantities....I was tempted to go into the dancing room for a short time, to witness the performances of the young people in this most delightful & most appropriate of all useful amusements. I here met Mrs. Calhoun,[44] with whom I held some conversation & then retired to my cabbin for the night. After the dance the young men were a little noisy & riotous for some time & prevented me from sleeping –

Wednesday 4....Several families are leaving the spring this morning, some for home & others for Limestone [Springs][45] etc....Col. & Mrs. Preston accompanied me in a ride of some three miles on the road to Edgefield to meet Mrs. Brooks, but not meeting her, we returned to the Spring. The rains in Laurens, Edgefield and Newberry have been very abundant & the freshets in the creeks & small streams very high, washing away bridges, mill dams & causeways. The mail did not arrive last evening in consequence, it is supposed, of bad condition of the roads & loss of bridges by the late rains.

Thursday 5th....There is at present a large crowd at this place, I presume over 150 persons, a portion of whom, have been brought here by a regimental review of cavalry which is to take place to day & tomorrow in the vicinity. I have never been thrown among as many gentlemen, among whom politics either local or general, state or national, were so little discussed. These topics are rarely alluded to & in no instance have they been made the subject of warm or protracted controversy. This is all right at a watering place, where people meet for the improvement of health or the enjoyment of pleasure where exciting subjects should be avoided.

[Next two sentences written vertically near the left edge of the page]

About four o'clock my dear wife & daughter arrived in excellent health, bringing no other than good news from home. How could I forget to record the most interesting occurrence of the day.

Friday 6th....There was a regimental review of cavalry in three miles of the Spring at which most of the visitors were present, together with a considerable concourse of persons from the country. The regiment consisted of six companies, Several of which made a good appearance on the field & performed their marching & wheeling & forming in line exceedingly well. They were commanded by Col. Gest,[46] a striking looking officer & were reviewed by Genl. Wallace & Genl. Gadberry with

[44] Floride Bonneau Calhoun (1792–1866), 1st cousin once removed and wife of John Caldwell Calhoun. They had 10 children. Except during his time as Sec. of War and his 8 vice-presidential years, she lived at Fort Hill, their large plantation in Pendleton (later Pickens) Dist. During his second VP term, under Jackson, she snubbed cabinet wife Margaret "Peggy" Eaton. This caused a rupture in the administration, which helped make Martin Van Buren, not Calhoun, Jackson's successor.

[45] A popular therapeutic resort established in 1835, located in modern Cherokee County. In 1845 Limestone Springs Female High School (now Limestone College) opened there. In 1840 the spring was the site of an attempted settlement of the feud between PSB and Lewis Wigfall. See introduction.

[46] William Henry Gist (1907–1874), large Union Dist. planter. SC House 1840–1843; Senate 1844–1855. As governor 1858–1860, he initiated the state's secession.

their respective staffs. At night there was a large concourse of persons at the Spring from 200 to 250 (I presume) among whom there is at every meal, a scramble for seats, many having to wait for the second table –

Saturday 7th....I heard through Miss Parker from Edgefield, who reports unfavourably in regard to the rail road from that place to Aiken. The amount of subscriptions on Munday last disappointed the friends of the enterprise & rendered its success somewhat doubtful.

Sunday 8th....There was preaching in the vicinity & also in the boarding house but I felt too indisposed to attend either. I reposed on the bed the greater part of the day on account of a feeling of debility. I heard from home through Thos. Bacon, & that all were well. Judge Harper has been in a perilous condition for two days but is reported to be better at 9 ocl. P.M.

Monday 9th....About 2 ocl. we left the Glenn Spring, having bid farewell to our friends, & at the crossroad, Mrs. Brooks & I parted, She taking the road homeward & I the road to Spartanburgh Courthouse. I went by the Ceader Spring, to enjoy a draft of that bold & delightful fountain, which delayed my arrival in the Village for half an hour & caused me to be caught in a shower of rain, that began to fall a few minutes before I reached the tavern. I stopped at Walker's,[47] a good house with a rough landlord.

Tuesday 10th....I left Walker's after breakfast on my way to Limestone & was exposed to several light showers, without getting at all wet. I reached Limestone at 1 ocl. & stopped at a house, kept by a venerable old gentleman by the name of Perry, Just in time to escape a storm of rain & wind, that prevailed for several hours. I thought of my dear Wife & daughter with great concern, fearing that they might be exposed to the peltings of so pitiless a storm. In the afternoon Governor David Johnson called at the tavern & pressingly invited me to go & stay with him. I accepted his invitation & rode to his house about sunset, where I met Col. Dawkins & his lady, with whom I passed my time most pleasantly. At night several gentlemen called & we enjoyed a game of whist[48] until 10 ocl. The Governor lives in a handsome & genteel style & he dispenses a courteous & liberal hospitality, that seems quite in fine keeping with his generous & kind nature and that imparts a feeling of contentness & gratification to his guests. I do not recollect ever to have passed a more agreeable night in social intercourse & to have felt more at ease. He is an excellent gentleman & so esteemed by the whole State. The [L]imestone establishment is now the property of a Doct. [Thomas] Curtis, a minister of the Baptist church who purchased it for $10.000 for the purpose of establishing a female

[47] Rev. Newton Pinckney Walker bought a hotel near Cedar Springs, south of Spartanburg, in the early 1840s. After renovating it, in 1849 he opened a school for the deaf and dumb there. It became the SC School for the Deaf and Blind, whose main building is Walker Hall (*Adv.*, Jan. 31, 1849).

[48] A trick-taking card game, later to evolve into contract bridge.

seminary, which is at this time in successful operation, numbering over 100 pupils under his charge. It is a popular institution & enjoys the entire confidence of the Baptist denomination of Christians. Governor Johnson represents him as a gentleman of eminent piety, free from sectarian bigottry, liberal in his views & doctrines and well qualified to conduct such an establishment.

Wednesday 11th....About 8 ocl. I left my excellent friend the Governor for Wilson Spring in No. Carolina & after passing Broad river on a good bridge & stopping to rest my horses on the road & to partake of a most excellent dinner put up without my Knowledge by the Governor, I reached Wilsons about 4 ocl. I found him to be just such a man as he had been represented, unsocial & unaccommodating, a churl without manners, intelligence or breeding wanting visitors in order to make money out of them & yet not kindness enough in his nature to do any thing for their comfort or accommodation. For the night I took a room, with a young gentleman by the name of Lewis from Newberry District. I had a good bed but the room was comfortless and dirty in many respects. Not more than 7 or 8 persons at this Spring & they of the second order of society....

Tuesday 12th....After breakfast I took the liberty to look over the old gentleman's premises & to inspect his sleeping apartments, when I found one, empty, which was both comfortable & roomy and well protected by a shade trees. Without any leave or ceremony, I ordered my man Cicero to take possession of it & to transfer my baggage to it without delay, to which I shortly repaired & where I am now comfortably seated, making this entry at 12 ocl. Not a word has been said or question asked in regard to my removal. In the afternoon I rode about 2 miles on the Yorkville road to see the celebrated Kings mountain. From an old field near the road I had a good view of the entire country in the neighbourhood of the mountain which consists of a range of hills or knobs, running apparently from No. West to So. East, being four in number and considerably elevated above the adjacent land. The centre knob (supposed to be Kings mountain) is the largest & highest & resembles a huge castle, consisting of a centre building & two wings of less size & elevation than the centre. This mountain presented a pretty & interesting appearance, independent of its patriotic associations, which imparted to me its chief value. The road from the Spring to the old field is pretty good & offers a pleasant ride either in the morning or afternoon.

Friday 13th....After breakfast I rode to the little Village of Shelby, distant two miles, for the purpose of depositing some letters in the Post office. I was much disappointed on learning that the stage had departed for Spartanburgh early this morning & that my letters could not leave the Village before tuesday next, which will delay their arrival for some 5 or 6 days. Shelby or Shelbyville is a neat little Village & is the County town of a new county, called Cleveland which was established a few years since by the Legislature, out of portions of territory, taken from the adjoining counties Lincoln & Rutherford. We had at dinner a party on a visit of pleasure to the Spring, Doct. Jones & family & Doct. Ervin & family of Greenville So. Ca. I had an attack of headache after dinner & suffered a good deal of pain.

Saturday 14th....In passing from Spartanburg to this place, I found the country rather poor, & undulating as far as Broad river & the road rough and neglected, tho passable. I observed small fields of cotton along the entire way & some small portions, looking pretty well. The corn was good except . . . where it has suffered by rain & the want of work. I crossed the Broad river on Ellis Bridge, which is a well constructed & safe conveyance over the stream. On this [east] side of the bridge I took the Lincolnton road, which runs for 12 miles over a high & level range & through very poor land, on which there are no signs of improvement but on the contrary the farm houses seem to be neglected & going to decay. I saw on this road for the first time, what is called a bee palace. It is a regular, constructed house, ingeniously divided into apartments in which you may see the bees in all stages of their existence in their various employments and making honey. I was indisposed all day & confined to the bed the greater portion, tho not suffering much pain....There is a rumour in the papers that Genl. Scott has taken the City of Mexico with small loss of his troops. I trust the report may be true, tho I doubt it for I think it improbable, according to previous accounts.

Sunday 15th....[T]here was preaching at Shelby in the babtist church, but I was afraid to risk the Sun....

Monday 16th....I read yesterday a morning service of our Church & two sermons, delivered to the students at Chappel Hill University. To day I have read a third & written & sent a letter to my Son Preston.

Tuesday 17th....I left Wilson's Spring after breakfast & stopped at the little Village of Shelby to attend a meeting of the inhabitants of the County on the subject of the Columbia & Charleston Rail road— The meeting was addressed by the Honble Jas. A. Black of So. Ca. in a sensible & argumentative speech, which occupied ¾ of an hour in the delivery & which produced a favourable state of feeling towards the road. In the afternoon I traveled as far as Mrs. Blanton's on the road to Rutherford, where I remained for the night. A pretty good house-- –

Wednesday 18th....After an early breakfast I left Mrs. B. & stopped for dinner at a Mr. Wallace, a clean & comfortable house & in the afternoon came to Mr. Harris at the foot of the Blue ridge, where I met a large party of travellers. This is a good house –

Thursday 19th....I took my departure for Deavors Spring[49] after breakfast & commenced the accent of the mountain, the passage over which I found to be very interesting from the various attractive objects of sight on the road. The most interesting object was two high mountains to the So. West of the road, which are united to-

[49] In 1830 Robert Henry and his son-in-law Reuben Deaver began erecting a hotel at what became known as Deaver's Sulphur Springs, near Asheville. By the 1840s it had a ballroom, bowling alleys, shuffleboard, and other amenities.

gether near their summits by solid rock & between which there is a regularly cut passway for the water as smooth and regular as if executed by art. About the middle of the passway a stream of water was flowing down the mountain in the form of a straight white line, which appeared to rise from the very summit of the mountain. The two mountains were from 600 to 700 feet high covered with thick forest trees to within from 40 to 50 feet of the summit & crowned with a bald & a solid mass of granite, which seemed covered with the scars & marks of the tempests & storms of ages – what was peculiarly novel & striking to me, was the issuing of [vapor?] from the very crevices of the solid rock, which floated around and crowned the highest points and all the varied forms of the most fitful fancy. Another rock on the side of the road seemed to be sweating water. The gap through the mountain at this place is called the hickory nut gap & passes for some 10 or 15 miles up one branch of the broad river which is crossed some eight or 10 times before you reach the ridge or highest elevation.[50] The river, where you first approach it, is a considerable stream but continues to get less until it becomes a branch & finally you see its source in a field near the top of the ridge. The scenery is constantly varying in appearance & interesting, at one time presenting the river, with a belt of level land on its borders, with small patches of corn & a human habitation of very humble pretensions, with their patches of cabbage & other vegetables & a few domestic animals. At another time the mountains run down & jut to the water's edge, presenting high & stony cliffs on each side, on which the growth & vegetation & forest trees is rather stunted. Then the road will wind up the side of the hill, leaving the river some 40 or 50 feet below you & forming rich dells of luxuriant growth and trees & shade, where the sun does not send a ray of his refreshing light during the 24 hours. After passing the ridge you have an extensive view of mountains to the North, which rise above in the form of an amphitheater & spread before you in various forms. The descent from the mountain is easy & safe & not more than two miles long. The people living on the road from Rutherford to Asheville are generally poor & exhibit no improvement or enterprise. They live in huts, many of which do not appear to have felt the hand of repair for years – At 5 ocl I reached Col. Deavors by Way of the free bridge & obtained a very convenient & comfortable room with a fire place. The company varying from 50 to 75 among whom I found my old friend Judge Oneal, Lady & daughter and several other acquaintances –

Friday 20th....The company at this place are highly respectable in character & in manners courteous & sociable. The Water is like that of Wilson Spring but not nearly so highly mineral. It is pleasant to the taste. The house seems well managed & the Landlord polite & accommodating. The table is well supplied with the various meats & vegitables, which the Country affords & the cooking is not objectionable.

---

[50] Today this area is between Lake Lure and Bat Cave, with Chimney Rock State Park mid-way.

Saturday 21....At 10 ocl. most of the Visitors at this Spring left for Asheville to attend a meeting of the people on the subject of the Columbia & Greenville rail road. Judge Oneal addressed the meeting in a speech of some length, in which he laboured to show the advantages of the road to the people of this section of the Country & the interest they had in taking stock in the enterprise, in which he was quite successful but I am not prepared to say what effect was produced on the minds of these cautious mountaineers....

Sunday 22....A Methodist camp meeting is being held within 3 miles of this place but my health is too infirm to venture to set in the open air. Camp meetings are at best but dull & profit less places, where I fear the cause of God is not now promoted, altho the object is to promote religion. As a means for the promotion of piety they have worn out & become useless.

Monday 23rd. Still cloudy in the morning & the tops of the mountains covered with vapour. The weather is so uncertain as to render it unsafe to take exercise either in the morning or evening. I rode in the afternoon to the top of the mountain, called Mount Yeadon, so called in compliment to Mr. R. Yeadon[51] of Charleston. The ascent is pretty steep but not difficult & when you reach the summit, the view of the mountains and the surrounding country is picturesque & interesting. We visited it at a favourable time & saw the mountains under all the aspects, which sunshine & shade, rain & shifting clouds could impart to the prospect & they all apparent at the same time in different parts of the mountains. The clouds were running from North West to South East & while we were on the summit, passed at least two thirds round the horizon and diversifying the view as they passed. Alternate sunshine & showers prevailed all around us for an hour, during which, dark and heavy clouds would form, rest for a moment upon the top of some adjacent cliff like a dark pall & then pass away, & making room either for a bright gleam of sunshine or a beautiful & gorgeous rainbow or of shade in interesting contrast with other portions of the mountains, while we were favoured on the mount & enjoyed the scene without a drop of rain – We returned to the boarding house about sunset ....

Tuesday 24th. We were confined to the house the whole day [by rain].

Wednesday 25....The day passed away without a ray of Sunshine. In the afternoon I took a short ride for exercise notwithstanding the humid state of the atmosphere. I found the temperature of the weather quite cool. Several arrivals to day.

Thursday 26th....I rode both morning & evening and felt better than usual. There were a number of arrivals at the Spring & some departures, Col. Griffin among the latter –

Friday 27th....At 1 ocl. I was attacked with violent headache & confined to my bed until Saturday morning. I suffered much agony for about six hours. I had been free

[51] Richard Yeadon (1812–1870), lawyer, ed. of the Charleston *Courier* 1833–1844. A unionist and supporter of industry and internal improvements.

from pain for the last ten or twelve days and I am totally at a loss to account for this attack or to trace it to any cause....

Saturday 28th. [afternoon] thundershowers in various directions & sometimes while the sun was shining, forming rainbows in the direction of the East – I left Col. Deavor's after breakfast & passed up the West side of the Frenchbroad River until I passed Mills river, soon after which I crossed the Frenchbroad & arrived at the little Village of Henderson[ville] about 5 ocl, stopping at Mr. Ripley where I met Mr. Treadwell & Arthur with their families from Columbia – while I was there Col. Preston & lady passed by & seeing me, stopped & shook hands &C &C. On the road, which I traveled to day I saw little to interest me until I approached Mills river, on & near which I saw a large field of fine, rich bottom land. The valley of the French broad was still wider & furnished some rich fields of corn, small grain & meadow grass of great value. I presume the bottom land would sell for $15 or 20 pr. acre – The road would have been good but for the rain, which had fallen last night & which rendered it exceedingly muddy. I must not forget to mention that Col. Deavors, is a pleasant place to spend a few weeks, as the boarders are favoured with a good rooms, good table, excellent order, delightful climate & an obliging landlord at a moderate price –

Saturday 29th. Clear & mild. I attended church & heard a sensible sermon from Mr. Pinckney on the subject of missions. After sermon I accepted an invitation & dined with Judge King[52] by whom & his lady I was most Kindly & hospitably entertained. Col. Preston & his lady were on a visit to the Judge & his family & contributed much to the social enjoyments of the day. I also called in the afternoon with Col. Preston at the Mountain house to see Mr. Walker & E. Brown, who were there on a short excursion for health.

Monday 30th....I set out after breakfast for Col. Hagoods[53] at Caesar's head, which I reached about 5 ocl in the afternoon after a tedious days ride up the mountain & over a miserably poor country. I have rarely seen as poor houses & as much destitution as I found on this road. A little corn, potatoes & cabbages constituted the whole crop, both for sale & consumption, which these mountaineers cultivate. At night we had a large & jolly company at the Cols. – not less than from 30 to 40 persons –

Tuesday 31st....I passed the day in looking at the different points of view from this mountain height, many of which were really grand and imposing & none without its peculiar beauty & interest. I first in the morning walked to a point commanding a view of the Valley, which presented about 7 ocl a most picturesque & pleasing

---

[52] Mitchell King (1783–1862), Scots-born prof. at Col. of Charleston, lawyer, and judge. He had one of the largest private libraries in the South, and a summer home in Flat Rock NC.

[53] Benjamin Hagood owned c. 500 acres around Caesar's Head in upper Greenville District. In 1860 he would build a hotel there.

sight – in consequence of the great height of the mountain the valley below, altho consisting of high hills & considerable mountains, with glens & narrow valleys running between, looks like an immence plain stretched out at your feet of green verdure & rich forest growth, with small farms interspersed along the winding streams of water and in the coves of the mountains & hills. At the hour above mentioned the sun was shining on this immense plain & exhibiting various contrasts of light & shade & over all the farms, the vapour had collected & settled, presenting the appearance of lakes in the bosom of this great expanse of forest land. It was a lovely sight. After breakfast I visited Caesar's head & enjoyed the magnificent view from that point of at least one half of the horyson. The view is more remarkable for its extent & grandeur than for the variety of objects. The table rock is in full view, at the distance of 5 or 6 miles & seems to present her time worn & furrowed front, to attest the power & majesty of its mighty creator & and inspire the beholder with feelings of his own impotency & littleness. The day was pleasantly passed in riding to other points of less interest but still very beautiful. The old Col. is a sort of lyon of the Mountains & almost as great a curiosity in his way as Caesar's head.

September 1. 1847.

Wednesday 1....Again at 7 ocl. I went out to view the Valley below, which presented an entirely different appearance from the one of yesterday morning. The entire Valley was at this time covered with white vapour, which imparted to it the appearance of a wide spread sea, with here & there a mountain top peeping above the clouds & resembling islands in the Ocean. While I stood & gazed on this sublime & magnificent sight, I witnessed the clouds roll up like a scroll & pass away like a thing of nothing. Nothing in the way of mountain scenery can surpass Caesar's head & its adjuncts in some of its grandest features. Water & Villages or Towns are wanted to complete the view, in these it is greatly deficient. I left Col. Hagood's after breakfast & reached Greenville in the afternoon very much indisposed & was forced to take a bed. After tea my son Preston came down to the hotel & sat with me until after 9 ocl. I recd. a letter from my dear Wife, informing me that all were well for which I desire to return thanks to the father of all mercies.

Thursday 2. I was exceedingly indisposed this morning, notwithstanding I paid a visit to my much esteemed relative [John] Wesley Brooks & his family. I found them well & as usual glad to see me. My good cousin Mrs. Brooks[54] seeing me suffering from cough, made a mustard plaster for my chest which I applied & from which I derived great benefit. From this place I went to Genl. [Waddy] T[h]ompson's where I was overwhelmed by kindness both by the Genl. & my estimable cousin Mrs. [Emmala] Thompson. I dined here & passed a few delightful hours in social conversation. In the afternoon the Genl. went with me to pay a visit to Doct. [William] Butler & family, whom I found in good health. A very heavy

[54] Malissa Duncan (1810–1872) was J. W. Brooks' second wife.

rain fell while we were at the Docts. after which we returned & I went to the hotel altho my kind relations pressed me to stay with them. As I was very feeble I retired to my room at an early hour. The hotel was crowded & among the Visitors were Col. Pickens & family, Arthur Simkins & family, Jas. Lynch & family, Col. Yeadon & many more, many of whom I did not Know. The papers report the fact that Genl. Scott had marched upon the city of Mexico –

Friday 3rd. Cloudy & warm. After breakfast I took my departure for Glenn Spring & had the company of my son Preston for a few miles....I reached Spartanburg in the afternoon & took quarters at the Walker house, which was nearly full of visitors & travelers. No late intelligence from Mexico.

Saturday 4th....I reached the Glenn Spring at 11 ocl, at which place there was a company of 40 to 50 persons, among whom were several of my neighbors, Mr. & Mrs. Lipscomb, Mrs. Glover, Mrs. Baron & some others – in the afternoon I obtained a very comfortable cabin, where I have every thing, necessary to my comfortable accommodation....

Sunday 5....I started Cicero home at day light this morning with a letter to his Mistress. We had no preaching or other religious services & I passed the greater part of the day in my room.

Monday 6th. Clear & warm day & the first for many, which was without rain. I read a portion of the day, played a few games of whist with a party of grave & moral gentlemen and took a ride in the afternoon for exercise not neglecting the use of the mineral water....

Tuesday 7th....I passed the day as usual in reading, writing etc. & drinking water –

....

Thursday 9th....I met most unexpectedly at table this morning Ch[arle]s Cross & his wife [Cornelia Bird], to whom I had not spoken or scarcely seen in five years[55] – about dark my man Kitt arrived from home, bringing a letter from my Wife & another from my overseer. All well & no news –

Friday 10th....The temperature of the air and the rustling of the wind reminds us of the approach of Autumn & I trust this may be the harbinger of clear weather. There have not been more than four or five days without rain in the last two months and in fact I think it doubtful whether there has been one totally free from rain in the entire state. I learned this morning by a paper from the stage that Mr. Saml. Gillison[56] died at Spartanburg yesterday afternoon....I have not felt as well for many

[55] WB had been very upset about their marriage, thinking it both socially and financially unfortunate for his niece. His silence here likely indicates that his view had not changed, but it could mean that time and the couple's circumstances had softened his opposition somewhat.

[56] Samuel Gillison (1790–1847) m. Elizabeth Ann Smith of Edgefield. His relationship to the Gillison family that Mary Simpson Bird married into is not known.

months –

Saturday 11th....The papers by the mail this afternoon give the intelligence that Genl. Scott had reached the City of Mexico & had two engagements with the enemy the first with Genl. Valencia & the other with Santa Anna in both of which the Mexicans were routed without much loss on our part. Santa Anna had asked for an armistice & had called a meeting of Congress to confer with Mr. Trist[57] the American Envoy –

Sunday 12th....Our company here are reduced to something like forty or fifty persons. Preston arrived in the Stage yesterday afternoon from Greenville on his way to Fairfield.

Monday 13th....After breakfast I took my departure for home, & arrived at Laurens about five ocl in the afternoon after encountering a good deal of anxiety & fatigue on account of my poor old horse Vidor, refusing to draw, owing to the inflamed state of his breast. I have owned him from 5 to 6 years & he never failed me before either in harness or under the saddle but his breast was so inflamed & sore, occasioned by a cancerous wart, that he could not draw. There never was a more spirited or generous animal —

Tuesday 14th....I traded off my old & faithful horse for a young bay horse, aged 5 years & of good qualities & left the tavern of Mr. Simmons for my plantation at 8 ocl. When I arrived at Genl. [John?] Gillians, he placed in my hands an extra of the Edgefield Advertiser, giving an account of two bloody battles between the troops under Genl. Scott & the Mexicans, in which Col. P. M. Butler & [2nd Lt.] David Adams[58] of this District were killed & also Private [Benjamin] Tillman of the 96 boys – The Palmetto regiment out of 272 men, lost 137 and killed & wounded.

[In another hand, with pencil.] W. B. B. wounded!

I reached the plantation about sunset & met only our son Hampden, Mrs. Brooks being prevented by the dreadful intelligence from Mexico from leaving home. My negroes generally well.

Wednesday 15th....After breakfast I rode over my crop in a hasty way & saw that the corn is good, much of it excellent & the cotton very large & luxuriant in weed but I could form no satisfactory opinion in regard to the product. At half past 9 ocl. I started for the Village & reached home at 2 ocl. where I found all well. Several friends & neighbors called to see me. About night we received further intelligence from the army & among other matters, that our dear Son Whitfield was dangerous-

---

[57] Nicholas Trist (1800–1874) was confidential commissioner to Mexico sent to negotiate for a suspension of hostilities. Gen. Scott contested his authority and he made little progress. Ignoring an order to come home, he continued talks and signed the Treaty of Guadalupe Hidalgo, Feb. 2, 1848. Despite the cloud over his head, the U.S. Senate ratified the treaty on March 10.

[58] A close friend of Whitfield Butler Brooks.

ly wounded. I pray that God in his infinite mercy & goodness may spare his life & restore him to the arms of his family. May he avert from my house the heavy calamity, which the death of this dear child would bring upon it.

Thursday 16th....I rode to the Village & recd. the papers by the mail, but they contained no further intelligence of a private nature. I then called upon Mrs. P. M. Butler & and family & read to her a letter from Genl. Worth to Judge Butler, in which he pays a high & most flattering compliment to Col. Butler for his gallantry & noble bearing on the field of battle – the death of my much valued friend was a glorious one, being in the service of his Country & in the very arms of victory. I mourn his loss but I would not reverse his fate. It was a favorite idea among the ancients, that it was sweet to die for one's Country, how infinitely enhanced must this feeling become, to fall amidst the shouts of Victory & triumph – peace to his noble & generous spirit. I have also to mourn the death of the spirited & Gallant & true & honourable & gifted young David Adams, who fell, leading the 96 boys to victory & glory.[59] I know him well & loved him as a Son. My father came out to see me. His health is good.

Friday 17th....My father left us after breakfast & I then went to the Village & caused a meeting of a few friends, to arrange the proceedings of a public meeting, to be held on Monday next in relation to the two great battles with the Mexicans near the City of Mexico & with the view of paying some tribute of respect to the lamented dead. A meeting is to be held on Monday –

[written vertically at left margin: Shortly after this visit of my father, his health began to fail, & I fear it was the last visit that he will be able to pay us. He is now (Feby 1848) in very feeble health.]

I rode over my crop at the farm. The corn is very good considering the wet year & my inability to cultivate it properly, owing to the sickness & discharge of my overseer [Samuel? Lowery] & some sickness among my negroes – The cotton is only tolerable owing to the grass & rain. My cattle looked to be in good order, also the horses, the negroes are in good health & I have abundant cause to praise God for his great blessings & privileges, conferred upon me & my family. Our only source of affliction is the perilous condition of our dear child in a distant & hostile Country.

Saturday 18th....I rode to the Village in the morning but could obtain no further information from the army in Mexico & to my farm in the afternoon.

Sunday 19th....In consequence of the absence of our minister Mr. Walker, we attended preaching in the Babtist church & heard a sensible but tedious sermon by the Revd. Mr. Johnson from the text "Lord revive thy work in the midst of the years" etc.

Monday 20th....We received no intelligence from Mexico by the mail of this morning. We are still left in great uncertainty & anxiety in regard to the [illegible] as the

[59] In PSB's place while he was on leave recruiting volunteers.

realization of our worst fears – A public meeting was held in the Courthouse to pay a suitable tribute of respect to the memory of Col. Butler & others, who fell in the battle of Churubusco on the 20 of Augt. near the gates of the City of Mexico. Mr. Wardlaw was called to the chair, who opened the meeting with much feeling in an address, characterized by appropriate thoughts & generous sentiments. Col. Carroll then addressed the meeting with pathos & eloquence, which brought tears to all quarters of the house & submitted a series of resolutions, all of which were adopted with much solemnity. Judge Butler, Col. Carroll & Major Blocker & family dined with us. I passed a bad night, having suffered great pain in the head from 11 ocl until morning, which deprived me of sleep & produced a good deal of debility.

Tuesday 21. I was so indisposed that I did not rise until 9 ocl altho the morning was inviting by its clearness & brightness. The weather for the last week has been delightful ....

Wednesday 22....Preston, his Wife & child returned in the stage yesterday & our Son James having awaited his arrival, we have now under our roof all our children except our dear wounded boy, who lies in Mexico, without the comfort or assistance, which every member of his family would desire to render him. Poor fellow, I fear his fate is a hard one, I pray God in mercy to alleviate it by mitigating his suffering & sparing his life. I sowed yesterday a lot of rye & wheat for my cows & calves & am preparing another today.

....

Saturday 25....No intelligence by the mail from the army.

Sunday 26th....The Revd. Mr. Reed preached in the Episcopal church to an attentive & delighted auditory. This gentleman is always interesting in the pulpit.

Monday 27th....I went to the Village but could learn nothing from the army. At 12 ocl the stockholders of the rail road . . .[held a?] meeting in the Courthouse for the purpose of organizing the company. I was called to the chair & Geo. Addison appointed Sec.t. After the discussion & passage of several resolutions, introduced by Mr. Griffin, the stockholders went into an election of a President & 12 directors, which resulted in making N. L. Griffin President & John Lipscomb etc. etc. directors, myself among the number....

Tuesday 28th....I finished sowing a second lot of a small grain for pasturage –

Wednesday 29th....I commenced to gather corn at the Youngblood place & find that the product is good, exceeding my expectation. The peas are very promising –

Thursday 30th....By mail of this morning our Son Preston received an order to return to his command in Mexico, which he greeted with undisguised rapture. He had suffered great mortification at being ordered to remain on the recruiting service. We recd. rumours of the recommencement of hostilities in Mexico –

October 1. 1847.

Friday 1. This was as lovely as day as ever ushered and a new month....Our Son Preston took leave of us at 12 ocl & set out for Aiken on his return to Mexico – this is a new source of affliction to us all & augments our anxiety & unhappiness occasioned by the wounded condition of our Son Whitfield & the uncertainty of his fate – Doct. Laborde & two of his Sons also to leave us on their return to Columbia. In the afternoon we received confirmation of the truth that hostilities had recommenced between the American army & Mexicans before the city of Mexico & of severe loss in killed & wounded on both sides – Genl. Scott had succeeded in taking possession of the city & Santa Anna had retreated to Guadalupe. The same account furnishes intelligence of the death of Genls. Worth & Smith, which I trust, may prove to be untrue & also of a severe loss in the army of Genl. Scott.

Saturday 2nd....The papers confirm the statement in regard to the recommencement of hostilities & of Genl. Scotts possession of the city of Mexico. I was engaged in gathering pea vines & a small lot of corn near the stable –

Sunday 3....The Revd. Mr. Reed preached in the Episc. Church & the Revd. Mr. Walker administered the sacrament in a very solemn & impressive manner. I had a severe attack of dispepsia or indigestion during the performance of the divine service, which greatly annoyed me without much pain however....

Monday 4th. This was another clear & delicious morning....The Court of Common Pleas commenced its fall Session this morning, Judge ONeal on the bench – I employed an overseer at my farm for the balance of the year at $40. His name is Henry Coleman, who came recommended to me by Mr. A[vory] Bland.

Tuesday 5th....I am preparing to leave for the Glenn Spring, where I propose to spend a week. I reached my plantation at 1 ocl and in the afternoon I rode over my cotton crop which I found more inferior than I expected. The stalk is even too large & luxuriant but is badly bolled. The boll worm has done great injury to my crop as I saw thousands of imperfect & diseased bolls in every field. Many of the forms had fallen off in consequence of the dry weather, which prevailed in September. I cannot make more than two thirds of a crop. The corn crop is good. There were a few cases of chill & fever among my negroes.

Wednesday 6th....I left my plantation at an early hour & arrived at Laurens Ct. House about dark, somewhat fatigued by the day's travel....

Thursday 7th....I left Laurens at half after seven ocl on my way to Glenn Spring, which I reached at 4 ocl. The company at this place have principally disbursed to their respective homes, leaving only six persons at the time of my arrival, 5 young men & 1 lady. I selected a comfortable room with fire place in the boarding house, where I have every convenience, necessary to comfort. Doct. Moor[60] called to see

---

[60] Dr. Maurice Augustus Moore (1791–1871), Union Dist. planter and leader of a group of 15 investors that bought Glenn Springs from John Glenn about 1837. He lived at

me.

Friday 8th....The entire place has an air of loveliness, produced by the marked contrast exhibited between its present condition & that which existed when I was here in the Summer. There were then over 200 persons of all ages & sexes, who filled every room & cabin belonging to the establishment & among whom could be heard at all hours of the day, the earnest conversations or the thoughtless chit chat, the joyous laugh & the merry whistle, interspersed with the notes of the Piano, or violin or clarinet or french horn. All was life & animation at that time, now silence prevails over the entire establishment....

Saturday 9th....I am now in better health & more exempt from pain than I have been for a length of time. The water is both soothing & salutary & I trust in a week that I may leave the Spring for home with renovated health. At 3 ocl. Judge [John Smyth] Richardson arrived from Spartanburgh, where he had been holding the Court of Common Pleas. He shows age & infirmity and has greatly declined since I last saw him. He is evidently too old & infirm to discharge the duties of a Circuit Judge & should not hesitate to resign & let some active young man with a vigerous & improving mind take his place. To receive a salary when not capable of discharging the duties of the station office is a species of moral dishonesty at which a just & sensitive mind would revolt. How often does the love of money, cause men to compromise their true dignity of character & forfeit the good opinion and respect of their fellow citizens. It can only be explained upon the principle that age & and averice go together.

Sunday 10th. Very cold morning . . . – the afternoon temperate & delightful. I was a little indisposed after dinner by eating some rich custard & took a ride as far [as] Doct. Smith's to get rid of my bad feelings. The [*his*] lady was exceedingly courteous and affable with whom I remained some twenty minutes in conversation. Her garden was gay with flowers of various kinds but the rose, the daliah & the China aster predominated.

Monday 11th....I wrote three letters to day & read several pages in Combe's[61] book on digestion & diet, a very fascinating production & one which imparts much information in regard to our physical structure & constitution. In the afternoon I walked to the Spring & thence took a short ride, which gave me a good appetite for supper, of which I partook sparingly.

Tuesday 12th....I feel daily improving in health & strength. The water produces the most salutary effect....I paid an agreeable visit to the venerable Mrs. Nott & her

---

the springs from that time. His wife Sophenista Nott was a daughter of Judge Abraham Nott (1768–1830) of Union District, a Congressman 1799–1801, Circuit Court Judge, and trustee of the SC College.

[61] Dr. Andrew Combe, consulting physician to Leopold, King of the Belgians, was author of *The Physiology of Digestion, Considered with Relation to the Principles of Dietetics,* which went through many editions in the 19th century.

daughter Mrs. Moore, whom I found in health & fine spirits. Doct. Moore was absent.

Wednesday 13th....Nothing has transpired to break the dull, monotonous routine of this place for the last three days – my time is passed in reading, writing exercising on foot & on horseback, eating & sleeping, having little or no conversation, except at meals, where I meet the Landlord & three young men, with whom I carry on for a few minutes a light conversation. The daily improvement of my health enables me to bear this state of solitude with patience....The mail arrived this afternoon bringing papers from Charleston & Columbia but they contain no intelligence from Mexico nor news of any interest except the decline in the price of cotton. I read in the Mercury a most touching & affectionate letter from Genl. J[ames?] Hamilton to Judge Butler on the subject of the death of the gallant Col. Butler in Mexico....

....

Friday 15th....I set out at an early hour on my return home & passing through Laurens Village I arrived at Bowens about sunset much less fatigued than I apprehended....At Laurens I heard of the death of Judge [William] Harper at his residence. I also learned that Judge Richardson was indisposed & unable to hold the Court at Laurens for more than two days –

Saturday 16th....I left Bowens at an early hour, passed through old Cambridge & reached my plantation about 2 ocl where I found all in pretty good health. Mrs. Brooks & Ellen & Hampden arrived about 5 ocl from the Village, bringing papers & letters but no late intelligence from Mexico.

....

Monday 18th....After breakfast I rode to Freeman Martin's to attend the sale of the land of his father's estate, where I met some 20 or 30 of the neighbours. The tract was purchased by Col. R[ichard] Griffin at a fraction below $10 per acre, portions of which he afterwards sold at the same price to [James] Creswell & [Wash?] Holloway. In the afternoon I rode over my crop. The cotton was rather better than it appeared to be on my way to the Glenn Spring two weeks before & was much more mature than I expected. The weather has been so dry that my small grain for pastures has not come up & I fear it will be of no account. I have had erected a framed (negro) house with two apartments, a new framed corn crib with sheds on each Side[,] a new screw & frame & also repaired my negroe houses & stables.

Tuesday 19th....I rode to Col. Griffin's but did not find him at home. In the afternoon I received a note from him, asking me to meet him on the land, which he had purchased the day before, which I did & we agreed upon the price & also a dividing line of something like 100 acres, which I consented to take from the original tract....

Wednesday 20th....The light frosts & dry weather have caused a great change in the appearance of vigitation within the last four days....At one o'clock we set out for home & arrived at Sunset, where we were gratified with the intelligence that our friends & neighbours were well. Col. Carroll & lady called to see us.

Thursday 21....The papers this morning contain further intelligence in regard to the capture of the City of Mexico by Gen. Scott & they also convey the melancholy tidings of the death of my nephew William Blocker.[62] He fell in one of the engagements at the gates of the City, while acting as first Sergeant of the company of 96 boys. He was frank & fearless, noble & generous in his nature, but right & independent in his conduct, just & manly in his intercourse with men & as true a friend has ever professed a sentiment. I mourn his death as for my Son. The noblest spirits of the company have been killed & wounded.

Friday 22....A public meeting was held in the Village to express the sentiments, occasioned by the recent news from the seat of war & to pay some tribute of respect to Col. Dickerson, Lieutenant John Moragne,[63] Wm. Blocker & others, who fell in the late battles before the City of Mexico.

Saturday 23rd....I rode to the Village & gave my vote on a question, submitted to the citizens by the town council, whether licenses to retail shall be granted within the corporate limits of the Town. I then went with Mrs. B & Ellen to pay a visit of condolence to my sister Mrs.[Nancy] Blocker & the family. I found them well but in great affliction on account of the death of Wm. who was very dear to his family for his many virtues & dutiful attention to his parents.

Sunday 24th....The Revd. Mr. Reed preached in the Epis. church in the place of Mr. Walker, who is absent at present. I have been informed that on the question, submitted by the town council of. "licence or no licence" there was a tye vote, being 41 on each side....

Monday 25th....My hands are employed in removing the house from the Youngblood place,[64] to the new settlement.[65] No news by the mail except the fall in the price of cotton, which is now as low as $8 1/2 per 100. lb.

Tuesday 26th....My oxen ran away with the cart & my boy Sam was greatly injured by jumping off & the cart running over him. The waggons arrived from Roselands with 20 bales of cotton on their way to Market.

Wednesday 27th....I set out for Hamburg with Mrs. Brooks & Ellen about 10 ocl. to purchase groceries &C. Arrived about 4 ocl. We took lodgings at Mr. Ketchum's, who keeps a clean & comfortable house. His rooms & beds are not inferior in furniture to those of the Augusta hotels & his prices more moderate.

Thursday 28th....My waggons arrived with 20 bales of cotton, which I deposited in the Ware house without offering them for sale. I purchased a large bill of groceries & dispatched my waggons about 1 ocl. I then went to Augusta to join Mrs. Brooks & Ellen, who had passed over in the morning for the purpose of shopping. We

[62] William Butler Blocker, son of Bartley and Nancy Brooks Blocker.

[63] John B. Moragne, brother of William C. Moragne.

[64] A farm tract belonging to WB.

[65] Roselands? It would be over a year before they made it their residence.

stopped at the Mansion house,[66] which is but moderately kept at this time....I heard no news of the slightest interest, either local, political or military.

Friday 29th....we set out for home about 1 ocl. & arrived safely at dark—All well.

Saturday 30th....No news by the papers. I rode to my farm to examine the progress of my carpenters on a house for the overseer. It was nearly completed & very well done. Our estimable kind neighbour Mrs. Lipscomb[67] died about 12 ocl. of a long & painful illness, which she bore with much fortitude. She was an excellent lady & her death will be a loss to us.

Sunday 31st....We attended service in the Epis. church, in which Mr. Reed read the service & Mr. Walker preached – The funeral ceremonies over the body of Mrs. Lipscomb commenced near 4 ocl. in the Baptist church by the Revd. Doct. Johnson, at the conclusion of which she was interred in the adjoining burying ground. The concourse of persons at the funeral was very large, affording to her friends the gratifying evidence of the high estimation, in which she was held by their neighbours. Mr. Lipscomb is seriously indisposed & confined to his bed.

This day closes the month of October, which has been remarkable for the dryness, mild temperature & delightful & clear weather, which have prevailed throughout the month. There did not fall but one rain [in] the District during the month & this afforded what planters call a good season. Two or three frosts have fallen but they were so light as barely to scorch vegetation slightly in low situations & to kill nothing. Cotton & potatoe vines are still growing in some situations. There never was a more favourable month for gathering crops & especially cotton.

November 1, 1847

Monday 1....This was sale day & a large concourse of persons assembled from all quarters of the District. A considerable portion of property was sold in land & negroes but I was too indisposed to be present at the sale & do not know at what prices. Some measures were adopted to raise a fund, to be called the Butler fund intended for the benefit of Col. P. M. Butler's family. I trust that a large amount will be raised in this District. I recd. a letter from my Son Preston from Vera Cruse but it contains no public news, other than what is given in the newspapers – he had received no intelligence of his brother, nor from his regiment.

Tuesday 2....I rode to the Village but heard no news. Judge Butler, Genl. Thompson & Doct. Butler paid me a visit in the afternoon & the Revd. Mr. Walker took tea with us –

---

[66] One of several hotels in the city, it was operated by William P. McKeen at one period.

[67] Sarah Bonham Lipscomb (1814–1847), daughter of James and Sophia Bonham, wife of John Lipscomb (1789–1856).

Wednesday 3....I have never seen finer or sweeter weather.

Thursday 4th....I recd. a letter from our Son Preston in which he informs me that he had recd. the command of a company of 70 men of the regular army through the politeness of Col. [blank] & that his position in the march to Mexico would be in the van of the brigade under the command of Genl. Cushing, which would give him the chance of a fight, if they should be opposed on the route. He seems to be greatly rejoiced at this good luck as he calls it. Col. Jack Hayes[68] of Texas had also presented him with a six barrel revolving pistol. The Brigade was to march on the 20th of October. He had received no news from the army in the City of Mexico, nor had he heard of his brother –

Friday 5th....I went to my plantation to carry back my man Lewis, who had ran from the overseer, arrived there about sunset. At night I gave out clothing to the men & boys & also a talk to my negroes in regard to their behaviour & good conduct as the only mode of getting on in peace with the overseer.

Saturday 6th....My negroes well except my man George, who had an eye, very much inflamed. I caused a blister to be applied to his neck, also a dose of salts to be taken & gave directions to him to apply slippery elm to his eye & to eat nothing stronger than milk & mush or gruel – I saw my horses & cattle, which looked in good order. At half past 10 ocl. I set out for home & arrived at half past two & found all well. No news of a public character. My carpenters finished in the afternoon a very commodious & well constructed potatoe house etc....

Sunday 7th....We attended divine service in the Epis. church by the Revd. Mr. Walker, who administered the Communion. In the afternoon I was considerably indisposed & did not leave the house.

Monday 8th....I finished this morning hawling in my corn crop, which has yielded well & commenced digging the potatoes. I suffered most unexpectedly an attack of headache, which lasted from 12 ocl. till 3 at night, from which I experienced great agony....

Tuesday 9th....For the last week it has been as warm as Summer with cloudy morning but bright & clear afternoons.

Wednesday 10th....My overseer at my plantation began to sow wheat on Monday morning last & I hope will finish to day. I have got my potatoes dug & in the house.

Thursday 11th....Miss Eliza Bacon was married at 7 ocl in the Episcopal church by the Revd. Mr. Walker to Doct. Baker. The house was full of invited guests, all of whom after the ceremony, repaired to the house of Mr. E. Bacon, to pass the evening & partake of the supper. I remained until 9 ocl, when I returned home, leaving

---

[68] Col. John Coffee Hays (1817–1883) commanded the 1st Regiment, Texas Mounted Riflemen, under Gen. Zachary Taylor. He later fought Mexican guerrillas under Gen. Winfield Scott.

Mrs. B & Ellen to enjoy the pleasures & amusements of the occasion. I saw all the supper tables. They were beautifully & tastefully prepared. Doct. Baker is very young but of good appearance.

Friday 12th....At 9 ocl. I set out for the Village to learn what intelligence had been brought by the mail & met on the way young Mr. W. Lipscomb, who informed that my precious & noble Son Whitfield had died of his wounds in Mexico. This information came through a letter [above the line beginning here is a row of + + + in pencil] from Genl. Bonham to his mother. In regard to this crushing & heart rending dispensation of Providence I can make no remarks. My prop, my right arm, my hope, my pride, the darling of my affections has been taken from us & I have nothing left in relation to this awful & heavy stroke but to pray to God, to give us grace & strength to bear it without murmuring or a feeling of rebellion agt. his divine will. May we be able to say in the spirit of meekness & truth that the Lord gave & the Lord hath taken away, blessed be the name of the Lord. No one but God knows, how near & dear this beloved dutiful & affectionate Son was to me or how heavy the blow has & will be to my lacerated heart. He was so pure, so virtuous, so manly, so generous & brave & so true & affectionate that all loved him, who knew him. I do not suppose that he has left an enemy behind him or one acquaintance, that will not regret his death. May God take his spirit to his own blissful mansions & prepare the hearts of his surviving family to follow him in God's appointed time & to be received in those mansions, where there is neither sorrow nor sighing.[69] The night was mild & clear with a bright moon.

....

Sunday 14th....We all feel badly this morning & I am suffering from a painful oppression about the head. Many of our friends called to see us & Major Blocker & family came down & passed the day.

Monday 15....I set out with the family for the plantation about 12 ocl at which we arrived before Sunset. The negroes are in pretty good health.

Tuesday 16....I attended the sale of Saml. Chappells property & purchased a negro fellow at the price of $805. Which is at least $150 above his value. I own his wife & [she?] begged me to purchase him, & these circumstances induced me to pay such a price. The other negroes sold equally high as I was informed, one man selling for $850.

Wednesday 17th....I rode over my plantation & pointed out a piece of land to my overseer to be cleared adjoining Mr. [Mathew?] Mims & gave other directions in regard to the business of the plantation. Our Son James arrived in the afternoon.

---

[69] According to an article in the *Adv.*, June 7, 1848, signed "Marlborough," WB had tried to dissuade his son from enlisting in the Palmetto Regiment, but yielded to PSB's sense of obligation and fervor. It is most likely that Mary shared his wish; he may have made the attempt on her behalf.

Thursday 18. I & James left the plantation after breakfast, for my fathers, where we arrived about 4 ocl. finding the old gentleman in his usual health but very feeble from age ....

Friday 19th....After breakfast we set out for my father's plantation near Saluda river, which I examined & also the tract of land belonging to Reuben Morgan. My father being so kind & liberal as to consent to let James have his place, during his life (for which I pray God to bestow upon him the richest gifts of his favour & love) I was induced to purchase the land of Morgan for a residence for James – I gave Morgan $1600 for his land, to be paid on the 15th of December. There are 476 acres in Morgan's tract and upwards of 600 in that of my father's with from 300 to 400 acres, cleared & now fit for cultivation. We returned to my fathers in the afternoon –

Saturday 20th....Morgan came to my fathers to breakfast & executed a title to his land & I gave him my note for $1500, paying him in a horse $100 – After breakfast I set out for home, at which I arrived about 4 ocl, having called to see my venerable Aunt Butler on the way. I found all at home well except my daughter who was a little indisposed....

Sunday 21....We attended church as usual –

Monday 22....I have finished my crop & have put my hands to cleaning up the stubble land & clearing a piece of new land. Nothing of great interest in the papers. Mr. Clay is expected to have addressed the people of Lexington Kentucky and to have offered a series of resolutions in relation to the war with Mexico. He takes the Whig ground of opposition to the war but regards it now as national in consequence of the vote of Congress, recognizing a state of hostilities between the two governments --

....

Wednesday 24th....My waggons arrived on their way to market with 20 bales of cotton.....

Thursday 25....I employed my hands in gathering manure throughout the day. The news from Europe is still of an unfavourable character & further reduction in the price of cotton.

Friday 26th....This is the first truly winter morning that we have yet felt & the only one on which ice abounded. We received no news by the mail –

Sunday 28th....We attended service in the Episcopl church. We heard in the afternoon that Mr. Saml. [S.] Tompkins [Tomkins] was elected Comm.r of the Court of Equity, beating Mr. Kerry, his opponent by 13 Votes. I regret this result as Thompkins could live comfortably without the office & to Mr. Terry [it] is almost indispensable. The one is in moderate circumstances with a large family of children & the other independent in his pecuniary matters & only one child –

Monday 29th....I sent my carriage this morning to Newberry to meet our daughter Mrs. Martha Brooks, on her way to visit us & shortly after the departure of my servant, we recd. a letter by the morning's mail from our Son Preston to his Wife, in which he informs her that he had reached the national bridge with Genl. Patterson's train on their March to the City of Mexico. He was in good health but greatly distressed on account of the mournful losses in his regiment & particularly in his own company.

Tuesday 30th....I killed 9 hogs that were raised in the lot & their average weight was about 170 lbs. Pork is selling in the Village at 4 ½ cts pr. lb. Our daughter Martha arrived in excellent health in the afternoon from her mothers in Fairfield. The month of November has been remarkable for its mild & agreeable weather, only one or two light rains having fallen during the time & only a few frosts & they are very light until the past week, when two killing ones fell. I have never known a fall, so favourable to gathering crops & most planters have already finished both the corn & cotton crop & are preparing for another crop. The general health of the Country is good, the provision crops abundant & altho cotton has greatly fallen in price, yet the country has been rarely more prosperous or in easier circumstances in regard to money. The price of land, negroes & mules has fallen very little, that of mules & horses more than any other property. Corn is selling at 40 cts pr. bushel & flower from $4.50 to 5 pr. barrel. All other articles at corresponding rates. "Man is justified by the free grace of God, through the redemption, which is in Jesus Christ." *[Romans 3:24, possibly added due to receiving letter below]*

[in pencil] Letter of W.B.B. December 1. 1847. [*in pencil:*] to Father x Mother [likely written by Preston, who as eldest son may have received the diary at his father's death]

Wednesday 1st....Rain throughout the day & the temperature cold.

Thursday 2. This was a cloudy & inclement day. We received by the mornings mail three letters from our dear Son Whitfield, two from Puebla before the army marched to Mexico [City] & the last a short one from the City of Mexico after he had recd. his fatal wound but when it was thought that he was recovering and would get well.

[Copy of his letter]. September 2. 1847.

My dear Parents,

For fear you should be more alarmed with regard to myself, I will attempt to give you a true statement of my condition. I am shot in the center of the Chest, the ball entering in a slanting direction and coming out under the left shoulder. When I was first shot, every one thought I would die in 4 or 5 hours but I have, thank God, been improving ever since & now hope to be up in 5 or 6 weeks. I was shot in making a charge on the enemy – Fifteen minutes before, Genl. Shields[70] rode in front of our regiment & asked who would follow him. I jumpt from the ranks & said I would follow him to death if necessary – After the men returned from the charge, he came immediately to where I was lying, said with tears in his eyes, My poor brave boy, you must not die. I asked him if I had discharged my duty? His reply was, "like a man" that I was an honor to myself, to my family and to my Country." He has been to see me repeatedly. I must now close.

Your affectionate Son

W. B. Brooks-

In these pleasing anticipations of recovery & improving health, how sadly was he disappointed. He lived about 40 days & died in the full possession of his faculties & with a perfect knowledge of his approaching dissolution. He was calm & composed to the last & only yielded for a moment to filial grief in the act of sending his last dying message to his family. Rest in peace my noble boy; faithfully did you discharge your duties in this life, in all its relations & May a merciful God assign to you a place in his kingdom above among the redeemed of his Son, our Lord & Savior Christ.

[The following is the message to his family through Lieut. Davis –]

Copy – [pencil:] W.B.B. last message

"My dear Mother, my father, my brothers, my sister! I shall never see them again!!! If I have done them any credit on the battle field, if I have shown myself to be in every way worthy of them, write & let them know it. One thing more & I shall die contented." He made an effort to continue, uttered a few half broken words but I could not understand them. In a few minutes he was speechless etc. – this is the statement of Lieut. Jon. R. Davis[71] – Thus has fallen one of the noblest & dearest of Sons on the very threshold of life – Mysterious are the ways of God.

Friday 3rd. Somewhat cloudy & cold. No news.

Saturday 4th....I learned that Lieutenant Moragnie [William C. Moragne] had reached New Orleans on his way home but in such a feeble health has to be compelled to stop there.

Sunday 5th....Service & the administration of the ceremony of the Lord's Supper were had in the Epis. church by the Revd. Mr. Walker. The afternoon was mild & clear. I took a ride for exercise.

Monday 6th....I set out at an early hour to visit my father & went to Judge Butlers to

---

[70] James Shields (1810–1879), born in Northern Ireland. Challenged Abraham Lincoln (who chose large swords) to an aborted duel in 1842. Commanded the 3rd Brigade at Vera Cruz, Cerro Gordo, and Churubusco, being wounded in the latter two. Promoted by Lincoln for his tactics against "Stonewall" Jackson in 1862.

[71] Jonathan Rutledge Davis (1816–1890) of Fairfield Dist. was twice wounded during the same battle.

breakfast, where I met Genl. Thompson, with whom I held a long & interesting conversation. I reached my fathers about 4 ocl. & found him in a feeble State, suffering in one foot & leg great pain, from inflammation. I am mistaken in the foregoing statement. Monday was sale day & I passed a portion of it in the Village. The concourse of persons was large and a good deal of property was sold, consisting of lands and negroes. I was quite sick at night from head ache....

Tuesday 7th. Clear & cold....I slept at my fathers & about 11 ocl three of his neighbours came in from a Sale somewhat intoxicated. After listening to them for some time I at length spoke, when one of them informed me that he had heard, his brother was dead in Mexico, that he was anxious to procure his body & that he would "give $100 for it as freely as he ever gave money for bacon for his family." The sentiment in this remark is the very perfection of the bathos. At about 12 ocl they took their departure, after having exhausted a decanter of whiskey.

Wednesday 8th....Finding my father on the recovery & willing for me to leave him, I set out after breakfast & went to the place, which I purchased from Morgan & thence to my plantation, passing by Guignard's & Butlers plantations. I had not passed over this road in thirty years & the general appearance of the Country had greatly altered since I had last seen it. I reached my plantation at dark & found all well. My overseer had just killed upwards of 6000 lbs. of pork.

Thursday 9th....I rode to the Village but heard no news –

....

Saturday 11....I recd. the President's message. It is an able . . . document, especially on the subject of our relations with Mexico. An entertainment was given at night by the Villagers to three of the Volunteers, who have returned from Mexico, to wit Delong, [Jeff?] Whitaker & [Francis?] Posey, all of whom were severely wounded.

Sunday 12....We attended service in the Epis. church.

Monday 13th....There was a sale at Major Jeters plantation but the day was too inclement for me to attend....

Tuesday 14th. Clear & cold ....I rode to my farm & gave directions to my servants to make preparations for Killing hogs.

Wednesday 15. Cloudy & very cold....Mrs. Carroll, My Wife, Ellen & Martha Brooks set out to pay a visit to Major Blockers family. A sudden change however took place . . . & the appearance of the heavens indicated snow or sleet. It continued to freeze during the entire day & about 2 ocl. snow began to fall in small quantities. My good Mother[in-law] & Wife could not have selected a worse day for visiting for it was difficult to keep warm by the fire. A heavy fire of canon was heard this morning at Hamburg & Augusta, from which we infer that Genl. Shields had arrived on his way to Washington. He has been invited to visit Columbia by Governor Johnson as the guest of the State & also by the citizens of Charleston to participate in a public dinner. I killed 14 hogs at the farm....

Thursday 16th....again cloudy & a light fall of snow by 8 ocl. Therm.t 25°. which continued at intervals during the forenoon but clear in the afternoon & at night. My waggons arrived with 20 bales of cotton on their way to Market. My overseer reports that the negroes are well.

Friday 17th....Therm.t down to 24°. Genl. Shields was received in Augusta with every declaration of public respect & admiration for his gallantry & noble bearing in the battles in Mexico. He was also recd. by a committee from Hamburg, attended by them to the town & partook of a breakfast given by the citizens –

Saturday 18. Still cold & clear. Therm.t 25°. It is reported that Col. Frazier has lost or at least will sustain great loss in a lot of pork from the killing of 90 hogs on tuesday the 7th. instant. My overseer killed 30 hogs at my plantation, on the same day and he writes me, that he does not think it is injured[?]. I fear that he is mistaken. I received a letter from a Judge Mays of Alabama, informing me that Mr. Moragnie was at his house & that his health was in improving. My servant Joseph was with him & in good health. Mr. Moragnie expected to set out in a few days for home....

....

Monday 20th....The intelligence from Mexico is of an interesting character. Anaya[72] has been elected President of the Republic & is in favour of peace. He had sent three commissioners to treat with Mr. Trist on the subject of peace but on their arrival at Mexico, they found that the powers entrusted to Mr. Trist had been recalled. It is reported that Genl. Scott had arrested Genls. [Gideon Johnson] Pillow & [William J.] Worth, which for the honor of the army will (I trust) turn out untrue.[73]

Tuesday 21....Genl. Quitman had arrived in Augusta by the cars & also Lieut. Moragnie of this place. Col. Carroll & lady returned from Columbia & called to see us.

Wednesday 22nd....I rode to my farm to direct the plough hands in regard to their work.

Thursday 23rd....My old & faithful servant Joseph arrived last night at 10 ocl from Mexico but we did not see him until this morning. He gives many interesting details in regard to the great battles in Mexico, to the various officers & men in the company of 96 boys & particularly in regard to the wound and death of our dear Son Whitfield. He is grave & serious & does not indulge in the least degree in the marvelous, but corroborated the various statements, which we have heretofore received in regard to all matters, on which he professes to have any knowledge. He was faithful & attentive to my Son & mourned his death with a depth and sincerity

[72] Pedro Maria de Anaya (1795–1854), commander at Churubusco, was twice interim president, the second time Nov. 1847–Jan. 1848.

[73] Hypersensitivity, intrigue, and distrust had led to Scott's arrest of the two officers, both of whom had Polk's ear to Scott's disadvantage.

of grief that is rarely manifested from a servant to his young master. It will be my pleasure to take care of him the balance of his life & to see that he shall want nothing, that may be necessary to his comfort. He is in good health.

Friday 24th....I paid a visit to my Sister Mrs. Blocker & passed the day with the family. I met my niece Mrs. Julia Reed & her husband there. He had been the pastor of the church at Grahamville [Beaufort Dist.] for some two years or more but owing to his feeble health had resigned the office some months since & had come to the District to pass the winter in the family of his Wife....

Saturday 25....So far we have a dull Christmas. The weather was too inclement for services . . . which had been appointed to be held at the Epis. church. We dined with our Mother Mrs. Carroll & partook of a most excellent dinner ....

Sunday 26th....Mrs. Carroll, Mr. Reed[,] Col. Carroll & lady dined with us. I did not attend church in consequence of the cold weather.

Monday 27th. Clear & very cold. I went to the Village about 11 ocl & altho I thought that I was cautious against any exposure yet I took a violent cold & about 2 ocl returned home with a severe chill upon me. During the afternoon & night I suffered great pain & was truly ill.

Tuesday 28th....In the forenoon I was free from suffering but in the afternoon the fever returned & I underwent a good deal of suffering.

Wednesday 29th....I was confined to my bed the greater part of the day, more from debility than pain. Our Son James arrived [from Barnwell] with his family on their way to his [new] residence on [the] Saluda.

Thursday 30....Very little change in my feelings or the condition of my health. I applied bats of cotton with suet to my breast on going to bed. Our daughter Martha Brooks left us this morning on her return to Fairfield. She has been with us about a month & has been a source of great comfort. And nothing could be sweeter or more interesting than our incomparable granddaughter[74] whose absence we shall feel most sensibly.

Friday 31....James & his family left us this morning for their new home. I must here note that the Revd. Bruce Walker was united to Miss Caroline Jeter[75] by the Revd. Mr. Reed in the Episcopal Church at 7 ocl. P.M. Several families were invited to witness the ceremony. This match has excited a great deal of remark & even animadversion but I trust for the interest I feel in both parties that it will eventuate to the happiness & prosperity of both. There is certainly no reason why it should not. This is the last day of the old year & it departs with a mild & temperate atmosphere. I trust that during the year-I have made some progress in the attainment of piety & of the knowledge of those great foundational truths, on which mans hopes

---

[74] Sally Means Brooks, born April 6, 1847. She would die on July 17, 1851, about two months after WB's journal-keeping apparently ended.

[75] Charles Bruce Walker (1817–1875); Caroline Simkins Jeter (1828–1898).

of eternal happiness depends – In short I do hope that I am a better man and a more devout & humble follower of our Savior Christ than I was at the beginning. I have suffered a great, an irreparable loss, a loss which crushes me to the Earth & yet I pray for submission to God's will.

W.B.B.

This is the only place in his journals where WB may indicate that he had a middle name, Butler. However, it seems equally likely that this was his confirmation that his lost son was on his mind and heart as he looked back on 1847.

[In a different hand, in pencil:] Arrival of remains

IX

January 1, 1848

Saturday 1st....Feeling much better & desirous of taking fresh air I rode out in the carriage to my farm with my Wife & daughter & on our return we went to the Village for a short time. I recd. a letter from Judge Butler & Sundry papers, but they did not contain any political news of any importance. I also received a letter from Col. Tro??[1] of Barnwell, informing me that he was in possession of two Silver cups, which had been awarded to me by the State agricultural Society from the exhibition of Stock at a meeting of the Society at Aiken last Summer.

Sunday 2....The Revd. Mr. Reed & Lady came down to church & dined with us. Mr. Reed preached morning & evening. In consequence of the cold I did not go to church until near the conclusion of the services during the administration of the sacrament of which I partook. Just a year from this day we parted with our Sons Preston & Whitfield at Camp Johnson near Hamburg on our return to this place. The Battalion was striking their tents, when we left, preparatory to their departure for Mexico. The day proved chilly & drizzly. What sad & momentous events have followed in rapid succession since that morning & how many family alters have been bathed in tears of anguish & lamentation, for sons slaughtered in battle or who have died of loathsome & protracted disease? Where are the thousand brave & patriotic men who at this time crossed the Savannah River on their way to the theater of war to maintain the flag of their Country in a foreign land. Alas! Three fourths have fallen[2] & now lie buried in the soil of Mexico, among the number of whom, were some of the most gallant spirits, that ever appeared upon the battlefield. History will chronicle their names & perpetuate their memories throughout all time.

Monday 3rd....I went to the Village & remained a short time viewing the large crowd of busy attendants on the Hill who seemed engaged in all sorts of Court day business. The assemblage was unusually large – The Village had the appearance of a market town & the public square was literally filled with men of all classes & descriptions, with horses & waggons & carts & carriages, some in one place attending to the sale of a horse, others bartering for tobacco & apples, others laughing at the gyrations of a stud horse, others attending the sales of the Sheriff while a large crowd was listening to a bombastic description of the great merits of a razor strap by a bold Vendor of the article. I gave my vote for several District officers & returned home.

Tuesday 4th....I rode to my farm and was pleased with the order in which my overseer was placing my fields. Four ploughs were engaged in sowing oats –

---

[1] Likely Francis John Andrews Trotti (1813–), owner of Briarwood plantation.

[2] One thousand forty-eight members of the Pal. Reg. went to Mexico, and 441 returned. The vast majority of the dead succumbed to disease (*SC Encyclopedia*, 699).

Wednesday 5th....I again rode to the Village & learned that Thos. G[lasscock] Bacon was reelected Clerk of the Court of Common Pleas. Simeon Christie was elected Sheriff and Col. Hill[3] was reelected Ordinary by large majorities. I voted for each of these gentlemen.

Thursday 6th....I went to the Village in the morning & transacted some business & in the afternoon I rode to my farm.

Friday 7th....I learned from Col. Pickens, that the bodies of Col.s Butler & Dickerson passed Aiken in charge of a committee of officers, who had been sent by the Governor of the State, to meet them at Augusta & to convey them to Columbia. I also learned that the bodies of my Son Whitfield and David Adams had been shipped from New Orleans to Charleston & might be expected to arrive in a few days –

Saturday 8th....The news by the papers not very interesting. There was a debate in the Senate of the U. States of some interest between Genl. Cass[4] & Mr. Calhoun in regard to the postponement of the consideration of a bill to increase the army etc. I finished this afternoon, sowing oats & I wish that I may not have put them in the ground at a bad time, being too late for Fall & too early for Spring oats.

Sunday 9th....I was prevented from attending Church by indisposition. The afternoon was milder & nearly clear, at which time I rode out in the carriage as far as Pottersville, to see Joel Hill,[5] one of the 96 boys, who had just returned from Mexico. Poor fellow! He exhibits the appearance of having suffered greatly from protracted and wasting disease. He says that he is indebted for his discharge to his Capt. P. S. Brooks, who on his way through Puebla to the City of Mexico, visited him & others in the hospital & procured their discharge.

Monday 10th....I sent for young [Gafford?], & he confirmed the information, previously received, that the remains of our Son were brought by a steam vessel to New Orleans & thence shipped to Charleston. He gives the credit for his discharge to his Captain & thus confirms the Statement of Hill. The day was very cold.

Tuesday 11th....Abraham Mitchell died a few days past & was buried in the Baptist church yard. I saw with great pleasure in the Charleston Courier a series of resolutions, passed by the officers of the Palmetto regiment at the City of Mexico, complementary to Capt. P. S. Brooks & welcoming him back to the Regiment. Col.

---

[3] John Hill (1801–); 1850 census: $3,000 real estate, 22 slaves. The Ordinary was abolished and replaced by the Probate Court under the Constitution of 1868.

[4] Lewis Cass (1782–1860), Territorial Gov. of MI, Jackson's Sec. of War, Senator from Michigan. Democratic presidential nominee 1848, Sec. of State 1857–1860.

[5] Joel Pittman Hill (1828–1854) was discharged from the army on Nov. 2, 1847, due to disability. The 1850 census showed him married to Margaret Parr Hill with three stepchildren. His real estate was worth $9,300.

Gladden presided & the resolutions were introduced by Major Donevant,[6] former Capt. of the Chester company, and seconded by Lieut. Jos. Abney[7]....

Wednesday 12th....I have no recollection of a period when at this season of the year the earth was so dry & the roads in such admirable order. The creeks and water courses are unusually low for the want of rain [.] I have never seen the small grains so indifferent & unpromising. Lots of rye & wheat sowed in September furnish no pastorage even for calves ....

Thursday 13th....Mr. Jas. Lipscomb was married to Miss S. Pickens[8] by the Revd. Mr. Walker. It was rather a private wedding [at Edgewood, the Pickens' home.]

Friday 14....I rode to my farm & found the temperature very pleasant –

Saturday 15th....I rode to the Village & transacted some business but heard no news of any kind....Col. J. E. Calhoun[9] of Abbeville called to see me.

Sunday 16th. The temperature is as mild as an April morning....The day was so mild, that I attended church in the morning & heard a sensible sermon by the Rev. Mr. Walker.

Monday 17th....I received a letter from the Misses Caldwells of Charleston informing me that the remains of my dear Son had been shipped from New Orleans on the 8 instant and were expected in Charleston about the 22nd. This certain information was a great relief to my feelings for I had been kept in a state of uncertainty in regard to them for the last two weeks – We paid a visit to Judge Butler to see our relation Mrs. [Emmala Butler] Thompson, who is very ill, so much so, that Mrs. Brooks did not see her. She was however represented to be better. I received from Mr. Calhoun a copy of his speech on his resolutions in regard to the war with Mexico. It is able but not satisfactory to me in respect to his defensive line. Judge Butler was never more correct, than when he stated that the situation (inserted: of the government) was in reference to the Mexican war, like that of the farmer who had the Wolf by the ears and was unable to decide, which was the safer course to let go or to

---

[6] Robert Gill Mills Dunovant (1821–1898), Chester Dist. native, physician in Texas who gave up his practice and raised a company for the Pal. Reg. Ended the war as Lt. Col. He would marry WB's daughter Ellen on May 21, 1849. Commanded SC forces on Sullivan's Island during the siege and battle of Ft. Sumter, April 1861.

[7] Joseph Abney (1819–1870), brother of Rev. Mark Abney. Lawyer, temperance supporter. Secretary to Col. P. M. Butler during the war. Wounded at Churubusco. Married in 1858 Susan Miller, cousin of Mary Boykin Chesnut. Daughter Agatha Abney Woodson became local historian.

[8] James Nathan Lipscomb (1827–1891) m. Susan Wilkinson Pickens (1830–1866). They would live on his plantation near Chappels Depot in Newberry Dist.

[9] Senator Calhoun had a brother-in-law (1798–1889) and a son (1826– 1861) named James Edward Calhoun. The former lived at Millwood plantation in Abbeville Dist. The son moved to California after graduating from SC College. Thus, WB's visitor was the elder Calhoun.

hold on. The line policy[10] would lessen the expenses of the Government, require a much smaller army to defend it than what will be necessary to prosecute the war & possibly in the end protect this country against the consequences, which may follow from any political connection with Mexico, yet the order to withdraw our troops will cover the army with shame & be equivalent to a severe rebuke to the administration for having brought on a State of hostilities unnecessarily with the Mexican Government. I have always thought the war just & unavoidable & therefore have uniformly supported the administration . . .[11]

Tuesday 18th....Yesterday morning the roads were as dry & dusty as they usually are in the month of July & in better order than I ever knew them at this season of the year. This is the day appointed for the funeral ceremonies over the remains of the gallant Col. Butler in Columbia ....A more propitious day . . . could not have been desired. Our woman Adrene had an infant.

Wednesday 19th....I killed a few hogs, which I purchased.

....

Friday 21....I saw & conversed with my old friend Doct. [William] Butler, who was on a short visit to his mother & on his return from the Village called & passed some time with me –

....

Sunday 23 – A continuation of the fair & mild weather. I attended service in the Epis. Church – Revd. Mr. Reed dined with us –

Monday 24th....

I rode out to meet Col. Huitt[12] to show him the line between his & Loyd Mitchell's[13] land. Returned with head ache & went to bed, suffering unspeakable pain in the head & nausea at the [stock?] until 10 ocl. at night. Night warm & cloudy – Genl. Thompson called to see me.

....

Wednesday 26th....A meeting was held in the Village, during the last week, at which a committee was appointed of the citizens to act with the military committee in the ceremonies, attending the reception & enterment of the remains of my noble Son Whitfield. He is to be buried with military honors – Col. [Giles] Mims[14] is chair-

---

[10] The Rio Grande as international boundary.

[11] WB here seems to support the Manifest Destiny vision of a full annexation of Mexico.

[12] John Huiett (1809–), a Major during the Seminole War, SC House; 1850 census: $12,000 real estate, 42 slaves. Chapman spells his name "Huiett." The census taker wrote "Huit."

[13] Lloyd Mitchell (1819–); 1850 census: $300 real estate, 22 slaves.

[14] Giles Mims (1815–), Sgt. in Seminole War, 1836; 1850 census: $6,000 real estate, 13 slaves.

man of the military committee & Maj. Thos. G. Bacon of the Citizen's committee. Mr. James Lipscomb was appointed to deliver a eulogy in the Courthouse on the day of his enternment & accepted the appointment. I hope that he will acquit himself handsomely & gratify the expectations & wishes of the public. My friend Col. Pickens called to know if I had any [commands?] in Charleston. I received letters from Charleston informing me of the arrival of the vessel in Charleston, conveying the remains of my dear Son & also the vessel bringing the bodies of David Adams & others – The remains of my Son & David Adams will reach Hamburg tomorrow night by the rail road cars, at which time I propose to reach Hamburg, to attend to their reception. Rain continued to fall through the day....

Thursday 27....I set out for Hamburg after breakfast & arrived there about 4 ocl. The cars from Charleston brought the remains of our beloved son Whitfield with those of his devoted friend David Adams, under the care of a committee of the Society of Oddfellows[15] from Augusta & of my young friends Wm. Huger & Radcliff Wilson. The coffins were taken to the house of Mr. [Goluthan?] Walker, where I went to enjoy the melancholy gratification of looking upon the enclosure containing the precious body of my dear boy – I wished to enjoy the evidence of my senses that his dear remains had returned to his native state & were on their way to the home of his birth. I saw his coffin & that of David Adams, returned humble thanks to God, for his great goodness in permitting his remains to be restored to us & returned to the boarding house. I regard the return of these young men to Hamburg at the same time & by the same car, as a remarkable coincidence in the short history of these interesting youths. They were united in life by the strongest & purest tie of friendship and the same bond served in death to bind them together & to forbid their separation.

Friday 28th....I was not very well & it did not go about much but attended to the purchase of a few articles – In the afternoon I went home with Major [Benjamin] Yancy & passed the night at his house. The Major is courteous & hospitable and his lady renders herself exceedingly interesting by her affable manners & conversation. I was much pleased with her deportment & the hospitality with which she entertained us.

Saturday 29th....At half past 1 ocl. the procession for the funeral ceremonies of D. Adams was formed in front of Mr. Walker's house & the body removed to the Baptist church, where a sermon was preached by the Revd. Mr. Evans of the methodist Church. The procession, composed of the military, the odd fellows & the citizens then reformed & marched in order to the burial ground, near the residence of Mr. D. L. Adams, where the last mournful ceremonies were performed over the remains of my gallant young friend. He & my Son Whitfield had both fallen at the battle of Churubusco in Mexico on 20 August last, Adams dying instantly & my Son surviv-

[15] A fraternal order begun in England and introduced into the U.S. in 1819. Its main purpose is providing assistance to those with particular needs.

ing upwards of 40 days. I passed the night with my friend Mr. David L. Adams at SummerVille [above Augusta] –

Sunday 30th....By the advice of several friends I returned home at which I arrived at 4 ocl, finding all well. At several times rain fell in slight sprinkles before reaching home & at night there was a heavy fall of rain....

Monday 31....About dark the remains of our dear Son reached our residence in charge of a committee & a few personal friends, who were met near the Village by the greater part of the citizens of the vicinity & accompanied to my house. Our friends could not be kinder or more considerate of our feelings, for which I return them my sincere thanks. They manifest the most earnest desire to show every demonstration of respect for our dear departed one, that the occasion will admit. May God bless them for it. Col. Carroll, Maj. Thos. Bacon, Major Meggs, [Charles G. Meigs?] Mr. William Huger and Mr. Radcliff Wilson & some others attended the remains from Hamburg. The two last were the personal friends of my dear boy & accompanied him from Charleston as a mark of their esteem and consideration for his memory. Joseph [H.] Gassaway died during the night at the house of Mr. F. Nicholas. He was a member of Capt. Brooks company of 96 boys & had only a few days returned from Mexico, having been discharged at Puebla on account of sickness. The poor fellow . . . just arrived in time to have his remains committed to his native soil & to [repose?] under the protection of his own Palmetto.

[In another hand] Burial of WBB

<u>February 1. 1848</u>

Tuesday 1st....The day was appropriated to preparations for the interment of our beloved Son and that of poor Joseph Gasaway, who died the night before. He will be placed in the funeral procession & buried at the same time with his fellow soldier & companion in arms.

Wednesday 2....At 12 ocl. the military formed the line of procession in Front of my house, composed of four uniform infantry companies & two cavalry companies under the command of Col. Giles Mims. At half past 12 ocl. the coffin, containing our idolized Son was placed in the hearse & joined the procession with 12 young men in charge of it as pallbearers, followed by the family and a large concourse of citizens in carriages & on foot at the sound of Solemn music by a band from Augusta. The procession then moved to Goodman's [Hotel] piazza, where a handsome & appropriate eulogy was delivered by Mr. James Lipscomb to a large Auditory. The upper gallery was crowded by ladies & the Piazza & the public square were almost filled by the military and citizens in carriages & on foot – At the conclusion of the address the procession proceeded up Main Street, through the cross street to Mrs. Bacons lot & thence to the Burial ground belonging to the Episcopal & [Methodist?] churches. Here the burial service was performed in a solemn manner by the

Revd. E. Reed & his body committed to his mother Earth, over which the Military performed their part in the last Solemn ceremonies, which were paid to the remains of this lamented & much loved youth – It was damp under foot, otherwise the day was not disagreeable. The demonstration by the entire District of respect for our dear boy & of regret for his death, of kind sympathy & condolence with his family for their loss & of the universal willingness to pay marked honors to his remains were very gratifying to our feelings but they offer no compensation for the great loss, which we have Sustained in the death of a noble, beautiful & affectionate Son. I thank God for his great mercy in allowing us to repossess the remains of our dear child, of having him under our roof for a short period & for the unspeakable gratification of being able to deposit his precious person in the soil of his birthplace among his kindred & friends, where he will repose in quiet under the guardian care of his family & where they will have an opportunity of repairing to drop the tear of sorrow for his early death. His body is near us & we hope & believe that his pure & manly spirit is with his God in Heaven.

Thursday 3rd. Rain through the night & the day gloomy & humid. No news by the papers except rumors of peace with Mexico....

[*in another hand, in pencil:*] Eulogy by J[ames] N. Libscomb

Friday 4th....Our young friends Huger & Wilson left us to day at 12 ocl. on their return to Charleston in the Hamburg stage – James & his family also left us on their return home. I learned with pleasure that the address of our young friend James Lipscomb gave general satisfaction & greatly exceeded public expectation. I rode to Pottersville to see Joel Hill, one of the members of the company of 96 boys, who was discharged at Puebla on account of protracted ill health & whose health is still precarious.

Saturday 5th....On examining my oats, I observed that they had come up very well & looked promising. The earth is now thoroughly wet & the watercourses full of water, which has not been the case since Christmas. Yesterday I saved a quantity of manure & today I am hawling straw & litter into the horse lot. This is my birthday. I am now 58 years of age and I return devout thanks to God, that my health is better than it was at the same period last year & that every member of my family are enjoying excellent health....

Sunday 6th....The Revd. Mr. Reed preached in the Epis. church but in consequence of the cold, I did not attend....Our young relation John Laborde[16] (who had come up to attend his cousins burial) left us in the Stage for Columbia on his return home. By him I sent $16 to be credited on the note of P. S. Brooks in the hands of Doct. Laborde.

---

[16] Maximilian Laborde, WB's brother-in-law, had a brother named John who died unmarried in 1822, and no sons named John. ML's brother Pierre Fabien (1807–1850) was unmarried. Thus, this J.L. is unidentified.

Monday 7th....There was a large concourse of persons in the Village & some property in negroes, lands & horses sold. Negro men sold from $650 to 675. I heard nothing of interest except the prevalence of a fatal endemic at Vaucluse factory from which several have died & by which the working of the factory had been suspended....

Tuesday 8th....I examined my oats & was pleased to see that they had come up well & presented a "fine stand."

Wednesday 9th....I set out for my plantation about 10 ocl. with Mrs. Brooks & Ellen[,] leaving Hampden with Mrs. Carroll, to go to school....

Thursday 10th....I rode over my plantation & examined my ditches & the preparation for a crop. The stock of cattle, hogs & horses looked to be in good order & the servants fat & well clothed.

Friday 11th....We paid a visit to Doct. Barrett & passed the day with the family. We saw & had a good deal of conversation with our relation Richard Watson, who had returned, badly wounded from Mexico. He is recovering from his wounds & I hope will be able to use his leg in walking. He repeated & confirmed much that we had heard in regard to the battles & of the individuals of our family who were wounded & killed near the City of Mexico.

Saturday 12th....I rode to my new ground, of something like 20 acres that I was clearing near Mr. M[athew] Mims It is a piece of choice land & will produce either corn or cotton. I again inspected the ditches, a new house for the negroes in the plantation and also the digging a well at the horse lot.

Sunday 13th....We left the plantation for my fathers and reached his house about 3 ocl. We found him exceedingly feeble & unable to move without assistance yet enjoying a good appetite & good digestion. He is failing in all his faculties.

Monday 14th....My father sent for Major Huet & Wife, Mr. Culbreath & Wife & James Brooks & his lady[17] to dine with us. The day passed off pleasantly & we found our friends both social & agreeable. In the afternoon we went home with James Brooks.

Tuesday 15th....After dinner I rode over a part of James' fields to see what progress he had made towards a crop. He is rather backward with his work tho seemingly getting on pretty well. In the afternoon we returned to my father's whom we found cheerful & free from pain.

Wednesday the 16th....After breakfast we left my father's & reached home at 2 ocl. where we found all well. We called at Judge Butlers & learned that Mrs. Thompson was very ill. No news except the failure of Tibbets, the Shoemaker, who had made an assignment of his property, during my absence to [sheriff] Col. Christie.

---

[17] Now living on ZSB's property but not in his house.

Thursday 17th....I rode to the Village & sold six stall-fed steers to Chs. Gray[18] for $120 & a cow & calf at $12.00. In the afternoon I rode over my farm and found everything equal to my expectation. In fact my overseer Mr. [Henry] Coleman surpasses my expectations for judgment & management. He had all the cotton land & two thirds of the corn land ploughed & the new ground is nearly ready for the plough.

Friday 18th....I caused a lot to be broken up for potatoes in the field, adjoining the garden.

Saturday 19th....I rode to my farm & observed that my overseer had broken up all the corn & cotton land (say 100 acres) except about 10 acres. I am more forward with my work than I have ever been at this period of the year.

Sunday 20th....I did not attend church in consequence of the inclemency of the weather.....

Monday 21....heavy showers of rain & thunder. The earth is now thoroughly wet & the roots very sloppy. The papers contained items of intelligence, favourable to peace with Mexico, which I sincerely wish, may prove to be well founded. The money market in Europe is reported to be in an easy condition. Int. 4 pr. centum –

Tuesday 22....repeated & heavy showers ....Genl. John Means arrived in the midst of one of the heaviest showers about 4 ocl. By him we learn that our daughter Martha Brooks & her little girl Mary are well. I suffered a severe attack of headache, which confined [me] to the bed from 12 ocl. till next day. The pain did not leave me until 2 ocl. in the morning.

Wednesday 23rd....Genl. Means & Col. Carroll dined with me. In the afternoon I took a ride with Mrs. E[Lizabeth] Carroll in her carriage & felt improved by the exercise. Rain . . . continued to fall throughout the entire night without intermission.

Thursday 24th....Genl. Means left us before Sunrise in opposition to all remonstrance to the contrary. He had engaged to take breakfast with Jacob Smith at Capt. Griffins & to return by his house on his way home. Rain continued to fall during the greater part of the day & night. The water courses are said to be high.

Friday 25th ....We received letters from our Son Preston from San Angel, Mexico, who was in good health. The belief prevails at Washington that a treaty of peace has been concluded with Mexico & was before the President & his cabinet for approval. We also recd. intelligence that the remains of my gallant nephew Wm B. Blocker had been sent from New Orleans to Charleston & they may be expected in this place in the course of ten days on their way to his fathers.

....

---

[18] Charles Martin Gray (1800–), remembered in later years as a fun-loving character who straightened up, married Ann Green in 1841, and became a constable, then door-keeper of the House of Representatives (Chapman, *History of Edgefield,* 191–96).

Sunday 27....The water courses both small & large have been full & small streams of water our running down every slope from the hills & along & across the roads. I felt the want of exercise & took a ride in the afternoon as far as my farm.

Monday 28th....I set out for Barnwell Courthouse in company with the Revd. Mr. Reed and reached Mrs. Swartz at Aiken in the afternoon, where we remained for the night. I met Bishop Gadsden at the public house & also a company of Yankees, amounting to some 6 or 8 (both men & women) & a more vulgar uninteresting set, I have rarely ever met. There was a statement in the papers, that the President had received a treaty of peace with Mexico & had Submitted it to the Senate for approval. The probability was that it would be ratified tho it will encounter opposition. Mr. [John Quincy] Adams was reported to be gradually sinking & no hopes entertained for his life. The little town of Aiken exhibits every sign of decay & dilapidation.

Tuesday 29th....Mr. Reed took the cars for Charleston & I the road to the [Barnwell] courthouse, at which I arrived about 4 ocl. in the afternoon, so sick as to be forced to take a bed, from which I did not rise till next day. The paroxysm of headache was severe & painful. I saw no person on the day of my arrival.

March 1, 1848

Wednesday 1st....About 9 ocl. Mr. Cave arrived in the Village & by 12 ocl. paid me the amount of his note, which he had given me for the purchase of a negro boy. So soon as I recd. the money I set out for Genl. Hammonds on my return home. The Village of Barnwell has greatly altered & improved since the date, when I practiced law in that District. The houses & lots exhibit the evidences of neatness & comfort – There is [a] new Courthouse now being built & nearly completed of brick. It is a handsome building & is an ornament to the public square. I put up with my old acquaintance Mr. Barny Brown & saw some 4 or 5 gentlemen, who called to see me. I arrived at Genl. Hammonds about sun set & found him at home and recd. a cordial reception from him & his excellent lady. In passing through two portions of this District I was struck with the want of improvement, everywhere apparent on the farms & plantations.

Thursday 2....I took my departure at 9 ocl. & passed through Augusta & Hamburg & reached home at dark. The death of Mr. Adams is announced in the papers as having occurred on Wednesday the 23 of Febr. in the Capitol. No other news of any interest. Cotton in Hamburg was slow & dull of sale – Price from 5 ½ to 7. extremes....I paid a note in bank for $600.

Friday 3rd....I went to the Village & met many of the gentlemen, with whom I held social converse for some time but heard no news. Every body seemed to be preparing for Court which convenes its session on Monday next. In the afternoon I rode to my farm. The oats look well & the new ground being plowed, has much improved the appearance of the field. There does not remain more than two acres yet to break up of all the corn & cotton land, which are designed to plant & that will be plowed tomorrow. My farm was never in a better state of preparation for a crop.

Saturday 4th....I rode to the Village in the morning & purchased a few articles for my negroes. The speculations of the Politicians at Washington are in favour of a ratification of the treaty with Mexico by the Senate. In the afternoon I rode over & inspected the condition of my fields at the farm, in order to be able to give directions in regard to the work of the following week....I returned home, feeling very unwell.

Sunday 5th....I was too unwell to attend church & was on the bed for several hours....I learned that my father was again very ill & that the Doctor had visited him.

Monday 6th....The Spring session of the Court of Com Pleas commences this morning, under Judge [Edward] Frost & the state of the weather indicated a favourable week for the transaction of business. I called at Counttee's [Compty's Hotel] to see the Judge but he had walked into the Village. There was a crowd of persons on the hill with waggons, carts, horses, mules, cakes, apples & various other articles for sale. Some property was sold by the Sheriff. A bill of indictment was given to the Grandjury against Charles Glover[19] for a nuisance in directing a stable near the heart of the Village & (as was alleged) partly on the public Street but it was not sustained, the jury returning no bill by their finding. The erection of this building is an outrage against taste, decency & good feeling & manifests a bad spirit on the part of Glover.

Tuesday 7th....The news by telegraphic dispatch is that cotton has advanced an 1/8 of a penny in Liverpool. A white man was publicly whipped at the jail under the sentence of the Court for stealing a horse....

Wednesday 8th....In the morning I paid a visit to Col. Pickens & on my return, attended divine service at the Epis. church. I attended in my carriage our good friend Mrs. Willie Williams,[20] formerly Miss Berrien to Col. Carrolls, where she is staying on a visit to her Sister....

Thursday 9th....The advance in cotton from a 1/4 to 3/8. No additional news by the papers & the fate of the treaty with Mexico still doubtful in the Senate tho the probabilities are in favour of its ratification.

Friday 10th....I had a horse on trial & rode him some three or four miles but was not pleased with him & returned him.

Saturday 11th....The morning was clear & spring like & tempted me to take exercise on horse back. I rode as far as my farm in company of Doct. Jones and returned by

[19] On July 7, 1836, Charles J. Glover bought from Benjamin Frazier a 12-acre tract "beginning on the corner of the public square and the main street…leading toward Augusta."

[20] Williamina Moore Berrien Williams (1820–1882) of Savannah was a sister of Eliza Berrien Carroll, wife of James Parsons Carroll. She married Henry Williams (1818–1878).

way of Pottersville. About 1 ocl. the body of my gallant nephew W. B. Blocker passed through the Village on its way to his paternal home for interment. There was a procession of carriages & persons on horseback, which attended the coffin, as far as Pottersville. My family & Mrs. Carroll accompanied the escort to Major Blockers. He was a frank, generous, true & noble boy & died gloriously at the gate of the City of Mexico. He & his cousin Whitfield Brooks were devoted to each other & met the same fate this on the battle field. Their bodies will soon rest in their native District & I trust that their spirits are with God.

Sunday 12th....I went to church in the morning but was so much indisposed, that I was forced to leave the house & return home. I was very unwell throughout the day & suffered a good deal from nausea & coughing. Major Yancy & Mrs. Williams with Col. and Mrs. Carroll called to see me. In the afternoon I rode as far as Log creek[21] for exercise & fresh air.

....

Tuesday 14th....At 10 ocl. we set out for Major Blockers to attend the funeral ceremonies of Sergeant Wm. B. Blocker & reach[ed] there about 11 ocl. There was a considerable concourse of persons & a tolerable turnout of the Militia. A procession was formed at 12 ocl, which marched to the family burying ground at the sound of music, where an address suitable to the occasion was delivered by Mr. Wm. Adams[22] to an attentive & large auditory. At the conclusion of the address the funeral ceremony of the Epis. church was read by the Rev. Mr. Reed in a solemn & impressive manner & the body was then committed to its last earthly resting place with the usual military honors. Among those present on the occasion I was glad to meet Lieut. Wm B. [C.] Moragnie, [Moragne] the gallant leader of the 96 boys in the battles of Contreras & Chururbusco, who was forced to return from Mexico in consequence of ill health. He has & is improving & if the war continues he proposes to return to Mexico, so soon as his strength will authorize him to undertake the journey.

Wednesday 15th....I was very unwell & did not leave the lot during the day. In the evening Judge Frost & Mr. Yancy called to see me but I was too unwell to leave my room....

Thursday 16th....There have been but few mornings as cold, during the Winter. I was confined to the house the entire day & for a great part of the time on the bed, with sick headache yet I felt & suffered from the cold....From the private correspondents of Newspapers, intelligence has been received that the treaty with Mexico had been ratified by the Senate by a vote of 35 to 15. I trust that it may eventuate in peace.

---

[21] WB probably rode out Meeting Street Road northward from ECH about a mile. Log Creek flows northwest, emptying into Stevens Creek.

[22] William Wright Adams (1820–1876), lawyer.

Friday 17th....I rode over my farm, which I had not seen for the last three days on account of a distracting attack of my old disease, & was much pleased with the manner, in which my overseer had planted about 30 acres of corn at the Youngblood farm. Mrs. Yancy arrived from Georgia to join her husband at this place. They passed the night with us.

Saturday 18th....I felt much recruited by rest & diet & after breakfast, rode to the Village, paid my tax $98.44 transacted some business & returned to dinner, at which we had Mr. & Mrs. Yancy, Col. & Mrs. Carroll, Mrs. W. Williams & our Mother Mrs. Carroll. In the afternoon I rode to the farm for exercise & to try a horse, which I am in treaty for....

Sunday 19th....Service as usual in the Epis. church, which I attended with no great inconvenience. I rode for exercise in the afternoon.

Monday 20th....I purchased a plow horse of John Mays[23] . . . at $75 and my overseer swapped my Fitzsimmons mare to Caleb Mitchell for a young horse, giving $40 to boot. Mr. Sevier[24] of the Senate has been appointed by the President & confirmed by the Senate commissioner to Mexico to conclude the treaty of peace with the Government of that Country. I transacted some business in the Village.

Tuesday 21....I was confined to the bed from ten ocl in the morning with an attack of headache & nausea at the stomach, which I shall long have occasion to remember. My suffering was indescribable.

Wednesday 22....Vegetation looks revived by the rain & the birds are caroling their morning hymns most sweetly in the flower garden. In fact all creation seems gladdened by the rain & mild temperature of the morning & to participate in a new pleasure. I alone seem out of tune & not in harmony with the scene around me. I felt much revived in the afternoon & went to the Village where Mrs. B. purchased something like $30 worth of merchandise from Cohn[25]....

Thursday 23rd....The vegetable kingdom has received a fresh impulse from the rain & is rapidly advancing. We visited our venerable Aunt Butler, particularly with the view of ascertaining the situation of our relation Mrs. Thompson, who lies exceedingly ill, & for whose life no hopes are entertained. We found the whole family in great affliction.

Friday 24....I omitted to state, in the minutes of yesterday, that a revolution had taken place in France & that Louis Felipe had abdicated the throne in favour of his

---

[23] Probably John P. Mays (1796–); 1850 census: $8,000 real estate, 41 slaves.

[24] Ambrose Hundley Sevier (1801–1848), Democrat, led the movement for Arkansas statehood and was one of that state's first U.S. Senators in 1836. A strong backer of "manifest destiny," he was picked by Polk to negotiate the final war treaty with Mexico, but poor health forced him to resign.

[25] Jacob Cohn, born in Hamburg, Germany, c. 1816 (*Adv.*, Jan. 31, 1845): J. Cohn & Co. Cheap Cash Store.

grandson. The people, however, had rejected the proposition of a regency & demanded a republican government. Both the palace and Tuilleries had been taken and five hundred persons killed. A republican government has been formed provisionally with Lamartine & others at the head.[26] We set out for Columbia on a visit to Doct. Laborde & family & reached Mr. John Lee's—

Saturday 25th....We arrived in Columbia early in the afternoon & received a hospitable reception by Laborde & all his family –

Sunday 26th....I was indisposed and did not attend church in the morning. In the afternoon I heard a sensible sermon from Mr. Young from Camden in the new Epis. church.[27]

Monday 27th....I rode into Town & examined the unfinished portrait of my dear Son Whitfield by Scarborough & made such suggestions as occurred to me to be proper and necessary—I rode over the town & saw that it was in a state of rapid improvement, many new buildings have been erected within a few years and many more in a state of completion. This is one of the prettiest towns in the Southern Country. The trade is also increasing.

Tuesday 28....I remained pretty much in the house....The treaty of peace was ratified by the Senate of the United States & Col. Sevier of Arkansas sent out as Commissioner etc.

Wednesday 29th....I again rode into Town & saw some of my old acquaintances. I purchased some jewelry & gave it as a present to my niece Miss Ellen Laborde –

Thursday 30....I rode with Dr. Laborde to his farm four miles out of town [Columbia] & was pleased to find, that he had made as good a selection of land as could be found in that quarter & within that distance of Columbia –

Friday 31st....In the forepart of the day I was in the streets for a short time & at Scarborough's painting room. In the afternoon we dined with Col. [William Campbell] Preston & passed a few delightful hours in his society and a few choice friends – the ladies visited Mrs. [Wade] Hampton's garden after dinner while I was forced to take a bed on account of headache. Many of my old friends called to see me & asked me to dine with them but the indifferent state of my health forced me to decline their tendered hospitality & attentions which I much regretted. In company with Col. & Mrs. Preston we paid a visit to Col. Hampton's residence, to see his pictures & grounds & called on our return at Mr. John Prestons. Neither of the families were at home so we had leisure to examine the paintings. The Brigand by

[26] These events touched off a series of revolutions in Europe throughout 1848. The outcome in France was the election of Louis Napoleon Bonaparte as president of the Second Republic, and then as Emperor Napoleon III in 1852.

[27] Trinity Episcopal Church had built a new sanctuary, which is still in use.

Devor[28] was the best I saw. It is a fine painting both in conception & execution.

April 1848 ---

Saturday 1st....In the afternoon I was unwell, & by way of experiment Doct. [Robert W.] Gibbs made an application of cloroform.[29] The sensation & excitement were very pleasant & the effect was to relieve the head entirely during the active operation of the medicine & to mitigate the pain afterwards – It put me to sleep –

Sunday 2....I attended divine service in the College chapel in the morning & listened attentively to a sermon by Mr. [James] Thornwell. As a speaker he is more distinguished for close, logical reasoning than for eloquence. He is an able man –

Monday 3. We rose early this morning, preparatory to our departure for home. We parted with our brother & Sister & the family about 7 ocl. & took the road, after spending with them most delightfully eight or 10 days. We reached at night Mr. John Bates, by whom we were well accommodated & entertained –

Tuesday 4th. We set out at an early hour from Bates & reached home before 1 ocl. Here I met a summons to attend my dear Father, who was represented to be exceedingly ill. I borrowed a fresh horse & after eating a light dinner set out for my father's & reached his house at sunset. He was in his perfect mind and recognized me. I here met my Sister Ms. Blocker & the Major, also James Brooks & his Wife in attendance on my father – I felt considerable fatigue from the day's ride, being upwards of fifty miles –

Wednesday 5th....About 9 ocl, my father enquired for me & upon going to his bedside, he asked some questions in regard to his affairs, then caused his pocket book with his money and valuable papers to be handed to me, gave a few directions in regard to a note of hand & then crossed his hands & seemed to be engaged in prayer. This was the last conversation I held with him although he attempted afterwards on two or more occasions to communicate something but I could not understand him – In the afternoon my Wife & children arrived & were known & recognized by my father – He however hourly grew weaker.

Thursday 6th....My father continued to get weaker & his approaching dissolution became evident & inevitable. He seemed to retain the full possession of his mind & to understand, what was passing around him. During the day he would frequently call on the name of those servants who habitually had attended him but was not able to express his wants. He also took notice of our Son Hampden & opened his hand to shake hands with him, regarding him with great earnestness. He gradually sunk

---

[28] James DeVeaux (1812–1844), Charleston-born artist who trained in Philadelphia under Thomas Sully and studied in Europe. Wade Hampton II was his patron, and Dr. Robert W. Gibbes published DeVeaux's memoir soon after his death.

[29] Scottish obstetrician James Simpson first demonstrated the anesthetic property of chloroform on humans in 1847.

during the night & at half past four ocl. in the morning his pure & noble spirit, parted from the venerable body & I trust, winged its way to the bosom of his God. He died ripe in years, full of good works & respected by his neighbours & beloved by his family. He was in his 83rd year. [added]: How I venerate his memory. 17 Feby 1849 –

Friday 7th....The day was devoted to preparations for the burial of my dear father....I was confined to my bed the greater part of the day.

Saturday 8th. A continuous & uninterrupted rain from morning until night, in consequence of which we postponed the interment of my father until next day.

[vertically on the left margin in pencil: death of our grandfather]

Sunday 9th....During the night a considerable freshet prevailed in all the creeks & the larger ones were impassable this morning. At 11 ocl a procession was formed & the remains of my venerable & venerated father were conveyed to the Butler family burying ground & deposited near the grave of his departed friend Genl. Butler in the presence of a large collection of his neighbours. The Revd. Mr. Reed read the funeral service in a very impressive manner.

Monday 10th....I devoted the morning to the business of the plantation, employing an overseer for the home place & giving directions to the overseers at the two other places in relation to their management & soforth – I was kept very busy until 12 ocl at which [h]our we set out for home, at which we arrived before sunset. I was sick the entire way & scarcely was able to raise my head –

Tuesday 11th....After breakfast I rode to & over my farm, returned & was forced to go to bed by headache.

Wednesday 12th....I went to the village & saw Several of my neighbours. I also purchased a horse of Thomas Bleas[30] at $83.50. During my absence in Columbia, several sales & changes of property took place. Goodman sold his public house to Burt & Dobey.[31] Chs. Glover sold the Ryan public house to a Mr. Jennings,[32] & Saml. Goode & Tompkins made an exchange of property etc.

Thursday 13th....I finished this afternoon, manuring & planting the lots near the house in corn. By Saturday night I expect to finish planting my crop at the farm. I have never seen my corn look better or show a better stand. I have also about 20 acres in cotton well planted.

Friday 14....I took leave of my family at 12 ocl & set out for my plantation at which I arrived in good time & learned that the negroes were generally well –

---

30 Thomas Wainwright Blease (1823–1880); 1850 census: $250 real estate, 52 slaves. Uncle of Coleman Livingston Blease (1867–1942), of Newberry. SC governor, U.S. senator.

31 John Harwood Burt, M.D. (1798–1861), a respected brother of two other doctors. John L. Doby had a hotel in Hamburg sometime during this period.

32 Mr. Jennings is probably not Dr. William Dickenson Jennings (1820–1897), "a prominent local physician" (*Story of Edgefield*, 58), but Jennings was a common name.

Saturday 15th....I rode over my plantation and inspected the state of the crop. The entire plantation is in fine order & the land better prepared for a crop than I have ever seen it. The corn looks well & exhibits an unusually good stand. The cotton crop was planted with the exception of 30 acres, which was a little too wet for the plow. The wheat was in head & promised a better crop than I expected. The oats were promising. Stock of all kinds looked pretty well.

Sunday 16th....Not feeling well I left the plantation at 10 ocl for the late residence of my father, at which I arrived near 2 ocl, most deadly sick with nausea & headache. I got no relief until night –

Monday 17th....I rode to the Whitehall plantation[33] & made all necessary inquiries of the overseer in regard to the number of workers & horses under his charge & also a number of acres in cultivation. I gave such directions as I considered necessary & returned again very sick & again forced to go to bed. In the afternoon my Wife & children arrived, bringing letters & papers. A letter from my Son Preston informs us that he had suffered from diarrhea for four weeks but was at the date a little better. I recd. a letter from Lieut. Jon Davis from Mexico.

Tuesday 18th. I rode in the morning to the Wheeler plantation & performed the same routine of duties, that I had done the day previous. I was not as well pleased with the condition of things at this place as I was with that at Whitehall – I again returned sick & was forced to bed. In the afternoon we went to my Son James, whose family we found well. I rode over a part of his crop & made sundry suggestions to him in regard to it –

Wednesday 19th. At an early hour we took leave of my Son & family & crossed into the District of Newberry at Huitts ferry. At 10 ocl. I parted with my family in the Village of Newberry, they directing their course to Fairfield & I taking mine for the Glenn Spring. In the afternoon I reached Mrs. Boyce's, with whom I remained until next day.

Thursday 20th....I left Mrs. Boyce at an early hour & reached the Glenn Spring about 1 ocl. I recd. a welcome reception by my friend Zimmerman[34] & was assigned to a very comfortable room. I met two young men of [??] & education on a visit to these Waters –

On reading the newspapers I was surprised to discover that a revolutionary spirit was pervading the whole of Europe & that the Kings of Prussia & Austria have been forced to make large concessions in favour of the liberties of the people. All

---

[33] A plantation near the intersection of SC 156 and US 221 was named Whitehall by Rev. War General Andrew Williamson. Closer to the Brookses was a house named Whitehall built in Saluda SC in 1893. Was WB referring to Zachariah Brooks' plantation, which other records call Brooks Hill?

[34] John Conrad Zimmerman (1802–1875) bought a part ownership of the Glenn Springs Hotel in 1842, and was sole owner 1844–1853. He built "a fine Greek Revival house" there c. 1854, which still stands.

the German principalities were progressing in the same work of reform and amelioration. Ireland was partially quiet but evidently kept down by the arm of power – She would blaze out in revolution, if she had the least hope of success. In examining the progress of vegetation & the oat crops, I am satisfied that this part of the State is from two to three weeks more backward than Edgefield. Vegetation was as far advanced in Edgefield on the 5th of the month as it is here at this time....I drank the Water with a great avidity.

Friday 21....In the morning I read the newspapers & played a game of billiards with Doct. [Maurice] Moore. At 12 took the headache & went to bed. In the afternoon Doctors Moore & Smith called on me, with whom I held an agreeable conversation for half an hour. I wasn't able to set up & entertain them.

Saturday 22....I felt entirely relieved from pain this morning, for which I desire to return thanks to God. I walked to the Spring & took a drink from the fountain about 10 ocl....

Sunday 23rd....I remained in my room, during the greater part of the day & read the lessons of the day in the Epis. prayer book.

Monday 24th....I finished & caused to be mailed three letters to day, one to Judge Butler, one to Mrs. Brooks & the other to my Son Preston in Mexico....I am entirely free from pain & feel improving in health....I took exercise on horseback. Doct. Erwin & Mr. McCullough called to see me & passed a half hour in social conversation –

Tuesday 25th....I paid a visit to Mrs. Doct. Moore & took a considerable ride for exercise in the forenoon. Feeling dull & heavy in the afternoon I remained in my room....

Wednesday 26th....I took a ride of four or five miles & returned by Mr. Cunningham, whose dwellinghouse & kitchen on the 19th instant with their contents were destroyed by fire while the family were at church. He had for temporary use two cabins which will answer with no great discomfort until he can rebuild. The good lady in telling me of her loss shed tears copiously. In the afternoon I played a game of billiards with Doct. Moore....

Thursday 27th....In the afternoon I rode to examine a portion of the land of a Mr. Cunningham with a view to the selection of a lot to build a house for a Summer residence, but I did not find one to please me.

Friday 28th....I passed the day as usual in reading, writing, riding, & in social conversation with Doct. Moore & others. I read with much gratification in the State banner [*The Banner,* Abbeville, SC] an obituary notice of my father, prepared I presume, by my friend Doct. Laborde. It gives a true & faithful portraiture of his character. I also read portions of the evidence in the trial of Genl. [Gideon] Pillow, from which I formed a very favourable opinion of Pillow's skill & ability as a lawyer. He conducts his own defense & does it with great dexterity. I have a most contemptuous opinion of Mr. [Nicholas] Trist [ex US emissary to Mexico]. He is a poor, malignant & presumptuous creature, with some talent but greater pretention.

Saturday 29th....I rode three or four miles in the morning for exercise & returned with a headache, which confined me to bed until next morning –

Sunday 30th....a moderate fall of rain, thoroughly wetting the earth near the surface & affording a good season. My horse has strayed off. He got loose & ran off, pursued by my servant & one of Mr. Zimmerman's but up to 2 ocl. nothing has been heard of him. The last papers abound with statements of the great excitement, which was prevailing in Washington in consequence of an attempt to inveigle & carry off some 78 slaves from the District of Columbia. The statement is that a vessel arrived, with a load of wood, which the Capt. soon sold & at night received on board 78 slaves, who had left their owners, stealing & carrying with them silver & other valuable articles. The boat was pursued & overtaken & carried back to Washington where three white men & the negroes were committed to jail. Public indignation ran so high that it was difficult to prevent the mass of the people from forcing the jail & taking summary justice in their own hands. The excitement in Congress was also great & the debates exhibit a high sense of indignation on the part of Southern members & of evident delight among a portion of the Northern abolitionists, such men as Palfrey & Geddings.[35] Toombs[36] of Georgia spoke like a true & devoted Southern representative & I thank him for his denunciation of the aiders & abettors of these mischievous & unprincipled plunderers. I attended the reading of the Epis. Service by Mr. McCullough. Horse brought back about 11 ocl.

<u>May 1. 1848</u>

Monday 1st....I wrote a letter to my wife & played a game of billiards with Doct. Moore in the afternoon. Read in the afternoon a portion of De Tocqueville on Democracy in America[37] & also the evening service in the prayer book....

Tuesday 2....I have rarely seen a more favourable rain than the one, which fell on Saturday night & Sunday morning....I rode a few miles for exercise & returned by

---

[35] John Gorham Palfrey (1796–1881), Unitarian clergyman, U.S. representative from MA, 1847–1849. Harvard graduate and professor. Freed 16 slaves inherited from his father. After his censure in 1842 for violating the "gag rule" by discussing slavery in the House, he resigned and was easily reelected.

[36] Robert Augustus Toombs (1810–1885), a Whig of Wilkes County GA, was a major figure in U.S. House, then Senate. He opposed secession until 1859. Briefly Confederate Sec. of State, then army general.

[37] Alexis de Tocqueville (1805–1859) was a French intellectual and politician best known for his 2-volume work *Democracy in America* (1835–1840) and *The Old Regime and the Revolution* (1856). The former was based on research he and Gustave de Beaumont did during a 9-month tour of the U.S. in 1831–1832. Examining the country's political life, it noted positives and negatives and issued warnings based on observed trends. WB may have chosen to explore it because of his concerns about the revolutions occurring in Europe at this time.

way of the Spring. About 12 ocl. a dark cloud began to form in the West, attended by heavy thunder and . . . a heavy fall of rain & hail. I have not seen such a hail storm for several years. The hail was small & I presume has not injured the crops but the rain must wash the land.

Wednesday 3rd....I rode in the morning to look at a tract of land, which I desire to purchase for a summer residence, & in the afternoon to examine the premises of a Mr. Alexander, who desires to rent his house & furniture for the summer. I was not pleased with the house. It is small & has no good sleeping apartments. Recd. two papers from home & also several belonging to our landlord, which furnish additional accounts of the agitations in Europe & of the probable contingency of a general war on the Continent. The condition of England is critical & the determination of the Chartists [labor rights group] to persevere in holding a meeting, which the government has forbidden, may involve that nation in a bloody struggle. The insurrectionary spirit is prevailing over the whole of Ireland, which may be rendered furious by opposition & the want of food. It may end in riots & bloodshed but not in emancipation. A free government is not suited to the turbulent character of the Irish people, and any attempt to establish one will gradually lapse into anarchy & then into despotism. I read a long letter from my Son in Mexico to a friend in Edgefield, which was published in the *Advertiser*. Also an obituary notice of my father prepared by Col. Carroll.

Thursday 4th....After breakfast in company with Mr. Kennerly I paid a visit to Doct. & Mrs. Smith. We found the lady at home, by whom we were courteously received & agreeably entertained for a short time. The flower garden presented a neat and pretty object for the eye & exhibited the tasteful hand of the owner in its order & arrangement. The grounds around & in front of the house in particular have been greatly improved by the Doct. in the last two or three years, both in their appearance & productiveness. Again rode in the afternoon for exercise. Col. H[enry] Thompson of Spartanburg, (one of the candidates for a seat in the Congress in the place of Jas. A. Black, decd.) arrived at the hotel about dark from an electioneering tour.

Friday 5th....Col. [William Henry] Gist took dinner at the hotel on his way to a cavalry muster in Spartanburg. Recd. a letter from my dear wife, who informs me that my family are well & that both overseers[38] report favourably of the state of the crops --

....

Sunday 7th....Mr. Zimmerman returned this morning, bringing the intelligence of the death of his Aunt Mrs. Murf, who had been in a dying state for the last three days. By her death Zimmerman gets an estate, valued at $50.000. I am making preparations to take my departure so soon as I get dinner, with the expectation of

[38] His and ZSB's former overseer?

attending the services of the church by Mr. McCullough, at present a lay reader, which are to commence at 11 ocl. I paid this morning to Zimmerman a bill for $27.50 for eighteen (18) days board without making any objection or complaint, solely for the reason that I omitted to make any bargain with him in regard to the price of board on my arrival. I had been informed by Mr. Kennerly that he was paying at the rate of $10 per month and eating at his family's table, with a servant to wait upon him. I was also carried to his private table & par took of the plainest & simplest country fare, with desert only occasionally & then a mere preparation of potatoes. We had for three days in succession the following dishes, Bacon and squirrel, bacon and blackbirds, bacon & a few doves. I did not complain of this for I eat but little & that principally of bread & rice. Not a servant of his, was interrupted from their work for a single moment to attend upon me, or my room & my horse. I had my own servant & he performed all these duties & prepared a part of my food. Yet Mr. Zimmerman charged me his summer prices, at which time he has a number of hired servants to wait upon his table, a house keeper & manager & a band of music at high prices. He has also to furnish servants to bring water & to attend to the tables, not one act of which did I require. He would not have felt that I was on his premises but for my presence at meals. I regard the charges as being against all notions of equity & in fact against conscience & common honesty. I intend at some future moment to read this entry to Zimmerman, for I think he is disposed to act correctly but his love of money warps his understanding & sometimes his sense of fairness is a little obscured. I left Zimmerman at 3 ocl. & arrived at Mr. Brags about sunset....

Monday 8th....I left Mr. Brag's at 6 ocl. & after traveling on the Laurens road for six or seven miles, I turned to the left & took a road leading to Milton....I stopped at Griffin Williams & rested some two hours but it did not relieve my headache. I was very sick on the road & on arriving at Mr. Vaughn's, I ask for a bed, where I rested an hour & enjoyed a refreshing sleep. Upon rising I was measurably free from pain & resumed my days travel. I reached my plantation about half after 8 ocl. & met my Son Hampden, from whom I learned that my family were well. The negroes at the plantation were well....Tuesday 9th....I rode through my plantation & inspected the larger part of my crop. As a whole it never has been better at this period of the year. The negroes were employed in running round the cotton & working it over the first time. I think that they began to day to chop out for the first time. A portion of my corn is near knee high & a better stand of cotton I could not desire. After dinner I set out for home & arrived about Sunset. I had not been in the house five minutes when I took a chill, which was succeeded by fever which lasted until after 11 ocl. at night. I was quite sick both by fever & dysentery, which troubled me during the night....

Wednesday 10th....I was so indisposed that I did not rise until 8 ocl. & not until I had sent for Doct. Williams & consulted him. I suffered a good deal during the day with pain in the bowels & took burnt bandy [whiskey] as a remedy. I confined myself to a thin gruel diet & remained on the bed the greater part of the day ....Saw Col. Carroll, who informs me that the Court of appeals had reversed the Circuit deerse in the case in which I was complainant as trustee for my Sister Mrs. Blocker so far as Elsy & her children were concerned & confirming it in regard to the trust deed. This is a great triumph. He also informed me that Mr. Geo. McKie[39] has lost his Wife & child, his overseer & fifteen negroes by pneumonia & measles.

Thursday 11th....I rode over my Youngblood farm & was pleased with the prospect of a crop there. I also rode by & saw a portion of the crop at Mount Parson's, which is superior to that at the Youngblood place. In the afternoon I rode to the Village & saw a few of the Villagers....

Friday 12th....After breakfast I rode to Judge Butlers, to see him. He is on a flying Visit to his sick sister Mrs. Thompson who is still declining & cannot survive many days. The Judge was a little indisposed but not in bed. The whole family are in great tribulation & my poor friend Thompson is almost distracted by the magnitude of the loss, he is about to sustain in the death of one of the best of women & devoted Wifes. She is in truth a noble specimen of a superior woman & her death will be mourned by thousands. On my return I was attacked by headache & confined to my bed until Saturday morning.

....

Sunday 14th....I attended church in the forenoon & heard a good sermon by Mr. Walker. In the afternoon I rode for exercise & found the sun oppressively warm.

Monday 15th....I rode to the Village & saw a large portion of the inhabitants & transacted some business. The accounts from Europe represent the Provisional Government of France as more stable & stronger than was anticipated and as having suppressed a demonstration on the part of the factious mob in favour of insurrection. The different governments of Europe were still at peace with each other, except Austria & some of her Dependencies. Ireland was kept in check altho ready for revolt & civil war. No news from Mexico of much interest. I took a long ride with Mrs. B. in the buggy in the afternoon & called upon poor Mrs. McClintock[40]....

....

Wednesday 17th....I rode over my farm in the morning & was pleased to see that the crop was growing & improving every day. I have plowed the second time about 35 acres of corn & planted the ground in peas – in the afternoon I went to the Village but heard no news –

Thursday 18th....No recent intelligence from Mexico. I was very sick for 12 hours

---

[39] George A. McKie (1802–); 1850 census: $12,000 real estate, 21 slaves.

[40] Juliana Vardell, wife of Henry King McClintock, who died April 30, 1848, in Monticello GA while returning from the health resort Indian Springs. She took in boarders in her home near the "Academy" after his death (*Adv.*, June 7, 1848).

with headache –

....

Saturday 20th....After the arrival of the mail I set out for my fathers old residence, calling at Judge Butler's to see Aunt Butler & to enquire about Mrs. Thompson. While there a copious shower of rain fell, which extended more or less as far as Saluda River, as I afterward learned. I parted with Judge Butler at my house, who was on his return to Washington. I reached my fathers at 4 ocl. The crops on the road were small but looked well & more generally in good order.

Sunday 21....I was indisposed through the day & exceedingly sick at night with a violent paroxysm of headache. My Son James came down and spent the day with me.

Monday 22nd....Having appointed this day to make an appraisment of my father's estate four of the gentlemen came about 8 ocl & being qualified by the Magistrate entered upon their duty & by 5 ocl. in the afternoon had got through with the entire estate at three plantations. The four gentlemen were very obliging & attentive & I passed an agreeable day with them. Several of the neighbours called to see me. The crops were represented to be pretty good & in pretty good order. The personal estate was valued at about $25.000.

Tuesday 23rd....I set out for home about 7 ocl....I reached home at 2 ocl. & found all well except Hampden, who was suffering from cold & pain in the eyes. No news in the last papers either from Europe or Mexico.

Wednesday 24th....I am engaged in transplanting the potatoe slips....Mrs. Emela [Emmala] Thompson died at 4 ocl today after a protracted illness of more than four months at the residence of Judge Butler, which she bore with exemplary patience & christian resignation. She was a lady of eminent virtues & of very high character. Her equal can rarely be found in any Society however intelligent & refined, & few persons in this life commanded so large a share of the kindness, respect & even admiration of her acquaintances while living or whose death will be more sincerely lamented.

Thursday 25th....At 2 ocl. we set out for Judge Butlers to attend the funeral ceremonies of our relation Mrs. Thompson. The Revd. Doct. Johnson preached a short and appropriate sermon in which he gave a faithful portraiture of her life & character.

Her remains were deposited in a temporary brick vault, from which her husband [Waddy Thompson] intends to remove them to Greenville.

Friday 26th....I recd. a few days hence a letter from my Son Preston in which I had the gratifying intelligence, that his health was restored & that he was getting fat....I took a ride in the afternoon with the family to the farm to examine the State of the crop, the condition of the poultry yard etc. & on our return one of the horses refused to pull up a hill, the carriage ran down the hill & broke one of the front wheels, so badly as to render it necessary to walk home, which was very fatiguing to me....

Saturday 27th....I went to the Village to get the papers & letters by the mail & to learn the result of the Convention at Baltimore in reference to the selection of a Candidate for the Presidency....At 9 ocl. I set out with the family to spend the day with my Sister Ms. Blocker. We passed our time agreeably & returned home in the afternoon.

Sunday 28th....light rain . . . continued to fall throughout the entire day which has made it dull & gloomy. The earth appears to be thoroughly wet & altogether there could not have fallen a more gentle and favourable rain....The day was too inclement to leave the house, so there was no service in any of the churches.

Monday 29th....I rode to the Village & received my papers & letters among the number was one from my Son Preston, who was at San Angel in good health & spirits. He writes that he has no confidence that the Mexican Congress will ratify the treaty & that the Puros or war party will do every thing to defeat its ratification. Such was the last report from Queretaro [a state in north-central Mexico]....I rode to the farm in the afternoon & found the earth too wet for the plough....

....

Wednesday 31. Clear & mild morning the earth very wet & the roads muddy. At 10 ocl. I set out for Augusta & reached Hamburg about 4 ocl. very unwell & was forced to take a bed. I saw very few persons during the afternoon & was unable to attend to business. I caused fifty one bales of cotton to be weighed to be ready to offer it for Sale next morning. The price of cotton was from 4 ½ to 6 ¼, principally at 5 ½ & six cts. when at the same period last year, Cotton readily commanded from 11 to 12 cts. I sold in May [1847] a lot for my father to Sibley & Co. at 11 ¾ cts. Cotton is now worth very little more than half that price. From the partial view of the crops as I passed on I came to the conclusion that I had rarely ever seen them better this season or in better order. Rye & oats look well & the corn & cotton in fine growing condition. The cotton crop is too good. All agricultural products are now at low prices & money scarce.

<u>June 1. 1848</u>

Thursday 1....I sold fifty one bales of cotton to Sibley & Co. at 5 7/8, purchased a few articles in the grocery line, paid both on & my fathers a/c in Hamburg & then went over to Augusta. I however felt so unwell & wanting in animation that I returned to Hamburg before 11 ocl. & lay down. In conversing with the gentlemen of Hamburg, I discovered that the nominees for President & Vice Pres at Baltimore are not very acceptable to the politicians especially Genl. Cass. Woodberry[41] would

[41] Levi Woodbury (1789–1851) of New Hampshire, governor and U.S. senator, and loyal cabinet member under Jackson and Van Buren. Polk appointed him to the Supreme Court after Lewis Cass got the presidential nomination.

have been more acceptable to So. Carolina. Between 2 & 3 ocl. I set out for home & after suffering great agony from sick stomach & headache I reached home at 8 ocl. & went immediately to bed.

Friday 2....After breakfast Mrs. Brooks & I went to the Simkins family burying ground to see the specimen of monuments there. We also paid a visit to Aunt Butler, whom we found in pretty good health & spirits. On our return we called at Col. Pickens & recd. a cordial reception from him & his lady. In the afternoon I rode over my crop at my farm and examined it pretty thoroughly. It is equal to any that I have ever had.

Saturday 3....I examined a ditch, which I had employed an Irishman to dig & found it badly done. Mr. Peurifoy & wife [Louisa Ann Bird] called in the morning on their return to Georgia. In the afternoon I purchased a large bill of articles for my negroes & while in the Village heard an account of the Battalion review at the Pinehouse[42] & of a speech, made by Mr. Yancy to the Sovereign people, defending his course in the last Legislature.[43]

Sunday 4th....I received a letter last night from my overseer Mr. Lowry, giving me an account of a severe rain, which had fallen at my plantation & of the injury, which it had caused to my fences & land. Also the death of a young & large mule by bots.[44] One or two of my negroes were sick & the grass threatening to get the upper hand of him. On the whole it was rather a discouraging report. We attended church and recd. the administration of the sacrament. The evening was clear & mild. I called to see my old friend & neighbour Mr. [John] Lipscomb, who had just returned from Florida.

Monday 5th....Intelligence reached us of the ratification of the treaty of peace by the Mexican Congress by a large majority. The Court of Equity began its session this morning Chancellor Caldwell presiding.[45] The assemblage of persons in the Village was not large, owing to the busy season in regard to crops. Some 6 or 8 negroes were sold at high prices as I was informed. I traded for a horse with Mr. E[lbert] Devore,[46] with which I am much pleased as he is gentle in harness & easy under the saddle.

---

42 A prominent residence about 6 mile south of ECH on Augusta Hwy. A stop on Washington's southern tour in 1791. Gen. John R. Wever (1820–1874) bought it in 1847. The current structure was built after a fire in 1868.

43 Benjamin Cudworth Yancey, Jr. (1817–1891), of Hamburg, was an Edgefield member of the SC House 1846–1850, after which he moved to Alabama. His speech was not mentioned in the *Adv.* in June 1848.

44 Bots: female bot flies that deposit eggs in the noses of large animals.

45 James John Caldwell (1799–1850) was Chancellor, 1846–1850.

46 Elbert Devore (c. 1810–); 1850 census: $5,000 real estate, 22 slaves.

Tuesday 6th....I called to see the Judge & Mr. Thos. Pope[47] at Counties, [Charles Compty's] transacted a little business & returned home. In the afternoon I rode over my crop, which I think a very good & in fair order. While riding through the field my [new?] horse snagged himself in his forefoot & became very lame.

Wednesday 7th....My horse is still very lame, which will (I fear) disappoint me in setting out for the Glenn Spring at the time desired....I had a long conversation with the Revd. Mr. Reed & my Sister Mrs. Blocker & affected the purchase of a negro girl from him for my Sister at $500....

Thursday 8th....I went to the Village & met my old friend John McGahee of Florida, who has lately arrived in the District from the Democratic convention at Baltimore, to which he was a delegate. He is in very excellent health – we had a few friends to spend the evening with us but I was too unwell to leave my bed.

Friday 9th....I was too indisposed to leave the house until the afternoon, when I went to my farm to give directions to my overseer. My crop looks promising.

Saturday 10th....I am making preparations for going to the Glenn Spring for which place I set out at 9 ocl. & reached my plantation about 2. In the afternoon I rode over a part of my crop. The corn was excellent & in good order. The cotton looked promising but was in a grassy condition. Wheat & rye cut & the oats looked to be good. A severe rain some 10 days previous had fallen & washed & injured my plantation very much –

Sunday 11th....After breakfast I distributed among my negroes about forty dollars worth of Sunday shoes, clothes, hats, caps, buckets &C & then took my departure for my father's old residence, at which I arrived at 2 ocl. I passed the evening in rest & reading the bible. I ascertained that the negroes were in pretty good health –

Monday 12th....Capt. Coleman came down & with him, James Brooks & Burk [Buck?] Culbreath. I rode over the tract of land, on which my father lived & pointed out where the dividing lines should be run so as to throw it into three tracts for Sale. I also designated a dividing line between this & the Butler tract, attaching the greater part of the swamp land & Creek to the tract on which my father lived – In the afternoon I went home with James Brooks, a portion of whose crop I saw, which was very good.

Tuesday 13th....I set out for the Glenn Spring & arrived at Newberry Courthouse at 10 ocl. I stopped a few minutes at Fair's office to get the latest intelligence & learned that the Senate of Mexico had confirmed the treaty of peace by a large majority & that our troops were on their way to Vera Cruz, on their return home. I thank God that this hitherto bloody war has been terminated & peace restored between two coterminous Republics. I also learned that Genl. [Zachary] Taylor had

---

[47] Thomas Herbert Pope (1803–1851), Edgefield Dist. native. Read law with John B O'Neall, later his brother-in-law. Moved to Newberry 1832. Comm. in Equity 1836–1840, SC House.

been nominated by the Whig convention at Philadelphia for the Presidency & [Millard] Fillmore of New York for the V. Presidency. I reached Mrs. Boyce's early in the evening. The crops on the road very good & in good order.

Wednesday 14th....I arrived at the Glenn Spring about 12 ocl. & found only four or five visitors here.

Thursday 15th....About 12 ocl. I was attacked with headache & was confined to the bed the balance of the day. In the afternoon Elizabeth Smith escorted by Doct. & Lewis Youngblood arrived on their return home from an excursion to Limestone Spring & Harris at the foot of Hickory nut gap....

Friday 16th....The young people from Edgefield set out for home before sunrise & I did not see them. This is a holy day with me for on this day thirty years ago I consummated the most important act of my life by my intermarriage with Mary Parsons Carroll of Charleston. We then took each other for weal & woe, for better, for worse. Our lives have been somewhat checkered & yet we have prospered in worldy goods & enjoyed as large a portion of happiness as falls to the lot of the most favoured. She is now a more affectionate & devoted Wife than she ever has been & is at this moment dearer to my heart than the day, we were united. She has now the worst of the bargain, for my health is bad & I fear that temper under it is sometimes irritable – Her health is good, her temper well regulated & all her feelings & sentiments chastened by a sincere & heartfelt piety. May God in his infinite mercy grant her many years yet of health & happiness & if it be consistent with his benign purpose, I also pray him to restore me to better health that I am [better?] able to cherish & comfort her as age approaches.

Saturday 17th....I rode a few miles in the morning for exercise....The papers report a further decline in the price of cotton and general langor in the markets. It is expected that the Palmetto Regiment will Sail direct for Charleston & will be landed at Fort Moultrie where they will be paid & discharged.

Sunday 18th....I sent Cicero to meet Joseph to exchange horses at Doct. Teags. I read the morning & evening prayers & also the Church service.

Monday 19th....My servant returned with my horse just before the rain bringing me a letter from my overseer, in which he makes a favourable report of the State of affairs at my plantation.

Tuesday 20th....I rode over the Dean tract of land with old Mr. Moore with the view of making a purchase. The old Gentleman and I agreed to divide it provided I could bargain for it.

Wednesday 21....I rode in the morning with Mr. Owens again to examine the Dean tract of land. In the afternoon I suffered for a few hours with headache. In the evening Mr. C[harles] Pinckney arrived and called on me at my cabbin, with whom I held a half hour of pleasant conversation.

Thursday 22nd....After breakfast I rode for exercise & on returning called to see Mr.

Hill, who is very sick & also Genl. Gilliam, who arrived yesterday....A gentleman by the name of Harris from Mississippi arrived at the Hotel, with whom I held a short & interesting conversation in relation to the soil & crops of his State & of the process of cultivation in that State. He also gave me some information in regard to Genl. Taylor & his opinions especially on the subject of abolition.

Friday 23rd....After breakfast I set out for the Village of Spartanburgh, where I remained the entire day, being confined to the bed the greater part of the time. Mr. Cottrel called to see me with whom I had some conversation. The public men of this District have not yet decided, whom they will support for the Presidency. Many are inclined to each candidate but the majority are not satisfied with either.

Saturday 24th....Mr. Bobo[48] called on me at the Walker house & sold me the Brick-house tract of land, lying near the Springs. The land is thin but it will answer my purposes for a farm, on which to raise provisions, & to keep a small stock of cattle, hogs & sheep, to raise poultry & vegetables for the summers consumption & also for fire wood & building timber &C. I find that my health requires that I should live at or near this mineral spring & to pay board at the hotel for myself & family will be too expensive – I left Spartanburgh at 8 ocl & returned to the Glenn Spring....There are now only half dozen boarders at the hotel....

Sunday 25th....The Protestant Methodists held divine service in the Academy at 11 ocl but I did not attend in consequence of the heat of the Sun. The minister was a Doct. Crumly, originally from Kentucky and a gentleman of moderate capacity & limited information.

Monday 26....I went out this morning to the Dean tract of land, to lay off a portion of it for Mr. Jas. Moore, who had agreed to purchase it in copartnership with me but he did not make his appearance nor did I hear from him. How to account for this act of bad faith I am entirely at a loss unless the old gentleman has been influenced by officious neighbours. In the afternoon I attended to the survey of a lot 4 acres of land, which I purchased of Zimmerman at $100. It is a very eligible lot & affords a handsome building Site.

Tuesday 27....I rode in the morning for exercise & returned with symptoms of headache, which finally confined me to the bed until about 6 ocl in the evening, when my head became uneasy & I eat [ate?] a hearty supper.

Wednesday 28th....I rode to see Mr. James Moore, to whom I sold a part of the Dean tract to wit 149 ½ acres for $525. I also entered into written articles of agreement with Mr. Zimmerman for the purchase of a 4 acre lot at $100. on which I propose to build a neat cottage for a Summer residence. I also conditionally bargained for the crop of Mr. M. C. Owings & the delivery to me of the Dean tract of land for the sum of $150. The possession to be given to me between the 15 & 20th

[48] Simpson Bobo (1804–1885), lawyer, Methodist leader, trustee of Wofford College, investor in manufacturing, signer of Ordinance of Secession.

of July next. I am making preparations for my departure home in the morning, at which I expect to arrive on Saturday evening. Very few persons at this Watering place, not more than a dozen, & I look for a small company during this Summer. The scarcity of money will deprive many of the means of leaving home. Our host is a good honest & clever man & I wish him success in his house. His table is always well furnished –

Thursday 29th....I left the Glenn Spring at 6 ocl & reached Laurens Village about 5. In passing through I saw Genl. [Waddy] Thompson & Capt. Cunningham at Simmons tavern, with whom I stopped and held a half hour's conversation. The Court of Equity was being held for that District by Chancellor Caldwell – I remained for the night at Mrs. Boyd's –

Friday 30th....I resumed my journey at 6 ocl & passing through old Cambridge arrived at my plantation about 1 ocl in the midst of a refreshing shower of rain. At & near Cambridge rain is much wanted ....I learned on my arrival that my negroes were well with the exception of two women who were suffering under some chronic disease. In the afternoon I rode over my crop, & saw the greater part of it. The corn is very good & a large portion of the cotton is promising. The oat crop seems to be very abundant but the wheat & rye ordinary. I have a new ground of nearly 30 acres in corn as rank & luxuriant as I ever saw growing in the low lands of the Savannah River. The crop is by no means free from grass. I have reason to be satisfied with it & to be thankful for it.

July 1. 1848

Saturday 1....I set out for home at 6 ocl & arrived about 1, where I found my family well & much rejoiced to see me. A child of our woman Sally died in a few hours after my arrival from an injury which it had received by a fall from the nurse. I heard a good deal of news, none however so unexpected & revolting as the rude & insulting conduct of Doct. Jones to his Wife in the Episcopal church within the view & hearing of the congregation, which occurred a few Sabbaths past. Great indignation is felt by the Citizens on account of this brutal conduct & universal sympathy for his Wife, who is represented to be an amiable lady & devout Christian. The health of the Village is good altho there are several cases of alarming symptoms but they are the results of some constitutional defect in the parties. The continued rains & moisture have created more mosquitoes than I have ever known & at night they are more annoying. They literally drive away sleep. I heard of a rather ludicrous personal rencoutre between Ch[arle]s Gray & [H. R?] Spann about some sheep killing dogs, that Gray was endeavoring to shoot....

Sunday 2nd....We attended divine service in the Epis. church & partook of the body & blood of Christ in the holy sacrament instituted by him....

Monday 3rd....A public meeting was held in the Courthouse to make arrangements to receive with some mark of distinction the Volunteers to Mexico from this District, being the company under the command of Capt. Brooks, called 96 boys. Col. Pickens introduced resolutions & made a few eloquent remarks, adapted to the occasion. He was followed by Mr. B[enjamin] Yancy in a neat address. A public dinner will be given to the company, and a military procession to be formed on the day. Col. Mims was appointed chairman of the military committee & Col. Frazier of the civil to make arrangements for a grand display &C – not many persons, in the Village, & very little property sold by the Sheriff –

Tuesday 4th....I went to the village & called on young Mr. Patterson, who has been employed by our trustees to take charge of our Academy, since the death of my old & valued friend Mr. McClintock. Every thing wore a dull appearance in the Village & not a sign was to be seen or a note of preparation heard to observe with suitable thankfulness this national anniversary of a free people. There were fewer persons in the Village than usual & they were sitting in the Piazas in listless groups, utterly unconscious of the obligations of the day. No intelligence of the 96 boys.

Wednesday 5th....I rose this morning unrefreshed in consequence of the annoyance of the mosquitoes during the night....[*Inserted:*] P. S. Brooks reaches Hamburg.

Thursday 6th....The intelligence from Europe represents France in a more excited State than at the time of the meeting of the Convention.

Friday 7th....I had an attack of headache from which I suffered considerably.

Saturday 8th....I received by the mail a note from Preston informing me of his arrival in Hamburg & requesting me to send for him. I set out in my carriage at 10 ocl & reached Hamburg at 5 ocl, where I met my Son in pretty good health. After resting for one hour & a half we left Hamburg & reached Doct. Guiger's [W. W. Geiger's] at 9 ocl, where we remained during the night....The good people of Hamburg gave a cordial reception to the members of the Palmetto regiment, who passed through their town.

Sunday 9th. We set out at day light & arrived at home at 9 ocl. where we met all the family in health. In the forenoon I took rest & sleep & in the afternoon went to Church.

Monday 10....I went to the Village with Mrs. Brooks to purchase sundry articles for our Glenn Spring establishment. In the afternoon suffered from headache & was confined to the bed.

Tuesday 11....I set out with Preston for the old residence of my Father on Big Creek, calling on my venerable Aunt Butler on the way, whom we found in pretty good health. On reaching the paternal residence I met James & several of the neighbours, who were engaged in running out the land. After dinner I rode to the White Hall place & inspected the crop &C.

Wednesday 12....After breakfast I rode to the Wheeler place & over the crop of corn & cotton. The crop is a good one. On returning to the house, I was forced to take my bed in consequence of headache. At 2 ocl. I rose from the bed & set out for home, suffering great pain for the first two hours, after which my head became comparatively easy & I reached home at dark. All well....

Thursday 13th....After breakfast I rode with Doct. Laborde & Preston to my farm & over my crop with the view of showing my crop to them but they seemed to enjoy the site about as well as a blind man would a beautifully executed picture or a deaf man, one of Mozart's best pieces of music. They were certainly not in an agricultural frame of mind....Lieut. [Joseph] Abney & Doct. [Elbert] Bland reached the Village on their return from Mexico & spent the evening with me.

....

Saturday 15th ....Preparations making in Columbia & Charleston to give an entertainment to the Volunteers of the Palmetto regiment.

Sunday 16th....I was indisposed during the day & did not leave the lot.

Monday 17th....We set out about 9 ocl for my plantation on our way to the Glenn Spring & reached the plantation at 2 ocl. In the afternoon I rode over a part of my crop & was grieved to find that it was suffering greatly for the want of rain, particularly the corn.

Tuesday 18th....I rose & inspected my entire crop, which I regret to record was hourly suffering for the want of rain. The corn was fireing & in some places the tassel seemed to be dieing. I conjectured that I was loosing at the rate of 50 bushels per day. The crop was in pretty good order in regard to work & the cotton was good. The overseer had put undercover the wheat & oats. The health of the negroes good.

Wednesday 19th....We left the plantation after early breakfast for the Glenn Spring & arrived Laurens Ct. House at 6....light showers in the afternoon.

Thursday 20th....I read at Laurens the account of bloody insurrection in Paris, in which 10.000 were killed, the Arch Bishop among the number. The rebellion was finally put down after five days fighting in various parts of the City. The National Guard behaved well & faithful to the Government....[49] I was exceedingly sick on the road & stopped for two hours to take a rest but derived but little benefit. We reached my new purchase the brick house tract of land, about 2 ocl & after giving directions to the Servants, who had preceded us, we went to the Glenn Spring. Not many persons at the hotel & therefore very little society.

Friday 21....We passed the greater part of the day at the brickhouse, cleaning up & repairing houses &C. Dark clouds & light showers in the evening & again at night.

Saturday. Cloudy & showery through the day. We were engaged again at the brickhouse.

Sunday 23rd. A continuation of . . . showery weather. We had no service at the hotel & the day passed away slowly & dull.

---

[49] Another episode in the ongoing revolutions of 1848 throughout much of Europe.

Monday 24....I went through the regular routine of visiting the brickhouse & preparing for our removal. Also rode into the country & purchased butter & enquired for a cow & calf. Few persons in the hotel.

Tuesday 25th. No change in the weather nor in the employment of my time.

Wednesday 26....After breakfast we removed to the brickhouse, having obtained tables, pots, ovens, chairs & a large portion of the et ceteras necessary to house keeping. Mr. Zimmerman & lady were very kind & have placed us under many obligations. We passed a pleasant day & night at our new home, with which I am greatly pleased. It is a pleasant residence, elevated & cool & having an abundance of water, fruit &C.

....

Friday 28. The same kind of weather & the usual routine of riding & drinking water.

Saturday 29....I had headache and was confined to the house the greater part of the day.

Sunday 30th....We attended the performance of divine service in the hotel by the Revd. Bruce Walker, who as usual read the service in good style & preached a sensible sermon.

Monday 31st....I was in the neighbourhood in search of a cow when the rain began to fall. The earth is now dry....The corn crop promises to yield in this District a most abundant product provided rain should fall in time but a continuation of the drought will greatly lessen the production.

August 1. 1848

Tuesday 1....I rode to Mr. Peaks [Pecks?] & purchased a cow & calf at $11. Went from his house to Smith's saw mill & engaged meal & lumber. Then to Glenn Spring & home.

Wednesday 2....In the morning I went to Spartanburgh, with Mrs. Brooks and my daughter. We purchased sundry articles, took dinner at the Walker house and returned home in the afternoon. I was informed that it was in contemplation to hold a Taylor meeting & also a [Lewis] Cass & [William O.] Butler meeting on Monday of sale day. The adherents of Cass are 5 to 1 of Taylor men.

....

Saturday 5th. Partially cloudy in the morning. Rain at 12 ocl & light showers until 2 ocl but barely enough to lay the dust.

Sunday 6th....We attended divine service in the new [Calvary] Episcopal Church now in a state of creation near the Spring. The Revd. Mr. McCullough read the service & delivered a very sensible & well written Sermon. After which the Revd. Bruce Walker administered the sacrament in an impressive manner. Some 15 to 20 persons partook of the bread & wine....

Monday 7th....After breakfast I went to the village of Spartanburgh & purchased a few articles for present use. At 12 ocl a meeting of the Democratic Party was called in & near one of the piaza's near the Courthouse, when Mr. Tucker one of the delegates to the Yorkville Cass convention addressed the crowd in a frank, honest & rather able manner, giving a statement of the proceedings of that meeting & of the ratification by the convention of the nominations of Cass & Butler for P. & V. President. He was followed by some six or seven candidates for the Legislature upon local subjects & the discussion was closed by Mr. Thompson, a candidate for Congress. The Speakers acquitted themselves rather better than is usual on such occasions. The proceedings of the Yorkville convention was ratified by a unanimous Vote. The auditory consisted of 400 or 500 persons. The Whigs held a meeting in the Courthouse at the same hour for the purpose of passing some measure favourable to the election of Genl. Taylor. The members of this meeting were few, not more than from 75 to 100 as I was informed. The Supporters of Cass & Butler are as from 4 or 5 to one in favour of Taylor. Such is the majority of the Mountain Districts generally as far as I am informed. I trust the majority over the entire State may be as great & that Whiggery & Taylorism may be finally rebuked & put down. I regret that some of my personal friends have declared in favour of Genl. Taylor, particularly Gen. Hammond. I think it the greatest error of his political life which he will himself regret in a few months.

Tuesday 8....I was engaged about my buildings.

....

Thursday 10. Thunder clouds but very light showers barely sufficient to lay the dust.

Friday 11....I went to Esquire Harris to purchase a cow & calf. On my return I was attacked with headache, from which I suffered a good deal.

Saturday 12....I again suffered from a paroxysm of headache ....

Sunday 13th....We attended divine service in the Hotel morning & afternoon & heard two sensible sermons by Mr. McCullough.

Monday 14th....I went to Smiths mill & got some plank for my stables &C. On my return was caught in a rain, of which I had none at my house....We went to the Hotel in the evening & remained until 10 ocl. Col. Donavin, Doct. Griffin, Messrs. Styles and Postell called on us in the afternoon – At the hotel I met Col. Davie, Col. Gladden,[50] Major Eves & several other gentlemen, who had arrived during the day.

Friday 15....Col. Carroll & lady arrived at night.

Wednesday 16th. The weather unsettled & occasional showers. Col. Carroll left us

[50] Probably Col. Adley Hogan Gladney (1810–1862) of Fairfield Dist. He took command of the Pal. Reg. upon the death of P. M. Butler.

after breakfast on his return to Edgefield, leaving Mrs. Carroll & her youngest child with us –

Thursday 17th....The company at the hotel daily increasing. The number at this time is about 100 persons.

Friday 18th....a good deal of rain, during the day. I was busily engaged on the stables & making fences. Company from the hotel called in the morning & afternoon –

Saturday 19th....Alternate showers & sunshine. The earth pretty thoroughly wet & vegitation & the crops much revived –

Sunday 20th....We rode to the hotel to attend preaching but there was none, the Rev. Mr. Johnson having gone to the Village of Spartanburgh after preaching a sermon in the morning.

Monday 21....I was occupied in opening a way for a new fence about which I became much fatigued. Visited Col. Gladden at the hotel, whom I found indisposed. In consequence of his indisposition we agreed to defer our departure for the mountains until Wednesday.

Tuesday 22....On this day I removed some houses & marked out the line for a new fence. Visited the Spring, drank water etc. etc.

Wednesday 23rd....Our Son Preston & his family arrived at our house about 12 ocl & he consented to join our party in a short excursion to the mountains, for which we set out at 3 ocl, meeting Col. Gladden & family, Col. Dunovan & Mr. Stiles at Whitmores store, from there to Spartanburgh Courthouse –

Thursday 24....We left the Walker house after breakfast for Greenville, at which we arrived about 4 ocl in the afternoon & took lodgings at the Mansion house....[51]

There were few Visitors at Greenville & we learned that there [were] comparatively few persons in the mountains this summer, which is owing (I presume) to the low price of cotton & the scarcity of money.

Friday 25th....We passed this day at the hotel, receiving the visits of our friends & in the afternoon took a ride to visit my worthy relation Wesley Brooks & his family. A dancing party was given at night to Col. Gladden, Col. Dunovan & Capt. Brooks – a transparency was prepared for the occasion with the names of these three gentlemen in large letters. The party filled the room & was composed of a handsome & neatly dressed collection of young ladies & a respectable class of young gentleman. The dancing continued until after 12 ocl.

Saturday 26th....After breakfast our party set out for the table rock & reached Sutherland's in the afternoon.[52] I was exceedingly sick on the way & did not get relief

[51] Erected by William Tomey on Courthouse Square. A starting point for trips into the NC mountains. It had 23 rooms, a piano, bar, ballroom, and "the only sofa in the village."

[52] William Sutherland opened the Table Rock Hotel in Pumpkintown, Pickens Dist., in 1845. Table Rock State Park was built by CCC workers in the 1830s.

until after night....

Sunday 27th. Cloudy but very little rain. We went to the rock in the morning with the base & summit of which the company was much delighted. In the afternoon the company took rest. I had a return of headache & past a few hours in suffering --

Monday 28th....After breakfast we set out for Caesar's head,[53] at which we arrived at 12 ocl. We found the ascent of the mountains laborious but not difficult. At the hotel we met Col. [Christopher?] Orr[54] & family & the wife of Mr. Sprawl of Abbeville. I was forced by a violent paroxysm of headache to retire to a room immediately upon my arrival & saw nothing during the day. The company were in raptures with the scenery & distant views from the mountain eminence & enjoyed themselves very much. At night we had good music on the Violin. Some hunters returned in the afternoon bringing with them two Pheasants & a rattle snake of some size, which had been taken in the mountains. Col. Hagood had a bear, a deer & a groundhog, which presented an assemblage of living animals, rarely to be met with at one place.

Tuesday 29th....Mrs. B. & I rose early for the purpose of viewing the valley & Mountains at Sunrise, which we did from a spot near the houses & also from Caesar's head. The prospect was beautiful & variagated & richly rewarded us for the early rising & the walk. About one year past I visited this place & gave at the time a description in this book of the Valley & mountain Scenery. After breakfast we set out for the flat rock settlement & reached Summie's hotel at 4 ocl. We found only four grown persons staying at the hotel & a few children. There are comparatively but few persons in the mountains this Summer. The Honl. Mr. [Mitchell] King & his son Doct. [Mitchell Campbell] King[55] called at the hotel to see us and gave the entire party a pressing invitation to dine with him, which we declined in consequence of a want of time.

Wednesday 30th....At 8 ocl we left the Flat rock for Col. Deavers[56] sulphur Spring which we reached in the afternoon – The company here was neither large nor select. We were provided with comfortable rooms but found the table only tolerable & the bread indifferent.

Thursday 31st....I was indisposed & remained in my room the entire afternoon. The ladies & young members of our party amused themselves with nine pins, music &

---

[53] Caesar's Head, a rock formation atop a promontory that, for some, resembles the profile of a man. Also now a state park.

[54] Christopher Orr was father of Congressman James L. Orr, later to provide support for PSB as a national Democrat in congress.

[55] Mitchell King (1783–1862), Scots-born prof. at the College of Charleston, lawyer and judge. Had one of the largest private libraries in the South, and a summer home at Flat Rock NC. His son Mitchell Campbell King was a physician.

[56] Col. Reuben Deaver built a wooden hotel, and expanded it to 250 rooms, above Asheville Sulphur Springs. Guests included the social elite of SC. It burned in 1862.

cards. At night they were able to make up a cotillion in which dance they participated for about one hour. I drank the mineral water in moderate quantities for an experiment & found that it was both too stimulating & indigestible. It disagreed with me so much that I was forced to abandon its use. It may be salutary in many cases of disease in other persons but to me it is injurious. The location of this watering place among the mountains & the cool temperature of the atmosphere make it a desirable place of sojourn for a few weeks during the hot Summer months & the only thing that detracts from the house, is the indifferent bread. The Landlord is sufficiently obliging & his charges are not unreasonable. My old acquaintance Chas. Warley & Major Lovel were staying here for a part of the Summer.

September 1. 1848

Friday 1....[I]n the afternoon there arrived from Warm Springs some ten or fifteen persons, which added to our numbers but without improving the character of our Society. At night the young folk again repaired to the dancing room & went through two or three cotillions.

Saturday 2....At 8 ocl we took our departure for Harri's (sic?) at the foot of the mountain, where the hickory nut gap terminates at which we arrived about Sunset. We were here thrown among a large crowd of Visitors of the mediocre class, with none of whom did I become acquainted – our party was delighted with the Scenery down this mountain pass – the cooking at this house was decidedly bad & all the means of accommodation rough & and in disorder. I was anxious to get away –

Sunday 3rd....We took our departure about 8 ocl & reached Rutherford Village at 12 ocl. We stopped here for dinner & a most excellent one did we receive at the hotel of Mr. Twitty. In the afternoon we passed Broad River & took lodgings for the night at a Mr. Camp's – he is a plain & unpretending planter, who gave us very substantial & well dressed breakfast & supper.

Monday 4th. We rose at an early hour & took breakfast at 6 ocl....At half past 12 we reached the Walker house in the Village of Spartanburgh, where we dined. In the afternoon we reached home in good time & our friends went to the Glenn Spring hotel. I found my negroes well & every thing in good order. I received sundry papers & letters but no news of any importance. Several deaths have occurred in Edgefield, among the number was old Mrs. Mitchell & [??] Wife – I received a letter from our Son James – informing us that his Wife had sustained a miscarriage. This is the third or fourth, which in her state may be regarded as a mercy of God.

Tuesday 5th....We attended a regimental review of Cavalry near the Glenn Spring. Genls. Wallace [,] Gadberry & Canty were present & reviewed the Regiment. The day was warm & exceedingly dusty. At night the young people collected together & had a large dancing party, which passed off very agreeably.

Wednesday 6th....I rode to the Spring both in the morning & evening & called at the hotel.

Thursday 7th....We passed the day in visiting the Spring & in receiving the calls of our friends ....

Friday 8th....Several of the Volunteer officers of the Palmetto Regiment left the Springs for Limestone to attend a public dinner. The company at the hotel has become greatly reduced in numbers being now not more than from 30 to 40.

....

Sunday 10th....We went to the hotel with an expectation of hearing a sermon but the minister did not attend.

Monday 11. Mild & sweet morning. For the last week, the nights have been exceedingly pleasant in temperature, with a bright moon & clear sky. There are a few agreeable & sensible persons at the Hotel, among the number are Col. Gladden & lady[,] Mr. Villapeig [?] & lady & Mrs. Flinn, who constitute an agreeable society.

Tuesday 12th....I passed the day as usual & at night we went to the hotel & attended the dancing of the young folk for a few hours –

Wednesday 13th....After breakfast I rode with my Son Preston to the Spring & on our return while the horse was in a full trot, the buggy wheel ran over a root & became entangled in some way, by which it was dashed to pieces & other parts broken & by which he & I were thrown out of the buggy but without serious injury. I was considerably bruised on my legs & hand, while he escaped unhurt.

Thursday 14th....I was indisposed & was confined to the house the greater part of the day....

Friday 15th....I rode to the Spring & drank freely of the Water. This hastened a paroxysm of headache by which I suffered great agony the whole afternoon. Doct. Pratt tried cupping on the stomach & also gave me a mixture of mauphine, ether & pepper mint to allay the irritation of the Stomach, but it aggravated the attack & increased my suffering.

Saturday 16th....I was measurably free from pain but felt feeble & out of order. Chancellor Dunkin & his daughter Mrs. Huger called out to see us. The Chancellor is a good friend of mine and on all occasions manifests anxiety about my health.

Sunday 17th....We attended divine service at the hotel & heard a sermon by a Mr. Johnson, a young divine of the Episcopal Church.

Monday 18th....Our Son Preston & family left us after breakfast for my plantation in Edgefield & thence to the Village. I accompanied them about 2 miles & returned by way of the Spring. At night we went to the hotel to take leave of Col. Gladden & family, who had assigned the following morning for his departure home. The young folk danced until 9 ocl. when we returned home.

Tuesday 19th....I rode this morning...for exercise & to look at a small tract of land & thence by the Spring. I saw a very superior crop of corn, the product of the labour of one man, who lived as lonely as a hermit with no living thing about him except a horse, a few fowl & a dog.

Wednesday 20th....I rode to the Spring & on my return bargained for a mare & mule colt for $115. In the afternoon we rode to the Spring & made calls on Sundry friends, among the number of whom were Chancellor Dunkin & his daughter Mrs. Huger.

Thursday 21....I took a long & circuitous ride through the neighbourhood in the morning & in the afternoon we went to West's Spring about 3 miles from my house....Doct. Pratt passed the morning with us.

Friday 22nd....I never saw a brighter morning or one more animating to the feelings. The world could not show a lovelier sky than that, which now hangs over us.

Saturday 23rd....About 6 ocl. P.M. Doct. Laborde's servant Edward arrived, bringing a letter, to inform us of the dangerous situation of our brother Col. Carroll by typhoid fever & requesting our immediate return, preparations for which we commenced without delay –

Sunday 24....After early breakfast we set out for home & arrived at night at Mr. F. Nance's. I was delayed on the road two hours to have a tyre put on one wheel of my carriage, which broke after our departure from EllenDale. I suffered during the whole day, great pain from headache & took a bed so soon as I arrived at Nance's. –

Monday 25th....We reached my plantation about 12 ocl. where I was forced to remain in consequence of a continuation of my headache, during the day – the family however came down to the Village, which they reached before night. I found Col. Carroll very ill but not as dangerously so as he had been —

Tuesday 26th....I rode before breakfast over a part of my crop, which I found as good as I expected. Both corn & cotton crop will equal my expectations. I arrived at home at half past 12 ocl. & on calling at Col. Carroll's, learned that he was considered a shade more out of danger. All well at home.

Wednesday 27th....I rode to my farm & inspected my crop. It is a good one & in every point of view equal to my hopes – I was gratified to find my negroes in good health & my stock of hogs, horses & cattle in good condition – [John?] Gallman seems to have managed well & to have been industrious – I directed him to commence to gather corn. He had picked out about 9000 lbs. of cotton in good order.

Thursday 28th....I passed a few hours in the Village in the forenoon & in the afternoon rode to Pottersville & to my farm. My corn is yielding a good crop per acre, equal to my anticipations.

Friday 29th....Major Blocker & my Sister came down to see us & also Judge Butler & his daughter. At 12 ocl we repaired to the Epis. Church to attend the baptism of Doct. Laborde's youngest child called Sophia L. Laborde by the Revd. Mr. Walker. I & Mrs. Brooks were selected as Godfather & Mother & joined in the ceremony –

Saturday 30th....I finished hawling corn from the Youngblood place & made by the measurement of the waggon 360 bushels to thirty acres, equal to 12 bushels to the acre.

October 1. 1848.

Sunday 1....The rain of last night has settled the dust & caused the small water courses again to run but enough did not fall to set the mills to running. We attended divine service in the Epis. church & participated in the sacrament. Cloudy & heavy thunder in the afternoon & a copious rain at night. Judge Wardlaw & Solicitor Edwards arrived to hold the Court of Appeals.

Monday 2....[T]he Court of Common Pleas commenced its fall session, Judge Wardlaw presiding. About 12 ocl a large concourse of citizens convened in the Courthouse, to hear an address from our Senator in Congress Judge Butler & also from Major Burt, the representative from this Congressional District, upon the condition of the Southern States in relation to the Legislation in Congress on the Slave question in connection with the territories etc. – I attentively listened to each Speaker & was rather pleased with the address of each. They concurred in the belief that the South could expect but little aid in the great slave question from either of the Candidates for the Presidency & that on unanimity at home was our only dependence. Both favoured the call of a Southern convention and indicated a preference for Cass for the Presidency.

Tuesday 3rd....I visited the Village & mixed for a short time with the crowd, whom I found considerably excited on the election of members of the Legislature –

Wednesday 4th....In company with Ms. Brooks & Ellen I set out for Hamburg about 10 ocl, at which we arrived at 5 in the afternoon. I had headache & was forced to bed & therefore had no opportunity of conversing or seeing any of the inhabitants.

Thursday 5....I sold 20 bales of cotton to Sibley &Co. for 5 ¾ cts & expended in groceries & negro shoes upwards of $200. Mrs. B. & Ellen passed the day in shopping in Augusta. I joined them in the afternoon & purchased furniture to the value of $195. I also received & sent by my waggons tombstones for my Father, Mother & Whitfield.

Friday 6th....We left Hamburg at 10 ocl & reached the Village at 5 when we heard of the deaths during the day of Matt Mims[57] & Mr. Chs. Meigs. Both died of some chronic disease under which they had been suffering for several years. Mr. Mims had been a useful citizen & for 30 years a member of the church and was in many respects a good man. Meigs was of amiable temper, kind hearted & obliging but he suffered temptation to seduce him into the ways of sin & transgression against both the laws of God and of the State. By death he escaped the penalty.

Saturday 7th....I paid a visit to the family of Mr. Mims & then went to the Village but heard no news. Mr. Mims was buried at four o'clock in the family cemetery. In

---

[57] Mathew Mims (1780–1848) lived near WB's Edgefield home. He was clerk of court starting in 1814 and a charter member of Edgefield Baptist Church.

the afternoon I went to my farm & learned from my Overseer that I should make over 1000 bushels of corn & a fair crop of cotton.

Sunday 8th....We attended preaching in the Epis. church by the Revd. Bruce Walker, our pastor. The congregation was small but attentive.

[*summarizes the rest of October:*]

Early in the week I went with my family to my plantation & thence to the Glenn Spring. I was exceedingly unwell for a week after my arrival at the Spring but upon the weather becoming open, warm & clear I began to improve. I passed upwards of a fortnight at the Brick house now called Ellendale with both pleasure & profit. While at Ellendale I engaged Mr. West to add to & repair my house. We returned to Edgefield about the last of the month by the way of the old residence of my father on Big Creek. The entire month was mild & generally clear with three or four light Showers, which only wet the surface of the Earth. I have never seen a fairer month for picking out cotton & gathering in the crops –

November 1848

On my return to Edgefield we remained a few days at home and then went down to Hamburg to allow Mrs. Brooks & Ellen an opportunity of making some purchases. Mr. Walker [*overseer*] had during my absence to the Glenn Spring sold forty bales of cotton at 5 cts & paid the proceeds over to me. I returned home & spent a few days here & then went to my plantation, where I was detained by bad weather until Sunday the 21. on which day I went down to my father's residence, feeling in better health than I have done for several days. On tuesday the sale of his estate commenced & closed on thursday. The land sold at very low prices but the negroes & other properties sold at a fair Value. On friday & part of Saturday I delivered property & took notes of hand & at 12 ocl on Saturday set out for home, which I reached about Sunset finding all well. Early in this month Mr. Cruise [?] commenced adding a new building to my house at the plantation, under whom I put four hands at $60 per month. On thursday the 30th of this month Mrs. Brooks set out for Columbia on a visit to Mrs. Laborde, her Sister, taking Ellen with her. The month of November was generally clear & mild with the exceptions of a few days of very cold weather when there was ice. During this cold weather I killed a portion of my hogs – the month was favourable to picking out cotton & gathering crops – during this month there was an extra meeting of the Legislature to elect Electors of President & Vice President.

December, 1848

I have occasion to remember Monday the 3 of December from the fact, that I had one of the most distressing headaches, with which I have ever been afflicted & from which I suffered inexpressible pain – On tuesday I was feeble but went to my plantation. Here I found the workmen busily engaged in framing my house. I remained tuesday at the plantation, attending to my business. On Thursday I went to James Brooks, on my way to Columbia, where I arrived in the afternoon....

Thursday 7. I left James Brooks before sunrise for Columbia, having dressed and breakfasted by candle light & arrived at Doct. Labordes in Colombia at 7 ocl. I received from my good Brother & his excellent Wife a most warm & cordial reception. I remained in Columbia until the thursday following & then set out for home on as gloomy a day as any man ever traveled. It was showery throughout the day & somewhat cold. We reached Mr. Lee's in good time, where we passed the night.

Friday 8th....We left Lees after breakfast & arrived at home about 3 o'clock where we found all well. No news –

Saturday 16th. Somewhat cloudy & cool. I was too indisposed to leave the house. Recd. the papers from Columbia, giving an account of the inauguration of Gov.[Whitemarsh] Seabrook & of his address which was highly complimented. Also of the passage of a resolution by both branches of the Legislature against the policy of rechartering the bank of the State. The commercial news from Europe of a favourable character.

Sunday 17th....I was confined to my bed the entire day, I suffered immense agony. I took an emetic, [*to induce vomiting*] which relieved me after an active operation.

Monday 18....I went to my plantation, where I found all well. My wheat had come up & presented a beautiful appearance.

Tuesday 19th....I paid a visit to Col. Griffin. I have still upwards of 20 bales of cotton in the field, to be picked out.

Wednesday 20th....I rode to Doct. Lelands & took a general examination of his land with the view of purchasing it. The land is valuable & would suit me but the price is high.

Thursday 21st....I returned home, where I found the family well.

Friday 22....I sent off this morning Betsy & her children from the Farm to my plantation with my stock of cattle, so that now Preston is in full possession –

Saturday 22nd....Capt. Bird and family & Col. Dunovant were with us.

Sunday 24. Cloudy & Misty in the morning which kept me from attending Church. Partially clear in the afternoon, when I attended church & heard a most interesting sermon by the Revd. Mr. Reed. Our Son James arrived at night.

Monday 25th....We attended service in the Epis. church & partook of the sacrament. We passed the day with our good mother & partook of a good dinner. We spent the day very pleasantly, having at table Capt. [Daniel] Bird & family Preston & Wife, my family & our son James & Col. Carroll. Also Col. Dunovant –

Tuesday 26th....Several of the Villagers are engaged in killing hogs, this being the first day when the temperature of the atmosphere would allow it. The entire month of December up to this period has been almost unprecedentedly warm & cloudy. There was one week of constant clouds with a humid atmosphere with only occasional visits from the Sun. It has been warm enough to plant corn or even cotton & all seeds have been vegetating.

Wednesday 27. Cold & rainy at day light with a damp atmosphere during the day. I had three waggons to pass by on their way to market with 24 bales of cotton.

Thursday 28th....I killed about 30 hogs at my plantation which but for the warm weather ought to have been killed two weeks past. Capt. Bird, Wife & daughter left us this morning on their return to Florida. They arrived at my house about six weeks since on a visit to their relations. They remained with us the greater part of the time, making our house headquarters, & passing their time in great harmony & in the interchange of affectionate offices with our whole household. I was much pleased with their visit and enjoyed much gratification & pleasure in their Society. Capt. Bird is an excellent man, having a warm & sincere heart. His daughter Sally is pretty & intelligent & altogether an interesting girl. May happiness abide with them.

Friday 29....I had a severe attack of headache & remained in the house, during the entire day. I dispatched Hilliard to Chester with letters, postponing a certain event, which was weighing upon my mind with the weight of a Mill Stone & pressing upon my feelings with such intensity as to deprive me of sleep & rest. To have suffered it to be consummated would have very nigh cost me my reason & I have therefore resolved on suspending it. Semper erit.[58]

Saturday 30th....I was again indisposed & did not leave the house. My waggons returned from Augusta with Windows for my new house but I did not see them.

Sunday 31....I was able to attend church & heard a sensible sermon by Mr. Walker. Time may wear away & mitigate the severest grief which either death or misfortune can cause but a daily & subsisting affliction, which is irremediable, is too hard for weak human nature to bear. I pray God to give me patience & resignation under any dispension [*dispensation*] with which it may be his pleasure to visit me or mine & while I cannot forbear to indulge in painful regrets, on account of sore disappointment, in a very tender point, I trust that I may be favoured with grace sufficient to preserve me from rebellious opposition to the Divine will. May I always preserve that frame of mind, which is necessary to the truly honest declaration, "thy will & not mine be done.[”]

---

[58] Sic semper erit: thus it has always been, thus shall it ever be. Since Chester Dist. was the home of R. G. M. Dunovant, it appears that WB was intervening in the potential marriage of his only daughter, Ellen. They would be wed on June 21, 1849, but WB was concerned about this prospect. Since Ellen was born Jan. 23, 1829, her age was not likely a factor. In any case, WB's action did not end Dunovant's visits (see 2/17/49).

X

<u>January 1849</u>

Monday 1st....The crowd of persons in the Village was unusually large & all seemed busily engaged in some business or interest. There was a good deal of land sold at fair prices & also a number of negroes at very high prices. It was a busy day for the officers of Court & the various boards, who convene here on the first Monday of every new year.

Tuesday 2....I & Mrs. Brooks went to my plantation to attend to the repair of our house & to lay off gardens. We arrived late in the afternoon & found all well.

Wednesday 3rd....I rode over [James] Beans land & made him an offer for it but he declined it, which was the result of great want of judgment & which I predict he will repent for years to come. The land is very poor but as it lay in my way, I was willing to pay a liberal price for it. The workmen are progressing with my new house, tho rather slow.

Thursday 4th....I was occupied in riding over and examining my various interests on my plantation.

Friday 5.... I rode to look at a tract of land in the piney woods, belonging to [James] Attaway, lying in the vicinity of Good hope church. The land is more fertile than I expected but the timber not so good and valuable. I did not purchase it.

Saturday 6th....I paid a visit to Col. Griffin but did not find him at home. I then went to Doct. Lelands, where I met Col. Griffin & Mr.[James] Creswell. I purchased the tract of land of Col. Griffin on which Doct. Leland lives at four thousand, three hundred & sixteen acres [*dollars*]. Number of acres 437. The price is high but the land joined my tract & I wanted it; therefore I consented to pay a good price for it. I am not dissatisfied with my bargain nor do I regret having made the purchase. My only concern now is to meet the payment of any notes for the purchase money. I dined with Doct. Leland & passed a few agreeable hours with the gentlemen among whom was Doct [*Col.*] Griffin. I returned home in the afternoon, having drawn & procured title to the land.

Sunday 7th....[S]mall particles of snow. I rode in the plantation until dinner & passed the afternoon in reading &C.

Monday 8th. Very inclement . . . day. Set out some fruit trees & superintended the work in the flower garden but was confined to the house the greater part of the day. I caused 25 hogs to be killed this morning. The temperature was favourable to the saving of pork.

Tuesday 9th....a light fall of snow, which was visible this morning. The day was cold & inclement. It was impossible to do much work of any kind & the day may be counted as lost to the labourer....The cold was extreme.

Wednesday 10th....The earth was frozen & the ice abounded wherever there was water. I set out to see Mr. Jno. Trap[1] but did not ride over two miles before I turned back upon learning that he had left home in the morning. The temperature of the air was cold & cutting to the face. The Bricklayer Mr. Comb was engaged in putting up a chimney for me & I fear that I erred in allowing him to work on it during such cold weather. We had a number of fruit trees set out during the day.

Thursday 11. No abatement of cold. We left the plantation at 10 ocl. on our return home.

....I was unwell & scarcely saw anything on the way home at which we arrived at 4 ocl where we found all well & glad to see us. I now learned from the papers of the election of Louis Bonaparte as President of the French republic by an immense majority over Genl. Cavignac. The papers also report a rise in cotton & the intelligence from Hamburg is that the article had advanced. Walker had sold 64 bales for me but a few days before the arrival of the news at 5 cts. The lot would now command $100 more than he recd. for it.

Friday 12th....The therm.t for 3 days has been below 20° in the morning. I went to the Village & transacted a little business & purchased a few articles for my negroes –

Saturday 13....Mr. Jas. Ransford[2] called & paid me $640. on his note. I went to the Village & paid several small accounts & returned to dinner. I heard no news....My ill health disinclines me to exercise & I am therefore not a fourth part as active as formerly. I must exert myself when I get to my plantation –

....

Monday 15th....mild & cloudy. There was an auction sale of the remains of Roberts stock of goods he had at which some things sold a very low & others at full prices. The only news of the day was that Cholera had made its appearance in Augusta, of which four persons had died & among these our old acquaintance James Gray, Atty at law – This gentleman had been returned but a few months from a tour to Egypt, Syria & Palestine & had passed through the dangers of sea & land in safety, to die in a few hours illness in his own house & so suddenly that his friends were not even allowed to gather around him.

Tuesday 16. No change in the weather. We sent this morning two waggon loads of furniture to Roselands for which place we set out at 10 ocl & arrived there at four. Some indisposition among the negroes but not serious....

---

[1] Rev. John Trapp (1799–), schoolteacher, pastor after conversion in 1829. From 1840 to 1856 he pastored Damascus Baptist near Phoenix, and 1850–1874 Bethany Baptist. "Greatly beloved" (Chapman, 313).

[2] James Beale Rainsford (1799–1868) came to Edgefield from England in 1833 to claim his share of his grandfather's estate; 1850 census: $14,000 real estate, 20 slaves. Burton, *In My Father's House,* 175, has $85,000.

Wednesday 17....The carpenter and brick layer are engaged in repairing my house but they have so mutilated the old building by alterations, that it is hardly habitable. I have a feeling that I shall not only be contented with my residence on my plantation, called Roselands, but that I shall enjoy much quiet & satisfaction. I am anxious to be permanently settled for at present it is unpleasant to be passing to & from the Village, superintending the removal of our furniture ....I set out to visit Col. Griffin for the purpose of paying him some money in payment of my note for the Martin tract of land. I tendered him $500 which to my surprise, he refused to receive upon no other ground, than that he wished the money paid to the Commi.s in Equity, who held his bond but who had no demand agst me. From his house I went to Doct. Leland's & purchased his stock of hogs at $65. I returned home to dinner & passed the afternoon in superintending some hands in cleaning up the yard & planting out shrubbery & rose bushes & id onsue genus [probably and all that sort]–

Thursday 18th....I rode over a part of my plantation & gave directions to Mr. Gallman in regard to the removal of some fences & sowing oats. I did not leave the yard in the afternoon but devoted the time to reading –

Friday 19th....I was confined to the house the greater part of the day, in reading & writing. In the afternoon we received a visit from the Revd. Mr. Hill, who is traveling to make collections in aid of the Baptist [institution?], established at Greenville[3]....Saturday 20th....The servants state that about day light, there was a small fall of snow & sleet. A gentle mist is now falling at 8 ocl. About 12 ocl I was attacked with headache & did not leave my bed except for a few minutes until Sunday morning, so the day was lost to me.

....

Monday 22....I rode over my plantation & gave directions to Mr. Gallman in regard to the fields to be cultivated & the order of work during my absence at the Glenn Spring.

Tuesday 23....I parted with my Wife at Roselands & set out for Glenn Spring at 9 ocl taking Hampden with me & Mrs. B returning to the Village. I arrived at Finny's before sunset, feeling much drowsiness & lassitude. I had a good supper & a comfortable bed & rested well during the night.

Wednesday 24....I reached my Summer residence EllenDale early in the afternoon & found my old trusty servant Barnett in good health & also his Wife & the children with them.

Thursday 25th....I rode over my grounds & inspected the work of my servants. The plowing was good & equal to my expectations but my man Barnett had committed one error, which would have proved vastly injurious if I had not arrived in time to correct it. He had undertaken too much without thoroughly contemplating any

[3] Furman University, a Baptist-related institution, which began its life in Edgefield, was to open its campus in Greenville SC in 1851.

part.

Friday 26th....I was engaged in directing the making of a fence & did not leave the place during the day –

Saturday 27th....I left home for the Village of Spartanburg at an early hour & suffered severely with cold before I reached the Village. I transacted my business with Mr. Bobo & return to EllenDale by 3 ocl. At night Doct. [Winsmith], Perry West & Mr. Wofford[4] called & took tea with me....

Sunday 28th. About day light I was attacked with sick stomach & headache & suffered great agony during the entire day. About sunset the pain became intolerable & I arose & drank upwards of a quart of warm water which caused me to cascade & to throw off the stomach a quantity of acrid bile and other offensive matter by which I got relief & was able to sleep....I was confined to the bed during the whole day without eating or drinking a mouthful of any kind. In fact I was in bed for 36 hours.

Monday 29th....I arose greatly enfeebled & depressed yet I determined to leave for home which I did at 9 ocl. The system reacted during the day & I felt better . . . in the afternoon. After an easy days travel I arrived at Finn[e]y's at 5 ocl & was well accommodated.

Tuesday 30th....I set out at 8 ocl & reached Roselands at 3 ocl. Here I heard of the sudden & unexpected death of [brother-in-law] Major B. M. Blocker in the fifty ninth year of his age. Major Blocker had a warm heart & was a zealous friend, ready at all times to render such services & sacrifices as friendship demands. About 4 ocl Mrs. Brooks & Ellen arrived bringing with them my papers & letters & the news from the little Town of Edgefield.

Wednesday 31st....I was engaged in riding over my plantation, inspecting the work & giving directions & Mrs. B. was setting out shrubs & flowers, which she brought up from our old residence – With my present overseer I have as yet no fault to find. He is attentive & manifests judgment and arranging & carrying on his work – He had sowed & plowed in about 140 acres in oats & the work was faithfully done. I have some 20 acres broke up for the new crop & several fences repaired but my new building interferes with my work in the plantation by taking from 3 to 5 fellows –

February 1st. 1849

....

Friday 2....I left Roselands after breakfast & reached my Sister's, Mrs. Blocker at 1 ocl, with whom I passed the afternoon and night – it was our first meeting since the death of her husband Major Blocker, whom I missed as the head & father of the

---

[4] Benjamin Wofford (1780–1850), Spartanburg Methodist minister, invested in cotton mills and willed $100,000 to build the college that bears his name. It opened in 1854. Dr. John Winsmith built a large house, "Camp Hill," in Glenn Springs in 1835.

family & for whose death the family manifested a becoming sensibility.

....

Sunday 4th....I attended church in the morning & heard a good sermon from the Revd. E. Reed. About 12 Ocl. I was attacked with headache & suffered throughout the day with pain in one eye & nausea at the Stomach.

Monday 5th....I was very feeble from the attack of yesterday yet I went to the Village & collected over $1300 for the estate of my father and about $900 for myself – The assemblage of persons in the Village was large & all seemed to be engaged in some kind of business. Land & negroes sold high. John Hollingsworth paid about $11 per acre for the Wall tract, lying on log creek of 180 acres, which was above its value. I was this day 59 years old.

Tuesday 6th....I set out for Hamburg after breakfast with Ms. Brooks in company & reached Ketchums[5] at 4 ocl. The cotton market a little dull & not much offered for Sale. Before leaving the Village I paid to Aunt Butler $800 on my fathers note – to N. L. Griffin $500 on my own note to his father for the Martin tract of land & also to Col. Carroll & Mr. Wardlaw $100 to each as a part of a fee in the suit in Equity vs the Penns to protect the trust property of Mrs. Blocker –

Wednesday 7th....I was busily engaged in laying in a large bill of groceries, paints, iron salt & necessaries for the plantation, all of which I was able to get to my entire satisfaction. I was in Augusta for a short time but heard no news. This Town is represented to be advancing in its prosperity under the influence of the canal & the various branches of manufacture, to which it has given existence while Hamburg has been & will continue to be injured by the same cause & especially by a diversion of the river trade, which is now carried through the canal.

Thursday 8th....We returned this morning from Major Yancy's (with whom & his estimable lady we had spent a pleasant night) to Hamburg & after attending to the loading of my waggons we set out for the Village about 12 ocl. I was exceedingly unwell & rode home almost without opening my eyes – We found all well at home.

Friday 9th....I went to the Village & made a number of purchases for my negroes – My sister Ms. Blocker came down & passed the day with us –

Saturday 10th....We took our final departure from the Village to Roselands and brought with us our negroes, all cooking utensils and a portion of our furniture. We had five wagons full & yet left all of the fine furniture – My Son Preston has now full possession of my old & pleasant residence & I pray God that the change may be for the good & benefit of us all. I am persuaded that it will improve my health & convenience without (I hope) interfering or diminishing the enjoyment of my wife & further that it may promote the welfare of my Son in his worldly prospects.

Sunday 11th....We passed the day quietly at home.

---

[5] William Ketchum (1812–) had bought or was now running Hubbard's hotel.

Monday 12th....In consequence of the rain the earth was too wet to allow of plowing & I sent two waggons to the Saw Mill for lumber for my house. Yesterday morning I threw up a good deal of blood from the stomach (I think) & not from the lungs and again a small portion this morning. It was caused by cold, at least I hope so. In looking over my fields, I discover that my oats are coming up & exhibit a good & regular appearance. I finished sowing about the last of January. The wheat & rye look quite promising.

Tuesday 13th....I rode to examine the condition of the public road, leading from Edgefield to Cambridge & found it in bad order & wanting repair. I returned by the Martin place & suffered from cold before I reached home. I directed the overseer to start 9 ploughs this morning.

Wednesday 14th....I rode over at the Martin place & examined the work of the negroes there & returned to dinner. I put both carriage horses to the plough and nobly they did their work....

Thursday 15th....I sent under the overseer this morning 20 hands to work on the road & in consequence of this diversion I was able to send two waggons back to the Saw Mill for lumber. I have thirteen ploughs running to day when I ought to have 23. I rode to the public road, where the hands were at work.

Friday 16th ....I took a long ride by Holloways & up the old Charleston road as far as the bridge across 96 Creek & thence home by the Martin place. Here I met my neighbor [James] Creswell & agreed to unite with him, in making a pasture fence at the lower end of my land on the Creek –

Saturday 17th....The Therm.t was as low as 22° at 7 ocl. Several negroes complained of cold & sore throat, to whom a dose of salts & pepper tea was administered. I was attacked with headache & did not leave the house. Col. Dunovant arrived in the afternoon on a visit.

Sunday 18. This was one of the coldest & most windy days that I have ever seen. The therm.t was about 20° in the morning and did not rise above 28 at any period of the day.

It was too cold to leave the house & I only walked as far as the Vegetable garden.

Monday 19th....The Thermt at 7 ocl stood at 17°. The earth frozen & nothing but the dryness of the atmosphere prevented most serious injury to the grain crops. I fear that the oats are injured to some extent. In consequence of the frozen condition of the earth I was enabled to send my waggons back to the Saw Mill....

Tuesday 20th....I rode with Col. Dunovant over a part of my plantation & to the Martin tract of land – The earth was in good order for the plough....

Wednesday 21....I rode to Wiley Adams & then by Jas. Matthews to enquire about the State of his health. The poor man is suffering a great affliction in having a cancer on his tongue. He said that he was better. Col. Dunovant left us this morning on his return home.

....

Friday 23rd....About 12 ocl set out for my Son James Brooks, & Mrs. Brooks & Ellen for the Village. I arrived at James before Sunset & passed a very agreeable night with him & his family. He has two promising & interesting little boys. I observed that he was very backward with his preparations for a crop.

Saturday 24th....I left James at 11 ocl for James Perry's, where I had been ill [naturely?] summoned by G. Yarborough[6] for a small account against the estate of my father not exceeding two dollars, which he had paid in order to sue upon without having presented the account or given me an opportunity to pay it. He was not ready for trial & the magistrate postponed the trial until the 3 Saturday in April. I was not well & returned home, where I passed a solitary night.

Sunday 25th....I rose unwell & soon after breakfast went to bed, where I remained for the balance of the day without seeing any person or eating or drinking the least particle of food or water. It was a day of suffering & lost to me entirely for I was too sick even to think. From 12 ocl until night the wind blew with violence from the NoWest. It was like a gale in March....

Monday 26th. Clear & cold with white frost. I rose free from pain but feeble and uncomfortable. After making a light breakfast of gruel & a little tea, I felt better & able to sit up & read. I took some medicine but in consequence of the spasmed State of my Stomach, it could not operate & it made me deadly sick. I at last had an enema administered but it afforded no relief. Finally I threw up a large quantity of bitter black bile which relieved me from my dreadful suffering. Mrs. B. & Ellen returned from the Village, bringing the intelligence that our relations & friends are well.

Tuesday 27th....I was able to ride after breakfast and rode into the plantation. I have the ploughs, breaking up corn land.

Wednesday 28th....For forty eight hours high winds have prevailed from the North which made it unpleasant to be out of the house....The Earth is becoming dry & will soon be too hard for the plough....I have broken up all the stubble land & a portion that was in corn, making from 175 to 200 acres broken up on this place. I have from 50 to 60 acres broken up at the Martin place, yet I feel that I am rather backward.

<u>March 1. 1849</u>

Thursday 1. Cloudy & cool....the wind is still prevailing from the North. I went to the late residence of a Mr. Upson to attend the Sale of his property by his assignee Mr. Stephens. The crowd was large for such an occasion & the anxiety to bid for

---

6 Dr. George M. Yarborough (1821–), related to the Butlers. Born on Big Creek. WB regarded him highly; 1850 census: $3,000 real estate, 22 slaves. He and family moved to Walhalla in 1868.

every sort of thing offered for sale was as keen as I ever saw it at a public Sale. All kinds of properties sold at high prices. I left about 1 ocl before the land, horses or negroes were sold....

Friday 2....I rode to the Martin plantation & examined the progress of the work – Hampden returned this afternoon on a short visit from Greenwood where he is at School.

....

Sunday 4th....Pres. Polk is out of office today & Genl. Taylor will not be inaugurated until tomorrow, this day being Sunday (dios non juridious) & so there will be an interregnum for 24 hours, when 20.000.000 of human beings will be without an executive head or chief officer. The term of office of President expires on the 4 of March under the Constitution & Genl. Taylor cannot be sworn into office until 12 ocl tomorrow the 5th of the Month....

Monday 5th....In the afternoon I rode into my plantation.

Tuesday 6th....In the afternoon I rode to the Martin Place to see the progress of preparation for a crop & was pleased with the addition, which I am making to the field on the Creek –

Wednesday 7th....Early this morning I shall finish ploughing the fields, allotted for corn. The low grounds are in fine order and break up better than I have ever known them with fewer clods or bracks[7] – It is very common to pronounce any irregularity in the weather as a remarkable season but for the last 8 or 10 days the State of the weather has been peculiar indeed. For 4 or 5 days the wind prevailed from the North point with cold temperature, the thermometer being from 32 to 36. It then gradually veered round to the East & gradually became warmer. It now comes from a point a little South of East & is charged with moisture with a gradual rise in the Therm.t – I left home at 8 ocl for the Village at which I arrived to dinner, finding Preston & family & our relations well. In the afternoon I rode to the Village, made some purchases at the stores & returned with sick headache.

Thursday 8th....my suffering from sick stomach & headache was almost intolerable. I took an emetic.

Friday 9....I was very feeble & much indisposed yet I determined to return home [meaning the plantation] & took leave of my children at 10 ocl....rain . . . continued to increase as I advanced toward home, upon my arrival at which I found my wagons ready to set out for the Sawmill for lumber, the earth being too wet to plough. I was very incredulous of the truth of the Statement but upon examination, I found it very wet & heavy....James & his family arrived at night on a visit.

Saturday 10th....I rode with James to the Martin place & then to N. Moore's to meet the tax collector, where I met several of the neighbours. I learned that some of them

[7] OED: Breaks, fragments.

were planting corn & others were laying off their land, with the purpose of planting next week – The inauguration of Genl. Taylor had taken place & his Cabinet appointments made & confirmed by the Senate. Congress broke up in a row....

Sunday 11....On taking a short ride I discovered that my small grain had grown more in the last three days than it had done in the last two weeks. The earth is quite wet & roads muddy whereas at the Village not more rain has fallen then was necessary thoroughly to settle the dust. Spring is making its appearance & the grass begins to look green in places, especially the greensward on the banks of the ditches –

Monday 12th....We learn that the notorious Russ Harden was tried the second time for the murder of his own slaves and acquitted in opposition to the charge of Judge Evans & also to public opinion. A man by the name of Butler is to be tried for the killing of a Slave, over whom he had control as an overseer. Martin Posey is suspected of having an agency in the murder of his Wife but I trust for the honor of human nature that he is innocent. His negro has not yet been taken, & both he & Master are yet at large....[8] Tuesday 13th....I began this morning to lay off corn land in the large field, called Goode field. I was confined during the afternoon by headache.

Wednesday 14th....I rode to the Martin place, where I met my neighbour Jas. Creswell. On my return I was caught by a rain about 12 ocl and forced to take refuge in a fodder house in the plantation....I was again sick & forced to take my bed at 1 ocl. Rain was heavy –

Thursday 15th....The water courses are running freely but are not fuller than ordinary. I went to the Martin place & superintended the work of my negroes until 1 ocl & returned to dinner through a light mist. Heavy thunder & rain at night.

Friday 16th....The earth is very wet & soft. I finished ginning & packing my cotton crop this morning, in all 178 bales agreeably to recollection. Their general average was from 370 to 380 pounds. There can be no ploughing except upon elevated & hard hills until Monday....

Saturday 17th....Vegetation is progressing most rapidly & the weather in temperature is truly Spring like....in the afternoon . . . heavy showers of rain fell for several hours, attended with much thunder & hail. The night warm notwithstanding the fall of hail.

Sunday 18th....On riding to the [Ninety Six] Creek I discovered that the rain was much heavier than I had supposed. The Creek had overflowed its banks & the entire surface of the Earth was full of water.

Monday 19th....The earth had dried very much since yesterday morning & I am able to plough on some high lots.

[8] Posey was convicted on October 3, 1849, and hanged for murder. His slave, App, had killed Posey's wife Matilda on his order, and Posey then killed him.

Tuesday 20....I began this morning to plant corn in the Goode field & by night had planted about 50 acres. The balance of the field assigned for corn was too wet for the plough. Corn in the field has been planted after cotton & the preparation of the land consisted of five furrows one way, which were crossed by four rows 3 feet apart, then opened & covered by the plough, running a furrow on each side of the corn. I plant all my land 3 by 5 feet except that which is planted in [using] the [seed] drill....

Wednesday 21. Upon examination I found my other field too wet to plant corn & I therefore commenced bedding for cotton on some dry land....I rode to the Martin place & was sorry to see that my man Toney had been delayed by rain & want of judgment in his preparation for planting corn. He will not be ready before tomorrow. I do not recollect ever to have been so late in commencing to plant my crop. My new house & rain have combined to retard me. About 5 ocl in the afternoon . . . [there was] a heavy shower of rain, accompanied with loud thunder and violent wind. It was truly an equinoctial storm.

Thursday 22....Overseer & neighbours were engaged during the day and putting up fences, blown down by the storm of last evening. Part of my hands were engaged in planting sweet potatoes [,] cleaning out ditches, hawling wood & leaves & cleaning up a small new ground near the house. My man Phill spayed & altered my stock of young hogs about 30 in No. During the previous night my young mare Ebba had a colt of good size & appearance, the product of my young stud Argile Jr.

Friday 23rd....Therm.t About 23°. Began to plant corn at Oaklands and on my arrival there I discovered that the corn was so carelessly dropped, that it will be impossible to plough the field the narrow way. A negro cannot be trusted to do any act or duty without supervision....

Saturday 24....I finished in the afternoon bedding Prospect field for cotton in a way that pleased me very much, the ploughing being thoroughly done....

Sunday 25....rain from early morn until 5 ocl in the afternoon. The earth again exceedingly wet....I was indisposed for a large portion of the day with nausea & headache....

Monday 26th....I set out for the residence of the late Mr. W. Hill to attend the sale of his estate & Mrs. Brooks & Ellen for the Village. The property sold at high prices. In the afternoon I went home with Stanmore Brooks, at whose house I met my Aunt Brooks now in the 83rd year of her age. She was in good health & when walking, carries herself as erect as a girl....

Tuesday 27th...frost...killed both young corn & vegetables. I went to Greenwood to visit my Son Hampden, whom I found in excellent health & well pleased with his school. I passed a part of the day at Capt. Tarrant[9] & became acquainted with the teacher of the Furman Academy Mr. Dederie, a young gentleman of good appear-

[9] John Robert Tarrant McKendree (1808–1891) lived in Greenwood, Abbeville Dist.

ance & considerable intelligence. From our short acquaintance I should suppose that he was well qualified for his vocation....In the afternoon I went to Butler Brooks & passed the night – Soon after my arrival I was attacked with violent headache & was forced to take a bed, & saw but little of the family –

Wednesday 28th....After breakfast I set out for home, where I arrived about 12 ocl & took my bed, again suffering with headache. My overseer was planting corn. Mrs. Brooks & Ellen returned about night from our Son Prestons [in ECH] –

Thursday 29th....I rode over my plantation, inspecting the small grain etc. which grows finely. The overseer finished planting the Everly field in corn about 80 acres. The land was in excellent order. In the afternoon I rode to Benj. Connoly's[10] for my papers & as I passed I saw Doct. Andrew's negroes planting cotton. I employed two men to work upon my well at $30.

Friday 30th....I was engaged in planting corn both here and at Oak forest –

Saturday 31....I planted near 50 acres of corn during the day, in the Corley field & low ground, which added to the Goode & Everly fields, make upwards of 200 acres now planted. At Oak forrest, my man Toney finished planting his corn, about 45 acres, except about 6 acres of new ground, which is not broken up. The weather is favourable & I hope by strict attention & continued effort to get my crop planted in due time, altho I have been put back very much by my various engagements in moving & building. For the last four days the weather has been pleasant & favourable to the operations of the planter.

<u>April 1. 1849</u>

Sunday 1st....We passed the day at home, in reading etc.

Monday 2....Finished planting the Corley field & low grounds in corn. I rode to Oak Forrest & inspected the manner in which my corn was planted there. The land had been plowed in pretty good order & the corn put in tolerable order. I called up & fed my sheep and upon counting them I found that there were over 100 old sheep & upwards of 40 lambs – I saw in Jas. Mims plantation corn up & replanted but it looked badly, having been injured by the frost.

Tuesday 3rd....I am engaged in planting the last field in corn, in cleaning up the land for cotton on the ditches & branches, and hawling out manure, which I find a laborious task & working on my Well. My carpenters are putting up a small building in the Vegitable garden, the Smith is in the shop, one hand at gates and another repairing bridles & harness. The flower and vegetable gardens, the yard & house are receiving their portion of attention & two hands are getting laths for the Plasterer. I was very sick in the afternoon. I employed a Mr. Heaferdon to do a job of work for me at the Glenn Spring. I am not very favourably impressed with this gentleman

---

[10] Benjamin Connoly [census: Conoly] (1805–); 1850 census: $2,000 real estate.

from the observations which a few hours conversation enabled me to make of his disposition & character. [added later]: I afterwards changed my opinion. He is a right good old fellow, very obliging but not over industrious.

Wednesday 4....I commenced planting cotton in the field next to Kemps, called Prospect field, this morning with Six plows. I rode out before breakfast to give directions in regard to the mode of planting etc. Rain fell in light showers from 11 until 1 ocl putting the earth in first rate order for planting. At 1 ocl I finished planting my corn crop except some 15 acres in the low grounds, which requires rebedding & which I propose to plant after the cotton crop shall have been planted....

Thursday 5th....Vegetation presents a most inviting appearance this morning & the young foliage of the forrests looks green & animating.

Friday 6th....The first planted corn, coming up & looking well. The day devoted to bedding land & planting cotton. Preston & his family arrived on a visit.

Saturday 7th....I planted about 14 acres in cotton at Oak forrest. The earth is becoming dry and hard. Col. D[unovant] arrived to dinner.

Sunday 8th. This was a summer day. Therm.t Up to 80°. We passed the day quietly at home except that Preston & I took a short ride after breakfast.

Monday 9th....I commenced this morning to shear my sheep & also turned my strong cattle in the range, keeping those that are poor & weak in the pasture, to be fed & salted for some time before turning them out. I put 40 in the pasture and turned out [blank]. The ladies with Col. Dunovant & Preston took a ride by Doct. Lake's and round by Oak Forrest, where I met them & returned with them....

Tuesday 10th....Preston & family with Col. Dunovant left us this morning taking Ellen with them on a short visit. I have about 150 acres planted in cotton.

Wednesday 11....I rode to N. Griffin's plantation & learned that he had finished planting cotton & was ploughing over his corn. I finished shearing the sheep, upwards of 100 in number & turned out about 40 lambs. On my return I observed that my man Toney was getting on very well with his work.

Thursday 12th....distressingly dry. I rode to Revd. Mr. [John] Trapps to get some lumber and returned very much fatigued. In the afternoon I rode over a part of my plantation & a portion of pasture lands to examine into the condition of the fences.

....

Saturday 14th....I have replanted about 70 acres of corn & by night shall have planted upwards of 200 acres in cotton. The earth dry & hard.

[*added in a different hand:* Snow 1849 on the 15th]

Sunday 15. This was an extraordinary day. Cold and cloudy at daylight with high wind from the No.E. At 8 ocl the Therm.t stood at 40°. By 10 ocl it fell to 38° when snow began to fall. By 12 ocl it had fallen to 36° & the whole earth was partly covered with snow. The forests presented a singular contrast in the verdure of the leaves, with their partial covering of snow....By 9 ocl at night the clouds had become dispersed & the stars shone brightly & cold. At 10 ocl the Therm.t had fallen to 36°.

Monday 16th. This was like a December morning. Clear & bright & cold with a frost almost as large & white as the snow of yesterday. Therm.t below 30°. So unusual & unexpected an occurrence of cold weather has not taken place in 30 years & in fact not in my memory, particularly in the late season of the year & in such an advanced stage of the vegetation. The leaves of the forrest trees are fully grown & peaches as large as bird eggs – I fear that all young vegetation will be killed with all the crops of wheat, corn & cotton, that are up. I now find that my backward state of planting is a decided advantage as I shall loose less corn & cotton than most of my neighbours.

Tuesday 17th....Upon examining my fields, I find that corn & cotton & all vegitables are entirely killed. So also all that fruit that I have examined. My wheat is injured but I hope not very materially. Young vegitation is totally killed in exposed situations & looks as if burnt by fire. I was sick the whole afternoon & night. Rose's Child died at night from an injury recd. by a fall from the bed. I regretted its death very sincerely as it was her first child.

Wednesday 18th. Cold & capricious weather with shifting wind....I have never seen a more unfavourable weather. In everything but dryness it offers a perfect contrast to the two preceding weeks which were warm & clear. It seems that the wind is determined to destroy what the frost has spared.

Thursday 19th....I rode in my fields & returned at an early hour to take my bed from which I did not rise till dark – Our Mother Mrs. Carroll & our daughter Ellen arrived from the Village about 4 ocl. My overseer & servants report that the corn, that was killed to the ground, is beginning to sprout & they think it will not require to be plowed up. I hope it may be so –

Friday 20th....my servants report that there was frost in the swamp. I have made my arrangements for going to the Glenn Spring & expect to set out about 12 ocl. I have two well diggers engaged in digging a well in the yard – I arrived at my Son James in the afternoon & found his family well. Unwell in the night.

Saturday 21....I attended before a Magistrate Jas. Perry[11] to a suit agt. me as Exor by G[eorge?] Yarborough. I succeeded on the main point. After the trial I returned to my Son James to dinner & after dinner I went on my way to the Glenn Spring beyond Newberry Courthouse to a Mr. Kellars, where I passed the night & was hospi-

[11] James Perry (1810–); 1850 census: $1,500 real estate, 22 slaves.

tably entertained by Mrs. Kellar who is a large, fat, kind and obliging lady – She advised me to eat fat bacon for my complaint and held up to me as encouragement, the fact that such diet had cured a relative of hers, who has suffered from dyspepsia for years –

Sunday 22. I left Mr. Kellar's at 7 ocl & reached the Glenn Spring at 6 ocl in the afternoon. I was glad to find my negroes in health and every thing appertaining to them or my farm in good order. I found Mr. Heafernon at Ellen Dale, plastering my house according to our agreement. He seemed to desire to manage everything to the best advantage & I approved of his acts –

Monday 23....Upon examining this morning the work of Mr. Perry West on my house I never was more disappointed. The materials were bad & many of them worthless & the workmanship worse and more uncarpenter-like than any that ever saw. In the language of Heffernon it was "scandalous". I discharged him so soon as I saw him & procured the services of two Carpenters to decide upon the amount that I should pay him for such portions of his work as were admissible. We settled in conformity with [these] computations without any ill feeling.

Tuesday 24th....I devoted the day to the repairs of my house & forwarding the plastering. I also visited the Spring & saw many of the Citizens, who seemed glad to see me.

Wednesday 25....I was again busily employed on my house –

Thursday 26....I went to the sawmill for plank & lumber which I obtained and got Mr. Owens to consent to assist me in raising my piazza on Friday. I sent for the lumber & traded for a waggon giving $40 and an old carryall for it. I also engaged 100 bushels of corn at 45 cts. purchased oats at 12 ½ pr. doz bundles & fodder at 50 cts.

Friday 27....I was very busy with my house & had not time even to feel sick – My workmen are progressing very well & please me much –

Saturday 28....I had another busy & laborious day. We succeeded in raising the piazza & of uniting it with the main building by iron bolts before Sunset – Mr. Heffernon also finished plastering the house about Sunset very much to my Satisfaction. The cleverness of Mr. Owens and the other workmen and the fidelity of their work in some degree made amends for my vexation with West & his botching. Late in the afternoon I rode over my corn & examined also the oats, all of which were improving under the influence of the gentle rains – The ravages of the frost & cold have been very destructive to crops & gardens & young vegetation –

Sunday 29th....I set out from Ellen Dale at 7 ocl on my return home & reached Mr. F. Nance's before Sunset. The crops on the road of wheat & corn & cotton much injured by the frost. The forest trees in many belts of Country on the road suffered the entire loss of their young foliage & now looked...brown as in Winter, while in higher situations, the leaves are green and almost untouched.

Monday 30th....I reached home at 12 ocl & found my dear family well. All my negroes were also in good health—In the afternoon I rode over part of my crop. It has sustained much injury by the frost. I had not time to make a thorough examination & barely saw that my corn was recovering from the blight of the frost & my cotton beginning to come up in places. My white wheat seemed much injured tho I did not examine it thoroughly—

May 1. 1849

Tuesday 1....I rode over my crop of corn & cotton & examined my wheat. The cotton will be up in a few days. I think, equal to a stand – The corn has commenced to grow & looks pretty well, so also do the oats, but the wheat will be almost an entire failure – That portion which was in head, when the frost fell is blighted & instead of grain there is nothing but chaff. Much of that, which is in the boot state, has turned yellow & will produce nothing. I calculated a few days before the frost on making 500 bushels & now I may not make 50 bushels....It is too early to be out of heart – Industry & perseverance may remedy all the discouraging difficulties, that now alarm the planter –

Wednesday 2nd....The grain crops have greatly improved by the late rain & cotton is coming up. I am ploughing over my corn, which begins to have a growing appearance. I ploughed up & planted over about 15 acres at Oak Forrest –

Thursday 3rd....Ploughed up & we planted about 10 acres of corn in the Indigo field.

Friday 4....James & his family arrived on a visit about 4 ocl.

Saturday 5. This was a summer day. I attended the battalion review at Col. [Oliver] Towles & saw & conversed with many of my neighbours....

Sunday 6th....We had no preaching nearer than Goodhope & we did not attend, but contented ourselves with reading the Bible & other religious books –

Monday 7th....My negroes are engaged in replanting corn[,] a good deal of which has been destroyed by worms & the frost. It continues to die, from various causes & requires constant attention and replanting. I began this afternoon to plough over cotton, the first time.

Tuesday 8....I started my waggon to market with the last of my cotton. I was much indisposed yet set out for Hamburg at 2 ocl & after much suffering, reached Edgefield at Sunset. I instantly went to bed & barely saw my children –

Wednesday 9th. I left my Son Prestons after breakfast for Hamburg, having Mrs. Brooks & [Nell?] in company. I suffered much on the road & also in Hamburg after my arrival....

Thursday 10th....I was too feeble to go about much & did not go more than 100 yards from the tavern. Mrs. Brooks & Nell went to Augusta & purchased the articles on their bill & returned at an early hour, while I procured our groceries etc. in Hamburg – Very heavy rain from Sunset until in the night. Cotton from 5 ½ to 7 cts. Groceries cheaper than usual. The corn on the road was small but looked in a healthy and growing state. Cotton was up in great quantities in every field, where seed had been planted but was small. Planters had barely made a beginning to chop out. Wheat & rye looked badly much being killed but oats were promising –

END OF VOLUME 3

APPENDIX

Report of the Cambridge Agricultural Society, On the situation of Whitfield Brooks' Plantation, and its claims for the Premium to be awarded for the best managed Plantation

At the request of Mr. Whitfield Brooks, of the District of Edgefield, we have examined his plantation with all the minuteness and accuracy, which circumstances would allow, and submit the following Report:

The land in cultivation is represented to be about 700 acres, of which one third may be denominated swamp and second low grounds, and the remaining two thirds, high land, under one continuous line of fence, with dividing fences at convenient distances, separating the whole into fields, varying from 30 to 120 acres. The high land is in a clean condition, free from trees, logs, briars or gullies, and in a state of progressive improvement by the rotation of crops, and the application of manure. The low land has been thoroughly drained by two main ditches of large size and many smaller drains, where the condition of the land required them. Cultivation extends to the border of the ditches and branches, the latter having been straightened and cleared out, to admit the free passage of water. The land in cultivation, presents the appearance of an undulating valley, formed by the junction of several small streams, from an elevated point of which the eye commands a view of the whole area of the plantation, with the crop of cotton, corn and small grain, in their present condition. There is a raised and well made road, passing nearly through the centre of the fields, and branching off in various directions, as necessity or convenience required. Gates are erected at every cross fence, which afford an easy passage to all parts of the plantation. We saw about 200 acres in corn, 250 in cotton, from 125 to 150 acres, which had been in wheat, oats, rye and barley, and about 90 acres in wheat, rye and oats, for the fall sowing of small grain, all of which is in a state of apparent gradual improvement and skillful cultivation, having yielded a good crop the present year, notwithstanding the severe drought which prevailed in this section.

We next directed our attention to his houses, fixtures and lots, of various kinds and sizes. – The stable lot is of good size, well shaded and supplied with water from a well, near at hand, which is worked by a pump, and from which the water is conveyed by troughs. In this lot stands a large two story frame stable, divided on the lower story into stalls, and affording a capacious repository in the second story for fodder and oats. On each side of the stable, is a framed shed, used as a shelter for the wagons, and for the feeding of horses in summer. At the north end of the staple (sic), another shed has been erected about 80 feet square, with a trough and rack in the centre, for the use of the mules in summer, having a large apartment above for fodder. These are substantial buildings, and well covered with shingles. – Besides these, there is a line of log buildings, extending from 40 to 50 yards in length, with stalls for separate horses, and oxen and apartments for harness, having in the rear a large shed for oxen. This lot has a communication by means of gates with various other lots, as appurtenant to the stable, one of which is appropriated to oxen, another with shade trees and a stream of water, into which the stock is turned for rest or gentle exercise. The third is a grove, neatly trimmed and cleaned, which is used for various purposes, occasionally for cows and pigs, for sheep, or for horses and mules that become either crippled or sick. His cribs are substantial and well arranged buildings, in a line with the stables, and covered with shingles. The stable lot communicates with the gin lot, in which stand two framed gin houses in a line, each thirty-two feet square, with a passage between them of 20 feet, all under one cover and well floored, the passage answering the purpose of drying cotton and small grain, or as a shelter in rainy weather for any kind of employment in such seasons. At one of the gin houses, and in connection with it, is a framed building, two stories high, in which are placed the threshing machine and fan, for the cleaning of small grain. These are propelled by machinery, and principally constructed by the mechanics of the owner. In the same lot is a two story framed barn, designed for grain, the upper story of which is ceiled, and divided into bins of 30 bushels each, for the reception of grain. On each side of the barn is a framed and enclosed shed with shingle roofs, for fodder, oats, &c. Near the gin house and cotton room, stands the screw, having a framed building around it, and so constructed, that one entire side may be removed, to admit repair of the screw.

In the rear of the gin house lot is another, (about one acre, now in small grain,) in which has been erected a row of substantial buildings, extending about two thirds of one entire side, in which is preserved provisions for the cattle, and immediately in the rear of this line of buildings, and fronting the south, is a covered shelter for the cattle in winter, with which is connected a winter lot, having trees and water, and also a large trough, made of poles or logs, to preserve the food from the feet of the cattle. In this lot the cattle are penned at night, both in winter and summer, and a supply of litter constantly applied around the trough for making manure. Much attention has been and is devoted to making manure, and the arrangements are well adapted to this purpose. We saw in the horse lot several large and substantial made pens, filled with manure, and three more in the cow lot, containing in all at this time no less than from 400 to 600 (500?) wagon loads. The negro houses have been erected in a shade lot, in a parallel line with the stables and corn-cribs, about 80 yards in the rear, but at a convenient distance from them, and extending to the east, and presenting a front to the south. They are either framed or hewed log buildings, with framed roofs, having double brick or rock chimnies (sic), plank floors, and stand from 30 to 50 yards apart. In front of these buildings is a shade lot, from 3(?) to 4 acres, enclosing the loom house and well, and in the rear, a garden and poultry house, for each family of negroes. – The house of the overseer is a framed building, with three rooms and brick chimneys; and with its appendages, occupy the crown of the hill and commanding a view of the blacksmith and work-shop, the negro houses, stable lot and houses, the gin house, lot and buildings, and the cow lot and its appurtenances. The dwelling house is a two story building, finished in a plain but comfortable style, with shed and piazza, having six rooms and a passage, and stands in a luxuriant grove of oaks about 400 yards from the overseer's house, with which it is connected by an avenue and lawn, containing from 10 to 15 acres. It has the usual appendages of a garden, kitchens, meat-house, fowl house and dairy. We were also shown various arrangements for raising and taking care of stock through different stages of its growth. These consist of various lots of different sizes under good fence, and an abundant supply of water. The first is a wood enclosure of near 500 acres, partly high land, and partly swamp, and so arranged as to be easily divided by a set of bars (sic). This is intended as a permanent enclosure for hogs, and occasionally for sheep and other stock. It has a direct communication with the stable lot, and cow lot, through a gate, by means of the lawn above referred to, and hogs are fed within 300 yards of the overseer's house, which commands a view also of this lot. Another was a lot of 75 acres, of which about one half is in woods and the other in small grain, intended for ewes and lambs and other young stock, and is connected with the lawn around the dwelling house by a gate. The third is a lot adjoining the dwelling house, containing about 15 acres, half in woods and the other in small grain, intended for calves and poultry. These are in addition to the lots above referred to, as connected with the stable lot, all of which constitute about 12 in number. There is also a shelter with stalls for the milk cows in winter, and a house for food and shelter for the calves. In short, there is a lot for all kinds of stock, adapted either to summer or winter use, with a shelter or covering for each kind. It is a rule of the establishment to put all food under cover, so that we found neither oats, fodder, straw nor shucks exposed to the weather, but all were stored away in substantial buildings. The overseer has an appropriate house or room for tools, ploughs, harness, and wagons, and no implement or vehicle is allowed to remain from under cover. The various lots adjacent to the stable lot and dwelling, are surrounded by good fences, neatly shrubbed trees trimmed, neat and substantial gates, and all supplied with water and shade. The stock on the plantation is as follows – about 90 stock hogs, 15 sows, with near 100 pigs, about 90 head of horned cattle, including three yoke of oxen, milk cows and calves – about 70 head of sheep, and from 40 to 50 hogs for the slaughter pen, all in a good and thriving condition. The horse power is 16 mules, and 7 horses, of which three or four are brood mares. The overseer reported that he manufactures clothing for the negroes, both winter and summer. – The supply of pork will be abundant for the wants of the plantation, amounting to 7 or 8000 lbs. That from the sale of wheat, rye, corn, peas and other surface products of the plantation, he is enabled to pay the current annual expenses, except his wages, besides furnishing a supply of flour to his employer.

In conclusion, we cheerfully bear testimony that for the arrangement of the plantation, for the reclaimed and highly improved condition of the land in cultivation, for the means provided for its permanent improvement, for the substantial and convenient character of the buildings of every description, and for the general economy displayed in its government, there is manifested a skill, judgment and industry, of no ordinary character, and which was indispensable to the accomplishment of the present improved condition of the plantation. We ought not however to omit some notice of the utensils and vehicles used on the plantation and of the present crop. These consist of the bull tongue plough, the common shovel, the half or twisting shovel, the barshare (sic), of Northern construction, the sweep or scraper, and iron tooth harrows. Several of these are used in breaking up and preparing land for cultivation, and all except the barshare, in the cultivation of the crop. There are three wagons and two ox carts, with their usual apparatus. The land seems to have been thoroughly broken up, and closely and skillfully ploughed and planted, ploughed and [lined?] by in the best mode to prevent washing. We were shown a field of 50 acres of corn, planted in the drill, which averaged over 25 bushels to the acre. The product was between 1300 and 1400 bushels. Another of 70 acres, which averaged about 20 bushels, and about the same product as the first. A field of 30 acres on an elevated ridge, yielded an indifferent crop, being cut off by an unusual drought. There remains from 30 to 35 acres of corn ungathered, which will yield between 400 and 500 bushels. The crop of cotton was greatly injured by drought and rust, and will only yield 130 bales of the average weight of 350 lbs. In a seasonable year, the same land, under the same cultivation, would have yielded 175 bales. In addition to the corn and cotton, there were made 250 bushels of wheat, 50 bushels or rye, a small quantity of barley, and the average crop of oats, an abundant supply for the plantation. 75 bushels of peas have been gathered and cleaned, and some 10 or 12 stacks of peas on the vine. The hogs are a cross from a Berkshire boar, and sow of the common stock.—The cattle are in a state of improvement from a cross, by a three year old Durham Bull, a very superior animal, bred by Col. B. F. Taylor, of Columbia. The sheep are a cross of the Bakewell breed, from a ewe and ram, a present by Major Thomas Means, of Fairfield. In making this Report, our only object has been to give a full, fair and impartial account of the state of the plantation, and if we have been tedious, the only apology we can offer is, that it was inseparable from a faithful discharge of the office committed to us. In certification of which, we have signed out names, this 21st of Nov. 1844.

R. C. Griffin, former Treasurer.
W. Andrews,
A. P. King,
James F. Lowry,
Thomas Paine,
James Dorn,
J. M. Walker,
Solomon Dorn.

Proceedings of the Agricultural Convention of the State Agricultural Society of South Carolina from 1839 to 1845. Columbia: Summer and Carroll, 1846, 285-289.
(Transcribed from Google Books by James O. Farmer, Jr.)

BIBLIOGRAPHY

Manuscript Collections
Perkins Library, Duke University
Richard Singleton Papers
South Carolina Dept. of Archives and History
Governors' Messages – John Lyde Wilson, 1824
Land Records – Whitfield Brooks; Z. S. Brooks
Manuscript Journals of the South Carolina House of Representatives, 1832-1835.
Miscellaneous Communications to the General Assembly – Report of the Commissioners to Consider Dividing Edgefield District, Nov. 12, 1828
Revolutionary War Pension Applications – Zachariah Smith Brooks
State [land] Grants; State Plats - Zachariah Smith Brooks land records; Whitfield Brooks land records

South Caroliniana Library, University of South Carolina, Columbia
Milledge Luke Bonham papers
Brooks Family Papers
Preston Brooks Papers.
Cantey Family Papers
Hiram Hutchinson papers
Francis W. Pickens Papers
William Campbell Preston papers
Henry Shultz papers
Eldred Simkins Papers
Waddy Thompson Papers
Williams-Chesnut-Manning Papers
John Bauskett Papers

Southern Historical Collection, University of North Carolina, Chapel Hill
John Forsythe Talbert Plantation Journal, 1838-1868
Benjamin Cudworth Yancey, Jr. papers.

Manuscripts in private hands.
Whitfield Brooks Journals and miscellaneous papers, Mary Jane Brooks Mobley and Emmett F. Brooks.
Brooks family Bible, genealogy pages. Photocopy in Bettis C. Rainsford collection.
Trinity Episcopal Church records, Dorothy and Lovick Mims, Edgefield, SC
Sermons of Rev. Arthur Wigfall, Bettis C. Rainsford
Bond, $30,000, Ker Boyce et.al. to Whitefield (sic) Brooks, Commissioner in Equity. 1830. photocopy in the editor's files.

Published Papers, Journals, and Diaries
Agricultural Society of Cambridge, SC*: Report of the Committee Appointed by the Society on Corn.* Np., 1842, 67-70.
John C. Calhoun Correspondence. *Fourth Annual Report of the Historical Manuscripts Commission of the American Historical Association, in Annual Report of the AHA, 1899.*
Calhoun, J. C. The Papers of John C. Calhoun, ed. R. L. Meriwether, Edward Hemphill, and Clyde N. Wilson. Columbia: USC Press, 1959 – 2003. Vols. 17-18.
Ruffin, Edmund. *The Diary of Edmund Ruffin,* Edited by William K. Scarborough. Baton Rouge: LSU Press, 1972.
Simms, W G. *The Letters of William Gilmore Simms.* 5 vols., Edited by Mary C. Oliphant et. al. Columbia: USC Press, 1955.
Newspapers
Edgefield Advertiser, 1836- 1852. Courtesy Center/Tompkins Library, Edgefield, SC, MF; Jessie Ball duPont Library, University of the South, Sewanee, TN. Six bound volumes (1836-1847).
Newspapers.com.
Chronicling America, Library of Congress

Genealogical Materials
Tompkins Library, Edgefield.
Biographical files
Brooks family files
Burt, Armistead file
Butler family files
Tompkins, Waddy file

Public Records
Edgefield County, Records of the Clerk of Court
Wills – Zachariah Smith Brooks, Whitfield Brooks, Mary Parsons Carroll Brooks
Probate Records
Land Records

US Bureau of the Census. Censuses for 1830 (5th), 1840 (6th), 1850 (7th). 1850 census for Edgefield District compiled by Vernon Burton and Terrance Finnegan.

U S Bureau of the Census, Heads of Families at the First Census of the United States Taken in the Year 1790: South Carolina (Wash. DC 1908)

Books
Bailey, Harris, Jr., Bernice Bennett, Ellen Butler, Ethel Dailey, and Vincent Sheppard. *Our Ancestors, Our Stories.* Suwannee, GA: The Write Image, 2014.
Bass, Robert D. *Ninety Six: The Struggle for the South Carolina Back Country.* Lexington SC: Sandlapper, 1978.
Benson, T. Lloyd, ed. *The Caning of Senator Sumner.* Belmont Calif: Wadsworth/Thomson, 2004.
Berry, Stephen II. *All That Makes a Man: Love and Ambition in the Civil War South.* New York: Oxford University Press, 1995.

------ *Princes of Cotton: Four Diaries of Young Men in the South, 1848-1860*. Athens: University of Georgia Press, 2007.
Berwanger, Eugene H., ed. *William Howard Russell: My Diary North and South*. New York: Knopf, 1988.
Biographical Directory of the American Congress, 1774-1949. US Government Printing Office, 1950.
Bleser, Carol, ed. T*he Hammonds of Redcliffe*. New York: Oxford University Press, 1981.
------ ed., *Secret and Sacred: The Diary of James Henry Hammond*. Columbia: USC Press, 1988.
------ ed., *In Joy and in Sorrow: Women, Family, and Marriage in the Victorian South, 1830-1900*. New York: Oxford University Press, 1992.
Boney, F. N. *Southerners All*. Macon GA: Mercer University Press, 1984.
Brannon, Rebecca. *From Revolution to Reunion: The Reintegration of the South Carolina Loyalists*. Columbia: USC Press, 2016.
Brooks, U.R. *South Carolina Bench and Bar*. Vol. I. Columbia: The State Co., 1908.
Bruce, Dickson D. Jr. *Violence and Culture in the Antebellum South*. Austin: University of Texas Press, 1979.
Burton, O. Vernon. *In My Father's House are Many Mansions: Family and community in Edgefield, South Carolina*. Chapel Hill: UNC Press, 1985.
------ *The Age of Lincoln*. New York: Hill & Wang, 2007.
Butterfield, Fox. *All God's Children: The Bosket Family and the American Tradition of Violence*. New York: Knopf, 1995.
Cash, Wilbur J. *The Mind of the South*. New York: Knopf, 1941.
Cashin, Edward J. *The Story of Augusta*. Spartanburg, SC: The Reprint Co., 1991.
Censer, Jane Turner. *North Carolina Planters and Their Children, 1800-186*0. Baton Rouge: LSU Press, 1984.
Chapman, John A. *History of Edgefield County, South Carolina*. Greenville, SC: The Southern Historical Press, 1994. (1897)
Chesnutt, David R. ed. *The Papers of Henry Laurens. Volume 11 (Jan.5,1776-Nov. 1, 1777)*. Columbia: USC Press, 1988.
Clinton, Catherine. *The Plantation Mistress: Woman's World in the Old South*. New York: Random House, 1982.
Collins, Bruce. *White Society in the Antebellum South*. London: Longman's, 1985.
Davidson, Chalmers. *The Last Foray: South Carolina Planters of 1860, A Sociological Study*. Columbia: USC Press, 1987.
Dean, Lewis S., ed. *The Papers of Michael Tuomey*. Spartanburg: Reprint Co., 2001.
Derrick, Samuel. *Centennial History of the South Carolina Railroad*. Columbia: The State Co., 1930.
Devereaux, Anthony Q. *Life and Times of R. F. W. Allston*. Georgetown, SC: Waccamaw Press, 1976.
Donald, David. *Charles Sumner and the Coming of the Civil War*. New York: Knopf, 1960.
Downey, Tom. *Planting a Capitalist South: Masters, Merchants and Manufacturers in the Southern Interior, 1790-1860*. Baton Rouge: LSU Press, 2005.
Edgar, Walter B. ed. *Biographical Dictionary of the South Carolina House of Representatives*. Columbia: USC Press, 1974.
------ ed. *The South Carolina Encyclopedia*. Columbia: USC Press, 2006.
------ *South Carolina, A History*. Columbia: USC Press, 1998.

Edgefield County Historical Society. *Edgefield Remembers the Mexican War*. 1948. (no author)
Edmunds, John B. Jr. *Francis W. Pickens and the Politics of Destruction*. Chapel Hill: UNC Press, 1986.
Elliott, Katherine B. *Early Settlers of Mecklenburg County Virginia*. Southern Historical Press, 1965.
Faust, Drew Gilpin. *James Henry Hammond and the Old South: A Design for Mastery*. Baton Rouge: LSU Press, 1982.
Fede, Andrew T. *Homicide Justified: The Legality of Killing Slaves in the United States and the Atlantic World*. Athens: UGA Press, 2017.
Fischer, David Hackett. *Albion's Seed: Four British Folkways in America*. New York: Oxford University Press, 1989.
Ford, Lacy K. Jr. *Origins of Southern Radicalism: The South Carolina Upcoumtry, 1800-1860*. New York: Oxford, 1988.
------ *Deliver Us From Evil: The Slavery Question in the Old South*. New York: Oxford University Press, 2009.
Fox-Genovese, Elizabeth. *Within the Plantation Household: Black and White Women of the Old South*. Chapel Hill: UNC Press, 1988.
------and Eugene Genovese. *The Mind of the Master Class: History and Faith in the Southern Slaveholders' Worldview*. New York: Cambridge University Press, 2005.
Freehling, William W. *Prelude to Civil War: The Nullification Controversy in South Carolina, 1816-1836*. New York: Harper, 1966.
------ *The Road to Disunion: Secessionists at Bay, 1776-1854*. New York: Oxford, 1990.
------ *The Road to Disunion: Secessionists Triumphant, 1854-1861*. New York: Oxford, 2007.
Friedman, Jean E. *The Enclosed Garden: Women and Community in the Evangelical South* 1830-1900. Chapel Hill: UNC Press, 1985.
Friend, Craig Thompson, and Lorri Glover, eds. *Southern Manhood: Perspectives on Masculinity in the Old South*. Athens: UGA Press, 2004.
Fuller, James A. *Chaplain to the Confederacy: A Biography of Basil Manly, 1798-1868*. Baton Rouge: LSU Press, 2000.
Genovese, Eugene D. *Roll, Jordan, Roll: The World the Slaves Made*. New York: Vintage, 1976.
Glover, Lorri. *Southern Sons: Becoming Men in the New Nation*. Baltimore: Johns Hopkins Press, 2007.
Greenberg, Kenneth S. *Honor and Slavery: Lies, Duels, Noses, Masks, Dressing as a Woman, Gifts, Strangers, Humanitarianism, Death, Slave Rebellions, the Proslavery Argument, Baseball, Hunting, and Gambling in the Old South*. Princeton: Princeton University Press, 1996.
Harris, J. William. *Plain Folk and Gentry in a Slave Society: White Liberty and Black Slavery in Augusta's Hinterlands*. Middletown, CT: Wesleyan University Press, 1985.
Helsley, Alexia Jones, and Michael Stauffer. *South Carolina Court Records: An Introduction for Genealogists*, South Caroling Dept. of Archives and History, 1993.
Heyrman, Christine Leigh. *Southern Cross: The Beginnings of the Bible Belt*. New York: Alfred Knopf, 1997.
Hobson, Fred. *Tell About the South: The Southern Rage to Explain*. Baton Rouge: LSU Press, 1983.
Hoffer, Williamjames Hull. *The Caning of Charles Sumner: Honor, Idealism, and the Origins of the Civil War*. Baltimore: Johns Hopkins Univ. Press, 2010.

Hollis, Daniel W. *The University of South Carolina*. Vol. 1. Columbia: USC Press, 1951.
Horne, Catherine H., ed. *Crossroads of Clay: The Southern Alkaline-glazed Stoneware Tradition*. Columbia: McKissick Museum, *1990.*
Howe, Daniel Walker. *What Hath God Wrought: The Transformation of America, 1815-1848.* New York: Oxford University Press, 2007.
Kibler, James Everett, *Our Fathers' Fields: A Southern Story*. Columbia: USC Press, 1998.
King, Alvy L. *Louis T. Wigfall: Southern Fire-Eater*. Baton Rouge: LSU Press, 1970.
Klein, Rachel N., *Unification of a Slave State: The Rise of the Planter Class in the South Carolina Backcountry, 1760-1808*. Chapel Hill: UNC Press 1990.
LaBorde, Maximilian, *History of the South Carolina College from its Incorporation Dec. 19, 1801 to Nov. 25, 1857.* Columbia: Peter Glass, 1859.
Lander, Ernest M., *Reluctant Imperialists: Calhoun, the South Carolinians, and the Mexican War*. Baton Rouge: LSU Press, 1980.
Logan, John H., *A History of the Upper Country of South Carolina From the Earliest Periods to the Close of the War for Independence.* 2 vols., 1859. Spartanburg: Reprint Company, 2009.
Lucas, Gloria Ramsey, *Slave Records of Edgefield County, South Carolina.* Edgefield County Historical Society, 2010.
Lumpkin, Henry. *From Savannah to Yorktown: The American Revolution in the South.* New York: Paragon House, 1981.
Mathew, William M., ed., *Agriculture, Geology, and Society in Antebellum South Carolina: The Private Diary of Edmund Ruffin, 1843.* Athens: UGA Press, 1992.
Mathews, Donald G. *Religion in the Old South*. Chicago: University of Chicago Press, 1977.
Mayfield, John, and Todd Hagstette, eds. *The Field of Honor: Essays on Southern Character and American Identity.* Columbia: USC Press, 2017.
McArthur, Judith, and O. Vernon Burton. *A Gentleman and an Officer: A Military and Social History of James B. Griffin's Civil War*. New York: Oxford University Press, 1996.
McWhiney, Grady, Moore, Warner O. Jr., and Pace, Robert F., eds. *'Fear God and Walk Humbly': The Agricultural Journal of James Mallory, 1843-1877.* Talladega: University of Alabama Press, 1997. [Google Books]
Meriwether, Coyler. *History of Higher Education in South Carolina*. Washington, D.C.: US Government Printing Office, 1889.
Meriwether, Robert L., *The Expansion of South Carolina, 1729-1765.* Kingsport TN: Southern Publishers, 1940.
Meyer, Jack Allen. *South Carolina in the Mexican War: A History of the Palmetto Regiment of Volunteers, 1846-1917*. Columbia: SC Dept. of Archives and History, 1996.
Mills, Robert. *Statistics of South Carolina. Charleston,* 1826.
Mitchell, Broadus. *William Gregg*: *Factory Master of the Old South.* Chapel Hill: UNC Press, 1926.
Motes, Jesse H., and Margaret P. Motes. *Laurens and Newberry Counties South Carolina: Saluda and Little River Settlements 1749-1775*. Greenville, SC: Southern Historical Press, 1994.
Nisbett, Richard E., and Dov Cohen. *Culture of Honor: The Psychology of Violence in the South.* Boulder, CO: Westview Press, 1996.
O'Brien, Michael, ed. *An Evening When Alone: four journals of single women in the south, 1827-67.* Charlottesville: University Press of Virginia., 1993.

------ ed. *All Clever Men Who Make Their Way: Critical Discourse in the Old South.* Athens: UGA Press, 1982.
------ *Conjectures of Order: Intellectual Life and The American South, 1810-1860.* 2 vols. Chapel Hill: UNC Press, 2004.
O'Neall, John Belton. *Biographical Sketches of the Bench and Bar of South Carolina,* Volumes I and II. Charleston: S. G. Courtney, 1859.
Pease, Jane H., and William H. Pease, *A Family of Women: The Carolina Petigrus in Peace and War.* Chapel Hill: UNC Press, 2014.
Phillips, Ulrich B. *Life and Labor in the Old South.* Columbia: USC Press, 2007. (1929)
Pope, Thomas H., *The History of Newberry County South Carolina.* Vol. 1, 1749-1860. Columbia: USC Press, 1973.
Proceedings of the Agricultural Convention of the State Agricultural Society of South Carolina, from 1839 to 1845. Columbia: Summer and Carroll, 1846.
Puleo, Stephen. *The Caning: The Assault that Drove America to Civil War.* Yardley, PA: Westholme Publishing, 2012.
Rainsford, Bettis C. et. al., *The Story of Edgefield.* Edgefield County Historical Society, 2009.
Rainsford, Bettis C. *Celebrating Darby Plantation.* ECHS, 2012
------ *Celebrating Halcyon Grove.* ECHS, 2011.
------ *Celebrating Holly Hill.* ECHS, 2015
------ *The Story of the Pine House.* ECHS, 2013
Roland, Lawrence S., Alexander Moore, and George C. Rogers, Jr. *The History of Beaufort County, South Carolina.* Vol. 1. Columbia: USC Press, 1996.
Rosengarten, Theodore. *Tombee: Portrait of a Cotton Planter.* New York: Morrow, 1986.
Rouse, Parke, Jr., *The Great Wagon Road from Philadelphia to the South.* Richmond, VA: the Dietz Press, 1995.
Scarborough, William Kauffman. *Masters of the Big House: Elite Slaveholders of the Mid-nineteenth Century South.* Baton Rouge: LSU Press, 2003.
------ *The Allstons of Chicora Wood: Wealth, Honor, and Gentility in the Carolina Lowcountry.* Baton Rouge: LSU Press, 2011
------ ed., *The Diary of Edmund Ruffin,* 3 vols., Baton Rouge: LSU Press, 1972-89.
------ *The Overseer: Plantation Management in the Old South.* Baton Rouge: LSU Press, 1966.
Schweiger, Beth Barton, and Mathews, Donald G., eds. *Religion in the American South: Protestants and Others in History and Culture.* Chapel Hill: UNC Press, 2004.
Sellers, Charles. *The Market Revolution: Jacksonian America, 1815-1846. New York: Oxford University Press, 1991.*
Simkins, Francis Butler, *Pitchfork Ben Tillman, South Carolinian.* Columbia: USC Press, 2002 (LSU 1944).
Simms, William Gilmore, *Lays of the Palmetto: A Tribute to the Palmetto Regiment in the War with Mexico.* Charleston: John Russell, 1848.
Sinha, Manisha, *The Counter-revolution of Slavery: Politics and Ideology in Antebellum South Carolina.* Chapel Hill: UNC Press, 2000.
Stallworth, Thomas Arrington. *History of the Brooks Family, the Butler Family, the Caldwell Family, the descendants of Margaret Rebecca (Caldwell) Stallworth.* Chester, SC, self-published, 1993. Copy in Tompkins Library, Edgefield.
State Agricultural Society of South Carolina, "Report of the Cambridge Agricultural Society on the situation on Whitfield Brooks' Plantation, and its claims for the premium to be awarded for the best managed plantation. *Proceedings of the State Agricultural Convention*

and of the State Agricultural Society of South Carolina from 1839 to 1845, Columbia, 1846, 285-89.
Stokes, Thomas L., *The Savannah.* Athens: U Ga Press, 1951, 1979.
Stowe, Steven M., *Intimacy and Power in the Old South: Ritual in the Lives of the Planters.* (Baltimore: The Johns Hopkins University Press, 1987).
Taylor, Rosser H. *Ante-bellum South Carolina: A Social and Cultural History.* Chapel Hill: UNC Press, 1942.
Tillman, Mamie Norris, *Inscriptions from Edgefield Village Baptist Cemetery: Including Trinity Episcopal Church Section.* Edgefield County Historical Society, 1958.
De Tocqueville, Alexis. *Democracy in America.* (1835, 1840) Translated and edited by Harvey C. Mansfield and Delba Winthrop. Chicago: University of Chicago Press, 2000.
Todd, Leonard, *Carolina Clay: The Life and Legend of the Slave Potter Dave.* New York: W. W. Norton, 2008.
Wallace, David Duncan. *The History of South Carolina,* 4 vols. New York: The American Historical Society, 1934.
Watson, Margaret J., and Harry L. Watson. *Greenwood County Sketches.* Greenwood, SC: Attic Press, 1970.
Watson, Ritchie D. Jr., *Normans and Saxons: Southern Race Mythology and the Intellectual History of the Civil War.* Baton Rouge: LSU Press, 2009.
Weiner, Marli. *Mistresses and Slaves: Plantation Women in South Carolina, 1830-1880.* Champaign: University of Illinois Press, 1999.
Wender, Herbert, *Southern Commercial Conventions, 1837-1859* Baltimore: Johns Hopkins University Press, 1930.
Williams, Jack Kenny, *Dueling in the Old South: Vignettes of Social History.* College Station: Texas A&M University Press, 1980.
------ *Vogues in Villainy: Crime and Retribution in Ante-Bellum South Carolina.* Columbia: USC Press, 1959.
Wood, Kirsten E., *Slaveholding Widows from the American Revolution through the Civil War.* (Chapel Hill: UNC Press, 2004).
Woodson, Hortense. *Giant in the Land: A Biography of William Bullein Johnson, First President of the Southern Baptist Convention. Nashville: Broadman Press, 1950.*
------ *History of the Edgefield Baptist Association.* Edgefield, SC, Advertiser Press, 1957.
Wyatt-Brown, Bertram, *Southern Honor: Ethics and Behavior in the Old South.* New York: Oxford University Press, 1982.
------ *The Shaping of Southern Culture: Honor, Grace, and War, 1760s-1880s*
Chapel Hill: UNC Press, 2001.
Yarborough, Donna. "It All Began With Moses" typescript, Tompkins Library, Edgefield, SC.

Dissertations and Theses

Balcerski, Thomas J. "Intimate Contests: Manhood, Friendship, and the Coming of the Civil War," PhD dissertation, Cornell University, 2014.
Gettys, James M. "To Conquer a Peace: South Carolina and the Mexican War," PhD diss. USC, 1974.
Graden, Harlan J., "Losing Control: The Caning of Charles Sumner and the Breakdown of Antebellum Political Culture." PhD diss. UNC, 1991.

Hanson, Eleanor Mims, "The Edgefield Advertiser and its Editors" MA Thesis, USC, 1930. Updated in 1980 and published by The Advertiser Press, Edgefield, SC.

Robertson, John C., "The Reactions of South Carolinians to the Brooks-Sumner Affair" MA Thesis, USC, 1982.

Welborn, James Hill, "Drinkin', Fightin', Prayin': The Southern White Male in the Civil War Era," PhD diss., University of Georgia, 2014.

Articles, book chapters, encyclopedia entries, book reviews:

Adger, J.[ohn] B. *Wigfall's Sermon upon Dueling,* 1856. *Southern Presbyterian Review,* X (1858), 126-137.

Aldrich, Alfred P., "Memoir of Judge A. P. Butler," Ulysses Robert Brooks, *South Carolina Bench and Bar* (Columbia: The State Company, 1906), Vol. I, 9-20

Ayers, Edward. "Everyman as Master," review of *Tombee: Portrait of a Cotton Planter*, by Theodore Rosengarten. Charlottesville: University of Virginia Press, 1987, in *Virginia Quarterly Review,* 63, Issue 3 (1987), 528-532.

__________ "Honor," *Encyclopedia of Southern Culture.* Chapel Hill: UNC Press, 1898: 1483-1484.

Barney, William. "Brooks, Preston Smith," *American National Biography*, ed. John A. Garrity and Mark C. Carnes. New York: Oxford University Press, 1999, 628.

Bell, Larry S., and Marvin L. Cann, "Silver Spoons and Spyglasses: The Lifestyle of the Abbeville Gentry, 1820-1860." *South Carolina Historical Magazine* [hereafter *SCHM*] 115, No. 4, (Oct., 2014): 304-324.

Berry, Stephen, and James Hill Welborn, "The Cane of his Existence: Depression, Damage, and the Brooks-Sumner Affair." *Southern Cultures* 20, No. 4, (Nov., 2014): 5-21.

Bonham, Milledge L. Jr., "A Carolina Democrat on Party Prospects in 1844," *American Historical Review* 42, No.1, (Oct. 1936): 79-82.

Breen, T. H. "The Great Wagon Road." *Southern Cultures*, 3, No.1 (Spring 1997): 22-57.

Brown, Richard Maxwell, "South Carolina Extremism and its Violent Origins: From the Regulator Movement to the Edgefield Tradition, 1760-1960." Ch. 3 of Brown, *Strain of Violence: Historical Studies of American Violence and Vigilantism.* New York: Oxford University Press, 1975.

Byron, Matthew A. "Thou Shalt Not Duel: Some Observations Regarding the Impotency of Dueling Laws in South Carolina." *Proceedings of the South Carolina Historical Association* 2013: 29-40.

Campbell, Richard, "Patriotism, Poetry, and Personalities: 'A Pasquinade of the Thirties'." *South Carolina Historical Magazine* 115, (January, 2014): 4-34.

Cashin, Joan E., "'Decidedly Opposed to the Union': Women's Culture, Marriage, and Politics in Antebellum South Carolina." *Georgia Historical Quarterly* 78 (Winter, 1994): 735-59.

_________ "The Structure of Antebellum Planter Families: 'The Ties that Bound us was Strong.'" *Journal of Southern History*, 56, No. 1, (February, 1990): 55-70.

Chaplin, Joyce E., "Creating a Cotton South in Georgia and South Carolina, 1760-1815," Journal of Southern History 57 (1991): 171-200.

Cheatham, Kate Wigfall. "The Old South and Beloved Old Edgefield." Copy in files of Bettis Rainsford, Edgefield SC.

Cordle, Charles G. "The Bank of Hamburg, South Carolina." *Georgia Historical Quarterly* 23 No. 2 (June, 1939): 148-153.

Cox, M. Ron. "From Democrat to Whig: The Senatorial Career of William Campbell Preston, 1833-1842," *Proceedings of the SCHA*, 2001: 19-38.

Crowther, Edward "Holy Honor: Sacred and Secular in the Old South." *Journal of Southern History*, 58, No. 4 (Nov. 1992): 619-36.

Dale, Elizabeth. "A Different Sort of Justice: The Informal Courts of Public Opinion in Antebellum South Carolina." University of Florida Leven College of Law, Spring 2003.

Deitreich, Kenneth. "'Ever Able, Manly, Just and Heroic': Preston Smith Brooks and the Myth of Southern Manhood." *Proceedings of the SCHA*, 2011: 27-38.

_________ "'The Sly Mendacity of Hints": Preston Brooks and the War with Mexico." *SCHM*. 113, No. 1, Oct. 2012: 290-314.

Durrill, Wayne K., "The Power of Ancient Words: Classical Teaching and Social Change at South Carolina College, 1804-1860," *Journal of Southern History*. 65 no. 3 (Aug. 1999): 469-98.

Faust, Drew Gilpin, "The Rhetoric and Ritual of Agriculture in Antebellum South Carolina." *Journal of Southern History*. 45, no. 4 (1979): 541-68.

Ford, Lacy K. Jr. "Origins of the Edgefield Tradition: The Late Antebellum Experience and the Roots of Political Insurgency," *SCHM*. 98 (Oct. 1997): 328-348.

------ "Self-Sufficiency, Cotton, and Economic Development in the South Carolina Upcountry, 1800-1860," *Journal of Economic History*, 45, Issue 2, (1985): 261-67.

------ "The Tale of Two Entrepreneurs in the Old South: John Springs III and Hiram Hutchinson of the South Carolina Upcountry." *SCHM*, 95 (July 1994): 198-224.

Forret, Jeff. "Conflict and the 'Slave Community': Violence among Slaves in Upcountry South Carolina," *Journal of Southern History* Vol. 74, No. 3 (Aug., 2008): 551-588.

Fox-Genovese, Elizabeth, "Religion in the Lives of Slaveholding Women in the Antebellum South," in *That Gentle Strength: Historical Perspectives on Women in Christianity*, ed. Lynda L. Coon, Katherine J Haldane, and Elisabeth W. Sommer. Charlottesville: Univ. Press of Virginia, 1990, 207-229.

Gallivan, Fielding C., "Episcopalians and Baptists in the South Carolina Upcountry: A Comparative Study of Christ Church (Episcopal) and Greenville Baptist Church, Greenville, South Carolina, 1820-1858." *Proceedings of the SCHA*, 1988-1989: 39-49.

Gienapp, William E., "The Crime Against Sumner: The Caning of Charles Sumner and the Rise of the Republican Party." *Civil War History*. 25 (1979): 218-245.

Gorn, Elliott, "Gouge and Bite, Pull Hair and Scratch, the Social Significance of Fighting in the Southern Backcountry." *American Historical Review*. 90. No. 1 (Feb. 1985): 18-43.

Grinde, Donald A., "Building the South Carolina Railroad" *SCHM*. 77 (April 1976): 84-96.

Holcomb, Brent H. "Petitions for Land from the South Carolina Council Journals, Vol. VI, 1766-1770," *South Carolina Magazine of Ancestral Research*. (1999).

Jennings, Thelma, "South Carolina Leadership in the Southern Unification Movement, 1849-1850," *Proceedings of the SCHA*, 1978: 31-41.

Jervey, Theodore D. "The Butlers of South Carolina" *South Carolina Historical and Genealogical Magazine*, 4, no. 4, (October 1903): 296-311.

LaBorde, Maximilian. "Hon. Preston S. Brooks," *Southern Quarterly Review*, 2 (1857): 348-70. Note: Though anonymous, LaBorde is named as its author in the preface to his *History of the South Carolina College*.

Lander, Ernest M., Jr. "The Calhoun-Preston Feud, 1836-1842." *SCHM. 59 (January 1958): 24-37.*

Loehr, Rodney C., "Farmers' Diaries: Their Interest and Value as Agricultural Sources," Agricultural History, XII, No. 4, (1938), 313-325.
Lord, C. W. "Young Louis Wigfall, South Carolina Politician and Duelist." *SCHM*, 59 (April, 1958): 96-112.
Mactavish, Bruce. "'O Sir He is From South Carolina:" Migration and the Establishment of Community; South Carolina and Mississippi as a Case Study" *Proceedings of the SCHA.* 1993: 57-68.
Martin, Thomas P. "The Advent of William Gregg and the Graniteville Company." *Journal of Southern History*. 11 (August, 1945): 389-423.
Mathis, Robert Neil. "Preston Smith Brooks: The Man and His Image," *SCHM.* 79 (Oct. 1978): 296-310.Meriwether, Robert L. ed., "Preston S. Brooks and the Caning of Charles Sumner," *SCHM.* 52 (Jan. 1951): 1-4.
Moon, David T. Jr., "Southern Baptists and Southern Men: Evangelical Perceptions of Manhood in Nineteenth Century Georgia," *Journal of Southern History.* 81 No. 3 (Aug. 2015). 553-606.
Moore, Andrew Charles. "Roll of Students of the University of South Carolina College, 1805-1905." Digital.tcl.sc.edu/cdm/compoundobject/collection/hsn/id/2298/rec.15 accessed Nov. 15, 2018.
Neuffer, Claude H., ed., *Names in South Carolina*, vols. 1-30 (1954-1984), Spartanburg, SC: The Reprint Company. Photocopies in Bettis C. Rainsford's library.
Richards, Miles S., "Pierce Mason Butler: The South Carolina Years, 1830-1841" *SCHM*, 87 (January, 1986): 14-29.
Rogers, Tommy W. "The Great Population Exodus from South Carolina, 1850-1860," *SCHM.* 68 (Jan. 1968): 14-21.
Sinha, Manisha "The Caning of Charles Sumner: Slavery, Race, and Ideology in the Age of Civil War," *Journal of the Early Republic.* 23, No. 2 (Summer, 2003): 233-262.
"The Colorful History of Glenn Springs" National Trust for Historic Preservation, 2019.
Stokes, Allan. "South Carolina and Drought – 1845" *Proceedings of the SCHA.* 1987: 44-52.
Stowe, Steven, "The 'Touchiness' of the Gentleman Planter: The Sense of Esteem and Continuity in the Antebellum South," *Psychohistory Review* 8 (Winter, 1979), 6-15.
"A Tourist's View of Glenn Springs, 1847," in "Upper South Carolina Genealogy and History," XX, No. 1, Feb. 2006.
Towles, Louis P. "A Matter of Honor at South Carolina College, 1822." *SCHM,* 94 (Jan., 1993): 6-18.
Walker, Melissa, "Mineral Water, Dancing, and Amusements: The Development of Tourism in the Nineteenth-Century South Carolina Upcountry," in Timothy P. Grady and Melissa Walker, eds., *Recovering the Piedmont Past: Unexplored Moments in Nineteenth-Century Upcountry South Carolina History.* Columbia: USC Press, 2013.
Weir, Robert M. "The South Carolinian as Extremist." In Weir, ed. *"The Last of American Freemen': Studies in the Political Culture of the Colonial and Revolutionary South.* Macon GA: Mercer University Press, 1986. 213-230.
Williams, Jack Kenny. "The Code of Honor in Ante-Bellum South Carolina." *SCHM.* 54 (1953): 113-128.

INDEX

NOTE: There are two indexes. The first is tha NAME index followed by a GENERAL index.

GENERAL INDEX